THE
ANCIENT GREEKS

THE
ANCIENT GREEKS
A CRITICAL HISTORY

□

John V. A. Fine

The Belknap Press of
Harvard University Press
Cambridge, Massachusetts
and London, England
1983

Copyright © 1983 by the President and Fellows of Harvard College
All rights reserved

Printed in the United States of America

10 9 8 7 6 5 4 3 2 1

This book is printed on acid-free paper, and its binding materials have
been chosen for strength and durability.

Library of Congress Cataloging in Publication Data

Fine, John V. A. (John Van Antwerp), 1903–
 The ancient Greeks.

 Includes index.
 1. Greece—History—To 146 B.C. I. Title.
DF214.F5 1983   938   82-23283
ISBN 0-674-03311-6

To My Son
John V. A. Fine, Jr.

Preface

WHILE WRITING THIS BOOK I was often asked for what audience it was intended. The answer, beyond trying to satisfy my own curiosity and questions, is that I was thinking of those seriously interested in Greek history, whether they were undergraduate or graduate students, teachers of Classics or of other humanistic fields, and the general reading public. My aim has been not to produce a smoothly flowing narrative which can lull a reader into unthinking acceptance of the views presented, but to try to make him think. One should never forget that we, as our predecessors were, are constantly being misled because we accept too readily the views that have become sacrosanct through tradition. A history which does not constantly cause one to reflect on what he is reading and to be cognizant of the nature and ambiguities of the evidence is hardly performing the function that a historical work should. Accordingly, references to Greek art, literature, philosophy, and religion are made only as the narrative demands, for any discussion, because of the problem of space and the author's inadequacies, could be little more than a summary of the work of experts.

After finishing a book on which he has worked for years, the writer is acutely aware of the magnitude of his indebtedness. The remarkable holdings of Princeton's Firestone Library are a superb aid and inspiration to a scholar in his work. Colleagues and former students have been generous with their suggestions and criticisms. Professor Glen Bowersock I wish to thank for suggesting that I submit my manuscript to Harvard University Press. Mrs. Mary Roberts Craighill was kind enough to undertake the thankless task of preparing an index. My wife with her keen literary and scholarly mind has rescued me from many an impasse. To my son, John Fine, I owe more than it is possible to express. Despite his responsibilities to his family and to an academic field very different from mine, he found time to read my manuscript in its various stages and to give me many sound historical criticisms. No matter how discouraged I became on occasions, he always revived my spirits with never-failing encouragement and convinced me that the work must be completed. Most recently, his assistance in reading proof, both galley and page, has been invaluable. My gratitude to him is very deep.

A statement is necessary about the translations of sentences or passages from the ancient authors and inscriptions which appear frequently in this book. For Homer the translations are mine, but often blended with those of the numerous existing prose translations. The translations of Herodotus are mine, but sometimes colored by those of Aubrey de Sélincourt in his Penguin rendering of the Greek historian. For several longer passages I have borrowed de Sélincourt's wording, although sometimes slightly adapted. For Thucydides I have consistently used the translation of R. Crawley, which first appeared in 1876. The several quotations from Aristotle's *Politics* are indebted to Ernest Barker, *The Politics of Aristotle* (Oxford: Clarendon Press, 1948). For the great majority of the ancient authors, I have used, with occasional slight changes, the translations given in the various Loeb editions. In the case of three rather long inscriptions, the *Pact of the Founders of Cyrene*, the *Themistocles Decree from Troezen*, and the *Oath of Plataea*, I have used respectively, as stated in the text, the translations of A. H. Graham and of A. R. Burn. With a few exceptions, the spelling of names and places is that of the *Oxford Classical Dictionary*.

Contents

Abbreviations and short titles used in the text

Barker   *The Politics of Aristotle,* trans. Ernest Barker (Oxford: Clarendon Press, 1946)

Bengtson   Hermann Bengtson, *Die Verträge der Griechisch-Römischen Welt von 700 bis 338 v. Chr.,* 2nd ed. (Munich: Beck, 1975)

Dindorf   William Dindorf, ed., *Demosthenes,* 9 vols. (Oxford: Oxford University Press, 1846–1851)

Hellenica Oxyrhynchia   *Hellenica Oxyrhynchia,* ed. Vittorio Bartoletti (Leipzig: Teubner, 1959)

Hicks and Hill   E. L. Hicks and G. F. Hill, *A Manual of Greek Historical Inscriptions* (Oxford: Clarendon Press, 1901)

I.G.   *Inscriptiones Graecae* (Berlin: de Gruyter, 1924–   ). The superscript 2 or 3 added to the volume number signifies second or third edition.

Jacoby   Felix Jacoby, *Die Fragmente der Griechischen Historiker,* 3 vols. with many fascicles (Berlin: Weidmann; Leiden: Brill, 1923–   ). The historians included are numbered consecutively.

M&L   Russell Meiggs and David Lewis, *A Selection of Greek Historical Inscriptions to the End of the Fifth Century B.C.* (Oxford: Clarendon Press, 1969)

S.E.G.   *Supplementum Epigraphicum Graecum* (Leiden: Sijthoff; Amsterdam: Gieben, 1923–   )

de Sélincourt   *Herodotus: The Histories,* trans. Aubrey de Sélincourt (Baltimore: Penguin Books, 1954)

S.I.G.   W. Dittenberger, *Sylloge Inscriptionum Graecarum,* 3rd ed. (Leipzig: Hirzel, 1915–1924; reprint ed., Hildesheim: Olms, 1960)

Tod   Marcus N. Tod, *A Selection of Greek Historical Inscriptions,* vol. II, *From 403 to 323 B.C.* (Oxford: Clarendon Press, 1948)

THE
ANCIENT GREEKS

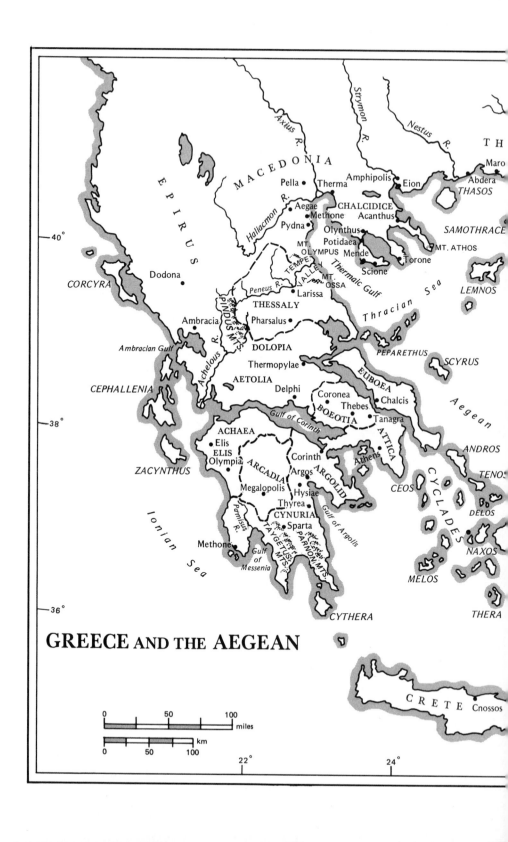

GREECE AND THE AEGEAN

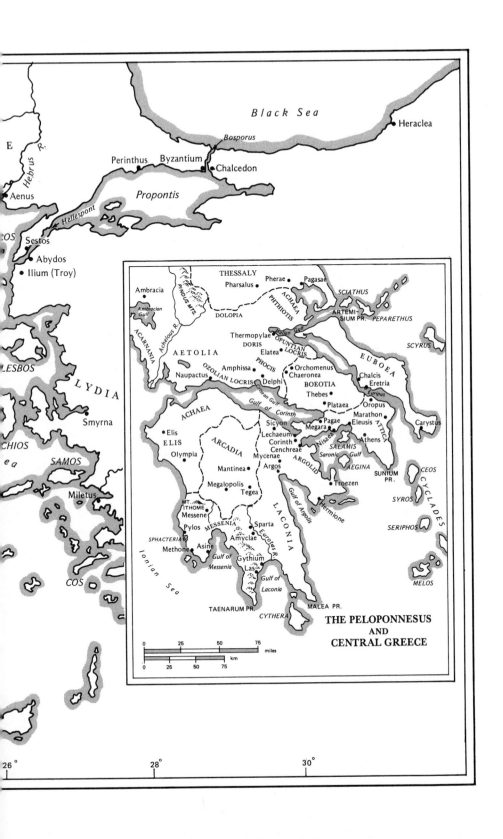

Black Sea

Heraclea

Bosporus

Perinthus   Byzantium   Chalcedon

Aenus   Propontis

Hebrus R.

Hellespont

Sestos

Abydos

Ilium (Troy)

LESBOS

LYDIA

Smyrna

CHIOS

SAMOS

Miletus

COS

Ionian Sea

THESSALY
Pharsalus   Pherae   Pagasae
Ambracia   SCIATHUS
PINDUS MTS.   ACHAEA
Ambracian   DOLOPIA   PHTHIOTIS   ARTEMI-   PEPARETHUS
Gulf   SIUM PR.
ACARNANIA   Thermopylae   SCYRUS
Achelous R.   DORIS   OPUNTIAN
AETOLIA   Elatea   LOCRIS   EUBOEA
Amphissa   PHOCIS   Orchomenus
Naupactus   OZOLIAN LOCRIS   Chaeronea   Chalcis
Delphi   BOEOTIA   Eretria
Crisaean Gulf   Thebes   Euripus
ACHAEA   Gulf of Corinth   Plataea   Oropus
Sicyon   Marathon   Carystus
Elis   Lechaeum   Megara   Pagae   Eleusis   ATTICA
ELIS   Corinth   Nisaea   Athens
Olympia   ARCADIA   Cenchreae   Saronic   SALAMIS
Mycenae   ARGOLID   Gulf   AEGINA   SUNIUM   CEOS
Mantinea   Argos   PR.   CYCLADES
Megalopolis   Troezen   SYROS
MT.   Tegea   Gulf of Argolis   Hermione   SERIPHOS
ITHOME   Sparta
Messene   MESSENIA   Eurotas R.
Pylos   Amyclae
SPHACTERIA   Asine   LACONIA
Methone   Gythium
Gulf of   Las   MELOS
Messenia   Gulf of
Laconia
TAENARUM PR.   MALEA PR.
CYTHERA

THE PELOPONNESUS
AND
CENTRAL GREECE

0   25   50   75
miles
0   25   50   75
km

26°   28°   30°

1
The Early Aegean World

T O THE ANCIENT Greek the earliest history of his land was enshrined in the great Homeric epics, the *Iliad* and the *Odyssey*, in the other heroic tales which had descended to him from the remote past, and in the ancient ruins, still visible, of places like Mycenae and Tiryns. If pressed, the educated Greek would have admitted that these epics contained much mythical and fanciful material, but they were so much a part of his heritage that they satisfied whatever curiosity he may have had about centuries long past. They entered into the very fabric of his being, for Homer played a basic role in his education, and, to the artists, poets, and orators by whom every Greek was deeply influenced, the epic tradition was a source of endless inspiration.

The modern mind has been more critical. When historians in the late eighteenth century and particularly in the nineteenth century turned to the study of Greek history, they usually began their books with a section devoted to legendary Greece, to which they relegated all the epic tales and also the ancient legends recounted by later Greek authors. The beginning of historical Greece was placed in the eighth century B.C., for the traditions and available information from that time on seemed more reliable. If one wanted to pick a particular time for the beginning of Greek history the year 776 B.C. was considered appropriate, since this traditional date for the establishment of the Olympic Games seemed to mark symbolically the transition from the realm of myth and legend to that of actual history. Not until modern times did startling archaeological discoveries, beginning in the last third of the nineteenth century and continuing ever since, reveal that great and completely unsuspected ancient civilizations had existed in the Aegean world.

Even before these discoveries tremendous advances had been made in the understanding of the early history of Egypt and of the peoples of the Near East. The Rosetta stone, found on the Rosetta arm of the Nile in 1799, recording in Greek, hieroglyphics, and the current demotic a decree honoring Ptolemy V Epiphanes in 196 B.C., enabled scholars, led by Jean François Champollion, to decipher the ancient Egyptian language and thus render intelligible records going back into the third millennium B.C. In the Near East in the first half of the nineteenth century the

1

famous Behistun (Bisitun) Monument, engraved some 225 feet above ground level on a precipitous cliff in the Zagros mountains, yielded its secrets. At great personal risk the Englishman Henry Creswicke Rawlinson managed to copy the long cuneiform inscriptions which accompanied the relief sculpture. Subsequently he and various scholars were able to decipher the inscriptions, which proved to be a proclamation of Darius the Great recorded in three separate languages: Old Persian, Elamite, and Babylonian (Akkadian). This brilliant and difficult achievement provided scholars with the necessary clues for interpreting other languages written in cuneiform scripts which were current at different times in the first three millennia B.C. in Asia from the Mediterranean Sea eastward into the Iranian plateau.

In the Aegean area it was the German Heinrich Schliemann who first demonstrated the existence of civilizations long before the traditional date of 776 B.C. This amazing and indomitable man, after amassing a fortune in business, set out to prove the soundness of his boyhood conviction that the Homeric poems reflected a historical and not a mythical civilization. His excavations, beginning at Troy in 1870, at Mycenae in 1874, at Orchomenus in 1880, and at Tiryns in 1885, revealed that powerful states had flourished centuries before the accepted beginning of Greek history and that some of the remains corresponded closely with descriptions given by Homer. Influenced by a tradition, persistent throughout antiquity, that King Minos of Crete had once ruled as master of the Aegean, the Englishman Arthur Evans began to excavate at Cnossos in 1899. The remarkable results of his excavations soon proved that there had existed in Crete a civilization in many ways more magnificent than the one on the Greek mainland, a civilization by which the mainland had been greatly influenced in the second millennium B.C.

Archaeological excavations have been very numerous in the twentieth century in Greece and the Aegean islands, in the Balkans, in Asia Minor, and in the Near and Middle East. Since the subject of this book is the history of the Greeks, the first question to be faced is whether the inhabitants of Greece, the islands, and Crete, whose early civilization was being revealed by archaeology, were the ancestors of the historical Greeks and the speakers of the same Indo-European language. The later Greeks, steeped in the Homeric epics, never doubted that the heroes fighting the Trojan War under the command of Agamemnon of Mycenae were their ancestors, but modern scholars had to consider the possibility that Homer had taken over a saga which Greeks, arriving at some unknown time, had inherited from their predecessors. The fact that in historical times many place names in Greece, the islands, and

Asia Minor ended with non-Indo-European suffixes like *-nthos* and *-ssos* (for example, Corinthos and Cnossos) suggested strongly that immigrating Greeks had adopted the names used by earlier inhabitants. If, then, the Indo-European-speaking Greeks were immigrants, when did they appear in the Aegean world? Linguistics and archaeology alone can attempt to answer this question.

The linguistic evidence is provided by clay tablets inscribed with linear scripts which excavators, beginning with Evans, have found in various parts of Crete. Of these seven scripts the significant ones for the present question are those known as Linear A and Linear B. Examples of Linear A, few in number, were found throughout Crete in archaeological levels stretching from ca. 1750 to ca. 1400 B.C.; some 3,000 examples of Linear B, of a more cursive style, were found only in Cnossos in a stratification of ca. 1400 B.C. Subsequently about 1,250 Linear B tablets were found in Pylos on the west coast of the Peloponnesus (1939) and some 50 at Mycenae (1952), dating about 1200 B.C., and around 20 in Thebes (1964) in a stratum of about 1320 B.C. Over the years many linguists have endeavored to decipher these tablets. The Linear A tablets have so far defied interpretation because of inadequate material with which to work, but in 1952 the Linear B tablets succumbed to the genius of the young English architect Michael Ventris. He proved that these tablets contained an archaic form of Greek, hundreds of years older than the earliest Greek formerly known, that of the Homeric poems. Linear B may well have developed at an early time from Linear A and other scripts in a more cursive form suitable for recording data on materials such as wood, leather, and papyrus as well as clay. When the scribes encountered speakers of Greek, whether in Crete or on the mainland, or both, they adapted some of the syllabic signs of Linear B—or devised new ones—to record their understanding of the Greek language.

These tablets, therefore, have proved that towards the end of the thirteenth century Greeks were living in Mycenae and Pylos and, presumably, elsewhere in Greece, and that some 200 years earlier they were present in Cnossos. Why is the evidence limited to these two approximate dates? The explanation probably is somewhat as follows. The decipherment of the tablets has shown that they were concerned mostly with annual inventories. At the end of the year any record which seemed of permanent importance was transferred from the sun-dried clay tablets to materials such as papyrus or wood while the tablets were softened in water so that they could be used again. The paradox of the situation is that the great conflagrations which consumed Cnossos ca. 1400, Pylos and Mycenae ca. 1200, and Thebes ca. 1320, by baking the tablets, transformed the supposedly ephemeral records into permanent ones, whereas the supposedly permanent records of papyrus and the like perished in the fires or, if in some places they escaped burning, gradually succumbed to the ravages of time.[1]

The Linear B tablets prove that Greeks were in the Aegean area by ca. 1400 but give no information on the time of their first arrival. Since no earlier documents exist, archaeological evidence alone is available for answering the question of the coming of the Greeks. Archaeology has shown that the unknown inhabitants of Greece lived under a neolithic civilization from at least the sixth millennium B.C. The transition from the later Stone Age to the Bronze Age occurred in the Aegean area about the beginning of the third millennium. It is probable that migrants from Asia Minor brought the use of metal—first copper and then, with the addition of tin, bronze—to the Greek mainland, the Cyclades, and Crete. This early Bronze Age lasted for approximately a millennium. It was towards the end of this period, or early in the next millennium, that most scholars now think that the first appearance of the Greeks should be placed. The evidence is scant and ambiguous, but unless one accepts the theory believed only by a minority that the Greeks were indigenous, no other time seems more logical.

These centuries also provide evidence for the appearance of certain Indo-European languages in Asia Minor. In 1906 the Germans began to excavate at a Turkish village, Boghazköy, in the bend of the Halys (Kizil Irmak) River, where remains of a large fortified city and of many sculptures were visible on the surface of the ground. Within a short time some 10,000 cuneiform tablets were unearthed, and it became evident that the archives of the Hittite Empire had been discovered. Among these tablets, which date chiefly from the fifteenth, fourteenth, and thirteenth centuries, three Indo-European languages were represented: Hittite, the closely related Luwian, and Palaic. In 1925 excavations at Kültepe (ancient Kanesh) in central Anatolia brought to light a large number of cuneiform tablets written by Assyrian merchants who for some three generations in the twentieth and nineteenth centuries B.C. lived and transacted business in this area. Since various Indo-European names of Hittite and Luwian types are listed in these documents, they provide proof that in the twentieth century, if not earlier, "Indo-Europeans" were living in central Asia Minor. These speakers of Indo-European languages probably entered Asia Minor by crossing the Caucasus mountains. The "original" homeland of the "Indo-Europeans" cannot be fixed precisely, but their wandering area seems to have stretched from the steppes north of the Caspian westward to the region of the Danube. From the closing centuries of the third millennium these wanderers of

"Indo-European" speech began to migrate, for various reasons and at different times, into India, the Iranian plateau, Asia Minor, the Balkans, including Greece, Italy, and many other parts of Europe,[2] their languages naturally developing differently as the groups lost contact with one another.

The arrival of proto-Greeks in Greece in the years around 2000 B.C., then, would be in conformity with what little is known about the wanderings of other Indo-European-speaking peoples and particularly with the appearance of the Hittites and Luwians in Asia Minor. For several centuries these proto-Greeks spread over much of Greece, destroying various settlements and gradually blending with the natives. Archaeology has revealed the existence in this period of many communities in the Peloponnesus, central Greece, and Thessaly, but here it will be sufficient to comment only on the better-known Mycenae. In the course of his excavations there, which began in 1874, Schliemann unearthed six royal shaft graves containing nineteen skeletons of men, women, and children, and a staggering amount of treasure, largely of gold, including golden masks on the faces of the men. The finding of these graves caused Schliemann to send his famous telegram to the king of Greece announcing that he had discovered the graves of Agamemnon, Cassandra, and their companions, killed by Clytemnestra and Aegisthus on their return from Troy. This emotional reaction is certainly more understandable than that of a learned scholar who, outraged by Schliemann's flamboyant character, insisted that one of the gold masks was a product of Byzantine art representing a portrait of Christ. Archaeologists have subsequently proved that these shaft graves and another grave circle discovered later should be dated to the late seventeenth and the sixteenth centuries. The wealth revealed was, and still is, startling, for little information is available on early Mycenae, but it shows clearly that the Mycenaeans at that time, through trade or possibly piracy, were familiar with products from the north (amber) and artifacts from the Cyclades, Crete, Anatolia, Syria, Mesopotamia, and Egypt.

In the first half of the second millennium Crete was by far the most civilized region in the Aegean area. In the early centuries at sites like Cnossos and Mallia in the north and Phaestus in the south, regular cities began to develop and large palaces were built. With the introduction of the potter's wheel, probably from Anatolia, ceramics made remarkable advances, and some of the most beautiful Cretan vases which have been discovered belong to this period. Metalworkers and gem cutters also produced excellent work, and before the middle of the millennium painters were decorating the walls of palaces with wonderful frescoes. In the course of the seventeenth century many Cretan cities suffered severe damage from earthquakes, but recovery was rapid, and the palaces were rebuilt and greatly enlarged.

The Cretans, or Minoans as they are often called from the mythical king Minos, had considerable influence on the emerging Greeks of the mainland, as the shaft graves revealed. Archaeology discloses that the Cretans had many contacts with the old civilizations of the east in Egypt, Syria, and Anatolia. The French excavation of Mari (Tell Hariri) on the middle Euphrates is particularly interesting in this connection.[3] In this Sumerian and Semitic city the palace of the king, a huge complex containing the royal quarters, administrative offices, workshops, and storerooms, was surprisingly similar to the palace at Cnossos in its general plan and in many architectural features; in addition, the frescoes which miraculously were preserved at Mari are reminiscent in technique and style of the famous Cretan frescoes. Since the palace at Mari was destroyed by Hammurabi about 1759, and the great palace at Cnossos with its remarkable frescoes was not built until the seventeenth century, it seems clear that the influence ran from east to west. Other buried cities might yield similar or even more telling evidence.[4] These influences and the personnel to execute them presumably reached Crete through Ugarit (Ras Shamra) on the northern Syrian coast, which French excavations in the 1930s proved to have been an important meeting place for Egyptian, Hittite, Mesopotamian, Syrian, Cretan, and Mycenaean products and ideas.

In the seventeenth and sixteenth centuries Crete attained the acme of its greatness. So far as one can tell from the silent records of archaeology, it looks as if some sort of cultural, and possibly even political, union was achieved in the island under the leadership of Cnossos. Archaeological finds, especially the pottery, reveal the spread of Cretan influence over the Cyclades, the Peloponnesus, and areas of central Greece. It is difficult, if not impossible, to disentangle the relationship between Crete and the mainland in this period. There is no necessity, however, to postulate a Cretan conquest of Greece as Evans did. The lords of Mycenae and other mainland communities were powerful figures, much impressed by Cretan culture and glad to employ Cretan artists and craftsmen and to have them teach the local population, but they apparently were proto-Greek rulers. Actually the evidence seems to suggest that by the fifteenth century, Mycenaean (that is, mainland) power was waxing whereas Cretan power was on the wane. This tendency can be illustrated from the excavations at two sites. At Miletus, on the west coast of Asia Minor, and in Rhodes Cretan colonies of the sixteenth century had, to judge by the quantity of mainland pottery, become Mycenaean settlements by the end of the following century.

A dramatic change in the relations between Mycenaean Greece and Crete seems to have occurred in the fifteenth century. About 1450 many cities in Crete were destroyed, although Cnossos was only slightly damaged. This destruction has often been linked with the tremendous volcanic explosion which shattered the island of Thera (Santorini) about eighty miles north of Crete—a disaster similar to that of Krakatoa in 1883. Since the latest Minoan pottery found at Thera can be dated to about 1500, the presumed time of the volcanic upheaval, it is evident that the resulting tidal waves and volcanic ash could not directly have leveled the Cretan cities, which survived for another fifty years, but they could have crushed ships in the shallow water of the northern harbors and killed vegetation for a number of years. Since primarily Greek Linear B tablets were found in the wreckage of the palace at Cnossos which was burned down in the period 1400 to 1375, it is easy to argue, thinking of the legend of the mythical Athenian hero Theseus, that Mycenaean Greeks, taking advantage of the weakening of Crete and the loss of its *thalassocracy* (control of the sea), invaded the island about 1450, destroyed many cities, and established themselves in Cnossos. When for reasons completely unknown Cnossos was destroyed in 1400 or shortly thereafter, the surviving Mycenaeans may have returned to the mainland. Thereafter Crete continued to play a role in Aegean affairs—Homer speaks of Idomeneus of Cnossos and his eighty ships—but archaeological evidence demonstrates that the center of gravity in the Aegean world in the fourteenth and thirteenth centuries had shifted from Crete to the Mycenaean mainland.

Although settlements similar to Mycenae existed throughout the Peloponnesus, Attica, Boeotia, southern Thessaly, the Ionian islands, and elsewhere, the term "Mycenaean" is used collectively to embrace them all since Mycenae was the strongest state and chiefly responsible for the cultural unity which prevailed and also, possibly, for some sort of political unity. The Mycenaeans were aggressive people both as traders and warriors. The extent of their trade is vividly emphasized by the wide area in which Mycenaean pottery has been found. This range stretches from the bay of Naples (the island of Ischia) and Sicily in the west to Macedonia and Troy in the north and northeast. Mycenaean pottery was common in the Cyclades and in some places on the west coast of Asia Minor, especially in Miletus where there was a flourishing Mycenaean settlement, and also in Rhodes, which had a large Mycenaean community. Many Mycenaean remains have been discovered in Cyprus, and Mycenaean pottery has been found in sites along the Syrian coast from Ugarit (Ras Shamra) in the north, where there is evidence for a Mycenaean settlement, down to the Egyptian border, and in Egypt in various places along the Nile as far south as Aswan. Trade naturally led to relations, both diplomatic and military, with other powers. Some tantalizing evidence possibly concerning these relations has been preserved in the Hittite documents unearthed at Boghazköy.

Among the thousands of Hittite cuneiform tablets there are about twenty fragments, primarily from the fourteenth and thirteenth centuries, which definitely or probably mention a land and people called Ahhiyawa and Ahhiyawans. As early as 1924 a scholar argued that Ahhiyawans was the Hittite way of writing Akhaiwoi—Achaeans—who, according to Homer, were the dominant people among the Mycenaeans. Since that time there has been intense scholarly argument about the legitimacy of this identification of names and also about the location of the region Ahhiyawa. Those scholars who accept the equation Ahhiyawans = Akhaiwoi find in the tablets evidence for some of the activities of the Mycenaeans in the period of their greatest power. Also since the last years of the thirteenth century (or, according to Greek tradition, 1192–1183) are generally assigned to the Trojan War, the presence of Mycenaean Achaeans in Asia Minor, it is hoped, may provide some background for the war immortalized by Homer.

Of the many suggestions for the location of the "kingdom" of Ahhiyawa, only one need be mentioned here: the region of northwestern Asia Minor subsequently known as the Troad. This proposal can be linked with the arrival of the proto-Greeks in the Greek mainland around the end of the third millennium. It is possible that at that time there was a dual push from the Balkans, one group migrating into Greece and the other across the Dardanelles into northwest Anatolia. Thus, those who entered Greece and those who established the sixth settlement of Troy could both have been proto-Greeks, one group or tribe of which was called whatever the current form of Achaean was, a form which ultimately became Ahhiyawans for the Hittites and Achaeans for the Homeric Mycenaeans. The conclusion from this theory would seem to be that the Ahhiyawans mentioned in the Hittite documents were not Mycenaean Achaeans but people who had long lived in the region of the Troad. This notion that the founders of Troy VI and the proto-Greeks entering Greece were originally the same or related peoples, speaking the same or closely related languages (a homogeneity maintained in the following centuries by regular trade relations), finds artistic confirmation in the epics of Homer, in which no language barrier seems to exist between the Mycenaean Achaeans and the Trojans. It is also interesting to note that in the Linear B tablets fifty-eight personal names have been recognized which appear in Homer, and that twenty of these belong to the Trojans and their allies.[5]

Knowledge of Troy is based on archaeological research beginning in 1870 with Heinrich Schliemann's famous excavations at the Turkish mound of Hissarlik, which, after a careful study of the terrain on the basis of the data provided by the *Iliad,* he decided must be the site of the city of Priam. As a pioneer, he naturally made many mistakes in archaeological methods. Subsequent work at Troy and particularly the excavations undertaken by the University of Cincinnati from 1932 to 1938 have corrected many of his conclusions, notably his belief that Troy II was the city of Priam. Archaeologists now divide the history of Troy into nine distinct phases, although to some of them they assign subdivisions. The first settlement can be dated to the last centuries of the fourth millennium. Troy VI was established by a new people about 2000 B.C., at roughly the same time as the proto-Greeks are believed to have migrated into Greece. In the ensuing centuries it had many commercial contacts with the Mycenaean world. This flourishing community was so thoroughly destroyed about 1275 that archaeologists are in general agreement that it was the victim of a violent earthquake.

The next settlement, Troy VIIa, was a cultural continuation of the preceding one, but on a more modest scale. This city was ravaged and burned by man about the end of the thirteenth century. Although archaeology furnishes no evidence, beyond the presence of some contemporary Mycenaean pottery, that the Mycenaeans were responsible for this destruction, most scholars agree that Troy VIIa was the city made famous by Greek epic.[6] Since the literary source for the Trojan War, from which the whole later tradition was derived, is Homer, and since Homer lived some five centuries after the supposed date of the war, a definitive decision on the actuality of the Trojan War will probably never be possible. The brief discussion of the nature of oral poetry in the final pages of this chapter will make some suggestions regarding the use of the *Iliad* and *Odyssey* as evidence. One point in support of the probable "historicity" of the Trojan War can be made appropriately here.

Scholarship on the Catalogue of Ships and the Catalogue of Trojan Allies at the end of book 2 of the *Iliad* has often emphasized their essential reliability in reflecting late Mycenaean conditions.[7] Most of the places listed in the Achaean catalogue are now known through archaeology to have been inhabited in Mycenaean times, while some were abandoned permanently at the end of that period. There is no mention of the Dorians, who became prominent in Greece in the early years of the first millennium. The supposition seems likely that Mycenaean oral poets composed catalogues of the heroes who joined the expedition against Troy, and that in the course of time catalogues of heroes in other exploits may have been added to the catalogue of the heroes against Troy as the Trojan War became a central theme in the evolution of Greek epic. Since the briefer Trojan Catalogue contains no hint of the post-Mycenaean Aeolic and Ionian migrations to Asia Minor, it is probable that oral poets originally composed it on the basis of inadequate Mycenaean knowledge of Anatolia. In view of the facts that one catalogue lists forces about to engage in an overseas expedition and the other enumerates forces which presumably were to oppose it and that both seem to be of Mycenaean origin, it is reasonable to assume that they are concerned with an actual expedition to Asia Minor. It may be perverse to deny that that expedition was the one against Troy.

According to the Greek tradition, which is confirmed by archaeology, the Achaeans did not settle at Troy after destroying it. The excavations show that for about a generation after the sack of the citadel, the survivors continued to live in the ruins. Early in the twelfth century some unknown people, bringing a crude "knobbed ware" pottery, appeared on the scene and apparently blended with the remnants of the Trojans. These two periods are now known as Troy VIIb, 1 and 2. For about four hundred years following 1100 the site seems to have been deserted, but in the Greek colonizing period of the eighth and seventh centuries Troy VIII, largely a Greek settlement, arose. This was the Troy visited by Alexander the Great at the beginning of his Asiatic expedition. Subsequently the site was extensively rebuilt by the Romans, and with this Troy IX the history of ancient Troy came to an end.

If the fall of Troy VIIa is correctly dated to about 1200, then its fate coincided with disasters which occurred in the Near East in the same general period. In these years the Hittite Empire in Asia Minor crumbled, many cities in Anatolia and Syria were destroyed, and Egypt was exposed to at least three serious attacks. The causes of all these disturbances are obscure, but they certainly are connected somehow with the Phrygian migration into Asia Minor and the activity of the so-called Peoples of the Sea. The Phrygians, who may have entered Anatolia by crossing the Bosporus or the Hellespont—it is worth noting that in Homer Phrygians are listed as allies of the Trojans—or equally possibly from the northeast, seem to have been chiefly responsible for the fall of the Hittite Empire and subsequently to have become the dominant power in Anatolia for several centuries. The Peoples of the Sea were a composite group;[8] some may have come from regions north of the Aegean, some may have been inhabitants of Aegean islands, and others undoubtedly were tribes which had been driven out of Asia Minor by the invading Phrygians. The evidence for these peoples comes from Egyptian documents. A great inscription in the temple at Karnak tells how the Pharaoh Merneptah (1225–1215) defeated a coalition of Libyans and northerners coming from all lands and Peoples of the Sea. Among these Libyan allies, whose names are difficult to transliterate from the hieroglyphics, were a group called Akaiwasha or Ekwesh. Some scholars have tried to equate them with the Ahhiyawans recorded by the Hittites, but the Egyptian statement—if interpreted correctly—that they were circumcised seems to rule out any identification with the Achaeans.

The invasions of these Peoples of the Sea and the northerners reached their peak in the reign of Ramses III (1198–1167). The most serious one occurred in the year 1191. Fortunately a vivid, if rhetorical and exaggerated, account of it is provided by the inscriptions and relief sculptures in Ramses' funerary temple at Medinet Habu. Numerous tribes, presumably starting from southern Asia Minor, moved southward by land and sea. They left a trail of devastation as they advanced through Syria. It was at this time that Ugarit was destroyed, never to be restored. Ramses led the Egyptian forces against the invaders and, in a naval and land battle, "utterly" defeated them. Among the members of this confederation, the inscriptions list the "Peleset" and the "Denyen." The Peleset were the Philistines, who, after their repulse by Egypt, established themselves along the southern coast of Syria and gave their name to the region—Palestine. The Denyen may possibly have been the Danaans, who in the *Iliad* are identified with the Achaeans and Argives. Menelaus' and Odysseus' stories in the *Odyssey* of their adventures and raids in Syria and Egypt may reflect some aspects of the unsettled conditions in the eastern Mediterranean in the early twelfth century.

In the years following the repulse of the attack on Egypt in 1191, there is little or no evidence for Mycenaean activity in the east beyond what can be gleaned from archaeological findings concerning the continued existence of Mycenaean settlements in places like Miletus, Rhodes, and Cyprus. The Near East in the last centuries of the second millennium and in the early centuries of the first was undergoing a great transition. The Hittite Empire in Asia Minor collapsed, but neo-Hittite kingdoms emerged in Cilicia and northern Syria, and a Phrygian kingdom gradually took shape in Anatolia. To the east an Assyrian kingdom was emerging in Mesopotamia; and to the south, with the Egyptians now confined to Egypt, first the Philistines and then the Hebrews developed their states in Palestine. The last major exploit of the Mycenaeans in these troubled areas seems to have been the Trojan War.

The appropriate word to describe the situation in Greece in this period is "obscure." Mycenaean civilization, which had reached its zenith in the fourteenth century and the first half of the thirteenth, began to decline thereafter. In the following generations Greece drifted into what is called the "Dark Age," dark both because of the low level of civilization and because of the extreme dearth of reliable historical information. This Dark Age comprises a period of at least four hundred years, for it is not until the eighth century that some reasonably certain historical data begin to become available. Obscure as these centuries are to the modern student, they were a vitally important era in the evolution of Greek history, for in that period the old Mycenaean order of things waned and a new order was born which ultimately developed into the Greece of recorded history.

UNTIL QUITE recently it was customary to attribute the disintegration of Mycenaean civilization and the advent of the Dark Age almost exclusively to the so-called Dorian invasion. Greek tradition associated the coming of the Dorians with the return of the Heraclidae. The basic theme in the different versions of this tradition was that Eurystheus banished from Mycenae the sons of Heracles and their followers, who, after many adventures and with the help of the Athenians, returned to the Peloponnesus and took possession of their rightful heritage. In this story, colored by patriotism and propaganda, the arrival of the Dorians was interpreted not as an invasion of newcomers, but as a return to the Peloponnesus of its legitimate rulers. It is interesting to note that this legend shows that the Dorians had appropriated the Mycenaean hero Heracles. The legend became accepted as fact, for even so scientific a historian as Thucydides (1.12.3) states that the Dorians with the Heraclidae took possession of the Peloponnesus eighty years after the Trojan War. Since in most Greek chronological schemes the Trojan War was assigned to what would be the equivalent of the early twelfth century, Thucydides' statement points to the end of that century for the arrival of the Dorians.

The ancients, then, described the coming of the Dorians as the return of the Heraclidae; the expression "Dorian invasion" is a modern invention, and an unfortunate one, for it implies an organized military movement. In keeping with this notion of invasion a rather romantic picture of the coming of the Dorians was developed, largely under the influence of "Nordic" theories. According to this interpretation, the Dorians, a Greek tribe which had remained behind in the mountainous regions north and northwest of Greece, migrated into the peninsula towards the end of the twelfth century. They were a vigorous, warlike people, and they had little difficulty in overthrowing Mycenaean civilization, grown soft from too much luxury, especially since the Dorians' iron weapons were far superior to the bronze weapons of the Mycenaeans. In addition to bringing iron, the Dorians also introduced the custom of cremation and a new style in pottery, which is known as geometric. After causing considerable destruction in central Greece they crossed into the Peloponnesus, apparently sailing from Naupactus, and soon became masters of practically the whole region except the mountainous Arcadia, where many of the Mycenaeans sought refuge.

Archaeological excavations in central Greece and the Peloponnesus have shown much of this picture to be false, but unfortunately, as often happens, the archaeological data themselves are hard to interpret. Archaeology points definitely to a decline in Mycenaean civilization towards the close of the thirteenth century, a decline which can be detected most easily in the deterioration in the quality, both technical and artistic, of the pottery. The building activity is also interesting and undoubtedly significant if one were sure of how to explain the facts. In the latter years of the century the walls of the citadels at Mycenae, Tiryns, and Athens were strengthened and elaborate steps were taken to ensure that there would be an adequate water supply within the fortifications. Such measures look like precautions against possible invaders, but who would the invaders have been? According to Greek tradition the Dorians did not arrive until over a century later. It is well to remember that this was the general period when the northerners of all lands and the Peoples of the Sea were causing havoc in the Aegean, Syria, and Egypt, and when a Phrygian invasion was threatening the Hittite Empire. Such widespread devastation could well have persuaded the rulers in Greece to strengthen their defenses at home. The general chaos in the Near East must have paralyzed the sea lanes; this would have had a crippling effect on Mycenaean trade, whose extent is revealed by the quantity of Mycenaean pottery found in regions as far apart as Thrace and Egypt. Trade was clearly essential to supply the necessary imports of foodstuffs and raw materials for the large population suggested by the number of Mycenaean sites detected in Greece. The decline of trade could have caused much distress, and this distress may have been one of the causes leading to expeditions such as the Trojan War.

The disturbances which were plaguing the Mycenaeans apparently reached a peak about the beginning of the twelfth century. Some time around 1200 various sites were abandoned, such as the houses outside the walls of Athens. Many of the great palaces were burned, including those at Iolcus in Thessaly on the Pagasaean Gulf, Pylos, Tiryns, and Mycenaean Sparta. At Mycenae the buildings beyond the walls were burned, and at a somewhat later time the citadel was destroyed. What was the cause of these devastations and abandonments of sites all over

Mycenaean Greece? The answer is still a mystery. If the Dorians were responsible, they left no identifying signs behind; and it should be noted that 1200 is about a century earlier than the traditional date for the coming of the Dorians. Feuds between cities—and also within cities—possibly contributed to the chaos. The depression caused by the disruption of trade with the East may have weakened what political unity existed in the Mycenaean world and caused one state to try to profit by despoiling another. One of the main themes in Greek epic tradition was the war of Argos against Thebes.[9]

The violent upheavals of these generations brought an end to the great days of Mycenaean civilization. All the people, naturally, did not perish, but the whole way of life must have changed greatly. The breakdown of the cultural—and possibly the political—unity is revealed by the emergence of various local types of pottery. It seems clear that with the destruction of the palaces, the great kingdoms collapsed. Some of the sites continued to be inhabited, but all aspects of civilization were on a much lower plane. The best example of continuity is provided by Athens. It was not destroyed as so many cities were around 1200, but the strengthening of the walls, the great pains taken to guarantee an adequate water supply within the area of the citadel, and the subsequent abandonment of the houses beyond the northeast walls—all to be dated in the same general period—suggest that Athens felt itself threatened by the same forces which were causing so much ruin in other parts of Greece. As a result of escaping the destruction which befell Greece as a whole, Athens became the chief city on the mainland for several centuries.

The development of Athenian pottery is interesting, for it reveals a continuous process with no violent breaks. In the twelfth century the pottery was of a debased Mycenaean type—good evidence that Athens was affected by the troubles harassing the Greek world—but from this there gradually evolved protogeometric, which in turn passed into Attic geometric and then proto-Attic. Protogeometric pottery is particularly important for the light it throws on the history of the period. Recent study has proved that Athens was the original home of this type of pottery and that in the course of the eleventh century it began to spread from Athens to other parts of the Greek world. Since tradition states and archaeology proves that Athens was not occupied by the Dorians, it seems certain that the old idea—that the Dorians either brought geometric pottery with them or created it after establishing themselves in Greece—must be abandoned. It is most probable also that the other innovations of the period—cremation burials and the use of iron weapons—which formerly were ascribed to the Dorians did not owe their origin to them. In Athens and various parts of Attica and also at other places in the Greek world which apparently had no connections with the Dorians, cremation burials and iron weapons have been discovered going back to the thirteenth century. On the basis of present evidence it is reasonable to assume that these two phenomena came to Greece from the East. In any case, it seems clear that three of the chief innovations of the period—protogeometric pottery, cremation, and iron weapons—do not, as formerly thought, imply the presence and influence of the Dorians.[10]

The notion that the invasion or migration of the Dorians was responsible for the collapse of Mycenaean civilization does not conform to either archaeological or traditional evidence. Archaeology places the destruction of many Mycenaean settlements in the beginning of the twelfth century, but Greek tradition dated the arrival of the Dorians and the Heraclidae about a hundred years later. A further difficulty is that so far archaeologists have found no material evidence for the presence of the Dorians before the tenth century. Scholars have emphasized how unrealistic it is to believe that the Dorians remained in isolation in the north for the best part of a millennium and then in the twelfth century burst into the Greek world still speaking a language basically the same as that of the other tribes long established in Greece. Faced with this dilemma, several scholars now argue that the "Dorians" were among those tribes which entered Greece about the beginning of the second millennium.[11] These tribes, speaking some Indo-European dialect, fought and blended with the earlier inhabitants for generations, and in the course of time their Indo-European dialect, by amalgamating with the native language or languages, gradually became Greek. These embryonic Greeks for centuries lived scattered throughout Greece from Thessaly to the Peloponnesus, and it is likely that in certain areas Greek dialects began to take shape for which there is no evidence until the period of the Dark Age.

The only Greek language for which there is proof in the second millennium is the one represented by the Linear B tablets of Cnossos, dated about 1400, and of Pylos and Mycenae, dated about 1200. These particular tablets, which are concerned primarily with governmental inventories, were preserved because of the respective conflagrations, but there is no reason to doubt that similar documents were in use from the time that states became sufficiently wealthy and strong to require some system of record keeping. The splendor of the shaft graves suggests that the Mycenaeans of the seventeenth and sixteenth centuries had so increased in power that their authority probably extended over neighboring settlements. It is likely that other great citadels developed in similar fashion. Since the administration of such kingdoms required the keeping of records and accounts, Cretan scribes were employed who, adapting the evolving Minoan Linear B script to the needs of the Greek language, produced the Linear B tablets. The similarity of the language found on the tablets at Cnossos, Mycenae, Pylos, and Thebes suggests that there was a common official scribal language. It seems obvious that these tablets and the language written on them were instruments only of the residents of the citadels—the kings, the aristocrats, and the bureaucrats. The rural and illiterate commoners, unaffected by the cultural changes taking place in the citadels, continued to speak the Greek language, which was developing and gradually assuming dialectical characteristics, such as Doric, Ionic, and Aeolic, which are known for the Greek world from the Dark Age on.

If the Dorians belonged to the population of the Mycenaean world, how does one explain the collapse of Mycenaean civilization, ordinarily attributed to the Dorian "invasion"? One must remember that the end of the thirteenth century and probably the entire twelfth century were times of trouble for the whole eastern Mediterranean. If the Trojan War occurred in this chaotic period, the war and its consequences must have contributed to the general confusion. Thucydides (1.12) remarks: "The late return of the Hellenes from Ilium caused many revolutions, and factions ensued almost everywhere; and it was the citizens thus driven into exile who founded the cities." If one keeps in mind the absolutism of the Mycenaean rulers, suggested by their palaces and citadels and by the contents of the Linear B tablets; the contemporary economic troubles; the rivalry and wars between Mycenaean states, such as Argos against Thebes; and possible natural causes like famine or plague, it is easy to imagine that conditions were ripe for an uprising of the downtrodden commoners. It is not necessary to visualize a general simultaneous uprising. The successful overthrow of the hated ruling class in one citadel may have sparked similar attempts elsewhere until the wave of destruction spread all over the Mycenaean world. Certainly the masses, who were workers or slaves in and around the massive citadels, were in a better position to wreck the mighty fortresses than new invaders from some backward northwest region.

In the Dark Age and thereafter the Dorians in Greece were located primarily in the Peloponnesus, which had been the chief center of Mycenaean power. Greek tradition about the early Dorians does not speak of their migration but of the *return* of the Heraclidae to their rightful home. If one accepts the interpretation that the "proto-Dorians" were among the "proto-Greeks" who migrated into Greece about the beginning of the second millennium, then the legend about the return of the

Heraclidae can be interpreted as a fanciful story of how native Dorians returned themselves to their rightful position by overthrowing a tyrannical ruling class, some of whom, according to legends, may have been aliens from Asia Minor, Phoenicia, and Egypt. This solution of the problems inherent in the concept of a Dorian invasion, although it treats rather cavalierly many of the colorful legends about the coming of the Dorians, does eliminate some of the difficulties present in the traditional account, such as the contradiction in dates and the strange phenomenon of Dorians, after centuries of isolation in the north, speaking a dialect intelligible to tribes long established in Greece. It explains also why archaeologists have been unable to find material evidence for the new destructive invaders, for if, instead of being invaders, the Dorians had been part of the population of the Mycenaean Peloponnesus, obviously there were no new artifacts to be discovered. What archaeology shows is a continuation of Mycenaean civilization on a much reduced scale, a condition which would have been the natural consequence of the destruction of the highly organized and centralized Mycenaean governments.

Everything about the collapse of Mycenaean civilization is obscure. The new theory of a general and continuing social upheaval against the ruling classes, based on archaeological and linguistic arguments, may be too imaginative, although it does eliminate some of the old dilemmas. One may expect heated debates among archaeologists, linguists, and historians on the validity or weakness of the proposal. The solution to the problem, if such a thing is possible, will have to come from specialists. Here it is necessary only to stress the appalling confusion which must have existed in Greece in the twelfth and eleventh centuries and even later as a result of the Dorian migration or of the social uprisings. There was much destruction, abandonment of sites, and shifting of populations before new settlements began to take shape. Since these events ushered in the Dark Age, they will be the subject of the next chapter.

With the fall of the mighty fortresses—Mycenae, Tiryns, and others—which symbolized the age, a phase of Greek history never again to be paralleled, although often glorified imaginatively in later Greek poetry and art, was over. Consequently, before turning to the period of the Dark Age, in which a new society developed out of the wreckage of the old, it will be useful to characterize briefly certain aspects of Mycenaean civilization.

THE SOURCES of information available for trying to gain some insight into the Mycenaean way of life are twofold: the material remains brought to light by archaeologists, including, of course, the Linear B tablets, and the Homeric poems. There has been, and still is, so much dispute about how the evidence furnished by the epics should be interpreted that it is essential to understand the nature of the problems involved in any attempt to use Homer as a historical source. The main problem can be stated simply. The *Iliad* deals with various events which are supposed to have occurred in the tenth year of the Achaean siege of Troy, while the *Odyssey* is primarily concerned with the adventures experienced by Odysseus on his return to Ithaca from Troy. The sack of Troy, however, should be dated to about 1180 according to Greek tradition and somewhat earlier according to many archaeologists; but Homer in the view of the Greeks lived in the ninth century, and on the basis of the internal evidence of the poems themselves he should be dated probably a century later. Four or five hundred years, therefore, separated Homer from the events which he was describing, and the question naturally arises concerning the accuracy of the tradition to which he fell heir. In the days before Schliemann's excavations the subject matter of the *Iliad* and the *Odyssey* was considered to be myth; after the startling discoveries at Troy and Mycenae the pendulum swung in the direction of accepting the two epics as basically historical accounts of real events. Researches carried on in this century in the field of oral epic poetry have demonstrated that whatever answer should be given to the question must be based on some understanding of the nature of oral poetry.

Oral epic poetry and its singers are phenomena characteristic of many illiterate or semiliterate societies.[12] Recent studies of the phenomena in Yugoslavia and in remoter parts of Greece, where oral poetry and its singers still exist (although they are rapidly disappearing with the advance of "civilization"), have provided many insights into the subject. These poets are definitely preservers of traditions, but they are far more than mere memorizers of traditional poetry which they have inherited from their predecessors. Through long years of apprenticeship and practice they have steeped themselves in the rhythms and basic themes of the poetry, and above all in the formulas. These formulas are phrases, running from half a line to several lines, which express in the appropriate rhythms many ideas basic to oral poetry. The apprentice, by listening constantly to older poets, learns hundreds of these formulas in much the same way in which a person can learn a new language by ear. The result is that after living with the poetry for years, the formulas, themes, and rhythms become so much a part of the poet that he instinctively thinks and composes in such terms. He does not consciously memorize a tale; he learns the basic facts—the skeleton—of many stories, but when he gives a performance, although he preserves the tradition in his subject matter, he also becomes an individual creator. That is, he does not deliberately change the basic story, since that would be to falsify history, but he feels free, depending on the occasion and the nature of his audience, to add or omit episodes, to introduce new characters, to change the order of events, to bring in humor or pathos—in short, to make the tale his own. This ability to embellish skillfully and to adapt the song to the requirements of the particular performance is the sign of an accomplished poet. Cases are known where a poet has heard a long story for the first time and then immediately sung it himself, remaining true to the basic facts, but embellishing it so much with touches of characterization and with different episodes culled from his own store of similar themes that his version is considerably longer than, and in many ways quite different from, the one he had just heard. Such feats and the endless variety that a good oral poet can add to the bare framework of a story fully justify the statement of a student of the subject that "the singer of tales is at once the tradition and an individual creator."

Readers of Homer will immediately recognize that the picture of the bard Demodocus in the eighth book of the *Odyssey* corresponds very closely to the brief characterization of oral poets just given. And when one realizes that a third of the verses of the *Iliad* and the *Odyssey* are repeated or contain repeated phrases—that is, formulas—then it is obvious that Homer himself was an oral poet. Oral poetry, however, is a cumulative thing to which each generation of bards makes a contribution. Clearly there had been a long tradition of such poets before Homer, but all the others are anonymous. The conclusion must be that he was the greatest of them all, and, since the *Iliad* and the *Odyssey* are indissolubly connected with his name, presumably he was the poet who, using the wealth of oral material available and under the inspiration of his genius, sang the epics in approximately the forms in which they have come down through classical Greece to the modern world. No information has been preserved as to when and how the Homeric poems were first recorded in writing, but a possible suggestion is that they were dictated by Homer himself. After all, since every oral poet is an original creator as well as a preserver of tradition, the poems, if dictated by a later oral poet, would have borne the stamp and hence, presumably, the name of that poet rather than of Homer. This was the period when, in the Near East, the Assyrian kings were collecting all the lore of the past for their great library and the Hebrews were recording those traditions of their early history which form the oldest strata of the Old Testament. In these generations many eastern cultural influences came to bear on the Greeks, and among them may have been the idea of preserving for all time the accounts of their great past, which had attained their finest expression on the lips of Homer.

When confronted with the Homeric poems, the historian, while admitting the basic literary unity of the *Iliad* and *Odyssey* as created by the genius of Homer, cannot fail to recognize that in the matter of historical data he is dealing with a mosaic built up through many generations and centuries. The language of the epics is a reflection of this mosaic quality. The dialect is predominantly Ionic, but there are many traces of archaic Aeolic and Arcadian. Presumably, therefore, the earliest songs about these subjects were sung in those dialects, but after the migration of many Greeks to the west coast of Asia Minor, the epic songs were developed in Ionic, which had many similarities with Arcadian. The presence in the largely Ionic *Iliad* and *Odyssey* of archaic Aeolic and Arcadian forms points to their retention from a much earlier period. This conclusion is confirmed by the fact that many of the Aeolic and Arcadian forms are preserved in formulaic expressions which, for metrical reasons, could not be changed to Ionic. Since it is the nature of oral poetry through all its mutations to preserve the basic facts of the story, the historian is probably not being too credulous if he believes that the story of an expedition to Troy is based on a true tradition, but he should be ready to admit that in the mouths of the oral poets one episode, out of possibly many similar ones, was magnified far beyond its inherent importance. Since songs about the expedition presumably began to be sung soon after the event, probably in the lifetime of the participants or at least in that of their sons, it is easier to believe that persons like Agamemnon and Achilles actually existed and took part in the expedition than that they are purely imaginary. But, in keeping with the nature of oral poetry, all sorts of additions could have been made. The shield of Ajax, for example, is always described by the formula "like a tower." Archaeology, however, has shown that such shields went out of use well before the time of the Trojan War. Possibly, therefore, the hero Ajax in reality belonged to an earlier age and another series of tales, but was incorporated into the Trojan story by the oral poets.

The Near East surely was the ultimate inspiration for some of the episodes which, in altered guise, found a place in the *Iliad,* and probably some tales in the *Odyssey* had an Egyptian origin.[13] Archaeology proves a considerable exchange of commodities between the Aegean world and the Near East, and it is only reasonable to assume that ideas accompanied commodities. The Sumerians had inaugurated an epic tradition far back in the third millennium, and that tradition, with changes and additions, had passed from the Sumerians to the Akkadians and to the Babylonians; and from the Babylonians to the people of Ugarit, to the Assyrians, and to the Hurrians; and from the Hurrians to the Hittites. When one compares the similarities between the story of Gilgamesh, his divine mother Ninsun, and his friend Enkidu in the orginally Sumerian *Epic of Gilgamesh*, and that of Achilles, his goddess mother Thetis, and his friend Patroclus in the *Iliad*, remembering that in each case the friend was killed in place of the hero by decree of the gods, and that the death was followed by the lament of the hero for his friend, then the evidence for oriental influence on Greek epic is hard to deny.

These remarks should be sufficient to suggest that a historian would be naive if he should try to base his picture of Mycenaean civilization on the evidence of the Greek epics. Homer preserves the memory of an expedition which undoubtedly took place and the names of various persons who probably played a role in the events. The formulaic epithets of some of the heroes are clearly old—in the case of Ajax going back earlier than the Trojan War. In places, especially in the catalogues of Achaean and Trojan forces in the second book of the *Iliad*, there seems to be a reasonably accurate memory of the location of the various tribes in the pre-Dorian period. Many other echoes of the Mycenaean Age are also embedded in the epics, such as the almost consistent description of weapons as made of bronze, but, as will become clear from a quick glance at the evidence of the Linear B tablets, the society—the way of life—depicted in Homer is very different from that suggested by the great Mycenaean fortresses. This should cause no surprise if one keeps in mind the nature of oral poetry and the fact that the oral poet is a creator as well as a preserver of tradition. As generations and centuries passed by, as memories of the realities of the Mycenaean Age grew dimmer, as poet after poet added his own contributions and observations to the mass of material which Homer ultimately welded into his masterpieces, more and more the picture of a way of life which was characteristic of the Mycenaeans was transmuted into a portrayal of the society familiar to the poets. Inconsistencies, anachronisms, archaisms abound, but, taking the epics as a whole—and that is what the historian with all due precautions must do—the picture of society which emerges is one that belongs somewhere in the Dark Age. Since the development of these oral epics, except for some rather obvious later accretions, ceased in the eighth century, that date can be taken as the latest possible time for the way of life presented. And since it is the nature of oral poets to try to achieve an archaic atmosphere, it is a logical inference that the way of life depicted by Homer is somewhat older than that current in his own generation. The ninth or tenth century has been suggested, and the suggestion seems reasonable.[14] The information on social, economic, and political conditions which can be gleaned from Homer, therefore, will be part of the evidence considered in the following chapter.

Since the Homeric epics can be used as evidence for the Mycenaean

Age (ca. 1400–1200) only in a very limited and dangerously subjective sense, any attempt to characterize that age must be based primarily on the archaeological findings, including, of course, the information provided by the Linear B tablets. The Mycenaean world covered a wide area, from Thessaly in the north to Crete in the south, and from Ithaca in the west to Rhodes and Cyprus in the east. A full account of Mycenaean civilization, naturally, would have to take cognizance of the finds from all the excavated sites, of which those with the most familiar names are—besides Mycenae—Argos, Pylos, Tiryns, Athens, Eleusis, Orchomenus, and Thebes; but since evidence of varying dates gathered from so many places is confusing even to the specialist, the few remarks made here will be restricted to Mycenae. This procedure seems justifiable, despite the revealing excavations at Pylos, for not only does Mycenae symbolize the age, but also the archaeological activity there has been unusually thorough.

The rocky hill of Mycenae had been inhabited at least since the third millennium. The remarkable shaft graves which Schliemann unearthed, now dated to the seventeenth and sixteenth centuries, are clear evidence that by that time powerful rulers were in control of the site. In the following generations there was much building and rebuilding, but it is very difficult to assign the shattered remains to a definite period or purpose. Most archaeologists, however, believe that the construction activity reached its peak towards the middle of the thirteenth century.[15]

Mycenae was a fortress rather than a city, likened by an excavator to the Kremlin or the Tower of London. Within the citadel were located the buildings which housed those essential to the functioning of the state: the huge palace of the king, the large houses of the higher military and civil officials, and smaller ones for soldiers, scribes, artisans, and slaves. The majority of the civilian population apparently lived in settlements below the citadel and in the adjacent low hills wherever water and fertile land were available. Probably many of these people could seek refuge within the citadel in times of danger. The citadel was surrounded by walls constructed from great blocks of limestone, so huge that the ancients believed that only the Cyclopes could have put them in place. The original height of these walls is unknown, but the thickness averaged some 20 feet. The main entrance to the citadel was the famous Lion Gate, about 10 feet wide and slightly higher, surmounted by a lintel of conglomerate weighing some 20 tons. Above this lintel in the "relieving triangle" was the relief—two lions rampant, one on either side of an upright pillar. This relief, almost the oldest example of monumental sculpture found in Greece, is amazingly effective. It almost certainly had a religious and heraldic significance—the lions as attendants of the

Mother Goddess (?) guarding the entrance to the citadel and to the palace of the reigning king.

From the Lion Gate the only street in the citadel that was more than an alley led to the palace, a street whose memory was preserved in the Homeric formula "wide-wayed Mycenae." As one walked along this street towards the palace, the remarkable Grave Circle lay on the right. This circle, about 85 feet in diameter, was surrounded by a double wall of vertical slabs. It was in this area that Schliemann, and later Stamatakes, unearthed the six royal shaft graves and found the splendid treasures. The graves, dating from the seventeenth and sixteenth centuries, were marked by stelae, some of them sculptured. The area must have been considered sacred, for a later king, who around 1250 had the citadel enlarged, caused the Cyclopean wall to run in such a way as to include the graves within the confines of the citadel. It was probably the same king who created the Grave Circle by erecting the circular wall around the graves. Since no buildings were subsequently raised over them, it seems that the area continued to be regarded as holy ground. The preservation of this Grave Circle provides strong, almost irrefutable, evidence that in the Mycenaean period there was a cult of the dead—at least, of those who had been mighty when living.

Among the wonders of the Mycenaean Age the *tholos,* or beehive, tombs, each the last resting place for a king and his immediate family, rank high, if not supreme. Of the approximately sixty-five *tholos* tombs which have been explored on the mainland of Greece, the most breathtaking is the so-called Treasury of Atreus, located a short distance to the south of the citadel at Mycenae. This tomb was approached by an entrance way *(dromos)* about 20 feet wide and almost 120 feet long, cut straight into the hillside and lined on either side with excellent stone work. The doorway of the tomb itself is over 17 feet in height. The huge stone lintel over the inner side of this doorway is about 26 feet long and is estimated to weigh about 100 tons. Architecturally it plays an important role in sustaining the tremendous weight of the vault rising above it. The *tholos* itself is approximately 48 feet in diameter and 43 in height, narrowing gradually as it rises to the summit, which is covered with one large stone. Since the style of the stonework in the Treasury of Atreus is very similar to that of the Lion Gate, it is quite possible that the king who was buried in this tomb was the same ruler who was responsible for the extension of the Cyclopean walls of the citadel, the Lion Gate, the Grave Circle, and also for the enlargement of the palace.

These remarkable buildings at Mycenae and elsewhere in the Mycenaean world bear eloquent witness to the power and wealth of the Mycenaean rulers. Because of the lack of historical documents, nothing can be learned about individual Mycenaeans beyond what one is willing to accept in the epic tradition, but the superb architectural and engineering achievements and the brilliant art revealed in frescoes, pottery, metalwork, and gem cutting, all influenced by Minoan Crete, prove that intellectual and aesthetic levels were high among some elements, at least, of the Mycenaean population. Such building programs, with strong emphasis on royalty, living or dead, suggest that the governments in the various kingdoms were thoroughly centralized, and this impression is confirmed by the information which can be obtained from the Linear B tablets.

Some 4,000 tablets have been found so far at Cnossos, Pylos, and to a lesser extent at Mycenae and Thebes. Most of them are fragmentary and many lack headings, which make decipherment and interpretation all the more difficult. The tablets from each site apparently refer to transactions of a particular year—the year in which the palace was destroyed—and, as noted before, they owe their preservation to having been baked in those conflagrations. Although the documents from Cnossos are probably to be dated about 1400 and those from Pylos and Mycenae about 1200, the script and the dialect of the three groups are almost identical. This conservatism suggests that the writing of accounts was the responsibility of professionals, but since about forty different "hands" have been detected in the Pylos tablets and about seventy in those from Cnossos, the suggestion has been made that the writers were bureaucrats in charge of different departments rather than full-time professional scribes.[16] Since all these tablets were found in or around the palaces and since they are concerned with such matters as inventories of materials, lists of personnel, assessments, distribution of commodities, and granting of rations, the inference seems sure that the whole economy of each kingdom—or certainly the major part of it—was under the direct control of the central government. The great palace complexes must have been like royal factories where all sorts of craftsmen—potters, bronzesmiths, goldsmiths, carpenters, bowmakers, carders, spinners, weavers, perfume makers—worked, divided into departments and supervised by bureaucrats whose tentacles stretched from the palaces themselves to the remotest districts of the kingdoms in their efforts to control the procurement and distribution of materials and commodities. The division of labor was highly developed, as can be seen from the large number of crafts and professions mentioned, and much of the work was done by slaves, including the as yet little understood slaves of the goddess (or god). Many of the documents are concerned with the working and status of the land. Unfortunately they are capable of different interpretations, but on the whole they give the impression that the holding of land by individuals was somehow conditional on the rendering of services or the furnishing of the necessary quotas of products.

At the head of these highly organized states stood the king, *wanax*, whose powers, civil, military, and religious, must have been very extensive, if not absolute. Beneath him, but not necessarily next in rank, was the *lawagetas*—literally, the leader of the people. Many scholars have argued that he was an army leader, which is quite possible, but his connection with the military has not yet been proved. Then there were various other officials, some of them clearly important, but it is rather rash to equate them with barons, counts, and the like, and the *lawagetas* with duke, for by introducing the terminology of feudalism with all its associations, the impression is given that much more is known about Mycenaean society than actually is the case. One other title should be mentioned, *basileus*, which in historical Greece came to mean king but in the Linear B tablets referred to a minor official, possibly the ruler of a village.[17]

The more one studies the information provided by these tablets, the more evident it becomes that they reflect a society very different from that depicted in the Homeric poems. The nearest parallels are to be sought in the Near East—in the contemporary Ugarit or older cities like the Sumerian and Semitic Mari—for the documents preserved from these places reveal the same type of control and monopoly over all aspects of life being exercised from the palace. When the Mycenaean kingdoms were destroyed, the whole elaborate and bureaucratic organization of government and society disappeared also. As that society faded away the vocabulary peculiar to it perished with it. Homer lacks most of the bureaucratic vocabulary present in the Linear B tablets. Down through the centuries, naturally, the oral poets kept certain recollections of things Mycenaean alive, especially by means of the traditional formulas, but by the time that Homer gave the *Iliad* and *Odyssey* their almost final forms, the memories had grown so dim and confused that the poems reflected the conditions of the Dark Age much more than they did the society which had existed in the great days of Mycenaean civilization.

2
The Dark Age

T HE DISCUSSION IN the preceding chapter of some of the problems concerning the decline of Mycenaean civilization and the migration or uprising of the Dorians should suggest why the period of Greek history which followed the Mycenaean Age is commonly known as the Dark Age. The term is justified both because of the lower level to which civilization sank and because of the difficulty, with the source material at hand, in penetrating the darkness which encompassed the whole Aegean world. It is not until the eighth century that more satisfactory information begins to become available and that occasional contacts between the Greeks and the Assyrians and Egyptians provide some welcome chronological landmarks. This long period, roughly from 1200 to 750, is one of great significance, for in it the Greeks, after the chaos caused by migrations or uprisings subsided, settled down in their historical homes and laid the foundations for their future remarkable civilization.

The basic sources for the study of the Dark Age are the Homeric poems. Although the *Iliad* deals with a short period in the Trojan War and the *Odyssey* with the return home of Odysseus and with the troubles his kingdom had been experiencing in his absence, the remarks made previously on the technique of oral poetry should assist the reader in recognizing that the conditions reflected in the poems are, on the whole, those with which Homer and his predecessors were familiar. One would probably not go far wrong, then, if he accepted the *Iliad* and the *Odyssey* as providing a picture of life primarily as it was in the ninth century and especially among the "Ionian" Greeks who had crossed to the coast of Asia Minor, for it was among these Ionians that the two epics developed into their final forms. It is well to remember, moreover, that a custom is not necessarily a static phenomenon. The custom of today is what it is because it has evolved from the custom of yesterday, and in turn it will develop into the custom of tomorrow. From this point of view, then, it is reasonable to consider the *Iliad* and *Odyssey* not as revealing the conditions of some arbitrarily selected date but as reflecting a way of life which not only had roots in the past but also was to continue largely unchanged into the future. Homer and his predecessors, of course, were poets and not historians, and consequently one will not find in the epics systematic discussions of historical problems, but the careful reader of these wonderful poems will discover that they contain a rich store of information on social, economic, religious, ethical, and political customs, especially as they prevailed among the upper classes.

Another contemporary source for the Dark Age—at least for its closing phases—is the Boeotian poet Hesiod. His precise date is unknown, but the internal evidence of his poems suggests that his *floruit* was around 700. Hesiod then presumably lived some half a century later than the largely arbitrary date (750) given above for the close of the Dark Age, but since Boeotia was a rather backward region and since Hesiod was in the tradition of the Greek mainland oral poets, it seems reasonable to believe that he gives an insight into ways and beliefs not only of his own time but also of earlier generations whose customs were similar. Anyone who reads the *Works and Days,* however, will almost surely get the impression from the earnestness of the tone that much of what Hesiod says had reference to his own personal experiences. The *Works and Days* is an invaluable source, for, in contrast to the *Iliad* and *Odyssey,* the emphasis is not on the upper classes but on the small farmer and his problems as he faces a hostile world. It is rare good fortune in the history of any period to have preserved among the records the words and thoughts of so articulate a spokesman of the nonruling class as Hesiod was. One other work which almost surely is correctly ascribed to Hesiod—the *Theogony,* a systematic treatment of the origin of the world and the genealogy of the gods—is also of great importance.

Other literary sources which in one way or another deal with the Dark Age are all posterior, some by many centuries, to the period itself. Many poets made use of early legends; some philosophers speculated on the early stages of Greek political and social life; and the first prose writers in the sixth and fifth centuries wrote works dealing with the genealogies of leading families and with the local histories, including the foundations, of various cities. The accounts of these prose writers —logographers—have not survived as separate books, but much of the material they assembled found its way into the works of later historians and especially into the writings of later travelers and geographers such as Strabo (ca. 64 B.C.–21 A.D.) and Pausanias (second century A.D.). These two men included accounts of the early history of many Greek cities; but since these accounts were largely in the form of legends which had been influenced in their growth by such emotional impulses as patriotism and the desire to claim some famous figure from the past as city-founder, and by the aetiological tendency—that is, the habit of inventing stories to explain the origin of obscure customs, institutions, names, and the like—obviously they must be treated with much skepticism. Nevertheless, they form an important part of the source material which the historian of early Greece must consider, for, even though they may be entirely or largely false, they are significant because they reveal what many Greeks believed about their early history.

The most objective evidence for the Dark Age is provided by archaeology—the settlements which have been excavated, unfortunately very few for this period, and the innumerable artifacts which have been unearthed. Of these, pottery, as usual, because of its almost indestructible nature, is the most abundant and important. Just as the general uniformity of the pottery in the Mycenaean Age is good evidence for the cultural and, to a certain extent, political unity which prevailed at that time, so the large number of local pottery varieties which can be dated to the period under consideration—especially to its earlier stages—points convincingly to the breakdown of that Mycenaean unity. Attic pottery is especially important, for—since the Ceramicus was used continuously as a cemetery—the development of the work of Athenian potters can be traced throughout this whole period. From the designs on these Greek vases various conclusions can be drawn about the way of thinking of the artists and the people among whom they worked, and about the different influences which came to bear on the Greeks. For example, the appearance of many oriental motifs in the latter half of the eighth century is sure proof that contact with the East had been resumed. Pottery also is important for providing information on the extent of trade; a considerable quantity of the pottery of one city discovered in another city is good evidence for trade connections between the two, if it can be proved that the pottery is not a local imitation. The very fact of imitation, moreover, would show that one city was being influenced by another. Pottery is such an important historical source for this period that a warning about accepting the evidence squeezed from it may be salutary. A vase is an objective fact, but the interpretation of its significance, even by an expert in ceramics and archaeology, is bound, of course, to be somewhat subjective.

Another type of evidence that the historian must constantly use in attempting to create some picture of the Dark Age is the survival of ancient institutions and customs in historical times. In many ways the Greeks were very conservative and clung to old names and rituals even though they were quite out of keeping with more modern times. In democratic Athens, for example, there was an annually chosen magistrate named *basileus* (king) whose duties were chiefly of a religious character. This office provides clear proof that at some earlier time Athens was ruled by a king who, among other things, was concerned with the religious life of the state. In any period of history the study of ancient survivals can disclose much about the past. An analysis of present-day religious and legal ritual and terminology could throw light on earlier stages in the development of religion and law if other sources were not available.

One other method for trying to gain an insight into the way of life of the Greeks in these early centuries should also be mentioned—the comparative or sociological approach, based on the drawing of analogies with other somewhat primitive societies, both ancient and modern. This method can be valuable for stimulating thought and clarifying problems, but obviously, if overworked, it can be very misleading. Australian Bushmen and American Indians did not necessarily have societies similar to those of the early Greeks. Nevertheless, the preceding chapter showed that a study of the technique of the Yugoslav oral poets could contribute much to an understanding of the method of composition of the Homeric epics.

W HEN A PERSON looks at a modern map of the ancient Greek mainland, he quite naturally derives the impression that the Greek world was divided into numerous well-defined states with fixed boundaries. It is more accurate, however, to think in terms of tribes than of well-established states, although Athens in Attica and Sparta in Laconia did develop effective central governments. The origins of these tribes and of their names are unknown, but in the years following the Dorian upheavals tribal groups, whether dating from the Mycenaean period or later, were involved in the general disarray. They ultimately succeeded in claiming or reclaiming certain districts, where they lived in scattered villages, united only by awareness of the tribe to which they belonged. The unsettled conditions of the period are well illustrated in one case by the fact that the movements of one such tribe, the Phocians, split the Locrian tribal communities so that thereafter they became two separate Locrian "states"—an eastern and a western. These tribal groups are the "states" which the ancient sources call Thessalians, Phocians, Boeotians, and the like. Many of them achieved centralized government only late when existing villages, often as a means of protection against outside enemies, united in some sort of league.

The chaotic conditions in mainland Greece from Thessaly in the north to the southern part of the Peloponnesus continued with varying intensity for several centuries, and it was not until roughly the ninth century that the various tribes finally settled down in the areas which were to be their homes throughout Greek history. Of the peoples not belonging to these ethnic tribes, many had been reduced to serfdom or some less burdensome inferior status, some had intermingled with the tribal groups, some had sought refuge in the mountains encircling Thessaly and in mountainous Arcadia, but many had tried to escape the dangers and chaos of this period by migrating to the coast of Asia Minor. Because this migration took place in the Dark Age, the information about it, just as in the case of the Dorian problem, comes largely from legends; but of the actuality of the migration there is no doubt since, when history began to emerge from the obscurity which followed the breakup of Mycenaean civilization, Greeks were found living on the west coast of Asia Minor and the adjacent islands from the Hellespont south to Rhodes.

The first immigrants settled along the northwest coast of Asia Minor as far south as Smyrna and the Hermus River and also on the neighboring islands, Lesbos and Tenedos.[1] Since their dialect was Aeolic, which may have started forming in the Mycenaean period, it seems clear that they had come chiefly from Thessaly, Boeotia, and other parts of central Greece, presumably fleeing from the Dorian "invasion" or upheavals. These Aeolians ultimately established twelve communities on the Asiatic mainland which were organized in some sort of religious league. The most important of these towns, Smyrna, was subsequently taken over by the Ionians. Much later, probably in the eighth century, colonists from Lesbos and also from the Aeolian league occupied the Troad, where, among other communities, they established Troy VIII. According to tradition, the original migrants from Greece had been led by Penthilus, the son of Orestes, and had finally settled in their new homes in the second generation after his death. The name of Penthilus may merely represent the desire of these eastern Greeks to connect themselves with the great Mycenaean traditions, but the story that they occupied their new lands only after three generations of wanderings could very well reflect the historical likelihood that various groups arrived at different times and that they had to struggle with the natives before they could take up residence. The archaeological evidence from the excavations at old Smyrna provides valuable chronological data and also largely confirms the dates given by Greek tradition.[2] The earliest Greek pottery—protogeometric—found at Smyrna dates from about 1000 B.C., and since Smyrna, as the most southerly of the Aeolian cities, was quite possibly the last to be established, it seems reasonable to assume that the others were founded considerably earlier, as the legends imply.

According to ancient tradition (Strabo, 13.1.3) the Ionian migration to that part of the west coast of Asia Minor extending from the

Hermus River southward to Miletus began four generations after the original setting out of the Aeolians.[3] It is impossible, of course, to give precise chronological data in such matters. There were various traditions that Athens played a prominent role in organizing and dispatching the colonists. Thucydides (1.2), presumably referring to the confused times of the Dorian migrations, records that Athens, because of the poorness of its soil, was spared from invasion and became a place of refuge for many displaced by the chaotic conditions. In the course of time, when the numbers of refugees became too great for the limited resources of Attica, the Athenians sent this excess population to Ionia. In later authors such as Strabo and Pausanias, the legends are presented in greater detail. The Neleid family, driven out of their kingdom of Pylos in Messenia by the Dorians, came as refugees to Athens, and subsequently its leader, Melanthus, succeeded in becoming king. His son Codrus in the next generation, by sacrificing his life, saved Athens from an attack by the Dorians. In the struggle for succession among the sons of Codrus, Medon won out, whereupon two other sons, Androclus and Neleus, led different groups of emigrants to Asia Minor, Androclus becoming the founder of Ephesus and Neleus, of Miletus. The very important role of Athens in these stories in furnishing the leaders and also in being the one place from which the emigrants set out undoubtedly owed much to fifth-century Athenian imperialistic propaganda, for the colonists almost surely departed from more than one place. Nevertheless, there is sufficient evidence to suggest that there is a firm substratum of truth in these legends. As early as the seventh century Mimnermus, a poet of Ionian Colophon, spoke of the founders of his city as having come from Neleian Pylos; in classical Athens the Medontidae were a prominent family, as the Neleids were at least in sixty-century Miletus; and in Ephesus the descendants of Androclus received certain special honors down into Christian times.

Despite their core of truth, these legends were in part the result of a later attempt to simplify and systematize what must have been a prolonged and confused chapter in the emigration of the Greeks to the coast of Asia Minor. The emigrants were partly from the Peloponnesus and partly from central Greece. Some set out directly from those regions, while others resided in Attica for an undetermined period of time before crossing the Aegean (Herodotus, 1.146). The migrations began probably in the eleventh century, but continued spasmodically in the tenth and ninth centuries. Some of the migrants settled in the Cyclades islands, some on the great islands of Samos and Chios, while the majority occupied parts of the coast of Asia Minor, some penetrating far enough inland to found Magnesia on the Maeander. Of the sites selected, Miletus had been the home of a Minoan and a Mycenaean community, and Mycenaean remains have been found at Colophon, Samos, and Chios. At the time of the Ionian migration, however, it is probable that these areas were occupied by natives—Leleges, Pelasgians, and Carians. There was a tradition that the Greeks who settled at Miletus had to war with the Carians and that they carried off Carian women to provide themselves with wives.

By the ninth century twelve of these Ionian communities had united in a loose league, called the League of the Ionians. The members were Miletus, Myus, Priene, Ephesus, Colophon, Lebedos, Teos, Clazomenae, Phocaea, Erythrae, Samos, and Chios. Since it had been Aeolian, Smyrna was not included, nor was Magnesia on the Maeander, which owed its origin to Magnesian emigrants from Thessaly. A common religious center in honor of Poseidon Helikonios was established at the Panionion on the promontory of Mycale. Little is known about the early history of this league, but it helped to give a sense of unity to these Greeks who were of very diverse origin. Another unifying factor among these cities was the celebration of the festival known as the Apaturia. In the course of time the celebration of this festival became a sign of membership in the Ionian branch of the Greeks, although for reasons which are obscure, Ephesus and Colophon were exceptions.

Just as there was an Aeolian and Ionian migration eastward, so also was there a Dorian migration to the east and to the southeast. When evidence becomes available at the end of the Dark Age, Dorians are found to be the dominant people in certain of the southern islands of the Cyclades such as Melos and Thera, in Crete, further east in Carpathos, and in various islands off the southwest coast of Asia Minor, of which Rhodes and Cos were the most important. They also took control of the Carian coast south of Miletus, where, among other places, they established settlements at Cnidos and Halicarnassus. Five of these communities, Cnidos, Cos, and the three towns on Rhodes—Lindus, Ialysus, and Camirus—formed a loose union known as the Dorian Pentapolis centering on the worship of Apollo on Cape Triopium. Originally this pentapolis was a hexapolis (Herodotus, 1.144), but at an early date Halicarnassus was excluded, probably because its population had a strong Carian element, and its dialect became Ionian. Halicarnassus remained famous, however, as the birthplace of Herodotus and the home of striking figures like Artemisia and Mausolus.

There is an even more difficult problem in dating this Dorian expansion eastward than there is in the case of the Aeolian and Ionian migrations. It will serve no purpose here to discuss the different dates which have been proposed. Since protogeometric pottery has been found on the sites to which the Dorians migrated, the most plausible time for their arrival would have been the tenth and ninth centuries, presumably after the upheaval which they had caused on the mainland of Greece had somewhat subsided. The lines in the Catalogue of Ships in the second book of the *Iliad* which speak of the son and grandsons of Heracles leading ships from Rhodes and Cos are surely late additions, since neither Dorian Rhodians nor Coans took part in the Homeric fighting at Troy. They may represent a later attempt to share in the renown of the Trojan War, a claim supported by the fact that there had been Mycenaean settlements on the two islands.

THIS BRIEF SURVEY of the establishment of the Greeks in their historic homes should make it clear that in the Dark Age the mainland of Greece and the west coast of Asia Minor witnessed prolonged confusion. There were migrations throughout Greece and eastward across the Aegean Sea, destruction and abandonment of cities, and, in varying degrees, expulsion, subjection, and blending of populations. The process was a long one, and it was not until the ninth century that almost all the Greeks were settled in the regions where the gradually increasing light of history finds them in the following century. It is obviously impossible to give a detailed and consecutive history of the Greeks in this chaotic age because of the lack of information and the confused nature of much of the information which is available; but, since this is the period in which the foundations of the later classical Greek world were being laid, it is essential to try to gain some insight into certain aspects of the social, economic, and political life of these early Greeks. Needless to say, it is hazardous to generalize about people who presented as complex a pattern as did the Greeks of the Dark Age, but since little understanding will be gained by a mere chronicling of the rather random assortment of facts which are known, it is necessary to point out what seem to have been the chief trends and characteristics in the Greek way of life in this period. The warning should be given, however, that as is true with all synoptic accounts, it would probably be possible to find exceptions to almost every general statement which will be made.

The first thing to emphasize is that the elaborate civilization of the Mycenaean Age, with its powerful centers of government and its bureaucratic control of agriculture and the crafts, collapsed at the beginning of the period. The decline was so great that most of the great centers were destroyed or abandoned; or if, as in the case of Athens, they survived, their scale of life was much reduced. The new communities—whether of the migrating or uprising Dorians, or of the displaced Mycenaeans, whether on the mainland of Greece or the coast of Asia

Minor—were small, unpretentious settlements, and for many generations all aspects of life were correspondingly simple. It was not until the
end of this period that the characteristic community of classical
Greece—the *polis*—began to take shape.

When historical information becomes more plentiful for the study
of the Greeks, it is clear that certain institutions of a social and semi-
political nature were fundamental to their way of life—*phylai* (tribes),
phratries (brotherhoods), *genē* ("clans"), and *oikoi* (households). Since evidence for these institutions before Homer is lacking, the question of their
origin and functions obviously is open to debate. For a long time it was
assumed that the Greeks who migrated to Greece around 2000 B.C. were
organized by kinship or fictitious kinship groups, the most comprehensive one being the tribe and the most basic and natural one the *genos*
("clan")—a grouping that seemed analogous with what was known of
migrating tribes throughout history.[4] When the decipherment of the
Linear B tablets revealed no mention of these groups, the usual argument was that although such bureaucratic documents were not concerned with "kinship" institutions, they continued to exist in some form
among the common people. There is an increasing tendency now, however, to maintain that these institutions first appeared in the Dark Age,[5]
a point of view which leaves one wondering how the migrating tribes
were organized. Since this controversy is probably unanswerable, it will
be avoided here except for a few remarks made below on the phratries.

The earliest definite mention of the three Dorian tribes, Pamphyli,
Hylleis, Dymanes, is in the seventh-century elegiac poet Tyrtaeus (fragment 1) in reference to the Spartans. In historical times these tribes were
found in all Dorian communities for which there is evidence, although
in certain cities, for example Argos and Sicyon, additional tribes were
created for the non-Dorian elements. There is no record for this tribal
organization in Thessaly, Boeotia, or in the Aeolian towns of northwestern Asia Minor,[6] a fact which might support the hypothesis that the migrating proto-Greeks of about 2000 B.C. did not enter Greece in tribal
formation. The four so-called Ionian tribes existed in Athens and in at
least four of the Ionian cities in Asia Minor, Samos, Miletus, Ephesus,
and Teos, although these eastern cities later added two tribes presumably as a means of giving civic rights to non-Ionian Greeks and to some
native peoples. It seems certain that the four tribes were transferred to
the Asiatic coast at the time of the Ionian migration, for there is no evidence in this period for a migration in the opposite direction. This conclusion, incidentally, supports the ancient tradition that the major part
of the Ionian migration set sail from Attica. It will suffice to say here

that these tribes served as administrative and military units for the gradually emerging communities.

A great scholar has said that the "phratries are the darkest problem among the [Greek] social institutions."[7] One can quarrel with this statement only to the extent of wondering if the *genē* do not present equally difficult problems. The importance of the phratries in the organization of Greek social life can be seen from the fact that they existed from early times to at least as late as the end of the second century A.D., when an inscription from the old Greek colony of Naples reveals a phratry still flourishing (*Inscriptiones Graecae,* XIV, 759). They also were widespread, for even though the available evidence associates them chiefly with the Ionian communities, it is clear that phratries, although sometimes under different names and in somewhat altered forms, played an important role in the social organization of Aeolian and Dorian Greeks as well.[8]

Linguistic evidence makes it almost certain that the proto-Greeks had phratries of some sort when they first entered Greece around 2000 B.C. The word *phrater,* with slight variations, signifies brother in the literal sense in many Indo-European languages. The fact that from Homer on the Greeks used the words *adelphos* and *kasignētos* and never *phrater* to express the idea of brother seems to prove that in very early times they abandoned using the word *phrater* in its literal sense and widened its meaning to something like brotherhood, that is, a group of people presumably connected by kinship—the meaning which it bore throughout Greek history.[9] The first mention of phratries in Greek literature occurs in two passages of the *Iliad* (2.362–363; 9.63–64). In each case old Nestor is speaking, once advising Agamemnon to divide his men by tribes and phratries so that phratry may bring aid to phratry and tribe to tribe, and the second time voicing the sentiment that "without a phratry, without law, without a hearth is that one who loves fearful civil war." If phratries had existed from early times, as the linguistic evidence suggests, it is strange that they are mentioned only twice in Homer. One would think that in the chaotic generations following the collapse of Mycenaean civilization, kinship groups would have been important for survival. The explanation may be that they were significant chiefly for the common people, the class largely ignored by oral poets. Homer, influenced by conditions with which he and his predecessors were familiar, may have been referring to a period, probably the somewhat more orderly ninth century, when aristocrats in their desire to increase their power began to gather scattered "kinship" groups of whatever kind into phratries which could be under their supervision. Certainly the evidence for the Dark Age shows the upper classes dominating all aspects of social, economic, and political life. In this connection it is important to emphasize Nestor's second remark, which reveals that a person in those times who did not belong to a group of some sort was in a highly precarious position.

Historians in the past generally believed that the Greek *genos* was the family in its most extended form—a so-called clan. They maintained that the *genos* was the basic kinship group of the proto-Greeks who migrated into Greece about 2000 B.C. Some scholars, however, rejected this concept, claiming that the phratries removed the necessity of postulating *genē*. Certainty on such a matter is probably unattainable, although recent scholarship is inclined to deny the significance of the *genos* ("clan") in the prehistoric period and the early Dark Age. In Homer, although the word *genos* occurs rather frequently, it never seems to have the specific meaning of clan or extended family. The prominent family unit in the *Odyssey* is the *oikos,* which, according to later Athenian law as gleaned from the Attic orators, was defined for inheritance purposes as a family embracing four generations. It was a unit in which it was theoretically possible for all the constituent generations to be living at the same time. In the *Odyssey* the *oikoi* which are conspicuous, those of Odysseus, Nestor, and Menelaus, include only two or three generations, but as wealthy households they comprise much more than the immediate family, for large numbers of retainers and slaves are included in the membership. Those scholars who believe in the early existence of the *genos* among the Greeks recognize in the *oikoi* a stage in the breakup of the original solidarity of the clan. To them the account of Priam living with his fifty sons and twelve daughters and their children all under one roof (*Iliad*, 6.242–250) would be a reflection of the nature of a *genos* before centrifugal forces began to cause its decomposition. Other scholars maintain that as far back as one can hope to penetrate the *oikos* had been the fundamental family unit and that it was only in the Dark Age that various *oikoi*, for political and economic reasons, began to unite in artificial kinship associations which came to be known as *genē*.[10] The problem is so murky that it will best be deferred to the chapter on early Athens where a certain amount of specific evidence on tribes, phratries, and *genē* can be examined. For present purposes it will be sufficient to think in terms of the *oikos*, but one should keep the *genos*, phratry, and tribe in mind, for their existence and importance in the eighth, seventh, and sixth centuries are unquestionable.

The *oikos* was a household rather than a family,[11] for, in addition to the several generations, if sufficiently wealthy, it included slaves and retainers. Most of the slaves were women, since in the raids which furnished the majority of the slaves, the attackers would kill the men and carry off the women and children. Many of the male slaves, like Eu-maeus in the *Odyssey*, had been kidnapped in infancy and then reared in the *oikos* which had purchased them or to which they were assigned at the distribution of the booty. "Retainer" is a word of rather general meaning, but it seems best suited to translate the Homeric term *therapon*. In both the *Iliad* and the *Odyssey* the *therapontes* include a wide variety of types, ranging from men like Phoenix and Patroclus who held privileged positions as retainers of Achilles to the many nameless *therapontes* per-forming various menial tasks in the establishment of Odysseus. The ori-gins of most of these retainers, except for a few who were refugees from their own *oikoi*, are unknown. Many must have been the victims of mis-fortunes which had wrecked their previous ways of life; rather than liv-ing the precarious lives of individuals, they had acquired security and some status by attaching themselves more or less as clients to some pros-perous *oikos*. In most cases the *oikos* must have welcomed them, for its prestige and military strength became greater as the number of its re-tainers increased.

The economy was a rural one, and pastoral more than agricultural. It is true that barley and some wheat were raised, that there were or-chards, vineyards, and vegetable gardens, but the real wealth of the households resided in their flocks—cattle, sheep, goats, and pigs. In matters of food supply and clothing, therefore, an *oikos* was largely self-sufficient. Metals, luxury articles, and slaves were procured chiefly by raids or from traders who were always foreigners, usually Phoenicians. That the occupation of trading was beneath the dignity of a member of one of these warlike households is clearly illustrated by the story of the insult inflicted upon Odysseus when one of the Phaeacians accused him of being a merchant interested only in greedy gains (*Odyssey*, 8.159–164). Nevertheless these Greeks had a strong acquisitive streak, and in their storerooms, besides jars of oil and wine and chests of clothing, they ac-cumulated as much gold, bronze, and iron as they could, sometimes in the form of bars and sometimes in the form of such utensils as cups, bowls, and tripods. The prestige of an *oikos* depended largely on the quantities of valuables of this type which it had. These objects were fre-quently obtained as gifts and then subsequently offered to others as gifts. As conditions in the Greek world became more settled, the idea that every stranger was an enemy was gradually replaced by the notion that "all strangers and beggars are from Zeus" (*Odyssey*, 14.57–58). Hence strangers often were hospitably entertained and on their departure pre-sented with valuable gifts. The *Odyssey* devotes many lines to the presents which were showered on Odysseus, Telemachus, and others in their trav-els. It is clear in most cases that the givers counted on receiving equal gifts when at some future time they or their sons should be guests of the men on whom they were now showering hospitality. Along with this giving of guest gifts there often was established a bond of friendship—guest-friendship—which became hereditary between the families concerned. Such relationships, particularly when they arose between prominent and ruling families, probably constituted an embryonic form of political alliances.

Since practically the whole economy of the Greeks in this period was rural, whether pastoral or agricultural, a knowledge of the system or systems of land tenure would be essential to a real understanding of their way of life. Once again, the fact that this was the Dark Age stands in the way of obtaining the desired certainty on these basic problems. When the proto-Greeks entered Greece in the second millennium it is reasonable to assume that, like many other peoples at a similar stage of development, they worked the lands on which they settled not as individuals but as kinship groups of some sort. The system may very well have been some variation of the Open Fields[12]—strips of land cultivated communally—a method which was widespread in early and medieval Europe. As Mycenaean civilization evolved, the great centers with their bureaucratic regimes must have brought about various changes in the status of land, but, as noted in the preceding chapter, it is still impossible to derive from the Linear B tablets a clear picture of land tenure in the fourteenth, thirteenth, and twelfth centuries. Then came the confusion of the Dorian "invasion" or upheaval and the migrations to Asia Minor. The Greeks in this Dark Age, whether on the mainland or the coast of Asia Minor, presumably reverted to the earlier way of working the land. For the ninth century the only "contemporary" literary source is Homer, and as always with the epics, there is the problem of whether certain relevant passages reflect the conditions of the ninth century or a later period, or whether there are embedded in them survivals from an older social and economic order. Nevertheless a few observations can be made with some assurance.

There is a famous passage in the twelfth book of the *Iliad* (421–423) in which the Achaeans and Trojans fighting across the wall separating them are compared to two men contending about boundaries, "having measuring rods in their hands, in a common field, and in a small space they struggle for an equal share." The picture here is clearly of an arable field possessed in common by some community—possibly a kinship group—in which an equal share, marked off by stones, was allotted to each man. An attractive explanation is that these lines refer to some type of Open-Field system of cultivation.[13] The same statement can be made about a few other passages, particularly the scene depicted on the shield of Achilles where many ploughers are driving their teams in a great, rich, ploughed field (*Iliad*, 18.541–543). The conclusion seems certain, therefore, that at some time in the Dark Age, probably early in the period, some arable land, at least, was occupied and worked in common by the community. The general impression derived from the *Odyssey*, however, is that much of the land was under the control of the various *oikoi*. It could be that earlier, when the Greeks settled in a particular area, more comprehensive groups divided the new land among themselves, and that in the course of time, as the solidarity of these groups weakened, the constituent households emerged from the collective organization as separate entities.

Whatever the proper interpretation of the "original" situation may be, by the ninth century the *oikos* seems to have become the basic social and economic unit. Each *oikos* possessed a certain amount of arable land, which was used for grains, gardens, orchards, and vineyards. As the size of an *oikos* increased, its members probably at times increased the holding by clearing parts of the adjacent wasteland. The custom was to leave the land assigned to the growing of grain fallow in alternate years. In addition to the land under cultivation, the *oikos* needed pastureland for its flocks. The question of the status of pasturage is a very obscure one. As is true of most early societies and even of more advanced ones, some of the pasturelands must have been common to all, or almost all, the inhabitants of a particular region. On the other hand, it seems clear that the *oikoi* claimed as their own certain lands on which their flocks grazed. Since the boundaries of these grazing lands must have been ill-defined, cattle raids undoubtedly were frequent, and many of the feuds which existed between different households probably owed their origin in part, at least, to the vagueness surrounding the demarcation of land used for pasturage.

Although the society represented by family groups such as the *oikoi* was far removed from any earlier hypothetical collective or communal organization of the population, nevertheless it would be a mistake to think of the property of the *oikos* as privately owned. The land belonged to the family as a whole. The living generation did not own the land in the modern sense of the word "own," for the land belonged equally to past and future generations. The living had only the usufruct and, joined with that, the sacred obligation to preserve the land on which their ancestors were buried and to transmit it unimpaired to succeeding generations. It is really an anachronism to speak of the land as inalienable, for the notion of disposing of the real property would never have occurred to the members of an *oikos*. How else in those days could a family live except from its land? On this land, then, all members of the household—several generations of men, women, and children, and whatever slaves and retainers there were—lived and worked for the collective welfare of the household. The word "collective" should be emphasized, for in this period the individual, except as representative of his *oikos,* was of little importance. The aim for which all members of the household consciously or unconsciously worked was a collective one, the self-sufficiency—*autarkeia*—of the *oikos.*

Although the greater part of the agricultural and pastoral land all over the Greek world was controlled by *oikoi* of the type just discussed, there must have been some independent farmers working holdings of their own. Homer, with his interest in the upper classes, gives little information on such men; it is not until the time of Hesiod when the Dark Age was coming to an end that it is possible to obtain a clear picture of how an individual as distinct from a family group sought to wrest a living from the soil. There is one passage in the *Odyssey* (5.489–491), however, which seems to refer to an isolated farmer. In a moving simile Homer likens Odysseus, cast up by the sea on the coast of Scheria and covering himself with leaves against the cold, to a man concealing a firebrand in the black ashes, a man living at the edge of the land with no near neighbors, preserving the seed of fire in order not to have to seek a light elsewhere. It is tempting to believe that here is an allusion to some homesteader who at the outskirts of the inhabited area has cleared a little holding for himself out of the waste. The lives of such homesteaders must have been appallingly lonely and also precarious, for, besides the dangers arising from wild beasts and starvation, what was to protect such a lone individual from the encroachments of the well-organized *oikoi?*

In the rural economy which prevailed in the Dark Age, the *oikoi,* sometimes with slaves and retainers, and the few isolated farmers counted for most of the population. The Homeric epics as well as Hesiod, however, mention two other elements of the population which, because of their importance for the future, merit brief consideration at this point. These were the *demiourgoi* and the *thetes.*[14] The *demiourgoi* were those who worked for the people—the *demos*—and included what nowadays would be called professional men and artisans or craftsmen. The professional men were the seers, bards, heralds, and doctors.

Seers, of whom Calchas and Tiresias were the most famous in the Homeric tradition, had the gift of prophecy and were useful in regulating relations with the gods. It was characteristic of the Greeks that, although seers existed throughout their history, it was only in sanctuaries such as Delphi and Dodona that they developed into what could be called a priestly caste. Bards were always in demand, for one of the most popular forms of entertainment was to listen to the singing of the glorious deeds of heroes. Some bards wandered from one community to another while others, to judge from Phemios at the court of Odysseus and Demodocus among the Phaeacians, resided permanently with some noble family. These bards, of course, kept alive the great traditions of an earlier age and passed them on to such men as Homer. Heralds were part of a king's staff. They were considered to be under the protection of Hermes, the messenger of the gods, and, carrying a herald's staff, transmitted messages, kept order at public meetings, and made official announcements. When not engaged in such public duties, they performed humbler tasks in the kings' households. Doctors were still uncommon, for within the families women often were reputed to have knowledge of healing herbs, and the warriors of necessity had to know how to bind up wounds; but some professional physicians had attained fame. In the *Iliad* there are several references to the renowned Asclepius and his two sons. Since these professions required specialized knowledge, it is not surprising that they were hereditary in certain families or developed into guilds. Guilds of Homeridae and Asclepiadae existed until late in Greek history, and at Eleusis, in Attica, one of the leading *genē* in historical times was named Kerykes, from the Greek word for herald.

The artisans, naturally, represented a larger proportion of the *demiourgoi* than the professional men, but even so they were not numerous. As is clear from Homer and the later Hesiod, the *oikoi* tried to be as self-sufficient as possible. Food and clothing were produced and made by members of the family—the women were responsible for the spinning, weaving, and sewing among many other duties—and most of the building, from wagons to the houses themselves, was the handiwork of the male members of the household. One need only think of Odysseus to be reminded of how a Greek in those times could turn his hand to almost any task. Nevertheless, and especially as society rose above the simplest levels, complete self-sufficiency became impossible, with the result that certain crafts developed to meet the growing needs. In Homer and Hesiod four types of craftsmen are mentioned, the *tekton*, probably best translated as carpenter; the potter; the leatherworker; and the smith. The fact that only four crafts are listed, when compared with the much greater number known from the Linear B tablets, proves that the elaborate division of labor which had been characteristic of Mycenaean society no longer existed and that the complicated bureaucratic system of earlier times largely disappeared in the Dark Age. This lack of division of labor is especially revealed by the *tekton*, for the "carpenter" included in his province such varied tasks as felling trees to procure the wood; building houses, furniture, and ships; and even working in stone.

Pottery was necessary for various purposes. In regions where there was good clay most of the pottery utensils were probably made at home, but potters were needed to bring their wares to districts which had no supplies of clay. Leatherworkers were in demand for only the more intricate articles, since the tanning of hides and the making of simple articles like sandals were done at home. The smith is a good example of the lack of division of labor, for although he was called *chalkeus* (worker in bronze), he also worked with iron, silver, and gold. Because of the rather complicated and heavy nature of a smith's equipment, it was necessary for him to have his own shop. The customer would supply the metal required for the desired object. Hesiod (*Works and Days,* 493–495) provides an interesting glimpse of a smithy and reveals that in the wintertime its warmth tempted men away from their assigned tasks.

Although there are many references to these craftsmen in Homer and in Hesiod, the artisan class was still a small one. The methods of work were simple, and there was no middleman between the producer and the user. In most cases the family supplied the craftsmen with the necessary raw materials. In later times, particularly in cities like Athens and Corinth, the artisans were to become an important element of the population, but in the Dark Age their role was minor because the economy was chiefly rural and because the households tried to be as self-sufficient as possible.

The *thetes* were the humblest and most downtrodden class in the social scale of the period, if class is an appropriate word to use for a group whose origins must have been very diverse. Although one can only guess at these origins—descendants of earlier inhabitants who had been dispossessed by immigrants, runaway slaves, people expelled from some kinship organization, refugees from a blood feud—their unhappy condition is well documented. In some ways their lot was worse than that of the slaves, for a slave, if he did his work faithfully, could count on security—food, lodging, and at times the affectionate concern of his master. Security, however, was precisely what the *thetes* lacked. In a world where one's welfare depended on belonging to a kinship organization or on possessing a profession or craft which was useful to the community, the *thetes* were people without land, a trade, or family connections. Some must have lived as beggars, to whom there are various references in the *Odyssey,* but the majority tried to earn a living as hired laborers. They were employed by the *oikoi* for various purposes, especially in busy agricultural seasons. Even a small farmer, as Hesiod reports, needed a hired hand (*thēs*) on occasions. They were available also for tasks which had no connection with the land. When the suitors of Penelope learned that Telemachus had sailed away in search of news of his father, Odysseus, one of them asked, "Did chosen men from Ithaca go with him, or his *thetes* and slaves?" (*Odyssey*, 4.643–644). This passage implies that a great household might have numbers of *thetes* on its staff on at least a semipermanent basis. In such a situation the *thetes* must have had approximately the same status as the more lowly of the *therapontes*. In most cases, however, the *thetes* were hired for a particular job. While working they were fed by their employers, and when the job was completed they presumably received a wage in kind. If the employer defaulted on the "contract," the *thēs* had no recourse, for what could an isolated individual do against an organized family group? In fact, there was nothing to prevent an employer from loading an objectionable *thēs* on a ship and selling him abroad as a slave. A striking commentary on the plight of the *thetes* is provided by a famous passage in the eleventh book of the *Odyssey* (488–491). When Odysseus meets the shade of Achilles in the underworld, Achilles, wishing to emphasize that the worst lot on earth was better than the grimness of the lot of the dead, says, "I would rather, working on the soil, be a *thēs* to another, a man without inheritance who has not much livelihood, than be ruler over all the dead." The general meaning of this comment could not be more clear, although the precise significance of certain Greek words in it is obscure.

This discussion on the way of life in the Dark Age has concentrated so far on social and economic conditions. Difficult as it is to acquire a satisfactory picture of social and economic organization, it is even more difficult to grasp the political structure, not only because of dearth of evidence but also because in this period city-states with definite political institutions had not yet taken shape. One fact is certain: powerful kings, such as those who ruled in the Mycenaean fortresses, no longer existed in the Greek world. A chieftain like Odysseus who boasts of his ability in using the scythe and plough, who works with leather and builds a house and his own bed, has very little in common with the great lords revealed in the Linear B tablets as masters of a far-reaching bureaucracy. Centralized government collapsed as a result of the migration or uprising of the Dorians, and almost everywhere, except at Athens where a Mycenaean kingship on a reduced scale may have continued, political life had to evolve all over again.

The Greeks, who gradually established communities on the mainland, the islands of the Aegean, and the coast of Asia Minor, were undoubtedly united by some kind of kinship or fictitious kinship organization. Their leaders were known as *basileis,* a term which in the Linear B tablets seems to have signified some minor village official, but which in Homer means kings or chieftains. The acquisition of the land and the subsequent development of the new settlements can only be imagined.

The occupation may often have necessitated the expulsion of natives or striking a bargain with them. The area acquired would usually include an easily defensible hill (acropolis) which could serve as a refuge for people and flocks in case of hostile raids and on which a simple shrine to some deity would be erected. The land would be divided among the various *oikoi*. The king, presumably the head of the most powerful household, would receive, in addition to his share of the allotted land, a demesne or *temenos*. This *temenos* may well have been near the acropolis. Certainly in the *Odyssey* the "palaces" of Odysseus and Alcinous seem to have been within the settlement. An area near the king's residence, or the acropolis itself, may have served as a central meeting place (agora). Adjacent to this meeting place many of the *thetes* and some of the artisans probably resided. The smith, at least, must have had a permanent workshop for his heavy equipment.

Since the households tried to be self-sufficient, the powers of the king were not very extensive. In fact, his authority was largely limited to military matters—leading the people in any offensive attack it might undertake and above all protecting the community from hostile raids. Thucydides (1.12) describes these early kings as hereditary. Undoubtedly each king hoped to pass the sceptre on to his son, but the case of Odysseus' son Telemachus, on his own admission, shows that succession to the royal power was not automatic. To maintain and transmit his position the king had to possess the necessary force and prestige, for the heads of many *oikoi* were only too ready to step into the role of king. It was no bad thing to be a king, as Telemachus (*Odyssey* 1.392) remarked. In addition to the *temenos,* the king was granted various honors and privileges, and he was the recipient of many gifts or benevolences from the people, and of an extra share in the division of booty. These prerogatives added to his wealth, and as his wealth increased he was able to exert more influence by increasing the number of his retainers, by establishing ties abroad through the marriage of female members of his household, and by extending the circle of his guest-friends.

The type of king depicted in the *Odyssey* could hardly hope to maintain his position unless he had some support from the great households which formed the dominant element in the population of the community. Consequently, when necessary, the king would consult with some, at least, of the heads of the *oikoi*. Among the Phaeacians the king, Alcinous, was constantly surrounded by twelve other men, called *basileis,* who presumably represented as many households. Any reader of the *Iliad* will remember that at Troy, Agamemnon frequently summoned various chieftains to a conference. There is no evidence that these leaders possessed any "constitutional" position, but a king could ill afford to flout their wishes too flagrantly. Although these chiefs apparently acted only in an advisory capacity, their role was important historically, for these gatherings were the seeds out of which developed the councils of nobles or of elders which formed the essential governing bodies when aristocracy supplanted monarchy throughout most of Greece in the eighth century.

In Homer the mass of people, as distinct from the leaders, played a small role, but they were always present in the background. In the *Iliad*, where wartime conditions existed, the people were called together on occasions only as an army assembly to listen to the words of their lords. In the *Odyssey*, however, there were several references to peacetime assemblies. These assemblies, which presumably could be attended by all the free adult males in the community, had no formal powers, but it is evident that the king or other leaders felt it wise in certain emergencies to test the state of mind of the people. Considering how important the assemblies of the people were to become in later Greek history, it is interesting to observe that even in the Dark Age the rulers found it necessary to pay attention to the demands of public opinion. Two examples of the power or potential power of the people are worth noting. When the suitors had failed to ambush and kill Telemachus, they were in great fear that he would so arouse the people against them that they would be driven from the land (*Odyssey*, 16.376–382). Many years before, the father of the chief suitor, Antinous, had had to flee for safety to Odysseus from the fury of the people because he had joined with some pirates in a raid on a tribe which was at peace with the Ithacans (16.424–430).

In these small communities which were developing all over the Greek world, political power, and all other power, lay with the king and the leaders of the more prosperous *oikoi*. The commoners were present, of course, but their role was mostly passive. If a commoner, forgetting his postition, made himself objectionable, there was always some chieftain to remind him harshly of his lowly place, as is illustrated by Odysseus' treatment of Thersites in the second book of the *Iliad*. The growth of many of these settlements into more organized cities (*poleis*) will be discussed in succeeding chapters.

3
The Age of Transition

THE DARK AGE CAME TO an end so gradually that it is arbitrary to set a definite date for its close, but since occasional contacts of the Greeks with Assyrians and Egyptians in the eighth century provide most welcome chronological data, it is customary to place in that century the dividing line between the Dark Age and the ensuing era, frequently termed the Age of Transition or, largely in terms of art, the Archaic Period (ca. 725–480). This period comprises the years in which the Greeks, after the chaos of the preceding centuries, settled down and gradually developed the way of life which is best revealed in the classical Greece of the fifth and fourth centuries. Although historical evidence is more abundant for the Age of Transition, the obscurity which shrouds the Dark Age still envelops many aspects of the evolution of the Greeks in the eighth, seventh, and sixth centuries. This obscurity is well illustrated when one tries to examine the most important development of these years—the rise of the city-state, the *polis*, the institution which more than any other is associated with Greek history.

There has been, and probably always will be, a great controversy among scholars concerning the date to be assigned to the first appearance of the polis among the Greeks. Suggested dates range from the ninth century to the late sixth century,[1] the latter dating advocated by those who refuse to recognize any community as a polis until the state had suppressed the power of the great family groups. In many ways the arguments about the time in which the polis emerged are rather futile, for there is inadequate evidence to pinpoint the period when a mere settlement of people became sufficiently aware of its community of interests and needs to think of itself as an organized state. Everybody, except those who insist on some unrealistically refined definition of the institution of the polis, would agree that Solon was thinking in terms of a polis early in the sixth century when he composed his poems on his reforms for Athens, as was his contemporary Alcaeus, the poet of Mytilene in Lesbos, when he wrote, "Not houses finely roofed or the stones of walls well-builded, nay nor canals and dockyards, make the city (*polis*), but men able to use their opportunity" (fragment 28). A century earlier the Boeotian poet Hesiod does not mention the polis specifically in his *Works and Days,* but his admonitions against the corrupt nobles and his insistence on the need for human justice suggest that he was familiar with at least an embryonic form of the polis. In Homer, scholars have been able to prove or disprove the existence of the polis depending on what passages they have selected to support their arguments. Certainly, in the description of the Phaeacian city of Scheria in the sixth book of the *Odyssey,* Homer seems to be giving an idealized picture of some polis with which he was familiar in Ionia, but the general impression derived from the *Iliad* and *Odyssey* is a way of life that did not yet know the true polis as distinguished from the mere settlement.

If one must try to be precise about the time of the first appearance of the polis, the middle of the eighth century will serve as a rough and reasonably satisfactory date, for Greek colonization to the west began about 750, and it is logical to assume that some stages in the formation of the polis preceded the beginning of the colonization movement. Two points, however, need to be emphasized: first, no settlement became a polis overnight by fiat, and second, in some parts of the mainland of Greece, especially in the west, the polis did not take shape until several centuries later. In Elis, for example, the city of Elis was not built until around 470, and even after its establishment the majority of the Eleans continued to live on their farms and country estates; and in regions like Acarnania and Aetolia cities were unknown until the end of the fourth century or even later.

Cities, of course, were not a new phenomenon in the Aegean world. Although the evidence is slight, considerable settlements probably grew up at the foot of such citadels as Mycenae, and it has been estimated that Cnossos in its prime may have had a population of many thousands. These settlements which gathered around fortresses or palaces, dominated by kings possibly considered semi-divine and by powerful bureaucracies, had little or no similarity to what the later Greeks meant by a polis, a city-state, an institution of which the members—the citizens—felt that they controlled its destiny, no matter how restricted in numbers they were on the basis of birth and wealth. With the collapse of Mycenaean civilization, the Mycenaean city system, if such it should be called, vanished. It may have lingered for a while in Athens, for there was continuity of residence there, but when evidence becomes available again, the acropolis is not the home of a more or less absolute monarch but of the goddess of the city, Athena. Elsewhere the growth of settlements had to start again from the beginning. The progress was slow, for the confusion and uncertainty caused by the Dorian migration or uprising, the ensuing conflicts and displacements of peoples, and the subsequent flight of various Aeolian, Ionian, and Dorian elements to the Aegean islands and the coast of Asia Minor kept the Greeks in a constant state of disarray. A long time had to elapse before inhabitants of straggling villages passed sufficiently beyond the stage of family loyalty and organization to think of themselves as belonging to a community greater than the family.

It would be a fascinating task to trace the evolution of these communities from their first appearance as precarious settlements to the forms which are recognized in the sixth century, but the evidence is so limited that the historian must be satisfied with a very general picture. Archaeology is helpful, but it is hampered by the fact that most of these communities were inhabited for centuries—some down to the present time—and hence most, or all, traces of the earliest habitation have been obliterated. Ancient legends and traditions are important, but obviously must be handled with care and skepticism. The comparative sociological method—drawing inferences from other societies, ancient and modern, at a similar stage of development—is useful and suggestive, but it cannot take full cognizance of the conditions which were peculiar to the Greeks and of the fact that presumably no two Greek states evolved in precisely the same way. Hence, in trying to explain the growth of settlements into cities, the historian frankly must have recourse to his imagination, which he should try to keep under reasonable control.

The remarks offered here will refer chiefly to central Greece, to the northeastern section of the Peloponnesus, and to the Aegean islands and the coast of Asia Minor. Athens and Sparta, for which there is more evidence, will be discussed in subsequent chapters.

By the tenth century some order, some recognizable pattern, was beginning to emerge from the chaos. Groups of displaced Greeks settled down permanently in regions where there seemed to be sufficient agricultural and pasture land for their needs. As was natural, considering the nature of the Greek terrain, the area occupied by a particular group frequently had more or less natural boundaries such as mountains, rivers, and inlets of the sea. At first the land may have been worked according to some type of open-field system, but before long each *oikos*—household—acquired control of definite amounts of arable and pasture land. Some pasture lands, particularly those on the slopes of mountains, were considered as common to all who possessed flocks. Since many cities in the historical period were built around a citadel, an acropolis, and since the word *polis* originally meant a citadel, it is reasonable to assume that the early Greeks, as they settled in a particular area, selected some easily defensible rocky hill as a place of refuge for themselves and their flocks. Such a strong place, when necessary, would be strengthened by the building of walls and from the very beginning it became the home of the tribal god or gods. In certain cities in Greece, where the acropolis was unusually large, the whole population lived within its confines. More commonly the people lived on the slopes of the hill or on the plain below.

In these early centuries one can imagine that, if the territory occupied by a tribal group was small, the various *oikoi* lived close to the place of refuge and that the men walked to their fields or pastures each morning and returned to their homes in the evening. If the territory was of considerable size, it is likely that, as conditions became more secure, many *oikoi* took up residence on their own lands. It is a natural assumption that the leader, the king, of each particular group resided in the citadel, but strangely enough there is no clear evidence for this. Aristotle's remark that an acropolis is suitable for oligarchies and monarchies (*Politics*, 7.10.4) suggests a connection between the king and the citadel, but against this one can set Odysseus' palace in the *Odyssey*, which definitely does not seem to have been located in a stronghold. It is probably best to visualize the king and his *oikos* as living close to the place of refuge and to recognize in this proximity one of the factors which encouraged concentration of population around the acropolis.

In the tenth, ninth, and eighth centuries, although the Greeks must have engaged in frequent border wars, cattle raids, and similar activities, their world was free from attacks by foreign powers. This comparative peace encouraged more settled conditions and presumably led to a growth of population. The number of *oikoi* must have increased as sons, on the death of their father, became heads of their own households. Various *oikoi* living close to one another tended to develop into villages. It is significant that in Attica many of the *demes*—villages which ultimately served as administrative units—were named after families or *genē* which at one time must have constituted most of the population of the community. Aristotle in the *Politics* (1.1.6–11) speaks of the village being formed from a union of *oikoi* and the polis arising from a union of villages. This is a theoretical statement, but it affords some help in visualizing how a polis developed. What is known about the older Greek cities suggests that they grew naturally without any conscious planning. Apparently various *oikoi* took up residence near the citadel and, as they increased in number, straggling villages began to take shape. At some time—probably in the eighth century—these villages merged into a polis. Various reasons can be imagined for such a union—a powerful or persuasive king, the need for greater protection against neighboring enemies, the prestige of the deity on the acropolis, and the feeling that the increasing population needed more organization. Also it is probable that many of the artisans and *thetes* lived more or less permanently in the vicinity of the citadel, which from the earliest times must have been regarded as the religious and "political" center of the area. The agora, at first a meeting place, gradually began to acquire some of the characteristics of a marketplace. As increasing population and a general rise in the standard of living resulting from more peaceful conditions made it more and more difficult for the *oikoi* to be self-sufficient, many households, or at least certain of their members, may have found it more convenient to live near the agora where, by bartering the produce of their estates, they could obtain the manufactured products and the articles of trade for which they felt a need.

In some of the larger territories, in addition to the growth of a capital city, villages took shape in the country districts. In Attica these villages were incorporated politically into the polis of Athens. A man living in a village was just as much an Athenian citizen as the man living under the shadow of the acropolis. For most other states in Greece it is impossible to obtain a clear picture of the status of the villagers, but it is probable that some lacked full rights of citizenship.

Formerly, the generally accepted view was that the Greeks who had migrated to the coast of Asia Minor—especially the Ionians—took the lead over the Greeks of the mainland in reviving civilized life and in developing the polis. The argument ran that these eastern Greeks did not experience as great a setback in civilization as the inhabitants of the mainland who had to struggle for generations with the confusion caused by the Dorian migration or uprising, that they were stimulated by contact with the advanced civilizations of the East, and that pressure from their eastern neighbors forced them to develop city-states in self-defense. More recent scholarship[2] and the excavation of places such as Miletus and old Smyrna have given good reason to believe that on the whole the Ionians were slower to develop culturally—with the exception of the epic—than Athens or the new Dorian states. The Greeks who migrated to Asia Minor had to struggle for a long time before they achieved a reasonable degree of security and prosperity. Their earliest settlements were made on the coast on sites as much surrounded by water as possible so as to reduce the extent of land frontier which had to be defended against the natives. To judge from the remains of old Smyrna, many such settlements had been established by about 1000 B.C. These early settlers were interested in land, and to obtain this they had to fight with the natives. The Greeks reduced some of the natives to serfdom, such as the Gergithes at Miletus and the Pedieis at Priene, but with others they came to terms in different ways. Since the Greeks had come to Asia Minor without women, or with only a few, there was much intermarrying with the natives; Herodotus (1.146) speaks of the new settlers at

Miletus seizing Carian women. An inscription from the Ionian city of Teos[3] suggests that some Asiatics were allowed to share in the division of the land that became the territory of the new settlement and that the descendants of these natives in the course of time adopted Greek names. The system implied in the document suggests some sort of "feudalism" which is inclined to adhere to the status quo rather than to fall in with more advanced proposals.

Certainty in the matter of the rise of the polis is impossible with the evidence currently available, but in view of the developments in Greek history in the seventh century, it seems reasonable to accept the eighth century as the period in which the self-conscious polis began to emerge from the mere settlement and to believe that this evolution started in the Greek mainland rather than in Ionia. Since Greek history from this point on is largely the history of city-states, which were numbered by the hundreds, it will be useful to emphasize here certain aspects of these characteristic Greek institutions.

The first thing to be noticed about these city-states is their small physical size.[4] Sparta, controlling Laconia and Messenia—the whole southern part of the Peloponnesus—and thus embracing about 3,200 square miles, was the most extensive of the Greek states. Athens, comprising both Attica and Salamis, was also from the Greek point of view unusually large; it contained 1,060 square miles, but even so it was smaller than the 1,248 square miles of Rhode Island. A few states in Sicily were as large as Athens, but in Greece and Asia Minor the average size of the city-states ran from about 30 to 500 square miles. Populations were correspondingly small. Athens in its prime, before the outbreak of the Peloponnesian War in 431, had some 40,000 to 50,000 adult male citizens. The total number of Athenians, then—men, women, and children—came to something like 180,000. Resident aliens and slaves are estimated to have been about equal in number to the Athenians, with the result that there was probably in Attica and Salamis a population in round numbers of about 350,000. Fifth-century Syracuse and Argos may have numbered about 20,000 adult male citizens each, although in the fourth century the citizen body of Syracuse may have increased to 50,000 or even more. The majority of Greek states, however, contained anywhere from about 2,000 to 10,000 adult male citizens. Greek political theorists considered 5,000 to 10,000 the ideal number. In such a state, ideally, every citizen could at least recognize by sight every other citizen.

Why were these Greek states so small? Geography provides a partial explanation. Both the mainland of Greece and the coast of Asia Minor are broken up into many districts, which are rather effectively separated from one another by the natural boundaries furnished by mountain ranges, rivers, and inlets of the sea. In the Dark Age one group settled in one clearly defined area, another in another, and, since the aim of these communities to be as self-sufficient as possible discouraged much communication among them, it was natural that each group developed largely in isolation. But geography was not the only reason for the exclusiveness of the Greeks. Sometimes neighboring states developed independently even though they were not separated by natural boundaries, as happened in the cases of Corinth and Sicyon and of the four distinct communities in the little island of Ceos to the southeast of Attica. Why did not such places—and also those which had natural boundaries—combine into larger units? It is easy enough to understand why the fully developed city-states of the fifth century had no desire to amalgamate. By that time each polis had developed its own traditions and way of life and a conviction that its way of life was the best possible one. The fierce patriotism engendered by that attitude led the citizens to feel that they did not want to jeopardize their precious heritage through having to share it with others or through having it weakened by the introduction of alien ways. The problem, of course, is to try to explain why larger groups were not formed in the early centuries of the first millennium before the intense chauvinism which was later characteristic of the Greek states had begun to take form.

Since the answer lies in the haze of the Dark Age and the early part of the Age of Transition, the historian must be satisfied with a solution based on probabilities. When the Greeks settled in these small districts they were organized by institutions based on kinship, real or imagined. Small as each area was, it was sufficient for the limited number of settlers and their pastoral and agricultural way of life. Generation after generation the people lived in the same way, tending their flocks, cultivating their fields, and occasionally being called together to repel some raid from beyond the borders. In these self-sufficient societies a deep love arose for the soil on which life itself was dependent. In these restricted districts, some of which were only a few miles in length and width, the inhabitants became familiar with every natural feature, with every hill and ravine, tree and stream. Shrines and altars to heroes, nymphs, and various vaguely conceived spirits gradually arose, making the land, which was already sacred from the tombs of the ancestors, more holy. And on the acropolis lived the protecting deity or deities of the community, which, although originally the same as the deities of the adjacent communities, gradually acquired distinguishing characteristics.

People living amid these intimate and familiar scenes generation after generation must have acquired a sense of belonging which is almost impossible for residents of today's urban monstrosities to understand.

Each community developed its own traditions and special ways of life which were intimately linked with the land, and the conviction grew that its ways were better than those of other communities. Thus by the time that increasing population rendered it no longer possible for the growing states to be self-sufficient and made it desirable for communities to combine their resources by uniting in larger groups, the inhabitants of each state were so passionately attached to their city and its lands and traditions that the idea of merging with another state and thus forfeiting part of their identity was unthinkable.

IF THESE city-states, which were to become the protagonists of Greek history, came into being in the eighth century, then their rise coincides roughly with a remarkable phenomenon—the disappearance of kingship from the Greek world.[5] Scholars are in disagreement on whether the creation of the polis should be considered an achievement of the kings, who shortly were discarded by the institution they had established, or whether the credit for founding the polis should be assigned to the nobles, who were in control of the city-states by at least the beginning of the seventh century. Either side of the argument can be defended, depending on the time at which one places the transition from mere settlement to polis. Even if the kings are denied credit for the establishment of well-defined poleis, it is obvious that they were responsible for many of the steps that led to that formation. It was under the kings that the Greeks settled in the various parts of the Aegean world where poleis ultimately developed. These kings, who in contrast to the Mycenaean dynasts should be thought of as minor chieftains emerging in the period of chaos and confusion, furnished the necessary military leadership in gaining control of the territory of the future city-state and in defending it from hostile attacks. They fostered the cult of the god or goddess on the citadel who was to become the patron deity of the polis. Their residence near the citadel naturally became a "political" center, and the first concentration of population which formed the nucleus of the subsequent town probably consisted of the kings' retainers and of numerous artisans and *thetes* who chose to live near the royal residence. Aristotle in the *Politics* (3.10.1) describes the kingship of the Heroic Age as "based on general consent but limited to a number of definite functions, with the king acting as general and judge and the head of religious observances." For this characterization of kingship Aristotle was drawing on the evidence provided by Homer and the other epics which were available to him, and also, probably, on his observations of the Macedonian kingship of Philip II.

In the *Iliad* and the *Odyssey* the king's judicial powers were greatly limited because justice on the whole was the business of the individual *oikoi*. It is quite likely, however, that in the tenth and ninth centuries the kings found it increasingly necessary to participate in the administration of justice. Populations were increasing, and the kings, to preserve order, must often have had to settle disputes arising among the growing numbers living around the citadel. Also, as life became more civilized, the ruinous feuds between various *oikoi* were becoming increasingly detrimental to well-ordered existence. It is probable that public opinion forced the kings at times to try to stop these feuds by acting as judges or arbiters in the quarrels.

In fact, the states were growing too populous for the old system of almost self-sufficient households to cope satisfactorily with the increasing complexities of life. More administration was needed, and the king must have turned more and more to his council—the heads of the chief families—for assistance and advice. Since he was basically only *primus inter pares,* he was not in a position to build up a powerful bureaucracy of his own immediate followers, as presumably his Mycenaean predecessors had done. Some of these family chiefs, who previously, at least in the larger territories, may have lived on their farms or estates at a considerable distance from the growing center, now probably began to reside more or less permanently in the neighborhood of the citadel and the king's residence. This tendency at first may have strengthened the kings' power and made the administration more efficient, but before long it spelled the downfall of kingship. The members of the council—the heads of the richer *oikoi*—considered themselves to be on almost the same plane of dignity and rank as the king. Certainly the suitors in the *Odyssey* showed no hesitation in having kingly aspirations, and among the Phaeacians, the king Alcinous was surrounded by twelve advisers who also were termed kings. All that was needed to bring about the end of kingship were the proper circumstances—kings who were unpopular, arrogant, incompetent in battle and administration; the throne falling to a minor; popular discontent; and the like.

Whatever the causes, the remarkable thing is that almost everywhere in the Greek world kingship disappeared in the course of the eighth century. The legends reflecting this phenomenon are unreliable, but their very scarcity confirms the notion that there was little difference between the power of the kings and that of those who supplanted them. The transition from the rule of kings to the rule of "nobles" occurred sometimes violently, sometimes peacefully. In some places kingship was totally abolished; in others it persisted as a magistracy with duties almost entirely religious or, as in Sparta, as a dual kingship, each king being able to act as a check on the other. Since the king's position had to a certain extent been rooted in religion, the nobles who usurped his place probably tried to obtain divine sanction for the change they were bringing about. This is an obscure subject, but the case of Sparta in particular seems to provide evidence for the part played by religion in this political revolution. In Greek terms the *theoi basileioi* became *theoi eleutherioi* (gods of liberty).[6]

Who were these "nobles" who, gaining control of the embryonic city-states in the eighth century, were to be the dominant ruling group for several generations and in some areas throughout Greek history? It is always difficult to give an adequate explanation of the origin and nature of a social class, and this difficulty obviously is magnified when the origin of the class in question must be sought in a distant past for which there is no adequate historical information. Some historians sidestep the problem by merely implying that the existence of a noble class in the Greek Dark Age is an ultimate fact which must be accepted. This is an attitude that begs the question. The standard approach is to point to the Homeric poems and the apparent distinction drawn there between the "nobles" and the common people. Oral epic poetry, however, is a slippery source on which to base conclusions; it is too easy to offer interpretations which are influenced by one's own preconceived notions. Certain scholars have been able to make a good case for the absence of any clearly defined, self-conscious noble class in the society depicted by Homer.[7] They argue that the standard epithets—like "well-born"—and the emphasis on and pride in genealogies which are characteristic of the later aristocracies are largely lacking in Homer. To them the society reflected in Homer is a simple one, organized by kinship groups, a type of society which antedates the separation into clear-cut social classes. The numerous petty kings—*basileis*—who are mentioned are merely heads of various families, and although many of them attend the king's council as elders, this does not set them off as a class apart. Only later, in post-Homeric times, did some of these *basileis* and their families become wealthy and powerful enough to form a self-conscious noble order. This point of view provides a salutary antidote to the usual assumption that the heroes in Homer constitute a well-defined noble order, but it does not take sufficient cognizance of the mass of men who are in the background in the *Iliad* and the *Odyssey*. The magic of Homer remains with its tantalizing enigmas, which stubbornly refuse to be neatly catalogued in orderly categories.

The nobles who supplanted the kings were members of *genē*, and it was as *gennētai* that they possessed the power and prestige to achieve their aims. By the eighth century the *genē*, whether old survivals from an earlier millennium or new creations of a more recent past, would have had approximately the same characteristics. It is necessary to assume that from the ninth century, at least, many *oikoi* were becoming economically and socially prominent. In order to increase their influence numerous *oikoi* combined into larger groups which became the *genē*. Some of these households may have been related, for frequently an *oikos* must have broken off from the parent *oikos* to form an independent group, but the newly formed *genē* seemingly included groups which had no apparent kinship with one another. The fiction of kinship was maintained, however, and the *gennētai* of each "clan" claimed to be descended from a common ancestor—often a figure from the legendary past. Special religious rites were adopted in which only members of the particular *genos* could participate. Before many generations had passed, these *genē* had acquired traditions which created the impression that the origin of the group belonged in the dim past.

Whatever may be the correct answer to the question of the origin of the *genē*, it seems certain that by the eighth century many such "clans" existed throughout the Greek world. By controlling the best land they increased their wealth and hence were dominant in all spheres of life— economic, social, military, and political. As they grew more powerful they became more class-conscious, and now, if not before, it is proper to speak of an order of nobility. To justify their status they placed great emphasis on their high birth and their distinguished ancestry. Because of their wealth and high birth, their genealogy often beginning with a hero or a god, they considered themselves the best—the *aristoi*—and the governments which they established in the cities therefore came to be termed "aristocracies."

The cities, then, whether some first began to take shape under the kings or only later under the nobles, were controlled from an early period by the nobles. One must emphasize, however, that these cities were still only in an embryonic state.[8] Nothing could be more misleading than to visualize these early towns in terms of the cities of classical Greece. They were little more than straggling agricultural settlements, for the economy was still almost entirely agricultural. The agora—the meeting place—was slow to develop into a market. The citadels, if some previously had been the dwelling places of kings, were now assigned to the gods of the state, although, of course, they could still be used as places of refuge. The people, both rulers and ruled, lived primarily in settlements which continued to grow in haphazard fashion around the foot of the citadel. Few cities were walled before the sixth or even the fifth century. In cities which possessed large tracts of land, some of the people lived scattered throughout the territory, either in isolated houses or in small villages.

Since hundreds of cities were taking shape in the course of the eighth century and passing from the rule of kings to that of nobles, it is obvious that there must have been considerable variation in the types of aristocratic governments which were established. There is more evidence for Athens and Sparta, which will be discussed later. Regarding the other cities, for which ordinarily only scanty items of information exist, if that, a few somewhat tentative generalizations alone can be made.[9] In some places all the *genē* took part in the control of affairs; in others, only a few of the more powerful ones. In certain cases the king and his particular family were supplanted by the royal "clan" as a whole. This is what apparently happened at Corinth, where the clan of the Bacchiads, claiming descent from a king Bacchis, held power for several generations—according to tradition for 200 years. At Miletus the dominant aristocrats were the Neleids and at Mytilene, the Penthilids, who claimed to be descendants of the earlier kings Neleus and Penthilus. At towns such as Chios and Ephesus the ruling nobles were known as Basilidae, a name which suggests that the governing aristocrats were descendants of the earlier royal families.

In every case the most important governing body was the council, which, with variations and restrictions, was an outgrowth from the Council of Elders which had advised the king. These councils were small and usually had an age requirement for admission. The Spartan Gerousia, which was probably an extreme case, consisted of twenty-eight members who became councillors only after they had reached the age of sixty. There were several magistrates, probably not more than two or three at first, who often were appointed by the council. After their term of office—usually a year—they became members of the council. It seems likely that these councillors, like Roman senators, held office for life; because of this long term of office, it is natural that the council was the dominant body in the government.

Although little is known about the government of these early aristocracies, there can be no doubt that the control lay with an exclusive council and a small number of magistrates who probably were not much more than annual executives for that council. One would like to know if these aristocratic constitutions included assemblies of the people and, if so, how the people should be defined. Unfortunately there is no contemporary evidence; the answer to the question must be inferred from later, and also from earlier, conditions. In the monarchical period assemblies certainly existed. In the *Iliad* there are various mentions of assemblies of the fighting men, and in the *Odyssey* there are passages dealing with assemblies in peacetime circumstances. In the *Odyssey* one would probably not go wrong by conceiving the assemblies to have consisted of men capable of bearing arms and of those who, now past that age, had once been capable of bearing arms. Such assemblies seemingly had no formal powers, but from their meetings the king and his advisers could test the temper of the people.

Under the aristocracies it is reasonable to assume that the dominant clans, whether few or many in number, would have attempted to eliminate or, at least, weaken any general assembly of the people. When later sources, referring to the sixth or seventh century, mention the Thousand at Cyme and Colophon, and the "hundred households" at Opus in east Locris, one can probably interpret these round numbers as referring to the number of adult males in the ruling clans. Assemblies of such men may very well have existed. Their functions would have been partly legislative and partly electoral—legislative insofar as they voted on proposals submitted to them by the councils and magistrates, and electoral in those cases where appointments to magistracies and councils were not under the control of the councils themselves. Needless to say, the candidates for any office had to be members of the ruling class.

It is most unlikely that any but members of the clans could participate in these assemblies. As the seventh century progressed, however, and the new phenomenon of the heavy armed foot soldiers (hoplites) began to supplant in military importance the previously all-important cavalry, it is probable that membership in the assembly was increased; but even so most of these hoplites presumably came from the clans, although possibly from the less prominent ones. The lower social elements of the population—the artisans and the day laborers—almost certainly were excluded from admission to the assemblies. To judge from later evidence, ownership of land was an essential prerequisite for any kind of political recognition. It is doubtful whether the small peasants had any political status, for their holdings would have been too insignificant to meet the property qualifications necessary for citizenship.

It may be anachronistic to apply the expression "citizenship" to this early period, but the ruling aristocrats, for their very survival, had to be acutely aware of who was and was not entitled to full privileges in the state. Those excluded from these privileges were part of the state from the very fact that they lived and worked there, but their membership was, so far as can be ascertained, purely a passive one. In the betterment of the position of the underprivileged in some states and their rise to complete control in the later democracies lies one of the most important themes in the internal history of Greece well down into the fifth century.

In ending this brief sketch of the nature of the early aristocracies, it will be useful to discuss the four chief bases on which the power and influence of the nobles seem to have rested. First, there was clan organization. By the eighth century the *gené* had become very cohesive groups. This solidarity was strengthened by the tradition of a common ancestor, by a religious cult in which all members shared, by the tombs of their dead,[10] and above all by the realization that their social, economic, and political interests were served by presenting a united front. Against such proud, organized groups the individual or the small family was powerless. Second, these clans controlled most of the arable land, and, if pasturage was still to some extent common, their flocks and herds monopolized the pasture land. In a society where the economy was almost exclusively agricultural and pastoral and in which wealth was estimated primarily in terms of land and its products, these *gené* were the only wealthy element in the community.

Third, the aristocrats from Homeric times down into the seventh century were supreme in the military field. They either fought as cavalry or rode to battle in a chariot and then dismounted and fought in single combat. The mass of the people were ill armed and hence ineffective as fighters. The nobles, who alone could afford to raise horses and own war chariots, were thus able to justify their privileged position, among other ways, by emphasizing that the responsibility of protecting the community rested on them. In the seventh century, however, the hoplites, partly as a result of improved techniques on the part of metalsmiths and partly because forms of wealth other than products of the land were becoming more common, began to make their appearance as heavy armed infantry. These hoplites were men of sufficient wealth to procure at their own expense the necessary equipment—metal helmet, round shield, corselet, and greaves, and as chief weapon a thrusting spear—and of sufficient leisure to indulge in the training which was necessary to produce a well-disciplined phalanx of hoplites in close order. By the middle of the century, to judge from the famous proto-Corinthian Chigi Vase and from the poems of Tyrtaeus concerning the Second Messenian War,[11] hoplite tactics had been adopted in many parts of the Greek world. This phenomenon weakened the almost total control over all aspects of the state which the aristocrats had enjoyed, for these new fighting men could not be denied some participation in the government. The granting of more privileges, however, affected only a comparatively small part of the population, probably members of the smaller clans and some of the wealthier commoners, for it is certain that the small peasants, artisans, and laborers could not have afforded to buy the necessary equipment to serve as hoplites. The widespread adoption of hoplite tactics, therefore, undermined the old exclusive aristocracies by forcing them to accept timocratic or plutocratic elements. The raising of horses and service in the cavalry, however, remained characteristic of aristocracies and oligarchies throughout Greek history, as Aristotle emphasizes in several passages in his *Politics*. Thessaly, where the terrain was particularly suited for cavalry fighting and where a largely feudal system persisted, is the obvious example.

The fourth basis of the power of the aristocrats which should be noted was their control of justice. In the monarchical period as depicted by Homer, with each *oikos* trying to be as self-sufficient as possible, justice was largely a matter of self-help. Recourse to voluntary arbitration was also common, but there is little or no evidence that the administration of justice was a state function. The picture presented by Hesiod, whose date can be placed presumably in the early years of the seventh century, is quite different. Hesiod was a native of the Boeotian village Ascra, which may have been included in the territory of the neighboring town of Thespiae. In the *Works and Days* (27–41) he tells how, after he and his brother Perses had divided their inheritance, Perses, not satisfied with the division, took the matter before the "bribe-swallowing" nobles and secured a larger share. The dispute was not finally settled, however, for Hesiod insisted now that they should not appear again before the nobles, but rather settle their disagreement by true (straight) judgments. The latter suggestion probably refers to voluntary arbitration, but the previous recourse to the nobles and Hesiod's warning not to listen to the arguments and quarrels of the agora certainly suggest that the governing authorities were taking an interest in the administration of justice. This is a natural development. As the cities gradually began to take shape, the governing bodies more and more felt called upon to maintain order, and public opinion must have exerted pressure on them to interfere in and settle disputes which were disruptive to social life. Although voluntary arbitration continued as it did throughout Greek history, the administration of justice increasingly became a responsibility of government.[12] Since the government was in the hands of the nobles, they, whether as magistrates or as committees of the council, assumed the role of hearing litigation and giving judgments. As there were as yet no written laws, their verdicts were based on the unwritten laws, the ancestral customs and ordinances (*themistes*). This lore, which was reputed to have divine origin, was the exclusive possession of the aristocrats, whose families in many cases claimed to be descended from gods or heroes. Hesiod, in his anger and frustration, denounces these rulers in their judicial capacity as bribe-swallowing princes; this denunciation may have been an exaggeration, but the totality of the evidence for this early period of Greek history makes it clear that the nobles, true to human nature, settled disputes and interpreted cases in conformity with the interests of their own class. The helpless victims had no recourse except to appeal to

Zeus and, conceiving of him as a god of justice, to predict that punishment would fall upon the wrongdoers. Hesiod's insistence on Zeus as a moral god to whom justice was a matter of vital concern was to have profound influence on the evolution of Greek religious thought.

The Greek aristocracies were weakened and altered in the course of the seventh century under the impact of the increasing importance of the hoplite infantry and the rising significance of other types of wealth besides land and its products, but in many places aristocracies, or oligarchies, or timocracies continued to exist for generations and in certain cases throughout Greek history. These aristocracies, with all their limitations, made great contributions to Greek civilization. Under their aegis culture flourished, especially in the areas of art and poetry. In the field of government they were responsible for many advances. When they succeeded the kings, the city-states were just beginning to take shape. The aristocracies developed the political machinery necessary for these new creations—councils, magistrates, and the beginning of state control of the administration of justice. And it was also under the supervision of the aristocratic governments that the great colonization movement began—a movement which spread the Greeks throughout the Mediterranean and Black Sea regions and affected the evolution of Greek civilization in countless ways. This colonization movement will be the subject of the following chapter.

4
Colonization

IN THE EIGHTH century the Greeks began to set forth from the homeland, the Aegean islands, and the coast of Asia Minor in what became one of the great colonizing movements of history. By the time this movement began to wane some two centuries later, Greek colonies had been established from the Crimea to the Nile Delta and from the Caucasus to Spain. Since these colonies were invariably founded on the shores of the Mediterranean, Hellespont, Propontis, Bosporus, and Black Sea or at the mouths of rivers flowing into these bodies of water, Plato's humorous comparison of the Greeks to frogs around a pond (*Phaedo*, 109b) was very apt.

Since hundreds of colonies were sent out by scores of cities in the course of two centuries, it is reasonable to assume that, except for special cases, there were similar underlying causes for such a widespread movement. By the eighth century the Greek world had had several generations of comparative quiet. Cities were emerging and aristocracies were taking over the responsibility of government from the kings. More settled conditions probably had caused an increase in population. The categories of population in the cities everywhere were roughly the same. Various *oikoi* controlled the best land. Many of these *oikoi*, especially the more prosperous ones, had become members of larger units, the *genē*, which contributed to the solidarity of "kinship" groups. Below these wealthy *oikoi* whose members, the *aristoi*, formed the ruling class were less successful *oikoi* with their plots of land of varying size and fertility—a group which presumably should be classified as peasants. There were also growing numbers of men without land—the *thetes*, or hired laborers, and a small artisan class.

In a society of this type, whose economy was almost exclusively agricultural and pastoral, growth of population presented a serious problem. If families produced more than one son, the land would subsequently have to be shared or divided. If this pattern continued for several generations, the available land would no longer be sufficient to support the increasing numbers. For the peasant with his smaller lot the problem obviously was more acute. Hesiod (*Works and Days*, 376–380), writing from the farmer's point of view about 700, advises that a man

62

should have only one son. Although the following lines, "But if you leave a second son, you should die old. Yet Zeus can easily give great wealth to a greater number. More hands mean more work and more increase," strike a more cheerful note, it seems certain that for both the upper and lower classes the division of land from generation to generation had caused many people to have insufficient land for their livelihood. Two general conclusions, therefore, seem valid concerning conditions in the period just prior to the beginning of the colonization movement: (1) there was not enough arable land in the existing Greek world to support the growing population by agriculture and pasturage alone; and (2) trade and industry were still too limited to afford adequate relief for people unable to live from the available land.

How did these men, both nobles and commoners, for whom the soil could no longer furnish adequate sustenance, manage to survive? Some took service as mercenary soldiers with the kings of the great oriental kingdoms, as Alcaeus' brother did in Babylon. Although this possibility must have been open from early times, the first documentary proof is an Assyrian record of Assurbanipal which states that Gyges, king of Lydia, sent Ionian and Carian mercenaries (about 655) to aid Psammetichus I of Egypt in throwing off the yoke of Assyria. Some Greeks certainly turned to piracy. Any reader of the *Odyssey* will remember the piratical raids in which men like Odysseus and Menelaus engaged. The greeting which old Nestor gave to Telemachus and his followers (*Odyssey*, 3.71–74): "Strangers, who are you? Whence do you come sailing over the watery way? Are you roaming over the sea on business or recklessly like pirates who wander risking their lives and bringing evil to others?" shows how common piracy was—so common and respectable that, as Thucydides (1.5) remarks, a host in asking a question like Nestor's was not insulting his guests. The Ionian (Iamani) mentioned in an Assyrian cuneiform tablet as having established himself as ruler in the Philistine city Ashdod in 711, only to be driven out shortly by the Assyrians, was presumably a Greek private adventurer. As cities developed and public authority grew, piracy gradually gave way to trade, but for a long while the same men probably could be either traders or pirates, depending on what the particular circumstances were.

Considering that the Greeks, through the Aeolian, Ionian, and Dorian migrations, had already established themselves on the coast of Asia Minor, it might seem natural for further Greek expansion to have occurred in the Near East. A brief glance at contemporary conditions in that area will explain why the Greeks, on the whole, turned in other directions.[1]

The chaos that ensued in Greece following the collapse of Myce-

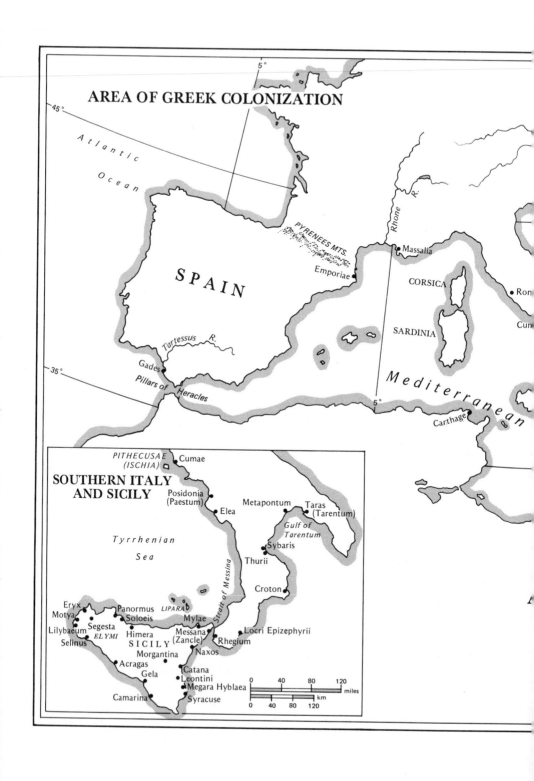

AREA OF GREEK COLONIZATION

Atlantic

Ocean

45°

5°

PYRENEES MTS.

Rhone R.

• Massalia

Emporiae

CORSICA

• Ron

S P A I N

SARDINIA

Cun

Tartessus R.

35°

Gades

Pillars of Heracles

5°

Mediterranean

Carthage

PITHECUSAE
(ISCHIA)

Cumae

SOUTHERN ITALY
AND SICILY

Posidonia
(Paestum)

Elea

Metapontum

Taras
(Tarentum)

Tyrrhenian

Sea

*Gulf of
Tarentum*

Sybaris

Thurii

Croton

Strait of Messina

Eryx

Motya

Panormus

Soloeis

LIPARA

Mylae

Segesta

ELYMI

Messana
(Zancle)

Locri Epizephyrii

Lilybaeum

Himera

Rhegium

Selinus

SICILY

Naxos

Morgantina

Acragas

Catana

Gela

Leontini

Camarina

Megara Hyblaea

Syracuse

0	40	80	120
miles

0	40	80	120
km

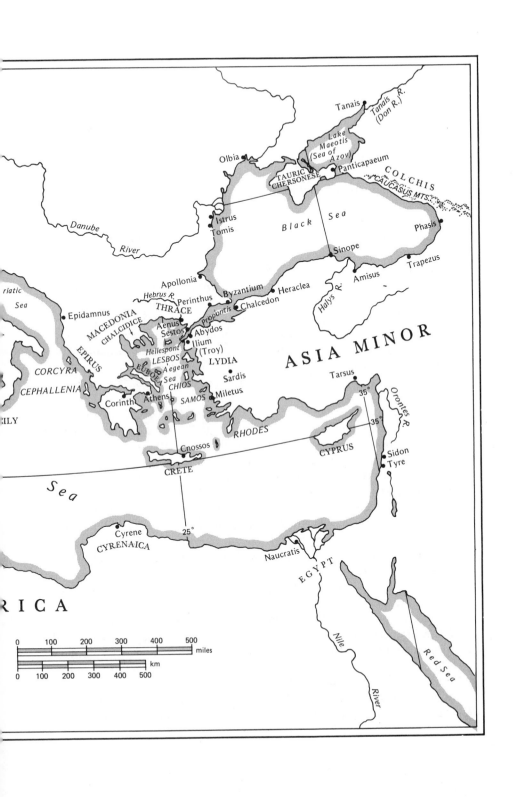

Tanais

Tanais R.
(Don R.)

Lake Maeotis (Sea of Azov)

Olbia

TAURIC CHERSONESE

Panticapaeum

COLCHIS

CAUCASUS MTS.

Danube

Istrus
Tomis

River

Black   Sea

Phasis

Sinope

Trapezus

riatic

Sea

Epidamnus

Apollonia

Hebrus R.

Perinthus

Byzantium

Heraclea

Amisus

MACEDONIA

THRACE

Propontis

Chalcedon

Halys R.

ASIA MINOR

CHALCIDICE

Aenus

Sestos

Abydos

EPIRUS

Hellespont

Ilium
(Troy)

LESBOS

LYDIA

Tarsus

CORCYRA

Aegean

EUBOEA

Sea

Sardis

35°

CEPHALLENIA

CHIOS

Orontes R.

Corinth

Athens

SAMOS

Miletus

35°

ILY

RHODES

CYPRUS

Sidon
Tyre

Cnossos

CRETE

Sea

25°

Cyrene

CYRENAICA

Naucratis

EGYPT

RICA

Nile

Red Sea

River

0	100	200	300	400	500

miles

km

0	100	200	300	400	500

naean civilization had its counterpart in the Near East. Great powers either disappeared or were so weakened that for several centuries their aggressive policies were curtailed. This fact is of great importance, for it meant that during their weak and formative period the Greeks were able to lay the foundations of their cities and civilization free from foreign interference. If in the Dark Age the Hittites, Babylonians, Assyrians, or Egyptians had been strong, it is most unlikely that the Greeks, at least those in Asia Minor, would have been able to develop as independent people.

By the eighth and seventh centuries, the great period of Greek colonization, the situation in the Near East, as it concerned the Greeks, can be summarized as follows. Early in the seventh century Phrygian power collapsed, and the Lydians, who may have been part of that realm, established under Gyges a kingdom in western Asia Minor which seriously threatened the Greeks living on the coast.

Syria to the southeast, as always, was playing an important role in history. In northern Syria the Minoans had had trade relations with Ugarit (Ras Shamra), and subsequently the Mycenaeans had settlements there and on the island of Cyprus. Ugarit was destroyed early in the twelfth century, apparently by the Peoples of the Sea. The return of the Greeks to this general region was demonstrated by Sir Leonard Woolley in his excavations between 1936 and 1949 at Alalakh and Al Mina.[2] Alalakh, some forty miles north of Ras Shamra, was on the Orontes, about twenty miles inland from the mouth of the river. This site, after having been inhabited for over 2,000 years, was utterly destroyed in the first decade of the twelfth century by the Peoples of the Sea, and was never really settled again. Woolley reasoned, however, that Alalakh must have had a harbor town at the mouth of the Orontes, and even though this harbor town was presumably destroyed also in the 1190s, its location would have been too important to be permanently abandoned. His reasoning was proved correct by his excavations at Al Mina, which revealed a city—almost certainly the Posideium mentioned by Herodotus—that had existed from at least the last half of the ninth century. The remains of the buildings—chiefly warehouses—and the pottery—Cypriote, Cycladic, Euboean, Rhodian, and, later, Corinthian and Attic—suggest that this was a trading post established by Greek merchants coming from many areas. Its significance as a place where Greeks and easterners met and where oriental products and ideas could enter the Aegean world is obviously very great. One would like to know whether occupation of Al Mina had been continuous from the close of the Mycenaean period, but unfortunately the area on which the earlier strata, if there were earlier strata, would have been has been washed away in the course of time by the current of the Orontes.

The Semitic people with whom the Greeks came most into contact were the Phoenicians, or Sidonians as they are called in Homer.[3] The Phoenicians were Canaanites—the name Phoenikes (red men) was given to them by the Greeks. Their cities, such as Berytus, Byblus, Sidon, and Tyre, were usually subject to the Egyptians in the latter centuries of the second millennium. It was only after the collapse of the Hittite Empire and the decline of Egypt in the twelfth century that the Phoenicians became really independent and began to play an important role in the eastern, and later in the western, Mediterranean world. This role involved chiefly trade, and the opportunities for expansion of this activity were obviously increased by the decline of the Mycenaeans, who had dominated the waters of the Aegean and the eastern Mediterranean in the fourteenth and thirteenth centuries. Evidence for Phoenician trade in these regions in the early part of the first millennium exists in Cyprus, Rhodes, and Crete, where Phoenician wares have been discovered, and also in the various references to Sidonian commerce and commodities in Homer. Except possibly at Citium in southeastern Cyprus, however, there is no evidence for a Phoenician colony. In the eastern Mediterranean area, then, it seems better to think of the Phoenicians as traders who were responsible for introducing the Greeks to many aspects of the Orient, but not as colonizers of permanent settlements. In the west the story was different, as will be seen later in this chapter.

Throughout most of this period the strongest power in the Near East was Assyria.[4] The Assyrians, the center of whose kingdom was at Assur and Nineveh on the upper Tigris, for centuries had been an important element in the history of Mesopotamia and eastern Asia Minor, but their early history is far from clear. In the eighth and seventh centuries they launched a series of attacks westward to gain control of Syria. In 721 the kingdom of Israel became an Assyrian province, and somewhat later the kingdom of Judah was reduced to the status of a vassal. Sidon was destroyed, the other Phoenician cities had to accept Assyrian overlordship, and about 671 Egypt succumbed to Assyrian armies.

During these years when the Assyrian empire was attaining its greatest size, a little evidence has been preserved of relations between the Assyrians and the Greeks. An Assyrian document of the year 711 records that "an accursed Iamani" (Ionian) who had become master of the Philistine city Ashdod was driven out. Two years later, after Assyria had taken control of Cyprus, tribute from seven Greek kings on the island came to Sargon II in Babylon. The Hellenistic Babylonian historian

Berossus states that under Sennacherib (705–681) there was a battle between the Assyrians and the Greeks in the Cilician plain, a fact which presumably should be interpreted as an Assyrian effort to prevent Greek colonization in that region.

For centuries after the repulse of the Peoples of the Sea in the early twelfth century, Egyptian power and prestige were at a low ebb.[5] The country was distracted by struggles between the priest kings of Ammon at Thebes and the various generals of the mercenaries who established themselves as pharaohs at Memphis. In the middle of the eighth century the Ethiopians established a dynasty (XXV), under which, in 671, Egypt became subject to Assyria. Soon thereafter, Psammetichus (663–609) from Sais in the Nile Delta, a man of Libyan mercenary stock, succeeded in founding the Saite dynasty (XXVI) and ridding the country of Assyrian domination. He was aided in his undertakings by Ionian and Carian mercenaries, including a detachment sent by Gyges, king of Lydia. Some of these mercenaries, at least, received grants of land as reward for their military service and were garrisoned in various parts of Egypt. Before long they were followed by Greek traders, for Psammetichus and his successors opened up Egypt to the Greeks, a subject which will be discussed later in this chapter. Here only one significant point need be mentioned: Psammetichus, in an effort to secure the support of the priests and the people, inaugurated a deliberate policy of imitating various aspects of the Old Kingdom, particularly in the realm of art and religion. Hence the Egypt which the Greeks first came to know and which influenced them so greatly was a deliberately archaizing one.

I T WAS THE Greek colonizing movement, beginning in the eighth century, that more than anything else caused the Greeks to emerge from the Dark Age; and their contacts with certain peoples of older civilizations, especially the Assyrians and Egyptians, furnish the first definite dates in Greek history. The commencement of the colonizing activity coincided largely with the period in which the poleis were beginning to appear. In fact, the phenomenon of colonization is one of the strongest reasons for dating the emergence of the city-states to the latter part of the eighth century, for, since the colonies seem to have been established as poleis, the logical inference is that they were sent out by poleis. In many ways the new foundations, to protect themselves in strange new lands, may have had to organize themselves more thoroughly than the mother cities. It is quite possible that the more regulated colonies and the success which many enjoyed had considerable influence on the development of the polis way of life in the homeland.

The conditions in the Near East certainly explain in part why the

Greeks, when they entered upon their colonizing activity, turned westward.[6] According to tradition, which in this case is supported by archaeology, the first Greek colonies in the west were at Pithecusae (Ischia), a little island off the Bay of Naples, and at Cumae at the northern end of that bay. The date for the founding of Cumae was about 750 B.C., but recent excavations have revealed evidence for Greek settlers at Pithecusae some twenty-five years earlier.[7]

These Greeks who migrated westward in the middle of the eighth century were not entering a totally unknown world. Sicily and southern Italy had to a certain extent been included in the Mycenaean sphere, as is revealed by Mycenaean sherds discovered in those areas, by some Mycenaean influence on native pottery, and also by the tholos-like tombs which have been discovered in Sicily at Thapsus and near Agrigentum. Evidence for Cretan connections with the west is much more tenuous, but one would like to know what to make of the legend that the inventor-craftsman Daedalus, fleeing the wrath of Minos, sought refuge with Cocalus, a king in Sicily, who murdered the pursuing Cretan king (Diodorus, 4.78–79). In the Dark Age, following the collapse of Mycenaean civilization, contact between Sicily and Italy and the mainland of Greece probably stopped completely. By the early eighth century, however, some sort of contact had been resumed, as is shown by the presence of a few Greek vases in Etruscan tombs. It is worth noting that fragments of eighth-century Greek pottery have been found in various native settlements over or near which the Greeks subsequently established their colonies.

The *Odyssey*, which probably was assuming more or less final form in the eighth century, also can be considered as evidence for a revival of knowledge of the west. Odysseus' account of his wanderings in books 9–12 presumably reflects some of the tales told by adventurers and traders. Scylla and Charybdis and the Cyclopes, no matter what they may have referred to in the earliest versions of the legends, certainly are to be associated in the *Odyssey* with the straits of Messina and Mt. Etna, respectively.

The colonists of Pithecusae and Cumae came from Chalcis and Eretria in Euboea and from Cyme in Aeolis, which gave its name to the settlement in Italy. One may well wonder why these first colonists did not settle on some spot nearer the Greek mainland, on the heel or toe of Italy or the east coast of Sicily, rather than boldly proceeding through the straits of Messina and up the west coast of Italy. Since various sites with fertile land were available to the colonists before they reached Pithecusae, it is probable that in this venturesome expedition the leaders were seeking a location which would be advantageous for obtaining metals—chiefly copper and iron—from the Etruscans, who, sailing probably from the east on several occasions in the tenth and ninth centuries, had settled and prospered in the region north of Rome. Excavations have unearthed the components of an eighth-century iron "foundry" on the island. Interest in trade is emphasized by the number of oriental objects found in the ruins, which reminds one that the Euboeans had shared also in the Greek activities at Al Mina from the end of the ninth century. Since Pithecusae and Cumae with their fertile land were also fine locations for agricultural colonies, the former protected from attack by land, the latter with an adequate citadel, it is probably a mistake, as with many other colonies, to think that settlements had to be either agricultural or commercial. Those settlers at Pithecusae who were interested in trade may also have realized that the island was an excellent base for piratical enterprises.

Cumae played a very important role in the history of western civilization, for, since it was the most northerly of the Greek colonies in Italy, it was the first Greek community with which the Etruscans and later the Romans came into contact. The Cumaeans used a Chalcidic form of the Greek alphabet, and it was this alphabet which the Etruscans adopted and later passed on to the Romans. The first example of this Chalcidic alphabet was discovered on a geometric cup found at a level in the Pithecusae excavations to be dated about 730 B.C. On this cup three lines, written from right to left, had been incised. Professor John Boardman's translation of these hexameters runs: "Nestor had a most drink-worthy cup, but whoever drinks of mine will straightway be smitten with desire of fair-crowned Aphrodite." Among the settlers at Cumae there was apparently a group from Boeotia called Graei. Since these were among the first Greeks whom the Romans came to know, it seems that these obscure people were the origin of the name "Graeci" which the Romans ultimately applied to all the Hellenes.

After Cumae, the next series of Greek colonies were founded first in Sicily and then in southern Italy. Thucydides in his sketch at the beginning of book 6 gives a valuable list of the colonies in Sicily which provides a relative chronology for their establishment. Herodotus also furnishes some useful data, and later authors like Pseudo-Scymnus (ca. 100 B.C.), Strabo (age of Augustus) in books 5 and 6 of his *Geography*, and the fourth century A.D. bishop-historian Eusebius of Caesarea contribute information, misinformation, and legends. Chalcidians from Euboea, apparently reinforced on occasions by other Ionians, were the most active colonizers. About 734 they founded Naxos on the eastern coast of Sicily; the name has led to the natural inference that some of the settlers came from the Aegean island Naxos. Sicilian Naxos itself remained small, but the original number of colonists must have been considerable, for six years later Naxos colonized Leontini and shortly thereafter Catana, both located to the south of Naxos. These two settlements, lying in rich agricultural land, soon outstripped their founder, but the Greeks in Sicily did not forget that Naxos was the earliest Greek foundation on the island. Thucydides (6.3.1) remarks that envoys on sacred missions (*theoroi*), before sailing from Sicily, first sacrificed on the altar of Apollo Archegetes, which in his time was outside the city of Naxos. A few years later the Chalcidians founded Zancle on the Sicilian side and Rhegium on the Italian side of the straits of Messina, thus gaining control of this important waterway. These colonies surely were founded for commercial and political reasons, for neither possessed adequate arable land. In fact the food problem must have been a serious one until Zancle about ten years later founded some twenty miles to the west Mylae, which controlled a fertile plain. Certain ancient accounts relate that some Messenians, driven out of Messenia in the First Messenian War because they were unwilling to come to terms with the Spartans, joined the Chalcidians in the settlement of Rhegium. This bit of information is welcome, for, although neither the founding of Rhegium nor the First Messenian War can be dated precisely, the synchronism of the two events suggests a date of 730 to 720 for the founding of Rhegium.

All the colonies so far mentioned—Pithecusae, Cumae, Naxos, Leontini, Catana, Zancle, Rhegium—were founded primarily by the Euboeans, and of the Euboeans, especially by the Chalcidians. It seems clear that the Chalcidians and others were suffering from overpopulation. In this connection it is interesting to note that one of the earliest wars (after the Trojan War) of which there is record in Greece was the one between Chalcis and Eretria for the Lelantine Plain, which lay between the two cities. This war probably should be dated towards the end of the eighth century. It is a logical inference, therefore, that it was land hunger more than anything else that drove many of the Chalcidians to seek new homes in the west.

Thucydides says that the Corinthians founded Syracuse a year after the Chalcidians had settled at Naxos—apparently, then, ca. 733. At the same time the Corinthians established a colony on the important island of Corcyra, driving out the Eretrians who had been there earlier, and thus acquired a dominant position on the route to Sicily. According to the tradition the majority of the Corinthian colonists to Syracuse came from the little plain of Tenea in the territory of Corinth. One would probably be justified in assuming that the people of Tenea went forth in search of land, but this assumption does not preclude the possibility that the Bacchiad oligarchy in Corinth was also thinking of trading opportunities. In any event Syracuse almost from the first had a trading population in addition to the farmers who received lots (*kleroi*) of land in the plain. The island Ortygia, the site of the original colony, was soon connected to the mainland of Sicily by a mole, and before long Syracuse, with its splendid harbor and control of good grain land, became the greatest city in Sicily. Corinthian wares, chiefly pottery and bronzes, came to Syracuse and other Sicilian cities in increasing amounts. Corinth's prosperity as a commerical city began with the founding of Syracuse.

The other chief colonies in Sicily need be mentioned only briefly. A few years after the founding of Syracuse, Corinth's neighbor on the isthmus, Megara, established a colony called Megara Hyblaea (Hybla had been a native community in Sicily) a short distance to the north of Syracuse. Because of the greater power of adjacent Syracuse and Leontini, Megara did not flourish, but about a century after its founding it established a colony, Selinus, in fertile land on the southwest coast of Sicily. Selinus was to play an important role in Greek history. Gela on the south coast was founded, according to Thucydides, forty-five years after Syracuse by colonists from Rhodes and Crete. It expanded greatly and in 580 established to the west the agricultural colony of Acragas, which before long outstripped its mother city in size and prosperity. On the north coast, west of Mylae, only one Greek colony was founded. About 648 some settlers from Zancle and elsewhere established the town of Himera, which brought the Greeks into close contact with the Phoenicians in the western part of Sicily. With this mention of the Phoenicians it becomes necessary to comment briefly on the various peoples whom the Greeks, as they expanded around Sicily, found living on the island.

T HUCYDIDES in the beginning of book 6 says that before the Greeks started coming to Sicily in the eighth century, the island was inhabited by Sicans, Elymians, Sicels, and Phoenicians. He believed that the Sicans were of Iberian stock and that subsequently they were driven into the southern and western parts of the island when the Sicels arrived in large numbers from southern Italy. Most scholars now believe that the Sicans and Sicels, as well as the inhabitants of southern Italy, were basically of an Illyrian stock superimposed on an aboriginal "Mediterranean" population. These people had received certain Mycenaean influences, as can be seen from the pottery and *fibulae* unearthed in the excavations and from the tholos-type tombs. If they were of an Illyrian stock, their language belonged to the Indo-European family, and they themselves were probably akin to many of the Illyrian peoples on the mainland of Greece. To the Greeks, however, they were barbarians, and they were regularly expelled from their settlements along the coast when the Greeks established their colonies. Those who remained were reduced to the status of serfs on the estates of the Greek colonists. Archaeology has been revealing that Greek influence penetrated inland much more than had been realized. The native town of Morgantina became thoroughly hellenized in the course of the sixth century; how much intermingling there was in such a site between natives and Greeks is still an obscure question.[8] The extreme west of the island, except for the coast, was the home of a mysterious people known as the Elymians. Their chief cities were Segesta and Halicyae, both of which became prominent in fifth-century Greek history, and they also had a sacred place on Mt. Eryx. Thucydides thought that they were Trojans who had sailed westward after the fall of Troy. This idea of Trojan arrival in the west was later taken up by the Romans and ultimately immortalized in Vergil's *Aeneid*. Whatever their origin, the Elymians were of a rather high culture which easily adapted itself to Greek and Phoenician influences—a characteristic which in itself may support the notion that they had come from the east.

In the same passage Thucydides records that the Phoenicians had been settled on promontories and small islands all around Sicily, but with the coming of the Greeks they had retired to the west, settling in Motya, and in Panormus and Soloeis in the northwest. Since there is no archaeological evidence for the presence of Phoenicians in eastern Sicily and no traditions preserved concerning struggles between them and the Greeks in the eighth and seventh centuries, it seems probable that Thucydides was misinformed. Possibly, as has been suggested, Thucydides, like all other Greeks, was under the spell of Homer; since Homer implied that the Phoenicians were more or less omnipresent, he took it for granted that they must have had stations all around Sicily. Because in the fifth century the Phoenicians were found only in western Sicily, the inference was that they had been driven westward by the Greeks.

The ancients, in general, believed that Phoenicians had sailed west early, founding Gades in 1110, Utica in 1101, and Carthage under the leadership of Elisa (Dido) in 814, and consequently were well established when the Greeks themselves turned westward in the last half of the eighth century. As will be seen below, the findings of archaeology do not confirm these early dates.[9] The ancient tradition also maintained that from their first appearance in the west the Greeks found themselves in hostile relations with the Phoenicians, and this view, presented in the fourth-century historian Ephorus, as preserved in Diodorus, and in Diodorus himself, is still prevalent to a certain extent. Ephorus, however, was probably influenced by fourth-century conditions, when relations between Greeks and Carthaginians were constantly bad, and Diodorus' thinking may have been colored by his knowledge of the long and bitter struggles between the Carthaginians and the Romans.

By the founding of Himera in 648 and Selinus in 628 the Greeks had come into proximity with the Phoenicians, but there is no evidence for hostility[10] until the events of about 580 mentioned in confused passages of Diodorus (5.9) and Pausanias (10.11.3). After the Gelaeans and Rhodians had established the colony of Acragas, which strengthened Greek control of southern Sicily, a Cnidian named Pentathlos with a band of Cnidians and Rhodians tried to settle at the site subsequently called Lilybaeum on the western tip of Sicily. A Greek colony at this place would have dominated the small Phoenician settlement at Motya. It seems that after founding his colony Pentathlos aided the people of Selinus in an attack on the Elymian town of Segesta. He was defeated and killed, and his surviving followers fled in their ships to the island of Lipara, where they established themselves. The victorious Elymians with the aid of the Phoenicians then destroyed the newly founded settlement at "Lilybaeum." This episode can be, and has been, interpreted as an effort by the Greeks to force the Phoenicians out of western Sicily.

Motya had been settled by the Phoenicians towards the end of the eighth century, about the same time or slightly later than the archaeological evidence for the founding of Utica and Carthage. From the point of view of the Phoenicians at Carthage, Motya was an important post, not only for trade in Sicily but also as a staging point for ships to and from the Etruscans, with whom the Phoenicians had many relations from at least the early seventh century. The Greek desire to dominate or destroy Motya, unless it is to be considered a chauvinistic move to make Sicily more Greek, presumably had a mercantile basis. In Greek eyes "Lilybaeum" was the best point in Sicily from which to launch ships for the metal wealth of Spain, and there is little doubt that the search for metals was a matter of great concern to both Phoenicians and Greeks. The poet Stesichorus, living in Himera in the first half of the sixth century, wrote of "the boundless silver-rooted springs of the river Tartessus."

Many different views about the nature of Tartessus have been expressed by authors, ancient and modern, but here the subject must be treated succinctly. Since ancient geographers often confused Tartessus with Gades, the city traditionally founded by the Phoenicians in 1110, it is not surprising that the belief arose that the Phoenicians had early learned of Spanish wealth in metals. This belief was strengthened among modern scholars by the frequent occurrence in the Old Testament of the expression "ships of Tarshish" in references, among others, to King Solomon and to Hiram, king of Tyre. These ships carried many products, including metals, and the identification of Tarshish with Tartessus was commonly made. It has been strongly argued, however, that the identification should be with Cilician Tarsus, and that Tarshish is akin to a Semitic word signifying mines or metallic ores.[11] Since the identification Tartessus-Tarshish is questionable, and since archaeology has revealed no traces of Phoenicians in the Cadiz (Gades) area before 550 B.C., it will be interesting to consider what Herodotus has to say about this mysterious place, Tartessus.

In his first book (chapter 163) Herodotus, after mentioning the Persian attack on Phocaea (c. 546), says: "These Phocaeans were the earliest of the Greeks to make long sea-voyages; it was they who discovered Adria and Tyrrhenia, Iberia and Tartessus, not sailing in round freight-ships but in fifty-oared vessels." On arriving at Tartessus they were treated well by the king, Arganthonios, who, on their departure, presented them with considerable wealth. This Phocaean voyage of discovery can be dated to approximately the middle of the seventh century. Herodotus mentions Tartessus again (4.152) in his story about the Samian merchant Kolaios, who, while sailing to Egypt, was driven by contrary winds through the Pillars of Heracles to Tartessus. This episode can be dated to about 638. Kolaios found there an untouched (*akēraton*) market and returned to Samos with incredible profits. The word "untouched" is interesting; presumably the Phocaeans had not acted as merchants, because they were exploring in a penteconter. If Kolaios found an untouched market, however, the implication is that he, and not Phoenicians years or generations before, was the first person to tap the metals of the region.

It seems then that the Greeks, particularly the Phocaeans and Samians, discovered the mineral wealth of Tartessus, which should be identified with the river called Baetis by the Romans, the present Guadalquivit. The Phocaeans continued their activities in the west by colonizing Massalia (Marseilles) about 600 and several smaller posts on the east coast of Spain. Since the Greeks were trying to maintain control of this valuable source of metals, it is quite possible that the attempt to found "Lilybaeum" had the aim of establishing a Greek port facing Spain and eliminating a Phoenician one. But the Greeks were too disorganized to retain the monopoly indefinitely. The survivors of Pentathlos' band who had sailed to Lipara found piracy on Etruscan ships so fruitful that they caused the Etruscans and Phoenicians to form an alliance. Another band of Phocaeans, fleeing from the Persian conquest of Ionia ca. 546, sailed to their colony founded some twenty years earlier at Alalia in Corsica, but they engaged in piracy so extensively that they were attacked by a combined Etruscan and Phoenician fleet and forced to evacuate the island. Corsica fell to the Etruscans, and Sardinia more and more came under the control of the Phoenicians. These Phoenicians were chiefly from Carthage, which, since the weakening of Tyre caused by the long siege of Nebuchadnezzar, 585–572, took over the leadership of the Phoenicians in the west.

The picture in Sicily is not clear, but it is probable that Carthage tried to strengthen the position of Motya and the other Phoenician communities. It was the increase of Carthaginian influence in west Sicily that may partially explain the actions of Dorieus in 511–510, as told by Herodotus (5.42–47). Dorieus, the younger brother of the Spartan king Cleomenes, received official permission to found a colony apparently directed against Carthage. He first went to the African coast between Cyrene and Carthage, but after about two years (ca. 514–512) he was driven out by the Carthaginians and natives. Then, following a brief return to Sparta, he set out on a venture (511–510) to establish a Greek settlement under Mt. Eryx. This aim was so clearly an aggressive Greek attempt to dominate western Sicily that the Carthaginians, Sicilian Phoenicians, and Elymians combined and in a battle, in which Dorieus was killed, put an end to the Greek undertaking. It is worth noting that in this struggle the people of Selinus who had been profiting from trade with Carthage did nothing to assist Dorieus.

To summarize this brief discussion of the relations between the Phoenicians and the Greeks in the west, the situation at the end of the sixth century can be stated as follows: the Carthaginians, succeeding to the role of Tyre, had strengthened themselves in Africa, had become leaders of the Phoenicians in west Sicily, and had gained a controlling position in Sardinia and the Balearic islands. It was at this time also that the Carthaginians succeeded in barring the Greeks from sailing through the Pillars of Heracles and having access to the metals of Tartessus by establishing a naval base at Carteia (Algeciras) in what is now the bay of Gibraltar.

W HILE THE Greeks were colonizing Sicily in the eighth and seventh centuries, a similar migration was finding its way to the boot of Italy, but, whereas in the former movement the Chalcidians and Corinthians were the most active participants, in the latter the small Achaean states on the south shore of the Corinthian Gulf took the lead. About 720 a group of Achaeans founded Sybaris on the Italian instep. This city grew so rich from its fertile lands and later also from commerce until its destruction in 511/10 by its southern rival Croton that the word "Sybarite" became and still is a term to describe a luxurious voluptuary.

Some twenty years after its founding Sybaris established an agricultural colony on the west coast of Italy, not far southeast of the Bay of Naples. The prosperity that this colony—Posidonia (Paestum)—attained is still revealed by the best-preserved temples from the Greek world. The Achaeans also founded Croton ca. 708; flourishing with its fertile fields, it became famous for its athletes, doctors, and its school of Pythagoreans. Another Achaean settlement was Metapontum, founded ca. 650 in the instep of Italy, whose prosperity from agriculture is symbolized by the emblem of an ear of barley on its coinage.

Some twenty miles east of the site of Metapontum, Taras (Roman Tarentum) was founded by the Partheniai from Sparta ca. 706. This was the only colony founded by Sparta in the west, for when other states were trying to solve the problem of land hunger by colonization, Sparta solved its similar difficulty by the conquest of Messenia. The motive for the colony has been obscured by legends which attempted to explain the term "Partheniai," but it is clear that the basic cause was political. The Partheniai apparently were men who were dissatisfied with their political position; according to legend they were sons born to Spartan women in the many years during which their husbands were absent fighting in Messenia. Gathering at Amyclae, the chief pre-Dorian town of Laconia, they organized a rebellion, but finally were persuaded to depart to Taras. Since the chief god of Amyclae, Apollo Hyacinthus, was also worshipped at Taras, it is possible that some of the rebels were pre-Dorians. The colony, however, was definitely Doric, as is proved by its dialect and institutions; and whatever were the true causes of its founding, it retained friendly relations with Sparta. During the seventh, sixth, and fifth centuries it was rather inconspicuous compared to the Achaean colonies, but in the fourth century it became the most powerful of the Greek cities in southern Italy. It should be mentioned that the stories placing its founding shortly after the end of the First Messenian War provide, as in the case of Rhegium, a welcome synchronism between events in the Peloponnesus and those in Italy and Sicily.

Only two other Greek colonies in Italy need be mentioned at this time. About 673 the Locrians, very possibly both the eastern and western branches, established Locri Epizephyrii near the toe of Italy on the eastern coast. About a generation later Zaleucus, known as the earliest of the Greek lawgivers, drew up a code of law for Locri. The last of the Greek settlements in Italy in this colonizing period was Elea, some twenty miles south of Posidonia on the west coast. The founders were Phocaeans from Asia Minor who had established themselves at Alalia in Corsica about 565, presumably as a stopping point on the westward sea route. Reinforced by Phocaean refugees from the Persians about 546, they soon were so threatened by combined Etruscan and Carthaginian resistance to their piracy that they abandoned their Corsican home and sailed to the future Elea, where they enjoyed a quiet prosperity and also gave rise to an important school of philosophy (Herodotus, 1.165–167).

The only Greek colony of great importance west of Italy and Sicily was Massalia (Marseilles), founded by the Phocaeans slightly east of the mouth of the Rhone about 600 B.C. Earlier than this the Rhodians apparently had explored the western Mediterranean, founded a colony, Rhode, on the northeast coast of Spain, and given their name to the river Rhone. Subsequently the Phocaeans (through Massalia) refounded Rhode, changing its name to Emporiae, "Market" (modern Ampurias), and established several other stations on the east and south coasts of Spain to secure the route for the metal trade with Tartessus. By the end of the sixth century, however, as mentioned earlier, the Carthaginians succeeded in barring the Pillars of Heracles to the Greeks. Massalia itself became a great trading city through which raw materials from the interior passed into the Greek world and Greek products reached the native Celts. The most famous of these products is the magnificent bronze krater, over five feet high, dated about 520 B.C., which was found in a royal Celtic grave at Vix. The depth of Massaliot influence on the Celts is emphasized by the fact that even to this day certain traces of Phocaean Greek seem to be detectable in some southern French dialects.[12]

Although the dates of the western colonies are not as exact as one would wish, scholars are in general agreement that after the founding of Ischia and Cumae ca. 750, the intense activity of the Euboeans, especially the Chalcidians, and of the Corinthians should be assigned to the last third of the eighth century. There is less unanimity, however, about the initial stages of the colonizing movement in the Aegean area. In the northwest corner of the Aegean, forming the eastern border of the Thermaic Gulf, lies the three-pronged promontory known in ancient and modern times as Chalcidice. It is almost certain that the region owed its name to the number of colonies founded there by Chalcis in Euboea. The Eretrians and the Aegean island of Andros also participated in this activity occasionally. The usual opinion is that most of these colonies were established by the Chalcidians either simultaneously with the founding of the western colonies or after their activity in the west had ceased. Another point of view argues that the total lack of traditional foundation dates for the colonies in Chalcidice—the only region for which such dates are lacking—in itself points to an early period for the colonizing of the region.[13] Fragment 98 of Aristotle states that in the Lelantine War the Chalcidian colonies sent aid to Chalcis. Colonies presumably would not have been in a position to send such help unless they had been established for a considerable period of time. If the Lelantine War is properly dated about 700, then the inference is that the colonies had been dispatched to Chalcidice two or three generations earlier. Since it is hard to believe that Chalcis had the population and strength to send out hundreds or thousands of colonists west and north at the same time, the more reasonable answer to the problem may be that the first colonies in Chalcidice should be dated to some time early in the eighth century. One colony in this region merits particular mention because of its subsequent importance in Greek history—Potidaea, founded about 600 B.C., as Corinth's only settlement in the Aegean area.

THE TREMENDOUS colonial movement which ultimately led to Greek settlement on the coast of Thrace, and in the regions of the Hellespont, Propontis, and Black Sea, was almost entirely the work of the Ionians and especially of the Milesians.[14] The history of the Ionians in the two or three centuries after their migration to the coast of Asia Minor is little known. By the end of the ninth century the various Ionian communities had organized themselves into some sort of league with a religious center at the Panionion, which was located on the promontory of Mycale. The settlements were ruled by kings who apparently were in some sort of feudal relation to a more powerful king, the king of Ephesus. The suggestion has often been made that the picture presented in the *Iliad* of the trouble Agamemnon had with his unruly subordinates may reflect the unsettled political conditions of Ionia in the ninth and eighth centuries. By the late eighth century the settlements began to develop into what can be called city-states, and kingship yielded to aristocracy. With the disappearance of the political kingships, it is likely that the feudal dependence of the small cities on Ephesus came to an end. By the beginning of the seventh century it seems certain that the population of these towns had increased greatly and that consequently the communities, which were still largely agricultural, were feeling the pinch of land hunger. Extension of their territory into the interior of Asia Minor was impossible, for by this time the consolidation of the Lydian kingdom had erected a formidable barrier against the Greeks. To ease their increasing economic difficulties, therefore, the Ionians had to seek relief beyond their immediate borders.

Their attention was naturally turned towards Thrace, for there the Euboeans, also Ionians, had already taken over the western section by colonizing Chalcidice, and in about 700 the Ionians of the Aegean island of Paros sent colonists, including the poet Archilochus, to Thasos and the adjacent Thracian coast. In the first quarter of the seventh century the island of Chios dispatched settlers to Maronea, about halfway between the mouths of the Nestus and Hebrus rivers. Towards the middle of the century Clazomenae established Abdera slightly east of the mouth of the Nestus. This colony apparently experienced many troubles and a century later was refounded by settlers from Teos. Towards the end of the seventh century a group of Aeolians founded Aenos at the delta of the Hebrus River. These colonies at first were mainly or entirely agricultural, but in the course of time they became important as centers through which products of Thrace reached the Greek world. They did not play a conspicuous part in Greek history, but it is worth remembering that Abdera was the native city of two of the most important fifth-century philosophers or sophists—Democritus and Protagoras.

The colonization of the Hellespont and of the Propontis, a prelude to the great expansion throughout the Black Sea, was undertaken in part, apparently, before the significance of the Black Sea region was realized. The dating of the foundation of these settlements can be only approximate, for the Eusebian chronology is almost universally admitted to be too high, and archaeology is only beginning to provide some scattered evidence. The first activity was associated with the Aeolians. Colonists, probably chiefly from Lesbos, established various small agricultural communities in the Troad on the south shore of the Hellespont in the eighth and early seventh centuries. Excavations reveal that the Greek settlement on the site of Troy, a settlement that was at least partially commercial, should be placed in the eighth century. Miletus became active about 700. That is the approximate date assigned to the founding of Cyzicus, with its excellent harbor and fertile land, on the south shore of the Propontis. Strabo (13.1.22) describes Abydos on the Asiatic side of the Hellespont as a Milesian colony founded with the consent of Gyges of Lydia. A suggested interpretation of this statement is that Abydos in its origin was a contingent of Milesian mercenaries posted there as a garrison against Thracians from Europe who had been raiding Asia Minor. In any case, the association of Abydos with the name of Gyges seems good evidence for the establishment of the town sometime in the first half of the seventh century. In the third quarter of that century Megara, the neighbor of Corinth, founded, among other colonies, Chalcedon and Byzantium on the Asiatic and European sides, respectively, of the Bosporus. According to Herodotus (4.144) Chalcedon was settled seventeen years before Byzantium. He and later writers (Strabo, 7.6.2; Tacitus, *Annals*, 12.63; see the long discussion in Polybius, 4.38–44) were amazed at the blindness of the Megarians in not colonizing Byzantium first, for Byzantium had a superb harbor and also, because of the nature of the currents, was able to dominate all shipping passing up or down the Bosporus. The explanation clearly is that at the time of the founding of Chalcedon, the great trading possibilities of the Black Sea were not yet fully realized. Chalcedon attracted the Megarians because of its fertile land and also possibly because the small island off Chalcedon, Chalcis, had copper deposits.

About the end of the seventh century the Samians, whose activity usually was directed to the south and west, founded several colonies on the north shore of the Propontis, of which the most important was Perinthus. Again, as in the case of Byzantium, the reason for the establishment of these communities should be sought primarily in the opening of the Black Sea region to Greek traders. The effect of these new commercial possibilities can be detected also in contemporary developments in the Thracian Chersonese (modern Gallipoli). Sestos, originally a Thracian town and later an Aeolian colony, now became important, like Abydos on the Asiatic side, for its strategic position on the Hellespont. More revealing is the activity of the Athenians. Until about 600 they had taken no part in any colonizing enterprises, but at this date, as will be discussed in a later chapter, they established Elaious on the tip of the Thracian Chersonese and made efforts to acquire control of Asiatic Sigeum, just opposite, at the entrance of the Hellespont.

Greek colonization of the Black Sea region was of great importance for subsequent Greek history. A huge area, rich in metals, timber, grain, fish, and many other products, was thus opened to a Greek world whose resources in raw materials and food products were inadequate for the constantly growing population. The necessity to pay for these imports stimulated the activity of Greek craftsmen—especially the potters and metalworkers. Greek civilization had considerable influence on the peoples living on the Black Sea, as has been revealed by excavations of various sites along the northern shore, and in their turn the Greeks received new ideas, particularly in the fields of religion and art. The earliest contacts between the Greeks and the Black Sea are shrouded in the same darkness which engulfs all early Greek history. It is possible that some Mycenaeans may have penetrated the area, but the few Mycenaean-type artifacts which have been discovered in the Caucasus region obviously do not prove the presence there of Mycenaean traders. The story of Jason and the ship Argo is referred to in the *Odyssey* (12.69–72), and certainly the legend of the Argonauts in its developed form reflected the adventures of early voyagers to the Black Sea.

Colonization proper apparently did not begin until the last quarter of the seventh century. The most accurate information for the establishment of the colonies in the seventh and sixth centuries seems to be that furnished by Pseudo-Scymnus, who links the foundations with various events in Median and Persian history. The data provided so far by archaeology largely confirm his dates.

Although other cities participated in this great colonizing movement, Miletus was by far the most active. Pliny in his *Natural History* (5.112) states that Miletus founded more than ninety cities in the general area. This number, even though one may consider it exaggerated, is significant, for clearly Miletus did not have an adequate population to establish that many colonies of an agricultural type. Most of the settlements, at least in the beginning, were trading posts. The Greeks were looking for commodities which were in short supply at home, and they settled in places where the supplies of fish, metals, timber, and grain were in abundance.

No attempt will be made here to enumerate all the colonies of which there is record, but it will be worthwhile to list and comment briefly on those which played an important role in Greek and, in some cases, in subsequent history. It is less confusing to list them by their consecutive geographical positions, starting with the west coast of the Black Sea, than chronologically by foundation dates, many of which are uncertain.

Along the west coast northward from the Bosporus lay Apollonia; Mesembria; Tomis (modern Costanza), where the exiled Ovid about 9 A.D. wrote his *Tristia;* Istrus, not far from the Ister (Danube) Delta; and at the mouth of the Dniester, Tyras (modern Belgorod-Dnestrovsk). On the north coast Olbia was founded in the last quarter of the seventh or in the first half of the sixth century on the estuary of the Bug River; it rapidly became the center of the grain trade to the Greek world, a position which it held until the fourth century B.C. Thereafter it slowly declined in importance and by the fourth century A.D. disappeared from history. Further to the east was the Tauric Chersonese (Crimea). Here about 600 the Milesians established Panticapaeum (Kerch) on the Cimmerian Bosporus. Within a century various other colonies were founded in this area and also across the straits—some sent out by Panticapaeum itself. In the fifth century these communities united to form the Bosporan Kingdom, with its capital at Panticapaeum. This kingdom, composed of Scythian and Greek elements, in the fourth century supplanted Olbia as the center of the grain trade; it continued in existence, but with many vicissitudes, until the fourth century A.D. The most northerly colony to be founded, which became part of the Bosporan Kingdom, was Tanais on the mouth of the Tanais (Don) River where it flows into Lake Maeotis (Sea of Azov). The chief remains of this town date from the third century B.C., but Soviet archaeologists have discovered traces of what was presumably an earlier stage of the colony only a few miles distant.

On the eastern coast, where the Caucasus mountains recede somewhat from the sea, the Greeks founded several trading colonies, the most important being Phasis and Dioscurias in Colchis, the land of the legendary Medea (west Georgia). On the south shore of the Black Sea, almost at the midpoint, the Milesians founded Sinope in the last quarter of the seventh century. Sinope, with its good harbor, became a flourishing trading city; among its distinguished citizens were the fourth-century Cynic philosopher Diogenes and the fourth- and third-century comic poet Diphilus. Sinope sent out many small trading colonies of which the best known was Trapezus (Trebizond), famous as the place where Xenophon and the remnants of the Ten Thousand first sighted the sea after their march back from the interior of Babylonia. Amisus, slightly east from Sinope, was established by either the Milesians or the Phocaeans about the middle of the sixth century. It soon became important as the chief center for the export of the iron which the neighboring natives—the Chalybes—smelted from the ore derived from mines in their territory. The last colony to be mentioned on the south coast was Heraclea in Bithynia. This city, founded in the first half of the sixth century by Megarians and Boeotians, provided a useful harbor on the voyage from the Bosporus to Sinope. It flourished because of the abundance of tunny fish in the waters and timber in the interior, and by the end of the century sent forth two colonies of its own, Kallatis on the west coast of the Black Sea and Chersonesus in the southwest corner of the Crimea near modern Sevastopol.

T HE COLONIZATION movement so far described was directed to the west, north, and northeast; in the south the activity was much less, but the colonies in Africa, Naucratis and Cyrene, although only two in number, were nonetheless very important in Greek history. Greek relations with Egypt in the Dark Age are obscure.[15] Odysseus' raid on Egypt (*Odyssey*, 14.245–286) and Strabo's statement (17.1.6) that Egyptians were posted at Rhacotis, near the Canopic mouth of the Nile, to prevent foreign raiders are evidence for the prevalence of piracy, presumably in the ninth and eighth centuries. The discovery of Egyptian bronzes probably dating from the early seventh century, especially in Crete and Samos, and Herodotus' story (4.152) that the Samian merchant Kolaios (ca. 638) had been sailing for Egypt before being blown westward to Tartessus, suggest that by the seventh century trading connections of some sort had been established.

The important evidence for the entry of the Greeks into Egypt is associated with Psammetichus I (663–609), the founder of the XXVI (Saite) dynasty. According to Herodotus (2.152–154), Psammetichus, in his successful effort to defeat the eleven other princes in the Delta, employed Ionian and Carian pirates who were raiding the area. Subsequently, as reward to these troops, he granted them land, known as the Camps, on either side of the Pelusian mouth of the Nile. These soldiers and their descendants continued to live there and apparently at the neighboring Daphnai until the pharaoh Amasis about a century later transferred them to Memphis to protect himself against disaffected Egyptians. Herodotus (2.163) says that when Amasis defeated his predecessor Apries and became pharaoh, 30,000 Ionian and Carian mercenaries fought in the army of the defeated monarch. The number may well be greatly exaggerated, but it causes one to suspect that the Ionians and Carians who fought earlier under Psammetichus were more than marauding pirates. It has been persuasively argued that these men must be understood in terms of the social and economic conditions which were sending forth thousands of colonists in these centuries. It is possible that Psammetichus, realizing his need of soldiers to achieve his domestic aims and to drive out the Assyrians, had circulated word in Ionia and Caria that those who came to serve under him would be rewarded with grants of land. The men who flocked to Egypt, then, were part colonists and part soldiers, and formed a continuing army which the pharaoh could employ in addition to the sometimes unreliable class of native warriors. The Greeks who scratched their names on the leg of a statue of Ramses II before the Temple of Abu Simbel in Nubia on the occasion of the invasion of Psammetichus II in 591 may have been descendants of these men (M&L, no. 7). These Ionians and Carians were granted the right of intermarriage with Egyptian women, which presumably explains why in Hellenistic times there were groups of foreigners in Memphis called Hellenomemphitai and Karomemphitai.

Little is known about these Ionians and Carians beyond the military role they played under the Saite pharaohs, a role which probably continued more or less unchanged after the Persian conquest of Egypt in 525. It was the traders and artisans following in the wake of the mercenaries who were responsible for establishing the colony of Naucratis on the Canopic arm of the Nile. Since archaeologists have found pottery on the site dating from the last quarter of the seventh century, it is probable that it was Psammetichus I who granted the Greeks permission to settle on this spot. Because Greek traders could easily turn into pirates, he may very well have considered it better for his kingdom that all these foreigners be assembled in one locality. Herodotus states in an important passage (2.178–179) that Amasis (570–526), being a philhellene, granted Naucratis as a city to live in to the Greeks who came to Egypt, and to the merchants not wishing to live there permanently he gave land for building altars and precincts to the gods. Ionians from Chios, Teos, Phocaea, and Clazomenae, Dorians from Rhodes, Cnidos, Halicarnassus, and Phaselis, and Aeolians from Mytilene (in Lesbos) combined to build a great temple precinct (*temenos*) called the Hellenion. Other Greeks—Aeginetans, Samians, and Milesians—established separate precincts to Zeus, Hera, and Apollo, respectively. Since some of the remains from Naucratis clearly antedate Amasis by several generations, Herodotus is definitely wrong in attributing the beginning of the settlement to his reign. Amasis, in view of the hostility of the Egyptians to the Greeks, may have insisted that Greeks who had strayed away from the original settlement confine themselves to the one site.

To judge from Herodotus' language it was the permanent settlers, presumably merchants and artisans, who formed the polis Naucratis. The transient traders, residing in the market (*emporion*) area, were not classified as citizens. When one contemplates the scattered and confusing information about Naucratis, one realizes that it was not at all a typical Greek colony. Since it was established by traders from numerous cities, there was no "mother city," although centuries later Miletus claimed that honor. The ordinary Greek colony was a free and autonomous city, whereas Naucratis was established only after permission had been granted by the pharaoh (presumably Psammetichus I, revised by Amasis), and it was attached to a native settlement in which archaeology seems to prove that there was a large fort. Efforts were made to keep the Greeks isolated from the natives, and, in contrast to the privileges granted to the mercenaries mentioned above, intermarriage with the Egyptians was forbidden. Also a fourth-century inscription reveals that the area of Naucratis then, as probably before, owed a tithe to an Egyptian deity.

Although much is, and perhaps always will be, unknown about Naucratis, its importance is obvious. It was the one Greek city in Egypt until the founding of Alexandria in 332–331, and for many years it was chiefly through Naucratis that Greek influences could enter Egypt and, what is more significant, that Egyptian influences, colored by the deliberately archaizing policy of the Saite dynasty, could penetrate into the Greek world.

Some five hundred miles to the west of Naucratis, Dorian settlers from Thera, an island in the southern Aegean, founded Cyrene on the north coast of Africa about 631 B.C. Since the unusually large amount of data concerning the founding and early years of Cyrene contained in ancient authors such as Herodotus, Pindar (with scholia), and Diodorus has been supplemented by the discovery at Cyrene of the very important "Stele of the Founders," a rather full account of this colony is indispensable.[16] Although no two Greek colonies evolved in identical ways, nevertheless the fuller information about Cyrene contributes to an understanding of the type of problems inherent in the founding and formative years of other colonies for which less evidence has been preserved. The reader is uged to read the account furnished by Herodotus (4.150–204), for there he will find a fascinating account in which fact, legend, and propaganda are all intermingled.

The island Thera, occupied by Dorians in the early part of the first millennium B.C., suffered severely, according to Herodotus, from a prolonged drought in the latter half of the seventh century. Under this story there is probably concealed the fact that at Thera, as elsewhere, the population had become too large for the limited arable land available. The Theraeans consulted the oracle at Delphi and were told to found a colony in Libya. They thereupon sent two penteconters to Libya under the command of Battus or, as he is called in certain sources, Aristotle. The name Battus presents a problem for which there are at least three possible solutions. It may actually have been the real name of the founder; or it may have been an epithet, meaning stammerer, applied to "Aristotle" because of a speech impediment; or, as Herodotus thought, the founder may have received that name because Battus was the native Libyan word for king. If the last hypothesis is correct, then the Greeks, including the Battiads, soon ceased to think of the word as a title and used it like a regular proper name. Since only two penteconters were dispatched, those selected to go could hardly have exceeded two hundred. The number is significant because it provides evidence for the smallness of some of the colonial undertakings.

Battus and his followers sailed to Itana on the eastern coast of Crete, where they hired a Cretan purple-dyer to serve as their guide. Possibly this episode about the Cretan guide refers to a preliminary exploratory voyage. In any case, the story about the Cretan is reasonable, for Cretan sailors were active at this time and a purple-dyer from Itana may well have been familiar with the dye-producing shellfish on the coast of Africa to the south. The colonists at first settled on a little island, Plataea (Bomba), near the coast. An initial settlement on an offshore island was probably a common procedure; the colonists were thereby provided with an easily defensible home while they tried to ascertain what the attitude of the natives was likely to be. Parallel examples are known from Syracuse, where the island of Ortygia was the first settlement, from

Ischia, which was colonized before Cumae, and probably from Chalcis, the little island off Chalcedon. After two years Battus and his followers moved to a site on the mainland, and then seven years later the Libyans led them to what became the future Cyrene, a place where, as the natives expressed it, the sky is perforated. Here the colony developed, growing rich from its grain, sheep, horses, and the native plant, silphium, which became noted throughout the Greek world for its medicinal value. Other settlements were founded so that by Roman times, at least, the area was known as the Pentapolis.

The name Cyrene (Cyrana in Doric) is apparently derived from the Libyan word *kura,* meaning asphodel; Cyrene, therefore, means the place where there are many asphodels. The date for the founding of the colony is usually given as about 631 B.C., the year mentioned by Eusebius, who presumably was basing his calculations on the work of the famous Hellenistic scholar Eratosthenes, a native of Cyrene. The oldest finds unearthed by archaeologists confirm this dating. Battus, the leader of the settlers, became the king of the new foundation and established the dynasty of the Battiads. So far as the evidence goes Cyrene was the only colony to have a monarchical form of government at first, just as its mother city, Thera, was the only state still under a kingship to send out a colony. During the reigns of Battus and his son Arcesilaus, further settlers presumably came from Thera, possibly including women, but since the original two hundred colonists must have been only men, it is almost certain that from the beginning there was intermarriage between Cyrenaeans and Libyan women.

The third king, Battus II, came to the throne ca. 580. Under him, and with the help of Delphi, many new colonists arrived in Cyrene, especially from the Peloponnesus, Crete, and the islands. To furnish them with "lots" of land, which had been promised as an incentive for migrating to Africa, the territory of the neighboring natives had to be encroached upon. This was the beginning of the hostility between the Cyrenaeans and natives which continued for centuries. The Libyans quite naturally appealed to Egypt for help, for the Egyptian army consisted largely of Libyan mercenaries, and also the Saite dynasty was probably of Libyan origin. Apries, the Egyptian pharaoh, marched westward but was badly defeated by the Cyrenaeans near their city. This battle can be dated to about 570 from its connection with Egyptian chronology, since Apries' disaster was almost immediately followed by the accession of Amasis.

In the reign of Arcesilaus II, the successor of Battus II, political troubles broke out in Cyrene. They were apparently caused by the resentiment of the wealthy landowners against the royal power and by the fact that the descendants of the original Theraeans and also the later arrivals from Thera alone were grouped in the three Dorian tribes, and hence held a privileged position. Arcesilaus' brothers, with a large following, left Cyrene and established Barca some sixty miles to the west. Dynastic feuds and trouble with the natives ensued. Finally under the next king, Battus III, Cyrene appealed to Delphi, and through the assistance of Delphi a Mantinean from Arcadia, Demonax by name, arrived to serve as arbitrator for the feuding Cyrenaeans. As far as can be ascertained, Demonax's reforms were chiefly twofold. First, he abolished, or removed political power from, the three traditional Dorian tribes and divided the free population into three parts, one consisting of Theraeans and the *perioeci* (presumably descendants of the original founders from the town of Thera and its *periocis*), another of Peloponnesians and Cretans, and the third of the islanders. Thereafter, either these three parts served as tribes, in which case the Theraeans would still have been exclusive, even though now controlling only one of these tribes, or, as has been suggested, each tribe consisted of a Theraean, a Peloponnesian and Cretan, and an island section. If this latter suggestion is correct, then Demonax, as Cleisthenes did later in Athens, made each tribe representative of the total population.[17] Second, he curtailed greatly the royal power, possibly reducing it largely to religious functions, and placed the real control of the state in the hands of what Herodotus called the *demos*—the people. Since at this time governing bodies such as magistracies and council must surely have been filled only from the upper and wealthy class, Cyrene, therefore, about the middle of the sixth century changed from monarchy to aristocracy or oligarchy, a transition which had occurred in most Greek states a century and a half or two centuries earlier.

In the 1920s a very interesting inscription, commonly known as the Stele of the Founders, dating from the fourth century B.C., was discovered at Cyrene (*M&L,* no. 5). In the first twenty-two lines, which refer to contemporary conditions, the mover of the decree, which was passed, was seeking to obtain citizenship for Theraeans, who had come to Cyrene to take up residence. In support of his proposal he produced a document called the Pact of the Founders which purported to be the agreement drawn up between the original colonists from Thera to Cyrene and those Theraeans who remained on their island. The Pact (lines 23–40 of the Stele of the Founders), if authentic, is so significant in terms of providing information on the preliminary stages in establishing a colony that it seems advisable to include here the translation offered by A. J. Graham.

AGREEMENT [PACT] OF THE FOUNDERS [line 23]

Decided by the assembly. Since Apollo has given a spontaneous prophesy to Battus and the Theraeans ordering them to colonize Cyrene, the Theraeans resolve that Battus be sent to Libya as leader and king: that the Theraeans sail as his companions: that they sail on fair and equal terms, *according to family;* that one son be conscripted *from each family; that those who sail* be in the prime of life; and that, of the rest of the Theraeans, any free man *who wishes* may sail. If the colonists establish the settlement, any of their fellow-citizens who later sails to Libya shall have a share in citizenship and honours and shall be allotted a portion of the unoccupied land. But if they do not establish the settlement and the Theraeans are unable to help them and they suffer inescapable troubles *up to* five years, let them return from that land without fear to Thera, to their possessions and to be citizens. But he who is unwilling to sail when the city sends him shall be liable to punishment by death and his goods shall be confiscated. And he who receives or protects another, even if it be a father his son or brother his brother, shall suffer the same penalty as the man unwilling to sail. [line 40; end of Pact of the Founders decree] On these conditions they made an agreement, those who stayed here and those who sailed on the colonial expedition, and they put curses on those who should transgress these conditions and not abide by them, whether those living in Libya or those staying in Thera. They moulded wax images and burnt them while they uttered the following imprecation, all of them, having come together, men and women, boys and girls. May he who does not abide by this agreement but transgresses it melt away and dissolve like the images, himself and his seed and his property. But for those who abide by the agreement, both those who sail to Libya and those who remain in Thera, may there be abundance and prosperity both for themselves and their descendants.[18]

Scholars at first were inclined to consider the Pact of the Founders (lines 23–40) and the following narrative section a forgery or at best an account based on the tradition preserved in some local chronicle. Since then a strong case has been made for accepting the Pact as authentic or, at least, as representing a slightly reworded version of the original document.[19] Certainly the proposer of the decree, since the decree was passed, was able to convince his fellow citizens in Cyrene that the Pact was genuine. It is worth noting that only the first part of the Pact (lines 23–40) is given in the form of a decree; the rest of the document (lines 40–51) is presented in narrative. If the proposer had been trying to pass off a forgery, one would expect him to have couched the whole document, given under the heading Pact of the Founders, in the more authentic-seeming form of a decree. Skeptics of the genuineness of the document have pointed to its heading: "Decided by the assembly." Without doubt it is surprising to find such a formula in use in Thera at a time when it was still governed by a king, but a similar phraseology can be cited from contemporary Dreros in Crete (although Dreros was ruled by an aristocracy): "The city has thus decided" (*M&L,* no. 2). On the whole, it seems reasonable to believe that the Pact of the Founders is a copy of an authentic document, possibly edited somewhat to modernize it, which had been preserved from the seventh century on either stone, wood, or some other material. If it is genuine, the importance of the Pact of the Founders for providing an insight into the procedures adopted in organizing a colony and into the mentality of seventh-century Greeks hardly needs to be emphasized.

IN THE preceding pages an attempt has been made to give some idea of the magnitude of the Greek colonization movement in the eighth, seventh, and sixth centuries. Only a few of the innumerable colonies have been mentioned. A complete enumeration would probably be impossible and certainly would be a complicated task, since the pattern, with some colonies failing and then sometimes being subsequently refounded on the same or different sites, and with many colonies themselves sending out new colonies, is very complex. It is necessary to emphasize, however, that the expression "colonization movement" when applied to the Greeks must not be associated in meaning with such modern terms as "colonialism," "colonial policies," or "colonial empires." A few of the early trading posts, some of Corinth's foundations along the northwest coast of Greece, and certain Athenian undertakings in the area of the Hellespont in the sixth century, which will be discussed in a later chapter, possibly could be included under a category of "colonial imperialism," but the overwhelming majority of Greek colonies from their earliest days were independent city-states, completely free from any political connection with, or subordination to, the mother cities.

There must have been considerable variation in the procedures followed in sending out and establishing a colony, especially in the early days before a pattern had been set, but evidence is lacking on just what those variations were. Certainly by the last third of the seventh century, as the data concerning the founding of Cyrene by Thera reveal, the whole undertaking was organized and supervised by the state. Possibly, particularly in the first phase of colonization, the initiative may occasionally have come from some leader, perhaps a disgruntled noble, who succeeded in collecting a band of followers and then set out on what was essentially a private undertaking. One should not eliminate the element of pure love of adventure from some of these enterprises, although it seems clear that in every case a certain amount of information was available concerning the region in which the colony was to be established. Usually, however, the ruling aristocrats or oligarchs in the state dispatched the colonists as a solution to social, economic, or political problems which were plaguing the state, such as overpopulation with its resulting land hunger, and political discontent or feuds. Subsequently the search for necessary raw materials and markets for local products, whether grown or manufactured, became an increasing motive for the founding of colonies.

When a city decided to send out a colony, it probably called for volunteers, but it is clear from the procedure followed in the founding of Cyrene that if enough volunteers were not forthcoming, compulsion, probably through some form of lot, was employed. The favor of the gods was essential for any such dangerous and important undertaking. Hence, by the seventh century at least, it became regular practice for cities on the mainland of Greece and for the Ionians in Asia Minor to obtain the blessing of Apollo at Delphi and Apollo at Didyma, respectively, on the proposed colony. The state appointed the leader of the colony, the *oecist*, under whose guidance the new community was established. After his death the *oecist* was buried in a prominent place in the town, and at his tomb he received the honors due to a hero, as the divine founder of the city. Since the majority of the early colonists wished to become landowners, one of the first tasks of the *oecist*, once possession of the new territory had been acquired, must have been to arrange for the allocation of the land. There is no definite evidence on how the assignments were made, and certainly there is no proof that the lots *(kleroi)* were all of equal size. It seems, however, that the descendants of the holders of the original lots became the aristocratic element, as contrasted with later settlers and members of the artisan class. These aristocrats, many of whose forefathers had been "have-nots," now belonged to the "haves"; and, true to human nature, they ordinarily exhibited little sympathy for the less fortunate who in the course of time emerged in all the colonies.

The colonies, although politically independent from their very foundation, usually—and naturally—maintained close ties with the mother cities. This relationship was symbolized by the sacred fire which the colonists took with them from the hearth of the city they were leaving to kindle the flame on the hearth of the new community. The colonists brought with them the political and religious institutions—the magistracies, the tribal division, the cults—of the mother city, and also the alphabet and calendar. Delegates from the colony were dispatched to attend the chief religious festivals of the founding city and, as trade developed, trade relations between the two communities were usually close. If a colony subsequently sent out a colony of its own, it was the custom to obtain the leader, the *oecist*, from the mother city. Corcyra, for example, when it founded Epidamnus, sent out the colonists under an *oecist* from Corinth.

The importance of the age of colonization for Greek and subsequent history can hardly be exaggerated. In the two centuries from approximately 750 to 550 the Greeks, who previously had been confined to the mainland of Greece, the islands of the Aegean, including Crete to the south, and the west coast of Asia Minor, spread over the whole Mediterranean and Black Sea regions. Throughout this wide area new city-states arose which, although somewhat influenced by local conditions, for the most part developed in similar fashion to the older poleis, reproducing all their good and evil features. The influence of this tremendous expansion on the social, economic, political, and cultural life of the Greeks will be discussed in the pages to come, but this chapter should end with a few observations on the effects of this widespread movement on the attitude of the Greeks towards themselves.

Colonization, by creating hundreds of new city-states, greatly furthered the innate preference of the Greeks to live in self-sufficient, parochial communities. In fact, it was the success of the new colonial settlements that, as much as anything, ensured that the Greek way of life would be that of the polis. But paradoxically, this colonial movement which had such a particularistic effect also contributed to a feeling of unity among the Greeks. On a small scale this resulted from the frequent partnership of inhabitants from two or more cities in the establishing of a colony, but much more from association with various strange peoples. As the Greeks came into contact with the natives of Spain, Italy, and Sicily, with the Thracians, Scythians, Anatolians, Egyptians, and Libyans, the different and seemingly strange ways and characteristics of their new neighbors made them realize more and more that the differences among themselves, if they existed at all, were insignificant. After all, whether men came from Sparta or Corinth, from Locris or Miletus, they all spoke the same language, possessed the same traditions coming down from the Heroic Age, and shared similar religious ideas and attitudes towards life. Although the Greeks probably intermingled with the natives more than is usually realized, especially in the interior of Sicily and with the Thracians, Scythians, and Libyans, on the whole they remained aloof. As the years passed and their city way of life developed in contrast to the tribal or nomadic cultures of the majority of their new neighbors, the Greeks came to think of themselves as different from these other peoples and increasingly to become aware of their own basic unity.

There is no certain evidence as to when the dichotomy between Hellenes and barbarians (that is, those speaking an unintelligible language) became an accepted concept. Thucydides (1.3) says it was late, and points out that Homer did not employ the term Hellenes to designate all the Greeks, nor the expression barbarians to refer to non-Greeks. Actually Homer (*Iliad,* 2.867) does use the term barbarian once, in the expression "barbarian-speaking Carians." Surely it is a safe inference to state that the unifying term Hellene with its opposite, barbarian, came into common parlance as one of the results of colonization. It is significant that the shrine built in conjunction by nine Greek cities in Naucratis in the latter years of the seventh century was called the Hellenion.

Colonization fostered a feeling of unity among the Greeks in another way, which is more or less a corollary to the tendency just described. The Olympian Games according to tradition were established in 776, but they did not acquire a Panhellenic significance until the following century. The other Panhellenic festivals—the Pythian, Isthmian, and Nemean Games, whatever their origin may have been, were little more than local celebrations until the sixth century. It seems clear that the colonies were very influential in transforming these festivals, especially the one at Olympia, into real Panhellenic occasions. The colonists were glad to return periodically to the ultimate motherland, and in August every fourth year they flocked to Olympia in great numbers to watch the athletic contests, to participate in the excitement of the carnival atmosphere, to negotiate some business deals, and incidentally to join in the religious ceremonies before the great temples of Zeus and Hera. The colonies sent their share of athletes to contend in the games, and the prowess of certain victors from the cities of Sicily and from Cyrene were celebrated in some of Pindar's finest *Olympian* and *Pythian* Odes. Hence it is important to bear in mind the significance of these great festivals in keeping the spirit of unity alive and of the colonies in contributing so much to their vitality.

5

Social, Economic, and Political Developments in the Seventh and Sixth Centuries

I N THE EIGHTH century when the age of colonization began, the Greeks were restricted to the Aegean world—the mainland of Greece, the coast of Asia Minor, and the Aegean islands between, including Crete to the south. Two centuries later when the great colonizing impetus subsided, hundreds of Greek colonies, and hence Greek poleis, had been established in the huge area from the Caucasus to Spain and from the Crimea to Egypt. It is obviously impossible, therefore, to write a comprehensive history of the Greeks in the sense of a work that would deal with all these innumerable new settlements as well as with the homelands that gave them birth. Even if source material were available, such a history could be nothing more than a confused jumble of disparate elements. To obtain any intelligible picture of the development of Greek history, it is essential to concentrate on general trends and on certain basic themes. For the sixth, fifth, and part of the fourth centuries emphasis can be focused on Athens and Sparta, which emerged as the leading states and as representatives of the democratic and oligarchic ideals, respectively; but their history, and especially that of Athens, cannot be isolated from that of the larger Greek world which the age of colonization brought into being. This present chapter, which is restricted to the seventh and sixth centuries, must be largely couched in general terms. Its aim is to provide some insight into the changing economic, social, and political conditions which resulted from the great expansion of the Greeks described in the preceding chapter.

In the early days of the Greek colonization movement, although motives such as interest in trade, political discontent, and love of adventure played their part, certainly the basic reason which caused so many people to leave their homes and venture into new regions was land hunger. The economy of the many city-states that were gradually taking shape was almost exclusively agricultural and pastoral, but as populations increased, the limited territories controlled by most of these states could not produce enough grain or rear enough flocks to feed the ever-growing number of mouths. Hence thousands of Greeks went forth in search of fertile land, and they found what they wanted in Italy, Sicily, Thrace, the Black Sea region, and later on the north coast of Africa at

Cyrene. Communications naturally were maintained between the new settlements and the motherland, and these communications soon developed into regular trade.

Greece is a land poor in natural resources; if it is to support a considerable population at a civilized level, imports of raw materials and foodstuffs are essential. Before long the colonies were in a position to supply many of the necessary commodities, either from their own lands or from the territories of neighboring natives. In the course of time many colonies were also founded expressly for the purpose of obtaining access to valuable raw materials. As the seventh century advanced, products in increasing amounts began to flow into the old Greek world from all parts of the Mediterranean and Black Sea regions. Grain was shipped from Sicily, Italy, the Crimea, through Olbia, and probably from Egypt through Naucratis. Metals, with which the Greek world as a whole is scantily provided by nature, were secured from many sources: gold from Lydia, Egypt, Thasos, and Thrace; silver from the latter two places and from Spain, which also was rich in tin; copper primarily from Cyprus; and iron from Cyprus, Cilicia, Etruria, and, from the end of the seventh century, especially from the southern shore of the Black Sea. Ivory came from Africa, and timber for ship building from Thrace and Macedonia. From stations in the Black Sea came dried or salted fish, presumably a luxury article. Cyrene provided silphium, a plant valued for medicinal purposes and as a condiment, and the East, various spices and, above all, incense, which soon became almost requisite in many religious observances. These and many other commodities became a regular part of Greek life as a result of the colonization movement.

To pay for all these imports, the Greeks had to develop products for export. They began to concentrate on viticulture and olive orchards, and soon were shipping throughout the ancient world large quantities of wine and olive oil. Another way in which the Greeks paid for all the imports brought in by the increasing trade was to expand the output of their various workshops, for the colonists and—ultimately through them—the barbarians became eager customers for all sorts of manufactured articles. Of the various manufactured products pottery was by far the most common, since it was used for a great variety of purposes: large amphoras as containers for the oil and wine which were exported, household wares of all types, and many utensils designed more for the luxury trade such as beautifully decorated mixing bowls, cups, and oil and perfume flasks. Pottery was made practically everywhere where there were available supplies of good clay, but in the seventh century Corinth became the pottery center of the Greek world, a preeminence which was gradually lost to Athens in the following century. After the potters the metal and textile workers were probably the most active craftsmen. Miletus became famous for its woolen products, and, of the various cities in which metal utensils and military arms and armor were made, Chalcis in Euboea seems for long to have been prominent.

In dealing with this trade and industry one must be careful not to exaggerate their importance and, above all, not to think in terms of modern industrialism with all its national and international ramifications. Nonetheless, trade and manufacturing from the seventh century on became increasingly important and offered many more opportunities for earning a livelihood than had the earlier, almost entirely rural, economy. In the society depicted in the Homeric poems trade was almost exclusively in the hands of the Phoenicians; such an occupation was beneath the dignity of a wellborn Greek, although the acquisition of plunder by piracy was common and honorable. Hesiod, writing about 700 B.C. and representing the point of view of a Boeotian farmer, recognizes that on occasions a man may have to load his surplus produce on a ship and dispose of it abroad, but this activity should take place only in July and August, the slack agricultural season and the time when the seas are safest. He admits that men in their desperation may have to go to sea with the beginning of spring, but this should be a last resort, for "it is a terrible thing to die amid the waves" (*Works and Days,* 687).

From Hesiod's time on, however, more and more men began to consider trading a full-time, and not just an off-season, occupation. As the colonies which were founded on the shores of the Mediterranean, Propontis, and Black Sea gradually began to develop characteristic patterns in conformity with their environments, it became generally known that one city usually had a surplus of grain, that another one was adjacent to good timber or near mines from which essential metals were being extracted, and that still another city had access to luxury goods such as gold and ivory. Because trade was based entirely on barter until the appearance of coinage around 600 B.C. and still to a great extent thereafter, a trader needed to know where he could exchange a cargo of one or more commodities for other commodities. Since no Greek city was self-sufficient, except perhaps in its most primitive stage, they were all possible markets for certain imports. As time went on traders must have acquired a good knowledge of what imports the various cities needed and also of what products they might have available for export.

Such traders probably were not very different in their methods from the Phoenicians. They loaded their ships where they could find useful cargoes and sailed to ports where they could hope to unload those cargoes and take on promising ones in return. Years may have passed before they returned to their native cities. Other traders, however, were more closely connected with the needs of their own cities. A shipowner (*nauklēros,* to use the term later in use) of Miletus, for example, would know that his city was always in need of foodstuffs. Accordingly he would load his ship with Milesian woolen garments and pottery and, if there was still space in his ship, take along a merchant (*emporos*) with his cargo. They would then sail to Olbia, where they would dispose of their commodities for a cargo of grain and preserved fish. There is no clear evidence as to how these traders disposed of their commodities. If they had to remain at the port of call throughout the winter season, they may have sold their wares themselves at retail; on the other hand, they may have had recourse to local traders (*kapēloi*).

In the course of time regular patterns of trade developed. Miletus and other Ionian cities traded especially in the Propontis and Black Sea regions, although they all had interests in Egypt through Naucratis, and Miletus and particularly Phocaea had interests in the west. For many years the Phocaeans seem to have had a monopoly on the silver and tin trade with Spain. Corinth traded especially with the west from the middle of the seventh century, and Chalcis with its colonies in Italy, Sicily, and Chalcidice. From the beginning of the sixth century there is evidence for Athenian trade in the area of the Hellespont and Propontis. Close ties or possibly some type of alliance may have been established between certain cities. In the Lelantine War (late eighth and early seventh century?) between Chalcis and Eretria in Euboea, Samos aided the former and Miletus the latter. Herodotus' statement (6.21) that Miletus mourned deeply over the destruction of Sybaris in Italy could suggest that there had been close commercial relations between the two cities.[1]

It is obvious that the new economic opportunities which were emerging in the seventh century must have had repercussions on the social system in the Greek world. The nobles were landed aristocrats, and wealth, so far as it affected political and social position, was estimated on the basis of land and its products. At least this was the case in Attica at the time of Solon's reforms, ca. 594, and there is no reason to doubt that the same situation obtained throughout Greece in the seventh century. Some of the nobles, however, probably were taking an interest in trade and were more and more frequently exchanging their surplus agricultural products for foreign luxuries which could be hoarded or displayed on occasions such as funerals and the providing of dowries, when conspicuous consumption was in order. When Sappho's brother sailed with a cargo of wine to Naucratis, he was playing the role of a Lesbian farmer disposing of surplus produce rather than that of a professional trader. Solon also engaged in trade, not as a regular occupation but presumably to finance his travels.

The land not controlled by the great families was owned and worked by the small farmers and peasants. Evidence concerning them between the time of Hesiod and that of Solon is almost entirely lacking, but to judge from conditions in Athens at the time of Solon's reforms, their plight by the end of the seventh century was an evil one. Colonization had helped relieve the pressure on the land, and those farmers who had gone out as colonists were now owners of the original lots (*kleroi*) in the new settlements and hence were in a privileged position. The peasants and farmers who remained at home, however, were apparently falling more and more into a situation where they were at the mercy of the nobles.

Despite these changes which were occurring to the population living on and from the land, it was in the cities, growing steadily larger as a result of the increase in trade and manufacturing, that the most significant innovations were taking place. Craftsmen (*demiourgoi*) had existed in the Greek cities from their beginnings, but now there was a much greater demand for the products of their skills. As owners of workshops in which commodities such as pottery, utensils, arms, and textiles were manufactured, many of these artisans must have done a thriving business. It is important to bear in mind, however, that these industrial establishments were not factories in any modern sense but merely workshops (*ergasteria*), small in physical size and with a very limited work force. The personnel of a typical shop consisted of the owner and possibly other members of his family with a few hired workers and probably several slaves, for slavery was steadily becoming a more important factor in social and economic life.[2] Many members of the artisan class must also have become traders. Since the approved sailing season lasted only from April to September, some of these *demiourgoi* may have worked as craftsmen during the major part of the year and then, when the seas became safe, they or some members of their families may have loaded some of the fruits of the winter's work on a merchant ship and sailed off to dispose of these commodities at a foreign port. The increasing prosperity of the artisan class must also have contributed to the betterment of the lot of the day laborers—the *thetes* of Homer and Hesiod—for employment in the shops and service as crew members on the trading ships provided working opportunities for more and more men.

The most important aspect of these new economic developments was that a certain part of the population in the Greek cities was acquiring wealth of a type different from that of land and its products. In this category of movable wealth, whether it was in the form of gold and silver bullion or manufactured articles, some of the *demiourgoi* were possibly becoming even wealthier than the nobles, and after the introduction of

coinage about 600 B.C. this tendency very likely became more pronounced. One significant consequence of this increase in movable
wealth, the new phenomenon of hoplite soldiers, was mentioned in an
earlier chapter. Until the end of the eighth century and even later the
military power of the state had rested on the nobles, who alone could afford the horses, chariots, and weapons necessary for war. This military
monopoly was one of the strongest bases of the privileged position of the
aristocracies. By the middle of the seventh century, however, as the famous proto-Corinthian Chigi Vase reveals, the hoplite formation was in
use, and the individual soldiers were accoutred in what became standard
hoplite gear—helmet, corselet, greaves, round shield, short sword, and
thrusting spear. The reliability of this representation is confirmed by the
poems of Tyrtaeus written in the last half of the century. The transition
to the new type of fighting equipment was presumably a gradual process. A late eighth century tomb at Argos contained a hoplite helmet and
corselet, and late eighth and early seventh century pottery exhibits both
old and new types of fighting. It is likely that the metalsmiths, aided by
improvements in technique and the increasing availability of iron, were
meeting growing demands for armaments from men now becoming
wealthy in movables. Much of this equipment may have been purchased
by those who subsequently sought employment as mercenaries at home
or abroad.

Since the hoplite shield, carried with the left forearm inserted under
a bar and the hand grasping a bracket at the edge of the shield, enabled
a warrior to use his right arm for manipulating his thrusting spear, the
result was that a hoplite fighting individually had his right side exposed.
The real effectiveness of the hoplite system arose when men were trained
to fight in phalanx formation, with each man in the line having his right
side protected by the shield of the hoplite on his right. It must have
taken considerable drilling to instruct men to fight efficiently in this
formation. The suggestion has been made that Pheidon, the tyrant of
Argos, was the first to develop this system and that his supposed victory
over the Spartans at Hysiae possibly about 668 was the first demonstration of the merits of the hoplite phalanx.

As the seventh century progressed, the hoplite army in most sections of Greece became the main military arm of a state, supplanting the
older tradition of nobles fighting more or less as individual champions
and whatever systems were employed in the intervening years. These
hoplites must have developed a strong group feeling, since they realized
that their effectiveness depended on the steadiness of the line and since
each man knew that his personal protection was provided by the man on
his right. Men such as these, who now could claim that they were the

defenders of the state, naturally posed a threat to the political and social prestige previously monopolized by the aristocrats. It is impossible to state precisely the social strata from which these hoplites came, but since it was Greek custom that a man provide his own weapons and armor, they must have been men of some economic substance. Probably some of them were aristocrats or at least successful farmers, but many almost surely came from the *demiourgoi* who had gained wealth in movables.[3]

This latter group presents an interesting and thorny problem. So far as one can ascertain, wealth, at least in relation to political and social status, was still estimated on the basis of land and its products. How did hoplites, whose wealth was based on movables, acquire the political recognition to which they felt their economic success and their new value as defenders of the state entitled them? The acquisition of land was difficult since little waste land remained to be occupied, and aristocrats and peasants were not inclined to sell any of their acres, even if tradition had allowed such sales, which, in many parts of Greece at least, is improbable. There is no certain answer to this problem—it will be studied in some detail later in its application to Athens—but somehow, in some or many cities, the wealthier non-nobles were acquiring political powers whereby governments gradually changed from aristocracies to timocracies. As confirmation for this conclusion one can cite the complaint of the Lesbian aristocratic poet Alcaeus, ca. 600, that "possessions make the man," and the ranting of Theognis of Megara some fifty years later against the habit of nobles marrying rich commoners (lines 185–190): "Yet in marriage a good man thinketh not twice of wedding the bad [that is, of low birth] daughter of a bad sire if the father give him many possessions, nor doth a woman disdain the bed of a bad man if he be wealthy, but is fain rather to be rich than to be good. For 'tis possessions they prize; and a good man weddeth of bad stock and a bad man of good; race is confounded of riches." As will be seen shortly, the tyrants may have had something to do with helping non-noble hoplites break down the exclusiveness of the nobility. In any case, there is no doubt that the new conditions provided by trade and manufacturing were undermining the props of the old aristocratic organization and creating a rather revolutionary atmosphere in the social, economic, and political spheres.

ONE OF THE great milestones in breaking down the privileged position of the aristocracies was the act of codifying the unwritten laws and reducing them into writing. Among the early Greeks, as among any early people, the laws were the ancestral customs—the customs, rules, and judgments which had gradually evolved from generation to generation for regulating society and making civilized life possible. In Homer they were called *themistes* or *dikai;* the earmark of uncivilized peoples, such as the Cyclopes, was that they had no *themistes.* Hesiod (*Works and Days,* 276–279) makes the same point when he says that Zeus gave *dikē* to mankind, but not to fish, beasts, or birds. In a society that was governed first by kings and then by aristocracies, it is natural that the knowledge, interpretation, and application of these unwritten laws became the exclusive prerogative of the nobles. This control over the administration of justice was one of the main bases of the power of the aristocratic governments, and it is known that they manipulated this control to their own advantage. A passage in the *Iliad* (16.386–388) speaks of Zeus's anger at men who make crooked judgments (*themistes*) in the assembly place and drive out *dikē* (here almost with one of its later meanings—justice); and Hesiod frequently denounces the bribe-swallowing princes for delivering crooked judgments (*dikai*). No wonder the victims of the maladministration of justice felt that the laws, no matter how harsh they might be, had to be wrested from the secrecy and mystery with which the nobles were shrouding them, for, as Euripides expressed it several centuries later (*Suppliants,* 433–434), "When the laws are written, both the weak and wealthy have equal justice (*dikē*)." It is often said, or implied, that it was the threatening attitude and the demands of the masses which forced the nobles to acquiesce in the publication of the laws. Certainly their discontent must have been a contributing factor, but the "masses" were probably still too unorganized, too powerless, and too illiterate to have assumed a leading role in any issue of such importance. It is far more likely that the initiative in this onslaught on aristocratic privilege came from that segment of the population which, through acquisition of wealth in movables and the consequent ability to give military service as hoplites, was now in a position to exert some influence on the policies of the state.[4]

A prerequisite for reducing the unwritten laws to writing, obviously, was that knowledge of writing be reasonably widespread in the Greek world. The type of writing mentioned in the first chapter, the syllabic Linear B script, apparently did not survive the collapse of Mycenaean civilization. At any rate, archaeology so far has revealed no evidence for the use of writing among the Greeks in the Dark Age. When writing appeared again in the Greek world, an alphabetic system had supplanted the earlier, cumbersome syllabic method. After generations of controversy, scholars are now in more or less general agreement that this momentous invention was made probably about the middle of the eighth century and almost surely on the Syrian coast. Since the Greeks adapted the north Semitic alphabet to the needs of their own language, a logical assumption is that this epoch-making event occurred in a trading post such as Al Mina, where Greeks and north Semites were in close association from at least the beginning of the eighth century.[5] This new alphabet, with slight variations, spread rather rapidly over the whole Greek world, as is proved by the cup found at Pithecusae, with the result that by the middle of the following century writing was sufficiently established among the Greeks to make possible the recording of the unwritten laws. In connection with the eastern derivation of Greek writing, the suggestion can be made that the Greeks may have obtained the idea of codifying and writing down their laws from the peoples of the Near East, among whom the practice of inscribing their codes on stone had been prevalent for centuries.

The loss of these early Greek codes is a serious blow to the understanding of the history of the seventh and sixth centuries. If they had been preserved, they would certainly provide solutions to many of the problems concerning social, economic, and political conditions in those centuries which perplex the modern historian. Many traditions about these codes and anecdotes about the lawgivers survive in Greek literature, as one would expect, but this type of evidence must be regarded with great caution. Particularly unreliable are the traditions which arose in the Hellenistic Age, for in this period, probably under the influence of such works as Plato's *Laws,* the notion spread that philosophy should concern itself with lawmaking. Philosophically minded writers did not scruple, in order to strengthen some moralizing point, to disregard chronological facts, to depict the early lawgivers under the influence of philosophers, especially Pythagoras, and to mingle inextricably the enactments of various lawgivers. Fortunately an earlier tradition preserves some isolated scraps of information which have the ring of authenticity. This type of evidence, when combined with what is known of the early Athenian lawgivers Draco and Solon, and with the famous Gortynian Code of Crete, which, although dating from the fifth century, is a revision of earlier laws, makes it possible to obtain some picture of the nature of the work of these early legislators.[6]

According to the universal tradition, Zaleucus, who made laws for Locri in Italy sometime around 650, was the first of the lawgivers. Charondas of Catana in Sicily, the legislator for his native city, was often associated with Zaleucus in tradition, although in fact he probably lived a generation or two later. Various other cities in Italy and Sicily claimed that their laws had been given to them by one or the other of these two lawmakers. This is quite probable, although the explanation may be that the laws of Locri or Catana were borrowed and adapted by these other cities rather than that Zaleucus or Charondas formally made laws for them. The tradition that it was in the western colonies that laws were first codified and recorded is a reasonable one, for the colonists had many new and unprecedented problems to face. Also, since many settlements consisted of colonists who came from different cities and thus were familiar with somewhat different customary laws, it was necessary for the lawgivers to formulate a code in which all would acquiesce.

Antiquity preserved the recollection of many early lawgivers, but because of the loss of much Greek literature down through the ages, most of them now are only names. At this point only four, besides Zaleucus and Charondas, need be mentioned, for they will be discussed later in this chapter or in subsequent ones. These four are Pittacus of Mytilene in Lesbos, Draco and Solon of Athens, and the Spartan Lycurgus, who was included among the early lawgivers by the Greeks despite the fact that he may have been a mythical or semimythical figure and that it was expressly stated that his laws were unwritten. Pittacus, Draco, and Solon all held some office, to which they had been appointed or elected, when they were serving as lawgivers; information is lacking about most of the others. Aristotle in his *Politics* (4.9.10) makes the interesting observation that most of the lawgivers came from the middle class. This statement seems to confirm the suggestion made earlier that it was the emerging hoplites who succeeded in forcing the aristocrats to allow the laws to be recorded.

The laws were inscribed in as permanent a form as possible on wooden, bronze, or stone stelae or on the walls of temples or public buildings. Since these laws to a great extent reflected the ancestral customs hallowed by age, it is natural that stories arose that many of the lawgivers were divinely inspired. This feeling of awe which the codes inspired helps to explain why the Greeks were reluctant to change their laws. Demosthenes (24.139) and other ancient authors report the well-known story that at Italian Locris, if a man wished to introduce a new law or amend an old one, he had to appear before a governing body with a halter around his neck; if his proposal was rejected, he was immediately strangled. According to this tale, in a period of two centuries only one law was altered.

Disappointingly little is known about the content of these early codes. They were primarily codifications of the old unwritten laws and, hence, in procedure the old customary methods presumably were followed. Because of new social, economic, and political conditions, however, certain innovations must have been introduced. One innovation apparently was the fixing of definite penalties for various offenses. In later times these penalties were considered extremely harsh—everyone knows the remark of the fourth-century Athenian orator Demades that

Draco's laws were written not in ink but in blood—but, savage as the punishments were, they were a gain over the previous arbitrary decisions of the aristocratic magistrates.

Certain other characteristics of these early laws, so far as they are known, should be mentioned for the insight they provide into the social and economic conditions of the seventh and sixth centuries. There were various regulations for maintaining the same number of households in a community, for preventing the alienation of the family lot of land (*kleros*), and for ensuring that an heiress marry her nearest male kinsman. These stipulations emphasize the importance which the early Greeks attached to the idea that land belonged to the family and must not pass out of control of the family, an important subject which will be discussed at some length in the chapters dealing with Sparta and Athens. The provisions about the treatment and status of slaves seem to prove that slavery was assuming an increasingly important role in the life of that period. The ancient sources also speak of sumptuary laws directed particularly against ostentatious displays at funerals and in female dress. Such legislation is often described as democratic in spirit, but a more reasonable explanation is that the lawgivers were primarily motivated by a desire to prevent rival families from ruining themselves by a competition in conspicuous spending. Finally, it should be noted that except in the case of the laws of the Athenian Draco, there is practically no evidence that these early codes contained provisions concerning homicide. This lack may be a result of the extremely fragmentary nature of the evidence, but it is more likely that in most Greek states in the days of these early lawgivers, homicide was still considered a matter to be dealt with by the kin of the slain rather than by any organ of the state.

Although evidence, naturally, is not available for every one of the hundreds of Greek city-states, it is probable that in the great majority of them the laws were codified and published in the seventh and sixth centuries. Evidence is also lacking on the manner in which this significant step was carried out. It is not known, for example, whether the nobles, in permitting this publication, yielded to peaceful pressure or to outbreaks of violence. The loss of the exclusive knowledge of the laws, like the rise of the hoplites, was a severe blow to the aristocratic monopoly of governmental powers—often exercised unscrupulously—against which Hesiod had protested so passionately.

OTHER developments in this period also contributed to the weakening of aristocratic privilege. By far the most important of these was the emergence of a group of men known in Greek history as tyrants. It would

be an oversimplification of history to maintain that the total explanation of the phenomenon of tyranny is to be found in the struggle against
aristocratic rule, but it is nonetheless true that in those cities which were
under the domination of tyrants for one, two, and occasionally three
generations, the noble families never again recovered their former exclusive and privileged position after the expulsion of the tyrants.

The subject of Greek tyrants is a fascinating one, but once again the
historian is thwarted by a lack of satisfactory sources of information—a
great loss, for a thorough understanding of these early tyrants would
provide answers to many of the baffling problems in the history of
Greece in the seventh and sixth centuries. So many tyrants arose in these
centuries that this period is sometimes called the age of tyrants. The
term is only partly acceptable, for tyranny was a recurring phenomenon
in the Greek world. In actual fact, there were two main periods in which
tyrannies were widespread in Greece: the age of the older tyrants lasting
from about the middle of the seventh century to the end of the sixth, although prolonged in Sicily until 461; and the age of the later tyrants,
which began with the rise to power of Dionysius I of Syracuse in 405 and
continued until the Roman conquest in the second century B.C. In general, therefore, one can say that tyranny was particularly prevalent in
periods of transition; in its earlier phase it contributed to the breakdown
of the aristocratic state, whereas in its later phase it was one of the
symptoms of the decline of the polis.

The words "tyrant" and "tyranny" did not originally have the evil
and sinister connotations which they acquired later for the Greeks and
which they have in the modern world. The first occurrence of the word
tyranny is in fragment 25 of Archilochus, referring to Gyges (ca.
685–657): "I care not for the wealth of golden Gyges, nor ever have en-
vied him; I am not jealous of the works of gods and I have no desire for
great tyranny." Here the word signifies absolute despotism, but since
Gyges obtained his position by overthrowing the preceding Lydian dynasty, there may also be a suggestion of usurped power. Since the term is
a loanword in the Greek language, it is quite possible that it was borrowed from the Lydians, with whom the Greeks were in close contact.
The poet Alcaeus, early in the sixth century, employed the word tyrant
to characterize his political opponent Pittacus. Since Pittacus was an
elected official and not a tyrant in any later technical sense, Alcaeus was
using the term as one of abuse. In the same century Solon and Theognis
used the word in their poetry to characterize anyone possessed of absolute power. In Athens after the overthrow of the Pisistratid tyranny, and
especially after the repulse of the Persian despotism with which the exiled Pisistratids had been cooperating, the idea of absolute power cen-

tered in one man became increasingly hateful. Nevertheless, in fifth-century literature, particularly in poetry, the term tyrant, although sometimes having an evil connotation, was often used as a mere synonym for the word king. It was not until the fourth century that the word, in the writings of philosophers like Plato and Aristotle, acquired a technical meaning: to them tyranny was an institution, a perverted form of government, in which a man seized power by force and ruled irresponsibly without regard to the laws of the state. Even earlier, if Thucydides (2.63) is to be trusted, the term was acquiring this special meaning, for in a speech delivered by Pericles in 430, the Athenian statesman is reported to have said to the people: "For what [the empire] you hold is, to speak somewhat plainly, a tyranny; to take it, perhaps, was wrong, but to let it go is unsafe." The philosophers in their analysis of tyranny usually depict the tyrant as a demagogue who, as leader of the masses, seized supreme power. In this concept they were influenced by the nature of tyranny, especially in Sicily, in their own times. It seems certain that it is an anachronism to speak of demagogues in the seventh and even in the sixth century for the very simple reason that the masses, the *demos,* were not yet sufficiently organized to provide followers for a demagogue.[7]

From the middle of the seventh century until the end of the sixth, and even later in Sicily and Italy, tyrannies were a common phenomenon in the Greek world. The western tyrannies form a somewhat special category and will be discussed in a subsequent chapter. In the Aegean world there is evidence for tyrants in Corinth, Sicyon, Megara, Athens, Mytilene, Miletus, Ephesus, Samos, and Naxos, not to mention various other cities for which only the name of a tyrant has been preserved. Many cities, of course, may have had tyrannies concerning which no information has survived.

In so widespread a movement, although circumstances naturally varied from place to place, it is reasonable to look for some general underlying cause. There is little reason to question the statement made earlier that in the great majority of cases the basic cause for the rise of tyrannies was opposition to the social, economic, political, and religious monopoly of power exercised by the aristocrats. When one tries to characterize these tyrants, however, and to describe the elements of the population which supported them in their rise to power, one becomes engulfed in a mire of controversies, as can be seen from the various answers which have been offered for these problems. Historians with Marxist leanings tend to see in these tyrants inspired leaders who led their proletarian followers in a successful uprising against their capitalistic masters, while historians tarred with a fascist brush eulogize them as benevolent despots who set their cities on the paths to their manifest destinies. Among less doctrinaire scholars opinions also vary widely; some see in the tyrants opportunistic nobles who seized power as a result of feuds between noble families, others argue that they were nobles, or occasionally commoners, who seized power as leaders of the masses—that is, as demagogues—and still others recognize in them men who championed the cause of the growing group of men wealthy in movables in the struggle to break down aristocratic privilege. The ironic fact is that the advocate of any one of these theories, or of numerous variants of them, can find some support in the ancient sources for his interpretation.

The sources are miserably inadequate and peculiarly susceptible to subjective explanations. Except for a few passages in contemporary poets, especially in the Athenian Solon, the first account of many of these tyrants is to be found in the pages of Herodotus. When Herodotus was writing his great work, ca. 450–430, two generations had already passed since the suppression of the Pisistratid tyranny in Athens and three or more generations since the disappearance of some of the earlier tyrants. Thus there had been sufficient time for all sorts of stories and anecdotes, many of them of the nature of folktales, to develop, especially since the tyrants as colorful and uninhibited individuals provided excellent material for the myth-making genius of the Greeks. Herodotus' accounts are obviously valuable, but they are exasperatingly anecdotal and devoted largely to the private lives of the despots.

Thucydides, later in the fifth century, makes a few passing comments on tyranny, but it is not until the fourth century, when a different type of tyranny was prevalent, that much was written on the tyrants. Of the historian Ephorus, unfortunately, nothing but fragments has been preserved; hence his account of and judgment on the tyrants have to be inferred from the use made of Ephorus by much later writers. In the writings of the philosophers Plato and Aristotle many discussions of tyranny are to be found, but they must be used with great caution. Both men were influenced in their conception of tyranny by the contemporary demagogic type of tyrant. Plato, in his political theory, was intent on representing tyranny as a perverted form of government; his vivid picture of the typical tyrant, if applied to the striking figures of the seventh and sixth centuries, would yield but a travesty. Aristotle tries harder to be objective and historical, but, although he records actions of certain tyrants which may be true, he usually is thinking of tyranny in a generic sense, and he lists the kinds of measures which a tyrant would be likely to take. Thus, while one can learn from Aristotle what a brilliant mind of the fourth century considered to be the essence of tyranny, there is no guarantee that any of the typical actions he mentions was ever taken by the particular tyrant one happens to be studying.

When the sources are of such a nature, it is easy to understand why the accounts and interpretations of the early tyrants given by modern scholars vary so greatly. In the brief discussion that follows of some of the better-known tyrannies, an effort will be made to see these men in the environment in which they lived. One will fail completely to understand them if one applies to them characteristics which belong to a later and more sophisticated period in Greek history, and especially if one thinks in modern terms of masses and capitalists and the like, a trap into which many historians have fallen.

One further word of caution should be given. Most of the ancient authors speak of the tyrants as champions of the *demos*. *Demos* means "people" and hence can have an ambiguous meaning just like the English word people. In fifth-century Athens, for example, *demos* could refer to all the citizens in Athens, rich and poor alike, or it could have a more restricted meaning, signifying the masses, the "democrats," as opposed to the upper classes. One's interpretation of the tyrants and their supporters, therefore, depends in large measure on how the word *demos* is to be understood when referring to their times. Those scholars who think of the tyrants as demagogues obviously are thinking of *demos* in the sense of the mass of the people as contrasted with the richer classes. It should be noted, however, that in the seventh and sixth centuries it may be an anachronism to think of the *demos* as including the masses in any political sense. The term may very well have had a much more restricted meaning, including only that new element of the population which was trying to gain political recognition—namely the emerging hoplites. Aristotle remarks in a passage of the *Politics* (4.10.10) that among the early Greeks the hoplite constitution was called democracy. Actually the word *demokratia* probably did not come into use until the fifth century, but this observation of Aristotle can be interpreted as meaning that in the seventh century the word *demos,* when used to denote a certain part of the free population of a city, referred not to the commoners, as would have been the case in the fifth century, but to those becoming rich in movables. Anyone who studies the early tyrants should bear this possibility in mind.[8]

I N GREECE proper the earliest tyrannies arose in Corinth, Sicyon, and Megara, according to the traditional or "higher" dating in the first two cities in the 650s and in Megara in the 630s. The uncertainty of these dates illustrates vividly how difficult it is to obtain a satisfactory understanding of this period. A sound chronology is obviously a basic need for the historian, but in the case of many tyrants that information is still lacking. Some scholars, probably incorrectly, advocate a "lower" dating for the tyrants of Corinth, suggesting that the tyranny began about 620. In Sicyon, where the tyranny is reported to have endured for a century, the "higher" and traditional dating is approximately 655 to 555. A papyrus, however, first published in 1911 and much discussed since then, provides interesting, but somewhat unconvincing, evidence for lowering these dates to about 610 to 510. Any dogmatism about the interrelation of these particular tyrannies clearly must be avoided.[9]

Corinth, since the overthrow of its monarchy about the middle of the eighth century, had been ruled by the clan of the Bacchiads, apparently the clan to which the royal family had belonged. The main difference between the old monarchy and the new oligarchy was that the chief power no longer resided in a hereditary king in one family but in a large *genos* from which annually a man was selected to serve as chief magistrate—*prytanis* or king. The strengh of the Bacchiads must have come from tradition and also from the wealth derived from their lands. Under their regime Corinth became prominent for the first time in Greek history. Colonies were sent to Corcyra and Syracuse ca. 734, a step which presumably settled the land hunger problem temporarily. In the third quarter of the eighth century, Corinthian late geometric pottery found its way as far as Al Mina in the east and Etruria in the west. With the beginning of the so-called orientalizing period, ca. 725, Corinthian pottery became dominant throughout the Greek world, especially in the west. The Bacchiads must have grown increasingly wealthy from the duties which were exacted on all imports and exports, but it is not necessary to think of them as engaging seriously in trade themselves or as being owners of various workshops. In the first half of the seventh century, however, the Bacchiads began to have troubles. An inscription (Hicks and Hill, no. 1), a second century A.D. copy of an epitaph from ca. 700 B.C., reveals that Megara recovered some land which had been appropriated by the Corinthians, and it is possible that the Corinthians suffered setbacks in a struggle with Pheidon of Argos. In the 660s they fought a naval battle with Corcyra, the first recorded naval battle in Greek history according to Thucydides (1.13). It is nowhere stated who won this battle, but the difficulty that Corinth subsequently had with Corcyra suggests that its colony was victorious. These failures in policy, which may very well have had a detrimental effect on Corinthian trade, combined with a natural resentment of the growing population towards this narrow and, according to tradition, oppressive oligarchy, paved the way for the rise of a tyrant and the collapse of the Bacchiads.[10]

The tyrant was Cypselus, who, according to the ancient sources, established a dynasty which endured for over seventy years. Cypselus was the son of a Bacchiad lady, Labda, who, rejected in marriage by the Bacchiads because of her lameness, became the wife of Aetion of Lapith stock, which presumably signified pre-Dorian stock. Herodotus (5.92) tells a fascinating story about the baby Cypselus. The Bacchiads, warned by an oracle that the offspring of Labda and Aetion would prove their undoing, resolved to kill the child but were frustrated by the mother, who hid her baby in a jar or chest (*kypselē*). The folktale nature of this story is clear, as is the attempt to find an aetiological explanation for the name Cypselus. Herodotus, who was more interested in Cypselus' son, gives little information about Cypselus himself. He merely says that after his babyhood escape, Cypselus grew to manhood, obtained the tyranny, banished many of the Corinthians, deprived many of their property and still more of their lives, and then after ruling for thirty years ended his life happily, leaving the tyranny to his son Periander.

A late source, Nicolaus of Damascus, probably following the fourth-century historian Ephorus, provides further data which are worth examining briefly. According to this account (fragments 57–60), Cypselus, after his escape as a baby, grew to manhood in Olympia. On returning to Corinth he became polemarch. This is an interesting statement, for in early Athens, at least, that office was a military one. As polemarch, Cypselus was required by law to imprison people who had been convicted by a court and to exact the appropriate fines, but by treating the condemned kindly he endeared himself to the people. Incidentally, the fact that he held office is sufficient to prove that he was considered to be of good family; in fact, because of his mother, his connection with the ruling *genos* was probably recognized. By employing such "demagogic" methods and exploiting the hatred felt for the Bacchiads as a whole, he organized a group of followers and killed the reigning Bacchiad. Then "the *demos* appointed him king."

This brief sentence has two points of interest. If the terminology is correct, Cypselus was not thought of as a tyrant but as a successor to the previously reigning Bacchiads. It is possible that his aim was to restore the kingship to the ancestral form it had had before becoming an annual office monopolized by the Bacchiad clan. Second, how should the word *demos* be interpreted? Earlier in the fragment Cypselus is said to have curried favor with the *plēthos,* the "masses," but his holding the office of polemarch and the later specific statement that he never had a bodyguard suggests that he had the backing of the army. Such evidence, obviously, is unsatisfactory, but it can be used to support the interpretation that *demos* in this passage refers to the hoplite group and that, accordingly, Cypselus became ruler as leader of the new type of warriors.

Only one other action of Cypselus need be mentioned here: he banished the Bacchiads and confiscated their property. One of these exiles, Demaratus, according to tradition, settled in Etruscan Tarquinii and sired Lucumo, who subsequently ruled in Rome as Tarquinius Priscus. The implication is that the confiscated Bacchiad property was divided among some of the Corinthians. Did the poor people, including struggling peasants, receive parcels of land, or were the landed estates of the Bacchiads divided among the hoplites, who may have been Cypselus' chief supporters? If the latter suggestion is correct, then it reveals a way in which men who may have been wealthy in movables only became landowners also.

Cypselus was succeeded by his son Periander who, in later times, was often selected as an example of the typical tyrant. This fact in itself suggests that he was an unusual person, no doubt brutal, but certainly able and colorful. In one tradition he was included among the Seven Wise Men (a list, varying over the years, of seventh and sixth century men noted for their pithy statements). In general the traditions about him are hostile; they reflect the sort of stories, largely dealing with his personal life, which would have been circulated by his enemies. A good example is the famous story of his relations with Thrasybulus, the tyrant of Miletus (Herodotus, 5.92). Wishing to learn how he could rule more securely and effectively, he sent a messenger to Thrasybulus to ask for advice. Thrasybulus said nothing to the messenger, but led him to a grain field beyond the city and, while walking through the field, cut off and threw away the tallest ears of grain. When this action was reported by the perplexed messenger to Periander, he immediately understood its meaning and proceeded to put to death or banish those leading Corinthians who had not been touched by Cypselus. One's confidence in the truth of this particular anecdote is not increased when one remembers that Aristotle (*Politics*, 3.8.3) reverses the characters, making Thrasybulus the one who was seeking advice, and that the Roman historian Livy (1.54) tells a comparable story about Tarquinius Superbus at Rome. Nevertheless, the picturesque tale may very well reflect Periander's policy. A second-generation tyrant was not likely to have the support which had put his predecessor in power, and there probably were many who resented seeing an irregular office, such as tyranny was, being regularized through a hereditary and dynastic principle. According to one tradition Cypselus had banished only the Bacchiads; it would not be surprising if his son had to turn against other nobles and influential people who did not want one-man rule to be perpetuated.

Although the Cypselids were in power for some seventy years, the nature of the source material concerning them is such that it is impossible to give a satisfactory account of their reigns. Their colonizing activity, however, is well authenticated. Cypselus and Periander founded colonies on the northern shore of the Corinthian Gulf on the cost of Aetolia, and along the northwestern coast of Greece from Acarnania to Illyria. The most important of these colonies were Leucas, Anactorion, Ambracia, and on the coast of Illyria, Apollonia and Epidamnus; the last of these, although a colony of Corcyra, had its *oecist* and probably some settlers from Corinth. The policy followed in establishing these settlements was different from that applied to Corcyra and Syracuse; these new colonies were founded and in certain cases ruled by sons of the Cypselids. Even Corcyra for a time was brought under Cypselid authority. The control over these colonies, which in the days of the tyrants was based on personal relations, survived the downfall of the dynasty, for as late as the end of the fifth century most of these communities were not independent city-states, as was the rule with Greek colonies, but were subject in one way or another to Corinthian rule. When these colonies began to issue coinage, apparently early in the fifth century, the coins were struck on the same standard and with the same types as those of Corinth. Even Potidaea, which Periander founded in the northeast in the Chalcidic peninsula, was still receiving annual Corinthian governors as late as the outbreak of the Peloponnesian War.

The establishment of the colonies along the west coast of Greece undoubtedly served various social, economic, and political purposes such as relieving Corinth of any excess population, whether rural or urban, and removing certain elements politically dangerous to the Cypselids. These settlements also provided ports of call for the voyage to Italy and Sicily, and bases for the embryonic Corinthian fleet in its effort to police the sea against pirates and to keep watch on hostile Corcyra. Since Ambracia was located at the beginning of the land route to the famous oracle of Zeus at Dodona in Epirus, one would like to know whether the Cypselids were trying to establish close relations with that ancient shrine. The colonies on the Illyrian coast are interesting, for they may have had a much more significant purpose than the obvious assistance they provided in obtaining the Illyrian iris necessary for the Corinthian perfume makers. Since Corinth began to issue silver coinage probably in the time of Periander or shortly thereafter, the question of the source of its silver supply naturally arises. Archaeologists so far have not been able to give a definitive answer to this problem, but Illyria, despite the fact that evidence for Corinthian penetration into the interior of that region is all post-tyranny, seems to have the strongest claim. If this hypothesis is correct it would explain, in part at least, why Corinth, contrary to the usual Greek custom, insisted on keeping its colonies on the northwest coast of Greece strictly under its control.

It is probable that the Cypselids, like most tyrants, were responsible for a large building program, but the Roman destruction of Corinth in 146 B.C. was so complete that few traces of the early city have survived. The temple of Apollo, of which some columns are still remaining, may have been erected in the time of Periander, although some scholars suggest that it was built to commemorate the fall of the Cypselids; the answer depends on whether the higher or lower dating for the dynasty is correct. In either case, it is an early temple, and hence Corinth deserves some of the credit for developing the Doric order in architecture. One can be almost certain that the Cypselids were responsible for various improvements to the city such as streets, drains, and the establishment of fountains, for it is axiomatic that tyrants had to find employment for the population. Excavations seem to prove that the *diolkos,* a runway paved with stone connecting the Saronic and Corinthian Gulfs, should be assigned to the time of Periander. On this, with the help of rollers, ships could be transported from one body of water to the other, thus giving shipowners an alternative to making the long voyage around the Peloponnesus.[11] The price paid for this convenience would have been another source of revenue for the tyrant.

Beyond the colonizing policy, this somewhat hypothetical building program, and Periander's activity as an arbitrator in a dispute between Mytilene and Athens concerning Sigeum, which will be discussed in the chapter on early Athens, the chief source of information about the Cypselids is to be found in the enumeration of typical tyrannical measures given by Aristotle in his *Politics* (5.9.1–9), some of which may refer to the Cypselids, and in statements in later authors derived probably from Ephorus. Three of these measures, which seem to be associated particularly with Periander, deserve brief mention if for no other reason than to emphasize that in enacting them the Cypselids may have had other motives than the derogatory ones attributed to them. The ancient sources imply that the prohibitions against idleness and the acquiring of slaves, and the various sumptuary laws, were all motivated by the desire to keep the people so poor and so busy trying to make a living that they would have no time or opportunity to conspire against the tyrants. Needless to say, the Cypselids, like any tyrants, would have attempted to prevent the formation of clubs and societies which could have become centers of dangerous discontent, but the motives which led them to pass enactments such as those just mentioned were hardly the childish and peevish ones attributed to them. They would have been interested in keeping the population busy, for the greater the output of the farms and the workshops, the greater would be the revenues, which were needed by the tyrants for projects such as sending out colonies and constructing buildings. Sumptuary laws may have been intended, among other things, to try to prevent the ruinous ostentation in which the wealthy were indulging, an aim similar to that envisaged by various more or less contemporary lawgivers. Periander's prohibition on the acquiring of slaves surely was not just an arbitrary measure directed against the rich. The fact that he and his father sent out various colonies is good evidence for overpopulation and unemployment in Corinth at the time. The attempt to curtail slave labor was probably intended to make employment easier for the free citizen.

The confused sources reveal that Periander's position towards the end of his life became increasingly precarious. He was succeeded by a nephew, who within a few years was assassinated by the Corinthians. Then, according to Nicolaus of Damascus, the *demos* razed the houses of the tyrants, dug up their graves, cast out the bones, and immediately established a new constitution. At this point the text unfortunately becomes corrupt, but from what is known of Corinth at a somewhat later time, it can safely be said that an oligarchy, but one much more broadly based than in the time of the Bacchiads, succeeded the fallen Cypselids. It is quite possible, therefore, that the *demos* which helped Cypselus to power and the *demos* which took control after the end of the tyranny in both cases should be understood as the upper classes, including those who could serve as hoplites.

ABOUT FIFTEEN miles west of Corinth, in the previously obscure town of Sicyon, another tyranny, known as that of the Orthagorids, was established towards either the middle or the end of the seventh century. The story of its rise, as in the case of the Cypselids, is largely withdrawn from view. According to a papyrus fragment of an author probably dependent on Ephorus, the founder of the dynasty, Orthagoras, was the son of a butcher (*mageiros*) named Andreas.[12] When one reads in Pausanias (6.19.1) that Myron, presumably the brother of Orthagoras, was victor in the chariot race at the Olympic Games in 648 B.C., an achievement possible only for a member of a well-to-do family, it becomes likely that the description of Andreas as a butcher was a deliberate calumny originating with the aristocratic opponents of the tyranny. The papyrus emphasizes the military prowess of Orthagoras, because of which he was made polemarch, and then unfortunately it breaks off with the words "the *demos* of the Sicyonians . . ." There seems little doubt that if a few more lines of the papyrus had been preserved, a statement would have been included that the *demos* enabled Orthagoras to become tyrant. Just as in the case of Cypselus, therefore, there is a strong suggestion that Orthagoras owed his rise to tyranny in part to the backing of the emerging hoplites. Another similarity between Cypselus and Orthagoras is that the information about them was chiefly restricted to their ascendancy to power. At Corinth it was Cypselus' son Periander who dominated the tradition, whereas at Sicyon it was Cleisthenes, who probably was the grandson or great-nephew of Orthagoras.

Cleisthenes clearly was one of the leading figures in Greece in the first quarter of the sixth century, and it is a great loss to the historian that the information about him is so scanty and anecdotal. An unfortunate result of the fragmentary nature of the sources is that any attempt to place his recorded activities in chronological order is bound to be somewhat arbitrary. One important event in which Cleisthenes seemingly played a major role was the First Sacred War concerning Delphi, which broke out in the 590s. A satisfactory explanation of this war will probably never be possible, for most of the evidence is late and, as is always true of "religious" struggles, distorted through hatred, intolerance, greed, and ignorance. Nearly contemporary evidence such as the *Homeric Hymn to Pythian Apollo*, "Hesiod's" *Shield of Heracles*, and vase paintings depicting aspects of the struggle for the tripod between Heracles and Apollo is allusive, symbolic, and sadly ambiguous to the modern mind. The earliest "historical" treatment is in Aeschines' Third Speech delivered in 330, but this represents the prejudiced point of view of the victorious side in the conflict. Since this war, however, marked a turning point in the history of Delphi and involved many Greek states, including Sicyon, Athens, and Thessaly, an effort must be made to grasp at least some of the complexities of the situation.

Delphi, which particularly in the sixth, fifth, fourth, and third centuries was the great Panhellenic center of Greek religion, had been inhabited in the Mycenaean period. The remains of the little village and of the votive offerings prove that even then it was a holy place—the shrine of some mother goddess. Destroyed in the period of the Mycenaean collapse, it revived in the Dark Age and continued as a small sanctuary to several goddesses and gods. When Apollo became the god at Delphi is unknown, but it was certainly by the seventh century. Archaeology has revealed that the settlement at Delphi had grown considerably by that time, possibly by absorbing the Apollos worshipped at other adjacent communities. In later times the general belief was that

Pythian Apollo had sponsored the great colonizing movement. If an oracle of Apollo was consulted by eighth-century colonists, it may well have been some other Apollo, but as Delphi grew its Apollo incorporated the traditions of other Apollos. Whatever the processes of growth were, by the end of the seventh century the reputation of Delphi had become so great that pilgrims to the sanctuary and the oracle were coming from all over Greece and probably from Asia Minor.[13]

Who controlled this thriving shrine? The *Hymn to Pythian Apollo* tells how Apollo caused some Cretan merchants to become his priests. This is a reasonable statement, since Crete was having a revival in the eighth and seventh centuries, and Cretan artifacts have been identified in the archaeological findings of that Delphic period. But could a small band of priests remain independent? The ancient tradition insisted that Crisaeans or Cirrhaeans, by controlling the route from the sea through the Crisaean plain to Delphi, interfered with the pilgrims by exacting tolls and committing outrages. The ancients apparently were confused about the distinction between Crisa and Cirrha, and the names were often interchangeable. Archaeology seems to have proved that Crisa was a Mycenaean community on a spur of Mt. Parnassus near the modern Chrysso. This site was destroyed in the period of the Dorian invasion or uprising and not restored until Byzantine times. Cirrha, located on the coast near modern Itea, probably served as a port for Crisa in the Mycenaean period. It survived the collapse of Mycenaean civlization and in the seventh century was a prosperous port.[14]

Aeschines (3.107–112) states that the Amphictions, angered by the conduct of the Cirrhaeans, sought an oracle at the shrine of Apollo and received the response to destroy Cirrha. Then on the motion of Solon of Athens the Amphictionic Council declared a Sacred War. Aeschines' account probably sounded reasonable in 330 B.C., but the historian must consider the likelihood that there was no Amphictiony at Delphi in the days before the war. The only relevant Amphictiony in the 590s of which one can be certain was the religious league which had long centered around the sanctuary of Demeter at Anthela near Thermopylae. This Amphictiony, having started to take shape before the development of cities, was comprised of tribes (*ethnē*) which ultimately were twelve in number. Many of these tribes in time became *perioeci* of the Thessalians, which enabled Thessaly to control the majority of the votes in the Amphictionic Council. Unfortunately there is no definite evidence concerning the time when these various tribes sank into that inferior status. Some scholars argue for the seventh century, but others maintain that Thessalian expansion was completed only in the following century.

Since Cirrha was destroyed and its population annihilated in this war, the accounts about the causes and results of the struggle as preserved in the scattered sources are those provided by the victors. Their claim was that Cirrha was interfering with the proper functioning of the shrine and oracle of Apollo at Delphi. If, as seems probable, Delphi was not yet under the supervision of the Amphictiony, the inference is that Cirrha itself was controlling the sanctuary. If, then, before the war the policy of Cirrha and Delphi was one, it is worth considering, as has been suggested, what the relations of those who launched the Sacred War were to the Cirrha-Delphi complex.

At Athens, Delphi had encouraged the attempt of Cylon to become tyrant ca. 632, and subsequently it had branded as accursed the *genos* of the Alcmaeonids, whose leader Megacles had been responsible for the slaying of Cylon's immediate followers. At Sicyon, although the chronological order of events is far from clear, Delphi had opposed Cleisthenes' policy against the Dorian cult of Adrastus. Since Cleisthenes paved the way for the collapse of Cirrha by his naval blockade of the port, and since Cirrha was so renowned for its maritime interests that for centuries the whole Corinthian Gulf was frequently called the Crisaean Gulf and a tradition arose that Cirrha-Crisa had founded Metapontum in Italy (Ephorus in Strabo, 6.1.15), it is reasonable to suspect that commercial interests, rather than religious indignation, were influencing Cleisthenes.

Regarding the Thessalians any statements are precarious. Scattered evidence seems to confirm that throughout the archaic period they were trying to push southward. Plutarch in his *Amatorius* (*Moralia,* 760–761) relates that in the Lelantine War—the long-lasting conflict between Chalcis and Eretria in Euboea allegedly for possession of the intervening Lelantine plain, in which Thucydides (1.15) says almost all Greek states were ultimately involved, a struggle which probably should be dated in the closing years of the eighth century and the first half of the seventh— the Thessalians contributed to the ultimate victory of Chalcis by serving with their cavalry. Since in the push south the Thessalians were constantly thwarted by the Phocians, it may be legitimate to believe that Thessaly was interested in crushing the Phocian city of Cirrha and thus obtaining more influence over Delphic policies. In view of such observations about Athenian, Sicyonian, and Thessalian attitudes towards the Cirrhaean-dominated Delphi, one may look with favor on the judgment of a scholar that "the Sacred War was fought for Delphi, but it was 'for the possession of' not 'for the sake of.' "[15]

The war seemingly was a long one, marked first by the leadership of the Athenian Alcmaeon, son of the Megacles who had caused the Alcmaeonids to be accursed, and the successful blockade of Cirrha by

Cleisthenes' fleet, and then by fighting in the mountains where the surviving Cirrhaeans, having established themselves in a fortress (a memory of Bronze Age Crisa?), were ultimately overcome by the Thessalians—according to one tradition through the poisoning of the waters of the Pleistos River by a doctor who had come from the island of Cos (*Hippocratic Corpus*, letter 27). The consequences of this war were significant for Greek history in many ways. Cirrha was razed to the ground, and the plain of Crisa was dedicated to Apollo with the solemn stipulation that it should remain uncultivated forever. This Crisaean plain with its sacred character was to play a leading part in the events two and a half centuries later which led to the victory in the Fourth Sacred War of Philip II of Macedonia over the Greeks at Chaeronea in Boeotia in 338. Following the First Sacred War, if not in its course, the sanctuary of Apollo at Delphi was placed under the protection of the Anthelan Amphictiony, henceforth called Delphic.

To commemorate the "deliverance" of Delphi, the games, which had been held there formerly on a minor scale, were reorganized. According to the Parian Chronicle, after the destruction of Cirrha a contest, in which the prize was a material one (*chrematites*), was established in 591. Following the conclusion of all the fighting, the contest, under the aegis of the Amphictiony, attained the prestige of being *stephanites*—that is, a contest in which the prize was a wreath. The new games, know as the Pythia, were held every four years and soon achieved fame second only to the Olympic Games among the great Panhellenic festivals. At the first celebration in 582 Cleisthenes was victor in the chariot race (Pausanias, 10.7.6).[16] It is interesting to note that apparently in the same year (582) the Isthmian Games in honor of Poseidon were also reorganized as a Panhellenic festival to be held every second year. Those scholars who accept the "higher" dating for the Cypselids see in this reorganization a celebration to commemorate the overthrow of the tyranny at Corinth; those who accept the "lower" dating consider the enhancing of the prestige of the Isthmian Games to be the work of Periander.[17]

Some years after the end of the First Sacred War the wooing and marriage of Cleisthenes' daughter, Agariste, occurred, a subject to which Herodotus devotes six very interesting chapters (6.126–131). Cleisthenes, like all the tyrants, believed in the grand, flamboyant gesture; he may very well have consciously been imitating the courting of Helen, but the fact that he had a famous model is no valid reason to doubt that he arranged a picturesque pageant for his daughter's marriage. The episode casts considerable light on the methods of the tyrants and, in particular, on the relations of various prominent Greeks towards them. Herodotus tells how Cleisthenes, after winning the chariot race at the Olympic Games of 576 (?), proclaimed to the assembled multitude that any Greek who considered himself worthy to become his son-in-law should come to Sicyon within sixty days. Thirteen suitors arrived, two from Athens and one each from eleven other cities. The fact that two came from Italy and several from western Greece may suggest, as does possibly also his previous attack on Cirrha, that Cleisthenes had particular interests in the west; in any case the absence of any suitors from the Aegean islands or the Greek cities in Asia might have considerable significance if enough evidence were available for interpretation. Cleisthenes entertained these aspirants magnificently for a year and carefully observed their prowess and conduct in athletic games and social intercourse. Two Athenians pleased him most, but on the day on which the selection of husband for Agariste was to be made, one of them, Hippocleides, son of Tisander, ruined his chance by dancing too indecorously under the influence of wine. Thus the choice fell on Megacles, the son of that Alcmaeon who had commanded the Athenian forces in the Sacred War. The other suitors were dismissed with thanks for the honor they had conferred on Cleisthenes by their presence, and each was presented with a talent of silver. Herodotus ends his account with some important genealogical information. The issue of the marriage of Agariste and Megacles was Cleisthenes, named after his maternal grandfather, who "established the tribes and the democracy for the Athenians." Another son, Hippocrates, also was born from this union; Hippocrates had a daughter Agariste, named after the daughter of the tyrant of Sicyon, and this Agariste, after marrying Xanthippus, gave birth to the great Athenian statesman Pericles.

Two observations, at least, should be made about this colorful episode told by Herodotus. First, even admitting that it contains picturesque embellishments, it provides a vivid glimpse into the brighter side of the luxurious life at a tyrant's court. Second—and far more significant—it emphasizes, more than any other item in all the preserved sources, how dangerously misleading it is to generalize about these tyrants. The usual, and natural, attitude of the historian is to think of them as men who climbed to power by murdering and banishing aristocrats, who consequently were consumed with a passionate hatred for their oppressors. In this brief story of Herodotus, however, young men of noble families from a dozen cities in the Greek world eagerly accepted a tyrant's hospitality and aspired to a marriage relationship with him. The Athenian suitors came from families—the Alcmaeonids and Philaidae—which became increasingly prominent in Athens. In this connection it should be mentioned that one member of the Philaidae bore the name Cypselus; this man, who was archon in Athens ca. 597 (*M&L*, no. 6), was almost certainly the grandson of the founder of the Corinthian tyranny. Herodotus expressly says that the distinction of the Alcmaeonids was enhanced throughout Greece by the marriage of Megacles to the daughter of the tyrant of Sicyon.

Herodotus (6.127), when listing the suitors who came to Sicyon at Cleisthenes' invitation, includes the following statement: "And from the Peloponnesus Leocedes, son of Pheidon the tyrant of the Argives, Pheidon who created measures for the Peloponnesians and committed outrages greatest of all Greeks by expelling the Elean managers of the games and himself holding the games at Olympia." Pheidon has been mentioned casually in earlier pages, but this seems an appropriate place in which to state the difficulty of dating this enigmatic man. Although Herodotus in this passage places Pheidon in the early decades of the sixth century, other ancient sources, all later than Herodotus, seem to write of him in the context of the seventh, eighth, or even ninth century. Ephorus, the fourth-century historian whose *Universal History* was very influential throughout antiquity, to judge from his fragments, depicts Pheidon as a powerful ruler of Argos who warred successfully against Sparta. One important event in this supposed early hostility between Argos and Sparta was the battle at Hysiae in the southwestern Argolid, in which the Argives defeated the invading Spartans in 669 B.C. Of extant ancient authors, Pausanias (2.24.7; 3.7.5), living in the second century A.D., is the only source to mention this battle, but he does not name the Argive leader. It has become rather common among modern historians to assume that Pheidon was the Argive general and that his victory resulted from his innovative use of hoplites in phalanx formation. The introduction of hoplite fighting in the seventh century is a well-established fact, although some scholars feel that the year 669 is too early in the century for such a large-scale encounter. One scholar, however, has argued rather effectively against the generally accepted view that throughout the Dark Age and the archaic period there was bitter enmity between Argos and Sparta.[18] His reasoning, in part, is that in the eighth and seventh centuries Sparta was too much engaged in establishing control over Laconia and Messenia, and in the first half of the sixth century too occupied with fighting Arcadian Tegea, to launch in these years an incursion into the Argolid.

The question of the date and activity of Pheidon is one of the key problems in the history of the archaic period. Because of the scarcity and contradictory nature of the evidence, conclusions have to be based on hypotheses, and it is only too easy for a hypothesis suggested on one page to appear somewhat later as a fact. Here it is sufficient to call attention to the dilemma that, although most historians place Pheidon somewhere in the seventh century and connect him with the development of hoplite warfare, an argument is also possible for assigning him to the early sixth century, as Herodotus states.

Herodotus (5.67–68) mentions briefly Cleisthenes' hostility to the Argives; his stripping of honors from the Argive hero Adrastus, who had a cult at Sicyon; and his attitude towards the Dorians. Since the cult of Adrastus was popular in Dorian Sicyon, Cleisthenes requested permission from the Delphic oracle to expel it, but was insultingly refused. If this episode happened when Cirrha was dominating Delphi, as is probable, it could have been one of the reasons leading to Cleisthenes' participation in the First Sacred War. In response to Delphi's insult Cleisthenes established in Sicyon, with Theban permission, the cult of Melanippus, the legendary enemy of Adrastus, transferring to him the honors and sacrifices which had belonged to Adrastus. In connection with this friction between Cleisthenes and the Argives, it is interesting to note that the Nemean Games in honor of Zeus were recognized as the fourth Panhellenic festival in 573 under the direction of Cleonae, a town in the northern part of the Argolid.[19] Since Cleonae almost certainly was under the influence of Argos, a logical conclusion is that the reorganization of the Nemean Games was some sort of propaganda move directed against Cleisthenes. It is quite possible that Adrastus, ousted from Sicyon, was awarded appropriate honors in the Nemean Games.

After his remarks on Adrastus, Herodotus states that Cleisthenes, in order that the Sicyonians and Argives should not share in common the names of the three Dorian tribes, Hylleis, Pamphyli, and Dymanes, changed these names in Sicyon to "Pigmen," "Assmen," and "Swinemen," while giving to his own tribe the designation Archelaoi, the rulers. This change of names, which Herodotus says remained in force for sixty years after Cleisthenes' death, was a strange way to achieve Sicyonian solidarity against Argos. Possibly they were nicknames popular among the disgruntled non-Dorians. The story, however it is to be explained, brings to the fore the important, but largely unanswerable, question concerning the relations in the Peloponnesus of the Dorians—whether one accepts the usual Dorian invasion interpretation or the concept of a Dorian uprising—with the rest of the population. Regardless of its truth, the legend of the Return of the Heraclidae had become orthodox by the end of the Dark Age, and an element of the population, whether descendants of the Mycenaeans in general or of the Mycenaean ruling class, was considered non-Dorian. In Sparta, as will be discussed in the following chapter, many of the pre-Dorians were reduced to serfdom, and there are various hints in the scattered sources that in other parts of the Peloponnesus a similar, but less stringent, fate befell the natives. Elsewhere than in Sparta, however, the passage of time brought an amelioration in the lot of the "serfs." In Sicyon, as this chapter of Herodotus reveals, a fourth tribe, consisting of the non-Dorians, either existed or was then created by Cleisthenes, in addition to the three traditional Dorian tribes. One wonders whether some of the Peloponnesian tyrants owed their rise, or some of their power, to the support of the non-Dorians. In the case of the Orthagorids there is no suggestion of this for the founder of the dynasty, Orthagoras, but the whole point of this chapter of Herodotus is that Cleisthenes was appealing to the non-Dorians in the population against the Dorians.

In this connection, it is worth remembering that in the case of the Cypselids, although there is no specific talk of a "racial" policy such as the one assigned to Cleisthenes, nevertheless it is stated that Cypselus on his father's side was of Lapith stock, that is, pre-Dorian. Unfortunately the evidence for this period of Greek history is too scanty to justify dogmatic statements, but this "preposterous" story told by Herodotus demonstrates that the existence of a somewhat underprivileged element in the free population had something to do in some places with the phenomenon of seventh- and sixth-century tyranny. Since in the fifth century there seems to have been much less—if any—gradation among the free peoples of the Peloponnesus (except at Sparta) on the basis of "race," it seems safe to conclude that one lasting achievement of the age of tyranny was the lessening or removal of this problem of privileged and underprivileged which had arisen from ethnic differences.

The Orthagorids, according to Aristotle (*Politics*, 5.9.21), ruled for about one hundred years. The traditional date for this dynasty is from ca. 655 to ca. 555; by this scheme Orthagoras would have seized power in Sicyon at almost the same time that Cypselus did in Corinth. A brief look at some of the evidence will reveal the difficulties inherent in trying to establish a chronology for these tyrants.

Because of his role in the First Sacred War, Cleisthenes can be assigned to the early sixth century. Since Nicolaus of Damascus (fragment 61) states that he ruled for thirty-one years, a reasonable approximation for his reign would be ca. 600–570. In view of the absence of information about Cleisthenes' predecessors (except for the rise to power of Orthagoras) and his successors, how should one date the roughly seventy other years belonging to this dynasty? Scholars have been looking for a solution by studying again a small, battered papyrus fragment, first published in 1911.[20] Whatever the nature of the work represented by the papyrus, the fragment does contain some historical data. Towards the end of the preserved section, one can read: "Chilon the Laconian, when ephor, and Anaxandridas, when general, put down the tyrannies among the Hellenes." Since it is known that Chilon was ephor ca. 556/5, Anaxandridas is surely the father of the Spartan king Cleomenes, prominent in the last years of the sixth and the early ones of the fifth century. Amid the wreckage of the bottom part of the papyrus, there is discernible "In Sicyon Aeschines [mutilated letters, but almost certainly the proper transcription] and Hippias" and then part of the name "Peisistratus." It seems logical to restore these last words as "Hippias at Athens son of Peisistratus." Hippias, tyrant of Athens, was driven out by Cleomenes and the Spartans in 510.

Plutarch (*De Herodoti malignitate*, 859D) reports that the Spartans ousted Aeschines from Sicyon. Some scholars argue that the lost part of the papyrus contained a list of tyrants expelled by the Spartans. Since the name Aeschines follows immediately after the statement about Chilon and Anaxandridas, they feel that his suppression should be related to Chilon and hence be dated to ca. 556/5. Thus the higher dating for the Orthagorids would be correct, roughly 655–555. Other scholars, because the names Aeschines and Hippias are juxtaposed, argue that Aeschines must have been suppressed at approximately the same time as Hippias, that is, 510. Plutarch seems to confirm this, for among the tyrants cast out by Sparta he lists, next to one another, "the sons of Peisistratus from Athens and Aeschines from Sicyon." This suggested late date should be considered in connection with Herodotus' statement that the derogatory names for the three tribes in Sicyon imposed by Cleisthenes lasted for sixty years after his death. Since it is reasonable to argue that the restoration of the names of the old Dorian tribes at Sicyon and the changing of the name of the fourth tribe from Archelaoi to Aigialeai in honor of the son of Adrastus would have been a natural step for the Sicyonians to take after Sparta had freed them from the tyranny, it would follow that the suppression of the tyranny came sixty years after the death of Cleisthenes ca. 570. Despite this logical inference it is hard to accept this late date, ca. 510, for the fall of the Orthagorids. As will be discussed at the end of the next chapter, Sparta in the last half of the sixth century, after making a treaty with Arcadian Tegea ca. 550, was very active in forming alliances in the Peloponnesus, thus establishing an organization which the ancients called "the Lacedaemonians and their allies" and the moderns, the Peloponnesian League. In view of the success of this Spartan policy, it seems contrary to the trend of the times to believe that the Spartans did nothing to subvert an "anti-Dorian" tyranny until ca. 510. Despite the tantalizing proximity of the names Aeschines and Hippias on the papyrus fragment, it is probably a sounder historical conclusion to work on the assumption that the Orthagorid line ended ca. 555 after enduring for about a hundred years. Herodotus' statement about the continued "use" of the derogatory names of the tribes for sixty years after the death of Cleisthenes, therefore, would remain unexplained.

Tyranny also emerged in the latter half of the seventh century in Megara, another Dorian community, located to the northeast of Corinth in a largely mountainous part of the isthmus. The only attempt in the extant ancient sources to interpret the rise of Theagenes as tyrant in Megara is a passage in Aristotle's *Politics* (5.4.5). In a discussion of how unscrupulous demagogues can subvert democracies, Aristotle remarks that in early times demagogues, who had military abilities or held military office, often became tyrants by convincing the *demos* of their hostility to the wealthy. As an example he mentions Theagenes at Megara, who slaughtered the flocks of the rich which he had found grazing beside the river. This story, probably based on a sound, if exaggerated, tradition, is not particularly enlightening as an explanation of basic causes leading to the rise of tyranny. Certainly the concepts of democracy and demagogues in the seventh century are anachronistic. One scholar, realizing that in the fifth century Megara had a considerable woolen industry, argues that the industry had begun earlier and that Theagenes was attempting to obtain a monopoly of it;[21] but there would seem to be more effective ways to achieve this aim than to destroy the sheep whose wool provided the basis for the industry. Theagenes apparently was an aristocrat; at least, he married his daughter to an Athenian noble who tried and failed to establish a tyranny in Athens (ca. 632). If he eliminated flocks which had been trampling down the crops on the plots of the peasants, it is quite possible that he became a hero to them and also furnished them with a much-appreciated ration of meat; but the fact that, after the overthrow of the tyranny, the aristocrats still seem to have been in control at Megara suggests that, although Theagenes' melodramatic action may have reflected quarrels and rivalries among the nobles, the tyranny at Megara was not a movement to overthrow the aristocracy.

Whatever may be the correct interpretation for the tyranny of Theagenes, it is evident from scattered sources and especially from the roughly 1,400 lines of elegies ascribed to Theognis of Megara (*floruit* 550) that Megara was the scene of great social disturbances and changes in the sixth century. Movable wealth was gaining recognition as a result of the earlier colonizing activity, and in the passage quoted earlier in this chapter Theognis laments that the landed aristocrats, for the sake of wealth, were intermarrying with this new, base-born class. In another poem addressed to his friend Cyrnus, Theognis writes (lines 53–58): "Cyrnus, this city is a city still, but lo! her people are other men, who of old knew neither judgments nor laws, but wore goatskins to pieces about their sides, and had their pasture like deer without this city; and now they be good men, O son of Polypaüs, and they that were high be now of low estate. Who can bear to behold such things?" It would seem that these lines refer to the betterment of the lot of the poor peasants, or possibly even serfs. One would like to know if Theagenes had had anything to do with such social measures. The only evidence is a story contained in the eighteenth of Plutarch's *Greek Questions* (295D) that some time after the overthrow of Theagenes, the poor managed to push through a measure by which they recovered the interest which they had already paid on their debts. Banishments and confiscations of property were probably common occurrences. Theognis himself experienced this fate, and his poem referring to this, in which he prays that he may be able to drink the black blood of his enemies (lines 341–350), reveals only too starkly the bitterness of the social and political divisions that could exist in the Greek world. In the case of Megara, as far as one can ascertain, a rather widely based oligarchy had control of the state by the end of the sixth century.

ACROSS THE Aegean Sea the Greek cities on the coast of Asia Minor and on the large offshore islands like Lesbos and Samos also had experiences with tyrannies towards the end of the seventh and in the sixth century. The history of Mytilene in Lesbos is especially interesting in this period; one can sense the contemporary passions in the poetic fragments of Alcaeus, who—with his almost contemporary Mytilenean, Sappho—was recognized as the greatest of the early Greek lyric poets. Additional bits of information about the state of affairs in early Mytilene can be found in a few later authors who probably had the whole body of Alcaeus' poetry to draw upon. When the monarchy was overthrown in Mytilene, presumably in the second half of the eighth century, the control of the government came into the power of the royal clan of Penthilids, reputed descendants of Orestes' son Penthilus, who, according to legend, had founded Mytilene at the time of the Aeolian migration. This narrow oligarchy became increasingly corrupt and brutal—Aristotle in a passage of the *Politics* (5.8.13) tells how they went about beating people with clubs—and was overthrown, and its members largely annihilated, about the middle of the seventh century by outraged nobles.

An aristocracy, consisting of leading noble families, now took control, but before many years had passed a tyrant was in power at Mytilene. This tyranny may have been established as a result of feuds between members of the ruling nobility, although Alcaeus' remark about possessions making the man suggests that another social class was beginning to acquire influence in the state. This tyrant (Melanchrus) was overthrown by a group of men including Alcaeus' brothers and Pittacus, the man who ultimately solved Mytilene's internal troubles. Before long another tyrant, Myrsilus, arose, and Pittacus, Alcaeus, and other nobles swore a solemn oath to destroy him. For reasons unknown Pittacus switched his allegiance to Myrsilus, thereby earning the hatred and scorn of Alcaeus. Somewhat later the tyrant died and Alcaeus exulted: "Now a man must get drunk, and drink violently, since Myrsilus is dead." The poet's joy was brief, for soon he and his brother had to leave Lesbos in exile; one wonders if they had been suspected of tyrannical aspirations. After a few years, during which the brother served as a mercenary in the Babylonian army, Alcaeus, his brother, and other exiles, well financed by the king of Lydia, tried to accomplish their return to Mytilene by force. The threat was so great that the Mytileneans (the nobles?) elected Pittacus to a special office to meet the emergency, a task which he successfully accomplished (Aristotle, *Politics*, 3.9.5–6).[22]

Alcaeus calls Pittacus a tyrant and heaps abuse on him, emphasizing, with typical aristocratic disdain, his low birth. Pittacus, however, was clearly a noble, for no commoner would have been accepted by Alcaeus and his fellow aristocrats as a sworn member of a group to slay the tyrant Myrsilus, as Pittacus had been. Also it is known that Pittacus married a lady from the survivors of the Penthilid clan. Aristotle says that Pittacus was elected *aisymnētēs*, an office which he defines as an elective form of tyranny; unfortunately the only example he provides for this office is Pittacus himself. When this non-Greek word is found elsewhere used in a political sense, it refers to an annual magistrate in certain of the eastern Greek cities. For all practical purposes apparently Pittacus was a tyrant, but after ten years (590–580) he voluntarily surrendered his powers. In that period, however, his statemanship was distinguished enough to earn him a place as one of the Seven Wise Men. Of his activity in his term of office, unfortunately, very little is known. Rather than establishing a new constitution, he contented himself with enacting special laws, including one aimed at curbing extravagant funeral expenditures. It is clear from Alcaeus' poetry that after the expulsion of the Penthilids a council and assembly (agora) had been part of the governmental machinery in Mytilene. Pittacus certainly made use of these bodies, probably opening membership in them to wider circles. Disgust with the excesses of extreme aristocrats like Alcaeus may have induced the Mytileneans to accept some sort of compromise. An oligarchy—in which, presumably, men possessed of movable wealth took part—became responsible for the management of affairs, and oligarchy remained the form of government at Mytilene until the last third of the fifth century.

Towards the end of the seventh century Miletus fell under the tyranny of Thrasybulus who, according to the ancient accounts, maintained close relations with Periander of Corinth. Aristotle in the *Politics* (5.4.5) cites Thrasybulus as an example of a tyrant who used the public office he was holding as a stepping-stone to the seizure of supreme power. In the case of the Asia Minor tyrannies, a special cause, in addition to whatever the internal conditions were, may have contributed to their rise. From the time of Gyges in the first half of the seventh century, the Lydians had been increasingly encroaching on the Ionian Greeks. The need for strong, centralized leadership against the Lydian threat could have caused various men to be entrusted with so much military power that the step to tyranny was an easy one. Certainly Thrasybulus devoted much of his energy to defending Miletus against the Lydians; similarly, it was the threat of returning exiles, backed by Lydian wealth, that led to the appointment of Pittacus as *aisymnētēs* by the Mytileneans.

Ephesus also had several tyrants in this period, probably aristocrats hostile to the old Basilidae clan which, like the Bacchiads at Corinth, had controlled the government since the abolishment of the kingship. Little is known about them except that they seem to have solved the Lydian problem by marrying into the royal Lydian family (Mermnadae). As a result Ephesus came under Lydian influence more than any other of the eastern Greek cities. At some period a significant change in the tribal structure took place at Ephesus;[23] since it is likely that the tyrants and the disorders leading to tyranny were at least partly responsible for the tribal reorganization, it should be mentioned briefly here, for something similar may have happened in various other Ionian cities.

In the early centuries of its existence the citizens of Ephesus had been organized in the four old Ionian tribes—Geleontes, Hopletes, Aigikoreis, and Argadeis—to which in the course of time two more were added, Boreis and Oenopes, presumably to include non-Ionian Greeks who came to Ephesus after the original migration. Later, and probably under the tyrants in the sixth century, five new tribes were substituted for the earlier six, and each of the new tribes was divided into at least six *chiliastyes*. The *chiliastyes,* theoretically groups of a thousand (but actually much fewer), were units which had been developed earlier for military purposes. Of the five new tribes, one was called Ephesians; it consisted of the former Ionian tribes and the two added later, Boreis and Oenopes, all now reduced to the category of *chiliastyes*. The four other new tribes, with their constituent *chiliastyes,* were apparently composed of Greeks who had not originally been Ephesians and of various native

Anatolian elements. The original Ionian Ephesians thus preserved the purity of the Ionian tribes, now reduced to *chiliastyes,* within the new tribe—Ephesians—but since the other four new tribes seemingly were made up of Greeks who had come to Ephesus from diverse places and of Anatolians, it is clear that the older Ionian element was no longer the dominant part of the population. Although on present evidence it cannot be proved, it is quite possible that the tyrants had been supported by natives and by Greeks who had not been accepted as citizens of Ephesus, and that this new five-tribe system was the way in which the tyrants rewarded their followers by making them full citizens of the city.

In this connection it is interesting to observe that the first temple to Artemis in Ephesus was built about 600. Ephesian Artemis was largely an oriental mother-goddess with whom the Greek Artemis was identified. Her acceptance as the patron goddess of Ephesus at this time emphasizes, as does the new tribal organization, the great increase of oriental elements and influences in the originally entirely Greek city of Ephesus. Herodotus (1.147) states that the Ephesians did not celebrate the purely Ionian festival Apaturia; it may very well have been at this time that the celebration of the festival was abandoned.

The most famous of the tyrannies among the eastern Greeks was that of Polycrates in the large island of Samos,[24] which lies close to the Asia Minor coast, about equidistant from Ephesus and Miletus. Samos, like many other Greek states, had shared in the colonizing activity of the seventh century. It was a Samian merchant who in the second half of that century opened up the profitable metal trade with Tartessus in southern Spain, and the Samians participated in the colonizing of Naucratis in Egypt. Subsequently they were active in the northeast, founding Perinthus on the north shore of the Propontis. It seems safe to assume that colonization and its stimulus of trade and industry, with the attendant increase in the importance of movable wealth, created social and political problems in Samos as in so many other parts of the Greek world. The first evidence of trouble is preserved in Plutarch's *Greek Questions,* 57 (*Moralia,* 303E–304C), where one reads that the landowners (*geomoroi*) took control of the state after the murder of Demoteles and the putting down of his monarchy. Since nothing more is known of this Demoteles, it is generally assumed that he had succeeded in establishing some sort of tyranny. Plutarch then says that when the Megarians sent an expedition against Perinthus, the landowners dispatched nine generals with a fleet to aid their colonists. Since Perinthus was founded about the year 600, it is reasonable to date this episode to a period when the colony was still in a formative stage. After achieving their purpose, the generals returned to Samos and with the help of their Megarian prisoners proceeded to massacre most of the landowners, who had assembled in the council chamber. What type of government was established after the overthrow of the "oligarchy" of the landowners is not stated, but this confused account reveals that Samos was experiencing social and political troubles in this period. The literary sources supply no further information about Samos until the emergence of Polycrates as tyrant, which is dated by the chronographers to 532/1. Herodotus (3.39) states that Polycrates, on seizing power, at first shared his authority with his two brothers, but subsequently killed one of them and banished the other. The report (3.120) that he gained ascendancy with the backing of only fifteen hoplites suggests that the path to power may have been somewhat prepared for him, possibly by his father.

'Of the many stories about Polycrates preserved in the ancient authors, the majority emphasize his naval power and his unfailing success—until his final reversal. Herodotus (3.122) speaks of his great fleet and his many victories, and adds that he was the first Greek, unless one counts Minos of Cnossos, who planned to become master of the sea. Polycrates undoubtedly increased Samian naval power greatly, but it is probable that the beginning of this dominance went back to the crushing of Phocaea by the Persian conquest of ca. 545. Since from that time the Persians had control over all the Greek cities of Asia Minor, it has been suggested that Polycrates owed his reputation and influence among the islanders, and possibly even in Greece proper, to his role as leader of the resistance against any further Persian advance westward. His alliance with Amasis, king of Egypt, can be interpreted as a defensive move against Persian aggression.

This alliance gave rise to one of Herodotus' famous stories (3.40–43). Amasis, fearing that the unbroken success of his friend would arouse the jealousy of the gods, wrote to him suggesting that, in order to avert divine anger, he throw away the object he treasured most highly. Polycrates, believing that the advice was sound, put out to sea in a penteconter and cast overboard a beautiful and artistic seal ring. A few days later a fisherman who had caught an unusually fine fish brought it as a gift to the tyrant, and when the fish was opened, the ring was found in its stomach. Polycrates immediately wrote to Amasis about this almost miraculous happening. After hearing the story, the Egyptian king, convinced that the tyrant was a marked man in divine eyes, broke off the alliance. Whatever one's attitude to this folktale may be, it is clear that Herodotus confused the ending, for Amasis, who was being threatened with a Persian attack, was in no position to cast off a powerful naval ally. Subsequent events make it certain that it was Polycrates who renounced the alliance and joined forces with the Persians; at least he sent a contingent, albeit of his political enemies, to accompany Cambyses, the Persian king, in his invasion of Egypt in 525. This failure to help Egypt and the apparent collaboration with Cambyses obviously militates against the concept of Polycrates as a champion of the Greeks against Persia. Polycrates himself, for reasons that are somewhat obscure, was captured and crucified by the Persian governor of Lydia in 522, the year in which Cambyses died. Some years later, in 517, the next Persian king, Darius, had Polycrates' exiled brother, Syloson, installed as tyrant in Samos.

Polycrates made a great impression on the Greek world, an impression that was still vivid almost a century later when Herodotus wrote. His sea power, often indistinguishable from piracy, and his unfailing success until the final dramatic reversal were remembered, as well as the splendor of his court, graced by men such as the poets Ibycus and Anacreon. Like many other tyrants, Polycrates was responsible for a building program. Herodotus (3.60) says that three of the constructions undertaken were the greatest yet achieved by the Greeks; it is very likely, however, that work on these undertakings had begun prior to his establishment as tyrant. One was the great mole, some 1,200 feet long, erected to provide safe anchorage for war and merchant ships, and another was the enormous temple of Hera. The most remarkable accomplishment, however, was the tunnel made by Eupalinus of Megara for bringing water into the city of Samos. An underground conduit, about half a mile in length, carried water from a spring to Mt. Ampelos, through which a tunnel of some 3,300 feet was dug; another conduit conducted the water to a fountain in the city. The digging of this tunnel was started simultaneously from opposite sides of the mountain, and when the diggers reached the middle they had missed a perfect join by less than twenty feet.[25]

Despite the considerable information and the numerous stories extant about Polycrates, the ancient authors nowhere discuss the fundamental causes of his rise to power. Polycrates was surely an aristocrat; no gossip has been preserved about his low or questionable birth, as it was in the cases of Cypselus and Orthagoras. As a man interested in sea power, he may have appealed to the new class of men wealthy in movables, but, if he seized control supported by only fifteen hoplites, one can hardly speak of him as a hoplite leader. Once in power, if one can trust the various stories, he treated the aristocracy harshly, but they remained strong enough to reassert themselves temporarily after his death. There is no reason to think of him as a demagogue, although it is obvious that his large fleet and the intensive building activity must have furnished jobs for many laborers and craftsmen. It seems necessary to admit, therefore, that one cannot explain the basis of the power of this man living so late in the archaic period unless somehow, despite the inexplicable vagaries of his career, he was able to capitalize on the very real danger of Persian aggression, as presumably Thrasybulus had done in the case of the Lydian threat.

Polycrates is the last of the seventh- and sixth-century tyrants that need be mentioned in this chapter, for the Pisistratids of Athens will be treated subsequently in the discussion of early Athens, and the tyrants established by the Persians in the Greek cities of Asia Minor owed their position to their Persian masters and not to the internal conditions of the cities.

THE AGE IN which these tyrants appeared—the seventh and sixth centuries—was clearly one of great social, economic, and political upheaval. Since most of the tyrannies arose in cities like Corinth, Sicyon, Megara, Miletus, and Samos, in which trade and manufacturing were on the increase, it is reasonable to conclude that the tyrants received support from the traders and artisans, who, as men wealthy in movables rather than in land and as potential hoplites, resented the exclusive control of the state held by the landed aristocracy. The tyrants themselves were not proletarians and should not be thought of as leaders of a proletarian revolution. They were usually ambitious nobles who probably had been feuding with other nobles, although some may have belonged to a lower social class. This is not to say that they may not have been supported by the "masses," whom they ultimately helped; it is merely a warning against viewing these tyrants as farseeing, idealistic social revolutionaries. Their rise to power was often, if not always, helped by their military prowess, presumably as leaders of the emerging hoplites. At the time of their seizing of power the tyrants probably were holding some influential office from which they refused to resign, and the actual coup apparently consisted of gaining control of the citadel, which was achieved with the support of their followers and possibly, at times, with the assistance of some mercenary troops.

Certainly once they had occupied the citadels, the tyrants must have worked fast against their enemies. Many nobles were murdered; others were driven out or fled into exile. How widespread this assault on the nobles was is unknown. The information concerning the Pisistratids at Athens and the evidence for good relations between tyrants and noble families of other cities are warnings against assuming any complete liquidation of the aristocracy. Some, or possibly many, aristocratic estates, however, were confiscated and divided among the tyrants' partisans. Although it is natural to assume that this land was assigned to the "masses" and to struggling peasants, there is no specific statement to this effect; hence it is quite possible that some—if not all—of this land was given to the non-landowning followers of the tyrants, thus enabling these men possessing only movable wealth to acquire landed wealth also.

The tyrants apparently did not produce any substantial change in the constitutional machinery of the various cities. The chief change lay in their own persons, for which there was no place in existing constitutions. It is not known what office, if any, a tyrant held. Some may have continued, unconstitutionally, in the office they held when they staged the coup. Orthagoras and Cypselus, for example, may have continued to be polemarchs. In general, however, their power was personal and was based on their successful leadership of the "middle class" and also of the downtrodden lower classes against the aristocratic monopoly of the state. The express statement that Cypselus had no bodyguard suggests that some tyrants, at least, had enough popular support not to have to rely on military force. The chief changes they effected in the governments probably consisted in a change of personnel. They undoubtedly saw to it that their followers held the important offices and became members of the council. The fact that these followers were largely members of the new business class—men of ability and experience—helps to explain why the tyrannies, in their early stages at least, seem to have been efficient.

The tyrants were men of great energy, and many activities can be credited to them. The Cypselids eased many social and economic problems by undertaking extensive colonization. All the tyrants, apparently, were great builders. In the various cities temples arose and harbors were improved; more efficient methods were provided for the water supply; streets were paved; and drainage systems were established. In fact, a real development towards urbanization occurred under the tyrants. They were also interested in cultural matters, as is revealed by their establishing, or reorganizing, festivals for various gods, and by trying to attract to their courts the most famous artists, architects, and poets of the time. One could continue to list many accomplishments of this kind, but such an enumeration is likely to sound like a eulogy of the tyrants. Granted that they did achieve much for their cities and certainly were responsible for economic life becoming more diversified, one would still like to have answers to questions such as the following: How many of these projects were financed by confiscations resulting from brutal murders and exiles? Under what labor conditions were some of the great building undertakings carried out, especially the digging of the aqueduct tunnel through a mountain for Polycrates of Samos? Unfortunately there are no certain answers to such questions, and a final verdict on the tyrants should be based on definite answers.

Tyranny has been described as a breakthrough of the individual into politics. This is a rather apt expression, for under the declining monarchies and under the aristocracies, government was largely a class affair. The tyrants, as individuals, undoubtedly gave increased direction to the domestic and foreign policies of their respective states. But the more the states were developed and organized, the less was the need for the tyrants.[26] In fact, their situation had an ironic characteristic: they owed their position as tyrants to the widespread need for the solution of certain social, economic, and political problems; but the more they succeeded, the less was there a need for this anomalous "office." It is not by chance that the second generation of tyrants is often represented as more oppressive than the first. Since tyranny was not an office in itself and since the tyrant relied largely on his energy, his daring, and his charismatic qualities, a successor, who had not won popularity by a successful coup, found himself in a much more precarious position than his predecessor, and usually had to maintain his position by the employment of bodyguards and by frequent resort to repressive actions. Tyranny was by nature transitional, and when it tried to become permanent, it collapsed. After it had performed its transitional duties, it was overthrown, sometimes by exiled aristocrats; sometimes by its own middle-class supporters, who had no desire to allow a transitional phenomenon to become permanent; and often, in Greece proper at least, with assistance from Sparta.

In summary, then, tyranny played an important role in the transition of many Greek cities from the regime of the closed society of landed aristocracies based on birth to that of the more open and progressive society characteristic of much of Greece in the classical period. The change might have occurred through the processes of natural evolution, but the crises in many states had become so acute that, as often happens in history, drastic measures were taken to expedite the slow workings of natural evolution. The tyrants by their drastic measures weakened the aristocracy and improved the social and economic conditions for city and country workers alike. In some Dorian cities they may have helped the non-Dorians to become equal members of the community. Although many cities apparently prospered, for a while at least, under the tyrants, it was not long before tyranny outlived the purpose for which it had been established, and then the tyrants, by trying to maintain themselves in power, became increasingly oppressive. Their overthrow was the work of the upper and middle classes; there is no evidence for a rising of the "masses" against them. This might suggest that the tyrants, as their position became more precarious, adopted demagogic methods in an effort to keep the support of the poor. In any case, the governments which succeeded them were not democracies, as is often said or implied, but oligarchies or aristocracies—much more broadly based, however, than in the days before the advent of the tyrants. Since the tyrants were overthrown by the middle and upper classes, the articulate segment of the population, the tradition which was recorded about them was hostile and redolent of the scandals which the Greeks loved to ascribe to their political foes. One would like to know whether the peasants and humble city workers, in the last analysis, had looked upon the tyrants as exploiters or benefactors.[27]

THE AGE OF tyranny was the period in which the concept of coinage made its appearance in the Greek world, a phenomenon which naturally increased the possibilities of accumulating movable wealth and gradually simplified earlier methods of transacting business. For people accustomed to the use of money, it strains the imagination to visualize life without it, but at all times of history people have lived, and do live, successfully, even though totally ignorant of a money economy. Before the introduction of coinage the chief form of wealth in the Greek world was land and its products, but, as has been emphasized in this and in the preceding chapter, movable wealth, especially as a result of the increase in trade and manufacturing following colonization, was steadily growing in importance.

Movable wealth, as can be ascertained from articles found in tombs and from descriptions in the Homeric poems itemizing contents of storerooms of the heroes, took many forms: beautiful pottery and metal vases; various objects of gold, such as cups and plates; jewelry; fine clothing; bronze and iron tripods and cauldrons; lumps or bars of gold, silver, bronze, and iron. The more movable wealth of this type that a man possessed, the greater were his prestige and his ability to make an impressive display. Since trade was based on barter, these articles could be given in exchange for others that seemed even more desirable. Purchases, however, were often made by using "tool money," for many utensils such as tripods and cauldrons of varying sizes gradually, from their familiarity to everyone, acquired more or less generally recognized values, and hence could be used as media of exchange. It was also customary in business transactions to make payments in gold, silver, copper, or iron bullion; in these cases the weight and purity of the metal had to be tested as far as was possible on each occasion. In certain parts of the Peloponnesus, at least, a type of iron coinage was accepted. This "money," about which little is known, was in the form of spits (*obeloi*), six of which constituted a handful (*drachma*). A tradition arose, reported in part by Strabo (8.3.33) drawing on Ephorus, that Pheidon of Argos had dedicated some of these spits to Hera after he had invented measures, weights, and coinage struck from silver, a tradition recorded by the Parian Chronicle under the year 895. For reasons that will be given below, it is now certain that Pheidon did not invent coinage. The attribution to him may have grown out of the probably erroneous belief that he established a system of weights in addition to one of measures. Since the various weight denominations (obols, drachmas, minas, talents, and so on) subsequently were used in many places also to designate coins or sums of money, the association of Pheidon's name with the introduction of coinage followed easily.

There is little doubt that Xenophanes (in Pollux, 9.83) and Herodotus (1.94) were correct in assigning the first striking of gold and silver coins to the Lydians, but it may be appropriate to give some credit to the Ionian Greeks also. The fully developed coin, as distinct from its prototypes, can be defined as a piece of metal of definite weight and shape which has been stamped with a particular mark by its issuer, whether public or private, as a guarantee of its weight and purity. The earliest and best evidence for such coins and their immediate forerunners comes from Ephesus. The foundations of the first temple of Artemis there were laid about 600 B.C. When the building was started, many objects of value were dedicated to the goddess, thus forming a "foundation deposit" below the base of the temple. Many of these articles can be dated by archaeologists to the last third of the seventh century, and among them are about a hundred coins and proto-coins, mostly of electrum, a natural alloy of gold and silver. The words of a distinguished numismatist are worth quoting in reference to these coins: "As one passes from the mere dump, through the punched dump, the punched and striated dump, the punched and striated dump with a type cut into it, to the normal coin, all lying in nearly contemporary deposits, little if at all affected in appearance or weight by wear, one has the feeling of assisting at the very birth of coinage. If the deposits may be dated about 600 B.C., then this great event can hardly have taken place much more than a generation earlier."[28]

The findings of archaeology have not provided similar evidence from other Ionian cities, but it is reasonable to assume that coinage made its appearance in them at roughly the same time as in Ephesus—that is, sometime in the last quarter of the seventh century. The invention was adopted, with silver as the metal, slightly later in Aegina and some of the islands, about 590. In Corinth, the first coinage probably should be assigned to about 575, whereas the first Athenian coinage seems to date from around 560. Thereafter its adoption passed throughout the Greek world. It produced many changes in social and economic life, for money could be put to work to produce more money in ways that were impossible for the older forms of movable wealth. Important as money economy became, however, it did not oust natural economy, which persisted in many backward parts of Greece and also continued in various forms even in the more progressive cities.

It used to be argued that the purpose of the invention and adoption of coinage was the desire to facilitate trade. Scholars have recently shown that the denominations of early coins refute this assumption.[29] The commonest type of the electrum coins found in the foundation deposit at Ephesus weighs slightly more than the early Athenian silver drachma. Since until the time of Alexander the Great electrum was estimated to be ten times more valuable than silver, the intrinsic worth of these Ephesian coins can be understood if one remembers that in fifth-century Athens a drachma was normal pay for a day's work. The early Greek coins were of denominations of two, four, or more drachmas. Such coins, almost like bullion, were useless for daily trading activities. The coins found at Ephesus, presumably guaranteed by the king of Lydia, could have been used for purposes like the payment of mercenaries. In the Greek world, since political and economic life was becoming more complicated as the cities developed, the high-denomination coins may have been struck, and guaranteed for weight and purity, by the city governments for the more accurate control of their expenditures on matters such as public works and distribution of surpluses among the citizens and of their income from harbor dues, taxes, fines, punishments, and the like. It was only late in the fifth century that fractional coins of small denominations, which could be used for everyday business, were minted; but until then, and even afterwards, barter remained common.

6
Early Sparta

GREEK HISTORY, by definition, should be an account of all the innumerable settlements of Greeks scattered over the Mediterranean and Black Sea worlds. For the centuries following the collapse of Mycenaean civilization the evidence is so scanty and fragmentary that the historian has little choice but to discuss the Greeks in general, utilizing the scattered data as best he can to characterize the most significant events, developments, and trends. For the sixth and subsequent centuries, however, the amount of evidence available is so great that it is essential to find a central focus, since no history can deal simultaneously with the affairs of countless separate states. A unifying theme is necessary, and that theme is provided by the histories of Sparta and Athens, the two cities which were foremost in the Greek world in the classical period. Ideally, the Greek historian should be cognizant of the development and attitudes of all the Greeks, but the obvious need to impose some unity on the medley of data available practically forces him to concentrate on Sparta and Athens and to deal with the other states chiefly as their histories impinge on those of the two leading cities. Although this concentration admittedly oversimplifies many aspects of Greek history and blurs many subtle nuances, it is justified by the demands of coherence and also by the dichotomy represented by Sparta and Athens, for the former became the symbol of the oligarchic and reactionary spirit and the latter, of the democratic and progressive point of view. This chapter and the next will be devoted to accounts of Sparta and Athens, respectively, from their obscure origins down to the close of the sixth century.

Laconia, the name usually applied to the territory of Sparta, forms the southeastern section of the Peloponnesus. Bounded on the east and the south by the sea, it is separated on the north from Arcadia and the Argolid by mountains, whose continuations in the rugged Taygetus range, extending to Cape Taenarum, form the western boundary and in the Parnon range culminate in Cape Malea. Between these two ranges and watered by the Eurotas River flowing from the Arcadian mountains lies the central plain of Laconia, cut off by a rocky ridge from the swampy, but fertile, delta of the river. According to surveys of archaeologists, over fifty sites in Laconia were occupied in the thirteenth century, most of which suffered devastation in the general catastrophe which struck Mycenaean civilization around 1200 B.C. Menelaus, Agamemnon's brother, had his capital at Lacedaemon, which may have been near the subsequent Therapnai on the east bank where in historical times the Menalaion was located, or on the west bank at Amyclae some four or five miles south of the future Sparta. From Homer's description it is clear that Menelaus' kingdom comprised a considerable part of Laconia. The lovely golden cups found in the *tholos* tomb near modern Vaphio, close to the ruins of Amyclae, are striking evidence that this general area belonged in the Mycenaean cultural world.[1]

As has been mentioned in preceding chapters, the reasons for the collapse of Mycenaean civilization are still a subject of scholarly discussion. Whether the responsibility should be attributed largely to a Dorian migration or to an uprising of Mycenaean "Dorians," there is no certain archaeological evidence for Dorian presence in the Argolid and Laconia until the closing years of the eleventh century. In the course of the following century four adjacent villages slowly developed on the west bank of the Eurotas, and from the union of these villages, probably late in the ninth century, historic Sparta began to evolve. The origin of the name is disputed; scholarly opinion is now inclined to explain it as derived from the prevalent plant *spartos* (Spanish broom) rather than from *spartē*, meaning, presumably, the sown land. Although the word "Sparta" was employed widely in literature, the Spartans themselves used the term "Lacedaemon" as the official name of their city and the territory it controlled. In all treaties and other similar documents which have been preserved, the Spartans were always referred to officially as Lacedaemonians.

The Spartan attempt to control Laconia was a slow and difficult process. This is illustrated by the fact that the Mycenaean town of Amyclae, some four or five miles south of Sparta, was not conquered until sometime in the first half of the eighth century. Amyclae must have come to satisfactory terms with Sparta, for it was not destroyed but was incorporated as a fifth village into the growing town of Sparta. The fall of Amyclae apparently weakened the resistance of the remaining Mycenaeans, and within a generation the Spartans had forced their way southward to the sea.

It is impossible to give a satisfactory account of the expansion of Spartan control in the eighth and seventh centuries, first over Laconia and then over Messenia. With rare exceptions the only information available consists of the inferences one can draw from archaeological findings and from the many legends included in the third and fourth books of Pausanias devoted to those two regions respectively. Since this expansion was completed by the end of the seventh century, the historian must work backwards from the comparatively known to the largely unknown in an effort, with the help of the fragments of Tyrtaeus, to identify those events which paved the way for creating the Sparta of the sixth and subsequent centuries.[2]

By about 750 Sparta had become master of all Laconia. This expansion was directed against the remnants of the Mycenaeans and also against Dorians who had settled in various communities throughout Laconia at more or less the same time that the town of Sparta was taking shape. The Dorian settlements, presumably, were not destroyed but became politically subordinate to Sparta. As *perioeci*—communities lying on the periphery—they retained a large amount of local autonomy but, at least in later times, owed military service to the Spartans. The Mycenaean survivors for the most part were reduced to a form of serfdom. Their land apparently was divided among the Spartan nobles, who, as absentee landowners, enjoyed a certain proportion of the revenues from the land to which the "serfs" were bound. This was the beginning of the helot system, which will be discussed later in this chapter.

In the second half of the eighth century the Spartans began the conquest of Messenia to the west, an undertaking which was to be decisive for their subsequent history. Since this was the time when the great colonizing movement, caused chiefly by land hunger, started in the Greek world, one can assume that the Spartans, beyond their lust for conquest, also felt that their growing population needed more arable land than the already appropriated fertile Eurotas valley. Messenia had been part of the Mycenaean world, as the excavations at Pylos on the west coast and the discovery of various *tholos* tombs have revealed. Readers of the *Odyssey* will remember that Telemachus and Nestor's son, Pisistratus, in their chariot journey from Pylos to Lacedaemon lodged for the night at Pherae. With the collapse of Mycenaean civilization towards the end of the thirteenth century, Messenia also entered a dark age. In the confused centuries that followed one can imagine the presence of various small communities—some Dorian, some Mycenaean, some mixed. From the end of the eleventh century there is evidence for settlements characterized by protogeometric pottery in the area of the Messenian Gulf.

The information available on the Spartan conquest of Messenia is very limited.[3] The closest approach to a contemporary source is the poetry, preserved in a few fragments, of the Spartan Tyrtaeus, who lived at the time of the "Second Messenian War," some two or three generations after the initial conflict. There is also a mass of legendary data preserved especially in the fourth book of Pausanias. To understand the nature of these legends, one should remember that Messenia, after subjection to Sparta for some three and a half centuries, regained its freedom in 369. This remarkable reversal of fortune naturally stimulated the curiosity of the Messenians, and other Greeks in general, to inquire into the history of this long-suppressed people. Little material, however, was available for this investigation, beyond the oral traditions passed down from generation to generation. Pausanias (chapter 6) states that he drew most of the data for his account of the Messenian wars from two third-century authors—Myron of Priene and Rhianus of Cretan Bene, the former writing in prose about part of the First Messenian War and the latter, in poetry, about aspects of the Second War. Rhianus was an Alexandrian scholar and poet who in his epic, *Messeniaca,* composed a work centering around the exploits of a hero, Aristomenes, as the *Iliad* was centered around Achilles. The epic is no longer extant, but if Pausanias drew chiefly from it and from the little-known Myron, the questionable authenticity of his "History of Messenia" hardly needs exposition.

On the basis of sources of this sort, it seems probable that even before the "official" First Messenian War the Spartans had crossed the Taygetus range and acquired some influence in the area of the Nedon River (Dentheliatis) and on the eastern and northern coast of the Messenian Gulf, possibly by imposing perioecic status on certain conquered settlements. The "official" war can safely be dated to the last half of the eighth century, for Tyrtaeus speaks of the Spartan king Theopompus as the leader. It also seems significant that in the preserved records of Olympic victors,[4] questionable as they are for the early period, seven Messenians are listed in the period 776–736 but none thereafter until the fourth century, with one exception, ca. 684, which can be taken as evidence that Sparta enslaved only part of Messenia in the first war. After long fighting the Spartans gained control of the plain through which the Pamisus River flows when the Messenians, according to Tyrtaeus, in the twentieth year fled from their fortress on Mt. Ithome. Those who were unable to escape to other parts of the Peloponnesus were reduced to the status of helots, "galled with great burdens like asses, bringing to their lords under grievous necessity a half of all the fruit of the soil" (fragment 6). Along the shores of the Messenian Gulf, Sparta organized more perioecic communities, presumably among those Messenians who were chiefly Dorian.

It is probable that the Spartan nobles, who were responsible for victory in the First Messenian War, alone received allotments of land in the newly conquered territory. The discontent felt by other segments of the Spartans at this exclusion from the fruits of victory was revealed by the rebellion of the Partheniai, which was mentioned earlier in the chapter on colonization. The term "Partheniai" (sons of unmarried mothers) may have been applied to a rebellious group of non-nobles to stigmatize their legitimacy and to justify their exclusion from a share in the Messenian land. The trouble was finally allayed by dispatching the malcontents to found Taras (Tarentum), the only Spartan colony in the west (ca. 706).

The "Second Messenian War" Tyrtaeus (fragment 5) implies was carried on by the grandsons of those who fought in the first war. In round numbers, then, it can be assigned to the middle of the seventh century or slightly later. The natural anger of the Messenians at their partial subjection to the Spartans seems a sufficient cause for their revolt, but many scholars assume that the "Second War" was started by the Messenians after the Argives defeated the Spartans at Hysiai in 669 (Pausanias, 2.24.7; 3.7.5) and after the Messenians had received promises of assistance from the Argives, Arcadians, and others. This picture of a united front against Sparta, based largely on a passage in Strabo (7.4.10) and various references in Pausanias, is too vague and controversial to require discussion here.

This war was a bitter struggle in which, according to ancient accounts, the poet Tyrtaeus aroused the flagging spirits of the Spartans. Certainly his poems, as can be seen from the surviving fragments, breathe the spirit of patriotism: "For it is a fair thing for a good man to fall and die fighting in the van for his native land" (fragment 10). It is also clear from Tyrtaeus that the Spartans by this time had adopted hoplite tactics, a change of great significance, as will be seen below, for the internal development of Sparta. In this war the mountainous fortress of Hira near the Arcadian border was the scene of the final unsuccessful stand of the Messenians, as Mt. Ithome had been in the first war. Pausanias in book 4, following Rhianus, tells various marvelous and romantic tales about the exploits of Aristomenes, the Messenian leader. After their complete victory the Spartans once again divided the fertile land of the Pamisus valley into lots for their citizens, and many more Messenians than previously were reduced to the status of helots. Subsequently the Spartans completed the conquest of Messenia by advancing to the west coast. Since this part of Messenia is mountainous and unfit for farming, it is unlikely that the scanty population became helots, at least in the sense of the agricultural serfs of the Pamisus region. To keep watch on the Messenians, the Spartans established various perioecic communities, some possibly peopled by Messenian Dorians and others by refugees from the Argolid towns of Asine and Nauplia which the Argives had destroyed. A new Asine rose on the western shore of the Messenian Gulf, and the Nauplians were settled at Methone on the south-west coast of Messenia.[5]

By the end of the seventh century Sparta, in control of Laconia and Messenia, had attained almost its maximum territorial expansion. Thereafter, extension of its political influence was usually achieved by a system of alliances.

IMPORTANT AS Sparta was in the political and military history of Greece, however, it was its institutions—constitutional, social, and economic, the so-called Lycurgan constitution—which made it unique in the Greek world and were responsible for the influence and fascination which Sparta has exercised from ancient times down to the present.

The sources for the development and the character of the Lycurgan constitution, as for the expansion of Spartan control over Laconia and Messenia in the eighth and seventh centuries, are limited and unsatisfactory. In addition to the archaeological evidence and the confusing and often contradictory legends preserved in late authors like Pausanias, the fragments of poets who lived and worked in Sparta in the seventh century—Tyrtaeus, the Lydian Alcman, and the Lesbian Terpander—are helpful, but pathetically few. Then for almost two full centuries no author who wrote about Sparta has been preserved. In the latter half of the fifth century Herodotus and Thucydides had much to say about the Spartans in their histories, but both were chiefly concerned with foreign relations, Herodotus concentrating on the period of the Persian Wars and the preceding generation or two, Thucydides on the Peloponnesian War. In the fourth century Xenophon wrote extensively on Sparta and the Spartans, but, like Thucydides, he was dealing primarily with contemporary events. Ephorus, existing now only in fragments, had great influence on subsequent writers and seems to have emphasized the themes of early Argive imperialism and of the continual hostility between Argos and Sparta. In the same century both Plato and Aristotle discussed Sparta at some length in their writings on political philosophy, Aristotle rather critically, but Plato usually very favorably. In fact, an early stage of the idealized picture of Sparta—what can be called the myth of Sparta—can be traced to some of the doctrinaire statements and conclusions of Plato.

In this summary it is unnecessary to list the numerous Hellenistic writers (Rhianus of Crete was mentioned above) who wrote about Sparta, since most of their works are not extant. It will be sufficient to call attention to Plutarch (ca. 46–120 A.D.) and Pausanias, whose *floruit* is placed about the middle of the second century A.D. Pausanias in book 3 provides much valuable information on the physical aspects of Sparta

and particularly on the cults, and he also m.   ·ical"
sketches and a great deal of legendary materiai.   ·h
Sparta has exerted down through the ages Plutar̖
portant, for in his *Life of Lycurgus* he presented what b̖
cal picture of the Spartan way of life, a picture which thor̖
lished the idealized myth of Sparta. Actually, none of thesȇ   ̖thors
knew much about early Sparta, and surprisingly little even about the
inner workings of the Spartan system in their own times. Thucydides
(5.68) gives the reason for this ignorance when in one passage he com-
plains that the Spartans tried to conceal all information about themselves. The Spartans, in fact, were very successful in erecting an iron
curtain between themselves and the rest of the Greek world.

Two other characteristics about the source material on Sparta
should be noted. First, Sparta was an aristocratic and conservative—or
better, reactionary—state. Consequently, democratically minded Greeks
distrusted it, whereas aristocrats and their authors idealized it and
helped develop the myth of Sparta. In reading an ancient writer on
Sparta, therefore, one must be aware of his social and political prejudices. The second characteristic is illustrated by Plutarch's *Life of Lycurgus.* In this biography, which is required reading for anyone seriously
interested in Sparta, Plutarch begins by admitting that no one knew for
certain either who Lycurgus was or when he lived, and then proceeds to
give a fascinating account of the Spartan way of life which was traditionally associated with the name Lycurgus. In writing this account
Plutarch was much influenced by the careers of two third-century reforming Spartan kings—Agis and Cleomenes—whose biographies he
also composed. These kings attempted to bring about a social revolution
involving such measures as the cancellation of debts and the redistribution of land in the belief that they were restoring Lycurgus' system. Plutarch, therefore, when writing his *Life of Lycurgus,* quite naturally and
probably unconsciously transferred certain third-century conditions to
the early days of Spartan history.

From sources such as these, beginning most logically with the constitution, one must derive his picture of the so-called Lycurgan institutions. Sparta had a dual kingship, one king belonging to the Agiad family and the other to the Eurypontids. According to the ancient tradition
this dual kingship had existed since the founding of Sparta. It was explained by the legend that the Heraclid Aristodemus who led the
Dorians into Laconia had twin sons, Eurysthenes and Procles, who both
became kings, the former being the father of the eponymous Agis, the
latter, the father or grandfather of the eponymous Eurypon. This is pal-
pably an aetiological legend to account for the fact of the double king-

ship. The ancient story that Eurysthenes was the firstborn of the twins probably contains a hint that the kingship belonging to his family—the Agiads—was the older one. Also there are suggestions in the ancient sources that the Agiad family had more prestige—presumably because it was the senior group. The best proof, however, that the Agiads were the original royal family lies in the king-lists which have been preserved. The genealogy of the Agiads from Aristodemus down appears to be perfectly straightforward, but the lists of the early Eurypontids are not consistent. The explanation almost certainly is that at some later date, imaginary names were inserted into the Eurypontid line in an effort to make its genealogy reach back as far as that of the Agiads. It is likely, therefore, that when the Dorians first settled at Sparta, they had one king. Like other Greek kings in the Dark Age, he presumably was surrounded by his companions, who formed a sort of council of elders. The common people, it may be imagined, were on occasions called into an assembly in ways similar to those described in Homer. When and how, then, did a second kingship come into existence?

Various answers have been offered for these questions.[6] One suggestion is that since the Dorians were divided into three tribes—Hylleis, Dymanes, and Pamphyli—there were originally three tribal kings of whom one was ultimately suppressed by the others. This interpretation, improbable in itself, seems to be ruled out by the fact that both Agiads and Eurypontids presumably belonged to the Hylleis tribe; at least, each claimed descent from Hyllus, son of Heracles. Another suggestion is that when Amyclae was incorporated into Sparta ca. 800–750, the old Mycenaean dynasty of the Agiads at Amyclae shared the rule with the Dorian Eurypontids of Sparta. Possible evidence for this theory can be seen in the fact that towards the end of the sixth century the Agiad king, Cleomenes, told a priestess at Athens that he was an Achaean (that is, Mycenaean), not a Dorian (Herodotus, 5.72). This startling statement may well suggest that there was more blending between Dorians and Mycenaeans in the early days than later Dorians and doctrinaire theorists, both ancient and modern, liked to admit; but in view of the certain Dorian domination in Sparta it is hard to believe that the senior royal family came from the pre-Dorian population. A variant of this suggestion has been inferred from the archaeological evidence. Since the excavations reveal that to the two original villages established on the site of Sparta two more were subsequently added, the proposal has been made that two separate groups of Dorians, each having a royal family, amalgamated at Sparta with the understanding that kings from each family should share the rule.

Another theory attempts to explain the establishment of the second kingship as a weakening of the royal power at Sparta at just about the same time that elsewhere in Greece monarchy was yielding to aristocracy.[7] It is true that the Eurypontids were the younger house and that the names of certain early representatives, even if subsequently inserted—Prytanis (roughly, "president") and Eunomos ("good law")—suggest an interest in civil government. The Eurypontids, thus, are considered as leaders of the aristocracy and the *damos* (Doric for *demos*), presumably landowners who could serve as fighting men, in an effort to restrict the arbitrary power of the Agiad kings. They achieved their purpose not by abolishing the kingship but by effecting a compromise whereby the Agiad king should always have a Eurypontid colleague. Granted that the early Eurypontid names Prytanis and Eunomos are suggestive, it is hard to believe that the aristocrats in their struggle against kingly power would have promoted a dual kingship, whose consequences might not have been a weakening of arbitrary power. One wonders also at the "altruism" of the aristocrats in agreeing to promote one of their number to a more exalted position.

In view of the almost total lack of information on the early development of Sparta, it is probably best to assume a dual kingship from an early period. The Eurypontids, however, may have had some responsibility for obtaining what one scholar has called the religious sanction for the new "republic." This sanction was secured in the form of an oracle from Apollo at Delphi; presumably the situation had previously been explained to the priests. Plutarch (*Lycurgus*, 6) quotes what purports to be the wording of the oracle, called a *rhetra*. The term *rhetra* here probably signifies an oracle which was enacted by the assembly. Plutarch writes that the *rhetra* was delivered to Lycurgus himself. This raises the probably unanswerable question of whether there ever was a real Lycurgus and, if so, when he lived. Regardless of one's attitude to this question, there seems to be no sound reason to doubt that Plutrach has preserved an ancient document, one that could be called the charter of "republican" government at Sparta. Needless to say, there has been endless argument on the significance and validity of this document. Those scholars who wish to date Lycurgus before the middle of the eighth century have to assume that the *rhetra* was preserved orally until the knowledge of writing became available. Even so, they are faced with the problem of when Delphi became sufficiently influential to issue such pronouncements. Those who date Lycurgus in the eighth or seventh century must deal with the tradition that Lycurgus forbade "laws" to be written down.

The text of the *rhetra*, as preserved by Plutarch, is corrupt at the end, and the wording, with its participles and infinitives, is so compressed that it is impossible to be sure what subject or subjects should be understood. The gist of the document, if one avoids certain technicalities, is the following: "Having erected a temple of Zeus Syllanios (Hellanios?) and Athena Syllania, having arranged(?) tribes and *obai*, having established thirty men, including the kings, as Gerousia, hold assemblies from season to season, then both introduce proposals and make final decisions(?)"—and then the corrupted line which probably means something like "and the power to belong to the *damos*."

This brief document, paraphrased here because of the difficulty of providing a generally acceptable translation, illustrates the nature of the material with which the historian of early Sparta must work. At this point it will be sufficient to say that the tribes presumably are the three Dorian tribes, while the *obai* refer to territorial tribes or regions of the town of Sparta, which will be discussed later; that the dual kingship is recognized; and that a Gerousia with a fixed membership was formed from the previous Council of Elders. Probably the kings and the Gerousia were responsible for introducing proposals, and the right of ratification lay with the *damos*. According to Plutarch, when the *damos* subsequently began to change and amend the proposals placed before it rather than merely ratifying them, the kings Theopompus (victor in the First Messenian War and surviving well into the seventh century) and Polydorus (ruling until after 669) inserted into the *rhetra* the words "if the *damos* should give its decision incorrectly, then the Elders and the kings shall make the final decision(?)." Tyrtaeus (fragment 4), writing at the time of the Second Messenian War, apparently included this amendment in the original *rhetra* as a device to control the *damos* if it should act otherwise than anticipated.

Whatever explanation one prefers for the origin of the dual kingship at Sparta, it is certain that the institution persisted for the long period from at least sometime in the eighth century until the closing years of the third. The nature of the kingship was similar to that depicted in Homer, but its powers were limited by its dual character and also by the constantly increasing importance of two other organs of the Spartan government—the board of five ephors and the Gerousia. Like Homeric kings, the kings of Sparta were leaders in war, and as was appropriate for men whose ultimate origin supposedly was divine, they had the priestly duties of acting as intermediaries between gods and men. In the field their powers were almost unlimited, although it is not clear how the two rulers shared the command. Towards the end of the sixth century a quarrel broke out between the two kings on campaign, and thereafter it was stipulated that only one king should be dispatched on a military expedition (Herodotus, 5.75).

From an uncertain date it became the custom for two ephors, like political commissars, always to attend the king on a foreign campaign. In various other ways, of which two should be mentioned, the ephors encroached upon the independence of the kings. According to Xenophon (*Constitution of the Lacedaemonians*, 15.7), each month the ephors on behalf of the state and the king on behalf of himself exchanged oaths, the king swearing to rule according to the established laws, the ephors swearing to maintain the kingship intact if the king abided by his oath. Also every ninth year the continuing tenure of office of the kings was at the mercy of the ephors. Plutarch (*Agis*, 11) describes the procedure as follows: "Every ninth year the ephors select a clear and moonless night, and in silent session watch the face of the heavens. If, then, a star shoots across the sky, they decide that their kings have transgressed in their dealings with the gods, and suspend them from their office, until an oracle from Delphi or Olympia comes to the succour of the kings thus found guilty." How often kings were deposed by this custom, which surely antedates the establishment of the ephorate as known in history, is unknown, but from this custom and that of the monthly exchange of oaths it seems that in the course of time the kings largely fell under the domination of the ephors. In fact, except when commanding armies on foreign campaigns, it seems that the kings more and more became figureheads in the Spartan government. Some scholars would object strongly to such a statement, however.[8] Certainly Agesilaus in the fourth century was an extremely influential man, but the ancient sources emphasize that as king he was extremely diplomatic in his relations with the ephors.

Although generalizations about the organization of the Spartan state are hazardous, and conditions naturally varied depending on circumstances, one could probably come closest to understanding the power structure by recognizing that ultimate authority lay with the ephors and the Gerousia. Nevertheless, as Herodotus (6.56–59) and Xenophon (*Constitution of the Lacedaemonians*, 15.2–5) point out, the kings had many prerogatives and honors—estates in the territory of the *perioeci*, special privileges at public sacrifices and games, and the right to receive a pig from every litter, presumably a survival from early times when the king lived surrounded by companions and attendants for whose maintenance he had to provide. When a king died his funeral was celebrated with much archaic ceremony, in which a free man and woman from every household had to participate as well as large numbers from the *perioeci* and helots.

There is even more uncertainty about the origin of the board of ephors than about the origin of the two royal families whose powers, in the course of time, they so greatly curtailed. Some scholars believe that the ephors were originally priests who, even after they became secular magistrates, retained one of their earlier religious functions—that of watching the heavens. This theory is possible, although it would be surprising to find a priestly caste which was willing to abandon most of its religious attributes and prerogatives. The ancient sources most commonly assign the establishment of this magistracy to Lycurgus (although it is noteworthy that it was not mentioned in the *rhetra*) or to Theopompus, the king during the First Messenian War. The fact that the Spartans had ephor lists supposedly going back to what would be 754/3 (the traditional date for the founding of Rome) might favor the attribution to Lycurgus, while the explanation given by Plutarch (*Cleomenes*, 10) that the kings, because of their long absences in the Messenian War, appointed deputies at home seems to point to Theopompus. One major difficulty stands in the way of accepting either of these suggestions. When information about the ephors becomes available they are always five in number, representing apparently the five territorial tribes (*obai*) into which Sparta was divided, each tribe being identified with one of the five component villages of Sparta. From a fragment of Tyrtaeus, however, it is clear that in the time of the Second Messenian War the Spartans were still organized according to the three old Dorian tribes. Organization of the Spartans by the five territorial tribes probably belongs to the end of the seventh century. The answer to this chronological dilemma may be that originally there were not five ephors—possibly only three to correspond to the three Dorian tribes—and that subsequently the number was increased to five. In any case, so far as the evidence goes, it was from the end of the seventh century that the board of ephors became an increasingly important part of the Spartan government.

The ephors were elected by and from the full body of Spartan citizens for the term of a year and apparently could not be reelected to office. As the supposed representatives of the Spartan people, they soon became the chief administrative officials of the state; the president of the board was the eponymous magistrate—that is, the man who gave his name to the year. Their power over the kings has already been mentioned—the monthly exaction of an oath, the watching of the heavens every ninth year for signs of divine displeasure with the kings, and the presence of two ephors with the king on a military campaign. The ephors were responsible for mobilizing the army and deciding what contingents should be called up. They received foreign ambassadors and, when necessary, introduced them to the assembly. They apparently alone had the right to convene meetings of the Gerousia and assembly, and they may have been the only ones authorized to introduce measures before these bodies. Their power over the lesser magistrates was almost unlimited. In the judicial field they heard the majority of civil cases, and in conjunction with the Gerousia they formed a court for all criminal matters. They seemingly had general supervision over the education of the young; as will be seen below, this education was the basic factor in the formation of the Spartan way of life. In fact, there were very few aspects of life in Sparta over which the ephors did not exercise some control.[9]

Many writers on Sparta, both ancient and modern, have claimed that the ephors, because they were elected from all the Spartan citizens, provided the democratic aspect of the Spartan constitution. This may have been true when they first became important magistrates at the close of the seventh century, but if so the situation soon changed, as it ultimately did with the tribunes at Rome. In this connection Plutarch (*Lycurgus*, 29.6) has an interesting statement which deserves to be quoted: "For the institution of the ephors did not weaken but rather strengthened the civil polity (*politeia*), and though it was thought to have been done in the interests of the people (*demos*), it really made the aristocracy more powerful." This rather startling judgment should be considered in conjunction with Aristotle's criticism (*Politics*, 2.6.14) that, since the ephors were chosen from the people in general, poor men were often elected to office who, because of their poverty, were particularly susceptible to bribery. Plutarch's mention of an aristocracy and Aristotle's reference to bribery (and surely the bribes were not always given by foreigners, as in the example adduced by Aristotle) furnish a good transition to a consideration of another important organ of the Spartan constitution—the Gerousia.

The Gerousia was a senate of thirty members, including the two kings who attended meetings *ex officio*. No satisfactory explanation has ever been found for the setting of the regular membership at twenty-eight. Plutarch (*Lycurgus*, 5–6) states that Lycurgus was responsible for the establishment of the Gerousia and that it was confirmed by the *rhetra* which Apollo of Delphi gave to the lawgiver. Plutarch is certainly wrong in attributing to Lycurgus the creation of an entirely new institution, for the early Spartan kings must have had some sort of Council of Elders similar to those which existed in all other early Greek states. It is quite likely, however, that at a particular time the membership and powers of the Gerousia may have been defined, and, as suggested above, that time may have been the occasion of the *rhetra*, which possibly should be considered the charter of "republican" government at Sparta.

The Gerousia had great powers in the state. No measure could be brought before the assembly until the senators had deliberated on the issues involved. This meant that the important right of initiative lay with them, although it was apparently exercised through the ephors. Criminal jurisdiction also lay within their province, but this was shared in some way, not well understood, with the ephors. The reasons for the great influence and prestige of the Gerousia are plain. No man was eligible for membership in the body until he had completed his sixtieth year and thus was no longer liable to military service. Election to the Gerousia was considered a reward for excellence—the highest honor that could befall a Spartan citizen. Once in the Gerousia, a man remained a member for the rest of his life and, so far as the evidence goes, he could not be held responsible for his words or deeds. Any permanent body of distinguished men in a governmental post can hardly fail to exercise great influence, and at Sparta, because of the age requirement, the influence naturally was conservative, if not reactionary. Aristotle's criticism of the Gerousia in the *Politics* (2.6.17) was very apt: "The mind, as well as the body, is subject to old age"; but the Spartans, needless to say, were more inclined to follow tradition than to heed the remarks of a philosopher.

The method of election to the Gerousia, which Aristotle called childish and Plutarch idealized, also was significant. Plutarch (*Lycurgus*, 26) describes the procedure in these words:

> An assembly of the people having been convened, chosen men were shut up in a room near by so that they could neither see nor be seen, but only hear the shouts of the assembly. For as in other matters, so here, the cries of the assembly decided between the competitors. These did not appear in a body, but each one was introduced separately, as the lot fell, and passed silently through the assembly. Then the secluded judges, who had writing tablets with them, recorded in each case the loudness of the shouting, not knowing for whom it was given, but only that he was introduced first, second, or third, and so on. Whoever was greeted with the most and loudest shouting, him they declared elected.

One need not be overly skeptical to suspect that such an electoral method easily lent itself to manipulation in favor of a special group or clique. What group?

Many scholars, apparently influenced by the myth of the equality of all Spartans, deny that there was any privileged group of Spartans and maintain that any Spartan who had passed his sixtieth year could stand for election to the Gerousia. There are various passages in the ancient sources, however, which clearly suggest that an inner clique or aristocracy did exist within the Spartan citizen body. Aristotle in the *Politics* (4.7.5) writes: "A second ground for describing Sparta as a democracy is the right of the people to elect to one of the two great institutions, the Senate, and to be eligible themselves for the other, the Ephorate" (Barker translation). This sentence certainly states clearly that the people could elect some people to the Gerousia, but not themselves. Again in the *Politics* (2.6.15), Aristotle, commenting on the need for all elements in a state to be satisfied with the constitution if it is to survive, remarks that this condition exists in Sparta, because the kings are content with the honors paid to their persons, the *kaloi kagathoi* (upper classes, gentlemen, aristocrats) with the Gerousia, for this office is the prize of excellence, and the people (*demos*) with the ephorate for which all are eligible.

In this connection one should remember the numerous references to rich Spartans which can be found in the pages of authors such as Herodotus, Thucydides, Xenophon, Aristotle, and Plutarch. All this talk about wealth and aristocracy is at complete variance with the notion of the equality of all the Spartans—a conception fostered by the myth of Sparta. It seems certain, therefore, that there existed in the Spartan state an aristocracy, an oligarchic group, or an inner clique—or whatever name one chooses to use. The origin and nature of this group will be treated below in the discussion of social and economic conditions; at this point it is sufficient to recognize its existence. It is probable that these wealthy members of the Gerousia were the ones responsible for the frequent bribery of the ephors to which Aristotle refers, and thus caused the ephorate to strengthen the aristocracy, as Plutarch states. These nobles, by controlling the Gerousia and exercising influence over the ephors and other magistrates, were the real power in the Spartan state; Demosthenes (20.107) commented in 355 that on election to the Gerousia a man becomes absolute master of the many. The nobles kept a jealous watch on the kings, who were their most dangerous potential rivals. Certain ambitious kings, like Cleomenes I and Pausanias in the early fifth century, irked at the supremacy of this oligarchic clique, tried to turn for support to the ordinary Spartans and even to the helots. As will be seen in subsequent chapters, they met a sorry end. Only in the third century was the corrupt power of these oligarchs temporarily broken. King Agis lost his life in the attempt. Cleomenes III succeeded briefly, and after him Nabis. The oligarchs had their ultimate revenge, however, for, thanks to them, Nabis was depicted in the pages of Polybius and Livy as a sadistic tyrant.

As in every Greek city, the Spartan government included as assembly of the full citizens—in this case of all who had reached their thirtieth year. Since there is no certain evidence that this body was called Apella, it will be better to use the more general term *ecclesia*. The *ecclesia* met apparently once a month, most likely on the occasion of the full moon (scholiast to Thucydides, 1.67). The ephors succeeded the kings as presiding officers. The *ecclesia* had electoral powers, electing the members of the Gerousia, the ephors, and various other magistrates, and, as a legislative body, had the responsibility of passing on measures proposed to it. Evidence is very scanty, but it seems that the introduction of business was the prerogative of the ephors and that debate may have been restricted to the members of the Gerousia, the ephors, and the kings. According to the "amended" *rhetra* of "Lycurgus" mentioned above, if the assembly decided incorrectly, the Gerousia and the kings (and certainly later, the ephors) could ignore the vote and make the final decision themselves. Unfortunately, beyond the wording of the amendment to the *rhetra,* in which the proper meaning of the verb, here translated as "make the final decision," is uncertain, no information is available which shows the assembly trying to act independently. One derives the impression, however, that it did not play a role comparable to the assemblies in democratic Greek states.

Despite certain peculiarities, the Spartan government in general was similar to that of many other Greek states. The uniqueness of Sparta lay in its way of life. Since the whole social, economic, and educational system was, in the last analysis, associated with the manner of land tenure, it will be necessary to examine this baffling and possibly unanswerable problem at some length.

THE FULLEST account of the Spartan land system is contained in Plutarch's *Life of Lycurgus,* especially in chapter 8, which is quoted here in its entirety because it is easier to discuss the problems involved by starting from a definite text.

A second, and a very bold political measure of Lycurgus, is his redistribution of the land. For there was a dreadful inequality in this regard, the city was heavily burdened with indigent and helpless people, and wealth was wholly concentrated in the hands of a few. Determined, therefore, to banish insolence and envy and crime and luxury, and those yet more deep-seated and afflictive diseases of the state, poverty and wealth, he persuaded his fellow-citizens to make one parcel of all their territory and divide it up anew, and to live with one another on a basis of entire uniformity and equality in the means of subsistence, seeking preeminence through virtue alone, assured that there was no other difference or inequality between man and man than that which was established by blame for base actions and praise for good ones.

Suiting the deed to the word, he distributed the rest of the

Laconian land among the *perioeci,* or free provincials, in thirty thousand lots, and that which belonged to the city of Sparta, in nine thousand lots, to as many genuine Spartans. But some say that Lycurgus distributed only six thousand lots among the Spartans and that three thousand were afterwards added by Polydorus; others still, that Polydorus added half of the nine thousand to the half distributed by Lycurgus. The lot of each was large enough to produce annually seventy bushels of barley for a man and twelve for his wife, with a proportionate amount of wine and oil. Lycurgus thought that a lot of this size would be sufficient for them, since they needed sustenance enough to promote vigor and health of body, and nothing else. And it is said that on returning from a journey some time afterwards, as he traversed the land just after the harvest, and saw the heaps of grain standing parallel and equal to one another, he smiled, and said to them that were by: "All Laconia looks like a family estate newly divided among many brothers."

This is a pretty passage, but the more one looks at it, the more one realizes that it represents the idealized picture of Sparta, the myth, rather than the reality. In writing it Plutarch was clearly influenced by the career of Agis, the third-century reforming Spartan king, who was aiming at the restoration of the "Lycurgan" system. In the *Life of Agis* (8) Plutarch says that Agis was planning to divide Laconia into 4,500 lots for the Spartans and 15,000 for the *perioeci.* These numbers are exactly half of those listed in the *Lycurgus,* the explanation being that in the time of Agis Sparta no longer controlled Messenia.[10] Plutarch, therefore, subconsciously at least, was thinking of a Lycurgan redistribution of land in both Laconia and Messenia despite the fact that in his *Life of Lycurgus* he dates Lycurgus to a period several generations before the conquest of Messenia. Other authors, like Isocrates (12.176–179) and Plato (*Laws,* 3.684), when referring to the Spartan land system, avoid Plutarch's chronological blunder, but their picture of the Dorians marching into Laconia and Messenia and, apparently simultaneously with their arrival, dividing the land into equal lots for the Spartans obviously has no historical validity.

There is no reason to doubt that Agis proposed to assign land to 15,000 *perioeci,* for in his day Sparta was desperately in need of manpower to fill the thinning ranks of the army. The doubling of that number for the time of Lycurgus, however, in the erroneous belief that Sparta then controlled Messenia is surely a fanciful picture of early Spartan history. In regard to the allotments to the Spartans, Plutarch evidently found conflicting data about the numbers and the period in his sources. This is not surprising, for the story of the assignment of equal lots to the Spartans at this early stage of their history is part of the myth, not of the reality, of Sparta.

Public land (*politikē chōra*) was divided among the Spartans, but the division took place at different times and not just once as the result of a legislator waving a magic wand. The process probably began in the first half of the eighth century when Sparta was acquiring control of the whole Eurotas valley; it was continued in the second half of the same century when the Spartans in the First Messenian War conquered a considerable part of the Pamisus valley. Since both these conquests occurred before the emergence of the hoplite army, it is likely that the nobles, who bore the brunt of the fighting, saw to it that the land should be divided among them and that conquered natives should be bound to the soil as helots to cultivate it. Then about the middle of the seventh century came the revolt of Messenia and the long, bitter Second Messenian War. As is clear from the poems of Tyrtaeus, the nobles, fighting as individual champions, were inadequate by themselves to handle the desperate situation. Hence Sparta, as was happening elsewhere in Greece, had to develop a hoplite army. This necessitated training in the new tactics not only the nobles but also other elements of the free population who could afford to equip themselves with the necessary weapons and armor—artisans, farmers, and possibly retainers of the nobles. When victory was finally achieved, the whole Pamisus valley was incorporated into Spartan public land. The nobles thus regained the lands they had lost, and the non-noble hoplites also received assignments of land which were worked for them by helots. When one considers the history of these Spartan conquests, it seems certain that there never was a single division of land into equal lots. The nobles, who presumably to begin with owned land in the environs of Sparta, acquired shares of state land in the lower Eurotas valley and then, later, shares in the Messenian plain. In terms of *kleroi* (lots), the nobles may have received several, while the non-nobles who participated in the Second Messenian War were assigned only one lot each from the newly conquered land.

Elsewhere in Greece the emergence of the hoplite army led to a weakening of the monopoly of the nobles and the rise of the "hoplite constitution" or, in those states where the aristocracy resisted stubbornly, to the phenomenon of tyranny. It is logical to assume, therefore, that a somewhat similar development occurred in Sparta. During the Second Messenian War, as can be learned from Tyrtaeus, the Spartans were organized according to the three Dorian tribes—Hylleis, Dymanes, and Pamphyli. By the beginning of the fifth century there is evidence that the Spartans, although the Dorian tribes still survived, were divided for political and military purposes into five territorial tribes (*obai*), each tribe apparently being identified with one of the five component villages of Sparta. No information has been preserved about the time when this new organization came into effect, but it is tempting to associate it with the results of the Second Messenian War and also to date the creation of a board of five ephors (in place of an earlier smaller board?) in the same period. What may have happened, therefore—although it must be emphasized that this is only a hypothesis—is that the nobles, who previously in combination with the kings had completely dominated the government, had to make certain concessions to the non-noble hoplites without whose help Messenia never would have been reconquered. These concessions consisted in granting to the "commoners" a more active citizenship than they had previously possessed—a citizenship which was protected and strengthened by assignments of public land in Messenia, by a more efficient organization in five territorial tribes (*obai*), and by the increased importance of the board of ephors, elected by and from the citizens at large.

Certainly from this time on, possession of a lot of public land was a prerequisite of citizenship. Theoretically, according to the idealized myth of Sparta, all holders of such lots of public land rated as equals. In the preceding pages, however, an attempt was made to show that although all Spartans were equals, some (to use Orwell's well-known phrase) were more equal than others. These "more equal" Spartans were the old nobility who, although forced by circumstances to increase the number of active Spartan citizens, were determined not to relinquish their earlier control of the state. They and their descendants managed to preserve this control by means of the prestige of their families; by their greater wealth, based in large measure on possession of several lots of public land and of private estates in the general territory of the *perioeci;* by their exclusive right to membership in the all-powerful Gerousia; and, in the course of time, by their success in influencing the ephors who, before long, seemed to represent the "oligarchy" rather than the "democracy."

The statement made above that possession of a lot (*kleros*) of public land was a prerequisite of Spartan citizenship is true and a simple one to make, but it involves the most baffling of all the perplexing problems about the Spartans. How did this system of each Spartan having a *kleros*—equal ones according to the myth—work? In any attempt to investigate this question two basic aspects of the Spartan way of life—the so-called Lycurgan system—must be kept constantly in mind. First, the Spartan state demanded lifelong service from every citizen. This service, which included, among others, military, governmental, and educational duties, left the citizen no time to engage in any private remunerative activity; in fact, participation in anything except public activity was prohibited by law. The state, therefore, had to provide complete maintenance for every citizen. The method devised was to assign to each citizen a portion of the public land—a *kleros*—cultivated by helots bound to the soil who had to turn over to the Spartan citizen a fixed amount of the produce of the land, an amount which in the judgment of the state was sufficient for his livelihood. Thus to be a citizen with full rights at Sparta, it was necessary to have the usufruct of a *kleros*. The second point which must be emphasized is that to retain that citizenship, the Spartan had to make from the produce of his *kleros* a monthly contribution to his military mess, the *syssition*, an institution which will be discussed below.

According to the myth this assignment of public land to Spartan citizens took place at one time and was believed to have been the work of the early lawgiver Lycurgus. Plutarch, in the passage quoted above, believed that the land was divided into 9,000 equal lots. According to Polybius (6.45.3), "the peculiar features of the Spartan State are said to be first the land laws by which no citizen may own more than another, but all must possess an equal share of the public land." Aristotle (*Politics,* 2.6.12) states it was thought that at one time there were 10,000 citizens. Assuming for the moment that the myth is reality, how could this system of the attachment of a *kleros* to a citizen have worked from generation to generation? There seem to be two chief possibilities. One is suggested by Plutarch in his *Life Of Lycurgus* (16.1), where he writes that if officials of the state, after examining a newborn boy, found him healthy, "they ordered the father to rear him, and assigned to the baby one of the 9,000 *kleroi.*" The inference here is that the state kept under its own control the management of the public land. Presumably the new baby did not have the usufruct of his *kleros* until he came of age. When his father died, the son, since he had already been assigned a *kleros,* did not inherit his father's allotment, which must have reverted to the state, for by the law of equality no one was supposed to have two *kleroi.* If a father had several sons, then one would think each should have been assigned a lot of land. If the number of legitimate claimants to the *kleroi* rose above 9,000, there is no hint in the ancient sources as to how this dilemma would have been met, for there is no suggestion in the myth that additional public land was acquired after the original division into 9,000 lots.

The second possibility in regard to the management of the public land is also provided by Plutarch, this time in his *Life of Agis* (5). Referring apparently to the early fourth century, Plutarch writes: "However, since the number of families instituted by Lycurgus was still preserved in the transmission of estates, and father left to son his *kleros* . . ." The clear meaning of these words is that, without any interference from the state, a son automatically inherited his father's *kleros*. Since later in the same chapter Plutarch says that it was the ephor Epitadeus (probably early in the fourth century) who first made it possible for a man to dispose of his *kleros* to whomever he wished, it is apparent that before that time the *kleros* was entailed in the sense that the citizen did not have outright ownership of it, but had only the usufruct of it on condition that he pass it on to his son. This possibility abounds in unanswerable questions, such as: If a man died without issue, did the *kleros* revert to the state? What happened if a man had numerous sons? According to the myth, each of the equal 9,000 lots was large enough to provide support for only one man and his family. Were some of the sons provided with *kleroi* which had reverted to the state when men who had no sons died?

It is idle to speculate further, for there obviously can be no meaningful answers to questions concerning a situation which never existed. As was seen above, it seems certain that the division of public land among the Spartans actually was carried out on several different occasions over a period of a century or more. Moreover, historical probability and the fact that the ancient sources contain so many references to rich as contrasted to poor Spartans lead to the sure conclusion that, although ultimately all full Spartan citizens shared in the public land, the amount assigned to individual Spartans varied greatly. Thus one must try to understand how the system of public land worked in reality rather than in myth. Unfortunately, it is more difficult to suggest explanations for the reality than for the myth.

In discussing this problem it will be best to begin with the available data concerning the decline in numbers of the full Spartan citizens (Spartiatai, often anglicized as Spartiates), for, since citizenship was based on possession of a *kleros*, it is clear that the decline in numbers must be intimately connected with the land system. According to tradition (and the tradition seems reasonable), there were at one time some 9,000 or 10,000 Spartan citizens to whom portions of public land had been assigned. This situation must refer to the period after the final conquest of Messenia, when Sparta had the maximum amount of public land at its disposal. By the year 480 there were, according to Herodotus (7.234), some 8,000 Spartan citizens. Definite figures are not available for the end of the fifth century, but the Spartan willingness to make peace with Athens in 425 to recover 120 Spartiatai who had been taken prisoner at Sphacteria (Thucydides, 4.38; 117) is clear evidence that the reduction in the numbers of full citizens had become a serious problem. By the time of the battle of Leuctra in 371, scholars have estimated that the citizen body may have sunk to 1,500 or 2,000 members. Early in 369

Messenia regained its independence. The chaos resulting from the loss of half of its territory must have wreaked havoc on the Spartan land system, particularly since it presumably followed on the measure of the ephor Epitadeus by which it became legal for a citizen to alienate his *kleros*. Thereafter, with the removal of all legal restraints on the *kleroi*, the rich began to acquire these portions of land by purchase, by foreclosure on mortgages, or by other methods, so systematically that, according to Plutarch (*Agis*, 5), at the beginning of the second half of the third century all the land was in the control of about 700 Spartiatai.

Since citizenship was based on possession of a *kleros* and since until probably the first third of the fourth century the *kleroi* were inalienable, how could the citizen body have declined from about 9,000 to some 2,000? A fragment from the fourth-century philosopher Heraclides Ponticus reads: "It is considered shameful for Lacedaemonians to sell land; but of the ancient part (*archaia moira*) it is not even allowed." If, as some scholars argue, the "ancient part" refers only to Laconia, it would be possible to assume that those citizens whose *kleroi* were in Messenia, despite the disgrace involved, sold their lots and hence ceased to rate as citizens. But it cannot be proved that this is the correct interpretation of the "ancient part," and also there would still be no explanation of the causes which induced Spartans to forfeit their citizenship by selling their *kleroi*. A definite answer to this problem of the astounding decline in the number of Spartiatai would illuminate one of the fundamental mysteries of ancient Sparta, but because of the lack of evidence, one must substitute speculation for an answer. Speculation usually centers around the system of military messes (*syssitia*). Each citizen had to make a monthly contribution from the produce of his *kleros* to his military mess. On two occasions (*Politics*, 2.6.21 and 2.7.4) Aristotle states that inability to meet this contribution requirement led to loss of citizenship.

Some scholars quote against Aristotle a sentence from Xenophon's *Constitution of the Lacedaemonians* (10.7): "For to all who satisfied the requirements of his code (*ta nomima*) he [Lycurgus] gave equal rights of citizenship, without regard to bodily infirmity or want of money." They then argue that "want of money" would include inability to meet the *syssitia* requirement, and hence this inability did not lead to loss of citizenship. In rebuttal of this argument one could maintain that satisfying the obligations of the code almost certainly would imply meeting the contribution requirement. Consequently this sentence does not prove that a man who did not contribute to the *syssitia* still retained his citizenship; it merely gives further evidence for the prevalence of economic inequality in ancient Sparta.

Why should any man possessing a *kleros* granted to him by the state

have been unable to meet the *syssitia* requirement? Again, more speculation is necessary. First, one must remember, as has been emphasized
above, that despite the myth of equality there were rich and poor Spartans. Second, one must admit that, despite the external simplicity of life
in Sparta, the rising standards of living elsewhere in Greece were also
penetrating the Spartan iron curtain. The poor Spartan citizen, however, had nothing to live from except the fixed income from his *kleros,* an
amount which had been set once and for all in days of simpler living. He
may very well have found it difficult, if not impossible, to meet the demands of an increased standard of living and still be able to pay his
contributions to the *syssitia.* On various occasions such a man may have
had to borrow. Since his only asset was his *kleros,* he would have had to
use it as security; but since it was inalienable, he could mortgage only
the produce of his *kleros.* Following this line of speculation, it is possible
to imagine many cases in which, after foreclosure, part or almost all of
the revenues of the *kleros* fell into the hands of the creditor. The Spartan
caught in this predicament would have been unable to meet his *syssition*
contribution and, therefore, according to Aristotle, would have ceased to
rate as a citizen. In Spartan terminology he would have ceased to be an
equal and would have fallen into the ranks of inferiors, who, to judge
from the ancient sources, became an ever-increasing element in the
state.

The above is pure speculation, and speculation must also be employed to try to explain what happened to the *kleros.* There seem to be
two main possibilities. One is that the *kleros* remained in the possession
of the family, being passed down from generation to generation, but so
beholden to creditors that it supplied little maintenance to the possessor.
The other possibility is that as soon as a citizen failed to meet the *syssitia*
requirement, his *kleros* reverted to the state. The ephors, as the chief administrative officers in the state, probably had the authority to dispose
of such lots. If one remembers Aristotle's emphasis on how subject to
bribery the ephors were, one wonders if the ephors, after receiving sufficient bribes, may not have allowed these vacated *kleroi* to be added to
the already large holdings of public land possessed by the rich—the ruling oligarchic clique in this paradoxical state of Sparta.

This suggestion that the ephors may have permitted *kleroi* to accumulate in the hands of Spartan oligarchs leads naturally to a discussion
of the controversial passage in Plutarch's *Life of Agis.* In chapter 5, after
speaking of the evil effects on the Spartans of the increase of wealth following their final victory in the Peloponnesian War in 404, Plutarch says
(presumably referring to this period of Spartan "hegemony") that Epitadeus, on becoming ephor, had a law enacted, with the support of the

powerful, making it possible for a man "to give his household (*oikos*) and his *kleros* to whom he wanted during his lifetime and to bequeath them by will." Since the *oikos* probably refers to a man's personal property, it is the *kleros* which is significant for the problem under consideration. In the rest of the chapter it is stated that the powerful, taking advantage of this law which soon must have signified the complete breakdown of the tradition of the inalienability of the *kleros*, continued to appropriate the land until by the time of Agis (in the 240s), only 700 Spartiatai remained as holders of *kleroi*. The Epitadeus in this passage, to whom the collapse of the "Lycurgan" system of equal *kleroi* is attributed, is mentioned by name in no other extant ancient source. Some scholars, therefore, have argued that he was only an invention of the revolutionary propaganda in the last half of the third century of Agis and Cleomenes, who advocated a return to the pristine Lycurgan institutions. This skepticism seems uncalled for when one examines Aristotle's remarks on the Spartan constitution, which, although not speaking of Epitadeus, seem to refer to the consequences of his measure.

In the *Politics* (2.6.10–12), written in the last half of the fourth century, Aristotle comments critically on the Spartan land system. He objects to the inequality in the holding of property, with some possessing a great deal and others very little. Therefore, the land had come into the control of a few. The laws have been at fault, for he (Lycurgus?) made it dishonorable to sell property, which was wise, but permitted those who wished to give or bequeath property. The result is that almost two-fifths of all the land belongs to women, because there are many heiresses and because the dowries are large. The heiresses can be given to any one who is pleasing. (In Athens, to keep the property in the family, the heiress was given to the next of kin). Thus a state which should have supplied many hoplites provided less than a thousand. The city consequently could not endure one blow, but was ruined by lack of men. (The blow surely is a reference to the Spartan defeat at Leuctra in 371.) Aristotle is therefore thinking of fourth-century Sparta, and although the only legislator he mentions in these pages is Lycurgus(?), it seems certain that with his talk of gifts, legacies of land, and large dowries he is thinking of the devastating effect of fourth-century legislation rather than of the mistakes of a "Lycurgus" far back in the dim past. The picture he gives of the concentration of wealth in a few hands is very similar to the one Plutarch draws in the *Agis,* although the Plutarch passage, of course, carries the account of Spartan decline into the century after Aristotle's time.

Because of the inadequate sources and the persistence of the idealized myth of Sparta, a definitive explanation of the *kleros* system and of the decline in the number of the Spartiatai will never be achieved. The foregoing remarks and arguments are merely an attempt to call attention to the problems and to suggest some possible answers. The results of the investigation can be summarized as follows. The "original" *kleros* system ran into difficulties in the fifth century as standards of living rose throughout the Greek world. As a result of borrowing on the security of their *kleroi,* many Spartiatai forfeited part or all of the produce of their *kleroi* and hence were unable to meet their contributions to the common messes. Early in the fourth century, as wealth flowed into the now imperial Sparta, the oligarchs in their drive for more power and property exploited every possible device of land-grabbing by means of gifts and bequests, by furnishing large dowries, and by arranging that heiresses marry men appropriate to their aims. The ephor Epitadeus, who was surely their tool, assisted their machinations through his *rhetra,* which legalized their probably questionable manoeuvres. Then came the disaster at Leuctra in 371, and two years later, with Theban help, Messenia regained its freedom. The social and economic effects of the loss of Messenia must have been enormous. Many Spartiatai who lost their *kleroi* would have fallen into the category of "inferiors." The oligarchs whose *kleroi* were in Laconia apparently offered no assistance. The efforts of this "inner clique" to get control of more and more land—which certainly no longer bore any resemblance to the idealized picture of the equal *kleroi* supposedly assigned by Lycurgus—continued until by the 240s only 700 men rated as Spartiatai. One of the greatest mysteries in Spartan history is how the men once classified as equals but subsequently reduced to the status of inferiors by the loss of their *kleroi* managed to stay alive. The only certain fact is that as the number of the "equals" decreased, that of the inferiors increased, and that these rejected men, who were still employed in the Spartan army, bitterly resented their humiliating position, as the conspiracy of the inferior Cinadon as early as 398 made very clear.[11]

THE REQUIREMENTS for Spartan citizenship, in addition to possession of a *kleros* of public land, were membership in one of the military messes and successful completion of the Spartan system of training (*agōgē*). As with everything else in their way of life, the Spartans attributed the introduction of their public meals—*syssitia*—to Lycurgus, but the prevalence of the custom in Crete and other parts of the Greek world and its obviously military character suggest that the institution developed in the confused and dangerous period following the collapse of Mycenaean civilization. The general name for the practice was *syssitia* ("common meals"). In Crete the name *andreia* ("gatherings of men") was usually employed, but in Sparta the most common expression was *pheiditia*, possibly a joke on the sparing quality of the meals—from the verb *pheidesthai*, to be sparing. Every young Spartan on attaining the age of twenty (or twenty-four) became eligible for admission to these messes, whose membership, according to Plutarch, was limited to about fifteen men each. In describing the system of election (*Lycurgus*, 12) Plutarch writes that one negative vote excluded a candidate from membership, for the aim was to have all members of the same mess be congenial. It is hard to believe, however, that in early times or in the period of Sparta's prime eligible candidates were ever refused admission to the *pheiditia*, for citizen soldiers were too desperately needed. Possibly Plutarch's description refers to much later times when—Spartan militarism no longer being possible under Roman domination—the *pheiditia* had degenerated into exclusive aristocratic clubs.

Except on the occasion of festivals, daily attendance at the *pheiditia* was compulsory, certainly for the evening and probably for the midday meal. Every member had to contribute monthly to his mess a fixed amount of barley meal, wine, cheese, figs, and a small amount of money for the purchase of meat—ten Aeginetan obols according to Dicaearchus in Athenaeus (4.19). Dicaearchus may have been referring to his own times (late fourth century), but since the Spartans had no regular coinage of their own until the reign of Areus in the third century, this passage is evidence that at least in the fourth century the Spartans made use of the coinage of a friendly state. Spartans who had brought home game from the hunt were expected to send a portion of it to their mess. The dish most commonly associated with the *pheiditia* was the "black broth," a concoction made of "pork cooked in blood and seasoned with vinegar and salt" which apparently only those born and bred on the banks of the Eurotas were able to enjoy. Since the amount of barley and wine contributed by each member was in excess of his needs, the suggestion has been made that the surplus may have been used for what has been termed the "junior *syssitia*" for the boys in training. On occasions these boys would be admitted to the *pheiditia*, where they had the chance to watch their elders and listen to their discussions.[12]

In a state that organized the lives of its adults so thoroughly, it was only natural that state supervision and control of the education and training of children should be exacting. The evolution of this system of training (*agōgē*) probably occurred over a long period of time, but the information preserved in the ancient sources refers almost exclusively to the fully developed stage. According to Plutarch (*Lycurgus*, 16), this supervision began at birth, for all babies, presumably both male and female, were checked by governmental officials to see if they were sturdy enough to justify rearing. Those who were found to be weak or crippled were exposed in a deserted chasm in Mt. Taygetus. For their first six years boys were raised at home under the care of their mothers; in the seventh year their lifelong service for the state began. For the next twenty-four years the boys lived in barracks, organized in herds (*agelai*). They were taught the rudiments of reading and writing, but the chief emphasis of the training was on physical and military exercises, with the aim of making them physically tough and totally obedient to commands. At six-year intervals they passed from one class to another, the training becoming more advanced and exacting with each change. In the second six-year period the boys usually had lovers from the more advanced class—the *eirens*. Xenophon and Plutarch try to idealize this relationship, emphasizing how the older boy would set an example for the younger one and how this one in turn would endeavor to live up to the expectations of his lover, but the brutal training and the barracks life obviously led to much homosexuality. In their nineteenth year the young Spartans passed into the class of *eirens*. They could now be used for fighting, but they were not considered full-fledged soldiers until they had graduated from this class. The *eirens*, as lovers and teachers, had many duties in connection with the training of the younger classes. This barracks life and constant training continued until the young Spartans had completed their thirtieth year. They were then considered men and, as citizens, could attend meetings of the assembly. Such home life as a Spartan had, now began, but until he had completed his sixtieth year every Spartan was eligible for military service and hence had to devote much of his time to military exercises and manoeuvres.

Much attention was also paid to the physical training of the girls, for the Spartans believed that women with well-developed bodies would produce correspondingly healthy and sturdy offspring. Not much is known about the exercises required for the girls, but Plutarch (*Lycurgus,* 14) writes that they practiced running, wrestling, and throwing the discus and javelin. Both boys and girls, and also adults, participated in many processions and festivals. On these occasions there were often contests between choruses of boys and girls or of boys, young men, and old men singing traditional songs and performing traditional dances. The Spartans placed much emphasis on music, especially that of the flute and the lyre—partly, perhaps, to alleviate the harshness of their lives, but certainly largely with the realization that performing the sometimes intricate steps in time to the music contributed to the development of bodily grace and coordination, qualities essential for the skillful hoplite.[13]

One of the most puzzling and sinister institutions in the Spartan system of training was the *krypteia,* often translated as "secret police" or "secret service." Plutarch writes about it as follows (*Lycurgus,* 28): "The magistrates from time to time sent out into the country at large the most discreet of the young warriors, equipped only with daggers and such supplies as were necessary. In the day time they scattered into obscure and out of the way places, where they hid themselves and lay quiet, but in the night they came down into the highways and killed every helot whom they caught. Oftentimes, too, they actually traversed the fields where helots were working and slew the sturdiest and best of them." Plutarch, who idealizes the "Lycurgan" institutions, cannot believe that such measures were part of Lycurgus' legislation. He suggests that this barbarous treatment of the helots should be assigned to a much later period, probably after the great earthquake in the middle of the fifth century when the helots, taking advantage of the havoc which had been wreaked on Sparta, rose up against their masters and threatened the very survival of the Spartans.

Scholars have offered numerous interpretations of the *krypteia.*[14] One of the most convincing ones tries to explain the institution by comparison with customs which have been prevalent among primitive tribes in Africa, Australia, and North America, whereby young men before they are accepted as full members of the tribe are sent out into the forest to prove their manhood by living through their own ingenuity and often by shedding human blood. According to this explanation, then, the *krypteia* would have been the final stage in the training of a Spartan youth, the last initiation before he was recognized as a man. This view envisages that all Spartan youths participated in the institutions of the *krypteia;* but it is also possible to infer from the words of Plutarch that this particular type of training was reserved for only an elite group. As with all institutions, the nature of the *krypteia* probably changed as the generations passed. This suggestion is confirmed by the last reference to it preserved in the ancient sources. At the famous battle of Sellasia in 222, by which time the Spartan state had experienced many vicissitudes, Plutarch (*Cleomenes,* 28) mentions the *krypteia* as forming a contingent in the Spartan army, and charged, among other duties, with that of reconnaissance.

F ROM THE discussion in this chapter of certain aspects of Spartan political, social, and economic institutions, it is clear that there are many problems about Sparta which can be answered only on the basis of probabilities. Plutarch and many other ancient authors assign the whole system with its resulting *eunomia*—the reign of good law—to the lawgiver Lycurgus, about whom they evidently knew nothing or little more than the institutions which went by his name. Modern scholars have argued at great length about whether there ever was a historical Lycurgus and, if so, when he lived, or whether he was some divinity to whom in the course of time the Spartans attributed their various institutions whose origin had long been forgotten. Certainly he was worshipped at Sparta in later times (Plutarch, *Lycurgus*, 31), apparently as a god, but the divine cult could easily have developed from an earlier hero cult, the type of worship which Greeks usually offered to founders or refounders of cities after their death. Certainty on this matter will probably never be attained. It may be most reasonable, however, to conceive of Lycurgus as an early lawgiver to whom, because of his fame, many subsequent measures were assigned. If one accepts a historical Lycurgus, the most likely time for his activity seemingly would be either the time of the great *rhetra,* which can be interpreted as the beginning of the aristocratic "republic," to be dated perhaps in the first quarter of the seventh century; or in the troubled period either during or immediately following the Second Messenian War. Regardless of how important Lycurgus may have been in introducing new institutions or in systematizing old ones, it would obviously be a gross oversimplification to attribute the whole Spartan way of life to the legislation of one man. Too many of the Spartan institutions are clearly an inheritance from earlier times. The government, except for the peculiarity of the dual kingship, developed from the type of government that was universal in ninth- and eighth-century Greece, and many of the strange aspects of the Spartan system—the division of the boys and young men by age groups; the segregation of the sexes in the long period of training; the *krypteia,* which was probably a rite of initiation; the flogging of young Spartans at the altar of Artemis Orthia, in which many scholars recognize rites of both fertility and initiation—were certainly survivals, however much altered in the course of time, from primitive customs.

For an understanding of Sparta it would be a matter of great interest to know when these "Lycurgan" institutions attained their full development. The ancients and some moderns who date Lycurgus early—in the eighth century or even earlier—imply that Lycurgan Sparta, with all its harshness, austerity, and totalitarianism, goes back to that period. This view is almost certainly wrong. It is true that from the fragments of the poems of Tyrtaeus, who wrote in the middle of the seventh century at the time of the Second Messenian War, one derives a picture of the patriotism and military discipline of the Spartans. But Tyrtaeus was followed by Alcman. Alcman, although apparently an Ionian Greek from Sardis in Lydia, lived for many years in Sparta at some period in the last half of the seventh century. A papyrus discovered in 1855 has preserved about half of one of his poems—a *parthenion* or hymn to be sung by a chorus of girls, presumably at a festival.[15] The love of nature and the appreciation of beauty, as well as the frequently jesting tone, reflected in this poem and in other fragments make it hard to believe that Alcman would have chosen to leave the comparatively luxurious Sardis to live in Sparta if the atmosphere in Sparta were already that of an armed camp. In the following century the Sicilian poet Stesichorus found a hospitable home in Sparta, and the Megarian poet Theognis apparently resided there for a while when he was exiled from his native land.

Archaeology provides even stronger evidence for rejecting the picture of Sparta as an austere and drab place in the seventh and a large part of the sixth century. Excavations at Sparta, supplemented by literary references, have revealed that in these generations ivory, scarabs from Egypt, amber from the north, and luxurious dresses and gold from Lydia were imported. Local artisans excelled in carving ivory and in working with gold and silver, and especially as potters and bronze workers. Laconian pottery dating roughly from 650 to 550 has been discovered by archaeologists at sites as far apart as Ephesus in the east, Etruria and Massalia in the west, and Naucratis, Cyrene, and Carthage in Africa. In the field of bronze work the most remarkable creation, if properly attributed, was the magnificent bronze krater, probably from the last half of the sixth century, which was found in the grave of a Celtic princess at Vix in France. These artisans were presumably *perioeci,* but their wares were not all made for export, for the Spartans also purchased and made use of many of these articles. By the end of the sixth century, however, all these activities of artists and artisans seem to have ceased, and the picture revealed by archaeology is reminiscent of Plutarch's statement (*Lycurgus,* 10) that under Lycurgus the unnecessary and superfluous arts were banished, foreign wares were no longer imported, no goldsmiths or silversmiths existed, and emphasis was placed on utilitarian commodities such as beds, chairs, and tables. What is the explanation for this change in the externals, at least, of Spartan living which, to judge from the excavations, apparently occurred in the latter half of the sixth century?

One explanation which has been advanced is that Sparta may have fallen behind in trade competition with other states when in the sixth century they adopted the use of silver and electrum coins while Sparta continued with its cumbersome and commercially useless iron bars and spits. This explanation may have some validity, but when one remembers how much Greek trade, even after the introduction of coinage, was still carried on by barter and realizes that Sparta, although minting no coins of its own (until the third century B.C.), did make use of the coinage of other states, it seems necessary to seek a more basic explanation. Hardly anything about Sparta can be stated with complete assurance, but there is no good reason to question the close connection between Spartan totalitarianism and austerity and the helot problem. The difficulty of trying to keep a population in serfdom had been revealed by the revolt of the Messenians in the Second Messenian War. The Spartans, on emerging victorious, decided to expand the system despite the warning they had just had of its dangers. It is true that Alcman flourished at Sparta after the Second Messenian War and that for a large part of the sixth century the artistic products of skilled craftsmen were popular there, but these facts need not have precluded the growth of militarism. As the years passed and the helots increased in number whereas the Spartan equals declined, a time must have come when the overwhelming numerical superiority of the helots, not to mention the *perioeci,* made it imperative to take drastic steps. Possibly the austerity and the requirement of devoting oneself totally to the welfare—chiefly military—of the state should be connected with the name of Chilon, ephor about 556, of whom little is known except that he was famous enough to be included among the Seven Wise Men. The details of the change in the Spartan way of life cannot be traced step by step, but by the beginning of the fifth century the "Lycurgan" institutions had certainly reached their full development, and the fears which the Spartans felt of the helots and, to a much lesser extent, of the *perioeci* in the fifth and fourth centuries justify the assumption that it was primarily the necessity to keep large populations under control which turned Sparta into a bleak and barren military camp.

THE RULING caste of the Spartan equals (Spartiatai) would have been unable to live according to the Lycurgan institutions had it not been for other elements in the population of the Spartan state: the *perioeci* and the helots.

In the Spartan state the citizens, although possessing *kleroi* in Laconia and Messenia, all lived in the city of Sparta. The *perioeci* lived in the numerous communities, one hundred in number according to tradition, which were scattered throughout the territory controlled by the Spartans. *Perioeci,* which means simply those living on the periphery, were not unique to Sparta; there is evidence for them in other states such as Thessaly, Argos, and Elis. In general *perioeci* were subjects or dependents of a Greek state, having their own communities and local governments, but owing allegiance and various services to the ruling state.[16] In Sparta the *perioeci* can be thought of as unequal allies or almost as inferior members of a federation, for, although they had no share in formulating Spartan policy, they were included, along with the dominant Spartans, in the designation Lacedaemonians. The origin of the Spartan perioecic communities is obscure. Presumably in the confused period following the collapse of Mycenaean civilization, Dorians established various communities in Laconia and Messenia, some of them probably on the sites of earlier towns and possibly in conjunction with survivors from the earlier inhabitants. Subsequently when the Spartans conquered all this territory in the ninth, eighth, and seventh centuries, they reached agreements with these Dorian communities by which they obtained "perioecic" status. It is also possible that in the course of their conquests the Spartans on occasion left garrisons in particularly strategic places— especially in Messenia—which, although originally Spartan in personnel, gradually fell into the perioecic category because of remoteness from Sparta. If all the perioecic communities became poleis themselves, as is probable, then even if some of the inhabitants had been Spartans they would have lost that citizenship, for a man could not be a citizen of his own polis and of Sparta simultaneously.

As far as one can judge from the scanty evidence, the perioecic towns ordinarily managed their local affairs without much interference from Sparta. They probably were not subject to the rigorous Spartan training, although they proved capable of supplying hoplites, but it can be taken for granted that the Spartans insisted that their governments be aristocracies. Their prosperity and independence were sufficient to enable them to participate in the contests at the Olympic Games. Whether they had to pay taxes to Sparta is uncertain, but it is known that part of the kings' revenues came from lands assigned to them in perioecic territory. There are a few references in the sources to Spartan governors and judges in perioecic towns, but it cannot be said whether this was regular procedure or caused by exceptional circumstances. The ephors could arrest *perioeci* in cases involving Sparta and bring them to Sparta for trial; ordinary cases affecting only *perioeci* almost certainly were tried by local magistrates. The chief obligation of the *perioeci* to the Spartans was military. In the army they served as hoplites, and at the battle of Plataea in 479 they furnished hoplites equal in number to those mustered by the Spartans. In later years, as the number of Spartan equals declined, they provided a higher proportion of heavy armed troops. For the navy, which ordinarily was small, the *perioeci* provided a considerable part of the skilled personnel, and they must have played the same role at Gythium where the Spartans had their naval base and dockyards.

Beyond their military services, the chief contributions of the *perioeci* to the Spartan state lay in the economic field. Since the Spartans were debarred by law from engaging in any utilitarian activities, all trade and industry were in the hands of the *perioeci*. In the eighth, seventh, and sixth centuries, when Sparta was producing fine pottery and metalwork, these products almost certainly were the handiwork of the *perioeci*. When Spartan austerity and isolationism began, the *perioeci* were the workers who manufactured such essential commodities as clothing, shoes, weapons, and furniture. Foreign trade must have been at a minimum, partly because of the lack of any real Spartan coinage and partly because of the institution of *xenelasia*, by which the ephors were authorized to expel foreigners. This custom may not have been as widely employed as Sparta's enemies claimed, but it is certain that the Spartan authorities were alert to see that no subversive foreign ideas penetrated their iron curtain.

The lowest caste in the Spartan system consisted of the helots. The name was probably derived from the Greek root *hel*, which denotes capture, although it might have come from the word *helē*—marshes—since the earliest people reduced to this status presumably were those dwelling in the swampy land near the mouth of the Eurotas. In Laconia the helots were probably "Mycenaeans" whom the Spartans reduced to serfdom; in Messenia some Dorians also may have been forced into this category when the Spartans conquered the Pamisus valley. This supposition, in conjunction with the greater distance from Sparta, may help to explain why the Spartans had more trouble in controlling the Messenian than the Laconian helots. The helots were bound to the soil, but they were the serfs of the state rather than of individual Spartans. It was the government that dictated how they should be employed and treated. A certain number of helots was assigned to each *kleros*, and it was their duty to supply enough produce from the land to their masters so that the Spartan citizens, free from any need to earn a living, could devote all their time and energy to the needs of the state. Apparently the helots paid a fixed rent in produce to the Spartan possessors of the *kleroi*. Tyrtaeus, referring to the end of the First Messenian War, says that they had to deliver to their masters half of what they produced. Plutarch (*Lycurgus*, 8) writes that each Spartan received from his lot 82 *medimni* of barley and a commensurate amount of oil and wine. Since there is no reliable information on the size of the *kleroi*, it is impossible to know how heavy a burden this payment was to the helots. What little evidence there is, however, suggests that economically the helots were not badly off. It may be, therefore, that the fixed rent was established early when the agricultural yield was small, and that subsequently, as improvements were made on the land, the helots were able to pay their rents easily and still have enough, and possibly a surplus, for themselves.

Legally and politically the helots were in a desperate position, for they had no rights whatsoever. According to Plutarch (*Lycurgus*, 28), who professes to be quoting Aristotle, the ephors, on assuming office, declared war on the helots. If this statement is correct, the consequence would have been that a Spartan could kill a helot with impunity and without incurring blood-guilt. Although it is difficult to accept literally Plutarch's description of the way the young Spartans in the *krypteia* (the Spartan secret police) systematically murdered helots, it is certain that the Spartans, who were tremendously outnumbered by the helots, often had to take drastic and brutal steps to keep their serfs under control. The constant worry of the Spartans that the helots, especially those in Messenia, would revolt and the various revolts which actually occurred are clear evidence of the hatred the helots felt for their masters. Nevertheless this hatred and fear can probably be exaggerated. At least the Spartans, when on campaign, were attended by helots who acted as their servants and apparently were allowed to have a share of the booty. Also the helots often served in the Spartan army as light armed soldiers and occasionally even as hoplites. If one can trust Thucydides (4.80), it did not pay the helots to show too much bravery. Referring to the year 424, Thucydides tells how the Spartans promised 2,000 of the bravest helots their freedom: "the Spartans, however, soon afterwards did away with them, and no one ever knew how each of them perished." Later remarks in Thucydides suggest that all may not have been murdered, but this horrible episode, even if it was motivated by wartime panic, reveals vividly how grim and danger-laden was the relationship between Spartan and helot.

A COMPLETELY coherent picture of Sparta will probably never be drawn because of the scanty, conflicting, and ambiguous nature of the available evidence. It seems certain, however, that in the eighth and seventh centuries as the Spartans conquered Laconia and Messenia, the land in the Eurotas and Pamisus valleys became public land which was assigned to the Spartan citizens in the form of *kleroi*. This process was completed by the end of the Second Messenian War, at which time, according to a reasonable tradition, some 9,000 or 10,000 Spartans were possessors of these *kleroi*, which had become a basic condition for enjoyment of citizenship. Helots assigned to these lots paid as rent to their masters a fixed amount of the products of the land, sufficient to provide a livelihood for the Spartans who thereby were free to devote all their time to matters of state. Excavations at Sparta which have revealed excellent products of artists and artisans, both local and imported, have made it clear that the famed "banishment of the unnecessary and superfluous arts" did not begin until towards the end of the sixth century. The explanation for the change to austerity is probably to be found in the increasing difficulty and danger the Spartans experienced in holding in suppression the ever-growing number of helots.

The impetus for this change may have come from the ephor Chilon, who, according to the fragmentary evidence, was a significant figure in Sparta in the middle of the sixth century. Chilon and his associates, in trying to put their measures into effect, may have believed or pretended that they were implementing or supplementing the work of the earlier lawgiver Lycurgus, who probably had been responsible for establishing the aristocratic "republic" a century or more earlier. The shrine at which Lycurgus received honors as either a god or a hero may already have been established. It is unlikely that many new measures were introduced at this time; it is more probable that various old customs, such as the division of youths into age groups for training purposes, the segregation of the sexes, and the initiation rites inherent in the *krypteia,* which had largely or partly fallen into abeyance, were once more strictly enforced. Since most of these customs were clearly ones that had been prevalent among the early Dorians, it was all the more easy to associate them with the name of Lycurgus and thereby to sanctify them. In some such way began the myth of Lycurgus and the Lycurgan institutions.

It is impossible to tell in what fashion the myth developed among the Spartans, for Sparta, having banished the superfluous arts, had no writers. The growth of the idealization of Sparta can be traced to some extent beyond the confines of Laconia. Oligarchs and aristocrats elsewhere in Greece usually looked with favor on Sparta, which, when possible, used its influence to support aristocratic regimes. In Athens, particularly in the closing years of the fifth century, the oligarchs, disgusted with what they considered the excesses of democracy, looked with longing eyes towards Sparta where no democratic "nonsense" was tolerated. In the first half of the fourth century, Plato, hating and distrusting democracy deeply and repelled by the selfish individualism which was so characteristic of his times, saw, or thought he saw, in Sparta much that was admirable—equality of all citizens, rigorous training of the young to be servants of the state, suppression of individualism and ostentatious luxury, absolute obedience to the laws—in short, an organization which had all the beauties of a geometric form. His *Republic* contains a strange medley of true and idealized Spartan elements. Aristotle, writing after the decline of Sparta following its loss of Messenia in 369, is more critical, but unfortunately in his *Politics* he discusses Sparta only occasionally.

In the generations following Alexander the Great, the Hellenistic philosophers, seeing the great social inequalities in their world and the constant threat of social revolution, contributed greatly to the myth of Spartan equality. It was Plutarch, however, writing in the late first and early second century A.D., who gave the idealized myth of Sparta its canonical form. His *Life of Lycurgus* is a fascinating document, and one can easily be swept along by the glowing, almost poetic, picture it presents. The critical reader, however, becomes more and more aware of inconsistencies, contradictions, anachronisms, and impossibilities in the account until he realizes that much of what he is reading has no relationship whatsoever with reality. Plutarch's *Lives* have had great influence through the ages, and not least the *Lycurgus*. To mention only one or two examples, in the eighteenth century French philosophers like Rousseau were greatly impressed by that biography, and leaders of the French Revolution were thinking of establishing a national school based on the ideas of Spartan training as depicted in the *Lycurgus*. The greatest evidence for the influence exerted by Sparta, however, both the idealized picture and the seamy side, is to be found in the tremendous interest which the Nazis and Nazi-minded German historians revealed for all things Spartan. The final sentence of an excellent book on Sparta published by a distinguished French scholar in 1939 on the eve of World War II deserves quotation: "And Sparta, mysterious and secret, after having nourished the thought of Plato and of Rousseau gives birth to a new mysticism."[17]

In this chapter an attempt has been made, as far as space permitted, to call attention to some of the realities which modern scholars have detected behind the facade of the idealized myth of Sparta. There is no need to repeat the arguments; it will be enough to emphasize that even at the "beginning" all Spartans were not equal, for among the so-called equals there was an aristocratic inner clique which through the Gerousia and the ephors managed to control the state. The "Lycurgan" system which they dominated was to be static: a privileged class of Spartan citizens who would be provided with all the necessities of life by inferior castes, the *perioeci* and the helots. The Spartans, thus freed from having to engage in any utilitarian occupations, could devote their lives from childhood on to the service of the state, and by acquiring supremacy in the profession of arms would be able to guarantee the permanence of this totalitarian structure. But institutions do not often remain static. The number of Spartan equals steadily declined, apparently chiefly from the inability of certain men to meet the requirements of the *pheidi-*

tia (military mess). These men fell into the category of inferiors, whose numbers increased in direct proportion to the decrease of the equals. The lot of these inferiors is one of the unanswered mysteries of Sparta, but their bitterness is vividly revealed by Xenophon's description (*Hellenica*, 3.3.4) of the abortive conspiracy of the "inferior" Cinadon in 398. Besides the inferiors, various other categories developed which marred and confused the symmetry of the "Lycurgan" constitution—sons of helot women by Spartan citizens, helots liberated as reward for some service (Neodamodeis), and the like. There is no evidence about how these hybrid groups, who certainly did not receive full citizenship, were integrated into the Spartan system.

The result of these developments is clear. From the beginning the Spartan citizens had had to defend themselves against the helots, but as time passed, other potentially dangerous internal enemies emerged—the inferiors, the various hybrid groups, and also the *perioeci*, who, as ideas of liberty and autonomy spread throughout the Greek world, probably often resented their somewhat humiliating status. These developments were gradual, however, and their full significance was revealed only by the great changes wrought by the Peloponnesian War and the subsequent loss of Messenia in 369. In the sixth century the efficiency of the Lycurgan institutions enabled Sparta to attain a position of leadership in the Greek world. Also, in fairness to totalitarian Sparta, it must not be forgotten that its prestige and the well-deserved reputation of its invincible hoplites caused it to be the center of the successful Greek resistance to the threat of Persian conquest. In conclusion to this chapter on early Sparta, therefore, it will be necessary to describe briefly how Sparta advanced to this position of leadership in the sixth century.

I N THE seventh century Sparta secured a firm hold on Messenia to the west. The next task was to try to settle matters on the northern frontier, where for generations Sparta had engaged in occasional fighting with the Arcadians and Argives. According to Herodotus (1.66–68), the Spartans, deterred from trying to conquer all Arcadia by an oracle from Delphi but encouraged to attack Tegea, the town in the southern part of the eastern Arcadian plain, marched out bearing fetters with which to enslave the Tegeans. They were defeated, however, and chained in the very fetters which they had brought. Herodotus reports that even in his day these fetters could be seen suspended as a thank offering in the temple of Artemis at Tegea. This defeat probably occurred early in the sixth century, and for some time thereafter Sparta was consistently unsuccessful in its expeditions against Tegea. Finally another oracle was obtained which promised victory if the bones of Agamemnon's son, Orestes, should be removed from Tegea to Sparta. Herodotus in one of his charming tales relates how a Spartan, in time of truce, managed to carry off to Sparta the bones of a huge man which had been unearthed in the shop of a Tegean blacksmith. Thereafter Sparta was always successful not only against Tegea but also against other parts of the Peloponnesus. In the case of Tegea Sparta inaugurated a new policy (ca. 560–550), for, instead of incorporating additional territory, it left Tegea independent but bound by treaty to furnish military aid whenever needed. The story of the bones of Orestes should not be dismissed as mere fancy. Pausanias (3.11.10) reports that there was a tomb of Orestes in Sparta, and it is most likely that he was worshipped there as a hero. By claiming that they had found the bones of Orestes, an old Mycenaean hero, which they buried with proper honors, the Spartans were launching a propaganda campaign by which they hoped to win the favor of the old "Mycenaean" population of the Peloponnesus in their intermittent rivalry with Argos.

Shortly thereafter the Spartans marched north into the region of the Thyreatic plain, which long had been in dispute between Sparta and the Argives. Herodotus' account (1.82) of the Battle of the Champions, in which 300 champions each from the Spartans and the Argives fought one another, may well have been derived from some old saga, but the final outcome was historical. Thyrea and its plain fell to the Spartans and were incorporated in their territory. The whole district of Cynouria also, the long, narrow coastal strip south of Thyrea on the eastern slopes of Mt. Parnon, and the island of Cythera to the south, for both of which the Spartans and the Argives may have been contending for generations, now became permanently Spartan. The date of these events can be placed approximately in 547, for Herodotus (1.83) relates that they occurred about the same time as the fall of Lydia and its king, Croesus, to Cyrus of Persia, which is usually assigned to that year.

Thyrea and Cynouria were the last territorial gains which the Spartans made. Thereafter Spartan policy was to extend its influence by means of diplomacy and alliances. In control of territory comprising two-fifths of the Peloponnesus and as victor over Tegea and Argos, Sparta enjoyed great prestige. In the remaining years of the sixth century Sparta employed that prestige to suppress tyrants when the opportunity arose, to support aristocratic and oligarchic regimes wherever possible, and to build up a network of alliances on the model of its treaty with Tegea. Among these allies were included numerous towns and villages of Arcadia, Elis, Corinth, Sicyon, Phlius, and various towns of the Argolid peninsula such as Hermione, Troezen, and Epidaurus—in fact, the whole Peloponnesus except Argos and the twelve small towns of

Achaea along the southern coast of the Corinthian Gulf. Out of these separate treaties between Sparta and the various individual states there gradually developed an organization which modern scholars call the Peloponnesian League, but which the ancient sources usually refer to as "the Lacedaemonians and their allies."[18] Sparta had allies beyond the Peloponnesus, such as Megara, but because of the usual usage of the term "Peloponnesians" in the ancient sources, it seems best to limit the membership of the League to the Peloponnesus and to consider extra-Peloponnesian states as allies in a different category. From the Spartan point of view it is clear that this league, among other things, was an attempt to weaken and encircle Argos.

The League was a permanent defensive and offensive alliance of cities under the leadership of Sparta. The first definite reference to it can be dated to about 500 (Herodotus, 5.91), but one can only say about its origin that it must have been subsequent to the agreement with Tegea ca. 560–550. Sparta alone had the right to call meetings of the League assembly, at which each member, regardless of the number of its delegates, had one vote. Only as a result of a majority vote could the League engage in a defensive or offensive war. The Spartans, because of their prestige and because they alone presided over meetings of the assembly and commanded the combined League army, were able to exercise great influence over the activities of the League. They could also refuse to call a meeting of the assembly if they did not approve of the matters which the members wished to discuss. The formation of this league was a great tribute to the statesmanship of sixth-century Spartans. It became one of the chief stabilizing factors among the Greeks—who always were badly in need of stabilizing influences—and in the first decades of the fifth century it played a major role in the defense of Greece against the Persian onslaught.

7
Early Athens

VERY DIFFERENT from the record of the closed society of Sparta was the history of Athens, which in the fifth century became the leading state politically, economically, and culturally among all the innumerable Greek states. So restless in mind and body that their enemies characterized them as "being born into the world to take no rest themselves and to give none to others" (Thucydides, 1.70), the Athenians, despite the many mistakes, excesses, and stupidities recorded in their history, have bequeathed to the world a fascinating vision of the potentialities of a truly open society. This chapter will trace the development of Athens from its almost unknown beginnings to the end of the sixth century, when Greece was on the eve of facing the great ordeal represented by the threat of Persian aggression.

Athens and parts of Attica had been inhabited for millennia before recorded history began. Remains of pottery produced by Neolithic man have been discovered on the northern and southern slopes of the Acropolis and also in the district which ultimately became the agora of historical Athens. There is evidence for habitation throughout the whole Bronze (Helladic) Age.[1] It is probable, therefore, that the metalworking immigrants who are believed to have come to Greece from Asia Minor early in the third millennium blended with the remains of the Neolithic population in Attica, and this process of mingling was presumably continued in the early centuries of the second millennium, when most scholars think that the proto-Greeks entered the Greek peninsula. In the late Bronze Age—the Mycenaean period—Athens was the center of one of the many kingdoms which flourished in those fascinating but obscure times. In these centuries an increase in Minoan influences can be detected. A palace arose on the Acropolis—Homer's strong house of Erechtheus—and, as at Mycenae and Tiryns, the fortifications were strengthened towards the end of the thirteenth century, presumably against some anticipated danger. Athens was spared from the general devastation—whether the result of a Dorian migration or uprising—which overwhelmed the Mycenaean world in the years following 1200. If the chaos was caused by invaders, it may be that they bypassed Athens because it was not on the direct route to the Peloponnesus or because its wealth was not as tempting as that of more renowned places like Mycenae and Tiryns; it is also possible that the Athenian boast of a later age that they heroically repelled the Dorians contains an element of truth. In any case, the Athenians took great pride in the fact that they were not "newcomers" to Greece like the Dorians of the Peloponnesus. Their orators never tired of emphasizing that the Athenians were autochthonous, earth-born or sprung from the soil itself; and archaeology confirms their contention at least in the sense that, despite interminglings with various elements in the course of the centuries, Athens had been inhabited continuously for several thousand years. The greatest blessing, however, which befell the Athenians from their escape from conquest by the Dorians was that they were not cursed with the problems arising from conquering and conquered populations, a situation which plagued the Spartans and, to a lesser extent, certain other Peloponnesian states for centuries.

For several centuries following the collapse of Mycenaean civilization, Athens was the chief city on the mainland of Greece. Contemporary evidence for the development of Athens in this period is restricted almost entirely to pottery. The debased sub-Mycenaean pottery of the twelfth and eleventh centuries reveals clearly that Athens also was affected by the chaos prevalent in the Aegean world. This was the time when, according to tradition, many refugees fleeing before the Dorians sought refuge in Attica, from where, after they became too numerous, they crossed over to the coast of Asia Minor in the so-called Ionian migration. Towards the end of the eleventh century a new style of pottery—protogeometric—began to evolve from the sub-Mycenaean, a development which may suggest that conditions were becoming somewhat more settled. Protogeometric and the succeeding geometric style of pottery span roughly the years from 1025 to 700, and throughout this period, except at its very end, Athenian pottery was the most abundant and artistic in the Greek world. Then for about a century the products of the Athenian potters were eclipsed by those of Corinth.[2]

In the Mycenaean period the various communities in Attica may have been under the general control of Athens, whose fortress was by far the most formidable and which alone of the settlements in Attica was mentioned in the Catalogue of Ships in book 2 of the *Iliad*. Many scholars, however, argue that the presence of fortresses at Eleusis to the west and at Thoricos, Brauron, and Marathon to the east and of a *tholos* tomb at Acharnae (Menidi) slightly to the north suggests the existence of princes possibly largely independent of Athens. Whatever unity there had been may have been weakened in the chaos attendant upon the collapse of Mycenaean civilization, necessitating a new attempt at unification. Thucydides' description (2.15) of this *synoecism* is worth quoting in full.

> Under Cecrops and the first kings, down to the reign of Theseus, Attica had always consisted of a number of independent townships, each with its own town-hall and magistrates. Except in times of danger the king at Athens was not consulted; in ordinary seasons they carried on their government and settled their affairs without his interference; sometimes even they waged war against him, as in the case of the Eleusinians with Eumolpus against Erechtheus. In Theseus, however, they had a king of equal intelligence and power; and one of the chief features in his organization of the country was to abolish the council-chambers and magistrates of the petty cities, and to merge them in the single council-chamber and town-hall of the present capital. Individuals might still enjoy their private property just as before, but they were henceforth compelled to have only one political center, viz. Athens; which thus counted all the inhabitants of Attica among her citizens, so that when Theseus died he left a great state behind him. Indeed, from him dates the Synoecia or Feast of Union, which is paid for by the state, and which the Athenians still keep in honor of the goddess.

In this account Thucydides gives an accurate picture of the results of the unification—*synoecism*—but in ascribing this achievement to the national hero Theseus, he and the tradition which he followed were adopting the common Greek practice of attributing measures or institutions of unknown origin to some great figure of the past as, for example, the "Lycurgan" institutions of Sparta were assigned to Lycurgus. The chronology also is perplexing, for the legends about Theseus place him primarily in the thirteenth century. Most scholars believe that in the troubled centuries of the Dark Age the possible unification of Mycenaean Attica disintegrated and had to be reestablished. Specific evidence is lacking, but one can imagine that some king or kings of Athens, under circumstances that are unknown, admitted nobles from other Attic settlements to the royal council. This may have been the beginning of the Athenian nobility—the Eupatrids—which Plutarch (*Theseus*, 25) ascribes to Theseus.[3] Thucydides and Plutarch in attributing the *synoecism* to Theseus were accepting the legend, promoted zealously in the sixth century by the Pisistratids, that represented Theseus as a great Ionian hero displacing the Dorian hero Heracles. The commonly accepted inference that Eleusis was not included in the *synoecism* until after 700, the proposed date for the *Homeric Hymn to Demeter* in which Eleusis seemingly was independent, is hardly convincing since the hymn, based on a Mycenaean legend, had no reason to mention Athens. The reference in the *Odyssey* (3.278) to Sunium as the promontory of Athens, however, suggests that by the end of the eighth century (?) the unification of Attica was well advanced. Nevertheless, particularism died hard and revealed symptoms in both the seventh and sixth centuries.

The importance of the unification of Attica cannot be overemphasized. It meant ultimately that every freeborn native of Attica, no matter where he lived in the territory, was just as much an Athenian citizen as the man living under the shadow of the Acropolis. The great majority of the people continued to live in the communities of their birth, for this was a political amalgamation and not a physical one involving the transference of all inhabitants to Athens itself—in Greek terms a *sympoliteia* rather than a literal *synoecism*. In the course of time effective systems of local government were developed, and a man could be proud of being an Acharnian or a Marathonian, but above all he was proud of being an Athenian. To realize the full significance of this *synoecism* it is enough to compare Athens with its neighbor to the northeast, Boeotia, whose territory was of approximately the same extent as that of Attica. In Boeotia in historical times there were some twelve cities, but they never united in a *synoecism* with the chief city, Thebes, so that all Boeotians became Thebans. At times the Boeotians were united in a league dominated by the Thebans, but such a league, in which force often had to be employed, was a far different and less effective means of achieving unity than the common Athenian citizenship enjoyed and prized by all the free inhabitants of Attica.

Athens is no exception to all the Greek states in that its early history is obscure. The reason everywhere is the same—lack of contemporary written sources. Knowledge of writing began to spread over the Greek world in the last half of the eighth century and by the middle of the next century was common enough so that in many states the ancestral laws and customs were codified and recorded on stone or wood. As the generations passed, writing was used more and more for governmental and business purposes and also by the lyric and late epic poets, but the great majority of this material has perished. In fact, except for the poetry and some law codes, it is unlikely that many written documents of the seventh and sixth centuries were available to the Greeks themselves when in the fifth and fourth centuries they became interested in trying to recover their past history. The modern scholar who is studying the early development of Athens has at his disposal as contemporary source material, in addition to the pottery and other archaeological remains, little except some rather extensive fragments of Solon's poetry from the beginning of the sixth century, a few of his laws quoted—and possibly altered—by later writers, and, from a generation before Solon, Draco's law on involuntary homicide, which, reinscribed on stone in the year 409/8, has fortunately been preserved, reasonably intact, to the present. Certain early dates recorded by ancient authors also inspire considerable confidence, for the Athenians kept a chronological list of their eponymous archons (the magistrate who gave his name to the year). Plato in the *Hippias Maior* (285e) implies that it would be easy to give the archon names beginning with Solon. It is possible, moreover, that the Athenians possessed lists of these magistrates going back to the year 682/1 when the annual archonship was established.[4]

Because of this lack of contemporary evidence for the early history of Athens, it is necessary to have recourse to Greek authors of the fifth and subsequent centuries. Herodotus, writing in the second half of the fifth century, obviously is important, for his narrative provides considerable data on the sixth and even earlier centuries. Thucydides contains a few references to earlier times. The Attic orators of the late fifth and the fourth centuries are a very important source of information, for they frequently drew on events from the past for political or ideological purposes. Their partisanship makes it necessary to be cautious about accepting many of their pronouncements, but even though they are often unreliable in their statements about early times, it is enlightening to discover the ideas and interpretations which were acceptable to a fourth-century audience. The orators derived much of their information about the past history of Athens from an important group of men known as Atthidographers—that is, writers of chronicles concerning Attica. The first man to write such an Attic chronicle was Hellanicus from Lesbos in the latter part of the fifth century, but in the following two centuries a goodly number of Athenians undertook the task. They followed a chronological method, providing dates by archons for the period after the establishment of the annual archonship. They were greatly interested in the origins of institutions—political, social, and religious—but since direct evidence was often lacking to them, they frequently had to reach their conclusions by analogies and by inferences from ancient survivals in the institutions of their own times. Like the orators, they were usually involved in contemporary ideological polemics, and consequently their interpretations were colored by their points of view—oligarchic, moderate, or radically democratic. Their writings unfortunately are largely lost except for fragments which can be gleaned from later authors like Plutarch, from the scholia to ancient authors, and from the lexicographers.

The extent of the influence of these Atthidographers can be illustrated by the last ancient source which needs to be mentioned in this context—Aristotle's *Constitution of the Athenians* (hereafter abbreviated as

Ath. Const.). This work, preserved on three papyrus rolls obtained by the British Museum in 1890 and first published in the following year, is of unusual interest. The work was written by Aristotle in the late 330s and revised in the years 329–322;[5] the latter part, chapters 42–69, contains an excellent and extremely valuable description of the contemporary radical democracy, while the first forty-one chapters provide a history of the development of the Athenian constitution. Aristotle clearly derived much of his material from the Atthidographers, particularly the moderate oligarch Androtion whose work appeared about 340, but he naturally exercised his own judgment, which was influenced by the political theories developed in his *Politics*. It has been maintained that, since he knew that the final result of the constitutional development was the radical democracy of his own time, Aristotle, following his teleological way of reasoning, arbitrarily selected or omitted material with that end product in mind.[6] Despite the many criticisms which can be leveled against this treatise, it seems unnecessary to assume that Aristotle organized the material to conform to his philosophical concepts.

IN THE DARK AGE Athens, like other Greek states, was ruled by kings, presumably hereditary, but what information has been preserved about them lies in the area of legend. Since Athens was spared the destruction and chaos which enveloped the Greek world in the late thirteenth and the twelfth centuries, it is possible that the Mycenaean type of king—the *wanax*—survived for some time. The gradual unification of Attica strengthened Athens, but the king's council and the addition to it of nobles from other settlements, some of whom acquired land in the Cephisian plain, caused the king ultimately to lose his position of preeminence and to become only *primus inter pares.* By the latter half of the eighth century the nobles, like their counterparts elsewhere in Greece, had seriously curtailed the powers of the kingship. They placed beside the hereditary king two magistrates, the archon (ruler) and the polemarch (leader in war)—probably annual rather than decennial as Aristotle (*Ath. Const.*, 3) says—to take over the most important functions of government. Because of the scanty evidence it is impossible to be certain which magistrate appeared first. Somewhat later the kingship ceased to be a hereditary lifelong office and also became an annual magistracy. It is tempting to assign this innovation to the year 682/1, apparently the date when it became customary to name the year after the (eponymous) archon. As long as the kingship was hereditary, dates presumably had been reckoned by regnal years.

Of these three magistracies the archonship was clearly the most important, as is proved by the fact that for many generations political strife centered chiefly around this office. The archon was the chief executive of the state. He presided over the council when it sat in a legislative or deliberative capacity and over meetings of the assembly. He also had jurisdiction in all litigation concerning the welfare of the family. The polemarch, in addition to his military duties, had jurisdiction in cases affecting aliens resident in Attica. The king, now an annual magistrate but still called *basileus* (king), retained only his supervision over the religious practices of the state; as religious conservatives the Athenians were afraid to risk antagonizing the gods by turning over to new magistrates the ancestral rites and sacrifices that had been associated for centuries with the office and name of king. The king also presided over the council when it sat as a judicial body to try cases involving religion.

In the course of the seventh century six other archons called *thesmothetai* (literally, "lawmakers") made their appearance.[7] Since their duties were exclusively judicial, recording judicial decisions and trying cases not in the jurisdiction of the other three archons, the explanation for their creation must be that the government was more and more trying to change the administration of justice from the dangerous system of family self-help to a regular governmental function. If Thucydides (1.126.8) was accurate when he spoke of nine archons at the time of Cylon's attempt to become tyrant at Athens, ca. 632, then clearly the *thesmothetai* were in existence before that date. Whether they were six in number originally or reached that number only after the need was demonstrated is unknown, although the fact that in later times they seemed always to function as a board may speak for the first alternative.

The information about the council in this aristocratic state is unsatisfactory, but there can be little doubt that it was the most powerful body in the government. Whether it was called the Council of the Areopagus before Solon's reforms as it was after is largely an academic question, for Solon clearly did not establish a new council of this type but regularized one already in existence. Membership naturally was restricted to the nobility—possibly to the heads of the leading families—although the system in effect after Solon that ex-archons automatically entered the council may have existed earlier. It appears that these councillors, consisting of the leading men in the state and holding office for life, were able to dominate any part of the government they wished, even if, because of lack of evidence, one may hesitate to spell out their particular powers. Aristotle (*Ath. Const.*, 8) says that before Solon the archons were appointed by the council, but this statement is questionable since the tradition about the reforms of Solon suggests that he was appointed to the archonship by the people—meaning presumably an assembly of landowners. It is safe to assume, however, that the council exerted at least indirect control over elections through the right to nominate candidates.

As the Athenians gradually emerged into the light of history in the seventh century, it becomes clear that, like other Greeks, their social and political structure was based on tribes, phratries, *genē*, and *oikoi*. As slightly more evidence is available for Athens, a brief discussion of these elusive institutions is necessary, for they were fundamental to the Greek way of life.

Since the Ionians who migrated from Greece to Asia Minor in the eleventh and tenth centuries were organized in the four so-called Ionian tribes, Geleontes, Hopletes, Aigikoreis, and Argadeis, the natural inference is that this tribal structure also existed among the Athenians in the early Dark Age. The origin of these tribes is unknown, although the Athenian tradition (Herodotus, 5.66; 8.44) claimed that they were named after the sons of Ion when he became the Athenian military leader. As Ion was believed to have given his name to the Ionians and, if he ever existed, to have lived sometime in the distant past, the tradition need not be taken seriously. Some scholars and ancient authors (Plutarch, *Solon,* 23.4) have suggested that the tribes may originally have been castes—possibly nobles, warriors, shepherds, and farmers respectively. This suggestion seems unlikely because in historical times there are no traces of such castes, and, moreover, each tribe had a king who was a noble. Since the components of each tribe were phratries and *genē*, theoretically based on kinship, the tribe also was considered to be a "kin" organization.

There is no definite information on how these tribes fitted into the governmental organization beyond the fact that they must have served some sort of military and political purpose. Probably each tribe had to furnish a contingent to the army. In the political sphere, if Solon in 594 did create a new council of 400, surely 100 councillors were selected from each tribe. At the head of each tribe there was a tribal king (*phylobasileus*). The relation of these four tribal kings to the hereditary king in the days of the monarchy is a complete mystery. Even after the substitution of ten territorial tribes for the four Ionian tribes in the reforms of Cleisthenes in 508/7, the tribal kings continued to exist; in the fourth century, and perhaps much later also, they were associated with the king archon in a homicide court in which, according to an archaic ritual, cases were tried where the murderer was unknown and where animals and inanimate objects had caused human death.[8]

Concerning the phratries and *genē* there is considerable contemporary information from the fifth and fourth centuries, and one can form some notion of their nature and functions in the two preceding centuries, but their origin and early history are as obscure as the beginnings of the tribes. Aristotle treated the problem in the first part of the *Constitution of the Athenians,* which was lost from the papyrus roll, but the following fragment, referring to the "Ion period," was preserved by a lexicographer: "And they [the Athenians] were grouped in four tribal divisions in imitation of the seasons of the year, and each of the tribes was divided into three parts, in order that there might be twelve parts in all, like the months of the year, and they were called thirds (*trittyes*) and phratries; and the arrangement of *gené* was in groups of thirty to the phratry, as the days to the month, and the *genos* consisted of thirty men." In this passage, which certainly is no credit to historical imagination, Aristotle—or his source, presumably some Atthidographer—seems to have visualized the ancient Athenians as a people on whom a whole set of institutions was imposed all at once. He is thinking in terms of a definite beginning, as when in classical Greece a colony was dispatched or a new city was founded according to specific regulations which had been formulated in advance. Since Ion is at best a hazy mythological figure, it is certain that Aristotle and the Athenians had no real information about him.

The proto-Greeks, when they first migrated into Attica, may have been organized by some type of kinship groups such as phratries, but there were not 360 *gené* and 10,800 *gennétai*. No information on these institutions is available for the Mycenaean period or the early Dark Age. The historical *gené,* of which some sixty are known by name,[9] were groups of families or *oikoi* who believed or claimed that they were descended from a common ancestor. It is likely that these *gené* were formed artificially in the tenth and ninth centuries by certain wealthy landowning families joining together so that through the joint resources of their united numbers they could increase their political, social, and economic powers. The members of these *gené,* or at least some of them, were the ones who weakened and then destroyed the hereditary monarchy and established the aristocratic republic at the end of the eighth or the beginning of the seventh century; hence they must be thought of as "nobles." Plutarch in his *Life of Theseus* (25) writes that Theseus at the time of his *synoecism* of Attica first established an order of nobility—the Eupatrids (those possessed of noble fathers). Some scholars wish to accept this statement, but any acceptance must be in a figurative sense.[10] Theseus is a mythical figure, most of whose "activity" belonged in the pre-Trojan War period, and the *synoecism* almost certainly was a gradual process. The creation of a nobility at one stroke is too reminiscent of the Greek fondness for attributing institutions of unknown origin to some famous figure of the past. In general, it is probably more reasonable to assume that the members of the *genē*—the *gennētai*—as they increased in power and prestige claimed for themselves the title of Eupatrids. Before the *synoecism* there must have been many local nobles who, after their communities were united to Athens, became Athenian Eupatrids. The members of the famous Eleusinian *genē*, the Eumolpidae and the Kerykes, for example, who presided over the Eleusinian Mysteries, surely were Eupatrids at Eleusis before their community joined Athens and strengthened the unification of Attica.

Did all the *genē* belong to the Eupatrid order? A final answer is impossible, although it is reasonable to assume that as some *genē* waxed stronger at the expense of others who waned in prestige, the more successful ones appropriated the title for themselves. Were all members of a noble *genos* Eupatrids? Again, a definite answer cannot be given, but since often one family or *oikos* within a particular *genos* was far more prominent than the other constituent families, it is possible that the title "Eupatrid," with its accompanying privileges, belonged only to the leading family. These *genē*, with their wealth and with the solidarity which each *genos* enjoyed through its organization and its own religious cult, dominated the state throughout the period of the aristocratic republic. It is sometimes stated that they had "no place in the civil or criminal law of Athens."[11] One wonders, then, why the Alcmaeonids, polluted from the slaying of the followers of the tyranny-aspiring Cylon, were banished, the bones of their ancestors were dug up and cast out, and the *genos* was termed accursed (Thucydides, 1.126; Aristotle, *Ath. Const.*, 1); and why before every meeting of the assembly, council, and law courts the official herald implored the gods to destroy utterly whoever deliberately deceived the people—the man himself, his *genos*, and his household (Demosthenes, 19.71; 23.67, 97). If in certain cases the phratries received legal recognition rather than the *genē*, the explanation may be that the former were considered as including the whole citizen body whereas the latter embraced only a limited number.

The first evidence for phratries in Athens is contained in an inscription of the year 409/8 (*M&L*, no. 86), which purports to be (and presumably is) a republication of Draco's law (ca. 621 B.C.) regarding homicide.[12] The law stipulated that a man exiled for unpremeditated homicide could return if relatives of the deceased—father, brother, or sons, or if there were no such relatives, then kinsmen as far as the degree of cousin's son and cousin—unanimously granted pardon; if no such relatives existed, then the decision was to lie with ten fellow phratry members of the deceased, selected on the basis of birth (*aristindēn*). From this statement, then, two important conclusions can be drawn: first, that phratries were recognized by law, and, second, since the term *aristindēn* clearly has a social significance, that a phratry contained both men of the upper class (that is, nobles or *gennētai*) and also "commoners" (presumably non-*gennētai*). For an understanding of the social structure of early Athenian society, it is obviously of great importance to know that by 621 at the latest, membership in the phratries was not restricted to Eupatrid *genē*.

Phratries may have existed among the migrating Greeks at the beginning of the second millennium, but there is no specific information about them until the inscription just mentioned and the two passages in the *Iliad* referring to phratries discussed in Chapter 2. A common, and probably correct, interpretation for their origin or recrudescence is that in the Dark Age the nobles, grouped in *genē*, organized their dependents for better control in phratries, each phratry being under the domination of one or more *genē*. A fragment of the third-century Atthidographer Philochorus (Jacoby, 328, fragment 35a), confirms the conclusion that phratries comprised more than *genē*. It reads: ". . . and the *phratores* by necessity are to receive both the *orgeones* and the *homogalaktes* (suckled with the same milk), whom we call *gennētai*." The fragment seems to be a quotation from a law, although the last four words are undoubtedly an explanation added by Philochorus. The word *orgeones,* to judge from its use in the fourth and third centuries, was a nontechnical term designating "partakers of rites." It seems clear that this term, as used in the quotation, referred to non-*gennētai* members of phratries (that is, to commoners).

The usual explanation that the *orgeones* included all the phratry members except the *gennētai* has been properly questioned by a scholar who argues that this interpretation makes no sense,[13] for it would mean that the *phratores* (the total membership) must receive the *orgeones* and the *gennētai,* namely themselves (all the members). A simpler explanation may be to imagine that there were other groups of non-*gennētai* in the phratries than only the *orgeones* who, originally at least, were dependents of the *gennētai*. These commoners, anxious for entry into phratries which, with their cults, were the foundation of "citizenship," could have exerted pressure by organizing themselves on the model of *genē* and *orgeones*. They would have been assisted in their endeavors by the new phenomenon of hoplite warfare; since many of them, possibly wealthy in movables, could afford to equip themselves as hoplites, they would have been able to use their military value to the state as a potent bargaining point. Once they gained admission to the phratries they would have been enrolled on the phratry registers and hence become "citizens," although clearly of a status inferior to that of the *gennētai*.

The quotation of Philochorus, then, possibly should be interpreted to mean that the *phratores,* including the new commoners (non-*gennētai*), had to accept the membership lists of the *gennētai* and the *orgeones,* who were clients somewhat bound to the *genē.* Fourth-century inscriptions reveal that the *gennētai* in a phratry had the right to scrutinize their own membership; the same privilege may have belonged to the *orgeones.* At some early period there was friction within the phratries. Possibly by strengthening their membership lists, the *gennētai* and *orgeones* were trying to dominate or expel the comparatively recent influx of commoners. When the commoners became recalcitrant and endangered the "harmony" of the phratries, the state interfered to support the privileges of the upper classes by passing a law that ordered the *phratores,* of whom many were commoners, to accept the lists of, and the candidates approved by, the *gennētai* and *orgeones.* The law is not dated, but historians have usually argued that its sponsor was either Solon at the beginning of the sixth century or Cleisthenes at the end of that century.

This discussion of tribes, *genē,* and phratries has raised more questions than it has answered, and unfortunately it has been based on speculation, but at least it should have emphasized how basic these badly understood institutions were to the social and political life of the early Athenians. Further discussion will be necessary in connection with Cleisthenes' reforms at the close of the sixth century. Only one other point needs consideration here: the problem of how many phratries there were. The fragment of the *Constitution of the Athenians* dealing with the "Ion period," it will be remembered, stated that the Athenians were divided into 12 phratries and 360 *genē.* Some scholars accept the number 12 even for fifth- and fourth-century Athens, but it seems certain that that number must be rejected along with the absurd figure of 360 *genē.* If the number 12 should be accepted, the consequence would be that in the Periclean Age, when Athens had a citizen body of some 40,000 to 50,000 adult males, each phratry would have had a membership of some 3,500 men. Even if the poorest class, the *thetes,* for financial or other reasons ceased to belong, the membership of each of the 12 phratries would have been in the neighborhood of 1,500. The evidence from literary sources, however, concerning the festival of the Apaturia, when fathers presented their children to their fellow phratry members for admission into the phratry, suggests much more intimate and informal meetings than would have been possible with a membership involving thousands. There seems little doubt that in the Periclean Age as well as in the period of the aristocratic republic the number of phratries far exceeded 12.[14] In the preceding discussion of phratries it was implied that the number of phratries was roughly equivalent to the number of *genē*. This suggestion is certainly closer to the truth than the rigid idea that phratries remained fixed at the figure 12 throughout Athenian history.

VERY LITTLE specific information is available on the history of Athens for the eighth and even the major part of the seventh century. The aristocratic government attained its full development about the middle of the seventh century when six new magistrates—the *thesmothetai*—were added to the three already in existence, the archon, the king archon, and the polemarch. The government was securely in the hands of the Eupatrids, whose position was based on their *genos* and phratry organization, their wealth in land, their military superiority, and their monopoly in knowing and administering the unwritten customary laws. To judge from the pottery, Athens was the leading state in Greece in the ninth and eighth centuries. The geometric pottery was of superior quality and was exported to various parts of the mainland, to the Cyclades and Crete, and as far east as Cyprus and Syria.[15] The so-called Dipylon vases, found near the Dipylon Gate leading to the cemetery of the outer Ceramicus, are of particular interest. These huge vases, standing about five feet high, sometimes were used as receptacles for the ashes of the dead and sometimes were placed as markers over the graves. In the latter case, the bottoms were often perforated so that libations could be poured into them for the dead below. The drawings on these vases, although partly reflecting scenes from the epic tradition, furnish some ideas on the life and customs of the upper classes—funeral processions and games, battle scenes with horses and chariots, and scenes of fighting between men on shipboard and men on land as in some raid. Presumably Athens had a navy of sorts at this time.

In the latter part of the eighth century and for most of the seventh, however, again to judge from pottery, Corinth surged ahead of Athens. This was the great period of Greek colonization, in which Corinth took a leading part whereas Athens did not participate at all. Because of the extent of its territory, Athens apparently was not yet afflicted by the land hunger which was distressing so many Greek states. As was seen in an earlier chapter, the establishment of colonies all over the Mediterranean and Black Sea worlds acted as a great stimulus to Greek trade and industry. Athens, although standing aloof from the movement, certainly felt some of its repercussions. One can safely say that movable wealth increased in importance among the Athenians and that in the military sphere the hoplites became more and more prominent.

In the latter half of the seventh century when tyrants were seizing power in various cities of Greece, an attempt to establish a tyranny was also made in Athens. The traditional date is 632. Cylon, an Athenian noble and Olympic victor, had married the daughter of Theagenes, the contemporary tyrant of neighboring Megara. With military help from his father-in-law, Cylon and a group of his friends seized the Acropolis of Athens. If they had expected support from the people at large, they were disappointed, for the Athenians flocked in from the countryside and laid siege to them. When the besieged were hard-pressed by lack of food and water, Cylon and his brother escaped, but their supporters, according to tradition, although they were promised pardon or at least the right to a trial, were slaughtered at the altars to which they were clinging as suppliants.

This episode, one of the very few for which there is evidence in the history of seventh-century Athens, casts some interesting light on the period. Since Cylon's attempt at tyranny received no support beyond his immediate circle, the inference is that neither the poor peasants nor the increasing number of hoplites as yet felt sufficiently aggrieved to favor a revolutionary method for improving their lot. Possibly, also, the presence of foreign soldiers on the Acropolis dampened whatever enthusiasm certain elements of the Athenians might have had for a change of regime. The violence with which Cylon's supporters were crushed suggests that the whole affair may have stemmed from rivalry among the powerful *genē*. Thucydides (1.126), correcting Herodotus (5.71), asserts that at that time the nine archons were the chief officials—thus giving a *terminus ante quem* for the existence of the nine archons—and he makes it clear that the blame for the sacrilege fell upon the Alcmaeonid *genos;* other ancient sources (for example, Plutarch, *Solon*, 12) give the information that Megacles, the head of the Alcmaeonids, was the (eponymous) archon at the time.

Because of the sacrilege the Alcmaeonids were considered accursed. According to the tradition that developed they were brought to trial before a body of 300 men chosen from the nobility, and, when found guilty, the whole *genos* was condemned to everlasting exile and the dead were exhumed and cast beyond the borders of Attica. The curse is historical, for it was resurrected against the Alcmaeonid Cleisthenes at the end of the sixth century and against Pericles, connected with the Alcmaeonids through his mother, on the eve of the Peloponnesian War, but one can properly be skeptical about some of the embellishments of the tale. The Alcmaeonids probably were banished, but in the first half of the sixth century they were back in Athens without, apparently, having suffered any confiscation of their real property. It seems clear that the story was exaggerated so as to become part of the propaganda against the Alcmaeonid *genos.* It is worth noting, however, how the story of the banishment of all the Alcmaeonids, living and dead, confirms the picture of the solidarity of a *genos* and of its collective responsibility for the acts of one of its members.

About a decade after the Cylon affair, Draco made the first codification of Athenian laws. The traditional date is about 621. His importance was similar to that of the other early Greek lawgivers, for, although the nobles retained the administration of justice, the publication of the laws made it more difficult for the magistrates to give "crooked" decisions of the sort that Hesiod had inveighed against so passionately. Little is known about his code because, except for the laws on homicide, it was superseded about a generation later by Solon's code. In later times, stories told about the severity of the penalties provided by his laws caused the Athenian orator Demades to comment that Draco's laws were written in blood, not in ink. In his laws on homicide, however, Draco made the very important distinction between premeditated and unpremeditated homicide. These laws were republished in the year 409/8, and, as mentioned above, the inscription bearing part of the laws on unpremeditated homicide has been preserved.[16] The publication of the laws on homicide represented a significant step in reducing the ruinous feuds which existed among the various *genē*. In fact, the bloody sequel of the Cylon affair and the growing conviction that the shedding of blood could bring pollution on the whole community may have been strong contributing factors in the demand for publication. Thereafter there was a carefully worked out procedure to be followed in the various types of homicide, but since the shedding of blood was still considered primarily a family affair, the prosecution had to be initiated by the kin of the victim.

When Cylon made his attempt to establish a tyranny about 632 he received no support from the Athenians as a whole. In 594 when Solon introduced his reforms, Athens was on the verge of social revolution. It seems likely, therefore, that in the interval conditions had deteriorated very rapidly in Attica. Because of the inadequacy of source material, any attempt to explain this deterioration has to be largely speculative and inferential, but a few observations can be made which partially elucidate the situation.

Throughout this period it is probable that Athens was fighting a desultory war with Megara for possession of the important island of Salamis. As long as the Megarians were in control of the island, they could interfere with Athenian trade and also launch destructive raids against the Attic coast. Until fairly recently the general assumption was that the adoption of a system of coinage in the latter decades of the seventh century by the predominantly agricultural Athenians caused various economic dislocations and, in particular, brought hardships upon the poor peasants. Numismatists, however, have lately argued persuasively that the "invention" of coinage should not be placed earlier than the last quarter of the seventh century, and that the first coins issued by the Athenians should be dated to about 560. The introduction of coinage, then, cannot be used to explain the evil conditions in Attica at the close of the seventh century. Nevertheless, with the expanding trade and industry which followed in the wake of the colonizing movement, movable wealth was becoming increasingly important throughout the Greek world. Before the actual appearance of coinage it is probable that precious metals and especially silver bullion, weighed out for each transaction, were more and more being employed as media of exchange. The significance of this is clear. In the days when trade consisted almost exclusively of bartering one natural commodity for another, the amount of wealth which one could accumulate in such commodities was obviously limited. Silver, however, is not perishable, and the more wealth of this type that a man could acquire, the greater would be his power and prestige. It is significant that the poems of Solon, which provide the earliest contemporary evidence about Athens, reveal that problems concerning debt had become acute. With the many new opportunities for the productive use of movable wealth, the wealthy probably became much harsher and more exacting as creditors than they had been in the days when borrowing and the repayment of debts were transactions carried out almost exclusively in terms of natural products.

One of Solon's acts, when he was in office as mediator and archon in 594, was to forbid the export of all natural products except olive oil (Plutarch, *Solon,* 24.1). A safe inference from this measure is that in that period Athens, while producing an excess of oil, was suffering from a shortage of grain. Inadequate supplies of grain, and hence a higher price, obviously caused hardships, especially for the poor unable to grow enough for family consumption. It was precisely in these years, ca. 600, that Athens, in a war with Lesbian Mytilene in which the Mytileneans Pittacus and Alcaeus both fought, acquired its first overseas possession, Sigeum in the Troad near the mouth of the Hellespont. Periander, tyrant of Corinth, had been called in as an arbitrator, and he awarded the town to Athens. This interest in the Hellespontine region, which is confirmed by finds of contemporary Attic black-figure ware there,[17] must mean that Athens was trying to get some share of the grain that was being exported from the Black Sea area, an attempt in which it presumably met resistance from its enemy Megara, whose colonies, Chalcedon and Byzantium, lay on either side of the Bosporus. The other half of Solon's measure—the permission to export olive oil alone—is particularly significant for the light it may throw on contemporary agricultural conditions in Attica: it suggests that olive culture had become the most profitable form of agriculture in Attica. Since olive trees do not bear a full crop until they are from fifteen to twenty years old, the raising of olives was a type of farming largely closed to peasants who could not afford to wait for years until the trees became fruitful, but it was an enterprise well suited to the larger landowners and one that probably caused them to try to extend their landholdings so that more and more acres could be devoted to olive orchards.[18]

The chief ancient sources for the study of Solon and his times and the steps he took to try to meet the pressing problems are, besides the fragments of his own poems, Aristotle's *Constitution of the Athenians* and Plutarch's *Life of Solon*. Both of these authors presumably had at their disposal the complete poems of Solon. From these sources it is clear that the poor were in great trouble, for many had fallen into some type of debt slavery or had become *hektemors* (sixth-parters), a term which in Aristotle's day was no longer understood. Aristotle (*Ath. Const.*, 2) emphasizes that all the land was in the control of a few. This statement is surprising, and his authority for it is unknown. It concerns the basic problem of what the Athenian system of land tenure was when Solon undertook his reforms. The problem can be phrased as follows: Was land owned by the individual, to do with as he saw fit, or was it held by the family with an obligation, whether legal, customary, or religious—or with all these sanctions combined—not to alienate it? Some scholars have answered the question by stating that private ownership of land in Attica was a late development, while others have asserted vehemently that the practice of private ownership of land among the Greeks was of great antiquity. This is not the type of question, considering the nature of the evidence, to which a definitive answer can be given.[19] The likelihood, however, is that land in Attica had the status of family land at least until the time of Solon and possibly considerably later.

The early Athenians, and the Greeks in general, had a passionate, almost religious, attachment to their land. One need only read the comedies of Aristophanes or the *Republic* and *Laws* of Plato to realize how deep that attachment was even in the full classical period. To ask whether an Athenian of the eighth or seventh century could alienate his land is really to ask an anachronistic question, for the conception would have been unintelligible to men of that time. The livelihood of a man and his family came from the land; how would they have lived if they lost it? It is true that from the earliest times there were artisans, who probably owned no land, and landless *thetes* or hired laborers who often worked on the land of others. These classes increased in number as the generations passed, but in the archaic Greek states these people were not considered to be regular members of the state, for citizenship was based on ownership of land and wealth was estimated for political purposes exclusively in terms of land and its products. The living family did not actually own the land in the modern sense of the word "own." Rather the family had the usufruct of it, and it had a solemn obligation to maintain that land intact for the dead generations who were buried on it and for the generations to come.

Beyond such statements, which admittedly run the risk of being subjective, two reasons of a more particular type can be given for believing that down to the time of Solon, at any rate, land was owned by the family and not by an individual, and hence was inalienable. First, Aristotle, while describing the wretched condition of the poor in the period before Solon's reforms, emphasizes that up to Solon's time all loans were secured on the borrower's person. Why would a needy person have borrowed on his personal security and thus, in view of the conditions of the time, run the almost certain risk of falling into debt slavery, if it had been possible for him to offer his land as security? The answer presumably is that there was something in the nature of the Attic system of land tenure—namely its family character—which did not permit land to be risked by being offered as security. Second, in the fourth century when Attic land could be bought and sold freely, there were elaborate regulations concerning intestate succession and various restrictions on testamentary rights. Since the aim of all these provisions was to prevent the real property from passing out of the ownership of the immediate family or relatives up to a specified degree, it seems only reasonable to interpret these provisions as survivals from an earlier time when land was the common possession of the family. The same argument applies also to the great care that was taken to see that an heiress married her nearest male kin.

These arguments all have to do with family land—land which had been hallowed by the traditions of the many generations who had lived on it. They do not preclude the possibility that an individual who had succeeded in clearing a little plot for himself out of wasteland could do with that plot as he wished, for that land would have been privately owned and not sanctified by family traditions.

If, then, it is probable that prior to Solon land was family land and hence inalienable, how is one to explain Aristotle's statement that all the land was in the control of a few? It is clearly naive to expect that a definitive answer will ever be found for this question. Even if some scholar should hit upon the right answer, there would be no possible way of proving that it was right. The best procedure here will be to quote in translation the two most pertinent passages from the ancient sources in order to illustrate the difficulties involved in reaching even a reasonably satisfactory solution to the problems concerned. Aristotle (*Ath. Const.*, 2), commenting on conditions in the latter part of the seventh century, writes:

> And after this it happened that there was friction between the "notables" and the common people (*plēthos*) for a long time. For the government was oligarchic in all other respects and in particular the poor were enslaved to the rich, both they themselves and their children and wives. And they were called *pelatai* and *hektemors*, for according to this rent they worked the fields of the wealthy. And all the land was in the control of a few. And if ever they did not pay the rents, they became subject to seizure, both they themselves and their children. And loans for everybody were secured on the persons of the borrowers until the time of Solon. This man first became leader of the people. Most harsh and bitter, therefore, of the affairs in the state to the many was the being enslaved. They were dissatisfied, however, also in other matters, for they happened, so to speak, to have a share in nothing.

In the twelfth chapter of the same work Aristotle quotes from a poem of Solon in which Solon, referring to his achievements, says:

> In the judgment of Time, the greatest mother of the Olympian gods would best bear witness to these things; Black Earth, whose markers (*horoi*) implanted in many places I removed, and she, formerly enslaved, now is free. And many sold abroad I brought back to Athens, to their god-built fatherland, one sold unjustly, and another justly, and those who had fled because of dire need, no longer uttering Attic speech since they were wandering in many places, and those having unseemly slavery here, trembling before their masters' tempers, I made free.

In these lines Solon lists the measures he took to rectify the evil conditions that had been in existence—the encumbrance of the land marked by *horoi*, the selling of many abroad, the flight from disaster to foreign lands, and the unseemly slavery of many at home. Nothing is said about the causes of these sufferings, but the passage makes clear that many—certainly many of the poor—had fallen into some type of slavery, a bondage which also had gripped the land.

Aristotle, living more than two and a half centuries after Solon, surely had these verses and perhaps others not now extant in mind when he wrote the first passage quoted above. He emphasizes the conflict between the powerful rich and the helpless poor, and by his remark that loans were secured on the borrower's person he implies that debt slavery was the root cause of the evil situation. Early in the passage, however, when he says that the poor were enslaved to the rich, he seems to be referring to a different type of bondage, for he says that they were called *pelatai* and *hektemors* (sixth-parters). Since *pelatai* is a word frequently used by Plutarch to designate the Roman *clientes*, the *hektemors*, grouped here with the *pelatai*, are usually interpreted as tenants who owed a sixth of their produce to the wealthy. The origin of this class of *hektemors* is nowhere explained in the ancient sources, and since the class was abolished by Solon's legislation, it seems certain that Aristotle and Plutarch were using a term long since abandoned which they did not really understand.

If Aristotle had difficulty in explaining the characteristics of the *hektemors*—enslaved to the rich, tenants on the fields of the rich, subject to seizure (as slaves) if they did not pay their rents—it is hardly surprising that modern scholars have speculated endlessly on the problem. Since Solon says that the *horoi* marked the enslavement of the land and then mentions people who seem to have been debt slaves, many scholars who believe that land was alienable argue that the *horoi* were similar to the stone markers of the fourth and third centuries, which are known to have been mortgage notices. Nevertheless, one wonders why there was need of *horoi* after foreclosure. Some scholars who believe that land was inalienable have tried to explain the situation roughly as follows. A peasant, in trouble, may have borrowed on the security of his person. When he was unable to repay the loan he faced enslavement, but the creditor, interested in exploiting more land and acquiring workers, and the peasant, anxious to avoid slavery, devised a compromise. By this agreement, the creditor took possession of the debtor's land while the insolvent peasant remained on his own land as a rent-paying tenant (*hektemor*), retaining the right to regain control of his land whenever the debt should be paid. This arrangement would have been the equivalent of a legal fiction designed to circumvent the inalienable character of the land—a forerunner of the common fourth-century type of real security known as sale with option of redemption. Legal students, however, have objected to this theory because a legal fiction has to be based on a possiblity, but if land was inalienable, sale under any conditions was impossible.

A definitive answer to the nature of the *hektemors* and of the contemporary debt slavery will probably never be attained. A scholar has recently made a valuable contribution to the problem by emphasizing that in the matter of slavery, the Greeks were familiar with various halfway statuses.[20] The simple antinomy, free man–slave, does not reflect accurately conditions in the Greek world. This scholar gives a good illustration of this situation by referring to a fragment in a play of Menander where a person in response to a question about whether a girl in debt bondage was a slave answers, "Yes, partly, in a way." Solon in the poem quoted above was certainly thinking of different types of bondage. Aristotle, writing several centuries later when debt and mortgages were common occurrences in Athenian life, may have put undue emphasis on the notion of debt.

In dealing with the times before Solon, where contemporary source material for Athens is lacking, one can only speculate on possible answers by drawing suggestions from seemingly similar situations in the ancient Near East, in the Old Testament, and in the many legends concerning the early history of the Roman republic. In such sources one can find cases of a borrower paying interest by working for his creditor, or guaranteeing the payment of the debt through working himself or having some member of his family work for the creditor for a certain number of years. If the creditor or debtor died, it is obvious that many problems about the debt would have arisen. In a somewhat similar way Heracles in the legend was sold as a slave to Queen Omphale for a definite period to earn the blood price for the kin of Iphitus whom he had slain.

Many of the situations which by Solon's time had grown into devastating debt problems may have originated from conditions having nothing to do with ordinary debt. In the unsettled period of the Dark Age, nothing would have been more natural than for a poor farmer to seek protection from a powerful landowner. In return for protection, he may have agreed to consign to the protector a definite percentage of his annual harvest. There may have been many cases of sons of peasants receiving permission to work on certain sections of the estate of a big landowner in return for a specified rent. As conditions became more settled, the peasant may have wished to abandon the tenant or client status his ancestors had had for generations, but the noble landowner, in need of a work force, could easily find ways to thwart the desire for independence of the weak and defenseless peasant. In such ways—and many others could be proposed, such as the present plight of the poor in India—it is easy to imagine how many types of bondage might have developed. It has been suggested that these vague statuses and obligations, including those of the *hektemors*, may have received legal recognition in the code of Draco. By reasoning along these lines it is possible to form some general notion of how the conditions faced by Solon had gradually developed—

conditions which could have included *horoi* marking the enslavement of inalienable land.

UNSATISFACTORY as the evidence is, it is clear that socially, economically, and politically Athens was in a deplorable condition at the beginning of the sixth century. The fragments of the poems of Solon are contemporary testimony to "Ionia's oldest land being slain," as he put it. Of all the evil conditions the worst was the ruthless exploitation of the needy, which had reduced many Athenians to actual slavery or to whatever form of bondage one wishes to recognize in the *hektemor* status. If the exploited poor had been the only discontented and outraged element in the population of Attica, they probably would have been too weak and downtrodden to bring about any improvement in their lot, and Athens would have been degraded into becoming a society based on the suppression of the disadvantaged. Fortunately for the fate of Athens, and of the world, other social elements in Athens were also dissatisfied, for the exclusive Eupatrids had a monopoly on all the organs of the state. Dissatisfaction was so widespread that Athens apparently was ripe for a tyranny as it had not been a generation earlier. It may have been fear of tyranny, which was at its height in the Greek world at this time, that convinced the nobles that concessions of some sort had to be made. The solution on which all classes finally agreed was, as Aristotle (*Ath. Const.*, 5) puts it, to appoint Solon mediator and archon and to entrust the government to him. There is no definite information on what body appointed him. Possibly, since this was an extraordinary situation, an assembly of all Athenians was called to elect the mediator. The position which Solon occupied must have been similar to that held at approximately the same time by Pittacus of Mytilene, who was known as an *aisymnētēs* or "elective tyrant." Pittacus, however, was in office for ten years, whereas in the case of Solon there is no good evidence, despite a statement in Plutarch (*Solon*, 16), that his tenure extended beyond the one year 594/3.

Thanks to the preservation of some parts of his poems, Solon is the first Athenian who can be visualized by the modern student as a distinct personality; in fact, he can be considered the first flesh-and-blood statesman of the western world, the first public figure whose policies and ideals can be at least partly understood. It is true that in the course of time legends became attached to his name and that fourth-century Atthidographers and orators confused the historical picture by interpreting and altering the traditions about Solon according to their own political ideologies, but with Solon's poetry and some of his laws as a touchstone it is often possible to discern what is mere propaganda or gossip. Solon was of noble birth but of only moderate means, which he tried to improve by engaging in trade. A consistent tradition represented him as traveling widely. Most of these travels—to Egypt, Cyprus, and Asia Minor—were assigned to the period after his legislative work at Athens, but it is probable that his early commercial activities took him at least to the Ionian coast. The breadth of understanding revealed in his reforms suggests that by 594 he had already seen something of the ways of the world. Certainly his poetry reflects the intellectual awakening which was occurring in Ionia at the beginning of the sixth century. One verse—"I grow old ever learning many things"—epitomizes the intellectual curiosity for which the Greeks in their best period were noted.

Solon obviously was a well-known and respected figure in Athens when he was appointed mediator. Successful leadership in the war with Megara over Salamis and the circulation of his poems, many of which were political tracts, contributed to the establishment of his reputation. These poems, some composed before his appointment and some afterwards to defend his measures, reveal his political and ethical thinking. Like Hesiod a century earlier, he was a passionate advocate of justice and believed that divine vengeance ultimately fell on the unjust. Although of high birth himself, he sympathized deeply with the sufferings of the poor and laid the blame for the evil plight of Athens squarely on the greed of the wealthy and powerful. Nevertheless, he believed that the wealthy upper classes, because of tradition and experience, should be dominant in the state, but under the restraint of law. *Eunomia*—the reign of good law—was his goal, under which each class would have its place in the state according to its aptitudes. The poor, therefore, although they should be treated with justice, were not qualified, because of inexperience and lack of leisure, to have an important role in government. What stands out above all else in Solon's poems, however, is the statesmanlike point of view in his insistence that the welfare of the community as a whole should take precedence over that of any particular class or individual.

Solon's first act after he had taken office was to strike at the fundamental evil in the state, the debt situation. His remedy was the famous *seisachtheia*—the shaking off of burdens. So far as can be ascertained, this measure consisted of the cancellation of all debts secured by the borrower's person. The measure was made retroactive so as to liberate all debtors who had fallen into slavery or into the status of *hektemors*. To ensure that there would be no recurrence of the miseries of debt slavery, he carried a law forbidding loans to be secured on the debtor's person. The removal of the *horoi* ended the enslavement of "Black Earth," and these lots of land apparently were returned completely unencumbered to their former owners. Solon states that he set free not only the debt slaves in Attica but also those who had been sold abroad. There is no reason to doubt his word, but one wonders how those sold abroad were tracked down and also how their masters, who presumably had bought these slaves in good faith, were remunerated for their liberation.

By the removal of the *horoi* and the elimination of the class of *hektemors,* the wealthy lost control over all the land on which the *hektemors* had toiled as tenants, but their own estates remained intact. One fragment of Solon's poems in which he said that the lower classes should not have an equal share of the rich soil of the fatherland with the upper classes is often interpreted to mean that there had been a clamor for a total redistribution of the land. If there was such a demand, Solon flatly rejected it. He believed too strongly in the dignity attached to position and wealth and in the privileges and corresponding duties which traditionally belonged to the upper classes to countenance any revolutionary procedure which would have abolished the social, economic, and political distinctions. Although he resisted any possible revolutionary hopes of this kind, his *seisachtheia* must have given birth to a period of bewildering confusion. Since the ancient sources provide no clear picture of the effects of this measure, one has to rely on his imagination to try to visualize some of the aspects of this unfolding social drama—the wealthy reluctantly relinquishing control of various plots of land and of the bondmen attached to them and worrying about an adequate work force for their own estates; the hundreds of liberated *hektemors* and other bondmen, including freed slaves returning from abroad, rejoicing in their newly gained freedom and trying to reestablish themselves on their own parcels of land; the painful realization that the land was inadequate to support them by the familiar grain culture, particularly since some of the land, when controlled by the wealthy, may have been converted to olive orchards; the need for farm equipment as they tried to maintain an independent existence; the necessity of borrowing and the worry that, although they were no longer required to offer their own persons as security for loans, they might fall again into some sort of dependence on their wealthy neighbors.

Specific information on these problems is lacking, but as they began to emerge, and possibly in anticipation of their emergence, Solon, realizing that the available arable land was too limited to support a growing population almost exclusively by agriculture, encouraged many poor country dwellers to come to the city and seek a livelihood as craftsmen and laborers. To promote a growth of industry and to establish it as efficiently as possible, he encouraged the immigration of foreign artisans.

According to the source followed by Plutarch (*Solon*, 24), he conferred citizenship on those who agreed to settle permanently in Athens. Since citizenship was based on membership in a phratry, this raises the difficult question of whether and how these aliens were enrolled in the phratries.

To stimulate Athenian trade and free it from too much dependence on the prosperous neighboring island of Aegina, Solon changed the system of weights and measures from the Aeginetan standard to one usually termed "Euboean," the standard which was also employed by Corinth. Throughout the sixth century, so far as the evidence goes, relations between Athens and Corinth remained on friendly terms, even though the export of Athenian pottery gradually began to exceed that of the formerly dominant Corinthian wares. The ancient sources say that together with the change in the standard of weights and measures Solon also shifted Athenian coinage to the Euboean standard, but this was a misconception since Athenian coinage did not begin until around 560. It was probably in conjunction with these various economic measures that he forbade the export of all agricultural products except olive oil. As was suggested above, this action seems to be clear testimony that there had been a great increase in olive culture in the final decades of the seventh century.

Athenians of later generations cherished the memory of Solon as the great lawgiver. His codification of the laws supplanted that of Draco except for the laws on homicide, although it is probable that he incorporated certain aspects of Draco's code into his own. His laws were inscribed on what were called *axones* and *kurbeis* (derivation unknown). In both ancient and modern times there has been much discussion on the significance of these terms. The most recent study[21] suggests that the *axones* were "four-sided pieces of wood mounted in an oblong frame" in such a way that a reader could rotate them so as to see the laws inscribed on each of the four flat surfaces. The *kurbeis* were either bronze or stone stelae with a pyramid-shaped top, three or four-sided with the writing going alternately from top to bottom and then from bottom to top or, as on the *axones,* from left to right and then right to left in the manner the Greeks called *boustrophedon* (as the ox plows). These monuments were located somewhere on the Acropolis, and since they were seen by writers in the third and second centuries B.C., it is clear that they were not destroyed when the Persians sacked Athens in 480 and 479. About the middle of the fifth century they were brought down from the Acropolis and placed elsewhere, the *axones* apparently in the Prytaneion, the *kurbeis* in the agora. In the last decade of the fifth century commissioners were instructed to recodify the laws, a task which necessitated searching out the laws that had been issued in the sixth and fifth centuries and eliminating any contradictions between them and the old laws of Solon. The new code was inscribed on marble. From it there remains a stele containing Draco's law on involuntary homicide; in addition several fragments, dealing with calendars of sacrifices, have been discovered in the agora.

For an understanding of Solon's legal contributions it would be very helpful to know how many of the laws which in the fourth century were quoted as Solonian were really his, for they were used by historians and antiquarians in their efforts to reconstruct and interpret Solon's work. Since some laws which were quoted were couched in archaic language, it is probable that these at least were basically Solonian. Others, however, although called Solonian, were enacted at a much later time. Solon's laws included various enactments which in later times would have been termed decrees; for example, according to Plutarch (*Solon*, 24.1) the prohibition of exporting all natural products except olive oil was included in the first *axon*. Solon's amnesty law also is probably better considered a decree. This amnesty, proclaimed in Solon's archonship, became the model for subsequent amnesty "laws" in Athenian history. Plutarch (*Solon*, 19.3) says that this law was contained in the thirteenth *axon* and that it restored citizenship to all who had been banished except those condemned for murder or seeking to establish a tyranny. It was under this amnesty that the Alcmaeonids may have returned to Athens, for they had been convicted probably on a charge of impiety. At any rate, in the First Sacred War, which ended about 590, the Athenian contingent was commanded by Alcmaeon, the son of that Megacles who had been responsible for the pollution arising from the slaughter of the suppliant followers of the would-be tyrant Cylon.

It is impossible here to mention all the laws attributed, with varying degrees of probability, to Solon. Two of them, however, deserve brief discussion because one has been commonly misinterpreted, whereas the other was basic for the development of Athenian legal procedure. The first is Solon's so-called testamentary law. Regarding this law Plutarch (*Solon*, 21.2) writes: "He was highly esteemed also for his law concerning wills. Before his time, no will could be made, but the entire estate of the deceased must remain in the family. Whereas he, by permitting a man who had no children to give his property to whom he wished, ranked friendship above kinship, and favor above necessity, and made a man's possessions his own property." On the basis of this passage, many scholars, who believed that Attic land was family-owned and hence inalienable until Solon's time, have argued that it was the testamentary law which first liberated land from the system of family tenure. Plutarch's language, however, clearly reflects conditions as they existed in his own time, and also it is reasonable to question the sentimental motives assigned to Solon. A study of the numerous fourth-century speeches delivered in inheritance cases reveals that Plutarch omitted three essential elements in his account of the law, for a man could will his property only if he had no *legitimate* and *male* children and if he *adopted* the heir. The testamentary procedure of Solon's law actually was as follows: If a man had legitimate sons, no testamentary right existed, for the property automatically devolved on them at the father's death. If a man, however, had no legitimate sons, he could appoint one heir, but this heir always had to be adopted into the testator's family. If there were daughters, the adopted heir had to marry one. This adopted heir was not allowed to adopt a son or to will the property. Thus he really only held the property in trust; his function was to beget sons who would carry on the testator's family. The whole point of the adopted heir clearly was, by means of a legal device, to ensure the preservation of the family and the family's land. If the adopted heir had no sons, then at his death the property automatically passed to the nearest of kin of the original testator.[22]

Solon, in his testamentary law, did grant a man who had no legitimate sons the freedom to select any man or boy he wished as heir. From the cases known in the fourth century it is evident that, despite this freedom, the heir chosen was almost always a close relative. Since, however, the heir, by becoming a member of his adoptive father's family, ceased to be a member of the family into which he had been born, it is obvious that Solon's law had nothing to do with releasing land from the system of family tenure. This point is important, for if Attic land was inalienable until Solon's time and if Solon did not legislate so as to permit alienability, the difficult problem remains concerning the period to which such a fundamental change in the system of land tenure should be assigned.

The other law of Solon which merits emphasis here is his creation of the public action (the *graphē*): He allowed any citizen ("he who wishes") to institute a public action to secure justice for himself or others. Formerly only the injured party himself or a kinsman could start proceedings, since access to the machinery of justice was linked with the family system and the notion of the collective responsibility of the family for each of its members. What Solon really did was to inaugurate criminal law, for criminal law begins when the right of action arising from a wrong is no longer restricted to the victim and his family but is granted to any citizen—when a community comes to the realization that an injury to an individual is also an injury to society as a whole.[23] It should be mentioned here, however, that in Athens and throughout most if not all of Greece, cases of homicide, for conservative religious reasons, remained within the province of the family system.

Solon's constitutional reforms are difficult to evaluate not only because of the scarcity of source material but also because of the tendentious nature of what does exist. In the fifth century and down to the middle of the fourth Cleisthenes was usually considered the founder of Athenian democracy, while Solon was spoken of respectfully as a poet, lawmaker, and one of the Seven Wise Men. According to extant evidence it was first in 356 that Solon, in Isocrates' speech *On the Areopagus,* was depicted as the founder of the moderate democracy. Since Isocrates was criticizing the contemporary radical democracy, it is not surprising that various good democrats, including Demosthenes (*Against Androtion*), retaliated by designating Solon as the father of the radical democracy. Solon thus became a figure in the political polemics of the time, and some 200 years after his death acquired the reputation of a constitution maker in addition to his other achievements.[24] Aristotle (*Ath. Const.,* 7.1) in his account of Solon says that he made laws and established a constitution (*politeia*). It is more probable, however, that Solon in his law and decree making touched on various matters relating to government than that he created a specific constitution. If, then, the accounts of Solon's constitution which have been preserved are to a considerable extent the products of ideological struggles, dogmatic statements on his constitutional measures would be rash. The best one can do is to use the ancient accounts judiciously and to make use of analogies and inferences drawn from survivals of old customs, as Aristotle himself did. The resulting picture may not reflect the constitution exactly as it was when Solon retired from office, but it should at least reflect sixth-century conditions. This warning should be kept in mind in connection with the following paragraphs on Solon's constitutional reforms.

When Solon came to power the Eupatrids completely dominated the state. The chief organs of government—the magistrates (the nine archons) and the Council of the Areopagus—were open only to these nobles. Solon, wishing to open the administration of the state to a wider group, made use of four census classes. At some earlier time in Athenian history, very probably in connection with the appearance of hoplites, the free population had been divided into these classes according to the military role they had to play. The two highest classes served as cavalry, the third as hoplites, and the fourth, when called upon, as light armed troops. The criterion for assignment to a class was the amount of grain or olive oil a man's land produced. The four classes were as follows (Aristotle, *Ath. Const.,* 7): *pentacosiomedimni,* those whose land produced annually 500 or more measures; *hippeis,* horsemen, whose land produced between 300 and 500 measures; *zeugitai,* hoplites (literally, "yoked to-gether"), whose land produced between 200 and 300 measures; *thetes* (lit-erally, "laborers"), whose land produced under 200 measures. By giving a political significance to these classes in addition to the military signifi-cance, Solon made a serious breach in the Eupatrid monopoly, for he admitted men, provided they had the requisite income, to various posts in the government even though they did not belong to the Eupatrid order. The following sketch of the organs of government will reveal the participation of the four classes in the administration.

The chief magistrates were the nine archons—the eponymous ar-chon, the king archon, the polemarch, and the six *thesmothetai.* The method by which they were appointed before Solon's reforms is not clear. Aristotle says they were appointed by the Areopagus, but since Solon himself seems to have been appointed to office by the people, pre-sumably the assembly, it is possible that previously the assembly had elected the archons from a list of candidates proposed by the Areopagus. According to Aristotle (*Ath. Const.,* 8), Solon established a system whereby each tribe elected ten candidates in a preliminary election, and then from these forty the nine archons were chosen by lot. Many schol-ars, with good reason, are skeptical about the employment of lot in the selecting of archons this early in Athenian history. They argue that the attribution of this measure to Solon was part of the fourth-century cam-paign to depict him as the founder of radical democracy. Unfortunately, the extant evidence is not sufficient to give a definitive answer to the problem. Before Solon only the Eupatrids were eligible for the archon-ship. Solon, by employing the timocratic principle, allowed men of suffi-cient wealth to be eligible whether they were Eupatrids or not. Once again there is a problem, for it cannot be stated with certainty whether he made members of both the first and second classes eligible, or only of the first class. One can argue that it would seem strange to have ex-cluded the *hippeis,* who fought as cavalry, but one can also wonder why the *pentacosiomedimni* class existed as distinct from the *hippeis* unless it en-joyed certain special privileges, that is, exclusive rights to the archon-ship. As happens so frequently in early Greek history, a final answer cannot be offered. It is known, however, that as late as Aristotle's own time the treasurers had to be selected from the first class. As for the ever-increasing number of minor magistracies, from Solon's day on they were open to members of the second and the third classes (and presum-ably not barred to the *pentacosiomedimni*).

The Council of the Areopagus clearly remained important after Solon's reforms as before. It is particularly difficult to characterize the early Areopagus with any assurance because most of the relevant evidence belongs to the fourth century, and the fourth century was precisely the time when the conservatives and oligarchs, in their desire to restore to the Areopagus the powers which (they thought) it had lost in the fifth century, muddied the historical tradition by painting the Areopagus as the supreme organ in the early Athenian state. It seems certain, however, that from Solon's time on, at least, it was composed of ex-archons who then served for life. Since Solon had opened the archonship to members of the first or of the first two classes, wealthy non-Eupatrids were able to gain admission to the council. As a permanent body consisting of men who had held the highest offices, it is certain that the Areopagus exerted much influence. A modern historian can do little more than quote Aristotle (*Ath. Const.*, 8.4), but with the warning that Aristotle probably had little other evidence at his disposal beyond the tendentious statements and interpretations of the fourth-century polemicists: "He [Solon] appointed the Council of the Areopagus to the duty of guarding the laws, just as it had existed even before as overseer of the constitution (*politeia*), and it was this council that kept watch over the greatest number and the most important of the affairs of state, in particular correcting offenders with sovereign powers both to fine and punish, and making returns of its expenditures to the Acropolis without adding a statement of the reason for the outlay, and trying persons that conspired to put down the people (*demos*), Solon having laid down a law of impeachment (*eisangelia*) in regard to them." In addition to these rather sweeping, but general, powers, the Areopagus definitely retained the particular prerogative of serving as the chief court for homicide and religious trials.

Both Aristotle and Plutarch state that Solon established a Council of Four Hundred, one hundred members being selected from each of the four tribes. Plutarch adds that its functions were *probouleutic*, which would mean that the councillors, after previous deliberation, were responsible for presenting the appropriate agenda to the assembly. Since no other responsibilities are assigned to this body and since its *probouleutic* functions for an assembly that presumably met only occasionally must have been very slight, some scholars have argued that the tradition about this council is merely an anticipation of Cleisthenes' establishment of the Council of Five Hundred.[25] Against this argument it has been suggested with some plausibility that the following statement of Plutarch, which can easily be turned into verse, is actually a paraphrase of several verses of Solon: "[Solon] thinking that the city with its two councils [Areopagus and the Four Hundred], riding as it were at double anchor, would be less tossed by the surges, and would keep its populace in greater quiet" (*Solon*, 19). Yet again, there is inadequate information to make a confident judgment in this matter; what little further evidence there is will be mentioned below in the discussion of Cleisthenes. If one accepts the existence of this Council of Four Hundred, then it is logical to assume that the first three classes were eligible for membership and that the term of office, as in the case of practically all Athenian organs of government except the Areopagus, was annual. There is no way to decide whether appointment to the council would have been by election or by lot. If this council did exist, then its *probouleutic* function must have reduced considerably the powers and influence of both the archons and the Areopagus. It can also be argued that the presence of such a council would help explain how Solon's reforms were able to survive subsequent Eupatrid opposition.

Concerning the fourth census class, the *thetes,* Aristotle says that Solon admitted them only to the assembly and law courts. Since the fourth class consisted of men whose land produced fewer than 200 measures of grain and olive oil, it is probably legitimate to conclude that men possessing no land and hence having no wealth to be estimated in terms of products of the land were excluded from all participation in the government, since they did not possess the minimum required income. Many scholars, probably the majority, reject this notion. To them it is inconceivable that a pragmatic man like Solon would have refused to recognize movable wealth for political purposes. The only evidence that can be mustered for this point of view is a rather unintelligible sentence in Plutarch's *Life of Solon* (23.3). Literally translated, this passage says: "In the valuations of sacrificial offerings he [Solon] reckoned a sheep and a drachma as the equivalent of a measure of grain (*medimnus*)."[26] To procure the desired meaning, some scholars change the word *thusiōn* (sacrificial offerings) to *ousiōn* (properties; in Greek the change is very slight), and then, disregarding the syntax, translate somewhat as follows: "In the valuations of properties, a sheep and (or) a *medimnus* of grain are reckoned at a drachma." Granted that the literal translation, which equates a sheep plus a drachma to a *medimnus* of grain, makes nonsense, it nevertheless is a rather high-handed method to amend "sacrificial offering" to "properties" and then to mistranslate the sentence to conform to one's own ideas of what Solon would have done. The truth is that no certain conclusion can be drawn from this passage, especially since Plutarch is committing an anachronism by having Solon compute in terms of drachmas, unless by that term the weight of unminted silver is designated. Numismatists have shown that Athens issued no coinage until some thirty years later. Strange as it may seem to the modern mind, it appears necessary to assume that in Solon's time wealth was reckoned officially only on the basis of land and its products.

The assembly, to which Solon admitted the fourth class, the *thetes,* was a primary body that could be attended by all male citizens. Prior to Solon there surely was an assembly of some kind, for such bodies were common to all Greeks from early times, as the Homeric poems reveal. In the time of the aristocratic republic in Athens there is no specific evidence for the existence of an assembly, but it is reasonable to believe that on certain occasions the magistrates convoked meetings of the people. It was Solon, however, who made the assembly an essential part of the governmental machinery by opening it to all citizens and by defining its role. This role, which was to increase greatly as the generations passed, was concerned under Solon with electoral, legislative, and judicial branches of government. If one rejects, as seems proper, Aristotle's statement that the archons were selected by lot after a preliminary election, it seems necessary to believe that the assembly elected all magistrates, but no evidence is available on the method used for nomination of candidates. In its legislative capacity, the assembly voted on all measures proposed to it; there is no information about the amount of discussion, if any, which at this time was permitted to members of the assembly.

It was by granting certain judicial functions to the assembly that Solon inaugurated a trend which ultimately was to be of fundamental importance for Athenian democracy. Before his time there had been no appeal from the verdicts of magistrates. Solon gave the right to all citizens to appeal to the assembly from the verdicts of all magistrates, although not from those of the Areopagus. When the assembly sat as a court of appeal, it apparently was called the Heliaea to distinguish it from the *ecclesia,* the assembly in its legislative and electoral capacities.

It is just possible that Solon bestowed another power upon the people when they were sitting as the Heliaea. In the *Politics* (2.9.4), Aristotle remarks that Solon granted to the people only the rights of electing and examining magistrates. To express the idea of "examining" or "scrutinizing" he uses the verb *euthynein.* In the fully developed democracy it is known that magistrates at the end of their term of office had to submit to an official examination (*euthyna*) of their administration; this was a rather complex process which will be described in a later chapter. In pre-Solonian Athens it is probable that the Areopagus conducted some sort of examination of retiring magistrates. According to the statement in the *Politics,* Solon transferred the conduct of this examination to the people in the Heliaea. Aristotle, however, committed various anachronisms in dealing with this early period; for example, when speaking of the right of appeal, he does not say that the appeal was made to the Heliaea but to the law courts (*dikasteria*), which, in this plural form, were not established until at least the time of Cleisthenes and probably later.

The ascription to the people of the right to conduct the scrutiny may also be anachronistic. Nevertheless, since the people at some early time did acquire the right to examine magistrates, it is possible that this practice in some simple form began with Solon—or perhaps with Pisistratus who, as tyrant, would have had more power to enforce regulations.

In ending this discussion of Solon's reforms, it is worthwhile to quote Aristotle's estimate of Solon's work (*Ath. Const.*, 9): "And the three most democratic features in Solon's constitution seem to be these: first and most important, the prohibition of loans secured upon the person, second, the liberty allowed to anybody who wished to exact redress on behalf of injured persons, and third, what is said to have been the chief basis of the powers of the multitude, the right of appeal to the law court [Heliaea should be substituted here for *dikasterion*], for the people, having the power of the vote, becomes sovereign in the government." Certainly these reforms were of great importance, for they guaranteed the freedom of the individual, recognized the individual as a legal personality distinct from the family unit, and granted to all an appeal to their peers against arbitrary verdicts of the magistrates. Although these measures were of fundamental significance for the development of the future democracy, to call them democratic is an anachronistic use of that term. The word *demokratia* probably did not come into use until after the time of Cleisthenes. Not only would Solon have failed to understand the term, but he would have been horrified by the concept if it had been explained to him. His ideal for Athens was *eunomia*—the reign of good law—which in his eyes meant that the wealthy landowners should have an honored position in and the real control of the government, but a control legally tempered by the necessity to recognize that the lower classes also had a legitimate and essential function in the state. Aristotle, in applying the term "democratic" to Solon's work, was clearly influenced by that fourth-century ideology which recognized in Solon the father of Athenian democracy.

ACCORDING TO the tradition, Solon, after stepping down from office, departed on his travels with the hope that the Athenians, left to themselves, would learn how to live in conformity with the laws he had made. Disturbances soon broke out again, however, for wide-ranging as Solon's measures were, with a judicious blend of the radical and conservative, they angered certain elements of the population while not fully satisfying others. The wealthy, of course, had suffered losses from the cancellation of debts. The non-nobles among them had been rewarded by gaining access to the highest offices, provided they owned sufficient land, but the Eupatrids were outraged at this breach in their monopoly of governmental control. For generations this monopoly of the aristocrats and of the kings before them had had a religious sanction, because the noble families all claimed descent from a god or hero. Now Solon had granted equal recognition to the secular claim of landed wealth. At the other end of the social scale, the liberated debt slaves and *hektemors* naturally rejoiced in their freedom, but the troubled generation following Solon's archonship suggests that his measures to help them fell short of what was needed to give them a secure economic and political position in the state. Those who abandoned their little farms to relatives and came to Athens to seek work as artisans and laborers, presumably now as landless men, ceased to rate as citizens.

Between these two social extremes, the third class—the *zeugitai* or hoplites—seems to have remained dissatisfied. In some of Solon's later poems, written in defense of his measures against mounting criticism, he rebuked the *demos* which in its hope for plunder had wanted him to become tyrant. The ambiguity of the term *demos* has already been discussed in Chapter 5, and the suggestion was tentatively accepted that in the seventh and sixth centuries the *demos* probably referred primarily to men of hoplite status rather than to the masses as a whole, and that this group formed the main support of the leaders who became tyrants. It may well be, therefore, that the *demos* chided by Solon also consisted chiefly of hoplites. Solon had benefited these *zeugitai* by admitting them to the minor offices and to the Council of Four Hundred and also by the cancellation of debts, for some, if not many, of them may have been in danger from the harsh debt laws. They apparently, however, had hoped that Solon would become tyrant so that they could profit from the distribution of nobles' land as their counterparts had in Corinth, Sicyon, and Megara, and they felt thwarted and aggrieved when Solon refused to resort to confiscations. It is also probable that those men who were wealthy in movables but not in land, and hence were excluded from a share in the government, were adding to the atmosphere of discontent.

In the decades following Solon's reforms the chief political disputes centered about the archonship, revealing, as Aristotle (*Ath. Const.,* 13) points out, the importance of that office. Twice conditions were so disturbed that no archon could be appointed, the year therefore being designated as *anarchia.* In 582/1 a certain Damasias became archon and managed to remain in office for two years and two months before he was driven out. Then, presumably for the remaining ten months, a compromise was reached by appointing ten archons, five from the Eupatrids, three from the *agroikoi,* and two from the *demiourgoi.* The *agroikoi* probably were non-noble landowners whose access to the archonship was opposed by the Eupatrids striving to regain their monopoly of that magistracy, but no satisfactory explanation has yet been offered for the *demiourgoi*. It is hard to believe that wealthy landless craftsmen would have been admitted to the archonship; moreover, if these particular *demiourgoi* were craftsmen possessed of adequate land, there does not seem to be a sufficient distinction between them and the *agroikoi*.

According to both Herodotus (1.59) and Aristotle (*Ath. Const.*, 13), three parties existed or took shape in these years: the Pedieis (men of the plain), the Paraloi (men of the coast), and the Hyperakrioi (men beyond the hills) or the Diakrioi (men of the hills). The significance of these topographical names has caused much dispute. Aristotle, by stating that they derived their names from the areas in which the members farmed, clearly gives a regional significance to each party. In addition, familiar with fourth-century political ideologies, he assigns a political aim to each group and its leader. The men of the plain under Lycurgus wanted oligarchy, the men of the coast under Megacles, grandson of the Megacles involved in the Cylonian affair, seemed to pursue a moderate policy (Solonian?), while Pisistratus, leader of the men of the hills, seemed to be recognized as a popular leader. Since it is unreasonable to believe that all the oligarchs lived in the plains of Attica and all the "moderates" along the coast—which, in its entirety, stretched from the boundary with Megara to that with Boeotia—it has plausibly been suggested that the names of these parties were derived from the locations where their respective leaders lived and formed the original nucleus of their supporters.[27] The assumption is usually made that Lycurgus, like the well-known fourth-century Lycurgus, came from Boutadai, slightly west of Athens. The original region of the men of the plain, then, would have been the plain to the west and north of the city. Concerning the men of the coast, it is known that the Alcmaeonids, later at least, possessed land in city *demes* (districts) to the east of Athens and extending south to the sea. From this land close to the Saronic Gulf and from a sixth-century inscription and *kouros* statue which may suggest Alcmaeonid residence near Anaphlystos on the coast near the southern extremity of Attica, the designation "men of the coast" could have been coined to distinguish this "party" from the men of the plain.[28]

Herodotus states that the third party was formed by Pisistratus when, as a result of the quarrels between the two other parties, he began to aspire to the tyranny. The Herodotean name for this group is probably the more authentic one—Hyperakrioi, the men beyond the hills. From the point of view of anyone standing on the Acropolis of Athens, much of eastern Attica is beyond Hymettus—beyond the hills. The employment of the alternate name, Diakrioi, is easy to explain. Diakria was an old name for the northeastern section of Attica, and near its southern border lay Brauron, the birthplace of Pisistratus. Diakrioi and Hyperakrioi thus became almost synonymous, and certainly the inhabitants of those regions lived beyond the hills—the Hymettus, Pentelikos, and Parnes ranges. It must be kept in mind that Athens in the first half of the sixth century, although the *synoecism* of Attica had been achieved, was not yet what one could call a unified state. The chief power still resided with certain great families rather than with the Athenians as a whole working through an orderly form of government. It is probable that the noble and wealthy families that had their estates near Athens itself were able to dominate the government. Pisistratus, therefore, with the support of the chief families living beyond the hills, may have to some degree represented the opposition of the remoter parts of Attica to the dominance of the great families resident in or near the city itself.

Although Pisistratus' original followers probably came from eastern Attica, he must have had supporters in Athens also, for, as will be seen below, he was able to seize the tyranny when the assembly voted him a bodyguard. No ancient source explains just who these supporters were or how they were able to outvote the adherents of Lycurgus and Megacles. One instinctively thinks of the "masses," especially the landless *thetes* working in the city, but then one is faced with the question of whether these *thetes* rated sufficiently as citizens to be able to attend the assembly. It is probable that Pisistratus, when tyrant, granted citizenship to many who had not formerly possessed it. This seems a safe inference from the fact that after the expulsion of the Pisistratids in 510, the Athenians revised the citizen rolls because, as Aristotle (*Ath. Const.*, 13.5) says, "many people were sharing the citizenship who had no right to it." But if these people received citizenship only after Pisistratus held the tyranny, how could they have helped him to attain the tyranny in the first place? A definite answer to this question seems impossible, for too little is known about the status of the landless *thetes*. Although possession of land was almost certainly essential for membership in the three upper classes, it is possible, of course, that this requirement was eliminated for the *thetes*, whose citizenship at the most granted them admission to the assembly and the Heliaea. Possibly in that early period there was no efficient way, when an assembly was held, to distinguish between those *thetes* who possessed their small plots of land and those who had none; or on that particular day large numbers of the landless poor may have forced their way into the assembly to vote on behalf of a man who had a reputation as a fine general and as a friend of the people. This reputation may have encouraged the struggling landowning *thetes* as well to look with favor upon Pisistratus. On such problems, where the key evidence is lacking, speculation could go on indefinitely.

Since Pisistratus became tyrant about 560, he obviously must have been forming his party of the Hyperakrioi in the preceding years. The reputation he gained at that time in the war against Megara by capturing the harbor of Nisaea on the Saronic Gulf surely added greatly to his following. The fact that he was either polemarch in that war or at least the holder of a high command is good evidence that he belonged to a prominent family. According to Herodotus (5.65), the family traced itself back to the Neleids, who, coming to Athens from Pylos in the distant past, had supplied Athens with two of its ancient kings, Melanthus and Codrus. Nestor, the well-known character in the *Iliad* and *Odyssey*, was a son of Neleus, and the future tyrant of Athens was said to have been named Pisistratus in memory of Nestor's son Pisistratus. An Athenian by that name was archon about 669/8,[29] and hence belonged to the Eupatrids, but there is no way of knowing whether he belonged to the same family or not. The only other item known about Pisistratus before his seizure of the tyranny is that Plutarch (*Solon,* 1) reports that his mother and Solon's mother were cousins.

The accounts given by the ancient sources of Pisistratus' seizure of the tyranny are picturesque, even if very sketchy.[30] While his reputation was high from his exploits against Megara, he wounded himself and his mules and, driving into the agora of Athens, asked the people for a bodyguard to protect himself against the enemies who, he claimed, had attacked him. Presumably a meeting of the assembly was held—whether then or on a subsequent day is not stated—and on that occasion a certain Aristion, clearly a fellow conspirator, proposed and carried a motion that Pisistratus be granted a bodyguard of club-bearers. The fact that club-bearers, presumably from the lower classes, and not "hoplite-type" spear-bearers were provided may suggest a picture of a disorderly mob rather than of an official assembly. With their help Pisistratus soon seized the Acropolis and established himself as tyrant. Both Aristotle and Plutarch record that Solon, then a very old man, tried to no avail to stem the tide. Their account is probably correct, for some late verses of Solon, in which he chides the Athenians, clearly refer to these events: "If you suffer bitterly through your own fault, blame not the gods for it; for you yourselves have exalted these men by giving them guards, and therefore it is that you enjoy foul servitude. Each one of you walks with the steps of a fox; the mind of you all is vain; for you look to a man's tongue and shifty speech, and never to the deed he does." For Solon, who, when trying to establish *eunomia* through his reforms, had spurned the tyranny which many wished him to take, Pisistratus' coup must have seemed like the destruction of his whole life's work.

Herodotus says that despite the good administration of Pisistratus, he was soon driven out by the partisans of Megacles and Lycurgus, who had effected a reconciliation. Pisistratus may have retired only to his native Brauron. Before long his two opponents quarreled, and Megacles, being worsted, made overtures to Pisistratus, offering to restore him to the tyranny if Pisistratus would marry his daughter. Agreement was quickly reached and the two leaders prepared a scheme for the return, the childishness of which outraged Herodotus (1.60), who liked to think that the Greeks were brighter than the "barbarians" and that the Athenians were the brightest of the Greeks. The ruse, as described by Herodotus, is so amusing that it is worthwhile to give a translation of his account:

> In the village of Paeania there was a handsome woman called Phye, nearly six feet tall, whom they fitted out in a suit of armor and mounted in a chariot; then, after getting her to pose in the most striking attitude, they drove into Athens, where messengers who had preceded them were already, according to their instructions, talking to the people and urging them to welcome Pisistratus back, because the goddess Athene herself had shown him extraordinary honor and was bringing him home to her own Acropolis. They spread this nonsense all over the town, and it was not long before rumor reached the outlying villages that Athene was bringing Pisistratus back, and both villagers and townsfolk, convinced that the woman Phye was indeed the goddess, offered her their prayers and received Pisistratus with open arms.

Herodotus and many other Greek authors are full of such colorful stories, and each one has to be judged on its own merits as to its possible veracity. In this particular case, since a majority of the Athenians wanted the restoration of Pisistratus and since the Athenians always loved a good show, one may be justified in accepting the story and believing that the people delighted in the spectacle and the irreverent humor just as much as the perpetrators must have enjoyed the situation.

Pisistratus' second tenure of power in Athens was also brief. Herodotus (1.61), as so often giving a personal cause, says that Pisistratus, because he already had adult sons and because the Alcmaeonids were considered to be under a curse, did not consummate the marriage with Megacles' daughter, whereupon Megacles in anger reconciled himself with the party of the plain. Pisistratus, fearing their combined forces, departed secretly from Athens and went first to Eretria in Euboea, with whose aristocratic government he apparently already enjoyed friendly relations. Determined to return to Athens, he spent some years—ten according to Herodotus and Aristotle—in building up his resources. He established settlements at Rhaecelus on the Thermaic Gulf and, east of the Strymon River, in the region of Mt. Pangaeus, rich in silver and gold. Since Eretria had settled many colonies in the general area of Chalcidice, it is likely that in his activities in the north Pisistratus had the support of the Euboean city. The precious metals from Pangaeus in the form of bullion or cast into coins—for the use of coinage was now spreading—enabled Pisistratus then and for the rest of his life to hire mercenaries. Various cities, especially Thebes, which somehow he had laid under obligation to him, offered contributions. At some stage in his career he had married an Argive woman, and when he launched his attack from Eretria about the year 546, a thousand Argive mercenaries were among his forces. He landed at Marathon on the eastern coast of Attica, well within the region either of the Hyperakria or Diakria, and soon was joined by his partisans both from the country districts and from Athens itself. Marching southwestward, he defeated the opposing forces at Pallene in central Attica, and thereafter entrenched himself in Athens where he ruled continuously until his death in 528/7.

Pisistratus' administration was a remarkable one. Aristotle, for all his denunciation of tyrants in the *Politics,* records in the *Constitution of the Athenians* (16) that his tyranny was spoken of as a Golden Age. Like any tyrant, however, Pisistratus was an extraconstitutional ruler who had seized power by force, and hence had to maintain his position by means of force and wealth. His wealth, which enabled him to hire the necessary mercenaries, came to him, according to Herodotus (1.64), from the Strymon River—that is, the mines of Pangaeus—and from Attica; this latter presumably refers to the 5 percent tax he placed on agricultural produce and possibly also to an early working of the Laurium silver mines in the southeastern peninsula of Attica which subsequently became so famous. Some of his opponents had been killed at Pallene and others, including Megacles, fled into exile immediately after his victory. In the case of opponents who did not flee, he seized their sons as hostages and deposited them with his supporter, the Naxian Lygdamis, whom Pisistratus had established as tyrant in Naxos.

Although Pisistratus had had to overcome—and continued to face—opposition from many of the aristocratic and wealthy families, his task had been made easier by the fact that Solon's reforms had broken the back of aristocratic privilege. Consequently, Pisistratus allowed Solon's laws and "constitutional" arrangements to remain in effect. He did, however, interfere in elections to the extent that some members of his family or trusted supporters always held certain of the key magistracies, that is, the archonships. Since the archons after their year of office automatically entered the Council of the Areopagus, the result was that in the course of time this important body consisted primarily of men who had met his approval. If, as is probable, Pisistratus had been polemarch when he took Nisaea, then he himself was a member of the Areopagus. He also established a system of rural judges. The purpose of these officials, in addition to facilitating the administration of justice, was to replace, or at least to weaken, the hereditary jurisdiction of the noble families. The more the influence of those families could be curtailed, the greater would be the unity and strength of the state.

Pisistratus clearly was much interested in the welfare of the small farmers. Besides establishing the rural judges, he himself often made trips into the country districts, inspecting conditions and settling disputes. He also granted loans to the peasants, presumably on easy terms. Historians usually say or imply that he benefited his followers by dividing among them the confiscated lands of his exiled opponents. This statement may be true, for it tallies with what little is known about the methods of tyrants elsewhere, but, strangely enough, there is no evidence to this effect in any of the ancient accounts of Pisistratus. Actually there is no specific information on the Athenian procedure followed in confiscations in this early period. Could it be that only movable property was confiscated? The history of the Alcmaeonids is pertinent to this problem. They were banished several times in the sixth century (the first time possibly was at the close of the seventh), but when they returned they apparently resumed possession of their land. In their case, and in others too, there does not seem to have been a confiscation and public sale or distribution of the lands of the exiled family. The obscurity of this subject makes it almost impossible to give a satisfactory account of agrarian conditions in the sixth century, for there is no way to be sure just how the credit should be distributed between Solon and Pisistratus for the creation of the satisfied peasantry, which was so basic to the stability and success of fifth-century Athens down to the time of the Peloponnesian War.

Pisistratus' conduct of foreign relations, which for the most part was peaceful, marked the transition from Athens' former isolation to its future active participation in the affairs of the Aegean world. In fact, it was under the tyrants that Athens first began to have what can be called a foreign policy, a policy which in many ways was a harbinger of the role Athens was to play in the fifth century. Both before and after his final establishment as tyrant, Pisistratus maintained alliances with various Greek states or with factions or tyrants in them. He was on good terms with both Argos and Sparta in the Peloponnesus, with Boeotian Thebes in central Greece, and in the islands with Euboean Eretria and with Lygdamis, tyrant of Naxos. In northern Greece his friendly relations with at least one faction in Thessaly and with Macedonia seem confirmed by the fact that both the Thessalians and Amyntas of Macedonia offered grants of territory to Pisistratus' son Hippias after his expulsion from Athens (Herodotus, 5.94). Also in the north, the mines of Mt. Pangaeus continued to be his chief source of revenue. Pisistratus' policy towards the little Aegean island of Delos was particularly significant. Delos, the reputed birthplace of Apollo, had since early times been a religious center for the Ionians. Pisistratus purified the island by digging up all the graves within sight of the temple and moving the bones to another part of Delos. By this symbolic act he anticipated Athens' future claim to be the "mother" of the Ionians, a claim to which there may be an allusion in Solon's description of Attica as the oldest land of Ionia.

Most important of all for the future political and economic development of Athens was the activity around the Hellespont that was carried on by or under Pisistratus. About the beginning of the sixth century, Sigeum, near the entrance to the Hellespont, for possession of which the Athenians and Mytileneans were fighting, was awarded to the former through the arbitration of Periander of Corinth. Subsequently Athens lost control of the town to Mytilene, and it remained under the rule of this Lesbian city until Pisistratus recaptured it, probably sometime in the decade 540–530. He emphasized the significance he attached to the place by installing one of his sons as governor there. Some years before this, probably in the same year (546?) in which Pisistratus established his lasting rule in Athens, Athens gained possession of a far more important strip of territory,[31] the Thracian Chersonese on the European side of the Hellespont. According to one tradition the Athenians had founded a colony, Elaious, in that region about the same time as their first seizure of Sigeum. If so, the colonists presumably returned home or were engulfed by the natives in the subsequent years.

Herodotus (6.34–36) tells a colorful tale about the Athenian acquisition of the Chersonese in the time of Pisistratus. The Thracian Dolonci who lived in that peninsula, hard pressed in war by a neighboring tribe to the north, sent envoys to Delphi to ask advice from the oracle. The oracle's reply was that the Dolonci should take with them as founder of a colony that man who first should offer them hospitality after they had departed from the temple of Apollo. The envoys walked through Phocis and Boeotia, and it was not until they were in Attica that they found a hospitable reception. Their host was Miltiades, the son of Cypselus, an Olympic victor in the chariot race, who, although Pisistratus had the supreme power in Athens, was a man of prominence. Worried by the government of Pisistratus, he, after obtaining the blessing of Delphi, set out for the Chersonese with those Athenians who wished to join in the expedition, and on arriving in the territory was made tyrant by the Dolonci. The historical reality behind this story presumably is that the Dolonci appealed to Pisistratus for the dispatch of an Athenian colony and that Pisistratus' choice of leader for the colonists was Miltiades.

The family of Miltiades claimed to be descendants of Philaios, son of Ajax (Herodotus, 6.35), and hence belonged to the Philaidai *genos*. According to Plutarch (*Solon*, 10.2), Philaios, leaving his native Salamis, granted the island to the Athenians and took up residence in Attica at Brauron. This statement of Plutarch has been the only support for the argument that Pisistratus and Miltiades, both as members of the Hyperakrioi party, were collaborators. The objection to this interpretation is that Miltiades, when he entertained the Thracian Dolonci, was not living in Brauron to the east but on the Sacred Way west of Athens, probably at Lakiadai, the home and *deme* of his heirs, Miltiades the younger and his son Cimon. If Miltiades the elder resided in Lakiadai, it is quite possible that he belonged to the plain party. A suggestion that Cleisthenes, an Alcmaeonid, in his reforms in 508/7 deliberately gave the *deme* name Philaidai to the Brauron area with the intent of emphasizing a link between the Philaidai *genos* and the then discredited Pisistratids, may be correct.[32]

The father of the elder Miltiades, Cypselus, had been archon about 597.[33] The prominence of the Philaidai *genos* was also revealed by the fact that another member, Hippocleides, was archon in the year 566 when the Great Panathenaea were established. About a decade earlier he had been second only to the Alcmaeonid Megacles in the famous wooing of Agariste, daughter of the Sicyonian tyrant Cleisthenes. The association of wealthy and noble families with the so-called aristocracy-destroying tyrants is an interesting aspect of the phenomenon of tyranny. The name of Miltiades' father, Cypselus, is clear evidence that there had been intermarriage with the Cypselids of Corinth. The wealth of the family is proved by the facts that Miltiades had been an Olympic victor in the four-horse chariot race and that his half-brother, Cimon, had had the unusual distinction of being a three-time victor at Olympia with the same horses in this most expensive contest (Herodotus, 6.103).

Miltiades is sometimes described as an opponent of Pisistratus. This is unlikely, for it is hard to believe that Pisistratus would have allowed an enemy to establish himself in a region as important as the Thracian Chersonese. It is more probable that Miltiades was not an active opponent of Pisistratus, but a man so powerful that it was less embarrassing and dangerous for each to have his own sphere in which to rule. The relationship between the Chersonese under Miltiades and Athens under Pisistratus is difficult to define in constitutional terms. It may well be that, since tyranny was an unconstitutional and personal phenomenon, there was no strictly legal relationship. That Athens maintained some sort of control over the Chersonese, however, seems proved by the fact that after the death of Miltiades the elder and his immediate successor, Stesagoras, the Pisistratids sent out Miltiades the younger, the nephew of the original colonizer, to take control of the region.

Athenian settlements on both sides of the Hellespont opened access for Athenian merchants to the rich world of the Black Sea. Importation of grain from this area undoubtedly increased in this period, and in exchange Athens exported the products of its craftsmen. Pisistratus' wide circle of connections and alliances must have opened many markets to the Athenians. As usual in these early centuries, the chief evidence for matters of economic history is provided by pottery. The export of Attic black-figure pottery, which had increased in the time of Solon, increased still more under Pisistratus—good testimony that both these statesmen were concerned with broadening the economy which had been almost exclusively agricultural. From about the middle of the sixth century Attic pottery began to oust Corinthian ware from many markets and clearly became the most popular pottery in the Greek world, a popularity which increased with the appearance of the red-figure technique about 530. The opening of new markets probably stimulated other crafts in Attica, although specific evidence is lacking. Pisistratus' great building program, however, certainly furnished employment to large numbers of artisans and laborers. Among these buildings were the temple of Athena on the Acropolis, the fountain house called Enneakrounos or the Nine Springs, the Telesterion (initiation hall) at Eleusis, and the huge temple of Zeus southeast of the Acropolis on the banks of the Ilissus, which remained uncompleted until the time of the Roman emperor Hadrian.

One of Pisistratus' greatest services to Athens—if not the greatest—was that for a whole generation under his rule and that of his son Hippias, the country enjoyed almost complete freedom from factional struggle. It is true that the tyranny suppressed political liberty, which would have been disastrous to the development of Athens if the absolutism of tyranny had become permanently rooted. Political liberty prior to Pisistratus, however, despite the reforms of Solon, had been largely a prerogative of the great families. The influence of these families, both aristocrats and wealthy non-nobles, had depended primarily on their local following, and the rivalry of these local groups prevented Athens from becoming a really united state. It was by capitalizing on these local and family animosities, of course, that Pisistratus had been able to establish his tyranny. As tyrant he contributed greatly to the growth of a united state. His motives undoubtedly were partly selfish—the desire to strengthen his own position—but it seems unjust to a truly great man to deny that he was also thinking of the welfare of Athens. On the basis of the limited evidence, it seems clear that there were three ways in which he attempted to foster a spirit of unity among the Athenians: his conciliatory attitude to some prominent families and his suppression of those stubbornly resistant to his rule by exile or seizing their sons as hostages; his building program, which not only provided employment to many but also must have increased the pride of Athenians in their city; and his religious policy.

The religious policy of Pisistratus, which can be detected only in general terms, was directed towards reducing the influence of various local cults by giving them a national significance, and by emphasizing those deities that had a more universal appeal. A precinct was set aside on the Acropolis for the cult of Artemis of Brauron. The Eleusinian Mysteries were brought under Athenian control, although two noble families of Eleusis, the Eumolpidae and the Kerykes, remained in charge of the ritual. The worship of Dionysus, always popular with the common people, was encouraged. Despite a legend concerning the mythical Athenian king Amphiction, it was probably under Pisistratus that the cult of Dionysus was transferred from the Attic town of Eleutherae on the Boeotian border to Athens and that a temple was built to this god for whom celebrations in various forms had presumably existed locally in Attica for generations.[34] It is very likely that Pisistratus was responsible for organizing the famous festival—the City Dionysia or the Great Dionysia—whose choruses in honor of the god ultimately developed into Athenian tragedy and comedy. Athena was honored with a new temple on the Acropolis, and her festival, the Great Panathenaea, first established in 566 under the archon Hippocleides, a kinsman of Miltiades, was developed to emphasize that she was the goddess of all the Athenians. In the same general period, as is evident from the remaining sculpture and vase painting, interest began to increase in the legend of Theseus, who ultimately was recognized as the great Athenian hero and the king reputedly responsible for the *synoecism* of Attica.[35] In still another way Pisistratus, or his son Hippias, succeeded in emphasizing the unity of Attica and glorifying Athena. The beginning of Athenian coinage is now usually dated to approximately 560 B.C. For some time the coins had no national type but were marked with what some scholars suggest were the devices of certain of the great families—the so-called *wappenmünzen*. At a date which cannot be fixed precisely, but which numismatists think should be assigned to the later years of Pisistratus or to the rule of Hippias (528–510), coins of the type which were to become the trademark of Athens began to appear—the famous owls, with the head of Athena on the obverse and her little owl on the reverse.[36]

Pisistratus died in 528/7 and was succeeded by his oldest son, Hippias, although at least one of the younger sons, Hipparchus, shared in the management of affairs. A fragment of an inscription discovered in the excavations of the Athenian agora and published in 1939 has added important information to the little that is known about the rule of Hippias down to the time of the assassination of his brother Hipparchus in 514. This stone, on which were inscribed six names in consecutive lines, clearly was part of a list of eponymous archons, inscribed, to judge from the letter forms, probably in the 420s b.c.[37] The second, third, and fourth names are Hippias, Cleisthenes, and Miltiades, and the sixth is almost certainly Pisistratus. Since it is known from Dionysius of Halicarnassus (*Roman Antiquities,* 7.3) that a Miltiades was archon in 524/3, it follows that Hippias was archon in 526/5, Cleisthenes in 525/4, and Pisistratus "the younger," the son of Hippias, in 522/1. The presence of the names Hippias and Pisistratus confirms Thucydides' statement (6.54) that, to secure their position, the Pisistratids tried to have one of their number always in office.

The appearance of the name Cleisthenes in this list reveals an error that Herodotus made in his account of the Alcmaeonids. Herodotus (1.64) says that after Pisistratus' victory at Pallene, which established him firmly in power, Megacles, the head of the Alcmaeonid clan, went into exile. The implication of his account is that the Alcmaeonids remained in exile continuously until a generation later, when Cleisthenes, the son of Megacles, in 511/10 succeeded in driving out the Pisistratids with the help of the Spartans. Herodotus' mistake is understandable. When he was in Athens in the 440s, the Alcmaeonids, with whom Pericles was connected by marriage, were very prominent, and it was from them that Herodotus derived much of his information about the earlier history of Athens. Since in the mid-fifth century tyranny was considered an abomination by the flourishing Athenian democracy, and the Pisistratids were damned both as tyrants and as collaborators with the Persians in the Persian Wars, it would not have been surprising if Herodotus' Alcmaeonid informants failed to mention to him that at one time their renowned ancestor Cleisthenes had cooperated with Hippias. There is no information concerning the time at which the Alcmaeonids returned from the exile into which they fled in 546, but the most logical inference is the beginning of Hippias' rule, when he might well have tried to strengthen his position by granting an amnesty to at least some of his father's enemies. Since the Alcmaeonids returned to Athens from exile again in 511/10, it is clear that their collaboration with Hippias was only temporary. It was probably after Hipparchus' murder in 514, which caused Hippias to become a tyrant in the derogatory sense of the term, that the Alcmaeonids were forced to flee into exile once again.

The name of Miltiades on the stone confirms the statement of Dionysius of Halicarnassus that there was an Athenian archon by that name in 524/3. A few words should be said about this archon, who can safely be identified with Miltiades the younger, the subsequent hero of the battle of Marathon, for the relations of the Pisistratids to him and his family illustrate the changing policies that tyrants had to adopt towards powerful family groups. This Miltiades was the son of Cimon, the half-brother of the Miltiades who, probably in 546, with the approval of Pisistratus, established himself and Athenian control in the Thracian Chersonese. Cimon, who was wealthy enough to win the four-horse chariot race three times at the Olympic Games, had been banished by Pisistratus. He achieved his return to Athens by having his second Olympic victory in 532/1 declared in the name of Pisistratus. Shortly after Pisistratus' death in 528/7, the year in which Cimon won his third victory at Olympia, the latter was murdered, according to Herodotus (6.103) by the sons of Pisistratus. If the story is true—and Herodotus' willingness to accept anti-tyrant scandal justifies doubt—the crime suggests a revival of the former Pisistratid hostility towards Cimon and jealousy of his wealth and Olympic fame. Cimon left two sons, Stesagoras and Miltiades. At the time of Cimon's death or murder, Stesagoras, the older son, was with his uncle, Miltiades, in the Chersonese, and on the death of his uncle he succeeded to his position in the Chersonese. The younger son, who was in Athens when his father was slain, was well treated by the Pisistratids and in 524/3 was allowed to become eponymous archon. About eight years later, after the death of his brother Stesagoras in the Chersonese, he was dispatched by Hippias to take control of that very important region.

In their domestic policy, as in their concern for the Hellespont, the sons of Pisistratus apparently followed the lines laid down by their father. The little information that is available relates chiefly to matters of a cultural nature.[38] Festivals such as the Dionysia and the Great Panathenaea were made more elaborate; according to one tradition it was Hipparchus, rather than his father, who added to the latter festival the recitations of the Homeric poems. Hipparchus was greatly interested in poetry, and it was he who attracted to Athens the best-known poets of the period—men like Simonides of Ceos and Anacreon of Teos. The younger Pisistratus carried on the tradition of erecting religious monuments by dedicating in his archonship an altar of Apollo in the precinct assigned to Apollo and the altar of the twelve gods in the agora. In the course of time this last altar came to serve as the central milestone for the Attic road system. Hippias and his brothers may well have thought that their rule was firmly established, when suddenly in 514 this sense of security received a rude shock in the murder of Hipparchus.

Herodotus (5.55–65), Thucydides (6.53–59), and Aristotle, in the *Constitution of the Athenians* (18), all refer to the slaying of Hipparchus, the latter two specifically stating that it resulted from a love affair. A handsome youth named Harmodius had as a lover a somewhat older man, Aristogiton. Hipparchus (in Aristotle, Thessalus, a still younger son of Pisistratus), who had the reputation of being erotically inclined, was also attracted by Harmodius, but his advances were repulsed. In anger, the Pisistratid decided to seek vengeance, while refraining from violence, by casting a stigma on Harmodius or his family. When Harmodius' sister was chosen to be a basket-carrier in the Panathenaic procession, Hipparchus caused her to be rejected on the grounds that she was unworthy of the honor (in Aristotle, her brother was termed unworthy). Harmodius and his lover were outraged by the insult; in addition, Aristogiton feared that Harmodius might be taken from him by force. They, therefore, with a few fellow conspirators, planned to assassinate Hipparchus, apparently hoping that after Hipparchus had been struck down, other citizens would join with them in an effort to overthrow the tyranny. The occasion of the Panathenaic procession was chosen for the deed. On the appointed day Harmodius and Aristogiton saw one of their accomplices talking with Hippias and, believing that they had been betrayed, without waiting for the appropriate moment, they fell upon Hipparchus and killed him. Harmodius was slain on the spot by the guards; Aristogiton escaped temporarily, but soon was captured and put to death under torture.

The deed of Harmodius and Aristogiton became part of the proud traditions of Athens. Before the end of the sixth century they were hailed by certain groups in Athens as the great tyrannicides. The sculptor Antenor made a group statue of them, which was carried off to Persia in 480, after the Persians had captured Athens. This group was restored to Athens many generations later by either Alexander the Great or one of his successors. In 477/6, after the Persians had been expelled from Greece, two other sculptors, Critius and Nesiotes, made another group statue which was set up in the agora. Harmodius and Aristogiton were honored by a tomb in the Ceramicus (similar to the American Arlington), where still in the last third of the fourth century—and probably also much later—the polemarch offered to them the sacrifices due to heroes (*Ath. Const.*, 58.1). Public maintenance in the Prytaneion (town hall) was voted to the oldest living descendant of each. At banquets they were toasted in drinking songs (*skolia*) such as the following: "In a branch of myrtle I shall carry my sword just as Harmodius and Aristogiton, when they slew the tyrant and made Athens free (*isonomos*)" (Athenaeus, 15.695).

To one familiar with the accounts of the slaying of Hipparchus in the ancient sources, the extravagant honors heaped upon Harmodius and Aristogiton and their heroization as tyrannicides seem totally illogical. Thucydides and Aristotle state flatly that Hippias as the oldest son of Pisistratus was the man who became the real ruler (tyrant) after his father's death, and that the murder of Hipparchus, far from overthrowing the tyranny and liberating Athens, actually, through the fear and suspicions it aroused in Hippias, turned his mild and enlightened rule into a cruel and vengeful despotism. Thucydides, in particular, protests against the commonly held view that Hipparchus was the successor in the tyranny to Pisistratus, and goes to considerable pains to prove by what seems to be irrefutable evidence that Hippias as the eldest son was *the* tyrant in Athens after his father's death. Herodotus, Thucydides, and Aristotle all agree that it was some three years after Hipparchus' assassination that the rule of Hippias, now become harsh, was overthrown by the Alcmaeonids and the Spartans.

If these three authors all insist that Harmodius and Aristogiton did not liberate Athens, with Herodotus saying specifically (6.123) that the Alcmaeonids rather than Harmodius and Aristogiton really set Athens free, why did the hero-cult of the tyrannicides take such firm hold on Athenian imagination? Many scholars have tried to answer this question. The remarks made here are merely an attempt to mention, in part, some of the most telling arguments.[39] A definitive answer to the problem is unlikely because of the inadequacy of the sources, but the subject is important for the light it casts on how propaganda can distort evidence and mislead the public. In presenting this summary it will be necessary to anticipate briefly certain matters that will subsequently be treated in some detail.

Hipparchus was murdered at the Panathenaic festival of 514. In the following three years, as Hippias became more "tyrannical," many noble families, including the Alcmaeonids, fled or were exiled from Athens. These nobles, apparently under the leadership of the Alcmaeonid Cleisthenes, made various unsuccessful attempts, costly in lives, to return to Attica. To the embittered and thwarted exiles it is natural that Harmodius and Aristogiton, members of the old *genos* Gephyraei, became a symbol of their anti-tyranny passions, for these two men had been pioneers in the attempt to eradicate tyranny. The names of Harmodius and Aristogiton probably were often celebrated in aristocratic drinking songs. When these noble families failed through their own efforts to "liberate" Athens, Cleisthenes succeeded in persuading Delphi to urge Sparta to oust Hippias. Following this expulsion of the Pisistratids, the aristocratic families became the dominant power in Athens for several years. It was in this period of their supremacy, apparently, that the glorification of Harmodius and Aristogiton began to take firm root. As the first heroes and martyrs in the struggle to destroy Pisistratid rule, they were honored as the men who restored equal privileges to the noble families. This idea is expressed in the *skolion* quoted above, for surely in an aristocratic drinking song the *isonomia* for which the heroes were responsible refers to the equal rights enjoyed by an aristocracy that is not endangered by some force above those rights, and not, as is sometimes argued, to the universal equality guaranteed by the Athenian democracy. For what the date is worth, Pliny the Elder (*Naturalis Historia*, 34.17) states that Antenor fashioned his statue of the tyrannicides in the year in which the kings were expelled from Rome (510/9).

The aristocratic supremacy in Athens was shattered in 508/7 when Cleisthenes, failing to obtain leadership among the nobles, turned to the people (*demos*) and with their support carried through a reorganization of the government which became the basic framework for Athenian democracy. Prior to this epoch-making political change of Cleisthenes it is probable that the Alcmaeonids had shared in the aristocratic movement to glorify Harmodius and Aristogiton, but with their swing to the people they must have begun to emphasize their own particular role in 511/10 in ousting the Pisistratids. In the ensuing generations the hostility between the conservative Athenian families and the maverick Alcmaeonids increased. Shortly after his governmental reforms Cleisthenes disappeared from the scene, possibly because of his alleged effort to effect an alliance with Persia. At the battle of Marathon in 490 the Alcmaeonids were accused of an attempt to betray Athens to the Persians and the aged Hippias, who had sought refuge with them. In the middle of the fifth century Pericles, connected with the Alcmaeonids through his mother, was largely responsible for establishing the "radical" democracy. His enemies, likening him to a new Pisistratus (Plutarch, *Pericles*, 7.1), increased their emphasis on the role of Harmodius and Aristogiton as the true tyrannicides, while the Alcmaeonids, naturally, stressed the fact that it was Cleisthenes and the Alcmaeonids who in reality ended the tyranny by expelling Hippias and the Pisistratids.

In the Periclean Age Herodotus spent some time in Athens in the 440s. It is obvious from his history that his account of earlier Athenian history was much influenced by Alcmaeonid traditions. In his discussion of the Pisistratids he states clearly that it was the Alcmaeonids rather than Harmodius and Aristogiton who liberated Athens. A generation later Thucydides, a great admirer of Pericles, expressed his convictions even more strongly. He asserts that the slaying of Hipparchus by Harmodius and Aristogiton was the result of a love affair and that the overthrow of Hippias and the Pisistratids three years later was the achievement of the Spartans and the Alcmaeonids. His careful research into the problem and his conviction that Hippias, the eldest son, was the actual tyrant may have been stimulated by the publication in the last decade of the fifth century of the first Atthidography, in which Hellanicus apparently repeated the popular version of Harmodius and Aristogiton as the tyrannicides. Aristotle about a century later, following Thucydides in general, emphasizes the three years of increased "tyranny" under Hippias after the murder of his younger brother. The glorification of Harmodius and Aristogiton, however, continued to flourish, and at some point in popular thinking Hipparchus replaced Hippias as the true tyrant and the three-year interval between 514/13 and 511/10 became part of the tyranny of Hipparchus. The vitality of this version is demonstrated, for example, by the fact that in the famous Parian Chronicle, erected in 264/3, one can still read under the heading for the year 511/10, "Harmodius and Aristogiton slew Hipparchus, successor of Pisistratus, and the Athenians expelled the Pisistratids . . . when Harpaktides was archon at Athens."

After his brother's murder Hippias executed or banished many who he suspected were a threat to his rule. It must have been at this time that Cleisthenes and the Alcmaeonids went into exile again. Under their leadership the exiles made various attempts to effect their return, but for several years these attempts all ended in failure. One would like to know if Hippias was able to use Athenian soldiers in opposing these attacks or if he had to rely entirely on mercenaries. If, as is probable, he had more confidence in mercenaries, he may have found it increasingly difficult to hire them, for the Persian conquest of Thrace ca. 513 must have prevented, or at least jeopardized, his access to the gold and silver mines of Mt. Pangaeus, which had been one of the chief sources of revenue for Pisistratus.

In fact, the expansion of the Persian Empire had already completely changed the complexion of the Near East. The conquest of Lydia in 546 had been quickly followed by the subjection of all the Greeks on the coast of Asia Minor, including the Pisistratid outpost at Sigeum on the Hellespont. As his position in Athens became increasingly insecure, Hippias turned to the eastern giant for support. He sealed an alliance with the Persian-supported tyrant of Lampsacus on the Asiatic shore of the Hellespont by giving his daughter in marriage to the tyrant's son. Thucydides (6.59) quotes the epitaph which was inscribed on her tomb in Lampsacus. Since Lampsacus and the Chersonese had been intermittently at war almost since the arrival of the elder Miltiades in that peninsula, this alliance must have strained or terminated Hippias' relations with the current dynast of the Chersonese, Miltiades the younger. In Attica itself, Hippias began to fortify Munichia, a steep hill in the eastern part of the Piraeus, thinking that it might be necessary to take up residence in a strong place which also had immediate access to the sea.

WHEN THE exiles failed by their own efforts to expel the Pisistratids, the Alcmaeonids took steps to win the cooperation of the priests of Apollo at Delphi. They obtained from the Amphictionic Council a contract to build a temple to Apollo in place of the older one which had burned down a generation earlier. They constructed the temple on a more elegant scale than the plans specified, for they used Parian marble rather than porous stone for the front part. Whether they met the extra expense from their own wealth or by skillful manipulation of the funds collected for the building is unknown; it was later said of them that they had bribed the priestess to tell the Spartans to liberate Athens. Herodotus (5.62–65) relates that whenever a Spartan arrived to consult the oracle, whether on public or private business, he always received the same reply: "Free Athens." The Spartans finally acquiesced, persuaded partly by their respect for the oracle, partly by their distrust of tyranny, and probably chiefly by their dislike of the friendship which existed between Argos and the Pisistratids. The first Spartan expedition was defeated, but the second, under King Cleomenes, marched on Athens and blockaded the Pisistratids in the Acropolis. Unfortunately for the Pisistratids, who were prepared to withstand a long siege which probably would have discouraged Cleomenes, their children were captured as they were being smuggled out of the country. To recover the children, they agreed to the terms imposed by the Athenian exiles accompanying Cleomenes that they leave Attica within five days. Hippias and the other Pisistratids went first to Sigeum, then to Lampsacus, and from there to King Darius of Persia. Twenty years later, as Thucydides (6.59) remarks, Hippias in his old age accompanied the Persians on the expedition which culminated in Marathon.

The Pisistratids were expelled in the archonship of Harpaktides, 511/10 B.C., through the efforts of the Alcmaeonids and the military power of Sparta. Although later Athenian sources tried to conceal the fact, it seems certain that part of the price Athens had to pay for its liberation was to become an ally of Sparta. Following the expulsion of Hippias, the noble families, long suppressed, became dominant again in Athens. In the struggle for power two men emerged as leaders: Cleisthenes, the head of the Alcmaeonids, and Isagoras, whom Aristotle, deceived by Alcmaeonid propaganda, called a friend of the tyrants, but who is more rationally to be thought of as one of the nobles who acquiesced sufficiently in the rule of the Pisistratids to have been allowed to remain in Athens. The archon for 510/9 was probably Skamandrios, under whom a decree was passed outlawing torture of citizens (Andocides, *Mysteries,* 43). This date is uncertain, but it is logical to place such a measure immediately after the overthrow of the tyrants when the memory of the torture of Aristogiton, and possibly of other citizens in Hippias' last years, was still vividly in the minds of the Athenians. In the rivalry for leadership, Cleisthenes, despite his important contribution to the expulsion of the Pisistratids, lost out to Isagoras—good evidence for the unpopularity of the Alcmaeonids with their peers among the oligarchically-minded upper classes. Isagoras was elected eponymous archon for the year 508/7.

At this point Cleisthenes took a step which was of incalculable significance for the future development of Athens (Herodotus, 5.66, 69; Aristotle, *Ath. Const.,* 20). This man, who formerly like all arisotcrats had disdained the *demos,* now won its support for his party by proposing a group of liberal reforms. The *demos* here clearly means the commoners in general, whose lot, bettered by the Pisistratids, had been jeopardized by the return of the aristocratic families to power. With their support he succeeded in carrying through a series of decrees which provided the framework for the future Athenian democracy. It is possible, of course, that Cleisthenes, exasperated by the reactionary attitude of the nobles, sincerely revolutionized his political thinking, but in the ancient sources the only motive ascribed to his actions was his rivalry for leadership with his fellow oligarch Isagoras. His reforms, however, were so well adapted to increasing the participation of all citizens in the workings of government that it is hard to believe that he had not given serious thought to the problem of liberalizing the state. If, on the other hand, the explanation for his actions offered by the ancient sources is correct, it is certainly one of the great ironies of history that these measures, which enabled an Athens based on a secular democracy to emerge from an archaic state still based largely on oligarchic principles and religious rites, were carried through by a man thinking entirely of winning out in a power struggle with his fellow oligarchs.

Since Aristotle (*Ath. Const.*, 21) dates Cleisthenes' program "in the archonship of Isagoras," it is almost certain that the reforms were proposals submitted to the assembly, which, when ratified, became decrees, dated by the archon under whom they were passed.[40] Since Isagoras, the bitter opponent of Cleisthenes and his proposals, was archon, the magistrate who at that time presided over the assembly, one wonders how motions concerning these measures ever reached the floor of the assembly. If Solon, as is probable, had established a Council of Four Hundred and that council year after year had continued to function even under the tyranny, then it is possible that Cleisthenes persuaded the councillors of the wisdom of his reforms, with the result that they, in their *probouleutic* capacity, included them in the agenda for the assembly. It is also possible, of course, that the procedure was less parliamentary. Cleisthenes would have seen to it that knowledge of his proposed reforms circulated widely among the people; on the day of the assembly, the people may have taken affairs into their own hands and demanded in such a threatening way that the proposals be submitted to their vote that Isagoras would not have dared to oppose them. In any case, the measures were enacted. The discomfited Isagoras then appealed to King Cleomenes of Sparta, since Athens was not behaving as a good oligarchic ally should. At the suggestion of Isagoras, Cleomenes sent a herald to Athens with instructions that Cleisthenes and many other Athenians, who were tainted with the hereditary curse incurred over a century earlier because of the sacrilege associated with the murder of the followers of Cylon, be banished. Cleisthenes immediately retired secretly from Athens (Herodotus, 5.69–72).

Shortly thereafter Cleomenes arrived in person with a small force and proceeded to expel as "accursed" 700 Athenian families whose names had been supplied to him by Isagoras. He then tried to abolish the Council and to entrust the government to Isagoras and 300 of his partisans. The aim clearly was to purge the more liberal elements and to establish a narrow oligarchy. When the Council resisted, Cleomenes with his troops, together with Isagoras and his partisans, seized the Acropolis. Thereupon the rest of the Athenians in anger besieged the Acropolis for two days. On the third day Cleomenes and the Spartans were allowed to return home under a truce while, according to Herodotus (5.72), the other captives were imprisoned and then executed. Aristotle (*Ath. Const.*, 20.3) says that Cleomenes and all those with him were allowed to depart under a truce, and this is apparently the correct version. Herodotus himself (5.74–76) tells of a subsequent attempt by Cleomenes to invade Attica for the purpose of establishing as tyrant Isagoras, who had departed from the Acropolis with him. This expedition proceeded as far as Eleusis, where dissatisfaction among the allies and friction between Cleomenes and the other Spartan king, Demaratus, caused the whole undertaking to be abandoned. Interesting evidence, based on a decree, is provided for this abortive campaign by the scholiast's comment on line 273 of Aristophanes' *Lysistrata,* which also proves that Herodotus' statement about the execution of all those besieged on the Acropolis except Cleomenes and the Spartans was misinformed. The passage reads in part: "Of those [Isagoras and his partisans] who had seized Eleusis with Cleomenes, the Athenians razed their houses, confiscated their property, and voted sentence of death upon them [*in absentia*]. And having inscribed this on a bronze *stēlē* they set it up in the Acropolis beside the ancient temple."

There has been a great deal of controversy concerning the identity of the council which resisted when Cleomenes tried to abolish it and establish Isagoras in power with 300 of his partisans. Of the three possibilities advocated, one can surely be ruled out. Since this episode occurred so soon after the enactment of Cleisthenes' program, the council could hardly refer to his proposed Council of Five Hundred, for there would have been insufficient time for the establishment of this new body. The Council of the Areopagus is a possibility, but more probable is the Council of Four Hundred, which may have been the body that brought Cleisthenes' proposals before the assembly. Certainty is obviously impossible when the evidence is so scanty and ambiguous that there are only three possible references to this Council of Four Hundred—first, when Solon is supposed to have established it; second, the passage under discussion; and third, Aristotle's statement (*Ath. Const.,* 21.3) that Cleisthenes made the council consist of 500 instead of 400 members.

Immediately after Cleomenes and his followers, both Spartan and Athenian, had been expelled from Athens, the Athenians, presumably the assembly, recalled Cleisthenes and the 700 families who had recently been driven into exile. It was then, apparently, that the necessary steps were taken so that the reforms of Cleisthenes, which already had been voted, could be put into effect.

To UNDERSTAND the purpose and significance of Cleisthenes' measures, which revolutionized the structure of the Athenian state to its very foundation, one must keep clearly in mind the framework of the previous Athenian state. The Athenians were grouped in the four Ionian tribes, each tribe consisting of a certain number of phratries, which in turn were composed of one or more *genē* and also the non-*gennētai* or commoners. These institutions were based on the kinship principle, whether real or fictitious, and the members were further united by the cults in which they participated. Since the *gennētai* and commoners belonging to a particular phratry were probably more or less neighbors, and since the several phratries which were the components of each tribe presumably were located in the same general area, it would seem to follow that the tribes also had territorial or regional characteristics. These four tribes, therefore, based on both the kinship and regional principles, were particularly susceptible to the domination of powerful and wealthy families. It is important also to remember that citizenship depended on membership in a phratry, an institution which, with its kinship and religious traditions, was not suited to the admission of new members beyond the children of the current members.

Although Solon at the beginning of the sixth century introduced many reforms and weakened the monopoly of the nobles (Eupatrids), the government as he left it was still based on the four Ionian tribes. The little that is known of the history of Athens in the first half of the sixth century reveals clearly that the "constitution" gave free play to the disruptive rivalries and combinations of the great families. This situation was accentuated by the emergence, apparently distinct from the four tribes, of the three factions of the plain, the coast, and the hill (Hyperakrioi), each having its nucleus in a particular region. It was largely by capitalizing on the feuds between these factions that Pisistratus had been able to establish himself as tyrant. The Pisistratids during their fifty years (with intermissions) as tyrants were able to suppress the centrifugal tendencies in Attica and to make the land a united whole as it never had been before. Under them, despite the tyranny, Athens was revealing its tremendous promise. No sooner were the Pisistratids expelled, however, than the struggles between the powerful families, with the old disruptive effects, began again. To curb these long-standing evils and the current chaos, Cleisthenes, after his return to Athens following the expulsion of Cleomenes, began to carry out his proposals which the assembly had ratified shortly before.

The most detailed description of the measures which Cleisthenes took is presented in chapter 21 of Aristotle's *Constitution of the Athenians*, but unfortunately many points are left unexplained. The core of the reforms was the establishment of ten tribes based on *demes* (townships) as fundamental units in place of the four old Ionian kinship tribes based on *genē* and phratries. These ten new tribes were not territorial in the sense that each represented one particular section of Attica, for ten such blocks would still have left too much scope for the operation of local influences, although less than under the previous four tribes. Each of the ten new tribes was composed of territory from the three different regions into which Cleisthenes divided Attica: the city and its surroundings; the coast, except for the area immediately south, southeast, and southwest of Athens, which was included in the city region; and the inland area. A tribe, accordingly, was composed of thirds (*trittyes*), a *trittys* from the city, a *trittys* from the coast, and a *trittys* from the inland area. In each *trittys* the basic unit was one which had developed naturally—the *deme,* the equivalent of a modern village, town, or township. Since the borders of the *trittyes,* especially in the country districts, sometimes conformed to natural phenomena, *trittyes* often varied considerably in size both of physical area and of population. Depending on the size of the *demes,* there might be one or several in each *trittys.* In the city region the *trittyes* naturally were smaller in area and larger in population. Some of the component *demes* of these ten city *trittyes* must have somewhat resembled the wards of a modern city.

The sketch just given should make clear that Cleisthenes, as Aristotle says, wished to "mix up" the population, for in each tribe there would be citizens from the city, from the coast, and from the inland area. Aristotle adds that Cleisthenes assigned the *trittyes* to the tribes, three to each, by lot. It is hard, however, to accept literally the statement that these assignments were made entirely by lot. Since the *trittyes* certainly varied in size of population, Cleisthenes, who wanted the tribes to have approximately equal numbers of citizens in view of military and political responsibilities, probably took steps to prevent any one tribe, for example, from consisting of three large or of three small *trittyes.* To secure tribes of more or less equal population, therefore, the assignment of *trittyes* to tribes could hardly have been left entirely to chance.[41]

The inadequacy of the source material makes it impossible to comprehend all the methods which Cleisthenes used in establishing this elaborate structure, or all the motives which influenced him, but the following observation of a scholar, although somewhat technical, will serve to illustrate his technique and purposes.[42] The coastal *trittys,* named Tetrapoleis, of the tribe Aiantis was located in the northeastern section of Attica. From prehistoric times there had existed there a religious league of four communties (known as the Tetrapolis), Marathon, Oinoe, Trikorynthos, and Probalinthos, and this league, even after it had been included in the *synoecism* of Attica, continued to survive as an independent cult organization, performing sacrifices and sending sacred embassies to shrines such as Delphi down at least to the first century B.C. These four *demes,* which formed a compact territorial group, had been an area of strong Pisistratid influence; it was at Marathon that Pisistratus landed when he returned from exile to establish his permanent tyranny, and Hippias led the Persians to Marathon in 490. Cleisthenes, when he set up the *trittys* of Tetrapoleis, detached the *deme* of Probalinthos and attached it not to the adjoining (on the south) coast *trittys* of the tribe Aigeis, for that contained Pisistratus' home town of Brauron, but to the coast *trittys* of the tribe Pandionis, which was still further to the south. Probalinthos, consequently, as far as the new tribal organization was concerned, was left as an enclave, separated from the *trittys* to which its fellow *demes* in the religious league belonged and serving as a barrier between Pisistratid influences in the neighboring coast *trittyes* of the tribes Aiantis and Aigeis. The place of Probalinthos in the coastal *trittys* of Aiantis was taken by the *deme* Rhamnous, a step that was logical from its adjacent location, but also advantageous, in Cleisthenes' eyes, because its cults were quite different from those of the Tetrapolis. In connection with this same tribe Aiantis it is significant to note that Aphidna, probably the name of the inland *trittys* bordering on the coast *trittys* with its Pisistratid influences, was the home of the *genos* Gephyraioi to which the tyrannicides Harmodius and Aristogiton had belonged. It seems clear, therefore, that these two *trittyes* had been established and organized with the definite purpose of trying to weaken the remnants of Pisistratid influence and also to break up old local religious cults, which always were an obstacle to the true unification of Attica. If such motives can be detected in the case of one tribe, Aiantis, it is a reasonable assumption that, if the evidence were adequate, somewhat similar motives might be found operating in the establishment of some of the other tribes.

The more one thinks about the *trittyes,* the clearer it becomes that these seemingly very artificial institutions were Cleisthenes' chief device in "mixing up" the people and in making citizens from the different regions of Attica—the city, the coast, and the inland area—cooperate in the various duties which as members of the tribes they owed, such as providing the personnel for the tribal regiment in the army and for the tribal representatives in the new Council of Five Hundred.

The *trittyes* were able to perform this essential function only because each *trittys* was composed of a certain number of *demes,* the fundamental units of the Cleisthenic system. Certainly one of the chief reasons why his reorganization of the citizen body in the new tribal arrangement endured for centuries was that at its foundation it was based on natural units, the *demes.* In the country districts—the coast and inland regions—Cleisthenes found *demes* already in existence, although it is possible, of course, that in a few cases he may have created one *deme* by consolidating several straggling settlements, or two *demes* by subdividing a settlement which might have seemed too large in area and population for his purposes. Only in the city did he have to establish *demes* arbitrarily by dividing the populous area into a sufficient number of units so that, by means of the *trittyes,* the population of the city could be distributed equally in the ten tribes.

Since people had their homes in their respective *demes,* Cleisthenes decided to use the criterion of residence rather than that of membership in a phratry for determining citizenship. All citizens who at the time of his reforms had their permanent residence in a particular *deme* became members and citizens of that *deme,* and their names were inscribed on the *deme* registers which, presumably, then began to be kept. Thereafter, sons of members, on becoming eighteen, were presented to the assembly of demesmen for inclusion, as adult citizens, on the rolls of the *deme.* Membership in a *deme* was made hereditary. Even if a man moved and took up permanent residence elsewhere in Attica, he still remained a member of the *deme* in which he or his forefather had originally been registered. The purpose of this hereditary regulation probably lay in the need to ensure as far as possible that, despite possible population shifts, the ten tribes should continue to have roughly equal numbers of citizens, for a man's tribal affiliation was dependent on the *deme* in which he was registered. Another motive may have been to keep a man, even though he migrated, legally tied to the district in which his family tombs were located.

The *demes* became centers of local government. Most of the available evidence comes from the fourth century, but local organs of government must have existed at least since Cleisthenes designated the *demes* as the foundation of the reorganized state. Each *deme* had an assembly (*agora*) of adult male citizens; an annual *demarch* (mayor), whether elected or appointed by lot is uncertain; other officials, including treasurers; shrines at which various festivals were held; public lands which were leased to produce revenues for the *deme,* and the like. In fact, each *deme* was, in a way, a microcosm of Athens, and it had a rather active municipal life in which its members could and did acquire experience for participating in the political life of Athens. Beyond their role in local affairs, the *demes* were essential for the functioning of the central administration of Athens, for it was from the data provided by the *deme* registers that the necessary provisions could be made for levying soldiers and for obtaining candidates for the various boards of magistrates, the Council of Five Hundred, and, from the middle of the fifth century on, for the law courts.

Although it is certain that Cleisthenes made enrollment in a *deme* the criterion for citizenship, there is an interesting problem concerning whether the implementation of this measure was accompanied by an increase in the size of the citizen body. Aristotle, in his discussion of

Cleisthenes' reforms, makes the following statement (*Ath. Const.*, 21.4): "And he made all the inhabitants in each of the *demes* fellow demesmen of one another, in order that they might not call attention to the newly enfranchised citizens by addressing people by their fathers' names, but designate people by their *demes;* whence it happens that Athenians address themselves according to their *demes.*" This passage explicitly states two things: first, that new citizens were enrolled when the reforms were carried out, and second, that calling a man by his demotic (Thucydides of the *deme* Halimos) rather than by his patronymic (Thucydides, son of Olorus) would conceal that he was a new citizen, a fact which would be evident to all from the use of the father's name, if that name was strange to Athens. The inference which Aristotle drew about the purpose of the demotics was wrong, as is proved by numerous fifth-century inscriptions and *ostraka* which reveal no standard usage in the system of names; sometimes the personal name alone was used, sometimes the personal name combined with either the patronymic or the demotic, or both.

But were new citizens admitted to the state when enrollment in *demes* became the criterion for citizenship? Some scholars answer this question with a flat negative, arguing that this is another example of an erroneous inference on Aristotle's part;[43] they claim that, since in Aristotle's political theory an increase in the citizen body was always accompanied by an increase in democracy, it would have seemed obvious to him that Cleisthenes, who apparently furthered democracy, achieved this aim by increasing the number of citizens. Many other scholars take the position that, although some new citizens probably were registered at this time, the numbers were too few to be of any real significance. As is true with so many matters in early Greek history, it is unlikely that a definitive answer will ever be given to this question, but since it is intimately connected with the whole problem of what constituted Athenian citizenship in the sixth century, the student of Greek history should at least be familiar with the nature of the evidence. Two other passages in Aristotle's writings are relevant to this discussion.

In an attempt to characterize the nature of citizenship, Aristotle (*Politics*, 3.1.10) remarks, "We may take as an example the action of Cleisthenes at Athens, when after the expulsion of the tyrants he enrolled in the tribes many foreigners and slave metics" (these last two words probably mean metics—that is, resident aliens—who formerly had been slaves). This statement should be studied in connection with a passage in the *Constitution of the Athenians* (13.5) where Aristotle, mentioning the motives of some of Pisistratus' adherents, writes, ". . . and, from the motive of fear, those who are not of pure descent; and this is proved by the fact that after the putting down of the tyrants the Athenians enacted a revision of the citizen lists (*diapsēphismos*) because many people shared the citizenship who had no right to it." This revision of the citizen lists is mentioned nowhere else in the ancient sources, but that is not sufficient reason for rejecting it, as some scholars advocate. If there was such an investigation into citizen status, it must have occurred shortly after the expulsion of Hippias when the Athenian oligarchs under Isagoras and Cleisthenes, backed by Cleomenes of Sparta, were in control. Who, then, were these men who, out of fear because of "their impure descent," had been supporters of Pisistratus and whose sons presumably had been supporters of Hippias?

In trying to find an answer, one must remember that down to the enactment of Cleisthenes' reforms citizenship had been based on membership in a phratry. As was pointed out earlier in this chapter, from the time of Draco (ca. 621), at least, phratries included in addition to the *gennētai* a certain, but unknown, number of "commoners." A generation later Solon was supposed to have attracted foreign artisans to Athens and to have granted citizenship to those who took up permanent residence in Attica. This tradition may be true, but one can only wonder how Solon managed to have these newcomers enrolled in the phratries, considering the "kinship" principle on which those institutions were based and their exclusive religious cults. In the following two generations the Pisistratids, using their power as tyrants, could have forced the phratries to admit new members, or they could have recognized various commoners who were potential supporters as citizens whether they were members of phratries or not. One can only confess ignorance and admit that in the sixth century there were probably many men in Attica, and particularly in Athens, whose citizen status was ambiguous. These men must have been primarily laborers and poor artisans—landless *thetes*—for the tradition probably still prevailed that ownership of land and citizenship went together. It would have been a natural reaction for the oligarchic forces, once the Pisistratids had been overthrown, to oust from their precarious citizenship and from any participation in the state these lowly men, who undoubtedly had been supporters of the tyranny.

Final answers in matters such as these, when the source material is so slight and vague, obviously are impossible, but it does seem probable that in 510 or 509 a revision of whatever citizen lists existed caused a considerable number of men to lose their citizen status, which at the best had been dubious. The new citizens whom Cleisthenes was said to have created were presumably those same men who were able to regain their citizenship because of Cleisthenes' reforms, and to have their citizen status guaranteed for the future through enrollment on the *deme* citizen rolls. Cleisthenes' reforms may also have been the occasion when official recognition was given to the fact that ownership of land was no longer essential for the enjoyment of citizenship.[44] Once again certainty is unattainable, but it is reasonable to assume that from this time on, whatever had been the case in preceding generations, landless *thetes,* as well as those *thetes* whose lands could not produce 200 measures of produce annually, had the right to participate in meetings of the assembly. These landless *thetes*—artisans and laborers—were probably chiefly inhabitants of the city and hence were enrolled in the city *demes.* As residents of the city they could easily attend meetings of the assembly and—although by means of the *trittys* system they were distributed among the ten tribes—could furnish support to Cleisthenes; it is important to remember that in the Athenian assembly questions at issue were decided by a majority of the voters present, not, as in Rome, by a majority of the tribes.

It was as a member of one of the ten tribes that an Athenian participated in the public life of the state. He was automatically a member of the tribe to which his *deme* belonged. The tribes were named after ancient, more or less legendary, Athenian heroes. Apollo of Delphi gave his blessing to these new tribes by selecting through his priestess ten names from a list of one hundred that had been presented to him (Aristotle, *Ath. Const.,* 21.6). Statues of these eponymous heroes were erected on the south side of the agora in Athens.[45] These tribes, although each one by means of the *trittys* system was composed of *demes* from the three regions of Attica, were organized like corporations. Each tribe had a shrine at which a priest officiated over the honors offered to the eponymous hero, and owned property which was leased to provide money for the tribal treasury. Tribal assemblies, presided over by annually elected officers, were held on occasion in Athens to transact tribal business. Each tribe was responsible for providing its quota of men for the army, for the Council of Five Hundred and various boards of magistrates, and later for the law courts. The tribes were also responsible for performing various public services (liturgies), especially in connection with the conduct of festivals, on both the state and tribal levels. In fact, there were few aspects of Athenian public life which were not linked in some way to these Cleisthenic tribes.

In his reorganization of the state, Cleisthenes erected a new framework without destroying the old. Understanding the hold that ancient institutions, consecrated by kinship and religious traditions, had on the Athenian people, he limited himself, by means of the new ten tribes based on *demes,* to strengthening the secular structure of the state at the expense of the religious. The *genē* remained influential, and for many years political and social leadership was provided primarily by men coming from the great families. Even the four old Ionian tribes were not officially abolished, although they faded away from desuetude until the only vestige left was an archaic homicide court composed of the king archon and the four "tribal kings." The phratries, in particular, retained an important place in social and religious life—and in political life also, at least to the extent that citizens were usually, if not always, enrolled in them. Inscriptions reveal that as late as the third century a foreigner granted Athenian citizenship was enrolled in a *deme,* tribe, and phratry. Membership in a phratry, however, although almost universal, was not obligatory for the citizen, as is proved by the fact that a newly appointed archon was not allowed to assume office unless he could answer in the affirmative the question of whether he belonged to a phratry (Aristotle, *Ath. Const.,* 55.3). Certainly the question would not have been asked unless there was the possibility of a negative answer.

The fact that it was customary for an Athenian citizen to belong to a phratry is one of the reasons why many scholars deny that Cleisthenes' reforms were accompanied by the creation of many new citizens, for they emphasize the difficulties Cleisthenes would have had in securing admission to the phratries for them. It is hard to believe that additional phratries were established at this time, for their members would have been immediately branded as new citizens. There is no satisfactory answer to the objections raised to the hypothesis that Cleisthenes' legislation involving the *demes* led to an increase in the number of citizens except the obvious one that, if the recognition as citizens of the landless *thetes*—the laborers and artisans—is denied to Cleisthenes, then it must be referred to the Pisistratids or to Solon, a suggestion which hardly solves the dilemma. If one employs the argument from probability, certainly it seems reasonable to attribute the increase in numbers of citizens to Cleisthenes, for his action in removing from the phratries their vital political role may well have had the effect of making them less exclusive. From this time on the activities of the phratries were largely social and religious, and only indirectly political. Beyond these roles they made an important contribution to Athenian life because the phratry records provided the only "official" lists of the numbers of women and children in the population. Since only citizens—that is, adult males from eighteen years on—were registered in the *demes,* the *deme* lists have been compared to modern voting lists, while the phratry rolls, containing men, women, and children, can be likened to the lists kept by departments of vital statistics or to the baptismal records maintained by some churches.

Beyond the new tribal system based on *demes* and *trittyes,* surprisingly little is known about the reforms of Cleisthenes. It is natural to attribute to him the various boards of ten which were so common later in Athens, but, of course, many of these may have come into existence subsequently as a consequence of his measures. Aristotle (*Ath. Const.*, 21.3) specifically states that Cleisthenes established the Council of Five Hundred in place of the Council of Four Hundred, with each tribe supplying fifty councillors. Nothing is known concerning the method of appointing these councillors at this time, and although one can be reasonably certain that men from the top three census classes were eligible for appointment, there is no direct evidence for this supposition in the early years of the council's existence. The discussion of this council, which soon became of extreme importance, therefore, will best be postponed to a later chapter dealing with the government in the fully developed democracy.

The change from a government based on four tribes and many phratries to one based on ten territorial tribes, thirty *trittyes,* and over a hundred *demes* was a revolutionary undertaking, but the ancient sources provide little or no information on how, or in what sequence, the various stages were carried out. A scholar has recently suggested that the first step was to order men to register in the villages in which they lived,[46] thus avoiding the time-consuming task of fixing boundaries for the individual *demes.* Then subsequently these groups of men were assigned to *trittyes* and tribes. Certainly haste was important to forestall oligarchic opposition. The second century A.D. lexicographer Pollux (8.110) states that the ten Athenian tribes came into being in the archonship of Alcmaeon. Since Alcmaeon, to judge from his name, was surely an Alcmaeonid, it is reasonable to assume that Cleisthenes, who had been archon in 525/4 and hence could not hold that office again—if the same prohibition against two tenures of the archonship existed in the sixth century as was the case in the fifth and later centuries—used his influence to have a kinsman elected archon. The archonship of Alcmaeon is usually assigned to 507/6, and thus this year is considered to have marked the inauguration of the new Cleisthenic system.[47] Aristotle (*Ath. Const.,* 22.2-3) states that in the archonship of Hermocreon the Athenians introduced the oath which the 500 councillors had to take, and then the Athenians began to elect the generals (*strategoi*) by tribes, one from each tribe, although the polemarch still continued as commander of the whole army. The date of Hermocreon is unknown, but, since Aristotle says in this passage that in the twelfth year after this the Athenians were victorious at Marathon (490), the archonship is usually placed in 501/0. It is puzzling that these two measures, so intimately connected with Cleisthenes' program, should not have been taken until seven years after the reforms had been voted. The delay may be evidence for the time required to work out the details of the program. Because of these chronological dilemmas, one can only say with assurance that it was sometime in the period 508/7–501/0 that the Athenian government began to operate according to Cleisthenes' reorganization.

One further law of Cleisthenes requires discussion here (although many scholars have expressed doubt about its ascription to Cleisthenes): the law of ostracism, by which an Athenian who was deemed dangerous to the public welfare either as a potential tyrant or, in later times, more generally as an obstacle to the will of the majority could be sent into "honorable" exile for a period of ten years. This institution played an important role in fifth-century Athenian political history. In the sixth prytany each year (the official Athenian year was divided into ten prytanies, running roughly from July to July), the question was placed before the assembly of whether or not an ostracism should be held (Aristotle, *Ath. Const.*, 43.5). If the decision was in the affirmative, the voting to decide who was to be ostracized apparently took place in the following prytany. In that interval one can imagine that Athens was deluged with a wave of political propaganda. Since the election of *strategoi* normally occurred in the seventh prytany (*Ath. Const.*, 44.4), it can be assumed that the matter of ostracism was decided first so as to avoid the possibility of the absurd situation that a man who had been elected as one of the ten *strategoi* should a few days later be expelled from Athens for a decade.

On the day appointed for the decision by *ostraka* (potsherds), the agora was fenced in with planks, with ten entrances, one for each tribe, left in the fencing.[48] The members of the tribes passed through the appropriate entrances, and each man deposited an *ostrakon* on which he had scratched the name of the man he wished to be ostracized. When the voting was completed the archons first counted all the *ostraka*, because, according to Plutarch (*Aristides*, 7), the voting was considered invalid unless at least 6,000 *ostraka* had been cast. In this tradition, 6,000 ostraka formed the necessary quorum to make an ostracism legal. Another version (Philochorus; Jacoby, 328, fragment 30) states that to make the ostracism valid, 6,000 *ostraka* had to be cast against one man, but in view of the large "scatter vote," this interpretation seems unlikely. The man whose name was on a plurality of the *ostraka*, provided a quorum of 6,000 votes had been cast, had to leave Athens within ten days for an exile of ten years, but since this was an "honorable" exile his property was not confiscated.

Aristotle in the *Constitution of the Athenians* (22.1) specifically assigns the law concerning ostracism to Cleisthenes, but a little later in the same chapter he says that two years after the battle of Marathon "the people, now being full of courage, then first put into effect the law concerning ostracism, which had been enacted from suspicion of those in power, because Pisistratus, being leader of the people and general, had established himself as tyrant. And first to be ostracized was one of his kinsmen, Hipparchus, son of Charmus of the *deme* Collytus, on account of whom especially Cleisthenes had made the law, wishing to drive him out." The date of this ostracism was 488/7, and many scholars argue that it makes no sense to have a law that was made with a view to one particular person not be invoked for some twenty years. To support their objection they quote a passage from Androtion, an Atthidographer writing about 350 B.C. to whom Aristotle was greatly indebted. In a passage preserved in the second century A.D. lexicographer Harpocration, Androtion is reported as saying that Hipparchus, a kinsman of Pisistratus, was the first to be ostracized, the law about ostracism *having been enacted then for the first time.* The text of Harpocration is uncertain, and in place of this reading which seems to suggest the beginning of a series of enactments of laws on ostracism, emendations have been suggested, one of which gives the reading: the law about ostracism *having been enacted before this time.*[49] In view of the uncertainty concerning the proper text of Harpocration it seems inappropriate to let a questionable reading of Androtion, dealing with a little-known period, jettison the definite statements of both Aristotle and the third-century Atthidographer Philochorus, who credit Cleisthenes with instituting the law on ostracism after he had put down the tryants.

It has been suggested recently that Cleisthenes' motive in proposing the law on ostracism may actually have been directed against his opponent Isagoras, and that it was this threat which caused the latter to appeal to Cleomenes.[50] The failure of Cleomenes' intervention and the flight of Isagoras removed the need to resort to an ostracism at that time. On further consideration Cleisthenes may have perceived that an ostracism was an unpredictable venture in which the man urging recourse to ostracism might be hoist on his own petard. Actually a late tradition, almost certainly apocryphal, preserved by Aelian (*Varia Historia,* 13.24), states that Cleisthenes himself was ostracized.

It is surprising that the first recorded ostracism did not occur until 488/7, but one should realize that the Athenians may often have had recourse to ostracisms which never were mentioned in the sources, because, the quorum of 6,000 votes not having been obtained, they remained abortive.[51] In this connection it is worth mentioning that some of the *ostraka* representing "scatter votes," usually attributed to the ostracisms which certainly did occur in the 480s, could, as far as the archaeological strata in which they were found are concerned, be dated equally well to the last years of the sixth or the first decade of the fifth century. After the battle of Marathon in 490, however, the feeling of exaltation which had been aroused in the Athenians, combined with their revulsion against Hippias who had been with the Persians and their suspicions, whether true or false, that certain friends of the Pisistratids in Athens had tried to play the traitor, resulted in a series of ostracisms of which the first was that of Hipparchus in 488/7.

Early IN THE course of adjusting itself to the governmental and social changes initiated by Cleisthenes, Athens had to face a serious external threat. It was probably in 506 that Cleomenes, resentful at his recent treatment by the Athenians and also wishing to make Athens behave as a respectable ally should, made arrangements for a threefold attack to be launched on Attica simultaneously: a Peloponnesian army was to invade Attica from the southwest while the Thebans attacked from the northwest and the Chalcidians of Euboea from the northeast. Thebes had been hostile to Athens ever since the occasion, several years earlier (519 or 509), when the little Boeotian town of Plataea on the northern slopes of Mt. Cithaeron had refused to join the Theban-dominated Boeotian League and had requested and received Athenian protection (Herodotus, 6.108). The reason for Chalcis' enmity is not known, unless it was a result of the friendship between Athens and Eretria, Chalcis' old rival in Euboea. The Peloponnesian army had advanced as far as Eleusis when the Corinthian contingent, becoming dissatisfied with the undertaking, returned home, to be followed shortly by the second Spartan king, Demaratus, and also by the other allies. Corinth may have decided that it was foolish to weaken Athens, whose hostility to Aegina could be serviceable to Corinth in its competition with a commercial rival. The quarrel between Demaratus and Cleomenes led to a new law at Sparta which stipulated that thereafter the two kings could not jointly conduct a foreign expedition. With the departure of his Peloponnesian allies, Cleomenes had to abandon his plan of restoring Isagoras to power in Athens as tyrant (Herodotus, 5.74–76).

The Athenians had marched out to meet Cleomenes at Eleusis thinking it best to face this menace before turning against the Boeotians, who had already crossed Cithaeron, and the Chalcidians, who were raiding northeast Attica. Freed from the Peloponnesian danger, the Athenians immediately hurried against the Chalcidians. Before they had joined battle with them they learned that the Boeotians were hastening to the support of their allies. To prevent the joining of the two forces, the Athenians turned against the Boeotians and won a complete victory, killing many and taking 700 prisoners. Then, according to

Herodotus (5.77), they crossed the Euripus straits on the same day and defeated the Chalcidians, who had returned home. They followed up this victory by taking possession of a large part of the Lelantine plain where the Chalcidian aristocrats had their estates, and, dividing this land into 4,000 lots (*kleroi*), they settled a corresponding number of Athenian citizens there. Herodotus calls the men who were sent to the Lelantine plain *cleruchs*, a term which should imply, if used officially, that these settlers retained their Athenian citizenship. There is no evidence concerning what class of Athenians was dispatched, but it is logical to assume that many of them would have come from the "new citizens" who had been landless. Thus these men became landowners and at the same time were able to act as an Athenian garrison to keep watch on Chalcis. The Chalcidians captured in the battle, as well as the 700 Boeotian prisoners, were kept in chains until they were later ransomed at 200 drachmas apiece. The fetters were subsequently hung up in the Acropolis, where Herodotus some two generations later saw them, and with a tithe from the ransom the Athenians dedicated on the Acropolis to Athena a bronze four-horsed chariot which bore the proud inscription in elegiac couplets: "In gloomy iron chains the sons of the Athenians quenched their arrogance, having subdued the nations of the Boeotians and Chalcidians in the deeds of war; as a tithe from them they dedicated these mares to Athena" (*M&L,* no. 15).

Athens won these victories and preserved its new constitution unaided, but Herodotus (5.73) relates that after Cleomenes' ignominious departure from the Acropolis and the recall of Cleisthenes and the 700 banished families, the Athenians, realizing that they had incurred the enmity of Cleomenes and the Spartans, sent envoys to the Persian satrap at Sardis in Lydia with the hope of concluding an alliance with Persia. The satrap replied that only if the Athenians would signify their submission by the symbolic gift of earth and water would King Darius make an alliance with them. The envoys on their own responsibility acquiesced in these terms, for which they were greatly blamed when they returned home. If this story is true, presumably Cleisthenes was responsible for this policy since, under whatever title it was, he was the leading man in Athens at this time; but Herodotus conceals the identity of the proposer of this policy under the general word "Athenians." Possibly Herodotus' informants in the mid-fifth century, the Alcmaeonids, in view of the stigma then attached to "medism" (treacherous cooperation with Persia), deliberately withheld from him the name of their ancestor. One should realize, however, that the validity of this story is suspect for two main reasons: first, it is questionable whether before the Ionian revolt of 499 an appeal to Persia would have been condemned as "medism," and second, it is hard to believe that the envoys could have made an alliance without obtaining the subsequent approval of the Athenian council and assembly. Whether Cleisthenes did fall out of favor because of this supposed appeal to Persia, therefore, is unknown.

Cleisthenes remains one of the great enigmas of Greek history. The man who established the secular state at Athens and laid the framework for the future democracy so well that that framework endured for centuries turned to the people only after he had lost out in a struggle for power among the oligarchs. At the height of his powers he disappeared totally from the stage, whether from death or loss of favor cannot be said. Although he was remembered in the fifth century as the founder of a democratic constitution, in the fourth century he was more and more ignored, except by Aristotle, and in the popular mind and in political propaganda Theseus and Solon became the great democratic heroes. The measure of his genius, however, can be judged from the simple fact that Athens would not have been what it was in the fifth and fourth centuries had Cleisthenes not carried through his remarkable reorganization of the state.

8

The Greeks and the Persians

T HE FIFTH CENTURY began with the revolt of the Asiatic Greeks
from the Persians, to whom they had fallen subject following the
Persian conquest of Lydia in 547 or 546. Soon after the suppression of
this "Ionian" revolt, the mainland Greeks were fighting desperately to
avoid absorption in the huge eastern empire. Since Greek and Persian
history collided constantly until the overthrow of the Persian Empire by
Alexander the Great in the last third of the fourth century, it is essential
at this point to try to obtain some idea of who the Persians were and how
it had come to pass that in a period of some thirty years they had become masters of almost all Asia, from the Indus River to the Mediterranean and Aegean seas, as well as of Egypt also.

Persia at the beginning of the fifth century, with its "world empire"
presided over by an absolute monarch ruling by divine right and surrounded with all the pomp and ceremony of the ancient Orient, formed
such a total contrast with the small, quarreling, independent Greek
states, in many of which the rights of the individual were more and more
finding expression, that it is easy to forget that the ultimate origin of
Greeks and Persians was the same, or at least similar. Since both Greeks
and Persians spoke languages belonging to the Indo-European family,
their linguistic ancestors were those hypothetical Indo-Europeans who
far back in the third millennium had left their "original" home and
started migrating in different directions. The future Greeks, however,
after the collapse of the Mycenaean world, had had several centuries in
which to develop their civilization largely in isolation, whereas those
Indo-European-speaking tribes whose final stopping place was the Iranian plateau, and particularly those who came into the western part of
this area, were greatly influenced in the course of time by the old, highly
developed civilizations of the Near East.

The Persians and the closely related Medes belonged to the Aryan
or Indo-Iranian branch of the Indo-Europeans.[1] In the second millennium some of these Indo-Iranian tribes migrated from the Eurasian
plains of southern Russia and, crossing the Caucasus mountains, came
into upper Mesopotamia, while others, moving east of the Caspian Sea
and then over the Hindu Kush mountains, arrived in the Indus River

area. They became the founders of the Aryan Sanskrit civilization and probably caused the final collapse of the great Indus valley culture, which excavations have revealed particularly at Harappa and Mohenjo-Daro.

In the following millennium more "Iranian" tribes moved out from the southern Russian plains. Those migrating eastward, when prevented from entering the Punjab by the earlier Aryans who were in the process of becoming Indians, settled in Sogdiana, where Soviet excavations have disclosed extensive irrigation works going back to the seventh century, in Bactria, and on the Iranian plateau. Other tribes crossed the Caucasus and then moved slowly southward along the Zagros mountain range. For several centuries while they were living in the valleys of the Zagros, these Iranians, in war and in peace, were strongly influenced by the Assyrians, Elamites, and Babylonians. Assyrian records refer frequently to the Iranian tribes, to the Persians as early as 844 and to the Medes first in 836.

Early in the seventh century the various communities of the Medes in the northwestern part of the Iranian plateau began to coalesce into a united kingdom. Herodotus (1.96–106), in a picturesque story, assigns the initiative to a Mede whom he calls Deioces, but it is probable that the major part of the work of organization fell to his successors, Phraortes and Cyaxares. Ecbatana (modern Hamadan), meaning "place of assembly," became the capital. In 614 the Medes marched against Assyria and destroyed the religious capital Assur. Then Cyaxares made an alliance with the founder of the neo-Babylonian kingdom, Nabopolassar, who had revolted from Assyria. This alliance was sealed by the marriage of a Median princess to Nebuchadnezzar, the son of the Babylonian king. It was for his wife that Nebuchadnezzar subsequently was supposed to have built in Babylon the "Hanging Gardens," which came to be considered one of the Seven Wonders of the ancient world. In 612 the Medes, aided by the Babylonians, marched again against Assyria and captured and destroyed the mighty capital Nineveh. Readers familiar with the Old Testament will recall the savage joy expressed by the Hebrew prophet Nahum at the destruction of the hated city.

Following the fall of Assyria, which, despite vicissitudes, had been dominant in the Near East for some three centuries, a rough balance of power existed among the four chief nations of the area: Egypt, the neo-Babylonian kingdom, the kingdom of the Medes, and that of the Lydians. The neo-Babylonian kingdom was the true heir of Assyria, for its territory included Babylonia, Assyria, Syria, and ultimately Palestine. It was Nebuchadnezzar who, after several campaigns, destroyed Jerusalem in 586 and led the Jews into the Babylonian captivity. The Medes, after the fall of Assyria, pushed northwestward into Asia Minor. In Cappadocia Cyaxares found his progress blocked by the Lydian army under Alyattes. According to Herodotus (1.74), after five years of indecisive fighting the combatants agreed to a peace when the battle in which they were engaged was interrupted by an eclipse of the sun. This eclipse, either of 585 or 582, was reputed to have been forecast by Thales of Miletus. The Halys River was established as the boundary between the two realms, and the treaty was confirmed by the marriage of Alyattes' daughter to Cyaxares' son, Astyages, the heir to the Median throne.

The Lydians, apparently a native people of Asia Minor whose language has not yet been deciphered, may have been under the general control of the Phrygian kingdom. When Phrygian power disintegrated under the onslaughts of the Cimmerians, either Iranian or Thracian nomads who swept over Asia Minor and Syria at the end of the eighth and early in the seventh century, the Lydians became independent. It was probably the need to resist the Cimmerians that led to the formation of the historical Lydian kingdom with its capital at Sardis on the Hermus River. Herodotus (1.7) says that its rulers were Heraclids, which suggests that they at least were of Indo-European speech like the Phrygians. Candaules, one of these rulers, was overthrown in the first quarter of the seventh century by Gyges, who then became the first king of the Mermnad dynasty.

Gyges was clearly a historical person, for he is mentioned by the contemporary poet Archilochus and also in Assyrian documents, but the story of his seizure of power lies in the realm of legend. Herodotus (1.8–14) in one of his most delightful stories, which may have been derived from an early Athenian drama,[2] portrays Gyges as one of Candaules' bodyguards who gained the throne as a result of a palace revolution involving the queen. Plato (*Republic*, 2.359–360) preserves the legend that Gyges had been a shepherd who, after finding a magic ring capable of making its wearer invisible, succeeded in seducing the queen with whose help he seized the throne. As king he ruled until about 652.

After becoming king, Gyges was faced with dangerous opposition from the supporters of the murdered Candaules. The two factions finally agreed to leave the settlement of the dispute to Apollo of Delphi. Apollo proved obliging to Gyges, and in gratitude he sent great dedications of silver and gold to the god, the first foreigner after the Phrygian king Midas, says Herodotus (1.14), to send gifts to Delphi. Gyges set the pattern followed by his successors of trying to control the Greek cities of the coast, presumably desiring both tribute and access to the sea. After failing in his attacks on Miletus and Smyrna, he achieved some success at Colophon. A few lines have survived from a poem of the Colophonian

Mimnermus celebrating the bravery of some citizen of an earlier generation while fighting against the Lydian cavalry.

Gyges' third successor, Alyattes, after carrying on the war begun by his father, came to terms with Miletus and signed a treaty of alliance. In bringing about this cessation of hostilities, Periander, the tyrant of Corinth, who maintained close relations with the Milesian tyrant Thrasybulus (Herodotus, 1.20), apparently acted as mediator, a role he also played at approximately the same time in the dispute between Athens and Mytilene concerning Sigeum on the Hellespont.

Alyattes' attention was soon directed to events in the east. Nineveh fell in 612, and within a few years Assyrian power was totally destroyed. The Median victor, Cyaxares, then pushed on westward into Cappadocia in the eastern part of Anatolia, a move which caused Alyattes to march out with the Lydians to stem the advance. This was the war mentioned above which, because of the eclipse of the sun, ended with the acceptance of the Halys River as the boundary between the two kingdoms and a matrimonial alliance.

Alyattes was succeeded about 560 by his son Croesus, the last and, in Greek eyes at least, the most famous of the Lydian kings. Croesus began his reign by taking Ephesus, although he treated the temple of Artemis with great respect. He then proceeded to subdue the rest of the Ionian cities as well as the Aeolian and Dorian ones, and to compel them to pay tribute. Miletus, however, was spared because of the alliance it had made with his father. It was under Croesus that Lydia achieved its greatest prosperity and its widest territorial expansion. Herodotus (1.28) says that he subjected all the peoples west of the Halys River except the Cilicians and Lycians.

About 549 word reached Lydia that Cyrus the Persian, by overthrowing Astyages, had become ruler of the Median kingdom. This report raised both fear and hope in the mind of Croesus—fear that this unknown aggressive figure might advance beyond the Halys and hope that, since the deposition of Astyages signified the end of the Halys boundary treaty, he could now, in the role of avenger of his brother-in-law, extend his conquests eastward. Wishing to obtain divine approval for his ambitious plans, Croesus devised a scheme for checking the veracity of various oracles, and after convincing himself that Apollo of Delphi spoke the truth, he sent enormous gifts of gold and silver to Delphi. When he asked the oracle through envoys if he should march against Persia, he received the famous reply that if he campaigned against the Persians he would destroy a great empire. The story that, on the advice of Apollo to ally himself with the strongest Greek state, Croesus made an alliance with Sparta is probably apocryphal,[3] for the Spartans, engaged then in establishing the Peloponnesian League, were in no position to take part in hazardous overseas ventures.

In 547 Croesus began to march eastward. After crossing the Halys River he treated Cappadocia as enemy territory, ravaging the land and enslaving the people. Cyrus hurried to meet him, and late in the summer a battle occurred which by nightfall was still undecided. On the next day Croesus, realizing that the defeat of his army was likely, began to retire to Sardis, the Lydian capital, with the intention of attacking Cyrus again in the following spring with increased forces. On reaching his capital he sent word to his allies—the Egyptians and Babylonians— to be present with their troops at Sardis in four months' time. Convinced that he would not have to fight Cyrus again until spring, he dismissed his mercenaries for the winter. Cyrus, however, figuring that Croesus would disband his army, waited the appropriate length of time and then marched westward so rapidly that he arrived at Sardis without any reports of his movements preceding him. The Lydians, greatly disconcerted, went out to meet the Persians. Against the Lydians, who relied chiefly on their excellent cavalry, Cyrus placed in the first line his pack camels, on whom armed men were mounted. It had apparently been noticed in the summer battle that the Lydian horses were frightened by the sight and smell of camels. The ruse was successful, for the Lydian horses became so unmanageable that their riders had to leap from them and fight on foot. The battle was a savage one, but finally the Lydians were driven back to the protection of their citadel, which Cyrus immediately began to besiege. Frantic messages were sent to Croesus' allies to come to his assistance at once, but before they could make a move, Sardis had fallen, on the fourteenth day of the siege. The citadel was very strong, and one section was considered so impregnable that it was only lightly guarded. As happened frequently in Greek history, the enemy scaled the supposedly inaccessible cliffs and seized the citadel. Thus the Persians won control of Sardis late in 547, and Croesus himself was captured (Herodotus, 1.46–85).

The fate of Croesus is uncertain. The contemporary Babylonian Chronicle, the so-called Chronicle of Nabonidus, states that Cyrus marched against Lydia, killed its king, took his possessions, and installed a garrison. Greek accounts of the fate of Croesus, both in art and literature, furnish a valuable insight into the growth of a legend. The earliest evidence is provided by an Attic red-figure vase now in the Louvre. The scene depicted on this amphora, which can be dated shortly after 500, shows Croesus sitting on a throne placed upon a pyre which already has begun to burn. By 468 when the Greek poet Bacchylides composed a victory ode for Hieron, tyrant of Syracuse, the legend had grown greatly.

In this account Croesus, unable to endure the degradation of captivity, had a pyre erected before the palace, which he, his wife, and his daughters ascended. As the flames rose to the shrieks of the maidens, Zeus sent a shower of rain which extinguished the fire. Apollo then carried Croesus and his daughters to the land of the Hyperboreans, the mythical worshippers of Apollo, "because his gifts to Pytho were greater than all men's gifts."

Some two or three decades later Herodotus wrote his version of the fate of Croesus, a version which, with alterations and additions, was followed by later writers throughout Greek history. In Herodotus' account (1.86–89) Cyrus had Croesus in chains placed upon a great pyre with fourteen Lydian boys. As Croesus stood on the pyre waiting for the flames to engulf him, he remembered how the Athenian Solon on a visit to Sardis, scorning all the royal wealth and magnificence, had declared that no man could be called happy until he was dead. Recalling this, Croesus thrice uttered the name of Solon. The curiosity of Cyrus was aroused, and through interpreters he extracted from Croesus the story of Solon's visit and how Solon, emphasizing the instability of all things human, had insisted that no life could be considered happy until one knew how it ended. Cyrus was impressed and began to repent the fact that he, a mortal, was burning alive another mortal who had once been as prosperous as he now was. He therefore gave orders that the flames should be quenched, but they proved to be too strong to be extinguished by human means. Then Croesus called loudly upon Apollo, begging the god to save him now if his gifts to him had been acceptable. Immediately clouds appeared in the clear sky, and the ensuing rain put out the fire. Thereafter Croesus received a place in Cyrus' retinue as an honored adviser, a role which he continued to play with Cyrus' successor, Cambyses.

This account, even if one removes the miraculous aspects, can almost certainly be rejected, for what is known about Persian religion, whether before or after Zoroaster, excludes the possibility that Cyrus would have polluted the divine fire by burning a human victim. The probability is either that the Babylonian Chronicle is correct when it said that Cyrus killed Croesus, or that Croesus committed suicide—possibly by cremation on a funeral pyre—in order to escape the indignities and execution which were customary in the Orient when one monarch fell into the power of another. It is also conceivable, of course, that Cyrus showed mercy. How and why, then, did these legends grow up around Croesus? There is little doubt that they originated with Delphi. Croesus had heaped fabulous wealth upon Delphi, and his reward had been an oracle that led him to his doom. To exonerate their god, the priests disseminated various tales showing that Apollo did not forsake a man so pious and generous as Croesus—tales, moreover, which also emphasized a favorite Delphic doctrine that nemesis was bound to overtake any man who rose so high and became so full of pride (*hybris*) as to forget that he was a mere mortal.

The famous story of Solon's visit to Croesus, although it presumably originated in Athens, is infused with the spirit advocated by the maxims inscribed on Apollo's temple at Delphi—"Nothing to excess" and "Know thyself." Only the gist of the story can be given here; it should be read in its entirety in Herodotus (1.29–33), where it is told in the historian's inimitable manner. When Croesus was at the peak of his prosperity, various Greek wise men visited Sardis, including Solon who had set out on his travels after completing his work of providing laws for the Athenians. Croesus entertained him hospitably for a few days and then had some of his attendants conduct the visitor through the royal . treasuries, which were bursting with riches of all sorts. When the tour had been completed Croesus, with the arrogance that attends great wealth, asked the Athenian sage who was the happiest man he had ever seen. Solon in his answer mentioned an Athenian, Tellus, who, after living to see children born to his fine sons, died gloriously while helping his city to victory against the enemy. Croesus then asked who was the second happiest person Solon had known. Solon thereupon told the tale of two young Argives, Cleobis and Biton, who, when no oxen were available to drag their mother's wagon to the festival of Hera, harnessed themselves to the cart and brought their mother in time to the temple, six miles away. When the assembled crowd congratulated the mother on her noble and strong sons, she, in great joy at their renown, prayed to Hera to grant them the greatest blessing which can befall a man. Soon thereafter the young men fell asleep in the temple and never awoke. In recognition of their excellence, the Argives had statues wrought of them which they dedicated at Delphi (and which now stand in the museum at Delphi). When Croesus expostulated that he, the mighty king, was ignored in favor of ordinary private citizens, Solon gave a lecture emphasizing the jealousy which divinity felt for human prosperity, pointing out the mutability of all things human, and ending with the words, "In every matter one must look to see how the end will turn out, for the deity, after giving a glimpse of happiness to many, destroys them root and branch." It was these maxims that Croesus remembered when he called aloud the name of Solon from his funeral pyre.

This story is almost certainly apocryphal, for chronologically it is hard to accept such an interview between Solon and Croesus, who probably became king only in 560. So many problems about the chronology of the sixth century, and particularly its first half, still exist, however, that one is tempted to sympathize with Plutarch's remarks (*Solon,* 27) which he prefaces to his version of the tale: "But when a story is so famous and so well-attested, and, what is more, to the point, when it comports so well with the character of Solon, and is so worthy of his magnanimity and wisdom, I do not propose to reject it out of deference to any chronological canons, so-called, which thousands are to this day revising, without being able to bring their contradictions into any general agreement."

The career of Croesus appealed to Greek imagination, and his fall from the pinnacle of prosperity to nothingness made a great impression on them. It was a perfect illustration of their favorite doctrine that the gods in the course of time would humble those who had become too mighty. The legends which grew up around Croesus, although they emphasized his pride (*hybris*), generally portrayed him sympathetically. The seamy side of Croesus, such as his cruelty in putting to death by torture a man who had supported a rival to the throne, was glossed over (Herodotus, 1.92). Although he was more responsible than any of his predecessors for subjecting the Greek cities of Asia Minor, exacting tribute from them, and probably establishing tyrants in many to act as his governing agents, these realities receded before the romantic legends. Why did Croesus and the Lydians in general fare so well in Greek tradition? Several reasons can be offered in explanation. First, the friendly propaganda from Delphi and from other shrines which had been the beneficiaries of the generosity of the Mermnads had great influence in shaping public opinion. Second, after the fall of Sardis it was Persia that became the enemy and remained so for many generations, and a natural sympathy arose for those who also had been victims of Persian might. To the Greeks under Lydian rule, although they surely objected to subjection, the Lydians were a familiar people, and the kings, no matter how exalted, had their residence only two or three days' journey inland, and hence were not completely inaccessible. Croesus' sister had even married a Greek, who was the tyrant of Ephesus (Aelian, *Varia Historia,* 3.26). The Great King of Persia, however, living so far away in the east that it took three months to reach his capital at Susa (Herodotus, 5.50) was little more than a terrifying name. The Asiatic Greeks under Persian control found themselves subject to a complex bureaucracy with its system of satraps, government agents, and local tyrants. Much more than when under the Lydians, the Greeks felt themselves to be little more than pawns in a game played by an absolute despot who was hopelessly remote and unapproachable.

Finally, the close proximity in which the Lydians and Asiatic

Greeks lived could scarcely have failed to bring about considerable interplay in the social, economic, and cultural spheres. Greek artisans found markets for many of their products at Sardis, and many Greeks probably were employed there. Certainly the Lydian kings made great use in their armies of "Ionians," who served either as mercenaries or at times possibly in fulfillment of a military obligation to the ruling power. Products of Lydian agriculture reached the coast as well as various luxury articles, including tapestries, whose designs had an influence on what is known as the orientalizing style of Greek art. The effect of oriental religious ideas can be seen clearly in aspects of the cult of Ephesian Artemis, a cult to which Croesus was very generous. Lydian music had considerable popularity among the Greeks, and also Lydian poetry after it had been transmuted into the Greek language. The Lydians, whatever the nature of their tongue, adapted the Greek alphabet to it, and revealed a great interest in the Greek language. It is probable that Greek was spoken by many people living in Sardis. The late-seventh-century poet Alcman, who lived for many years in Sparta, was reputed to be a Lydian; this must mean either that he had been a Greek living in Lydia or a Lydian who had mastered Greek. The poems of Hipponax of Ephesus, whose *floruit* was shortly after the death of Croesus, were filled with Lydian words and expressions, and in the fifth century the Lydian Xanthus wrote a *Lydiaka* in Greek.

In the generations before the emergence of Cyrus the somewhat nomadic Persian tribes, who had been mentioned in Assyrian documents since the ninth century, migrated southward into Persis east of the Persian Gulf, where they were partially under the control of the Elamites to the west. About 639 the Assyrians destroyed the kingdom of Elam and reduced the Persians to subject status. After the Medes and Babylonians had annihilated Assyrian power in 612, the Persians, now under the suzerainty of the Medes, succeeded in incorporating the old realm of Elam. The fact that many Persian inscriptions were written in Elamite side by side with other languages and the subsequent designation of Susa as one of their capitals suggest that the Persians had been greatly influenced by the ancient civilization of Elam.

CYRUS CAME TO THE throne of Persia in 559. One can accept Herodotus' statement (1.107–122) that his mother was a daughter of the Median king Astyages, even though the account of his birth and childhood is permeated with folktale motifs similar to those associated with figures like Moses and Romulus. Early in his reign Cyrus formed an alliance with Nabonidus, who had become king of Babylonia in 555. Nabonidus, the son of the high priest of the moon-god Sin in Harran in northwestern Mesopotamia, was anxious to recover Harran, which had been under Median control since the collapse of Assyria at the end of the seventh century. It is possible that Nabonidus encouraged Cyrus to aggressive action against the Medes so that he (Nabonidus) would have a free hand to recover Harran. Astyages, the Median king, received word of the negotiations between the Babylonian and the Persian, and summoned his grandson Cyrus to Ecbatana. When Cyrus refused to obey, Astyages took the field against him and was badly defeated in two battles, in the second (550) falling captive to Cyrus. Soon thereafter the capture of Ecbatana marked the end of the Median kingdom. The new Persian kingdom or empire signified a change in dynasty rather than the formation of a new, and the destruction of an old, kingdom. The Medes and the Persians were so closely related that the new kingdom was really an amalgamation of the two peoples. Ecbatana remained one of the capitals, and most of the Median officials were retained in their posts. To many western people the Persian kingdom was still the Median kingdom. This is well illustrated by the use of the word *medism,* meaning negotiating or intriguing with the Medes. Even at the time of the great Persian invasions, when intriguing with the enemy represented treason, the term that was used by the Greeks was *medism,* not *persism.*

After overthrowing Croesus, Cyrus was faced with the problem of the Asiatic Greeks who had been subject to the Lydians. No sooner had the Greeks heard of the fall of Sardis than they sent envoys to Cyrus requesting that they retain the same status under him as they had had under Croesus. Cyrus demanded complete surrender. At the beginning of the campaign against Croesus he had sent heralds to the Greek cities urging them to revolt, but they had paid no heed. Miletus alone was granted the same favored status that it had had under the Lydians, presumably because the city had responded favorably to Cyrus' original proposal and also because, with Miletus attached to Cyrus, Greek resistance would be handicapped from the start (Herodotus, 1.76; 141).

The Greeks decided to resist. The Ionians assembled at Panionion, their meeting place on Cape Mycale, and voted to send envoys to Sparta to request help, a decision in which the Aeolians also joined. The Spartans refused to send military aid but did dispatch a ship to Asia Minor so that they could see for themselves what the situation was. At this point Herodotus (1.152–153) tells a wonderful tale. A Spartan herald went up to Sardis and ordered Cyrus not to harm any Greek city, since the Spartans would not suffer it. Cyrus, somewhat startled, asked some Greeks who were present who the Spartans were. After receiving an answer Cyrus said to the herald, "I have never yet been afraid of men who have a special meeting place in the center of their city, where they swear this and that and cheat each other." Herodotus goes on, "This was intended by Cyrus as a criticism of the Greeks generally, because they have markets for buying and selling, unlike the Persians who never buy in open market, and indeed have not a single market-place in their whole country." It has been well said that in this probably apocryphal story Herodotus has clearly emphasized the "temperamental incompatibility" between the Persian and Greek social and economic systems.[4] The Persian point of view, except for its acceptance of absolute monarchy, was more akin to that represented in the *Odyssey,* in aristocratic poets like Alcaeus and Theognis, and in the "idealized" Spartiates with their contempt for anything mercantile. Greece in the sixth, fifth, and fourth centuries, however, with the trade and industry which had been stimulated by colonization, with the rise of the lower classes, and with the explosion of intellectual curiosity, was completely alien to the largely feudal Persian concept of the proper organization of society.

Cyrus, without further concern for the Ionians, placed a Persian in charge of Sardis, assigned to a Lydian named Pactyas the task of collecting the gold which had belonged to Croesus and other Lydians, and then set out for Ecbatana. Pactyas almost immediately persuaded the Lydians to revolt, and going down to the coast, he hired many of the Greeks as mercenaries, paying them from the gold now in his possession. With these troops he returned to Sardis and besieged the Persian governor in the citadel. When Cyrus heard of the rebellion he sent a detachment of his troops under a Mede to relieve the siege of Sardis, to deprive the Lydians of all their weapons, to sell into slavery all those who had joined with the Lydians in the march on Sardis, and to capture Pactyas alive. These orders seem to have been carried out. The Lydian martial spirit was so thoroughly extinguished that before long they acquired the reputation of being a nation of shopkeepers. Pactyas was hounded from Greek city to Greek city until he was betrayed to the Persians in return for a bribe. And then came the turn of the Asiatic Greeks. The inhabitants of Priene, who must have been especially active in the attack on Sardis, were sold into slavery. Although many of the cities resisted stoutly, they could not withstand the siege and assault tactics of the Persians, and in the course of several years all the Ionian and Aeolian cities were subjugated. About half of the population of Phocaea sailed westward and after various vicissitudes founded the city of Elea on the southwest coast of Italy. The inhabitants of Teos escaped and sailed to the coast of Thrace, where they established the city of Abdera. After these Asiatic Greeks, except the Milesians, had been subdued, the Persians, compelling the Ionians and Aeolians to serve with them, marched southward and subjugated the Dorian Greeks, the Carians, and the Lycians (Herodotus, 1.154–176).

Cyrus' career after he returned to Ecbatana had no further direct connections with the Greeks, but since he laid the foundations for the Persian Empire, which influenced Greek history so profoundly for two centuries, a few remarks on his subsequent achievements should be made. The chief sources for these exploits are the last chapters (177–216) of the first book of Herodotus and various Babylonian documents. In 539 Cyrus marched against Babylon. The great city was seething with discontent caused in large part by the indignation of the powerful priests of Marduk at the neglect of their cult by Nabonidus, the devotee of the moon-god Sin. This is the period depicted in the Book of Daniel with its feast of the crown prince Belshazzar and the handwriting on the wall, although the author seemingly confused Nebuchadnezzar with Nabonidus. In the autumn the city joyfully opened its gates to Cyrus, which enabled him to appear to the Babylonians as a liberator and legitimate successor to the throne.

In his first official year as king of Babylon (538), Cyrus issued a decree granting to the Jews permission to return to Palestine and rebuild their temple at Jerusalem. Actually it was not until the next century that a large migration to Palestine, under Ezra and Nehemiah, took place. In this proclamation about the Jews Cyrus was being true to his principle of religious toleration, but he was also showing sound statesmanship. Palestine lay on the threshold of Egypt, and a friendly Palestine would be useful to the campaign against Egypt which he was projecting. Already the kings of the Phoenician cities had come to him to pledge their loyalty and to place their fleets at his disposal. This meant that the Great King of Persia now had two fleets under his control, for after the subjection of the Asiatic Greeks their ships came under Persian command.

By the time of Cyrus' death in 530 the Persian Empire in the east extended to the frontiers of India, and the northeastern boundary had been set at the Jaxartes River. His last campaign, in which he was killed, was against the Massagetai, a Saca or Scythian nomadic tribe living to the east of the Caspian. His soldiers recovered his body, which was conveyed to Persia and buried in the plain tomb that he had had constructed in Pasargadae, the city he had built in the Persian highlands. Cyrus was one of the world's great conquerors, and he was also a great organizer. Darius the Great, who is recognized as the real organizer of the Persian Empire, built on the framework which Cyrus had established. Few if any conquerors have been remembered in history with a tradition so universally favorable. In all the territories that Cyrus conquered, he honored the native customs and religious beliefs and tried to play the role of legitimate successor to the former rulers, thereby setting a pattern which two centuries later may have influenced Alexander the Great. Among the Babylonians and Jews, and probably others, he was looked upon as a liberator. He was idealized by the Persians as the "father of their country," and in Greek tradition he was always treated with respect.

Cyrus was succeeded by his eldest son Cambyses, who in 525 began the conquest of Egypt which his father had planned. Egypt had been a region of importance to the Greeks since Psammetichus I (664–610), the founder of the twenty-sixth (Saite) dynasty, had opened certain areas to them. The next to the last pharaoh of this dynasty, Amasis (570–526), foreseeing an ultimate Persian invasion, had tried to build a defense against such an attack by gaining control of the cities of Cyprus and forming an alliance with Polycrates, the tyrant of Samos. By the time of the departure of Cambyses' forces, however, Persian might and influence had caused Cyprian ships, as well as those of a reluctant Polycrates, to join in the armada along with the contingents of the Ionian Greeks and the Phoenicians. After the Nabataean Arabs had guided the Persian army across the Sinai desert, the main struggle of the campaign took place at Pelusium on the most easterly branch of the Nile Delta. In this bitter battle Ionian and Aeolian Greeks were fighting under the Persians, while Greeks and also Carians were serving as mercenaries in the Egyptian army. Two generations later, Herodotus (3.12) saw the bones of the dead still lying scattered about the desert. The victorious Persians then advanced to Memphis, which they took after a brief siege. Cambyses had to abandon his plan to attack Carthage because the Phoenicians refused to fight against their kinsmen, but the Greek cities of Cyrene and Barca as well as various Libyan tribes acknowledged Persian suzerainty.

Although Cambyses acquired Egypt as another province (satrapy) for the Persian Empire and extended Persian control beyond the first cataract of the Nile, where on the adjacent island of Elephantine a colony of Jews served for many years as a garrison to protect the southern boundary, Herodotus (3.1–66) depicts him as a man who, becoming insane, committed atrocities and lost thousands of troops in mad campaigns. Cambyses may have become unbalanced—the matter cannot be proved or disproved—but the source of these hostile stories can probably be traced to certain priesthoods venting their fury because he curtailed some of the inordinate privileges which they had enjoyed at the expense of the Egyptian people.[5] It is also well to keep in mind that Darius, who became king a few months after Cambyses' death, was really a usurper from a different branch of the royal family; and usurpers, by their nature, are prone to vilify their predecessors.

The circumstances which brought Darius to the throne after the obscure death of Cambyses in 522 are one of history's great unsolved mysteries. Although these events belong to Persian rather than Greek history, nevertheless, because Greeks and Persians were so constantly embroiled with one another, because Herodotus (3.61–87) treats them at length, and because the problems are intrinsically interesting, a concise account of them and of the nature of the evidence will be relevant here. The official version of the events, provided by Darius and circulated by various means throughout the empire, has been preserved, inscribed in Old Persian, Akkadian, and Elamite, on the famous Behistun monument mentioned in the first chapter. On the first column Darius states that Cambyses had a brother, Bardiya, by the same mother and father, and that Cambyses murdered him secretly. After Cambyses had gone to Egypt a Magian by the name of Gaumata asserted that he was Bardiya, the son of Cyrus. When Cambyses died, Gaumata became lord of the whole kingdom until Darius with a few men killed him and his followers and became king by the favor of Ahura Mazda.

Herodotus' account is basically the same as the official version, although enlivened by many picturesque details. As he tells the story, Cambyses, disturbed by a dream he had in Egypt that Smerdis (the Greek rendering of Bardiya) would seize the throne, dispatched a trusted friend to assassinate his brother. Some time later a Magian whom Cambyses had left as guardian of his household in Susa, knowing that Smerdis had been secretly murdered, decided to revolt from Cambyses. This Magian had a brother who not only closely resembled the dead Smerdis in looks but also bore the same name. The Magians, then, with the brother sitting on the throne, dispatched proclamations throughout the empire that Smerdis should be recognized as king rather than Cambyses. This manifesto reached Cambyses in Syria in the spring of 522 as he was returning to Persia. Cambyses at first thought that his friend had failed to kill his brother Smerdis, but when he was persuaded that the murder had been performed and that consequently the man then reigning at Susa was a "false" Smerdis, his intention was to rush home to seek vengeance. While leaping upon his horse he accidentally wounded himself in the thigh with his sword, and shortly thereafter he died from the gangrene which had set in. Before his death, however, he called the leading Persians to him, confessed the murder of his brother, explained the usurpation of the false Smerdis, and implored them not to let control of the kingdom revert to the Medes.

The Persian leaders whom Cambyses had exhorted on his deathbed disregarded his admonitions, thinking that the unbalanced and vindictive king had merely been trying to foment trouble for his younger brother. Consequently the false Smerdis ruled in peace for seven months and gained popularity by declaring a three years' remission of taxes and military service. Before the seven months had elapsed, however, Otanes, a Persian noble living at Susa, began to be suspicious of the new king because he never left the citadel of Susa and never summoned any eminent Persian to an interview. Otanes was able to confirm his suspicions through his daughter, who formerly had been one of the wives of Cambyses but now was a wife of the false Smerdis. He instructed his daughter to ascertain, when her husband was asleep, whether or not he had ears, for it was known that years before Cyrus had had the ears of the Magian Smerdis cut off in punishment for some crime. The daughter in due course reported that her husband had no ears. Otanes informed a few trustworthy friends of the discovery, and soon a group of seven conspirators was formed, of whom the young Darius, who had been in Egypt with Cambyses (3.139), was the boldest and the most insistent on immediate action. The seven quickly entered the palace and, forcing their way into Smerdis' apartment, killed both him and his brother.

Five days later the seven conspirators met to discuss the situation and decide on future action. In a famous passage (3.80–82), which has been received with much skepticism both in antiquity and down to the present day, Herodotus gives the gist of the speeches made by three of the men, one (Otanes) advocating that a democracy (isonomia—equality before the law) would be the best form of government for the Persians; another, an oligarchy; and Darius, a monarchy. The four who had not spoken concurred with Darius. Since it was clear that the king must be selected from this group, Otanes withdrew his name on condition that he and his descendants should not have to submit to the man who became king and the dynasty which he established. The condition was granted, and Herodotus remarks (3.83) that down to his time the family of Otanes continued to be the only free family among the Persians, although bound not to transgress the laws of the Persians. The six contenders then agreed that they would meet in the suburbs of the city early the following morning on horseback, and that he whose horse should neigh first after the sun had risen should be designated as king. The story (3.85–87) of how Darius' groom succeeded in making Darius' stallion be the first to neigh is another example of the many inimitable tales to be found in Herodotus.

The differences between Herodotus' colorful account and the official one are not serious. In the course of a few generations the oral traditions on which Herodotus was dependent naturally diverged somewhat from speaker to speaker. The real problem is the reliability of the official account. Throughout history it is the victor who tries to establish the tradition that shall become orthodox. In the case under consideration it is quite possible that Cambyses murdered his younger brother; in a huge empire like Persia, it is possible, although hardly probable, that knowledge of the murder could have been effectively suppressed. The seizing of the throne by a Magian, however, and his success in escaping detection for seven full months strain one's credulity. It is also necessary to bear in mind how revolutionary Darius' actions were. Although his father and grandfather were both living, Darius, a young man of about thirty years of age, seized the throne and then spent nearly two years in bloody fighting throughout the empire, suppressing what he called rebellions. Despite the general acceptance of the official version of the relevant events down through the ages, there is much to be said for the minority opinion that the man who revolted from Cambyses was his real brother Smerdis, who, in Cambyses' absence in Egypt, seized the throne and held it for seven months with the aid of the Magians. According to this interpretation Darius would have overthrown and killed the legitimate occupant of the throne, for, since Cambyses had died childless, his younger brother Smerdis was next in line of succession.[6] This reconstruction would furnish an explanation for the widespread rebellions. Revolts like those of Elam and Babylon were clearly nationalist uprisings, taking advantage of the dynastic troubles of the Persians. Others, however, may well have been the work of Persians who resented the seizure of power by Darius because they felt they had as good a claim to the throne as he. Darius was an Achaemenian, as he boasts at the beginning of the Behistun inscription, but he was descended from the eponymous Achaemenes in a different line from that of Cyrus and Cambyses. Since the ancestor common to Cambyses and Darius was their great-great-grandfather, Teispes, son of Achaemenes, the question has been well asked whether there were not other Achaemenids as eligible for the kingship as Darius was, and hence prepared to challenge his seizure of the throne.

A large part of the text of the Behistun monument is devoted to an account of the suppression of the revolts which broke out in the empire after Darius became king. Darius claimed in the first year of his reign to have fought nineteen battles and to have taken prisoner nine kings. The beautifully carved relief forming the center of the monument represents Darius victorious over the rebels. Darius himself, with his foot on the prone figure of Gaumata, the "false" Smerdis, stands facing a line of nine conquered rebels, their necks linked by a length of rope and their hands pinioned behind their backs. Over the heads of the captives floats the winged figure of the god Ahura Mazda, who brought victory to the Great King. As one looks at this scene of merciless victory and abject defeat, one cannot forget the descriptions in the text of the punishments inflicted on these victims, which, with variations, are worded as follows: "Afterwards I cut off both his nose and ears, and put out one eye; he was kept bound at my palace entrance; all the people saw him. Afterwards I impaled him."

Darius suppressed the revolts with amazing speed. His success presumably can be attributed to his ability, determination, and ruthlessness; to his control of the "regular" army; to the steadfastness of certain loyal friends; and to the fact that the rebels, each with his personal ambition, were unable to unite. His next task, and the one for which he was particularly remembered, was to organize the empire, or rather to reorganize it, since Cyrus and Cambyses had paved the way. It will be useful at this point to mention briefly some characteristics of the nature and organization of the Persian Empire which confronted the Greeks during more than two centuries. Because of lack of space and also of evidence, it will not always be possible to distinguish between the empire of Darius' time and that of the post-Darian period.

IN SIZE THE Persian Empire dwarfed all its predecessors. In Asia it extended from the west coast of Asia Minor (including the offshore islands) and the Syrian coast to the Indus River, from the Caucasus mountains and Sogdiana, bounded by the Oxus and Jaxartes rivers, to the Indian Ocean. Of this huge section of Asia, Arabia alone remained apart. In Africa the empire embraced Egypt south at least to the first cataract of the Nile, and also Libya to the west with the Greek cities of Cyrene and Barca, while in Europe it possessed for some years a large part of the region called Thrace. This huge empire had been created in a single generation by a comparatively obscure kingdom in southwestern Iran. Even with the aid of the closely related Medes, the Persians were too few in number and still too backward culturally to attempt to establish a uniform civilization throughout an area which, to mention only the most obvious, contained Egypt, Syria, and Mesopotamia, with their age-old traditions; the Greeks on the coast of Asia Minor and the Lydians and Phrygians in the interior; the various Iranian groups, at different levels of culture; and the Aryans in India. The Persians, therefore, necessarily and probably in accordance with their temperament, had to adopt a policy of toleration towards the manifold social, economic, and religious institutions and customs prevailing among the innumerable nations and peoples which had been brought under their control. Ancient kingdoms like Egypt and Babylon continued to exist as kingdoms, with the Achaemenid rulers reigning as pharaohs or kings, until local efforts at recovering national independence made it necessary to try to discourage national consciousness. Small kingdoms like Cilicia were even allowed to retain their own dynasties.

Over all these peoples and nations stood the Persian king, sacred but not divine. In the first lines of the Behistun inscription Darius said, "By the favor of Ahura Mazda I am King; Ahura Mazda bestowed the kingdom upon me." By his victory over the "rebels" Darius established firmly the tradition that kingship was the prerogative of the Achaemenid family. By custom, the first son born after the coronation at Pasargadae was considered heir apparent, but since a king had several wives, there often were other aspirants to the throne. Herodotus (7.2) states that the king was required to name his successor before undertaking a military campaign. In theory, the king was absolute—the royal judges (under pressure) told Cambyses that there was a law that it was possible for the king of the Persians to do whatever he wished (Herodotus, 3.31.4)—but in practice his conduct was restricted by law and custom and by the privileges enjoyed by the Persian nobles, especially by the families of the six men who had assisted Darius in overthrowing the "false" Smerdis. From these six families only could the king choose his wives. In determining matters of law and custom, the king was advised by the royal judges. According to Herodotus, "The royal judges are men chosen from among Persians (who hold office) until they die or are convicted of some injustice. They settle cases between the Persians and are the interpreters of the ancestral ordinances, and all matters in dispute are referred to them."

Early in his reign Darius and his advisers prepared the King's Law, based largely on the famous code of Hammurabi which had dominated legal procedure in Babylonia and elsewhere since the eighteenth century B.C. Incorporated into Darius' lawbook presumably were concepts from early Iranian tribal law. Under various categories, specific cases were listed to serve as precedents for the judges in rendering their decisions. Since Darius intended that the "Law of the Medes and Persians" should apply throughout the empire, it can be assumed that copies of the law, inscribed on stone or clay or written in Aramaic on parchment or papyrus, were dispatched to the widely scattered appropriate officials. Side by side with the "Law of the Medes and Persians," however, local systems of law were also honored.

The Persians as the ruling people held the most honored position in the empire, and after them the Medes. The Persians alone were not subject to taxation, but their military assignments and responsibilities were heavy. Although in wartime contingents were levied from the whole realm—Herodotus (7.61–80) gives a vivid picture of these contingents in his account of Xerxes' forces in 480—the core of the army, both in peace and in war, consisted of Persians and Medes. The most effective divisions of the army were the Persian infantry, especially the ten thousand "immortals" (thus named because any losses were immediately replaced) and the Persian cavalry. The "immortals" are usually described as Persians, but it seems clear from the sculptures of Persepolis and from the colored glazed bricks at Susa that Medes and Elamites also served in that corps.[7] Commanding officers throughout the army were usually Persian, or at least Iranian.

For administrative purposes the empire was divided, exclusive of vassal kingdoms, into twenty or more satrapies (provinces); the number varied as internal troubles or revolts caused certain subdivisions to be made. Herodotus (3.89–95) lists twenty satrapies organized by Darius, some of which had been established by Cyrus. The Lydians and Ionians were assigned to a satrap (governor) residing in Sardis, while the Greeks in the Hellespont and Propontis regions were subject to one whose headquarters were at Dascylium. These Greek cities, ruled by tyrants favorable to Persia, were free from the interference of the satraps so long as they met promptly the requirements concerning tribute and military service. The satraps were appointed by the king, and if they proved satisfactory, they could hold office for many years. Usually they were Persian nobles, although in the fifth century the reigning dynast served as satrap in Cilicia, and a similar situation existed in Caria in the fourth century. The satrap was in charge of the civil administration of his province and also was the highest judicial authority in the area. In time of war he was responsible for mobilizing the Persians residing in his district as well as the required number of natives, of whom he took command. Since each satrap was governing a district which in most cases had formerly been ruled by a king, he was like a king himself and had a court staffed by a large bureaucracy. These governors had so much power that there was always the danger that they would act too independently or would actually revolt against the central authority. In the fourth century especially, these dangers, becoming realities, contributed greatly to the weakening of the empire.

From the time of Darius on, various measures were taken to meet this threat, but little information is available on the subject. Garrisons were placed in the satrapies and in fortresses along the royal roads; they were composed of Persians from the regular army and were commanded by officers personally appointed by the king. Deputies of the king—sometimes members of his family—and officials known to the

Greeks as the "King's eyes" and the "King's ears" made frequent tours of inspection to investigate conditions in the various provinces. Among other things, these inspectors would check to see that the tribute due annually to the royal treasury at Susa was properly collected. Darius assigned a fixed tribute in precious metals to each province. According to Herodotus (3.95), the annual total amounted to 14,560 Euboic talents, to which India, followed by Babylonia, contributed the greatest amount. Besides this tribute in money or in bullion, the satrapies also had to make contributions in kind for the courts of the various satraps, and for the maintenance of the king and his army when marching through the provinces.

Although the Persians were the ruling people in this gigantic empire, the Achaemenids realized that their country was too rugged and mountainous to provide a sufficiently accessible administrative center. Cyrus, to be sure, built his city Pasargadae in Persia, and Darius and his son Xerxes constructed Persepolis with its astounding buildings and sculptures, and many of the Achaemenids were buried in the rock tombs cut in a cliff west of Persepolis; but the kings chose as their capital the ancient Elamite city of Susa. In the heat of summer the king and his court usually moved to the cooler Ecbatana some 200 miles to the north, the former capital of the Median kingdom, while at times Babylon served as a winter capital. Since it was essential that there be good lines of communication between these cities and various parts of the empire, the Persian kings, and probably Darius in particular, devoted much effort to restoring old roads and creating new ones. The most famous, known as the Royal Road, extended from Susa across the Tigris and upper Euphrates through Asia Minor to Sardis and then to the Greek city Ephesus, a distance of about 1,700 miles. Herodotus (5.52–54) gives a detailed description of this road and remarks that it would take a man three days to travel from Ephesus to Sardis and ninety days from Sardis to Susa. Along this road there were one hundred and eleven post-stations maintained by the government, provided with couriers and swift horses for carrying imperial dispatches. "Nothing stops these couriers from covering their allotted stage in the quickest possible time—neither snow, rain, heat, nor darkness. The first, at the end of his stage, passes the dispatch to the second, the second to the third, and so on along the line" (Herodotus, 8.98). It was said that royal couriers, in contrast to private individuals and caravans, could cover this distance in a week. Other roads connected Babylon with Egypt and with Ecbatana, Susa with Persepolis, and Ecbatana with India via the Kabul valley. These roads, in addition to their importance for the movement of troops and for facilitating trade, were of great value in the administration of the empire, for they enabled the king to maintain communications with all parts of his realm and, through his agents, to keep the satraps under some sort of surveillance.

The Persians had a saying that Darius was a tradesman or shop-keeper (*kapēlos*), Cambyses a despot, and Cyrus a father (Herodotus, 3.89). Darius certainly made efforts to foster trade, both for economic reasons and for its unifying effects. The extensive road systems for which he was partly responsible and the safety which they provided to the traveler were great inducements to merchants. It was also Darius who inaugurated the first Persian coinage. His gold darics, with the emblem of the running archer, and the silver and copper coinage which satraps were permitted to strike were important for encouraging trade, but par-ticularly for the payment of mercenaries. Wishing to link Egypt more closely with the rest of his empire and also to facilitate communications between east and west, Darius completed the canal between the Nile and the Red Sea which a seventh-century pharaoh had begun. At some period in his reign, on his orders, a Carian Greek, Scylax of Caryanda, sailed down the Indus River, and some two and a half years later after considerable exploring arrived at the canal connecting the Red Sea with the Nile (Herodotus, 4.44).

One other factor should be mentioned which facilitated trade and contributed to consolidating the administration of the empire—the rapid spreading of the Aramaic language. The Aramaeans, Semites from Arabia, had become increasingly influential since the beginning of the first millennium. They established several small kingdoms in Syria, of which Damascus was the most important. The Aramaeans were great traders and, in contrast to the Phoenicians, traded mostly by land. Their caravans were constantly traversing the regions from Syria as far east as western Iran. Their language became so familiar that it was adopted as the basic commercial tongue, and by the time of the Achaemenids it was so much a *lingua franca* throughout the Near and Middle East that it was the language regularly employed in the Persian administration.

AFTER CAMBYSES' conquest of Egypt and Darius' suppression of revolts and reorganization of the empire, the Persian Empire included within its boundaries the four kingdoms—Media, Lydia, Babylon, and Egypt—which in the first half of the sixth century had maintained a general balance of power in the Near and Middle East. A unique situa-tion existed, therefore, in that part of the world, for never before, despite Assyrian might and aggressiveness, had all these nations and peoples been absorbed into one gigantic state. With order established in Asia and Egypt, Darius turned his attention to Europe. About 513 he crossed into Europe and undertook what, in imitation of Herodotus, has usually been termed the Scythian expedition. According to Herodotus (4.1), Darius' motive was the desire for revenge on the Scythians for the damage they had done to the Medes well over a century earlier. The Greeks used the term "Scythian" generally for all the nomadic tribes, apparently akin to Iranians, who roamed over the vast area from the plains north of the Danube eastward through the steppes north of the Black and Caspian seas and extending far beyond the Aral Sea. The Massagetai, against whom Cyrus had died fighting, were a Scythian tribe, and it was against these Scythians, east of the Caspian, that Darius fought victoriously in the campaign that was recorded on the Behistun monument. Since the Scythians who ravaged the Medes in the middle of the seventh century were almost certainly eastern tribes descending into the Iranian plateau from the Caucasus, the statement that Darius' campaign against the Scythians north of the Danube was one of revenge for the depredations of the more easterly Scythians a century earlier need not be taken very seriously. Modern scholars have suggested various motives for Darius' expedition—the search for more easily defended frontiers, the gold mines of what is now Rumania, and the like—but these suggestions do not carry much conviction. It is hard to see, for example, why the Danube would have been a better frontier than the Hellespont and the Bosporus, and certainly the Persians had sources of gold within their huge empire sufficient to render improbable a campaign in search of gold.

It may well be that the explanation for the campaign was very simple. Since Persian power had been expanding rapidly from the middle of the century and was still in full momentum, an explanation might have been more necessary for a cessation of the expansion than for its continuation. In official documents Darius called himself "King of kings, King of lands." If, however, one wants a specific motive for Darius' enterprise, a reasonable one can be found in the relations of the Persians with the Greeks. Persian control of Asia Minor included control also of the Aeolian, Ionian, and Dorian Greeks on the west and southwestern coast, as well as of the Greek cities located on the Asiatic side of the Hellespont, Propontis, and Bosporus. Although there is no specific evidence, presumably Persia laid claim to the Greek colonies on the south coast of the Black Sea. In addition, of the large offshore islands, Cyprus and Samos were under Persian domination, as were probably Chios and Lesbos. Since the Asiatic Greeks were his subjects, it may have seemed an obvious policy to Darius to subdue also the various Greek cities on the Aegean and Black Sea coasts of Thrace, for, among other things, the proximity of Greek cities still enjoying liberty was a constant reminder to the

Asia Minor Greeks of their subject status. In fact, in some way not mentioned in the sources, Darius had already begun to exercise his influence over the Greeks on the European side of the Hellespont and Bosporus, for the forces mustered for the expedition included Miltiades, the tyrant of the Thracian Chersonese, and Ariston, tyrant of Byzantium.

Darius and his army crossed into Europe by a bridge of boats constructed over the Bosporus by a Samian engineer named Mandrocles. One can believe that the Persian forces were large without accepting Herodotus' figures of 700,000 infantry and cavalry and 600 ships. The fleet, which was under the command of the Greeks, then sailed along the west coast of the Black Sea to the mouth of the Danube and through the delta to the main channel of the river. At this point another bridge of boats was constructed. In the meantime Darius proceeded northward through Thrace, receiving the submission of various tribes except the Getae, who had to be subjected. According to Herodotus (4.97–98), Darius, after crossing the Danube, ordered the bridge to be broken up and the personnel of the fleet to join his invasion of Scythia by land. When the general of the Mytilenean contingent, Coes, warned the Persian king of the danger of destroying the bridge and advised him to leave the fleet behind to guard it, Darius was persuaded, and undertook the campaign with his land forces only. The Ionian naval commanders were told to guard the bridge for sixty days and then, if Darius had not returned by that time, to sail home.

In Herodotus' account the great Persian army marched northward, hoping to bring the Scythians to battle, but the nomads, being mounted while most of the invaders were on foot, constantly eluded them and simultaneously drew them further and further into the interior through what is now Bessarabia and well into the Ukraine. Surprise cavalry attacks and constant employment of scorched earth tactics added to the woes of the Persians, until finally Darius and his staff realized the dangerous situation into which they had fallen. One night the Persians began a secret retreat, leaving behind in their camp the sick and the disabled. On the following morning, when the Scythians learned from the abandoned troops about the flight, they rode off in pursuit, but because there were no regular roads, they missed the Persians and, being on horseback, reached the Danube bridge well before the fugitives. They summoned the Ionians to a meeting and urged them, now that the sixty days had passed—for they had been informed about that provision—to break up the bridge, leaving the Persians to the vengeance of the Scythians, and thereby to strike a blow for their freedom. The Greek leaders debated the proposal, with the Athenian Miltiades, tyrant of the Chersonese, advocating acceptance of the Scythian suggestion and Histiaeus, tyrant of Miletus, maintaining the opposite. The Milesian won the other Greek leaders over to his point of view by emphasizing that their position as tyrants in their respective cities was dependent on the prosperity and goodwill of Darius. To deceive the Scythians, however, whom they feared, they answered that they would destroy the bridge, and as proof of their intentions they dismantled the sections on the northern side of the river. The nomads were convinced and rode off in search of the Persian army. After an unspecified length of time the Persians reached the Danube at night, and thinking that the bridge had been destroyed, fell into a panic. At Darius' order an Egyptian, notorious for his loud voice, shouted the name of Histiaeus the Milesian. The shout was heard, the dismantled part of the bridge was restored, and soon the terrified Persians gained the safety of the southern bank (Herodotus, 4.135–141).

Book 4 of Herodotus, which is chiefly devoted to the Scythians, is a fascinating document. Along with much that is fanciful, it contains a great deal of valuable anthropological information about the history and customs of the nomad tribes grouped by the Greeks under the comprehensive name "Scythian." Herodotus, however, clearly did not understand the purpose and nature of Darius' expedition. If Darius had been planning the conquest of "Scythia," certainly the fleet, rather than remaining at the Danube bridge, would have sailed along the northwestern and the northern shores of the Black Sea so as to maintain as close communication as possible with the invading army. Moreover, the period of sixty days which was allotted to the expedition was far too short a time to permit a large infantry army to march from the Danube into the Ukraine and then, after settling matters to Persian satisfaction, to return again. Possibly Darius was hoping by a demonstration of Persian power to intimidate the Scythians and discourage them from making destructive raids, a policy which he apparently had already attempted on his northeastern frontier, but speculation is rather idle when the necessary evidence is lacking. Herodotus' characterization of the "Scythian expedition" as a fiasco is surely misleading and exaggerated, but it is quite probable that Darius fell into unexpected difficulties and dangers. His subsequent intense gratitude to Histiaeus is clear testimony that the Milesian had performed a great service for him. The troubles which broke out in the Hellespont and Bosporus areas indicate that his difficulties with the Scythians had caused at least temporary damage to his prestige.

When Darius crossed to Asia Minor, he left a Persian noble, Megabazus, with a large force (80,000) as commander in Europe. Megabazus first subdued Perinthus, a Greek city on the northern coast of the Propontis which previously had refused to submit to Persia, and then marched westward to carry out Darius' order for the conquest of Thrace.

How far Persian control penetrated into the interior is unknown, but the new satrapy of Thrace that was established certainly included the coastal areas of both the Aegean and the Black seas as far north as the mouth of the Danube. Further west, Amyntas, king of the Macedonians, acknowledged Persian suzerainty by offering the symbolic gifts of earth and water. Megabazus found Histiaeus, the tyrant of Miletus, engaged in fortifying Myrcinus near the mouth of the Strymon River, a site which Darius had granted to him at his request in recognition of his loyalty during the Scythian campaign. When Megabazus returned to Sardis to report to Darius on his accomplishments in Thrace, he warned the king that an able man like Histiaeus might become dangerously independent if he were permitted to build a city in a strategic location like Myrcinus, guarding the crossing of the Strymon and near the gold and silver mines of Mt. Pangaeus, and in an area rich in timber for shipbuilding and thickly populated with Greeks and natives. Darius was convinced and recalled Histiaeus, hiding his suspicion under the pretext that he needed him as an adviser at Susa.

Before leaving for Susa with Histiaeus, Darius appointed his brother Artaphernes satrap with headquarters at Sardis, and a Persian nobleman, Otanes, commander over the people of the coast, presumably with his administrative center at Dascylium on the Propontis. Otanes took Byzantium and Chalcedon, which must have revolted, several places in the Troad, and the islands Lemnos and Imbros, important for their strategic position near the Hellespont (Herodotus, 4.143; 5.1–27).

In his account of the Scythian expedition, Herodotus (4.137) says that the only Greek commander at the Danube who recommended destroying the bridge and abandoning Darius to the Scythians was the Athenian Miltiades, tyrant of the Chersonese. Hippias had dispatched this Miltiades in 516 or 515 to take control of that important peninsula. Herodotus (6.40), while describing the Persian mopping-up operations after the suppression of the Ionian revolt in 493, digresses to say the following about Miltiades: "Two years after his arrival [in the Chersonese] he was obliged to take to his heels to escape a marauding party of Scythians, composed of nomad tribes which, incensed by the attack of Darius, joined forces and marched as far as the Chersonese. Miltiades did not await their attack, but fled, and remained away until they withdrew, when the Dolonci sent and fetched him back. This had occurred two years previously; on the present occasion . . ." (de Sélincourt). Since the present occasion was 493, something is obviously wrong with the reading "two years previously." It is probably best to accept a suggested amendment of the text which would read: "This had happened earlier; but now (in 493) . . ."[8] There are several puzzling matters about the activities of Miltiades in this period. If he really had advocated abandoning Darius by destroying the Danube bridge, a matter which would have been reported immediately to the king by his loyal Greek tyrants, then certainly Miltiades would have been fleeing not from the Scythians but from the wrath of Darius. Some scholars have argued that Miltiades' patriotic Greek proposal, as opposed to the *medism* of the tyrants, was an invention made to help Miltiades' defense when he was on trial for his life (on the charge of tyranny) at Athens in 493. This suggestion is plausible, but undemonstrable. Another possibility is that Miltiades did have to flee from the Persians and that, after some ten to fifteen years during which nothing is known about him, he returned to the Chersonese, presumably at or near the beginning of the Ionian revolt in 499.

It is clear that the sequel of the Scythian expedition was detrimental to Athenian interests in the north and northeast—the Strymon region, the Troad, and the Chersonese. Myrcinus on the Strymon was first given as a reward to Histiaeus and then taken over by the Persians themselves. Coes the Mytilenean, who had benefited Darius, was rewarded by being made tyrant of Mytilene and thus could be a menace to Sigeum in the Troad. At the same time, whatever Miltiades' conduct towards Darius had been, Athenian control over the Chersonese was either weakened or lost. Hippias, fearing for his position in Athens after the murder of his brother Hipparchus in 514, began to look abroad for support. He married his daughter to the son of Hippoclos, tyrant of Lampsacus. This Hippoclos was another of the tyrants who had been loyal to Darius at the Danube bridge. Since Lampsacus had had a feud with the Chersonese for years, Athenian influence in the peninsula (and that of Miltiades if he was there) suffered, because Persia naturally supported the tyrant of Lampsacus in his interests in the Chersonese.

To JUDGE FROM the silence of Herodotus, relations between the Persians and their eastern Greek subjects were outwardly, at least, untroubled in the last decade of the sixth century. In the year 499, however, the Asiatic Greeks broke out in what is called the Ionian revolt, an event of great importance, for from it the path leads directly to the Persian invasion of Greece. Herodotus, who is the chief and almost the only source for this revolt, describes it at length in books 5 and 6. In presenting the causes, he, as was his wont, emphasizes personal motives. The trouble started with a revolution in the prosperous Aegean island of Naxos. While the Pisistratids were ruling in Athens, Naxos had been governed by the tyrant Lygdamis, Pisistratus' protégé, until he was overthrown by the Spartans ca. 524 (Plutarch, *De malignitate Herodoti,* 859D). In the following years Naxos flourished under an aristocracy, or at least a wealthy class, and its fleet, after the death of Polycrates of Samos ca. 522, became one of the strongest in the Aegean. In or around the year 500, nevertheless, Naxos became the scene of internal strife (*stasis*), and the *demos*, very possibly influenced by what had happened at Athens a few years before, seized power. The ousted aristocrats fled to Miletus with whose tyrant, Histiaeus, they were on terms of friendship. Since Darius had taken Histiaeus with him to Susa, Miletus was then being governed by his son-in-law (or brother-in-law) and cousin Aristagoras. The exiles appealed to him to help them achieve their return to Naxos. Aristagoras, thinking he saw an opportunity for his own aggrandizement, enlisted the aid of the Persian satrap in Sardis, Darius' brother Artaphernes, explaining to him that if Naxos were captured, it would be easy to proceed from there to the conquest of the rest of the Cyclades and of the great island of Euboea also. Artaphernes was pleased with the suggestion and, after obtaining the approval of Darius, prepared a fleet of 200 triremes and a strong force of Persians and Ionians, under the command of his cousin Megabates. According to Herodotus (5.33) the plan to take Naxos by surprise failed when, as a result of a violent quarrel between Megabates and Aristagoras, the former, in anger, notified the Naxians of their impending danger. It is more likely, however, that this is the tale spread abroad later by Aristagoras to try to explain why all the plans went wrong. In any case, the expedition accomplished nothing. After a futile siege of four months the campaign was abandoned and the fleet returned to Asia Minor.

Aristagoras, who had been the original sponsor of this costly and humiliating failure, was obviously in a precarious position. Herodotus, continuing with his attribution of the outbreak of the Ionian revolt to personal motives, tells one of his more colorful stories. When Aristagoras in desperation was contemplating revolt, he received a message which confirmed him in his intention. Histiaeus, unhappy in his honorable captivity at Susa, decided that if a revolt should break out among the Ionians, Darius might send him down to the coast to quell it. Not daring to send a regular message because the roads were carefully guarded, he shaved a slave's head, tattooed the order to rebel on the skull, and then, after the hair had grown in again, dispatched the slave to Aristagoras. On reading the word "revolt," Aristagoras immediately took counsel with his partisans. All recommended revolt except the historian and geographer Hecataeus, whose objections were overruled. An envoy was immediately sent to sound out the attitude of the personnel of the fleet which, since its return from Naxos, was stationed at Myus, a few miles to the north of Miletus. The sailors and soldiers responded enthusiastically to the proposal of revolt and as a first step seized their generals, many of whom were tyrants. These men were sent back to their respective cities, where most of them were allowed to go free, but Coes of Mytilene had made himself so hated since his appointment as tyrant by Darius after the Scythian expedition that his fellow citizens stoned him to death. Aristagoras took the lead by giving up the tyranny in Miletus (which he really was holding as regent for Histiaeus), by assisting in the expulsion of other tyrants, and by advocating the establishment of democratic institutions (*isonomia*) throughout the eastern Greek cities (Herodotus, 5.35–38).

The enthusiasm with which the Greeks in the fleet responded to the idea of revolt and the rapid spread of the insurrection reveal clearly that the reasons for the outbreak were much more fundamental than the machinations of Aristagoras and Histiaeus. Beyond the hampering of Greek trade because of Persian control of Egypt, the Hellespont, and the Bosporus, the basic cause of discontent was the system of tyrants established by the Persians. Tyranny, as discussed in Chapter 5, had been a common phenomenon in the seventh and sixth centuries, but the Greek tyrants in that period had primarily been leaders of certain sections of the population in the overthrow of aristocratic privilege. By the end of the sixth century tyranny had become discredited in many parts of the Greek world, and constitutional governments of varying types had emerged. Under the Persians, however, a different type of tyranny was introduced at precisely the time in which the concept of arbitrary rule by one man was being rejected elsewhere. The Greek tyrants supported by the Persians were not men who through ability and initiative had acquired power in their respective cities through the support of parts of the population, but appointees of the Persians who had selected them in the hope that in return for power they would be loyal to their masters. These tyrants, protected by the Persian satraps and supported presumably by garrisons of mercenaries, ruled their cities absolutely, with no interference from the satraps provided they supplied the appropriate military levies, when called upon, and the allotted share of tribute. Such absolutism obviously could lead to various abuses, from which appeal to the distant satraps and the still more distant king was difficult and probably impossible. This total lack of any share in the governments of their cities combined with the requirement of paying tribute fostered growing discontent among the eastern Greeks, and the assembling of large Greek contingents for the Scythian and Naxian expeditions provided opportunities for the Greeks to exchange grievances and also to acquire more sense of unity. Certainly the discomfiture just experienced by the Persians at Naxos must have done much to create an atmosphere in which the notion of revolt seemed an attainable ideal.

Ultimately almost all the eastern Greeks joined in the revolt, but there is no satisfactory evidence on how they were organized in this common effort. About the Ionian cities in particular, however, a little information is available. For centuries there had been a loose league of these cities which, in addition to its religious character, had some jurisdiction in the political sphere. In the course of time with the growing independence of the cities, the functions of the league were reduced to little more than the holding of an annual festival at the Panionion, a temple of Poseidon on the promontory of Mycale. On occasions, though, the league could still play a political role. Herodotus (1.141, 170) refers to several meetings of the Ionians at the Panionion when they were threatened by Cyrus and before they had been subdued by the Persians. On one occasion they voted to send to Sparta for aid, and on another Thales of Miletus proposed that they should establish a federal center with one council chamber (*bouleutērion*) at Teos because of its central position. This statement is interesting, even if it is apocryphal as many think, for it shows that Herodotus saw nothing impossible about a proposal for a federal state in the sixth century.[9] At the time of the Ionian revolt now under consideration, Herodotus refers to the league (*koinon*) of the Ionians (5.109) and to delegates or representatives (*probouloi*) who gathered at the Panionion to discuss war strategy (6.7). It seems also that a federal coinage, as distinct from the issues of the individual cities, was struck for a while to ensure that soldiers and sailors be paid by a common standard.[10]

Once the gauntlet of rebellion had been thrown down, Aristagoras sailed for the mainland of Greece to try to obtain allies for the Ionian cause. He first went to Sparta, universally recognized as the strongest of the Greek states, and obtained an interview with King Cleomenes. Herodotus' account (5.49–51) of the failure of this mission is a gem of storytelling and should be read unabridged, even though he gives the erroneous impression that Cleomenes alone could make such a decision for the Spartans and that Aristagoras was proposing a march into the center of the Persian Empire.

After leaving Sparta, Aristagoras went to Athens where, apparently, he was permitted to address the assembly (Herodotus, 5.97). As he had at Sparta, he spoke of the wealth of Asia and the military inadequacies of the Persians, but he also emphasized that, since the Milesians were colonists of the Athenians, it was only proper for them in their need to receive aid from their founders. The Athenians were persuaded and voted to send twenty ships to help the Ionians. Herodotus, who reveals prejudices against the Ionians in general and Aristagoras in particular, remarks that it is easier to deceive many than one, for Aristagoras failed with Cleomenes but succeeded with 30,000 Athenians. Since census statistics do not exist for the Greek cities, this figure, surely referring to adult male citizens, is very welcome, although one would like to know Herodotus' authority for it.

The reasons for Athens' favorable response to Aristagoras are clear, although subsequent events revealed that the decision was not unanimous. Shortly before 500 the Spartans, disturbed by the growing power and independence of the Athenians and also convinced that Delphi had been bribed by the Alcmaeonids to give the oracle ordering the Spartans to liberate Athens from the Pisistratids, decided that the best way to render Athens subservient to them was to restore the tyranny. Hippias was recalled from Sigeum, and at a meeting of the representatives of the Peloponnesian League (the first recorded existence of this league), the Spartans explained their plans. The allies rejected the proposal, largely, according to Herodotus, because of an eloquent denunciation of tyranny by the Corinthian delegate in which he related the sufferings of the Corinthians under the Cypselids. One can suspect that fear of further increase of Spartan power influenced the allies as well as the ethical argument against tyranny. Hippias, therefore, had to return to Sigeum, although both Amyntas of Macedonia and the Thessalians offered him territory, Anthemus and Iolcus respectively. Once back in Asia Minor, he exerted himself to convince the satrap Artaphernes to restore him. When they heard about this, the Athenians sent envoys to Sardis urging Artaphernes not to listen to the Pisistratids. The reply they received was that if they wished to be safe, they should take Hippias back (Herodotus, 5.90–96). The Athenians refused, and their indignation against Persia was still prevalent when Aristagoras arrived in Athens. Aristagoras' appeal to Athens as the founder of Miletus also was effective, for, since Pisistratus' purification of Delos, at least, the Athenians had seen the value of Athens cast in the role of "mother of the Ionians." Economic considerations, too, influenced the Athenian decision. Control of the Hellespont and Bosporus by Persian-supported tyrants was detrimental to Athenian trade in the Black Sea, and it is likely that Athens was already interested in the islands Lemnos and Imbros so strategically located for safeguarding the approach to the Hellespont.

In the spring of 498 the Athenian squadron accompanied by five ships from Euboean Eretria, which had been aided by Miletus in the past, set sail for Miletus. At that time twenty ships probably represented a high proportion of the total Athenian fleet; the remaining vessels were needed to patrol local waters as protection against raids from hostile Aegina. The Eretrian contingent was surprisingly small, but it is possible, on the evidence of a story (whose reliability cannot be checked) preserved in one of Plutarch's essays (*De malignitate Herodoti*, 861B) that other Eretrian ships sailed to the neighborhood of Cyprus and there, presumably in conjunction with an Asiatic Greek squadron, defeated the Cypriot (that is, Phoenician) fleet. This battle, if historical, could have been a major factor in causing the Cypriot Greeks to join the revolt in the following year.

Meanwhile the twenty-five Athenian and Eretrian ships had transferred their base from Miletus to Corēsos, the harbor town of Ephesus. They disembarked and, joined by Ionian troops, marched inland to Sardis, which, except for the citadel guarded by Artaphernes and his garrison, they easily took. The lower town, consisting chiefly of straw huts, was burned, Herodotus says by accident. Unfortunately the temple of the native goddess, Cybele, went up in flames, an event which angered the Lydians and provided the Persians with an excuse for their subsequent burning of Greek temples. Learning that Persian forces were approaching, the Greeks retreated to Ephesus where they were overtaken and defeated by the Persians. The surviving Ionians scattered to their respective cities, but the Athenians sailed home; Herodotus (5.100–103) says nothing about the Eretrians at this point. Despite numerous pleas from Aristagoras the Athenians refused to participate further in the revolt. The election of Hipparchus, son of Charmos, as archon for 496/5 is good evidence that a group friendly to the Pisistratids, and hence to Persia, had temporarily gained the ascendancy—undoubtedly capitalizing on the fear of the Persians which permeated Athens after the defeat at Ephesus. Hipparchus presumably was the man whom, according to Aristotle, Cleisthenes particularly had in mind when he proposed the law on ostracism; he was a Pisistratid or a friend of the Pisistratids—one of those men allowed to remain in Athens after the expulsion of the tyrants because he had not shared in any of their offenses.

The burning of Sardis fanned the spirit of revolt, which by the following year had spread from Byzantium to Caria and Cyprus. There is no need to describe the course of the revolt in detail. By 497 Persian forces, both land and sea, were mobilized, and in that year and the next, after bitter fighting, Cyprus and Caria fell once again under Persian domination. It was probably in 496 that Aristagoras was killed. Herodotus (5.124–126) depicts him as a troublemaker who lost his nerve and fled to Myrcinus on the Strymon, where he met his end fighting against the Thracians. Some modern scholars have argued that his retirement to Myrcinus was to assist the revolt by exploiting the great resources of the Strymon region in foodstuffs, metals, timber, and manpower. Seemingly in these confused years Miltiades, wherever he may have been since the

Scythian campaign of Darius, returned and took control of the Chersonese once again. He also captured the islands of Lemnos and Imbros,
which soon were colonized by poor Athenians.

The great test of the revolt came in 494 when the Persians began to
besiege Miletus by land and also brought a large fleet against it. To
confront the Persians the Ionians marshaled a fleet of some 350 ships, of
which the majority were contributed by Chios, Miletus, Lesbos, and
Samos. The naval battle took place near Lade, a little island just off Miletus. The treachery of large sections of the Samian and Lesbian ships
doomed the rest of the Ionians, although they fought valiantly. By the
end of the year or early in 493 Miletus was taken by storm, and, except
for bloody mopping-up operations, the back of the revolt had been broken. Large parts of Miletus were ravaged, and the famous temple with
its oracle of Apollo at Didyma, some eleven miles from Miletus, was
plundered and burned. Miletus was not totally destroyed, however, for
Milesians continued living on the site, but the days of its greatness were
over, only to be partially recaptured in the Hellenistic and Roman periods.

The Persian fleet wintered at Miletus. In the spring of 493 it sailed
north and easily took the islands of Chios, Lesbos, and Tenedos, and
then the Ionian towns on the mainland. Herodotus' commentary on the
fate of the Ionians is grim (6.32): "The threats which the Persian commanders had uttered against the Ionians when they found them resolved
upon opposition were now carried into effect; once the towns were in
their hands, the best-looking boys were chosen for castration and made
into eunuchs; the handsomest girls were dragged from their homes and
sent to Darius' court, and the towns themselves, temples and all, were
burned to the ground. In this way the Ionians were reduced for the third
time to slavery—first by the Lydians, and then, twice, by the Persians"
(de Sélincourt). The Persian vengeance, no doubt, was frightful, but
Herodotus' picture is clearly exaggerated. Within a few years the cities,
although not as prosperous as before, were functioning normally and
providing tribute and military contingents to the Great King. In this
same summer of 493 the Phoenician fleet, by campaigning in the
Hellespont, Propontis, and Bosporus areas, brought back into the fold
those cities on the European side which had joined in the revolt. It was
then that Miltiades fled from the Chersonese and, after a narrow escape
from the Phoenicians, arrived safely in Athens.

A word should be said about Histiaeus who, according to Herodotus, was responsible, in conjunction with Aristagoras, for the outbreak
of the Ionian revolt. After the death of his son-in-law (or brother-in-law)
he obtained permission from Darius to return to the Aegean, supposedly

to help quell the rebellion. He stopped at Sardis, but when he found that the satrap Artaphernes suspected him of having fomented the rebellion, he fled to the coast. His activities for the next few years, as described by Herodotus, form so complicated a pattern that some scholars have depicted Histiaeus as a loyal servant of Darius throughout, while others have argued that he really was a Greek patriot, working for the liberation of the Ionians. The riddle of his intentions has little chance of solution, for, depending on whom he was associating with at the time, he had to play the role of friend of the Persians or friend of the Greeks. Ultimately he fell into the hands of Artaphernes, who had him impaled and his head sent to Susa. Darius, who seemingly never had lost confidence in him, had the head buried with the honors due to a man who had been a benefactor to him and to the Persians (Herodotus, 6.30).

Herodotus' account of the Ionian revolt is vitiated by his bias against the Ionians and by his inability to grasp the real nature of the rebellion. His prejudice arose from various sources, such as the fact that he was a native of the Dorian and Carian city of Halicarnassus; furthermore, he had many friends among the Samians, who probably distorted the history of the revolt to palliate their treachery at the battle of Lade; also he was a great admirer of Periclean Athens, which to justify its imperial rule over the Ionians maintained that Athens had freed the Ionians from Persia. With these prejudices and his habit of looking for personal causes, he depicted the revolt as the work of two irresponsible adventurers, and as doomed to failure because of the softness and lack of discipline which he attributed to the Ionians. He failed to realize that the revolt, because of deeply felt grievances, had almost universal support from the eastern Greeks. He was unaware of the basic incongruity in his account—that those despised Ionians had stood up against the might of Persia for six long years. After recording that Athens voted to send twenty ships to aid the Ionians, he remarks somberly (5.97): "These ships were the beginning of evils both for Hellenes and Barbarians." The implication of these words is that the Athenian action was responsible for the subsequent Persian invasions. The course of Persian history since about 550, however, suggests that the Persian drive towards expansion would have continued, provocation or no provocation. Darius had already shown his hand by his Scythian and Thracian expedition, by sending fifteen Persian officers in two Phoenician warships under the guidance of a Greek doctor, Democedes, who had been in his service, to make a reconnaissance of the Greek world as far as Italy (3.131–138), and by his approval of the proposal to take Naxos, the other Cyclades, and Euboea. In view of the predictability of Persian aspirations, assistance to the rebelling Ionians from the Greeks of the mainland logically would have seemed to be an enlightened policy of self-preservation rather than an irresponsible provocation.

After crushing the revolt, the Persians in the same year (493) took certain steps which Herodotus (6.42) describes as useful to the Ionians and conducive to peace. Artaphernes summoned envoys from the cities to Sardis and "compelled the Ionians to make treaties with one another so that they should abide by judicial decisions and not harry and plunder one another." He also had the land surveyed as a preliminary to a reassessment of the tribute. The assessment was approximately the same as the preceding one, but presumably was assigned more equitably. Herodotus remarks that it was still in effect in his time, a statement which, if correct, is usually interpreted to mean that in the time of the Delian League and the Athenian empire, the Athenian assessment for Ionia was based on the Persian model. In the following year, Herodotus says (6.43), Mardonius, the son-in-law of Darius, newly appointed as general, did a surprising thing, for he deposed all the tyrants in the Ionian cities and established democracies in their place. Since tyrants continued to rule in some of the islands, like Chios, as well as in some of the Aeolian and Dorian cities, this statement, if true, presumably refers to the Ionian cities proper of the mainland. Even for this restricted area, however, the statement raises a problem, for one wonders who these tyrants were and when they were established, since one of Aristagoras' first acts in the revolt had been the suppression of the existing tyrannies. Although one hesitates to prefer a later source (Diodorus, 10.25) to Herodotus, it may be justifiable here to accept Diodorus' remark that the Persians restored their laws to the Ionians. Under this interpretation, the surprising policy of the Persians would have been their willingness not to revive the system of tyrants in Ionia, which they realized had been one of the main grievances leading to the rebellion, and to permit—or to assist—the cities to establish constitutional governments of a democratic type.

In 492 Mardonius, after establishing "democracies" in Ionia, crossed the Hellespont and with both land and naval forces began the task of reconquering Thrace, which had broken away from Persia in the confusion attendant upon the Ionian revolt. This purpose was achieved, and Macedonia also once again recognized the Great King as overlord. Herodotus (6.43–45) implies that the real objectives of the expedition were Eretria and Athens, but this may well be an anticipation of the goals which were set for the campaign that followed two years later. In any case, a hard battle in Macedonia with a Thracian tribe in which Mardonius himself was wounded, and the wreck of many ships in a violent storm as they were trying to round Mt. Athos, the most easterly of the three promontories of Chalcidice, necessitated a return to Asia. Despite these setbacks, however, the expedition was successful, for with Thrace and Macedonia under its control Persian suzerainty now extended to the northern border of Thessaly, the most northerly of the mainland states which were recognized as Greek.

WITH THE Asiatic Greeks subdued and reorganized and with Thrace and Macedonia once again submissive to Persian authority, Darius was ready to begin his offensive against the Greek mainland. The first step in his program was to inflict punishment on Athens and Eretria for their audacity in aiding the Ionians in their revolt and to exact vengeance for the burning of Sardis. To emphasize the evil consequences of the "provocative" action of the Athenians, Herodotus (5.105) tells the story that after hearing of the burning of Sardis and being informed who the Athenians were, Darius ordered a slave every night at dinner time to repeat thrice to him, "Sire, remember the Athenians," an unlikely tale which would fill Athenians of later generations with pride. As a preliminary measure to the projected campaign, Darius is said to have sent heralds to the various Greek states to demand earth and water as a token of submission. According to Herodotus (6.48–49), the Aegean islands and many states on the mainland tendered their submission. Since the Persian expedition in 490 treated the islanders as enemies, despite their supposed submission (6.96–99), it seems clear that Herodotus erroneously attributed to Darius what Xerxes demanded a decade later. The story (7.133) that the Athenians threw the heralds into the *barathron* (a pit into which criminals were cast) and the Spartans, into a well, bidding them to get earth and water for the king from these places, surely can be regarded as apocryphal in part, for Darius was hardly likely to send envoys to Athens, a city he had marked out for punishment. The tale concerning Sparta, however, is more probable since Herodotus (134–137) tells of the two volunteers sent to Xerxes to atone for the violation of "the law of nations," but presumably the violation had been perpetrated on heralds sent by Xerxes himself.[11]

Very little trustworthy material is available about the internal political conditions and the various trends of public opinion prevalent in Athens in this period. Consequently, in trying to depict and analyze the situation, scholars have supplemented the scanty data by giving rein to their reasoning and imaginative faculties, and the results have been amusingly diverse. It is important to remember that there were no political parties in the modern sense of the word; the chief dichotomy lay between rich and poor, or oligarchs and "democrats." Between these two extremes there were many citizens belonging to no particular category whose vote could swing the political pendulum one way or the other. Since leadership resided with certain prominent families, the carrying out of policies often depended on the formation of alliances between such families and also on how effectively the leader of the combination could sway the assembly. Occasionally, as in the case of Themistocles, sheer genius and the ability to convince the assembly of the absolute need of a particular proposal could carry the day against all opposition. In the last years of the sixth century it seems reasonable to assume that the Alcmaeonids remained influential, both because of the general satisfaction with Cleisthenes' reforms and also because it is probable that many of the poorer adherents of the Pisistratids transferred their allegiance to the "democrat" Cleisthenes. It is true that Cleisthenes disappeared from history, but this need not imply that the embassy to Sardis requesting help against Athens' aggressive enemies—if there was such an embassy and if Cleisthenes was responsible for it—caused him or his family to fall into disfavor, for at that time no stigma was attached to seeking or maintaining relations with Persia unless these relations were to be the means of exploiting or conquering other Greeks.

With the outbreak of the Ionian revolt at the beginning of the fifth century the concept of *medism*—having friendly relations with, or seeking help from, Persia—had to be redefined, for now thousands of fellow Greeks from Byzantium to Cyprus were engaged in a life-or-death struggle against the Persians. As was seen above, in 498 the Athenians sent twenty ships to aid the Ionians. Herodotus in his account gives the impression that the Athenians in general approved of this step, but he says nothing about the man or men responsible for this momentous decision. After the burning of Sardis and the subsequent defeat at Ephesus, this Athenian contingent returned home and no further aid was sent to the Ionians despite their desperate need. The election of the "Pisistratid" Hipparchus as chief archon for 496/5 has generally been interpreted as evidence that a "peace party" had gained the ascendancy in Athens, and that the hope was that a "Pisistratid" could more effectively appease the wrath of the Persians, who seemed assured of victory. Hipparchus may have advocated noninterference in Asia, but he never would have been elected if he had openly favored the Persian-supported Pisistratid exiles. Possibly the defeat at Ephesus, a more firsthand knowledge of the might and the endless resources of the Persian Empire, and disillusionment with the lack of organization among the Ionians had temporarily daunted and silenced even those who had been most militant a few years earlier. One would like to know what stand the Alcmaeonids took at this time, but, because of lack of evidence, the answer could only be a conjecture.

The fall of Miletus in 494 with its attendant horrors made a deep impression on the Athenians. Their emotions presumably were a combination of guilt for not having sent effective aid to a friendly city and fear that they themselves might suffer a similar fate. It was possibly in the spring of the following year that the tragic poet Phrynichus produced his play called the *Capture of Miletus* at the Dionysiac festival. Herodotus (6.21) relates that "the audience in the theatre burst into tears, and the author was fined a thousand drachmas for reminding them of a disaster which touched them so closely." Since Herodotus gives no specific date, a scholar has recently argued, with some reason, that an audience hardly needed to be "reminded" of its grief so soon after the fall of Miletus, and that it is more logical to place the production of the play and the trial of Phrynichus some years later.[12]

In 493 two men who in their respective ways and on different occasions were to contribute most to preserving the Greek mainland from Persian conquest—Miltiades and Themistocles—became prominent in Athens. This Miltiades, the son of Cimon and nephew of the Miltiades, son of Cypselus, who had taken control of the Thracian Chersonese about the middle of the sixth century, had been sent to that region by Hippias about 516. He was one of the "Ionian" tyrants who accompanied Darius on the "Scythian" expedition. Subsequently he had to flee from the Chersonese, but it is uncertain whether his flight was caused by the Scythians or the Persians. In any case, he was once again in control of his realm during the Ionian revolt. It was presumably in this period that he acquired the islands Lemnos and Imbros for the Athenians. In 493, when the Phoenician fleet was reestablishing Persian control over the European coast of the Hellespont, Propontis, and Bosporus, Miltiades fled, for whatever his relations with the Persians had been in the last years of the sixth century, his activity in the Chersonese during the Ionian revolt and his seizure of Lemnos and Imbros had put him in the category of Darius' enemies. He arrived in Athens with four triremes, but instead of finding the safety that he had expected, he was brought to trial by his enemies on the charge of having ruled as a tyrant in the Chersonese (Herodotus, 6.104).

This seemingly straightforward statement by Herodotus raises at least four problems to which he gives no answers. First, who were the enemies? Since four years later Miltiades was prosecuted on a capital charge by Xanthippus, whose wife was an Alcmaeonid (6.136), scholars have generally identified his enemies in 493 also with the Alcmaeonids. This is quite possible, but since Miltiades belonged to a powerful Athenian family and since Athenian families were rivals for leadership, other families may at least have cooperated in the prosecution. Second, how could an Athenian be charged with tyranny in the Chersonese? This raises the problems, touched upon in the preceding chapter, of the relationship of the Chersonese to Athens, and of the status of the Athenians who went out with Miltiades the elder and the younger. Since Athenian occupation of the Chersonese took place when the Pisistratids were tyrants in Athens, it is probable that the agreements under which the two Miltiades operated were personal rather than "constitutional." Some Athenians in the Chersonese, however, must have retained their citizenship rather than acquiring the status of colonists, or the charge of tyranny—which surely in this case must have implied behavior towards Athenians—would seemingly have been meaningless. Third, before what body was Miltiades tried? Since Herodotus states definitely that the trial in 489 was before the *demos,* the same procedure may have existed four years earlier. If so, the assembly was playing the role of a court of first instance rather than merely of a court of appeal—an important development in the administration of justice at Athens, which will be discussed fully in a later chapter. And fourth, who presided over Miltiades' trial if, as is likely, it took place before the assembly?

The answer is that it could have been Themistocles, who was eponymous archon for 493/2.[13] This answer has to be qualified in various ways, however. Although it is likely that Miltiades was brought to trial immediately after his return to Athens, it is possible that the trial fell either in the year 492 or 491. If the trial did occur in 493, Themistocles could have been the magistrate in charge only after he had assumed office in July. Also it is not certain—although reasonable—that the archon in this period was the official who presided over the assembly. It makes a pleasing and dramatic picture to think that these two men of destiny may have been defendant and "judge," respectively, at this famous trial.

Little or nothing is known about Themistocles' previous career. He was the son of Neocles and belonged to the old family of the "Lykomids," but in the strangely and almost universally hostile tradition about this brilliant man, he was usually depicted as a lone individual. Although Plutarch (*Aristides,* 2) says that he belonged to a *hetaireia*—a name signifying an aristocratic or oligarchic political society—it seems that Themistocles had no following among the great families, but rose to prominence, and ultimately to a position where his vision saved Greece, by hard, persevering work and sheer genius. In his archonship or later when he held some other office, the Athenians began to turn the easily fortified rocky harbors of the Piraeus into a naval and commercial base in place of the open roadstead of Phaleron, a task not completed until after the Persian defeat at Plataea in 479. At some point Themistocles became convinced that Athens' future development and its chance to grow in power depended on control of the sea. In 493 this man, whom Thucydides (1.138) praised as a versatile genius with incredible ability to anticipate the future, may have sensed the aggression that was to come from Persia and hence looked with favor on the aristocratic Miltiades, a veteran soldier and a declared enemy of the Persians. Miltiades was acquitted of the charge brought against him and soon thereafter was elected general (*strategos*). If Themistocles was the presiding magistrate at the trial, one wonders whether a remark attributed to him by Plutarch (*Aristides*, 2) could refer to his conduct on that crucial occasion: "Never may I sit on a tribunal where my friends are to get no more advantage from me than strangers."

Mardonius' successful reestablishment of Persian control and influence in Thrace and Macedonia in 492 should have served warning that Darius' next enterprise would be against the mainland of Greece. As mentioned above, Herodotus (6.48–49), probably erroneously, states that Persian heralds traveled widely trying to intimidate the Greeks into medizing. Some scholars think that the island of Aegina, in particular, was susceptible to Persian pressure. In view of the splendid performance of the Aeginetans in the campaigns of 480, it is difficult to imagine that a decade earlier they had bowed to Persian threats. The Athenians, however, believed or suspected that they were medizing. Athens had long been on hostile terms with Aegina, whose strong fleet predominated in the Saronic Gulf. In the period around 506 in what was called the "unheralded war," the Aeginetans made various raids on Phaleron and other Attic maritime communities (5.80–89). In the 490s, one reason for the early return of Athenian ships from the Ionian revolt may have been the need to have them in home waters to protect the Attic coast from Aeginetan depredations. The thought that Aegina was medizing and might become a base for the Persian fleet was so alarming to the Athenians that they appealed to Aegina's ally Sparta.

One of the Spartan kings was Cleomenes, who, although some years earlier he had been humiliated by the Athenians when following the expulsion of the Pisistratids he had tried to establish an oligarchy under the leadership of Isagoras, now believed that the strengthening of Greece was all-important in view of the imminent threat from Persia. He clearly was a remarkable man, but since he tried to increase the royal power and initiative at the expense of the Spartan oligarchic group, represented by the ephors and the Gerousia, he was constantly thwarted in the execution of his plans. Under his leadership the Peloponnesian League, which was to be so important in the defense of Greece at the time of the great Persian invasion of 480–479, had gained in strength and solidarity. At the battle of Sepeia in 494(?) he had reduced Argos, recovered from her defeat at Thyrea ca. 546, to impotence for several decades.[14]

When Cleomenes heard from the Athenian envoys of the suspected medism of Aegina, he immediately went to Aegina and demanded hostages. His demand was rejected on the grounds that Cleomenes alone did not represent the will of the Spartan state. Cleomenes then decided that his fellow king, Demaratus, must be deposed, for he was always obstructing his (Cleomenes') plans, and also seemed to believe that the best policy was for Greece to accept Persian suzerainty as gracefully as possible. If Herodotus (6.61–66) is to be believed, Cleomenes' methods in ridding himself of Demaratus were to spread rumors that he was not really the son of the preceding king, Ariston, and to bribe Delphi to declare Demaratus illegitimate. The picture is not pretty, but one has the right to suspect gossipy evidence of this type, especially when the source for such stories was probably the oligarchic group at Sparta which was bitterly hostile to Cleomenes. In any event, Demaratus was deposed and soon fled to Persia, to return to Greece with Xerxes in 480. His successor at Sparta was Leotychides. The two kings then proceeded to Aegina, where objections were no longer voiced. Ten prominent Aeginetans were selected as hostages and deposited at Athens (6.73). Thus, thanks to Cleomenes' prompt, if unscrupulous, actions, Aegina caused no worry when the Persians descended upon Athens in the following year.

Early in the summer of 490 the Persian expedition set out from the coast of Cilicia in southern Asia Minor. Since the plan was to sail straight across the Aegean Sea, a large number of troop and horse transports was necessary in addition to the warships, which Herodotus (6.95), using his conventional figure (and exaggeration) for a Persian fleet, numbers at 600. The command was entrusted to Datis, a Median noble, and to Artaphernes, Darius' nephew, the son of the Artaphernes who had been satrap of Sardis during the Ionian revolt. Their orders were to take the Cyclades and then, in punishment for the destruction of Sardis, to enslave Athens and Eretria and bring the slaves to Darius himself. The fleet proceeded along the coast of Asia Minor to Samos and then headed west. Naxos, which had resisted the Persian attack successfully in 499, was taken, and the town and temples burned. Delos was spared and honored, for Apollo had often shown favor to the Persians, but the other islands, intimidated into submission, were forced to provide troops and hostages. Then the armada sailed to southern Euboea and, after compelling a defiant Carystus to capitulate, proceeded through the waters separating Attica and Euboea to Eretria. Athens, in response to Eretria's appeal for help, had ordered the 4,000 Athenian *cleruchs*, settled on the land confiscated a few years before from the wealthy Chalcidians, to go to the aid of the threatened city. According to Herodotus (6.100–101), a leading Eretrian, suspecting treachery within his own city, urged these Athenians to save themselves by returning to Attica, a suggestion which they followed. Eretria was assaulted for six days and on the seventh was betrayed by two prominent citizens. The Persians, in obedience to Darius' commands, pillaged and burned the temples, in revenge for the temples destroyed at Sardis, and enslaved the population. A few days later, directed by the aged Hippias, they sailed to the northeastern end of the plain of Marathon and disembarked in a region where their ships could be protected against bad weather by the promontory of Cynosoura. From the Persian point of view Marathon seemed to offer various advantages: the landing there would be unopposed; the terrain was favorable for cavalry action; there was a chance that adherents might flock to Hippias from a region where Pisistratid influence had been strong; and Athens itself would be left comparatively unprotected if the Athenians decided to dispatch their army to Marathon.

Immediately after hearing of the fall of Eretria, the Athenians appealed to the Spartans for assistance. A professional runner, Philippides (or Pheidippides) reached Sparta in the course of the second day after covering a distance of some 140 miles. The Spartans were anxious to march out, but it was only the ninth day of the month, and religious law forbade them to depart until the day after the full moon. At Athens, presumably while the Persians were still at Eretria, the decision had been reached not to await the enemy attack on the city itself, a strategy which would have enabled the Persians to block communications between the Athenians and the Spartans and to profit from any attempts at treachery. To judge from references preserved in some fourth-century authors, the assembly, on the motion of Miltiades, passed a decree authorizing the army to take provisions and to march out to wherever the enemy should land. When word reached Athens that the Persians were landing at Marathon, the army set out at once, and on reaching the southern end of the Marathon plain, some twenty-six miles away, they encamped in the foothills to the southwest. Soon after taking up their position they were joined by the total forces of the little Boeotian town of Plataea, which had been a loyal ally since the Athenians had protected it against the Thebans ca. 519 (Herodotus, 6.108); at the battle of Plataea eleven years later, the Plataeans were able to muster 600 men.

The story of the battle of Marathon should be read in Herodotus (6.102–120) whose account, although it has been the despair of military historians, will linger in the memory, because of the magic of his words and style, far longer than the many modern polemical interpretations.

In general the situation seems to have been as follows. The Athenians had no desire to join battle with the Persians because they were outnumbered by the invaders and were waiting for reinforcements from Sparta, which could be expected several days after the full moon. The Persians, who surely knew through deserters about the plans of the Spartans, were anxious for battle but hesitated to attack the Greeks ensconced in the foothills. On the night of the full moon, realizing that further delay might be disastrous, they embarked some troops and presumably their cavalry on part of the fleet with the hope that this contingent could sail around Sunium to Phaleron and make a dash on Athens before the Spartans could arrive or the Athenian army could return from Marathon. The rest of their army had moved to a position about a mile from the Athenians, with the plan of attacking them from the rear if they should start marching back to Athens either by the coastal road or the path over the hills. The Athenians, probably informed by some Ionians in the Persian forces, acted rapidly. Their commander-in-chief was the polemarch Callimachus, but each tribal contingent was under its own general, of whom Miltiades was one. From beginning to end of the Marathon campaign, according to all ancient accounts, Miltiades was responsible for the strategy, but Callimachus should receive full credit for being willing to accept the suggestions of this brilliant officer, his inferior in rank.

Early in the morning the Athenians, with Callimachus on the right and the Plataeans on the left, descended from their camp and advanced against the Persians on the run. In the hand-to-hand fighting that followed, the well-disciplined Greek hoplites proved far superior to the more lightly armed Persians, who were soon driven back to the shore where they had great difficulty in boarding their ships to put out to sea. Herodotus reports that the Persian dead numbered 6,400 and the Athenian, 192, figures which are moderate enough to inspire confidence; among the Athenian dead were the polemarch, Callimachus, and the brother of the Athenian tragic poet Aeschylus. Exhausted as the Athenians were, they could not pause, for they knew that the Persian fleet was heading for Athens. Leaving the contingent of one tribe under its general Aristides to guard the prisoners and the booty (Plutarch, *Aristides*, 5.5), the rest of the army marched back to Athens as rapidly as they could. On the following day when the first Persian ships arrived off Phaleron they found the victors of Marathon lined up to meet them, and they made no attempt to land. When the whole Persian fleet had assembled, Datis, after a campaign which had been partially successful, led it back to Asia. He then had the prisoners, of whom the Eretrians alone are mentioned, conveyed to Susa. Darius ordered them to be settled in a region about twenty-five miles from Susa, where Herodotus (6.119) reports they were living in his own day.

True to their word, immediately after the full moon 2,000 Spartans (probably an advance guard) set out and covered the 140 miles so rapidly that they arrived in Attica on the third day. They marched to Marathon so that they could see the Persian dead and then, having congratulated the Athenians, returned home. A historian has well observed that, although too late for the battle, the Spartans made a real contribution to the victory by giving encouragment to the Athenians and also by causing the Persians and their "secret friends" to try prematurely to accomplish their purpose.[15]

A few words should be said about these "secret friends" of the Persians. Herodotus (6.115) reports that after the Persians had boarded their ships following their defeat, a shield, presumably held by someone on a bare high hill, flashed a signal to them. In Herodotus' time the Alcmaeonids were accused of being responsible for the signal, a charge which Herodotus found incredible (6.121–124), although he admits that there was a shield signal. Historians, on the whole, have been inclined to accept Alcmaeonid guilt, but their reasons seem to be based on little more than suspicion of an able and rather unpredictable family, which, like too many other Greek families, could be unscrupulous in trying to achieve its ambitions. It is difficult to understand what these realistic men could have expected to gain from betraying their city to the Persians when the fate in store for Athens, if conquered, would have been to be placed under the old, vindictive Hippias, who would hardly have felt much enthusiasm for the family responsible for his expulsion twenty years before. If the Alcmaeonids had been suspected at the time, one wonders how Xanthippus, who was married to the sister of Megacles, a prominent member of the clan, could have succeeded in his prosecution of Miltiades, the hero of Marathon, just one year after the battle. If anyone or any group is to be considered as guilty of medism at this time, the Pisistratid Hipparchus and his followers would seem more likely candidates, especially since Hipparchus was ostracized in 488/7 and subsequently condemned to death for treason *in absentia,* according to the fourth-century orator Lycurgus (*Against Leocrates,* 117).

It is true that in the following year the Alcmaeonid Megacles was also ostracized, who according to Aristotle (*Ath. Const.,* 22) was a friend of the tyrants, but one cannot but wonder what Aristotle's authority was for placing Megacles in that category. When Aristotle mentions the ostracism of Xanthippus, Megacles' brother-in-law, in 485/4, he makes no such comment about his associations. Xanthippus was recalled in 481/0 and played a prominent role in the defense of Greece at the time of

Xerxes' invasion. Xanthippus was the father of the great Pericles, who thus was connected with the Alcmaeonids through his mother. When Herodotus was in Athens in the 440s, the oligarchs were conducting a vindictive campaign against Pericles, the leader of the democratic faction, and it is tempting to believe that the charge of medism against the Alcmaeonids at the time of Marathon was merely a part of the slander and abuse directed against Pericles. In any case, since the coup, whatever may have been intended, was not carried out, it probably is impossible ever to discover with certainty the identity of the would-be perpetrators.

The dead of Marathon were cremated and buried where they had fallen. Gravestones (stēlai) were erected bearing the names of the fallen, listed by tribes. Subsequently a monument was raised on the site, and other commemorative monuments were set up in Athens, Delphi, and Olympia.[16] Before long the traditions of the battle became enshrouded in legend. Marathon was not a decisive battle in the sense that it put an end to the threatened danger, for ten years later the Persians returned with vastly greater numbers. But the effect that the victory had on the morale of the Greeks, and especially of the Athenians, was boundless. One small Greek state with the help of 600 valiant Plataeans had dared to face the army of the greatest power on earth—had not only dared, but had conquered. The inspiration arising from that deed and from those of a decade later was to be a vital force in the life and thought of the Greeks for generation after generation. How a Greek felt about Marathon can probably best be illustrated by quoting a funeral epigram composed for the great poet Aeschylus.[17] His fame as an unsurpassed tragic poet found no place for mention:

> This tomb the dust of Aeschylus doth hide,
> Euphorion's son, and fruitful Gela's pride,
> How tried his valor Marathon may tell
> And long-haired Medes who knew it all too well.

The Persians had been thwarted in their plans to punish Athens and restore Hippias, but the campaign had been successful in destroying Eretria and bringing the Aegean islands under their control. Since these islands, and especially the Cyclades, could serve as convenient bases if the Persians should attempt another naval expedition, Miltiades decided it was necessary to force them to renounce their allegiance to the Great King. As the hero of the hour he succeeded in persuading the assembly to entrust him with the fleet to undertake certain missions whose nature, for strategic reasons, he did not specify very clearly. In 489, or possibly in the autumn of 490, he set out with seventy ships and after some initial successes sailed against Paros. According to Herodotus' account (6.132–136), which was based on a tradition hostile to Miltiades, the Parians refused to pay the huge sum of 100 talents demanded of them, whereupon they were besieged and assaulted for twenty-six days. At the end of that time, Miltiades, whose leg had been badly injured, sailed home having failed to carry out whatever promises he had made to the Athenians. His enemies, headed by Xanthippus, taking advantage of his momentary loss of popularity, brought him to trial before the assembly on a charge of deceiving the people. His friends, by emphasizing his services at Marathon and in winning Lemnos for Athens, managed to have the death penalty converted to a fine of 50 talents. Miltiades died soon thereafter from gangrene which had settled in his leg, and the heavy fine was paid by his son Cimon.

MILTIADES DIED probably in 489 with his fame tarnished by the victory of his domestic enemies over him. At approximately the same time Cleomenes of Sparta also died, in circumstances which make it almost certain that he too was a victim of his opponents at home. Herodotus includes his account of the last activities and death of Cleomenes before his description of the Marathon campaign, but modern historians are in general agreement that his death and the events resulting from it cannot be dated before 489. After telling about the deposition of Demaratus and the depositing of the ten Aeginetan hostages with the Athenians, Herodotus (6.74–84) continues, "Later on, when his machinations against Demaratus became known in Sparta, Cleomenes took fright and slipped away into Thessaly. From there he passed into Arcadia, where he began to stir up trouble and tried to win the support of the Arcadians for an attack on Sparta." A lot of history, unfortunately largely lost, is concealed in these few words. Cleomenes' journey to Thessaly presumably was concerned with the medizing tendency developing among the Aleuadae of Larissa, at that time the most powerful family in the still largely feudal organization prevalent among the Thessalians. When Mardonius in 492 reduced Macedonia to the status of a Persian vassal, it was clear to everyone and to the Aleuadae in particular that if the Persians should attempt an invasion of Greece by land, Thessaly would be the first Greek state to be overrun. The Aleuadae, who wanted to maintain their ascendancy among the Thessalians even if that would necessitate becoming vassals of Persia, were anxious to reach some understanding with the Persians. It is interesting to note that the first issues of Larissaean coinage, which can be dated to just about this period, were struck on the Persian standard.[18] Herodotus reports (7.6) that in 485 envoys came from the Aleuadae to Susa to urge Xerxes, who had succeeded to the throne on Darius' death, to invade Greece. There is no evidence that Cleomenes was able to accomplish anything while he was in Thessaly, but as an ardent believer in trying to defend Greece against Persian aggression, he naturally wanted to see for himself what the situation was in the most northerly part of Greece, which was bordered by Persian-dominated Macedonia.

From Thessaly Cleomenes went to Arcadia, where he tried to organize the Arcadians against Sparta. It was at this time, according to the best dating that numismatists can offer, that the first issues of coins were struck bearing the title—of Arcadians—as distinct from those bearing the name of a particular city. It is possible that Cleomenes was encouraging the development of an Arcadian league, thereby trying to frustrate Spartan policy which was to keep the Arcadian towns as disunited as possible.[19] There is some reason to believe also that Cleomenes, by holding out various promises, was inciting the Messenian helots to revolt. Plato in the *Laws* (3.692, 698) mentions that the difficulties caused by a Messenian war were responsible for the lateness of the Spartan contingent sent to help Athens at the time of Marathon. Cleomenes, then, may have been planning to acquire enough support in the Peloponnesus to overthrow the oligarchic government at Sparta and establish himself as some sort of national king. In any case his activities worried the Spartan authorities so much that, deciding it was safer to have him at home where he could be under surveillance, they sent envoys to him offering to restore him to his royal position in Sparta. Cleomenes accepted the offer, but soon after his return he became so insane that, according to the story, he was placed in confinement where, demanding a dagger from one of his helot guards, he proceeded to mutilate himself horribly until he died.

It is hard to form a proper estimate of Cleomenes, for most of the evidence about his career is provided by Herodotus, who uncritically followed the unfriendly and often vicious official version sponsored by the oligarchic Spartan government whose very existence Cleomenes had seriously threatened. It is clear, however, that he was an unusual man. Early in his reign when the Plataeans had appealed to him for help against the Thebans—at the time he apparently was in Megara, regulating certain matters about its relationship to the Peloponnesian League—he had persuaded them to "give themselves" to Athens on the grounds that Sparta was too distant to provide the immediate help which on occasions might be needed. By this diplomatic stroke he had achieved the useful end for Sparta that two important states in central Greece, Thebes and Athens, through their mutual hostility should serve as a check on each other (Herodotus, 6.108). Subsequently he had been chiefly responsible for the expulsion of the Pisistratids from Athens and for some years had tried, although unsuccessfully, to dominate Athenian policy. In 499, according to Herodotus, he rejected the Ionians' appeal for help, but one wonders how much he was curtailed by the cautious and conservative policy of the Spartan government as a whole. His crushing of Argos at the battle of Sepeia in 494(?) tremendously strengthened Sparta's control over the Peloponnesian League and stabilized that organization so much that it was able to be the bulwark of defense against Persia in 480–479. Athens' appeal to him about the suspected medism of Aegina in 491 is vivid evidence of the prestige enjoyed by Sparta at that time. Cleomenes displayed his statesmanship then by forcing an allied state to furnish hostages to an enemy, or at least a rival state, because he realized that the most serious current problem was defense against Persia.

Cleomenes' activities in his last years with the Thessalians, Arcadians, and helots can only very faintly be discerned, but they seem to reveal a man who would go to almost any extreme to free himself from the shackles imposed by the archaic, reactionary Spartan oligarchy. This oligarchy—and earlier the traditionalist king Demaratus—obviously were in great fear of his independence, ambition, and resourcefulness. It does not require much skepticism to reject Herodotus' account of his death as reflecting "official" propaganda and to feel as sure as one can in such matters that actually he was murdered by the Spartan government. One has the feeling that if Cleomenes had been a citizen of almost any other Greek state he would have emerged as a great man, but the closed society of Lycurgan Sparta had no place for imaginative greatness.

No sooner was Cleomenes dead than the Aeginetans appealed to Sparta to aid them in forcing Athens to return the ten Aeginetan hostages held there. The Spartans, only too willing to reverse the policy of the dead and discredited Cleomenes, sent king Leotychides in company with Aeginetan envoys to Athens to obtain the release of the hostages. The Athenians refused to liberate them, whereupon the Aeginetans in retaliation captured a number of leading Athenian citizens who were sailing to Sunium to participate in a festival there and held them as prisoners and hostages. War broke out immediately, and although little is known of its course, this conflict with Aegina exerted considerable influence on the political struggles in Athens in the decade of the 480s (Herodotus, 6.85–93).

FOR CERTAIN aspects of the intense political life of Athens in these years, Aristotle (*Ath. Const.,* 22) is the chief source, although his chronology is far from clear. In 488/7 the first recorded ostracism took place, that of the Pisistratid Hipparchus, because of whom Cleisthenes is said to have introduced the law. The presence of Hippias at Marathon and the suspicion that the Pisistratids still remaining in Athens might have hoped for a Persian victory furnish adequate reasons for this ostracism. Aristotle remarks that the Athenians continued to ostracize friends of the tyrants—he mentions by name only Hipparchus and Megacles—for three years, and then they began to ostracize men not connected with the tyranny who seemed to be too powerful. Those scholars who believe that the Alcmaeonids were responsible for the shield signal flashed at the time of Marathon naturally see confirmation for their arguments in this ostracism of Megacles and his characterization as a friend of the tyrants. In addition to what was said earlier against this view, it can be suggested that lack of success in the war against Aegina might have turned the people against a leader like Megacles. A similar reason, in conjunction with the rivalry of great families, may also explain the ostracism of Xanthippus in 485/4.

To the same year (487/6) in which Megacles was ostracized Aristotle assigns a change in the method of appointing the nine archons. Since Aristotle alone, and in a sentence that raises questions, mentions this change, discussion of the problem will be postponed to the chapter on the development of Athenian democracy.

In 483/2 Aristides, a prominent politician, was ostracized. In referring to ostracisms at Athens both ancient authors and modern scholars sometimes use expressions like "so-and-so had so-and-so ostracized." If one recalls the procedure in ostracism, one will realize that it is an oversimplification to say that one man had another ostracized. First a meeting of the assembly in the sixth *prytany* had to decide whether or not an ostracism should be held in that particular year. Only if the decision was in the affirmative did the actual voting on the *ostraka* occur in the following *prytany*, and no man could be ostracized unless he received a majority of the votes cast, for which the necessary quorum was 6,000. It is true that if some leader wanted to have a rival removed he might (and probably did) urge his followers to vote for an ostracism in the sixth *prytany*. Between then and the seventh *prytany*, however, he had to work hard to turn out the vote to be cast against his rival, for obviously that rival—or possibly several rivals—was doing his best to turn out the vote of his own followers.

It is quite possible, as has often been suggested, that Themistocles may have been behind some of the ostracisms in the 480s, but it is amply clear that his opponents were exerting themselves to have him ostracized. Of some 6,500 *ostraka* which have been found in Athens, chiefly in the agora and the Ceramicus, some 542 had the name of Themistocles scratched on them. An excavator discovered in an abandoned well a hoard of 190 *ostraka,* mostly of a similar type and inscribed by about fourteen hands, all bearing the name Themistocles.[20] It is clear that some opponent of Themistocles had prepared hundreds of such *ostraka* to be used by his followers against Themistocles—a useful service for those followers who may have been illiterate—but Themistocles must have been even more successful in getting his followers out to vote. The hoard of 190 *ostraka* presumably is evidence that Themistocles' opponent had more *ostraka* prepared than he had followers to use them. In the case of the ostracism of 483/2, it is certain that the primary targets were Aristides and Themistocles himself, and the issue was the building of a huge fleet which will be described below. This ostracism was the occasion of a famous anecdote about Aristides (Plutarch, *Aristides,* 7.5–6). While the voting was in process, an illiterate farmer came up to Aristides, whom he did not recognize, and asked him to write the name Aristides on his *ostrakon.* Aristides asked the man what harm Aristides had done him, and the answer was, "None; I don't even know the fellow, but I'm sick of hearing him everywhere called 'The Just.' " Aristides, true to his "title," took the *ostrakon,* wrote his name on it, and handed it back to the peasant.

In 483/2 some men who held leases from the state to work the silver mines in the Laurium region in the Sunium promontory discovered an unusually rich vein of silver at a place called Maroneia. The profits to the state amounted to 100 talents a year, far more than the normal governmental expenses required. When the proposal was made that the surplus beyond current needs should be distributed among the citizens at a rate of ten drachmas to each, Themistocles introduced a motion that the windfall should be used to build a large fleet of triremes. This was the policy which he had long favored, and he and his followers now succeeded in obtaining a favorable vote from the assembly. The continuing lack of success in the war with Aegina certainly was the factor chiefly responsible for the acceptance of the measure, but the news of extensive Persian military preparations and the start on the task of constructing a canal through the Athos promontory must have caused many thoughtful people to wonder if a strong fleet might not be a better defense than concentration on hoplites, as Aristides presumably advocated. The prospect of the creation of thousands of jobs in connection with the building and manning of the fleet must also have influenced the vote in the assembly, particularly if employment had been lagging. A hundred of the richest men in Athens were each made responsible for the building and equipping of one trireme—the first reference to what became the trierarchic system. The sources vary as to whether the decree specified 100 or 200 triremes (for example, Herodotus, 7.144; *Ath. Const.,* 22.7). The answer to the conflicting statements may be that there was a later decree authorizing a second hundred. At any rate, by 480 Athens had available 200 triremes, although this number may have included some of the ships in service before Themistocles' decree.

It is characteristic of the ancient authors to mention a matter as important as Themistocles' decree, but to say nothing about how it was carried out. Actually, all the activities concerned with the building of the ships and the training of the crews had a tremendous effect on Athenian social and economic life, for thousands of people had to learn new skills almost overnight. Since Athens was lacking in timber and pitch, these commodities had to be imported. Thrace, presumably, despite its riches in timber, was out of the question as a source of supplies, for the Persian fleet must have been patrolling the waters from Athos to the Chersonese. It is likely, therefore, that the building materials were imported from Macedonia, where Alexander, although a vassal of Persia, was also a friend and *proxenos* of Athens (patron of Athenians visiting Macedonia) (Herodotus, 8.136). The training of the crews must have consumed a great deal of Themistocles' time and energy. It is possible that on a training cruise Themistocles took the fleet, or part of it, as far westward as Corcyra, of which Thucydides (1.136) reports he was a benefactor. Such a supposition would require placing the peace between Athens and Aegina before the winter of 481/0, the date implied by Herodotus.[21]

SINCE THE NEW Athenian fleet did not begin to take shape until the end of the 480s, it was fortunate for Greece that Persia did not strike again until ten years after Marathon. Herodotus (7.1) depicts Darius as infuriated by the Persian defeat and determined to prepare an expedition which would overwhelm Greece, but this picture is clearly colored by the Greek assumption that the desire to conquer Greece dominated Persian thinking more than any other problem in the huge empire. Whatever Darius' plans were, they were cut short in 486 first by the revolt of Egypt and then by his own death after a reign of thirty-six years. He was succeeded by his son Xerxes who, because he was the protagonist in the great Persian invasion of Greece, was represented in the Graeco-Roman tradition as the very embodiment of the oriental despot—cruel, vindictive, luxurious, and cowardly. Herodotus' characterization of him, however, is surprisingly sympathetic in places, considering that Xerxes' role is made to illustrate a dominant theme in his history and in Greek thought in general—the *nemesis* that follows upon *hybris*. Prior to his accession Xerxes had been viceroy of Babylon for some twelve years. Immediately after becoming king he suppressed the revolt in Egypt in person (485), and, eliminating the special privileges formerly enjoyed by the land of the Nile and refusing to take an Egyptian name as pharaoh, he reduced it to the standard status of a satrapy. Babylon revolted in 482 and was promptly subdued. Like Egypt, Babylon lost its special privileges and, merged with Assyria, became a regular satrapy. The reasons for the revolts of Egypt and Babylon are not clear, beyond the desire for more independence and exasperation at the burden of taxation, but Xerxes' speedy suppression of them reveals him as a man of resolution, determined to stomach no insubordination within the empire which he had inherited.[22]

Meanwhile Xerxes had been making preparations for the campaign against Greece. Herodotus represents him as reluctant at first, but finally yielding to pressure from his cousin Mardonius and the arguments of envoys from the Thessalian Aleuadae and of the Pisistratid exiles. The fourth Achaemenid ruler, however, was in no need of persuasion to avenge Persian honor for the defeat at Marathon. It was decided that the expedition should be by land and sea, as Mardonius' had been in 492, but on a much greater scale, and with the conquest of all Greece as its goal. Since Mardonius' fleet had been wrecked in a storm off Mt. Athos, a canal, which took three years to complete, was dug through the isthmus of the Athos promontory. Once the ships had passed through this canal, they would be protected from the northeast winds by Mt. Athos as they sailed past the other two Chalcidic promontories. A bridge was thrown over the Strymon River, and deposits of food were established at various points along the route to be followed through Thrace. A double bridge of boats was constructed across the Hellespont from Abydos on the Asia Minor coast to Sestos on the European side. Herodotus (7.33–36), emphasizing the *hybris* of Xerxes, reports that when this bridge was destroyed by a violent storm Xerxes had the engineers beheaded and gave orders that the Hellespont should receive 300 lashes, be branded with hot irons, and have fetters thrown into it. Those responsible for building the second twin bridge saw to it that it was constructed more sturdily than its predecessor.

After the various contingents of the army had assembled in Cappadocia in the course of the summer of 481, they proceeded under the leadership of Xerxes to Sardis, where the huge host went into winter quarters. From Sardis Xerxes sent heralds to all the Greek states, except Athens and Sparta, demanding the signs of submission, earth and water. Early in the spring of 480 the army set out for Abydos, where the fleet presumably was gathering. After crossing the Hellespont by the bridge, an operation which, according to tradition, took seven continuous days and nights because of the great numbers, the land forces proceeded northeastward through the length of the Chersonese and then westward to Doriscus near the mouth of the Hebrus River, where they were joined by the fleet. Herodotus (7.61–99) takes this opportunity, when the total Persian forces were assembled in the same area, to list the components of the infantry, cavalry, and fleet. The foot troops were provided by forty-six nations, and by enumerating them and describing their costumes and military equipment, Herodotus presents a fascinating picture of the magnitude and heterogeneity of the Persian Empire—Persians, Medes, Cissians (Elamites), Bactrians, Sacae (Scythians), Indians, Parthians, Sogdians, Caspians, Arabians, stone-age Ethiopians in leopard and lion skins, Libyans, Paphlagonians, Cappadocians, Phrygians, Armenians, Lydians, Thracians with fox-skin caps, Colchians, and many others. The cavalry consisted of Persians, a nomadic tribe called Sagartians, Medes, Cissians (Elamites), Indians, Bactrians, Caspians, and camel-riding Arabians. The huge fleet was provided by the Phoenicians, Egyptians, Cyprians (both Greek and Phoenician), Cilicians, Pamphylians, Lycians, Carians, Asiatic Dorians, Ionians, and Aeolians, as well as the Greeks of the Hellespont and Bosporus regions and the Aegean islands. On this occasion and again in greater detail on the eve of the battles of Artemisium and Thermopylae, Herodotus (7.184–187) lists the manpower of the host brought from Asia, to which he adds the contingents levied in Thrace, Macedonia, and Thessaly. He concludes that the crews and marines of the 1,207 triremes and the 3,000 penteconters with the infantry and the cavalry numbered 2,641,610, a figure to be doubled when one included the servants, camp followers, and the like.

A possible, but only partial, explanation for this extraordinary estimate, beyond the obvious fact that all the fighting personnel were not attended by servants and concubines, is that Herodotus had seen or heard about a roster of the military manpower in the Persian Empire and naively identified it with the forces led by Xerxes. Total mobilization in all the regions controlled by Persia could well have produced troops to be numbered in the millions. Military experts have claimed that in view of logistical problems, especially those of providing food and water, Xerxes could have led through Thrace at the most an army of some 200,000. It is interesting to note that Herodotus graphically describes how some 400 Persian ships were destroyed by a storm off the coast of Magnesia (7.190) and another 200 off the southeastern Euboean coast (8.7, 13). He remarks, "Heaven was indeed doing everything possible to reduce the superiority of the Persian fleet and bring it down to the size of the Greek." It was more dramatic and more in keeping with the theme of *hybris* and *nemesis* for the gods to destroy hundreds of Persian ships than for the Persians to have sailed forth with a smaller armada.

In their accounts of these heroic days the Greeks were not concerned with prosaic accuracy. Their defeat of the might of Persia was almost a miracle, and the various episodes of the struggle soon passed largely into the realm of legend. Even Aeschylus in his drama *The Persians,* produced in 472, has the messenger, describing the battle of Salamis, say (338–343): "For the whole number of the ships of Hellas amounted to ten times thirty, and, apart from these, there was a chosen squadron of ten. But Xerxes, this I know, had under his command a thousand, while those excelling in speed were twice a hundred, and seven more." Obviously, for the Greeks, the greater the number of the Persians, the greater was the miracle and thus the glory in which they shared. To them, accustomed to the small levies of their city-states, the Persian forces were of titanic proportion, and it is only natural that they were described as countless. This point of view is well illustrated by an epitaph raised over the Peloponnesians who fell at Thermopylae (Herodotus, 7.228): "Four thousand here from Pelops' land/Against three million once did stand."

Long before Xerxes crossed the Hellespont in the spring of 480, the Greeks had learned that the Persians were planning an expedition against the mainland of Greece. Word of the elaborate preparations, in which the Asiatic Greeks were involved, could not have failed to filter across the Aegean in one form or another. In particular, the great activity of the Persians in digging the canal through the Athos peninsula must have become common knowledge from its start in 483. To judge from Herodotus, the Greeks as a whole took surprisingly few, if any, steps to strengthen their defenses against the imminent threat. Many may have comforted themselves with the thought that, in case of necessity, medism would save them from destruction. Themistocles, so far as the evidence goes, was one of the few who throughout the whole decade of the 480s was certain that the Persians would return in still greater force. In putting his famous navy bill through in 483/2 he may have used as his main argument the unsuccessful naval war Athens was waging with Aegina, but he knew that the great purpose of the fleet would be to provide the most promising means to meet and overcome the oriental invader.

It was not until the fall of 481, apparently, when Xerxes had already arrived at Sardis, that some Greeks began to take concerted action. Herodotus (7.145.1) relates that "representatives of the Greek states who were loyal to the general cause now met for a conference. Guarantees were exchanged, and the decision was reached that the first thing to be done was to patch up their own quarrels and stop any fighting which happened to be going on amongst themselves." The meeting was probably held at Sparta, and it is a safe inference that the initiative was taken by the Spartans, backed by the Athenians. This was the birth of the organization usually spoken of by the ancients merely as "the Hellenes," but which modern historians generally call the Hellenic League.[23] Although the Peloponnesian League provided a large proportion of the membership, the new league was definitely a separate organization from the former league. By the time of the battle of Plataea in 479 the membership consisted of thirty-one states, but before the arrival of the Persians in Thessaly and their breaking through Thermopylae, which forced many states to medize, the number of members was probably far larger. This Hellenic League—the first union of Greek states since the mythical times of the Trojan War—was the instrument through which the Greeks organized their successful resistance to Persia. The leadership, or as the Greeks called it, the *hegemony* of the league fell to Sparta in recognition of its generally admitted position as the strongest state in Greece. The hegemony included the right to preside at meetings of delegates from the member states, which usually were held at Corinth, and also the supreme military command over both land and naval forces. The Athenians were the strongest naval power, but when they realized that other Greeks resented the idea of serving under Athenian leadership as something too new and untried, they wisely acquiesced in the supreme command of the Spartans.

As a result of the first meeting of the Hellenic League the various quarrels between Greek states were reconciled, including the war between Athens and Aegina—if, as suggested above, those hostilities had not stopped even earlier. The delegates also voted to send envoys, with the hope of bringing them into the alliance, to Argos, Corcyra, Crete, and to Gelon, the tyrant of Syracuse (Herodotus, 7.148–169). The responses to these embassies were disappointing. The Argives, still suffering from their devastating defeat at the hands of Cleomenes at Sepeia some thirteen years earlier, offered to join the league only if they were promised a thirty years' truce with Sparta and were granted an equal share in the command of the allied forces with the Spartans. These stipulations, as the Argives must have expected, were rejected, and thus they remained neutral as the oracle at Delphi, whom they had previously consulted, had advised. The Cretan cities, although anxious to fight on the side of the Greeks, were also warned by Delphi to remain neutral.

The attitude of Delphi in these and other cases seemed clearly defeatist, which in the existing circumstances meant playing into the hands of Persia. This role of Apollo, which was the equivalent of medism, contrasted sadly with the grim determination of the members of the Hellenic League to fight to the death to preserve Greek liberty. Delphi lost a superb opportunity to enhance its prestige, for as a great Panhellenic shrine it could have had tremendous influence in encouraging and stiffening Greek resistance. The dilemma facing the shrine was difficult. Apollo was supposed to speak the truth, and to the priests, who were well informed in international affairs, a Persian victory seemed assured. Their role was certainly not heroic, but they may have thought that their advocacy of defeatism would spare the Greeks much suffering. It is also possible, of course, that cynically they were looking forward to rewards and favors from the Persians. It seems clear, however, that the Greeks as a whole did not consider Delphi's role treacherous, for after their final victory they offered many gifts and dedications to Apollo. Delphic propaganda, no doubt, was very effective then, particularly in trying to conceal the fact that Apollo had really been guilty of prophesying untruths.

In the west the Greek envoys were equally unsuccessful. The Corcyraeans promised to send a fleet to aid the alliance, but, according to Herodotus, they played a double game. In the following year their contingent of sixty ships lingered off the southern coast of the Peloponnesus, supposedly detained by adverse winds, until they learned of the Greek victory at Salamis. In Sicily the failure to obtain allies was a bitter disappointment, for the western Greeks, and especially Syracuse, had large military forces at their disposal. Sicilian history since the close of the sixth century had been dominated by the activities of a group of able and energetic tyrants.[24] Hippocrates, tyrant of Dorian Gela on the southern coast, succeeded in bringing under his control a large number of native Sikel and Greek communities, except Syracuse, in the central and eastern parts of Sicily. He was succeeded by his cavalry commander, Gelon, who pushed aside Hippocrates' sons and seized the tyranny himself. Gelon, taking advantage of civil war which had broken out in Syracuse, managed to add that city to his kingdom. He immediately made Syracuse his capital and strengthened it by transferring there the population of several cities including half the population of his native Gela, which was put under the control of his brother Hieron. In the same period a man named Theron became tyrant of Dorian Acragas west of Gela. Theron and Gelon worked closely together, and their alliance was cemented by dynastic marriages. The aggressive policies of these two men threatened the position of Anaxilas, tyrant of Chalcidian Rhegium in the toe of Italy, whose domain spread across the straits to include Messana in northeastern Sicily. Himera, a partly Chalcidian city on the northern coast of Sicily, was also threatened, and its tyrant, Terillus, struck an alliance with Anaxilas; and both tyrants when Theron seized possession of Himera turned to Carthage for aid.

The Greek envoys arrived at Syracuse when Sicily was in this explosive condition. In answer to their request for aid Gelon answered—and his reply illustrates the wealth and power of Syracuse at this time—"I am willing to help you by a contribution of 200 triremes, 20,000 hoplites, 2,000 cavalry, 2,000 archers, 2,000 slingers, and 2,000 light horsemen; and I undertake to provision the entire Greek army for as long as the war may last. My offer, however, is subject to one condition—that the supreme command of the Greek forces against the Persians shall be mine" (Herodotus, 7.158; de Sélincourt). This condition was indignantly rejected by the Spartan envoy. Gelon then compromised to the extent that he would be willing to accept only the naval command. The Athenian envoy promptly rejected this proposal—the Athenians were willing to serve under Spartan command but under that of no other state. Whereupon, according to Herodotus (7.162), Gelon closed the interview with the pungent remark, "My friends, it looks as if you have the commanders, but will not have any men for them to command."

Herodotus also reports the story current in Sicily that Gelon refused aid because of his fear of a Carthaginian invasion. As will be seen later, Carthage did stage an invasion of Sicily in the following year (480). Some modern scholars have argued that this enterprise had no connection whatsoever with the Persian assault on Greece. This seems incredible, although it may be true that there was no formal alliance between the Persians and the Carthaginians. Since the Phoenicians always retained close relations with the Carthaginians, their colonists, Carthage certainly was cognizant of Xerxes' plans. It was only elementary common sense for Persians and Carthaginians to attack simultaneously so that the western Greeks would be prevented from aiding those of the mainland, and the mainland Greeks, from sending assistance to their western kinsmen.

The year 480 was a momentous one for the Greeks and for subsequent Western civilization. In the spring Xerxes and the Persian army moved out from Sardis and proceeded to Abydos (Herodotus, 7.37). As far as can be ascertained from Herodotus' rather vague chronology, it was probably early June when the Persians, having crossed the Hellespont, began the journey which three months later brought their army and navy to Attica (8.51). When word reached Greece in May that the Persians were about to cross into Europe, the Thessalians, realizing that they were the first state in Greece into which the enemy would march, sent envoys to the delegates of the Hellenic League who were meeting at the Isthmus (7.172). They explained that unless their fellow Greeks sent them aid, they would be compelled from sheer helplessness to submit to the Persians. Up to this time, apparently, the Aleuadae of Larissa were the only Thessalians who had formally medized. The Greeks responded to the appeal by dispatching an army of 10,000 hoplites, of whom the Athenian contingent was under Themistocles. The troops went by sea, presumably largely on Athenian ships, through the Euripus to Halus in Achaea Phthiotis, and then disembarking marched north through Thessaly and took up their position in the pass of Tempe where the Peneus River flows between Mt. Olympus and Mt. Ossa. Soon after their arrival messengers appeared from Alexander of Macedonia, a Persian vassal but professedly well disposed to the Greeks, warning them not to remain in the pass where they would be overwhelmed by the Persians, whose numbers in men and ships they described. The Greeks, persuaded by the advice, abandoned their position and, after returning to their ships, proceeded to the Isthmus of Corinth.

This account of the failure of the expedition to Tempe or to the precinct of Heracles slightly to the north in Macedonian(?) territory, as stated by a later source, is hard to understand.[25] Why did the Greeks withdraw on receiving from Alexander information of which they certainly were aware? Was Alexander honestly solicitous, or was he concerned that a successful Greek stand could lead to a prolonged and disastrous sojourn of the Persians in Macedonia? Did the Greeks discover that Aleuad influence and the activity of Persian agents had made the mountain people favorable to Persia and potential guides to other passes? Separated from their fleet, were the Greeks having difficulty in procuring supplies, and were they worried about what unimpeded Persian ships might undertake? Was Themistocles protesting the stand at Tempe because it was contrary to his naval strategy? Questions such as these cannot be answered because of lack of evidence. All that can be said is that the Greeks returned to the Isthmus either at the end of May or the beginning of June, and that the Thessalians and their *perioeci*, thus deserted by the Hellenic League, submitted without opposition to Xerxes when he entered Macedonia.

The weeks that intervened between the Greek withdrawal from Thessaly and the battles of Thermopylae and Artemisium in the latter part of August were a critical and terrifying period for the Greeks, since, with Xerxes threatening from Macedonia and then from Thessaly, the delegates of the Hellenic League had to make the final strategic decisions concerning how and where the storm about to burst upon Greece should be met. For a proper understanding of the plans and activities of the Greeks, one should have a clear knowledge of the chronological order of events, but unfortunately Herodotus, although in books 7 and 8

he gives a marvelously vivid picture of Xerxes' invasion and its anteced-
ents, is often exasperatingly vague not only on absolute, but also on relative, chronology. To illustrate the difficulty the historian has in trying to
obtain a logical interpretation of Greek policies and strategies in this period, it will be worthwhile to summarize the order followed by Herodotus in his presentation of material (7.131–174). Herodotus states that
after Xerxes had arrived in July(?) at Therma in Macedonia at the head
of the Thermaic Gulf, the heralds he had dispatched to the Greek states
from Sardis to demand earth and water reported to him, bearing the
tokens of submission from the Thessalians, Dolopians, Aenianes, Perrhaebi, Locrians, Magnesians, Malians, Phthiotic Achaeans, Thebans,
and all the other Boeotians except the Plataeans and Thespians. Except
for the Locrians and the Boeotians the list was probably correct, for the
rest were Thessalians and their *perioeci* who presumably medized after
the Greek withdrawal from Tempe; it is unlikely that the Boeotians and
Locrians submitted until after the fall of Thermopylae. Against these
medizers the Greeks in the Hellenic League took an oath of vengeance,
which will be discussed later. Then, after explaining why the Persians
had sent no envoys to Athens and Sparta, Herodotus devotes a famous
chapter to the praise of Athens (7.139). Scholars are in general agreement that this passage was written late, about the time of the outbreak
of the Peloponnesian War in 431, when Athens, through its aggressive
imperialism, had become hated throughout large parts of the Greek
world. In this chapter Herodotus emphasizes that Athens saved Greece
in 480, for without the Athenian fleet, Spartan bravery and the defenses
on the Isthmus of Corinth would have been totally ineffective against a
Persia controlling the sea. Not even terrifying oracles from Delphi could
intimidate the Athenians into abandoning the Greek cause.

Herodotus then quotes two oracles which were given to Athenian
sacred envoys to Delphi. The first one stated unequivocally that Athens
was doomed and that its people should flee to the ends of the earth. The
envoys were naturally dismayed, but on the advice of a prominent Delphian—which makes one wonder about the manipulation of the oracle—they approached Apollo again, this time as suppliants. The prophecy of the Pythia (the medium) on this occasion is so famous and so
important for its influence on Athenian (and Greek) strategy that it
should be quoted in full.

Pallas [Athene] cannot appease Olympian Zeus, though entreating
him with many words and deep wisdom. But I will speak this second word to thee, having drawn near to adamant(?). When the
other places are taken, as many as the boundary of Kekrops [a
mythical Athenian king] and the secret place of divine Kithairon

enclose, Zeus of the broad heaven grants to the Triton-born [Athena] a wooden wall alone to remain unsacked, that shall help thee and thy children. Do not thou await the cavalry and the host of foot that come from the mainland, but withdraw, turning thy back; even yet shalt thou face him again, O divine Salamis, but thou shalt destroy the children of women, either, I think, when Demeter is scattered or when she comes together.[26]

When the envoys reported this oracle to the Athenians, some older people interpreted the reference to the wooden wall as a prophecy that the Acropolis would not be destroyed, for in ancient times it was fenced in by a thorn-hedge. Others believed that the allusion was to the ships, but they feared that the mention of women's sons dying at Salamis foretold an Athenian defeat there. Themistocles, however—now appearing for the first time in Herodotus' history—argued that the epithet "divine" attached to Salamis signified a favorable outcome for the Athenians, and his reasoning was accepted by the majority. Herodotus then proceeds to report another service which Themistocles had performed for Athens—the employing of the surplus silver from Laurium to build a fleet of 200 ships. Following this digression on the building of the fleet, which began in 483, Herodotus returns to the oracle and says that the Athenians, after having accepted Themistocles' interpretation, voted "to await the barbarian invading Hellas in full force on the ships, in obedience to the god, together with those of the Hellenes who so wished" (7.144). Next in order he deals with the topics mentioned above: the formation of the Hellenic League, the settling of disputes between various Greek states, the attempt to obtain alliances with Argos, Crete, Corcyra, and Gelon of Syracuse—negotiations which presumably should be dated in the latter half of 481. And then Herodotus comes to the appeal of the Thessalians to the Hellenic League and the expedition of the Greeks to Tempe in May 480, two months(?) before Xerxes arrived at Therma in Macedonia.

This digression on Herodotus' rambling, but effective, method of presenting his material should make clear the difficulty involved in establishing an exact chronology for the events described. Despite this difficulty, there is a general consensus among scholars that the oracles, and in particular the significant one about the wooden wall, should be dated to the period immediately following the return of the Greeks from Thessaly.[27] With the Tempe line abandoned and with the pressing need to formulate new plans promptly, it would have been a natural time for the Athenians to consult Delphi. The Athenian acceptance of Themistocles' interpretation of the wooden walls undoubtedly influenced the negotiations of the delegates of the Hellenic League, who met as soon as the

Greeks had returned from Thessaly. The decision of the delegates was to hold the pass at Thermopylae "in order to prevent the Persians from entering Greece" and at the same time to send the fleet to Artemisium at the northeast tip of Euboea so that land and naval forces could cooperate in trying to prevent the further advance of the Persians.

A glance at a map shows clearly why the Greeks, now that Thessaly had been abandoned, selected Thermopylae and Artemisium as the line they would try to hold. Since Persian strategy was based on close communications between land and naval forces, the Persian army would have to try to break through the narrow pass of Thermopylae between the mountains and the Malian Gulf, while the fleet had to sail from the head of the Thermaic Gulf along the rocky coast of Magnesia and then, turning westward, ultimately make its way into the channel between Euboea and the mainland. The Greek army, under King Leonidas of Sparta, which took up its position at the pass consisted of some 6,000 or 7,000 hoplites, of whom 300 were Spartiates. These troops were considered only a vanguard; after the Carnean and Olympic festivals were over (approximately 20 August), the Spartans and other members of the Hellenic League were expected to arrive in full force. The fleet, according to Herodotus (8.1–2), consisted of some 271 ships, of which 147 were provided by Athens, some of which were manned by Plataeans and Chalcidians (the Athenian colonists?). The Spartan Eurybiades held the chief command, but Themistocles, leading the largest contingent, was able to exercise predominant influence. The fleet sailed through the Euboic channel and took up its station off Artemisium.

The fame of Leonidas' heroic stand at Thermopylae loomed so large in Greek tradition that it overshadowed the significance of the fighting off Artemisium. The size of the Greek fleet, to which subsequently 53 Athenian ships were added, thus bringing the total, exclusive of penteconters, to 324, seems to prove that Themistocles' policy of concentration on war by sea was being followed. If the Greeks had succeeded in crippling the Persian fleet in the narrow waters off Artemisium and westward, reinforcements almost certainly would have been hurried to Thermopylae. Presumably the expectation, reasonable in itself, was that Leonidas and his vanguard would be adequate to hold the pass until a naval decision had been reached.

From Herodotus' account it is rather hard to understand why the Greeks were not more successful at sea. The Persian fleet, after leaving Therma, reached the Magnesian coast between Casthanaea and Cape Sepias supposedly by nightfall. Since there was only a small stretch of beach suitable for moorings, the majority of the ships had to anchor offshore. At dawn the next day a heavy storm—a Hellespontian—broke and continued for three days. According to Herodotus' exaggerated account (7.190), at least 400 warships and a huge number of supply vessels were destroyed, with a corresponding loss of life. On the fourth day the Persian fleet sailed around Cape Sepias and took up its position at the mouth of the Pagasaean Gulf, near Aphetai. During the storm the Greek ships, presumably, had sought shelter in the narrower waters of the Malian Gulf. Undoubtedly they were also somewhat battered by the weather and consequently slow in returning to their post at Artemisium, but it looks as if the Greeks failed to seize the opportunity to attack the disorganized Persian fleet as it rounded Cape Sepias. It was probably when the Persians were rounding Sepias that they dispatched a squadron of 200 ships with instructions to sail outside the island of Sciathus and then to circumnavigate Euboea so as to take the Greek fleet from the rear. Another storm struck these Persian ships as they were off the rocky southeast coast of Euboea and destroyed them all. This episode about the 200 Persian ships is denied by some scholars, however. It is impossible here to examine the complicated arguments; it is enough to say that at approximately this time 53 Athenian ships, which had been left behind in case the Persians should sail around Euboea, joined the main Greek fleet at Artemisium (Herodotus, 8.7–14).

It is difficult to form a coherent picture of the naval fighting off Artemisium. After two days of minor skirmishes it seems that a major encounter took place on the day following the arrival of the Athenian reinforcements. In this hard-fought battle, although the Greeks remained in possession of the dead and the wrecks, their losses were so serious that, according to Herodotus (8.18), they began to plan withdrawal that night. Since such a retreat would have meant abandoning the Greeks stationed at Thermopylae, one can assume with confidence that it was the report of the fall of the pass that drove the fleet to retire.

While the inconclusive fighting at sea was in progress, the Persian land forces were trying to break through the pass held by Leonidas and his small army of Greeks, both from the Peloponnesus and central Greece—four thousand Peloponnesians against three million, as one of the epitaphs expressed it. Two days of frontal attacks achieved nothing and were costly in Persian lives. Then in the evening a Malian Greek, by name Ephialtes, offered to lead the Persians over the mountains by a circuitous path which would enable them to attack the Greeks from the rear. A detachment of the "Immortals" was assigned to follow Ephialtes, and the next morning they closed in on the Greeks from the eastern end of the pass. Before their arrival Leonidas had been informed of this manoeuvre by scouts. Realizing that the situation was hopeless, he ordered most of his troops to withdraw so as to escape the massacre. True to the

Spartan ideal of staying at one's post until death, he chose to remain with the 300 Spartiates. The 700 Boeotian Thespians insisted on staying with him. The Spartan king's decision had also a strategic motive, for, by continuing the struggle throughout most of the day, the troops who had been ordered to withdraw were able to make their escape free from the dangers of pursuing Persians. The fighting in the pass was savage. The Greeks sold their lives dearly, but finally they were overwhelmed and cut down to the last man. Herodotus' account of the battle (7.202–238) is unforgettable. By his time, fact and legend had become indistinguishable. Thermopylae was a defeat, a bad one, which could have been prevented if the full Peloponnesian levies had arrived in time, but the heroism of Leonidas and his 300 Spartiates became a source of endless inspiration to the Greeks. It cast everlasting glory upon the Spartans, as Marathon had upon the Athenians. The simple epitaph raised over the tomb of the 300 Spartiates at Thermopylae movingly characterizes Spartan steadfastness: "Oh stranger, tell the Lacedaemonians that here we lie, obedient to their commands."

FOLLOWING THE fall of Thermopylae the Greek fleet immediately sailed through the Euboic channel and, at the request of the Athenians, put in at Salamis. According to Herodotus (8.40), the Athenians wanted the fleet to be stationed there so that they could remove their wives and children to safety. They had expected that the full Peloponnesian army would be in Boeotia, but to their dismay they discovered that the Peloponnesians were busy fortifying the Isthmus. The Athenians then returned to their own land and issued a proclamation that every Athenian should save his children and household in whatever way he could. Most of them were sent to Troezen, but some also to Aegina and Salamis. This picture of a hasty evacuation of Attica after Thermopylae and Artemisium, rendered necessary because the Peloponnesians had failed to take up a position in Boeotia through which lay the Persian route to Athens, is flatly contradicted by the wording of the "Decree of Themistocles" found at Troezen. Some years ago a farmer in Troezen in the Peloponnesus, across the Saronic Gulf from Attica, unearthed a small marble slab which, although inscribed, he used as a doorstep. In 1959 a school teacher persuaded him to contribute the stone to a collection of finds from ancient Troezen which he was displaying in a local coffeehouse. It was there that Professor M. H. Jameson, then of the University of Pennsylvania, saw it, and in the following year he published the text with a translation and excellent commentary.[28] This discovery has given rise to a heated controversy among scholars, some considering it an authentic decree of Themistocles, others, a reconstruction, and still others, an ancient forgery. A translation and brief discussion are given here, for if the inscription is an authentic decree proposed by Athens' greatest leader at the time of its greatest crisis, it is an unusually exciting historical document.

GODS

It was Resolved by the Council and People:
Themistokles, son of Neokles of Phrearroi, proposed:
To deliver the City in trust to Athena the Mistress of Athens and all the other gods to guard and ward off the barbarian from the land; and that the Athenians themselves and the foreigners who dwell in Athens shall deposit their children and wives in Troizen ... the patron of the land, and old people and goods in Salamis. That the treasurers and priestesses on the Acropolis remain guarding the things of the gods; and the other Athenians all, and the foreigners of military age, embark on the 200 ships which have been made ready and defend against the barbarian their freedom and that of the other Hellenes, with the Lakedaimonians and Corinthians and Aiginetans and the others who choose to share the danger. That there be appointed trierarchs two hundred, one for each ship, by the Generals, beginning tomorrow, from among those who have land and house in Athens and sons born in wedlock and are not over fifty years old, and that they assign the ships to them by lot. That they enrol marines ten to each ship from among those over twenty years of age and under thirty, and four archers; and that they allot the petty officers to the ships at the same time when they allot the trierarchs. That the generals also write up lists of the crews of the ships on notice-boards, the Athenians from the service registers and foreigners from those registered with Polemarch. That they write them up dividing them into 200 companies, by hundreds, writing over each company the name of the ship and of the trierarch and those of the petty officers, so that men may know in which ship each company is to embark. And when all the companies are made up and allotted to the triremes, the Council shall complete the manning of all the 200 ships with the Generals, after sacrificing a propitiatory offering to Zeus Almighty and Athena and Victory and Poseidon the Preserver. And when the ships are fully manned, with one hundred of them to meet the enemy at the Artemision in Euboia and with the other hundred of them off Salamis and the rest of Attica to lie and guard the land. And that all Athenians may be of one mind in the defence against the barbarian, those banished for the ten years shall depart to Salamis and remain there until the People come to a decision about them; and the ... [29]

Since epigraphic experts are convinced, on the basis of letter forms, that the stone was inscribed in the first half of the third century, the first question that arises is how a decree passed in 480 was preserved for some two centuries so as to be available for inscribing on the stone under consideration. As it was not customary in early fifth century Athens to inscribe administrative decrees on stone,[30] the decree of Themistocles was probably written on papyrus and placed in the archives. Since Athens was devastated and burned by the Persians both in 480 and in 479, one has the right to wonder whether this particular piece of papyrus escaped the conflagration.

The first specific reference in ancient literature to the decree of Themistocles is a remark of Demosthenes (19.303), who says that Aeschines in a speech delivered about 347 read the decree aloud. Throughout the long period from 480 to that date, although Herodotus and Thucydides wrote about Themistocles, and Aristophanes alludes to him several times in the *Knights,* there is no statement that can be positively identified with the decree of Themistocles as recorded on the inscription from Troezen. Obviously Themistocles, as the leading Athenian in 480, must have been responsible for various decrees, but the problem under discussion is concerned with one particular decree. Where did Aeschines find the decree which he read? It is known that at the end of the fifth century the Metroön in Athens became the official repository for state archives. Attempts were probably made to assemble those state papers which previously had been housed in various offices, and it is also possible that at that time certain decrees, famous in Athenian history and preserved until then only by oral tradition, were transcribed and placed in the archives. Their accuracy, naturally, depended on the reliability and integrity of the human memory. Aeschines himself had been secretary of the Council about the year 350, a position which gave him easy access to the state archives. This was the period when the aggressive activity of Philip of Macedonia was alarming the Athenians, and Aeschines and Demosthenes were stumping the Peloponnesus in an effort to build up an alliance against the "new barbarian." One of the most effective arguments that Athenian orators could and did use was to recall to the memories of their audiences those heroic days when Athens and the Peloponnesians stood shoulder to shoulder against the Persian bar)arian. Did Aeschines find *the* decree of Themistocles in the archives, one which may have been transcribed from oral tradition half a century earlier; did he find several decrees which he amalgamated into one; or did he give free rein to his imagination?

The decree on the Troezenian inscription orders evacuation of the nonmilitary population of Athens, and the immediate mobilization of all Athenians and foreigners of military age, to be followed by their embarkation on the 200 ships which had been made ready, 100 of which were to proceed to Artemisium. If the decree is authentic, one must assume that after the retirement from Tempe and the delivery of the oracle to the Athenians concerning the wooden wall and "divine Salamis," Themistocles and the Spartans, in conjunction with the delegates to the Hellenic League, decided on the overall strategy to be employed against the Persians. This decision must have been reached in June 480. Athens and Attica were to be sacrificed. Artemisium and Thermopylae were to be merely holding actions to provide time for the completion of the evacuation of Attica and of the fortified wall across the Isthmus. The salvation of Greece was to be staked on defeating the Persian fleet in the narrow waters between Salamis and Attica and on the strength of the Isthmus defenses.

Advocates of the authenticity of the Troezen inscription naturally find support for their position in the last two lines of the famous oracle, for they seemingly prove that Themistocles and the Greek leaders had decided on Salamis as the scene for the decisive battle. But was it so certain in June 480 that Salamis would be the site of the determining battle? It is true that once the Persian army broke through Thermopylae it would proceed directly against Athens, its primary objective, and that the fleet would hasten to Phaleron. What guarantee was there that the Persians would obediently do what the Greeks wanted? According to the ancient sources it required trickery on the part of Themistocles and stupidity on the part of the Persians before the Persians were trapped in the narrow channel. If, rather than falling into the trap, the Persian fleet had made a feint against Aegina or some part of the Peloponnesus—for example, against Cythera, the island just south of Laconia, which the exiled Spartan king Demaratus told Xerxes the Spartans always dreaded might fall into the hands of an enemy (Herodotus, 7.235)— what would have prevented the unruly contingents in the Greek fleet from sailing away to the protection of their respective cities? Oracles quoted in ancient authors are notoriously unreliable to use as evidence, for again and again an oracle was altered after the fact. These two lines easily could have been added or altered after the battle for the greater glory of Apollo and also, perhaps, to justify Themistocles against those who, angered at the destruction of Athens, may have felt that the city should have been defended. It should also be noted that, although the channel between Salamis and Attica furnished an admirable place for Greek strategy, there were bays and narrow channels in the Artemisium, Pagasaean Gulf, and Malian Gulf regions.

If the Troezen inscription does represent *the* decree of Themistocles, carried probably in June 480, then it bears witness to the almost superhuman influence which Themistocles had over his fellow citizens and to a marvelous "Hellenic" patriotism on the part of the Athenians, willing to sacrifice their homes, their properties, and the temples and shrines of their gods for the salvation of Greece as a whole. It seems, however, that even if the evacuation order was given in June, most of the Athenians, through optimism, procrastination, or inertia, postponed sending their families out of Attica. Hence, after the fall of Thermopylae and the withdrawal from Artemisium, with the arrival of the Persians in Attica expected very soon, there was an atmosphere of emergency, confusion, and panic that pervaded the whole procedure of evacuation. As the years passed and as Athens' relations with Sparta, Corinth, and Aegina became bitterly hostile, it may well have been this confusion and panic that lingered in the popular imagination, and as explanation for it there gradually developed the idea that Athens had been abandoned by its Peloponnesian allies, even though this "abandonment" had been part of the grand strategy. This version, although false if the Troezen inscription is authentic, was the one accepted by Herodotus and all subsequent writers; even though there are occasional passages in Herodotus, Thucydides, and Plutarch which possibly can be interpreted as being in conformity with the Troezen document, the overwhelming impression given by the literary sources is that the evacuation of Attica was an emergency measure carried out in desperation after the fall of Thermopylae.

An inscription is ordinarily a sound source, and advocates of the authenticity of the Troezen inscription feel that the burden of proof should rest on those who refuse to accept its stipulations. They are justified in saying that various anachronisms and the like which have been detected in its wording are not too significant, for the stone represents the version of the decree which was current in the third century, and the Greeks, when they dealt with documents, were likely to paraphrase them rather than to insist on verbatim accuracy as is demanded by modern historical research. Nevertheless, at least five objections can and should be raised against accepting the Troezen inscription as an accurate reflection of *the* decree of Themistocles.

First, it is known from Aristotle (*Ath. Const.*, 22.8) that the ostracized were recalled in the archonship of Hypsichides (either July 481 to July 480 or July 482 to July 481.). If the date 481/0 is accepted, it is startling to find that as late as June 480, when the emergency because of which the ostracized had been recalled was reaching its peak, the Athenian government had not yet decided on the policy to adopt concerning them. In fact, it is evident that the decree recorded on the inscription is at fault here. Two of the ostracized men who were recalled were Aristides and Xanthippus, and of these, Aristides probably, and

Xanthippus certainly, were generals (*strategoi*) for 480/79 (Herodotus, 8.95, 131). Elections of generals were usually held in the seventh *prytany* (February–March). It is inconceivable that in this critical year the election of the chief military officials would have been postponed. Consequently, Xanthippus and probably Aristides must have been recalled to Athens and elected *strategoi* some four months before the date of *the* Themistocles decree which records that action still was to be taken on the ostracized.[31] A similar difficulty exists if one assumes that the ostracized men were recalled in 482/1. This earlier date would have permitted the Athenians to locate the ostracized wherever they were spending their exile and bring them to Athens, where public opinion on their reliability probably differed considerably. Their presence in Athens for a year or more, however, was insufficient for a policy to be voted on them, for according to *the* Themistocles decree, in June 480 they were ordered to depart (from Athens) to Salamis and await there the official verdict on their status. These incongruities almost necessitate the conclusion that the Troezen inscription may represent the gist of several decrees promulgated by Themistocles at different times.

Second, the decree implies that in June 480 the necessary steps for manning the ships with officers and crews and appointing trierarchs were being taken for the first time. Lines 18–27 specifically state that trierarchs are to be appointed and that they and the petty officers are to be assigned by lot to the triremes. It is hard to believe that some of these new ships, at least, had not been manned earlier so that the raw crews could receive some training. It is almost certain, for example, that Athenian ships were employed to transport to Thessalian Halos the hoplites who were assigned to guard the pass at Tempe.

Third, if as the decree states, the Athenians were ordered to evacuate their noncombatants beginning in June, one would expect that the Euboeans and Plataeans, both more directly in the line of the Persian advance than the Athenians, would have been advised by the Greek generals to attend to their evacuation problems. Herodotus (8.19–20, 44) states explicitly, however, that it was only after Thermopylae and Artemisium that the Plataeans and Euboeans began to cope with such problems.

Fourth, it is difficult to believe that an official decree would order the treasurers and priestesses to remain on the Acropolis, thus clearly designating them as expendable.

Fifth, the decree states that 100 Athenian ships were to proceed to Artemisium and 100 to remain on guard off Salamis and the coast of Attica. Obviously, circumstances subsequently may have necessitated changes in these numbers, but Herodotus' figures, 147 ships at Artemisium and 53 arriving later, are very different, although, of course, in each case the total is 200. Moreover, according to the interpretation of advocates of the authenticity of *the* Themistocles decree, the actions at Artemisium and Thermopylae were to be merely holding actions. Certainly Herodotus' description of the fighting at Artemisium does not seem to belong in that category, and if Leonidas' stand was planned only to give the Athenians a little more time for evacuation and the Peloponnesians, for adding a few more stones to the wall at the Isthmus, then the futility of Leonidas' heroism makes a mockery of one of the most stirring events in the very stirring annals of the Greeks.

As is true with so many historical problems, there may never be a definitive answer to the question of the authenticity of the Themistocles decree from Troezen. In view of objections such as those listed above, however, it seems preferable to interpret it as an amalgamation of the gist of several decrees proposed by Themistocles in the years 482 to 480. The stipulations concerning the ostracized certainly should be dated prior to February 480, while those dealing with the evacuation, if they are to be dated before Thermopylae and Artemisium, probably proposed a plan which was to be put into effect only in case of necessity. One will never know the precise motivation for the setting up of this inscription, but since Troezen and Athens stood together against the Macedonians in the late fourth and the third centuries as they had against Persia in 480, it is possible to imagine that, in days darkened by threats from Macedonia, the people of Troezen may have wished to do honor to the memory of the great Athenian who more than any other Greek was responsible for the shattering of the Persian onslaught.

IT WAS apparently on the third day after the fall of Thermopylae that Xerxes and his army resumed their march southward. As they passed through Phocis, town after town was devastated at the insistence of the Thessalians, who had long been feuding with the Phocians. Herodotus (8.35–39) preserves the tradition that Apollo, by a series of miracles, saved Delphi from a marauding Persian contingent, a tradition that can safely be attributed to subsequent Delphic efforts to conceal Xerxes' friendly attitude to the shrine. From Phocis the Persians marched into Boeotia, which after Thermopylae had promptly submitted except for the Thespians and Plataeans. These towns, steadfastly loyal to the Greek cause, were destroyed by the Persians, who then entered Attica, burning and looting as they proceeded. At the same time the fleet, which had set out three days after the army, arrived off Phaleron, presumably having burned various coastal towns as it sailed around Attica.

In the approximately one week between the fall of Thermopylae and the arrival of the Persian army and fleet on the confines of Attica, the evacuation of Attica had been successfully carried out, except for some people who remained on the Acropolis and five hundred whom the Persians captured throughout the countryside. The occupants of the Acropolis provide a problem. Herodotus describes them as a few temple treasurers and poor people, and the Themistocles decree from Troezen ordered the treasurers and priestesses to remain on the Acropolis to guard the property of the gods. Neither of these groups sounds like a very effective fighting force, but Herodotus (8.51–53) writes that their defense was so effective that Xerxes was baffled for a long time until his troops finally scaled the north side of the Acropolis, massacred all the defenders, and looted and burned the temples. It looks as if the Athenians, despite the evacuation, had decided to garrison the Acropolis with seasoned warriors.

The Greek fleet, on retiring from Artemisium, had put in at Salamis. When the Athenian ships had completed their role in the evacuation they joined the main fleet, as did some ships which had assembled at Troezen. According to Herodotus (8.42–48), the total fleet, exclusive of penteconters, consisted of 378 ships of which 180 were Athenian. Nearby at Phaleron the Persian fleet had its base. There are no reliable figures for the Persian ships, but despite the severe losses by storms, the Persian naval forces were still formidable and considerably more numerous than those of their opponents. Since the most likely date for the battle of Salamis is about 20 September, when in ordinary times the Athenians would have been celebrating the Eleusinian Mysteries, it is probable that the two fleets lay watching each other in a war of nerves—and in a test of logistics—for several weeks. Scholars and military historians have endlessly discussed the tactics of this crucial battle, with very divergent conclusions. There is no need here to investigate all the suggestions, many of them subtle and subjective, which have been made. One should by all means read Herodotus' fascinating, but imaginative and unscientific, account (8.56–96) as well as the vivid poetic presentation in the *Persians* of Aeschylus, who was probably a participant in the struggle.

Herodotus, completely ignoring the strategy which is supposed to be inherent in *the* Themistocles decree, depicts the Peloponnesian contingents as anxious to retire to the Isthmus where the Peloponnesians were building a wall, and Themistocles as fighting against this policy by threatening the commanding officer, the Spartan Eurybiades, that unless the fleet remained at Salamis where the fighting could take place in narrow waters, the whole Athenian contingent would sail away to Italy.

The Aeginetans and Megarians, whose countries would have been abandoned to the Persians in case of a withdrawal to the Isthmus, sided with him. Finally the passion for retreat became so overpowering that Themistocles, to force the battle to take place in the narrows between Salamis and Attica, sent a trusted slave, Sicinnus, to the Persian fleet with the message that his master was well disposed to the Great King and that the Persians should attack since the Greeks were all quarreling with one another and were planning to retire to the Isthmus. The Persians, afraid that the Greeks would escape, sent at night a squadron (apparently the Egyptian one) to block the western end of the straits between Salamis and the mainland. In the morning, expecting to find the Greeks in chaos, the main Persian fleet approached the eastern end of the straits and by some incredible folly—or tricked by one of the many stratagems which modern ingenuity has suggested—allowed itself to be enticed into the narrow waters. The Greek ships were upon the Persians instantly and a desperate, bloody melee ensued, lasting for hours and ending with a stunning victory for the Greeks and a complete vindication of the policy Themistocles had been advocating for years.

The Greeks, who had suffered many losses in battle, did not comprehend at first the full significance of their victory, and made preparations for a renewal of the struggle on the following day. The Persian fleet, however, was too badly battered to fight again so soon and lingered at Phaleron while the crews made as many repairs as possible. Several days later, under cover of darkness, it secretly sailed away to the Hellespont. Xerxes, greatly worried over what effect the news of his defeat would have upon the Ionians, had ordered the fleet to proceed directly to the Hellespont to guard the bridges and keep watch over the activities of the eastern Greeks. When the Greeks discovered that the Persian ships had departed, they sailed in pursuit as far as Andros without overtaking them. According to tradition, Themistocles advocated that they should sail straight to the Hellespont and break up the bridges, but his proposal was voted down by Eurybiades and the Peloponnesian commanders, who argued that it was safer to let Xerxes escape to Asia than to have him confined in Greece. It was also the time of year when weather conditions made sailing dangerous. The Greeks, therefore, after extorting money from various islands and from Carystus in Euboea because they had aided the Persians, returned to Salamis. They first chose from the plunder various objects, including three Phoenician triremes, to be offered in gratitude to the gods and then proceeded to the Isthmus to select the man who had demonstrated the greatest excellence (*aristeia*) throughout the campaign. Herodotus (8.123) tells the famous story that each commander voted for himself but that the majority agreed in putting Themistocles in second place, an anecdote, whether true or not, that illustrates the intense competitive spirit of the Greeks.

In the meantime Xerxes and his army had left Attica and retired northward into friendly territory. Since the campaigning season was now over, it was decided that Mardonius with 300,000(!) select troops should spend the winter in Thessaly and undertake an expedition against the Peloponnesus in the following spring. Xerxes himself with the rest of the army set out on the march back to Asia, which, in the imagination of patriotic authors like Herodotus (8.115–117) and Aeschylus, turned into a journey of horrors. Food ran out so that the soldiers fed on the leaves and bark of trees. Thousands perished when the thin ice on the Strymon collapsed under their weight. Suffering from plague and dysentery, they finally reached Sestos and, since storms had broken up the bridges, they were ferried across in boats to Abydos. Here many more perished from overeating after a long period of starvation. The remnants of the great army then proceeded to Sardis with Xerxes. These accounts, representing the march as a desperate flight, obviously have little to do with historical reality. It is true, however, that the reports of Xerxes' defeat at Salamis, and the very fact that he was retiring with part of his army, caused some revolts from Persian rule. When Artabazus, a noble Persian who had escorted Xerxes as far as Abydos, reached Chalcidice on his return journey with a large body (60,000!) of select troops from Mardonius' army, he found Potidaea, a Greek colony at the head of the Pallene promontory, in revolt and also the neighboring Olynthus, a town inhabited by the Bottiaei (a partially Greek tribe), on the threshold of revolt. This latter place Artabazus quickly took and, after slaughtering all the inhabitants, turned it over to loyal Chalcidians in the area. Olynthus, thus, for the first time became a Greek community. Potidaea he besieged unsuccessfully for three months and then abandoned the attempt, for, with the coming of spring, he had to lead his troops back to Thessaly so that they could be at the disposal of Mardonius (Herodotus, 8.126–129).

Before turning to a discussion of the events of the year 479, it will be useful to comment briefly on developments among the western Greeks in the momentous year of 480. As was stated earlier, when Theron of Acragas seized Himera on the north coast of Sicily, the fugitive tyrant of that city, Terillus, and his ally Anaxilas, tyrant of Rhegium and Messana, appealed to Carthage for help. It was undoubtedly knowledge of an imminent Carthaginian attack which had caused Gelon of Syracuse to refuse the request for assistance made by the envoys from the Hellenic League. The anticipated invasion took place in the summer of 480. The

Carthaginian general, Hamilcar, sailed from Carthage with 200 warships and a large number of supply ships, including horse transports. These latter, being slow and unwieldy, were lost in a storm. The Carthaginians landed at the Phoenician town of Panormus, and then army and fleet moved to Himera. A siege of the city was begun at once, whereupon Theron sent an appeal to Gelon who quickly arrived with the large number of troops he had in readiness, including 5,000 cavalry. Hamilcar, at a disadvantage because of the loss of his horses at sea, sent messengers to Selinus on the southwest coast, which was in alliance with Carthage, requesting that a detachment of horsemen be sent to compensate for the losses he had suffered. It is interesting to note that, however much a potential menance the Carthaginians were to the Greeks in Sicily, the Greeks in their constant struggles with one another did not hesitate to appeal to Carthage. By a stroke of luck Gelon learned when this cavalry reinforcement was expected to arrive. At the appropriate time he sent his own horsemen to the Cathaginian camp, and they were admitted in the belief that they were the expected forces from Selinus. Once inside the camp, the Syracusan cavalry fell upon Hamilcar, who was engaged in sacrificing, and slew him, and simultaneously Gelon and Theron launched an attack. The battle ended in a total disaster for the Carthaginian forces, which consisted of mercenaries from Africa, Spain, Sardinia, Corsica, and other regions; thousands were slaughtered and thousands were captured and enslaved (Diordorus, 11.20–26).

The battle of Himera in the minds of Sicilian Greeks came to be regarded in the same way as the mainland Greeks thought of Salamis. According to Herodotus (7.165–167), the Sicilians believed it took place on the same day as the battle of Salamis; a later tradition synchronized it with Thermopylae. Peace with Carthage was made soon after the battle, with the Carthaginians paying the sum of 2,000 talents to Gelon to cover the total cost of the war. For seventy years thereafter Carthage did not interfere in Sicilian affairs, and when it did interfere again about 408 under the leadership of Hannibal, the grandson of Hamilcar, part of the motive was to seek vengeance for the death of the general who met his end at Himera. The Carthaginian tradition concerning his death was that all through the battle Hamilcar was sacrificing to obtain favorable omens, casting one victim after another into a huge fire, and that in a final desperate effort to avert defeat he threw himself into the flames as the ultimate victim to propitiate the gods.

IN THE SPRING of 479 the Greek fleet, consisting of 110 ships, assembled at Aegina under the command of the Spartan king Leotychides (Herodotus, 8.131–132). The Athenian contingent was under Xanthippus, which proves that he was *strategos* for the year 480/79, an office to which he was also elected for the following year. A confused passage in Plutarch's *Aristides* (10.6–8), which lists Xanthippus as an envoy to Sparta in the late spring of 479, might seem to refute this argument, but if one wishes to accept the statement of Plutarch, the logical explanation is that the envoy mentioned was another Xanthippus, possibly the man who was archon from July 479 to July 478. While the Greeks were at Aegina, an embassy came to them from Chios, where an unsuccessful attempt had just been made to kill the tyrant, urging them to undertake the liberation of Ionia. The Greek fleet did sail as far as Delos but refused to proceed further until more should be known about the movements of Mardonius. In the meantime the Persian fleet had assembled at Samos. It was a much weaker force than the one which had sailed the preceding year with Xerxes. Its orders were to keep watch over Ionia, where the Persians quite naturally suspected that revolt might break out if an opportunity presented itself.

Probably even before the Greek ships had gathered at Aegina, Mardonius, hoping to detach the Athenians from the Hellenic League so that he could use their fleet to circumvent the fortifications at the Isthmus, sent Alexander of Macedonia as an envoy to Athens, knowing that the Macedonian, although a Persian vassal, was well disposed to the Athenians. Alexander, as mouthpiece for Mardonius, was able to offer tempting terms which had been approved by Xerxes—restoration of Athenian territory and acquisition of further land, rebuilding of its temples at Persian expense, and local autonomy, subject, of course, to the overlordship of Persia. The Macedonian, emphasizing the unlimited power of the Great King and the fact that Athens lay in the most exposed position of all the Greek allies, urged the Athenians to accept Persian terms and save themselves from the danger of annihilation. It so happened that Spartan envoys were present at the same meeting of the assembly before which Alexander had spoken, for the Spartans, as soon as they had heard of the arrival of the Macedonian in Athens, had hastily sent their own ambassadors there, and the Athenians had deliberately postponed negotiations with Alexander until the arrival of the Peloponnesians. The Spartans urged the Athenians to refuse the Persian proposals and to remain true to their heritage and to the Greek cause, especially since, in a sense, they had been responsible for bringing this war upon Greece. Adding that they sympathized with the Athenians for the suffering and devastation they had experienced, the Spartans offered to provide support for all the nonmilitary inhabitants of Athens as long as the war lasted (Herodotus, 8.140–142).

The Athenian replies to the two embassies, as reported by Herodotus (8.143–144), rank among the noblest expressions in Greek literature. Herodotus ascribes them just to the Athenians; Plutarch, to Aristides. One would like to know whether these words were actually spoken or whether their particularly moving quality owes much to the genius of Herodotus. There can be little doubt, however, that Herodotus truly reflects the spirit of dedication which carried the Athenians through the ordeals of these years. To Alexander, they said, "You may tell Mardonius, therefore, that so long as the sun keeps his present course in the sky, we Athenians will never make peace with Xerxes." To the Spartans, the response was:

> Were we offered all the gold in the world, and the fairest and richest country the earth contains, we should never consent to join the common enemy and bring Hellas into subjection. There are many compelling reasons to prevent our taking such a course, even if we wished to do so: the first and greatest is the burning of the temples and images of our gods—now mere heaps of rubble. It is our bounden duty to avenge this desecration with all the power we possess—not to clasp in friendship the hand that wrought it. Again, there is the Hellenic nation—the common blood, the common language; the temples and religious ritual; the whole way of life we understand and share together—indeed, if Athens were to betray all this, it would not be well done. We would have you know, therefore, if you did not know it already, that we will never make peace with Xerxes so long as a single Athenian remains alive (de Sélincourt).

The subsequent history of Greece is a sad commentary on how this noble concept of brotherhood, called into being in the supreme crisis, withered away when the crisis passed. The Athenians ended by saying that, since the enemy would soon be on the march again, the Spartans should send an army at once into Boeotia before he could overrun Attica.

When Alexander returned to Thessaly with the report that the Athenians refused to medize, Mardonius moved out of winter quarters as soon as possible and marched south. After spending some time in Boeotia he entered Attica, which he found abandoned, and took possession of a deserted Athens ten months, according to Herodotus (9.3), after its capture by Xerxes, hence probably in June 479. The Athenians had remained in Attica until the last minute hoping for the arrival of a Peloponnesian army, but when they learned that Mardonius was in Boeotia and still no aid had arrived from the Peloponnesus, they had had to withdraw to Salamis. From Athens Mardonius sent an envoy to Salamis, thinking that, with Attica once again in the hands of the Persians, the Athenians might at last be ready to accept the offers which had previously been made to them through Alexander. When the envoy had explained his business to the council, one of the councillors, by name Lycides, suggested that the proposal be referred to the assembly for action. Enraged at this apostasy, his fellow councillors surrounded him and stoned him to death, and the Athenian women, not to be outdone, stoned his wife and children. The episode became famous in Athenian tradition and was used by patriotic orators of the fourth century to illustrate the fierce determination of their forefathers to remain free, but in their accounts a decree demanding the death penalty was substituted for the "lynching" reported by Herodotus (9.4–5), a good example of how the details of a story could be changed with the passage of time.

When the Athenians retired to Salamis they had sent envoys, along with representatives from Megara and Plataea, to Sparta to rebuke the Spartans for not having sent an army to Boeotia and to demand that now they dispatch troops immediately to Attica. The ephors postponed giving their answer from day to day. Herodotus (9.7–11) assigns as reasons for the delay both the celebration of the important festival of the Hyacinthia and also the fact that, with the Isthmus fortifications now completed, the Spartans felt secure. Events of the next few years, however, made it clear that Sparta had good cause to be disturbed about symptoms of discontent breaking out in Argos, Arcadia, and Messenia. Finally, the Athenian ambassadors threatened the ephors by saying that, since no help was forthcoming from Sparta, the Athenians would have to come to an understanding with the Persians. Thereupon the ephors informed them that before dawn that morning 5,000 Spartiates had set out for Attica. The Athenians, after expressing their irritation at being kept unnecessarily in the dark, hurried home, accompanied by 5,000 picked *perioeci*.

The fact that 5,000 Spartiates and 5,000 *perioeci* and, according to Herodotus, 35,000 helots all departed from Sparta, presumably on the same day, proves that despite the frustrations experienced by the Athenian envoys, the Spartan authorities must have been engaged in secretly mobilizing their forces for some time. These troops, under the command of Pausanias, son of Cleombrotus, acting as regent for Leonidas' son, Pleistarchus, who was still a minor, marched rapidly through eastern Arcadia so as to avoid hostile Argos, and halted when they reached the Isthmus. Here other Peloponnesian forces joined them. Meanwhile the Argives sent word to Mardonius warning that the Spartan army was on the march. Mardonius, realizing now that there was no hope that the Athenians would agree to his terms, destroyed whatever had been left standing in the city, burned the temple of Demeter at Eleusis, and then, hearing that the Peloponnesians had arrived at the Isthmus, retired into Boeotia. He took up his position in the territory of Thebes in the southern Boeotian plain through which the river Asopus flows. Just north of the river he constructed a fort or stockade to serve as a place of refuge in case of necessity. About five miles to the south of the Asopus on the northern foothills of Mt. Cithaeron lay Plataea. Since his most effective force was his cavalry, numbering possibly about 10,000, Mardonius hoped to be able to entice the Greeks into battle somewhere in the plain between the Asopus and Plataea where the terrain was favorable for cavalry action.

In the meantime the Peloponnesian forces had marched from the Isthmus through Megara to Eleusis, where they were met by 8,000 Athenian hoplites under the command of Aristides. Then the combined army, following the road to Thebes, crossed Mt. Cithaeron and encamped on some low hills about three miles east of Plataea. According to Herodotus (9.28–30), the total Greek forces numbered 38,700 hoplites, and some 70,000 light armed troops of whom 35,000 were helots. Since he gives the figures for the hoplites contributed by each of the twenty-four states participating in the campaign, it is probable that these numbers are approximately correct, whereas those for the light armed troops may be less reliable. The size of Mardonius' army is unknown. The Greek figure of 300,000 is certainly far too large; one can do little better than to assume that the two armies were of about equal size while remembering that the Persians had a tremendous superiority in cavalry. Considering the number of men involved, it is not surprising that each army had great difficulty in procuring the necessary food supplies.

Herodotus (9.31–70) devotes many pages to the Plataea campaign, but his account of the various manoeuvres is confusing, and nothing would be gained here by trying to analyze them. Reconstructions of the battle have been attempted by many modern scholars, and, as might be expected, interpretations have differed greatly. A few points are clear. The two armies remained facing one another across the Asopus for many days, possibly as long as three weeks. Mardonius hoped to draw the Greeks into the plain where his cavalry could be most effective against them, while the Greeks wanted to bring about a battle in rougher terrain. Each side hoped that shortage of supplies might cause the opponent to make a false move. Finally after the Persian cavalry had succeeded in riding around the Greek lines and obstructing springs essential to the Greek water supply, Pausanias decided to move during the night to a location nearer to Plataea. The next morning, before all the Greek contingents had taken up their new positions, the Persians attacked. The

Athenians towards the left of the line were hard pressed by the Boeotian hoplites and cavalry until they were rescued, at great cost to the rescuers, by the Megarians. The battle was decided, however, on the Greek right wing, where Pausanias and the Spartans and Tegeans sustained an attack of the main Persian army and then, attacking in turn, completely overwhelmed the enemy and killed Mardonius, riding a white horse, in the thick of the fray. The Persians ultimately broke and many fled to take refuge in the stockade north of the Asopus. This was stormed by the Greeks who, taking no prisoners, slaughtered their foes by the thousands. As far as one can ascertain from Herodotus' account, Mardonius' whole army was annihilated except for the troops under the command of Artabazus. The latter, when he saw that the battle was hopelessly lost, managed to withdraw his men and succeeded ultimately in escaping through Thessaly and Thrace to Asia Minor.

The victory at Plataea was a remarkable achievement for the Greeks. If Themistocles and the Athenians were primarily responsible for saving Greece at Salamis, Pausanias and the Spartans and other Peloponnesian contingents played that role at Plataea. When one tries to envisage the difficulties Pausanias faced in holding together for weeks an army consisting of over 100,000 men from some twenty-four cities, plagued by dissension, insubordination, and lack of food and water, as well as the difficulty of warding off the constant threat of the excellent Persian cavalry, one can only applaud Herodotus' judgment (9.64), rising superior to the anti-Spartan and anti-Peloponnesian propaganda which he heard during his residence in Athens, when he writes that Plataea, "the finest victory in all history known to me was won by Pausanias, the son of Cleombrotus, the son of Anaxandridas."

For ten days after the battle the Greeks remained in the vicinity of Plataea, burying their dead, dividing the spoils between gods and men, and fulfilling vows which had been made to the gods. On the eleventh day they marched against Thebes, determined to exact punishment from those leaders chiefly responsible for the medizing policy. After a siege of three weeks the Thebans surrendered those leaders to Pausanias. According to Herodotus, this was done at the suggestion of the men concerned, who felt that at a trial before the Greeks they would be able to win acquittal through bribery. Pausanias, however, suspecting their plans, dismissed the allied army, and, taking the prisoners to Corinth, put them to death. The Spartan commander may have acted on his own authority, but since Herodotus' account (9.86–88) is very brief, it is possible that the congress of the Hellenic League was consulted before the executions were carried out.

Of the various dedications made to the gods from the spoils of the battle of Plataea, one in particular deserves mention. At Delphi a golden tripod resting upon a tall bronze column representing three intertwined serpents was presented to Apollo. The tripod was melted down by the Phocians in the following century in the course of the Third Sacred War, but the column remained at Delphi until the fourth century A.D., when Constantine had it moved to Byzantium, which he was transforming into his capital, Constantinople. It still stands in Istanbul in the ancient Hippodrome. On the coils the simple words "These fought the war" were inscribed, followed by the names of thirty-one states. Although a few names are inexplicably omitted, it seems clear that the list was intended to record all the communities which had remained loyal to the Hellenic League and had participated in the fighting even after the fall of Thermopylae. Some of these states are familiar only to the specialist in Greek history, but the names of those Greeks who refused to submit to the Persian terror should be recorded. They are listed, possibly in the order in which they joined the Hellenic League, as follows: Lacedaemonians, Athenians, Corinthians, Tegeans, Sicyonians, Aeginetans, Megarians, Epidaurians, Orchomenians (from Arcadia), Phliasians, Troezenians, Hermioneans, Tirynthians, Plataeans, Thespians, Mycenaeans, Ceans, Melians, Tenians, Naxians, Eretrians, Chalcidians, Styreans, Eleans, Potidaeans, Leucadians, Anactorians, Cythnians, Siphnians, Ambraciotai, and Lepreatai (*M&L,* no. 27).

In the month of August while the Greek land forces were at Plataea preparing for the crucial struggle with Mardonius, envoys came from Samos to the Greek fleet stationed at Delos under the command of Leotychides and urged him to sail to Asia and liberate Ionia, since the Ionians were ripe for revolt. The Spartan king, who had rejected a similar proposal from the Chians several months before, now gave heed to the Samian appeal. As stated above, Herodotus says that in the spring the Greek fleet of 110 ships had assembled at Aegina under Leotychides, with Xanthippus commanding the Athenian contingent. Since the total number of vessels which he mentions is surprisingly small, it may be that additional ships from Athens and other cities joined the fleet only after Mardonius had retired from Attica, thus bringing the total gathered at Delos to 250 triremes, as Diodorus (11.34) says. The Greeks sailed to Samos where they expected to encounter the Persian fleet. The Persians, however, on hearing of their approach and thinking that their fleet was no match for the enemy, sailed to Mycale, the promontory on the mainland opposite Samos. Here they disembarked, dragged their ships onto the beach, and erected a palisade around them. Then, supported by a Persian army which had been stationed in that area, they awaited the expected attack. The Greeks, not finding the Persians at Samos, proceeded straight to Mycale where they landed and began an assault on the Persian positions. The Persians fought valiantly, but their doom was sealed when many of the Ionians and Aeolians in their forces turned against them. The struggle ended with a total victory for the Greeks, who, after killing many Persians in the battle itself and as they tried to flee into the interior, burned all the abandoned ships of the enemy.

In the battle of Mycale the Greeks passed from the defensive to the offensive against their enemies, and, as Herodotus (9.104) says, "Ionia revolted the second time from the Persians." In Greek tradition, which loved to emphasize the synchronization of great events, the belief arose that the battles of Plataea and Mycale occurred on the same day. Specific dates cannot be given, but it is probable that the battle of Mycale took place somewhat later in August than the decisive struggle near Plataea.

The Greeks returned to Samos, where the leaders met in council to try to decide what should be done about Ionia. The Peloponnesians, feeling that it would be impossible to give constant protection to the Ionians and that, if such protection were not given, they would be at the mercy of Persian vengeance, proposed that they should be transported to Greece proper and be settled on the lands of the medizing Greeks who, in turn, should be expelled. The Athenians objected strenuously to this proposal, not, according to Herodotus (9.106), emphasizing the tremendous difficulties that such transfers of populations would entail, but arguing that Ionia should not be depopulated and that the Peloponnesians had no right to determine the fate of "Athenian colonists." Since the Athenians were very insistent on this matter, the Peloponnesians acquiesced. Thereupon they enrolled in the Hellenic League the Samians, Chians, Lesbians, and other islanders who were now campaigning with them, binding them by the appropriate oaths.

The Greek fleet then sailed to the Hellespont with the intention of destroying Xerxes' bridges, but on arriving there found them no longer in place. At this point Leotychides, feeling that his assignment had been completed, sailed home with the Peloponnesian contingents, but Xanthippus and the Athenians decided to remain and make an attempt on the Chersonese—the region in which, since the time of Pisistratus, at least, the Athenians had been greatly interested. They crossed to Sestos on the European side of the Hellespont and laid siege to this town, which was held by a strong force of Persians and allies. The siege was long and hard, but by the end of the year 479 or the beginning of 478 the Athenians captured the fortress. Then, having heaped all sorts of riches on their ships, including the cables of Xerxes' bridges which had been stored in the town—fine spoils to dedicate in their temples—they sailed home. It is with the capture of Sestos that Herodotus ends his remarkable history, an appropriate ending since a new chapter in the relations between Greeks and Persians was about to begin.

ONE IMPORTANT and interesting problem has deliberately been postponed until now so that it could be discussed in the framework of Xerxes' invasion of Greece and its aftermath. The problem is concerned with what is usually called The Oath of Plataea, which, from its name, suggests an oath taken on the eve of the great battle. Several versions of this oath and allusions to it have been preserved, but the time and circumstances with which it is associated vary considerably. It looks as if in this matter, as in the case of *the* Themistocles decree, one is dealing with evidence for the Greek custom in post–Persian War generations of using and altering a historical document in whatever way would render it most effective for the particular purposes of the moment. Of the various references to an oath taken by the Greeks, only two specifically assign it to the eve of Plataea. Since many states were joined as allies in the defense of Greece, it is quite possible that oaths of similar content were taken on several different occasions and that only later, when it became clear how crucial the battle of Plataea had been, did tradition single out for fame one from several oaths, assign it to the time of the battle, and give it a composite form by including in it elements from other oaths sworn in the same general period.

The earliest ancient source that refers to an oath is Herodotus. In book 7, 132, he relates that when Xerxes was at Therma—in June 480—the envoys he had previously sent to Greece to demand earth and water returned to him bearing the tokens of submission from the Thessalians, Aenians, Dolopians, Perrhaebi, Locrians, Magnesians, Malians, Phthiotic Achaeans, and Boeotians (except the Plataeans and Thespians). He adds: "Against these the Greeks who determined to resist the invaders swore an oath to the effect that, once the war was fought to a successful conclusion, they would 'tithe' to the god at Delphi all Greeks who, not under compulsion, had given themselves to the Persians." Concerning this passage it should be noted that Herodotus has made a mistake either in the matter of the time—for him, between Tempe and Thermopylae—or in the list of medizers, for it is certain that the Locrians and Boeotians, at least, did not medize until after the Greek defeat at Thermopylae. The word here translated as "tithe" (*dekateusai*) can mean "to take a tithe from," but it also can signify "to treat as a tithe."[32] Scholars have convincingly demonstrated that the latter meaning is the appropriate one here and in the other references to the "Oath of Plataea." Tithing in this sense would involve dedicating a city to Apollo by destroying it and leaving its land untilled, but apparently available for pasturage, as was done to Crisa about 590 at the end of the First Sacred War and as the Thebans proposed should be done to Athens in 404 at the end of the Peloponnesian War. When Herodotus says that the Greeks swore this oath, he is presumably referring to the Greek delegates of the Hellenic League meeting at Corinth, but, as stated above, he is vague about a precise date. It has been suggested that the first Greek delegates who assembled in the winter of 481/80 to organize the Hellenic League may have formulated this oath about "tithing" in the hope that the threat might deter various states from submitting voluntarily to Persia. If this suggestion is correct, then, of course, at that time the oath was directed against possible medizers in general, not against any particular city or people.[33]

Of the two cases where the taking of the oath is connected with Plataea, one is provided by the Athenian orator Lycurgus, who, in a speech delivered in 330 (*Against Leocrates*, 80–81), while emphasizing the patriotism of their forefathers, quotes the oath which the Greeks took on the eve of Plataea in the following words: "I will not hold life dearer than freedom nor will I abandon my leaders whether they are alive or dead. I will bury all allies killed in the battle. If I conquer the barbarians in war I will not destroy any of the cities which have fought for Greece, but I will 'tithe' those which sided with the barbarian. I will not rebuild a single one of the shrines which the barbarians have burned and razed but will allow them to remain for future generations as a memorial of the barbarians' impiety." The clause about the shrines is interesting. Since no temples in the Peloponnesus had been destroyed by the Persians, it is hard to understand why the Peloponnesians should have sworn to this part of the oath. This stipulation would have applied only to the Athenians, Phocians, Plataeans, and Thespians, and provides part of the evidence for the suggestion made above that *the* Oath of Plataea was really a composite of various oaths, differing in detail, sworn by the Greek allies. It will be shown in a subsequent chapter that this stipulation had a direct bearing on the fifth-century building program at Athens.

The second document specifically linking the oath with Plataea (not by name, but from the context) is an interesting inscription discovered at Menidi (ancient Acharnae) in Attica in 1932.[34] The inscription, set up by the local priest of Ares and of Athena Areia, records first the oath sworn by Athenian *ephebes*—young men called up for military training—and then proceeds as follows:

The Oath which the Athenians swore, when about to give battle to the barbarians: "I will fight to the death, and I will not count my life more precious than freedom. I will not leave my officer, the commander of my regiment or company, either alive or dead. I will not withdraw unless my commanders lead me back, and I will do whatsoever the Generals order. I will bury the dead of those who have fought as my allies, on the field, and will not leave one of them unburied. After defeating the barbarians in battle, I will tithe the city of the Thebans; and I will never destroy Athens or Sparta or Plataia or any of the cities which have fought as our allies, nor will I consent to their being starved, nor cut them off from running water, whether we be friends or at war.

"And if I keep well the oath, as it is written, may my city have good health; but if not, may it have sickness; and may my city never be sacked; but if not, may it be sacked; and may my land give increase; but if not, may it be barren; and may the women bring forth children like their fathers; but if not, monsters; and may the cattle bring forth after their kind; but if not, monsters."

After taking this oath, they covered with their shields the sacrifical offerings and uttered the Imprecation at the call of a trumpet, invoking the curse upon themselves, if after swearing it they should transgress any of that to which they had sworn, and not keep well the oath as it was written.[35]

This inscription has been quoted in full to illustrate the liberties that the Greeks took with "documents," inserting, omitting, or altering sections so as to make a document conform to the needs of the particular occasion when it was being cited. The heading of this document states that it was the oath sworn by the Athenians before joining battle with the barbarians, but certainly the Athenians would not have been called upon to swear not to destroy Athens, although this may have been part of the oath taken by the Spartans. The linking of Athens, Sparta, and Plataea together and the singling out of Thebes alone for "tithing" are clearly an adaptation of the original oath to the conditions existing around the year 370, when those three cities were united in bitter hostility against Thebes. The omission of the stipulation about not rebuilding shrines that had been destroyed is interesting. Could it be that this temple of Ares had been rebuilt and that the priest did not want to call attention to this breach of one of the clauses of the famous oath? Other similar observations could be made, but these should be sufficient to demonstrate that although the gist of this document may be—and probably is—authentic, various liberties have been taken with the "original" oath, which, as a matter of fact, may have been known to this priest only in a rather general form.

It is known from other sources that the clause in the inscription about not cutting allies off from running water is derived from an old oath employed by the delegates at the council of the Delphic Amphictiony. This fact lends added weight to an interpretation of the "Oath of Plataea" which a scholar made some years ago.[36] In an earlier chapter reference was made to the fact that membership in the Delphic Amphictiony was restricted to twelve peoples or *ethnē*, which proves that the establishment of this Amphictiony predates the rise of the poleis. In historical times if, for example, an Athenian was sent as a delegate to the Amphictionic Council, he was considered to be representing the Ionians rather than Athens in particular. If one now returns to the passage of Herodotus discussed above where he lists the medizing people whom the Greeks swore to "tithe," it is interesting that he mentions *peoples* and not cities, and that the nine peoples recorded were all members of the Delphic Amphictiony. The other three members—Ionians, Dorians, and Phocians—were precisely the peoples who did not medize and bore the brunt of the war agaisnt the Persians. This observation leads to the suggestion that the "Oath of Plataea" may have been of Amphictionic origin.

In several places earlier in this chapter attention was called to the unpatriotic and defeatist—medizing, if one wishes—role of Apollo at Delphi in the early stages of Xerxes' invasion. Despite this shabby performance, however, Apollo was in high favor after the battle of Plataea, and Delphi was enriched by many dedications. It is probable that after Salamis the priests at Delphi decided that the Greeks, after all, would ultimately be victorious. They were obviously anxious to regain any prestige which their faltering conduct had jeopardized. The Greeks committed to resistance to the death against the Persians, on the other hand, would have been glad to have the support of Apollo, which could contribute greatly to the general morale. It is quite possible, therefore, that, with the encouragement of the Delphic priests, representatives from the three "loyal" Amphictionic peoples, the Ionians, Dorians, and Phocians, convened at Delphi in 479—they could reach it from the Corinthian Gulf—at the time when the spring meeting (Pylaea) of the Amphictionic Council normally was held, and voted to "tithe" the other nine members of the Amphictiony who had medized. By so doing they were in fact transforming the war against the Persians also into a sacred war under the aegis of Apollo against those Greek peoples who had betrayed Greece.

The Oath of Plataea, therefore, may have been an Amphictionic oath in origin, but an oath must have been sworn on various occasions and not just at Delphi in the early spring of 479. Surely the Peloponnesians and the Athenians who combined their forces at Eleusis in July(?) of that year must have sworn an oath to be loyal to one another. And possibly another oath was sworn in the long waiting period at Plataea before the battle was fought. On each occasion, depending on those who were participating in the ceremony, the actual wording of the oath may have varied to some extent. As the years passed by and the battle of Plataea became part of the glorious legend which developed about Greek victory over the barbarians, it was only natural that the oath which became *the* oath was assumed to have been sworn on the eve of the dramatic, heroic, and crushing defeat of the Persians at Plataea.

The oath declared that when victory had been won, the loyal Greeks would "tithe" those Greeks who, although not under compulsion, had yielded to the Persians. The members of the Hellenic League had taken this oath when, because of the grim danger overhanging them, they were in a highly emotional state, and when they were swept away with fury at those fellow Greeks who threatened to medize or had thrown in their lot with the enemy. After victory had been secured and the Greeks turned to fulfilling the vows which had been made, the enormous difficulty—in fact the impossibility—of carrying out the "tithing" stipulation of the oath must soon have become apparent. The attempt to destroy the majority of Greek communities in central and northern Greece would have involved the members of the Hellenic League in another desperate and bloody war which they were in no position or mood to undertake. There would also have been the problems of deciding in each particular case whether the medizing had been voluntary or done under duress, and within each community whether all had been guilty or only some dominant group. It was not long, therefore, before the whole project of "tithing" was tacitly abandoned, but in the meantime at least three attempts were made to carry out that provision either literally or in some modified form.

The first two attempts have already been mentioned. Shortly after the victory at Plataea the Greeks began the siege of Thebes, but their thirst for vengeance was satisfied when the leaders of the medizing party were surrendered to them for trial and punishment. Second, after the Persian defeat at Mycale the Peloponnesian leaders, presumably thinking in terms of the "Oath of Plataea," proposed that the medizing Greek peoples be expelled and that the Ionians be moved from Asia Minor and be settled on the land of the banished medizers. This proposal, which was quashed by the Athenians, would have carried out some of the implications of the "tithing," but not the basic one that the land, dedicated to Apollo, be left untilled.

The third attempt is described by Plutarch, who relates in his *Life of*

Themistocles, 20, that at a meeting of the Amphictionic Council the Spartans proposed that "all cities, which had not shared in the fighting against the Mede be excluded from the Amphictiony." This proposal clearly has some connection with the Oath of Plataea and may be considered as further evidence that the oath was an Amphictionic one. Unfortunately Plutarch's remarks are too brief to provide a satisfactory interpretation of this episode. No date is assigned; theoretically the passage could refer to any meeting of the Amphictionic Council beginning with the one in the fall of 479. Although it is not so stated, presumably only the Ionians, Dorians, and Phocians were represented at the meeting, for if the nine medizing Amphictionic peoples had sent their delegates, obviously they could and would have voted down the motion. According to Plutarch, Themistocles, fearing that the passing of the motion would enable Sparta to dominate the Amphictiony, was responsible for its rejection. In his argument he pointed out that only thirty-one cities, mostly small, had shared in the war, the inference presumably being that they were too few to be considered as representing all Greece. Although many aspects of this episode are obscure, it provides a clear illustration of a great power trying to exploit the importance and prestige of Delphi for its own political advantage.

9
Delian League and Athenian Empire

THE GREEK achievement in 480 and 479 was amazing. Under the dire threat of Persian conquest a group of cities, many hostile to and jealous of one another, joined in a Hellenic League in order to present a united front against the invader. The name used to designate this alliance—the Hellenes—and the emphasis on Hellas and common blood in the Athenian reply to the Spartan envoys early in 479, as reported by Herodotus (8.144), suggest that, confronted by the barbarian peril, the Greeks were almost thinking in terms of a Greek nation. The serpent column erected as a dedication at Delphi after Plataea listed thirty-one cities which, remaining faithful to "the Hellenes" to the end, "fought the war." Although Athens certainly was influential in convincing the Greeks of the necessity of a united defense, it was Sparta, with its high military reputation and its numerous allies in the Peloponnesian League, that was chiefly responsible for organizing the Hellenic League and, above all, for holding it together. Spartans presumably presided over meetings of the League's delegates, and in every campaign a Spartan held the supreme command—King Leonidas at Thermopylae, Eurybiades at Artemisium and Salamis, Pausanias at Plataea, and King Leotychides at Mycale. If the genius of Themistocles and the Athenian fleet, with Eurybiades having enough judgment to recognize their supreme value, were chiefly responsible for crippling the Persian navy, the genius of Pausanias and the bravery and discipline of the Spartan hoplites contributed most to the destruction of the Persian army in the crucial battle of Plataea. The prominence of these two leading states, however, should not blind one to the heroism and dedication of the other twenty-nine cities, large and small, some of which, like Plataea and Thespiae, were ravaged as ruthlessly as Athens.

The Greeks in the fall of 479 could offer thanks to the gods for their deliverance from the perils and terrors of the past two years, but they could not yet know how complete the deliverance was. The fact that the fleet of the Hellenic League was dispatched in the following year to fight in eastern waters is clear evidence that they felt the threat from Persia was still hanging over them. Nevertheless, with the passing of the immediate crisis, the unity which that crisis had forged began to weaken.

Friction and jealousies were not slow in appearing. After Plataea the Athenians brought back to Attica their families from the places where they had been deposited for safety and turned to the task of rebuilding their city and walls. According to Thucydides (1.90–93), allies of the Spartans—presumably primarily the Aeginetans, Corinthians, and Megarians—alarmed by the size of the Athenian navy and the valor and aggressiveness displayed by the Athenians against the Persians, induced the Spartans to try to take steps to curb the ambitions of the Athenians, which might be detrimental to them. The Spartans, therefore, sent envoys to Athens to argue against the rebuilding of the walls on the grounds that, if Athens were unwalled, the barbarian could not use the city as a fortified base in case he returned. They also added that, should it prove necessary, the Peloponnesus could always serve as a place of refuge and a region from which to launch an offensive. Such a policy, obviously, would have put the Athenians at the mercy of Sparta and its allies, something which the Athenians never, and particularly not after their recent heroic efforts and sacrifices, would have voluntarily accepted.

In the ancient sources the Athenian refusal of the Spartan suggestion is associated with an anecdote, which, although serving the purpose of illustrating the trickery of Themistocles, need not for that reason be rejected. At his suggestion the Spartans were dismissed with the answer that Athenian envoys would be sent to Sparta to discuss the matter. He then told the Athenians to send him as an envoy to the Spartans, but not to dispatch his colleagues until the whole population of the city, men, women, and children, using every available material, had raised the walls to a defensible height. Arrived in Sparta, Themistocles stalled the Spartans for some time by saying that he was waiting for his colleagues who had unexpectedly been delayed. When word reached the Spartans that the Athenians were building walls, Themistocles, emphasizing that rumors werre unreliable, urged them to send envoys to Athens to learn the real state of affairs. Simultaneously he secretly sent word to the Athenians not to let the Spartan emissaries go until he and his colleagues had returned, for these, including Aristides, had joined him with the information that the walls had been built to a sufficient height. Themistocles then told the Spartans that Athens was now capable of defending itself and that any city which had accomplished what it had against the Persians deserved to be a free and equal member of the Hellenic League. The Spartans, concealing their displeasure, had to acquiesce in what had been done, and the respective embassies returned home. Themistocles then persuaded the Athenians to complete the fortifications of the Piraeus which had been begun in his archonship (492/1), for he was convinced that Athens' future lay with its fleet.

In the campaigning season of 478 the fleet of the Hellenic League once again went into action. Pausanias with twenty Peloponnesian and thirty Athenian ships and with an unspecified number from the other allies sailed to Cyprus, an important naval base for the Persians, and subdued large parts of the island. The Greeks then sailed to Byzantium and after a siege became masters of this strategically located city. With both Sestos and Byzantium in their hands, they now controlled the straits by which the Persians had crossed from Asia Minor into Europe and also the important commercial route leading into the Black Sea. During the siege and subsequent occupation of Byzantium serious dissension broke out among the Greek forces. According to Thucydides (1.94–95)—and later authors largely followed him, with the addition of colorful details—Pausanias by his arrogant and arbitrary behavior outraged many of the Greeks serving under him, especially the Ionians and those who had recently become free from the Great King. The elements angered by Pausanias appealed to the Athenians, asking them on the basis of kinship to take over the leadership and to protect them from the violence of Pausanias. The Athenians, under the command of Aristides and Cimon, son of Miltiades, lent a ready ear to these complaints and suggestions and apparently used various propaganda devices to foment the dissatisfaction still more. Meanwhile, as a result of reports which had reached Sparta, Pausanias was called home to face an investigation. Thucydides reports that he was brought to account for some of his private misdeeds, but was acquitted of the major charge of medism. Another Spartan, Dorcis, was sent with a small force to Byzantium to take over the command of the fleet of the Hellenic League, but all the contingents except, presumably, the Peloponnesians refused to put themselves under the Spartans again since they had already decided to look to the Athenians for leadership. The Spartans thereupon returned home and abandoned all further participation in the struggle against the Persians. Thucydides, surely reflecting the Athenian version of events, says they were glad to be rid of the war and had confidence that the Athenians could conduct it satisfactorily.

With the withdrawal of the Peloponnesian contingent from eastern waters, Thucydides (1.96) states that the Athenians, having thus received the hegemony with the approval of the allies, began to establish an organization for these allies—an organization which modern scholars call the Delian League. Before discussing the early characteristics of this league, which within several decades evolved into the Athenian empire, it is pertinent to emphasize the confused situation in which it had its origins. Part of this confusion is exemplified by Thucydides' remark that the Athenians received the hegemony. Until this time (late 478) the only hegemony which had existed for the Greeks in their war with Persia was that of Sparta over the Hellenic League formed in the winter of 481/0. Under Spartan leadership this league had defended Greece in 480 and 479 and then had initiated offensive warfare in the east. This league, according to the serpent column erected after Plataea and Mycale, consisted of thirty-one members, a number that was increased after the battle of Mycale by the addition of the Samians, Chians, Lesbians, and other islanders (Herodotus, 9.106). In view of Peloponnesian reluctance to assume responsibility for the protection of the Ionian cities, the eastern campaign of the Hellenic League under Pausanias in 478 is surprising. Cyprus and Byzantium were not Ionian, but in the troubles which arose at Byzantium, Thucydides lists as participants "Ionians and as many as had recently been freed from the Persians." This statement presumably refers to Ionians other than just the islanders received into the league following Mycale. Despite Peloponnesian objections, it seems that some Ionian cities had been admitted to the Hellenic League in the summer of 478.

It is obvious that Athens did not become hegemon of the original Hellenic League. That league, in an emasculated form, continued to exist under Spartan leadership until at least 462/1. When Thucydides says that Athens received the hegemony, he is clearly referring to the new league that Athens began to organize in the winter of 478/7. What was the relationship of this Delian League to the already existing Hellenic League?[1] Some scholars have argued that it was a subdivision of the Hellenic League—its naval arm; one is to think of a comprehensive Hellenic League under the hegemony of Sparta which was divided into the Delian League with Athens as hegemon and the Peloponnesian League with Sparta as hegemon. This concept seems most unlikely. There is no evidence that many members of the original Delian League were participants in the Hellenic League, and it would be absurd to suggest that new additions to the Delian League in the 470s were enrolled also in the Spartan-dominated Hellenic League. It seems necessary to assume, therefore, that the Delian League was a new grouping under Athens of states interested in carrying on the war against Persia—a war for which Sparta was showing no enthusiasm. Some participants in the new organization, such as Athens and certain islands, had been members of the Hellenic League, but their ties to that association were now largely severed, and any new acquisitions were bound to the Delian League alone. The argument of this chapter will show that whatever unity had been achieved by the Hellenic League of 481/0 waned steadily and that the two leagues, the Peloponnesian and the Delian, divided the Greeks into two hostile camps, although the concept of the old Hellenic League lingered on like a shadow to be appealed to by individual states when convenient.

It was in the winter of 478/7, undoubtedly on the initiative of the Athenians, that those cities which were interested in continuing the war against Persia were invited to send delegates to Delos, the sacred island of the Ionians, to discuss matters of common interest. A large number of cities which were already liberated from Persia in the Aegean islands, on the coast of Thrace, in the Hellespontine (and Bosporus) region, and on the coast of Asia Minor either responded to the invitation, or in the immediately following years joined the new organization. The delegates agreed that their aims should be to seek vengeance and compensation, by ravaging the King's territory, for the injuries which their cities had received from Persia. Their aims probably included also their determination to protect those Greek states which had already revolted from Persia and to liberate those still under Persian rule, but Thucydides (1.96) and other sources mention only the desire for revenge and booty. To achieve their purposes, proper organization obviously was necessary. They therefore decided to establish a congress or assembly of delegates which should meet at Delos,[2] with each state, regardless of size, having an equal vote. Some scholars argue that the arrangement actually was a bicameral one, as in the fourth-century Athenian League, the vote of the Athenian assembly being equivalent to the combined votes of members of the allied congress. Despite certain ambiguities in Thucydides' language, however, it seems more probable that Athens voted in the Delian congress theoretically on a basis of equality with the other states, although obviously, because of its prestige and power, it could easily influence or intimidate smaller members. Athens, quite naturally in view of the great reputation of its fleet, was granted the hegemony, that is, it was to have the supreme command in war, to perform the chief executive duties, and, presumably, to preside over meetings of the league's assembly.

The always thorny problem of finances was faced squarely. A treasury was established in the Temple of Apollo at Delos, and Athenian magistrates known as *hellenotamiai* (treasurers of the Hellenes) were appointed to take charge of the league funds. The method of appointing these officials is obscure, but it is possible that in the early years of the league, at least, the congress selected ten men from a slate of candidates presented by the Athenians. Since a regular income was essential, Aristides, whose reputation for integrity was high, was given the task of determining what each member state could and should contribute. This difficult task may have been simplified by adopting the same rates of tribute as the Persians had imposed. Herodotus (6.42), when describing the arrangements made by the Persians after the suppression of the Ionian revolt in 493, says that the satrap Artaphernes "surveyed their lands by parasangs . . . and on this basis he assessed tributes on each of them; these tributes have continued to hold valid on the same scale from that time right down to my own day, just as they were assessed by Artaphernes." Although the brief accounts of Thucydides (1.96) and Aristotle (*Ath. Const.,* 23.5) suggest a rapid organization of the league, Plutarch (*Aristides,* 24) states that Aristides inspected the land and also the revenues of the allies, a task which would have required considerable time. If Plutarch is correct, Aristides' prolonged financial duties could explain why he did not appear as a leader in the league's military activities. Thucydides remarks that the first assessment of tribute (*phoros*) amounted to 460 talents and adds that the Athenians "assigned which cities were to furnish money against the barbarian and which, ships." Presumably Aristides, after completing his task, presented his recommendations to the council and assembly of the Athenians.[3]

There has been, and still is, much disagreement among scholars concerning the proper interpretation of Thucydides' words referring to the tribute. He speaks of the appointment of *hellenotamiai* "who received the tribute (*phoros*). For thus the payment of the money was called. And the first tribute was assessed at 460 talents." It has been figured from the annual tribute-quota lists beginning in 454/3, which will be discussed later, that in the years following that date the tribute collected probably never reached 400 talents. The actual assessment for 454/3 has been estimated by various scholars to have been about 490 talents.[4] Since by that time many more states had joined the league and some had shifted from contributing ships to contributing money, it is strange that, if the initial assessment had been as much as 460 talents, the totals collected in the 450s and afterwards were not much greater. One explanation for this dilemma, rather widely accepted, is that the 460 talents represented all contributions divided about equally between those rendered in cash and those rendered in ships, valued at one talent each, whereas the tribute-quota lists recorded only payments in cash.[5] This suggestion is ingenious, but it seems to contradict Thucydides' use of the word *phoros*. In the passage quoted above he links *phoros* with cash payments, and three chapters later, in speaking of causes of revolt, he makes a clear distinction between failure to contribute *phoros* and failure to contribute ships.

The truth is that many problems concerning the tribute and the financing and maintenance of the league's fleet, despite valuable information provided by the tribute-quota lists and other sources, are obscure. For example, it is not known whether the states that contributed ships supplied pay for their crews or whether the necessary pay was provided by the tribute. Since the league fleet operated year after year, the expenses obviously were high. Booty at times furnished welcome revenue; but there were also disasters which required repairing of ships and constructing additional ones. As this is not the place to discuss the complexities of the tribute system, it will be sufficient here to call attention to a new approach to the subject which a scholar has proposed.[6] He argues that Athens had at its disposal many military assets not recorded on the tribute-quota lists. As an example he speaks of the islands Naxos, Thasos, and Samos which, after the suppression of their revolts, had to surrender their ships. Since these islands had well-equipped dockyards and experienced workers, is it not reasonable to assume that Athens, rather than neglecting such facilities, exploited them in lieu of imposing heavy tribute requirements? Other cities with good harbors may on occasions have performed necessary services, a supposition which would help explain the frequent variations in the amounts of their tribute payments.

Rather than entering into a long and complicated discussion, it may be best to assume that the first assessment of 460 talents represented cash contributions, as Thucydides' language seems to imply. Such a suggestion would also make it somewhat easier to understand the mysterious accumulation, from tribute and booty(?), of 5,000 talents in the league treasury by the year 450/49.

When the delegates at Delos, for whom Aristides was undoubtedly serving as chairman, had reached agreement on all the necessary provisions, including the assurance that each state should be autonomous except insofar as membership in an alliance curtailed complete individual freedom in foreign policy, the alliance was sealed by an impressive oath. Aristides took the oath for the Athenians and then administered it to the Ionians and other Hellenes. All swore to have the same enemies and friends, the regular formula for a defensive and offensive alliance. The ceremony of oath taking was completed by dropping lumps of iron into the sea, a symbolic way of demonstrating that the alliance was to be permanent (Plutarch, *Aristides*, 25.1; Aristotle, *Ath. Const.*, 23.5, dating the occasion by the Athenian archon Timosthenes, 478/7). In connection with this "permanent" alliance, it is important to remember Thucydides' phrase (1.96) that the Athenians assigned which cities should furnish money and which, ships against the barbarian. Obviously a difficult problem would arise if at some future time peace were to be made with the barbarian. Despite the opinion of some scholars who argue that the founders of the Delian League were consciously envisaging the time when the struggle with Persia would be over and were deliberately trying to form a Greek nation,[7] it seems more probable that in 478/7, with hatred and fear of Persia still strong in their blood, a perpetual state of war with the barbarian, as a fact of life, was an unconscious assumption in the minds of the delegates and the Greeks in general.

The achievements of the Delian League and its evolution into the Athenian empire, a development attended by increasing hostility between Athens and Sparta and their respective allies, form the main theme of Greek history for many years in the fifth century insofar as the international relations of the Greeks were concerned. In 431 this hostility exploded into the Peloponnesian War, to an analysis of which the great work of Thucydides is devoted. Thucydides, realizing that the growth of Athenian power and the threat which the empire spelled for the independence of many Greek states were basic causes of the Peloponnesian War, devoted a brief but important section of his first book to an account of this growth, beginning with the aftermath of Plataea. Since the period from 479 to 431—in many ways the high point of Greek civilization—is roughly fifty years, it has been called since the first century B.C., at least, the Pentecontaetia. Another reason which Thucydides (1.97) gives for treating these years is that his predecessors had dealt with Greek affairs before the Persian Wars or with the Persian Wars themselves; only Hellanicus had touched on this fifty-year period in his *Attic History,* but with a faulty chronology. The implication, therefore, is that Thucydides was trying to establish an accurate chronology. Since in these chapters he does not offer specific dates, his chronological aim apparently was only to establish an accurate sequence of events. It seems reasonable, consequently, to accept the order in which he lists events, unless there is strong evidence to the contrary. Fortunately a few absolute dates are provided by other sources, and these, together with Thucydides' own statement that the Peloponnesian War broke out in the spring of 431, fourteen years after the signing of the Thirty Years' Truce, render it possible to insert some absolutes into the relative chronology.

These few chapters in book 1 of Thucydides (89–117) are the nearest thing to a contemporary historical account of the Pentecontaetia that is extant, but it is important to remember that his purpose in writing this sketch was to select from the confused and complicated history of the period only those matters which he considered basic to his theme—the growth of Athenian power. A large amount of historical or semihistorical writings of the fifth and later centuries dealing with this period have perished or been preserved only in fragments. Two later writers, however, are very important, although every statement they make must be scrutinized before acceptance—Diodorus of Sicily, living in the last half of the first century B.C., who in books 11 and 12 of his *Historical Library* makes much use of the popular fourth-century historian, Ephorus of Cyme; and Plutarch, whose prodigious literary activity fell in the latter part of the first century and the early part of the second century A.D. Of his "Lives" the particularly relevant ones for this period are the *Themistocles, Aristides, Cimon,* and *Pericles.* In reading and interpreting Plutarch one must remember that he was writing moral biographies, not history, and thus he did not necessarily follow a chronological pattern. His *Lives* and other writings are very valuable, for he drew his material from many authors no longer extant whose names he frequently mentions, thus rendering it possible to formulate certain historiographic ideas about men who helped to shape the historical traditions. One other source, the most basic of all, should be mentioned—the contemporary inscriptions on stone, unfortunately often fragmentary, whose numbers increase with the passing years of the fifth century.

THE FIRST activity which Thucydides ascribes to the fleet of the newly organized Delian League was the capture of Eion, a fortress held by the Persians at the mouth of the Strymon River. The scholiast to the second oration of Aeschines reports that Eion fell in the archonship of Phaidon (476/5). Since a papyrus fragment of, or based on, Ephorus states that the Athenians and their allies campaigned against Eion after sailing from Byzantium,[8] it is usually assumed that the league fleet in the summer of 477 was delayed because of the return of Pausanias to Byzantium, and hence did not begin the siege of Eion until that winter—a siege not ended until the late summer of 476. This operation was conducted under the command of Cimon, son of Miltiades, who henceforth for many years provided leadership in most of the achievements of the Delian League. Before continuing the discussion of these activities, it will be well to glance briefly at the fate of the three men who had dominated Greek history before the rise of Cimon to prominence—Aristides, Pausanias, and Themistocles.

Aristides, who had commanded the Athenian contingent at Plataea, was, as has been seen, the chief architect of the Delian League and the man responsible for the first assessment of the tribute (*phoros*). Although it was Themistocles' building and leadership of the Athenian fleet which had made the Delian League possible, he is mentioned by no source in connection with the establishment of the league. After Aristides' great activity in the winter of 478/7, so far as the scanty evidence goes, he practically disappeared from history. As an ex-archon he would have been a member of the Council of the Areopagus, and presumably his voice was heard on occasions at meetings of the assembly. He probably died shortly after 467 when, according to Plutarch (*Aristides*, 3.4), a tribute was paid to his reputation for justice on the occasion of the performance of Aeschylus' *Seven against Thebes*.

Pausanias, the hero of Plataea, has been damned by history as a traitor. Before accepting such a verdict one should consider the sources responsible for this damnation.[9] The earliest extant account of the "medism" of Pausanias is provided by Thucydides, whose rather circumstantial description is followed, with the addition of various details, by many later authors. Thucydides, presumably, was dependent for his information on the official versions offered by Athens and Sparta. Since the Athenians in 478 were obviously eager to acquire leadership over the naval forces of the Hellenic League, it was in their interests to represent the conduct of Pausanias, to which the Ionians were objecting, in as evil a light as possible. Pausanias' behavior, which could have been arrogant without being treasonable, furnished fuel for their propaganda. The Spartan version of the Pausanias affair was distorted by the fear the oligarchic government had of the regent who, in his desire to overthrow the established order, had apparently entered into revolutionary relations with the helots. It has recently been suggested that, to ensure the loyalty of the 35,000 light armed helots at Plataea, Pausanias may have made certain promises to them—promises which subsequently he could not honor because of governmental policy.[10] A charge of medism, however, would justify the action of the ephors in putting Pausanias to death. Both Athenians and Spartans, therefore, had motives for misrepresenting the conduct of Pausanias. The strange stories surrounding Pausanias' death are reminiscent of the mystery which enshrouds the death of King Cleomenes, who also had hoped to weaken or overthrow the oligarchic government at Sparta. The medism of Pausanias cannot be definitely disproved, but Thucydides' account (1.128–134)—probably the most uncritical section in his whole history, with its inconsistencies, melodrama, and frequent recourse to expressions like "it is said"—does not inspire confidence. One example should suffice to illustrate the improbabilities in the account. Thucydides professes to give the actual wording of a letter from Pausanias to Xerxes which was discovered later. How the Spartans or any Greeks could have learned the contents of a letter filed in the royal Persian archives at Susa stretches the imagination. In the letter Pausanias was alleged to have written, "I propose also, with your approval, to marry your daughter, and to make Sparta and the rest of Hellas subject to you," a proposal which Herodotus (5.32) questions.

An accurate chronology of Pausanias' actions in his last years would throw much light on the events of the 470s and possibly of the early 460s, but Thucydides gives no specific dates. He merely says in some detail that Pausanias, after his recall to Sparta in 478, returned as a private citizen with one ship to the Bosporus region and took possession of Byzantium, from which he was expelled by the Athenians. He then settled at Colonae in the Troad, from where, on reports that he was medizing, the Spartans summoned him and subsequently put him to death. It is generally assumed that it was his occupation of Byzantium in 477 which caused the fleet of the Delian League to devote that summer to ousting him rather than beginning their siege of Eion. How one man with a single trireme took possession of Byzantium is nowhere explained. Since Byzantium was a Megarian colony and hence had Peloponnesian ties, Pausanias may have had supporters there. A non-Thucydidean source, Justin, the third century A.D. epitomizer of the Augustan historian Pompeius Trogus, reports (9.1.3) that Pausanias occupied the city for seven years. This statement of a late and often erratic source has usually been rejected, but some scholars have used this passage, with interesting results, in trying to reconstruct the events of this period. If this chronology is accepted, then Pausanias may not have crossed to Colonae in the Troad until ca. 470, and he may not have been recalled to Sparta until early in the 460s. His death then may not have occurred until possibly the year 467/6, a date which fits well with the story of Themistocles' flight from Greece, which will be described below.

As corroboration of these dates for Pausanias, it has been argued persuasively that his three sons, of whom the eldest, Pleistoanax, became king in 459, were almost certainly born in the years between 475 and the early 460s.[11] As further confirmation for this late expulsion of Pausanias from Byzantium, one might mention the second of the fictitious, but sometimes perceptive, letters of Themistocles in which the latter, after his ostracism (not before 474), writes to Pausanias who is master of the Hellespontine region. This assumption that Pausanias was powerful in the Hellespont-Bosporus region until about 470 and was also possibly on friendly terms with the Persians would form background for Cimon's mysterious capture of Persians at Byzantium and Sestos mentioned in an anecdote about Cimon (Plutarch, *Cimon*, 9) and would also provide some explanation for the known activity of the Athenians in the Chersonese in 465.

It is hard to believe that Pausanias' return to Byzantium in 477 was really a private venture, for he was still regent for his young cousin, Pleistarchus, and also he carried a *skutale*, a cipher arrangement entrusted only to Spartan officials. It is possible that, with the secret approval of some Spartans, his aim was to disrupt Athenian plans in the

Hellespont-Bosporus area, if necessary even with Persian aid. The evidence is too uncertain to reach any clear conclusion. When Pausanias was recalled the second time, the ephors finally moved against him after eavesdropping on a supposedly treasonable conversation he had with a trusted slave. He sought asylum in the Temple of the Goddess of the Brazen House, which the ephors kept under guard in order to starve him to death. Just before he died he was dragged out into the open in an attempt to avoid the sacrilege of causing a man's death in a holy place. Apollo of Delphi commanded that he be buried honorably.

A final incongruity in the story of Pausanias is to be found in the words of the second century A.D. traveler also named Pausanias. Describing various buildings in Sparta, this Pausanias (3.14.1) says, "Opposite the theatre is the tomb of Pausanias, who commanded at Plataea: the other tomb is that of Leonidas. Every year speeches are made over the graves and games are held, in which none but Spartans may compete." In the course of centuries, obviously, men's ideas and points of view change, but the picture of the great hero and the supposedly great traitor honored equally hardly strengthens one's belief in the strange account recorded by Thucydides.

Themistocles, the man responsible for making Athens a great power and the savior of Greece at Salamis, is not recorded in the ancient sources as participating in the formation and early exploits of the Delian League, for which Aristides and Cimon alone receive credit. He retained his influence for some time, however, for in the fall and winter of 479 he succeeded, against the wishes of the Spartans, in carrying through his policy of rebuilding the walls of Athens and subsequently of fortifying the Piraeus. He also succeeded at some point in this period in thwarting the attempt of the Spartans to turn the Delphic Amphictiony into their political tool (Plutarch, *Themistocles*, 20). In 476 he was the *choregus*, or producer, for Phrynichus' drama *The Phoenician Women*, whose theme was apparently similar to that of Aeschylus' *Persians* produced four years later. Whether he was elected to the annual board of ten generals in these years is unknown, but it seems clear that he was having difficulty competing with the great families and their followers or clients. These political enemies succeeded in achieving his ostracism in 474, 473, or 472. The issue may have been primarily the question of policy towards Sparta. Cimon, as far as can be ascertained, consistently advocated cooperation with Sparta, whereas Themistocles was openly hostile to the hegemon of the Hellenic and Peloponnesian Leagues.

Forced to leave Athens for ten years, Themistocles took up residence in Argos, from where he traveled to various parts of the Peloponnesus in an effort to arouse anti-Spartan feeling. He may have been influential in persuading the Eleans in 471 to establish a city by uniting various scattered towns through *synoecism*. The formation of the city of Arcadian Mantinea by the same process at about this time may also have owed something to his encouragement. The Spartans, who found it easier to dominate allies living in scattered villages than in centralized cities, were disturbed by these movements. Convinced that Themistocles was a menace to their authority in the Peloponnesus, they claimed that in their inquiry into the treasonable conduct of Pausanias they had discovered evidence incriminating the Athenian. The charge that Themistocles was guilty of medism is absurd, but it is quite possible that he had been associated with Pausanias in "subversive" activities among the helots. When the Spartans demanded that the Athenians punish Themistocles as they themselves had Pausanias, the Athenians, on the urging of the Alcmaeonids and Cimon (Plutarch, *Themistocles*, 23; *Aristides*, 25.7), consented, and men were sent from both cities to try to apprehend him in Argos or wherever he might be found. The account in Thucydides (1.135) implies that the trial of Themistocles, if he had been caught, would have been at Athens, but later sources (Diodorus, 11.55.4; Plutarch, *Themistocles*, 23.4) may be correct in their statement that the trial would have been before the *synedrion* of the Hellenic League. Themistocles, realizing that his enemies would have no mercy on him, took to flight. He first went to Corcyra, whose government he had previously benefited, but the Corcyraeans, afraid to oppose Athens and Sparta, conveyed him to the continent opposite (Epirus), where he became the suppliant of Admetus, the king of the Molossians. Admetus defied the Athenian and Spartan pursuers when they arrived and then, at Themistocles' request, sent him overland to Pydna in the realm of Alexander of Macedonia. There the fugitive boarded a trading vessel which was setting out for Ionia. After a narrow escape when a storm drove the ship to the island of Naxos, which was being besieged by the Athenians, Themistocles landed at Ephesus and subsequently entered into communication with Artaxerxes, son of Xerxes, who had recently come to the Persian throne.

There is a notorious chronological crux concerning the time of Themistocles' flight across the Aegean and of his arrival in Asia Minor. The date of the revolt and siege of Naxos cannot be fixed positively, but for some years the consensus has been to select 470 as the most likely year. The accession year of Artaxerxes, however, is known by Babylonian documents to have been 465/4. How, then, is one to explain Themistocles' five-year delay before communicating with the Persian king? To overcome this dilemma, some scholars have suggested reading "Thasos" for "Naxos" in the text of Thucydides, supporting their suggestion by the variant "Thasos" which occurs in one manuscript of Plutarch. Since Thasos revolted and was besieged by the fleet of the Delian League in 465, this reading would eliminate the problem of Themistocles' five-year delay in Asia Minor, but, beyond the questionable legitimacy of altering the reading in Thucydides, it would necessitate downdating the death of Pausanias and the beginning of Themistocles' flight further than ordinarily has been considered possible. If the dating of Pausanias' death to ca. 467, as suggested above, is approximately correct, however, events fit more satisfactorily into a pattern. According to this arrangement, Themistocles took flight in 467. His reason for fleeing northwestward may be explained by the tradition that he planned to escape to Hieron, tyrant of Syracuse. When word arrived that Hieron had just died, Themistocles then thought of Persia as a refuge. In Thucydides' account he barely escaped from the Athenian fleet which was besieging Naxos. The date for that event, however, is not definitely fixed. In later pages the possibility will be mentioned of down-dating this siege to 467.[12] This chronological scheme, which is based on the uncertainty of the exact date for the Athenian attack on Naxos, would mean that Themistocles had to wait only two years in Asia Minor before communicating with the Persian king, a more comprehensible delay. Themistocles may well have felt that the risk of approaching Xerxes was too great. Certain later writers (Plutarch, *Themistocles,* 27.1), including Ephorus, avoid the whole chronological problem by stating that Themistocles, after traveling inland to Susa, had his interview with Xerxes, not Artaxerxes. Since it is only too probable that this version was motivated by the romantic desire to depict the dramatic confrontation of the two great protagonists of the Persian Wars, it can safely be rejected in favor of Thucydides' more prosaic, but more likely, account.

Artaxerxes treated Themistocles generously, possibly hoping at some time to be able to make use of his unusual talents. Themistocles was made governor of the district of Magnesia on the Maeander and was permitted to draw on the revenues of this region and also certain other places which were assigned to him. At Magnesia he died, from sickness as Thucydides says, although, in keeping with his supposed medism, a story circulated that he committed suicide when he realized that he could not fulfill the promises he had made to the king. The year of his death was probably about 459, but some scholars would put it ten years later. One of the strange aspects of the limited data about Themistocles is that for certain landmarks of his life, such as birth, archonship, and death, there are two distinct chronological schemes spaced ten years apart. Thucydides (1.138), after an impassioned assertion of Themistocles' genius, surely intended as a rebuke to the hostile and petty tradition which had evolved about him, ends his digression on Pausanias and Themistocles with the austere observation: "So ends the history of Pausanias and Themistocles, the Lacedaemonian and the Athenian, the most famous men of their time in Hellas."

THE FLEET OF the Delian League under Cimon took the fortress of Eion on the Strymon River from the Persian garrison in 476/5. In the same year the Athenians sailed against Scyrus, a rocky island east of Euboea, enslaved the Dolopian pirates who had inhabited it, and settled the place themselves. It was here, according to Plutarch (*Cimon*, 8.6), that Cimon miraculously discovered the bones of the ancient Athenian hero Theseus, which, transported to Athens and buried with great pomp, gave birth to a popular hero cult. At some time within the next few years an expedition was sent against Carystus in the southwestern part of Euboea, which had medized after the battle of Artemisium, and Carystus was forced to join the Delian League. The next event which Thucydides lists—to be dated probably in 467—is the revolt of Naxos and its subsequent suppression. It seems clear that Thucydides has selected for mention, out of many exploits, these four to illustrate the first examples of the different types of activities in which the league's fleet was engaged—the capture of a Persian fortress, suppression of pirates and acquisition of territory not controlled by the Persians, forcing of a Greek city to join the league, and the secession and suppression of a league member.[13]

The revolt of Naxos only ten years after the formation of the Delian League raised the fundamental issue of whether a member had the right to secede from the league. Athens, presumably with the approval of a majority in the assembly meeting at Delos, decided that secession, which violated the concept of a permanent alliance inherent in the oaths, could not be tolerated. The revolt was promptly crushed and, contrary to the original "charter" which guaranteed autonomy to the members, Naxos became subject, in some way not clearly defined, to Athens. Thucydides (1.99) remarks that the fate of Naxos subsequently was experienced by many other states, and, realizing the importance of the trend, he analyzes the causes of revolts and the reasons for their failures.

From the time of the establishment of the Delian League, the allies had been obligated to contribute cash (*phoros*) or to provide ships and to participate in the campaigns. When an ally was derelict in any of these obligations, Athens brought pressure on it to abide by its commitments, and this pressure, probably applied harshly, aroused so much dissatisfaction that often revolt ensued. Thucydides and Plutarch (*Cimon*, 11) point out that in many cases the allies had only themselves to blame. As the danger from Persia receded, many allies, reluctant to endure the hazards, hardships, and expenses of providing and manning ships for the campaigns, with the consequent neglect of farms and other occupations, had their contributions in ships commuted to payment of the appropriate amount of cash. With this *phoros* the Athenians built and manned more and more ships, with the result that the league fleet tended to turn into an Athenian fleet. The allies, on the other hand, became demilitarized, and hence if they failed in some obligation, especially in paying tribute, or displeased the Athenians in some other way, the league fleet, now increasingly an Athenian fleet, had little difficulty in subduing a city designated as rebellious whose citizens were unprepared and untrained for war. From the point of view of Athenian power and of efficiency in the management of the fleet, it was clearly advantageous to the Athenians to have the allies contribute money rather than ships. Plutarch is probably correct when he credits Cimon with the policy of not trying to force allies whose original assessment had been in the form of ships to continue in this obligation, but of encouraging them to make their contributions in money, thereby, as it were, paying for protection. This process of changing from payment in ships to payment in cash, sometimes occurring voluntarily, sometimes under Athenian compulsion, expanded so greatly that by 454, it has been estimated, only about seventeen states still furnished ships, and in the next decade, all members of the league—or empire as it was fast becoming—fell into this tributary category (that is, paying cash) except the three large islands, Lesbos, Chios, and Samos.[14]

After his remarks on the causes of revolt within the Delian League, the next item mentioned by Thucydides in his sequence of events is the victory of Cimon, commanding the league fleet, over the Persians at the mouth of the Eurymedon River in southern Asia Minor. The Persians had been assembling there a large land and naval force, presumably with the intention of launching an offensive against the Greek cities of the Asia Minor coast and of the neighboring islands. Cimon, learning of these preparations, sailed swiftly to the Eurymedon, defeated the Persian fleet, capturing and destroying 200 triremes, and then, landing, overwhelmed the Persian army. Subsequently, according to Plutarch's rather full and seemingly accurate account (*Cimon*, 12–13), he sailed eastward and annihilated 80 Phoenician ships which had set out from Cyprus to join the Persian armada.

If one assumes that Thucydides is following a chronological order, this victory must have occurred after the revolt of Naxos and before the next event mentioned, the revolt of Thasos, which can be safely assigned to the year 465. A commonly accepted chronological arrangement has been to date the revolt of Naxos in 470 and the battle of Eurymedon in 469. One reason for this dating of Eurymedon is Plutarch's story in his *Life of Cimon* (8.7–8) that when Sophocles in his first appearance in the contest of tragedies in the spring of 468 was competing with Aeschylus, the feelings of the spectators were running high. Consequently the archon, Apsephion (469/8), instead of appointing the judges by lot in the usual way, prevailed upon Cimon and his fellow generals, when they entered the theatre, to act as judges. This occasion became famous, and some scholars claim that it reflects the glamor of Cimon's recent great victory. It can be argued, however, that if the emotions of the audience were excited, the appointment as judges of well-known generals in a period of great military activity need not be associated with any one particular victory. In a work published in 1972 a historian has sensibly placed emphasis on the existing military situation.[15] If the Persians had been launching an offensive, why did not the Athenians follow up their stunning victory by sailing eastward to win over more of the cities of southern Asia Minor and in particular to revive Pausanias' campaign against Cyprus, an important Persian navel base, which apparently had been neglected since 478? Thucydides' next entry, however, is the revolt of Thasos in 465, to which must be attached some Persian activity in the region of the Thracian Chersonese revealed by the fragments of an inscribed Athenian casualty list.[16] It is reasonable, then, to assume that urgent dangers in the north prevented Athens from pursuing ventures in the east. Eurymedon, therefore, should be dated in 466, the year before the outbreak in Thasos. Following this line of reasoning, it is logical to think that the revolt of Naxos, which potentially could have led to great disorder in the Delian League, may have encouraged the Persians to undertake their offensive. The revolt of Naxos, accordingly, should be placed in 467, a date which fits in better than the usually accepted 470 with the problems concerning Themistocles' flight to Asia Minor.

After referring to the victory at the Eurymedon, Thucydides next lists the revolt of the important island of Thasos. The Thasians, who controlled some markets and a mine in Thrace, apparently resented Athenian encroachments from Eion on the mouth of the Strymon and also feared increased difficulties from the colony which the Athenians were planning in that region. This seems to have been an obvious case of economic imperialism on the part of the Athenians. They defeated the Thasians at sea and then landed and began a siege of the city. About the same time a colony of 10,000 settlers, both Athenians and allies, was sent to occupy Ennea Hodoi (Nine Ways), later called Amphipolis, on the Strymon. The colonists took possession of Ennea Hodoi, but when they or some of their troops advanced into the interior, they were destroyed at a place called Drabescus by the united Thracians, who were alarmed at the establishment of so large a settlement in their territory. The disaster at Drabescus is one of the few events in this period which can be positively dated. Several sources provide the information that Amphipolis was founded in 437/6, and Thucydides (4.102.3) states that that founding was twenty-eight years after the defeat at Drabescus, which, accordingly, can be dated to 465/4. Since Thucydides implies that the occupation of Ennea Hodoi and the Drabescus disaster followed closely on the Athenian attack on revolting Thasos, the beginning of that revolt can surely be placed either early in 465/4 or late in 466/5.

The defeat at Drabescus may have had a special significance in the development of Athenian democracy, although some scholars reject the interpretation reported here.[17] Pausanias (1.29.4), describing the tombs in the Ceramicus of those Athenians who had fallen in battle on land or sea, says: "The first buried here were the men who in Thrace, after conquering the country as far as Drabescus, were surprised and massacred by the Edonians [a Thracian people]." This apparently was the beginning of the democratic custom of burying together, without distinction of family or rank, all who had died in war for Athens. This practice must have been authorized by a decree of the people, which may well have been proposed by the emerging popular leaders Ephialtes and Pericles. The decree presumably also prescribed the ritual for public funerals and for funeral orations (*logoi epitaphioi*), of which the one delivered in 431 by Pericles, as reported in book 2 of Thucydides, is the supreme example.

In the winter of 465/4 the Thasians, hard pressed by the Athenian siege, appealed to Sparta, as hegemon of the Hellenic League, to assist them by an invasion of Attica. According to Thucydides, the Spartans, without the knowledge of the Athenians, agreed to send help, but were prevented from carrying out their promise by the occurrence of an earthquake and a revolt of the helots. This earthquake was a serious disaster, although one may question the statements of later authors (Diodorus, 11.63; Plutarch, *Cimon,* 16.4) that over 20,000 Lacedaemonians were killed and that all but five houses in the city of Sparta were destroyed. The Thasians, deprived of any hope of aid, withstood the siege of the Athenians until the third year (463/2), when they surrendered under the following terms: destruction of their walls, surrender of their ships, payment of an indemnity immediately and tribute (*phoros*) thereafter, and abandonment of the markets and mine in Thrace. This is the first mention of the confiscation of the ships of an ally after the suppression of a revolt; whether the same procedure had been followed after the subjection of Naxos is unknown.

Thucydides' account (1.101–103) of the helot revolt and of the sub-

sequent sending of aid by Athens in response to Sparta's appeal is so
compressed that it is somewhat misleading. From the information supplied by Plutarch in his *Life of Cimon* (16–17) and from other sources it is
possible to obtain a fuller and more intelligible picture of the course of
events. After the devastating earthquake, the helots in the Eurotas valley
rose against the Spartans; they were soon joined by the Messenian helots
and a few (two according to Thucydides) communities of the *perioeci*.
The Spartans, who had suffered numerous losses in the disaster, were
hard pressed and appealed for help, probably to various allies, but certainly to the Athenians. Many years later in the *Lysistrata,* produced in
412, Aristophanes has an amusing reference to this occasion (lines
1137–1144). Lysistrata is speaking: "And then, Laconians, for I shall
turn to you, don't you know when Pericleides, the Laconian, came here
once and as a suppliant of the Athenians sat on the altar, pallid in his
scarlet cloak, begging for an army? And Messenia then was attacking
you and the god shaking you up at the same time. And Cimon going
with 4,000 hoplites saved all Lacedaemon." It was presumably at this
time that a famous debate took place in the Athenian assembly, with the
democratic leader, Ephialtes, recommending that no help be sent while
Cimon, true to his policy of cooperation with Sparta, finally won over
the Athenians by urging them "not to suffer Hellas to be crippled nor
their city to be robbed of its yoke-fellow." Xenophon in the *Hellenica*
(6.5.33) refers to this dispatch of Athenian troops when he has the Spartans in 370 remind the Athenians of the zealous help the latter had furnished when the Spartans themselves were being besieged by the Messenians. At this time, then, the Spartans, with the help of their allies,
were able to defeat the rebels sufficiently so that thereafter the war centered around Mt. Ithome in Messenia, which the helots used as a base
and a refuge. After the Spartans had taken to the offensive, Cimon and
his men returned home. Even if the date for this expedition of Cimon
was 464, the fact that the Athenians were besieging Thasos then need
not militate against it, for it is unnecessary to believe that Cimon himself
had to remain continuously in Thasos throughout the long siege.

Plutarch (*Cimon,* 17.2) says that later (462/1) the Spartans again
called on their allies, including the Athenians, to aid them against the
Messenians in Ithome. It is at this point that Thucydides' account becomes pertinent. He reports that the Spartans had particularly called
upon the Athenians because of their reputation in siege operations.
When assaults on the mountain fortress failed, however, the Spartans
dismissed Cimon and the Athenians alone of their allies, saying that
they no longer were needed. Thucydides assigns as the real motives
Spartan worry about the revolutionary spirit of the Athenians and fear

lest they might be persuaded by the besieged Messenians to undertake subversive actions. The historian would give much to have a clear understanding of the friction which developed between the Athenians and the Spartans at this time, but he must be content with Thucydides' general statements. Nevertheless, it seems reasonable to suspect that the Spartans were influenced by memories of Pausanias' intrigues with the helots, in which Themistocles may have been involved, and also by rumors that democratic forces were currently attacking the conservative regime at Athens.

Many scholars reject the earlier expedition of Cimon to Sparta, claiming that he only went to Ithome in 462/1. Ancient sources do at times duplicate undertakings, but the *Lysistrata* passage and the reference in Xenophon's *Hellenica* clearly refer to an occasion when Sparta itself was in danger, whereas the expedition of 462/1 is concerned exclusively with the siege of Ithome in Messenia. Aristophanes, Xenophon, and Plutarch, therefore, mention an entirely different military situation from the one Thucydides records.[18]

When Cimon went to Ithome in 462, or on his unhappy return to Athens, his political opponents took advantage of the situation. In their efforts to increase the democratic elements in the Athenian government they had long been attacking the Areopagus, the most conservative body in Athens, and now, under the leadership of Ephialtes and the young Pericles, they succeeded in carrying through the assembly measures that stripped the old council of all authority except its jurisdiction in homicide cases and other matters of a religious nature. The great significance of this measure, which can be dated securely to 462/1 (Aristotle, *Ath. Const.*, 25.2), for the evolution of Athenian democracy will be discussed in the next chapter. The dismissal of Cimon and his troops by the Spartans, which emphasized the failure of the policy of cooperation with Sparta, played into the hands of Cimon's domestic enemies. On their motion the assembly broke off the alliance which the Athenians and Spartans had made against the Persians in 481/0 and contracted alliances with Sparta's chief enemy, Argos, and also with the Thessalians (Thucydides, 1.102.4). It is probably more logical to attribute the action of the assembly both concerning the Areopagus and the alliances with Argos and the Thessalians to the anger felt by the Athenians, including Cimon's disillusioned hoplites, on the return of Cimon to Athens with his pro-Spartan policy in disgrace.

Thus this year 462/1 marked the end, for all practical purposes, of the Hellenic League. That league, which had provided the organization for Greek defense against Persia in 480 and 479, had waned rapidly in significance thereafter, but its influence was still sufficient to explain probably the Thasian appeal to the Spartans, and certainly the Spartan appeal to the Athenians in their war against the rebellious helots. The breach between the Athenians and Spartans destroyed any feelings of unity among the Greeks which common action in 480 and 479 had inspired, and the Greek world soon was divided into two hostile camps, one dominated by Athens and the other by Sparta. One ironic aspect of this trend was that Cimon, the friend of Sparta, contributed greatly to the cleavage, for his naval policy tended both to make Athens more imperialistic and also to increase the influence of the common people in the government, and these were the very developments which inspired suspicion and fear among the Spartans and their allies.

When Cimon returned to Athens in the autumn of 462 he jeopardized his popularity, already at low ebb because of the ignominy inflicted upon the Athenians at Ithome, by a fruitless attempt to support the traditions of the Areopagus. The people, however, freed from the rather ill-defined powers of this archaic and conservative council, had little sympathy with its champion, and in the following spring (461) Cimon was ostracized. The antidemocratic extremists in Athens then sullied the political atmosphere by assassinating the man they considered their most dangerous opponent, Ephialtes.

The dating of the helot revolt is one of the great cruxes in fifth-century chronology. Although a definitive answer may be impossible, one should be familiar with the nature of the difficulties. Thucydides, who in the Pentecontaetia is presumably following a chronological order, lists events as follows (the dates have been defended above): earthquake at Sparta and revolt of helots (465/4); surrender of Thasos (463/2); Cimon's expedition to Ithome, his dismissal by the Spartans, the Athenian break with Sparta, and the Athenian alliances with Argos and the Thessalians (462/1). Thucydides next states—in chapter 103—that in the tenth year the helots on Mt. Ithome surrendered with the stipulation that they should be allowed to leave the Peloponnesus and never to return. The Athenians, now hostile to Sparta, settled these refugees with their wives and children in Naupactus, at the western end of the Corinthian Gulf, which they had recently taken from the Ozolian Locrians. If the helot revolt began in 465/4, the tenth year should be 456/5, but Thucydides does not reach that year in his concise narrative of events until the end of chapter 108, where he mentions the circumnavigation of the Peloponnesus by the Athenian general Tolmides—an event dated by the scholiast to Aeschines (2.75) to 456/5, a date which there is no reason to reject.

It would be futile to discuss in detail here all the interpretations which have been suggested to solve this chronological riddle. The truth is that the evidence from the sources is so conflicting that, depending on what points are emphasized or minimized, it is possible to obtain several more or less convincing solutions. In general there have been three types of interpretations, which can be summarized as follows: (1) The ordinal "tenth" represents a mistake in the manuscript tradition. Certainly the commonest mistakes made by scribes copying manuscripts of Thucydides concerned proper names and numerals. The emendation most frequently suggested for "tenth" has been "fourth." (2) The revolt really began about 469/8, possibly as a result of Pausanias' machinations, but became serious only after the earthquake mentioned by Thucydides. The fall of Ithome should be placed in 461/0. (3) The earthquake and revolt occurred, as Thucydides implies, in 465/4, but Ithome did not fall until the tenth year, 456/5. This solution assumes that Thucydides, anxious to complete his account of the helot revolt and fall of Ithome, violated his chronological scheme of listing events in order of occurrence. Since dating the fall of Ithome in 461/0 fits reasonably well with the rest of Thucydides' narrative, the emendation "fourth" for "tenth" is probably the most satisfying suggestion, but it should be noted that the scholiast to the passage of Aristophanes' *Lysistrata* quoted above dates the earthquake and the helot uprising to the archonship of Theagenides, 468/7.

With the ostracism of Cimon and the assassination of Ephialtes, Pericles, who apparently had served as an assistant to the latter, came to the fore. Pericles was the son of Xanthippus, the Athenian commander at Mycale and at the taking of Sestos in the winter of 479/8, and of Agariste, the niece of the great democratic reformer Cleisthenes. Pericles, therefore, was connected with the Alcmaeonids through his mother. The ancient sources imply that the mantle of Ephialtes immediately fell upon him. Since in 460 he was only about thirty-five years old, it is possible that, because of his subsequent fame, later authors depicted him as the leading statesman in Athens at a time when he was only one of several prominent public figures. It is certain, however, that his influence in the state increased rapidly.

I N THE YEARS following 460 the Athenians were extremely active. The war with Persia, of which nothing is known except for the activity in Thrace following the battle of Eurymedon ca. 466, was renewed; it lasted until the alleged Peace of Callias in 449. In 460, or possibly a year or two later—the exact chronology is obscure—the Athenians, abandoning the policy advocated by Cimon, also began hostilities with various allies of Sparta and soon with Sparta itself. In fact, the fighting in Greece from 460 until 445 (date of the Thirty Years' Peace between

Athens and Sparta), with an intervening five years' truce, can be called the First Peloponnesian War to contrast it with the Great Peloponnesian War which broke out in 431. In these years the Delian League definitely was transformed into an Athenian empire, and in Greece proper the Athenians established a short-lived land empire. At the same time, and continuing thereafter, Athenian democracy was swiftly developing, and also a remarkable intellectual life was flourishing. Although wars, imperialism, growth of democracy, and intellectual ferment, as contemporary phenomena, all obviously influenced one another, they must be treated largely separately so as to avoid the confusion that would arise from shifting constantly from one emphasis to another.

As stated above, it was probably in the year 461/0 that the Athenians settled the helot refugees at Naupactus. At about the same time the Megarians, because of a border dispute with the Corinthians, withdrew from alliance with Sparta and allied themselves with the Athenians. The latter immediately occupied Megara and Pagae, its port on the Corinthian Gulf, and began to build long walls from Megara to Nisaea, the port on the Saronic Gulf, which they garrisoned. The acquisition of Megara was very important for the Athenians, for it not only strengthened their frontier against the Peloponnesians, but possession of Pagae facilitated their communications with Naupactus. Athenian naval bases at Pagae and Naupactus, at the eastern and western ends respectively of the Corinthian Gulf, obviously were a threat to Corinthian western trade, and Thucydides (1.103.4) emphasizes that the violent hatred of the Corinthians for the Athenians had its origin at this time.

The next events listed in Thucydides' account are the revolt of Egypt from Persia and the Athenian participation in the enterprise. As usual, no specific date is provided, but since the Athenian expedition ended after six years of fighting, apparently in 454, its beginning can be placed in 460 or 459. The instigator of the revolt was Inaros, son of Psammetichus—a Libyan, according to Thucydides, but to judge from his father's name, probably related to the former Saite kings of Egypt. The revolt spread throughout Lower Egypt, and, as Herodotus (3.12, 15; 7.7) reports, at Papremis, somewhere in the Delta, Inaros defeated and slew the Persian governor, Achaemenes, Xerxes' brother, and destroyed a large part of the Persian army. At this point (or earlier, from fear of the Phoenician fleet), Inaros appealed to the Athenians for help. The Athenians, with 200 ships of their own and their allies, were campaigning in Cyprus; abandoning that island, they sailed up the Nile, took possession of two-thirds of Memphis, and began a siege, which was to last much longer than anticipated, of the fortress, known as the White Castle. The presence of so large a fleet of the Delian League off Cyprus is the first evidence, as preserved in the scanty sources, of a vigorous offensive against Persia since the battle of Eurymedon. As mentioned above, Persian activity in Thrace and the revolt of Thasos in 465 probably prevented the Athenians from capitalizing on their victory at Eurymedon by renewing the attack on Cyprus inaugurated by Pausanias twelve years earlier. Before his ostracism in 461, Cimon may have been advocating such an expedition, but it was undertaken only when his opponents presumably were swaying the Athenian assembly. Whether Pericles was one of the sponsors, although probable, is unknown. If word of the Egyptian revolt had reached Athens, this knowledge may well have encouraged the Athenians to believe that, with Persian attention directed elsewhere, it was a particularly favorable time to undertake a campaign in Cyprus. Thucydides' succinct narrative implies that Inaros' appeal for help was made to the Greek fleet off Cyprus, but certainly it must have been referred to Athens—or to the league congress at Delos—for it is hard to believe that the Athenian generals would have accepted the call on their own responsibility.

As with the Cyprus campaign, the sponsors of the Egyptian expedition are unknown, but their arguments in favor of intervention must have touched on such matters as the opportunities to weaken Persia, to acquire a naval base in Egypt, and to gain access to the abundant grain supply of the Nile Valley. One would like to know what the reaction of the allies was to this venture; possibly the Ionians dreamed of regaining their profitable sixth-century relations with Egypt. Thucydides writes as if all 200 ships abandoned Cyprus and sailed to Egypt, but it is unlikely that so large a fleet would have been removed from service elsewhere by being permanently confined to a siege which lasted several years. Since scattered evidence shows that several cities on the southern coast of Asia Minor and Dorus on the Phoenician coast joined the league, presumably in this period, it seems correct to suggest that part of the fleet continued to cruise in the eastern Mediterranean. The question of the ultimate fate of the Greeks sent to aid Inaros will be discussed below.

While Athens and other members of the Delian League were becoming involved in the Egyptian revolt, the First Peloponnesian War broke out in Greece proper. After the Athenian break with Sparta in 462/1 and the subsequent defection of Megara from Sparta to an alliance with Athens, with all the dangers that this signified for Corinth, the maintenance of peace must have been very precarious. Thucydides (1.105) implies that Athens began hostilities by naval attacks on allies of Corinth (Halieis on the southeast tip of the Argolid and Cecryphalea, an island in the Saronic Gulf). The immediate motivation may have been Athenian success in repulsing with the Argives a Spartan attack on

Oenoe (Pausanias, 1.15.1) in the southwestern Argolid, an attack launched to punish Argos for the recent alliance with Athens.[19] Then war broke out between Athens and Aegina, an old commercial rival of Athens, and in a great naval battle off that island between the Athenians and their allies and the Aeginetans and their allies, the Athenians were victorious, capturing seventy enemy ships. They thereupon landed and began a siege of the city of Aegina.

Two things are noteworthy about this struggle with Aegina. This was the first recorded time that Athenian allies—presumably members of the Delian League—took up arms against a Greek state in a quarrel which existed solely between that state and Athens. Second, since a statement of Pericles bidding the Athenians "to remove Aegina as the eyesore of the Piraeus" (Plutarch, *Pericles,* 8.5) was remembered, it seems safe to conclude that Pericles was one of the leaders who advocated this war. The Corinthians and their allies, wishing to aid Aegina, invaded Megara in the belief that the Athenians, with large forces occupied in Aegina and Egypt, would have to raise the siege of Aegina in order to bring support to their recent ally, Megara. The Athenians, however, in an action which became famous, dispatched under the general Myronides the oldest and youngest of those left to protect the city, and this force, in a more or less drawn battle, succeeded in protecting Megara.

These far-flung activities seemingly occurred in the years 460 or 459. The most vivid and moving comment on them is provided by a public monument erected by the Athenian tribe Erectheis (*M&L*, no. 33). On a plain stele one can read this heading: "Of [the tribe] Erectheis the following died in the war in Cyprus, in Egypt, in Phoenicia, in Halieis, in Aegina, in Megara in the same year." Beneath this statement 177 names are inscribed. The fighting in Phoenicia, although not mentioned in the literary sources, could well be connected with the addition of Dorus to the league. Similar monuments were presumably erected by the other nine tribes, but it is to be hoped that they recorded fewer casualties.

In these times, says Thucydides, the Athenians began to build the long walls from the city to the sea, one to Phaleron and the other to Piraeus. Since Athenian military and economic life was becoming more and more dependent on the sea, they had come to realize how disastrous it would be for them if an enemy should cut off the city from its harbors. As they were unwilling to abandon Athens with its associations of centuries, the solution they chose was to link the city with its harbors by a continuous line of walls. Then with no specific mention of time, but the year was probably 457, Thucydides refers (1.107) for the first time to Spartan entry into the hostilities.

According to Thucydides' account, the Phocians had attacked the three Dorian communities located to their northwest, which traditionally were considered the metropolis of the Spartans. The Spartans went to the aid of their metropolis with 1,500 hoplites of their own (presumably including *perioeci*) and 10,000 of their allies. After compelling the Phocians to desist from encroaching on these Dorian towns, the Spartans started to retire, but were afraid to cross the Corinthian Gulf (by which route they had probably come) because of the Athenian fleet, or to march through Megara since the Athenians were guarding the pass over the Geraneian mountains. When some oligarchs in Athens, who hoped to eliminate the democracy and also to halt work on the long walls, entered into secret communications with them, the Spartans proceeded to Tanagra in southeast Boeotia to await further developments. The Athenians, suspicious that an attempt against the democracy was impending, marched out against them in full force, accompanied by 1,000 Argives and an unspecified number of other allies. These combined troops, numbering 14,000, were later joined, in conformity with the alliance, by some Thessalian cavalry, who, however, deserted to the Spartans in the engagement. The battle took place at Tanagra; after heavy losses on both sides, the Spartans (who probably had been reinforced by Boeotian contingents) were sufficiently victorious to be able to return to the Peloponnesus through the Megarid, cutting down the olive trees as they proceeded. The Athenians were not daunted by the reverse at Tanagra, for on the sixty-second day thereafter they marched into Boeotia under the command of Myronides, and at Oenophyta near the Attic frontier they thoroughly defeated the Boeotians. As a result of this victory the Athenians, after tearing down the walls of Tanagra, won control of all Boeotia and also of Phocis and Opuntian Locris.

Since Thucydides, in his sketch of the Pentecontaetia, is concerned only with giving a chronological account of the growth of Athenian power as background for his study of the Great Peloponnesian War, modern historians have to try to explain the reasons for the events he records. Many suggestions have been offered to elucidate the situation just mentioned, which marks the beginning of the Athenian "land empire." It will be sufficient here to single out a few points which emphasize the complexity of international relations in this world of city-states aspiring to be independent—and dominant. Sparta's professed motive for marching into central Greece was to protect the Dorians of Doris, their "kin." Behind the piety of this action there was a very practical motive. One should remember that in the council of the Delphic Amphictiony the Dorians possessed two of the twenty-four votes. Doris controlled one Dorian vote and the Peloponnesian Dorians, exclusive of

Sparta, the other.[20] Sparta's chief hope for representation in the voting was to persuade Doris to vote as Sparta wanted. If Doris should be engulfed by Phocis, then, apparently, Phocis would have controlled three votes. That the Spartans had the Amphictiony very much in mind seems proved by the fact that they reduced the influence of Phocis by liberating the Delphians from Phocian control (Plutarch, *Cimon,* 17.3).

The situation in central Greece was further confused by activity among the Boeotians. There is some slight numismatic evidence that about this time Tanagra was aspiring to restore and lead the Boeotian League.[21] Diodorus (11.81), although with reference to the period immediately following the battle of Tanagra, states that Thebes, whose reputation had been at a low ebb since its medizing, requested Spartan help in reviving the Boeotian League under Theban control, thereby establishing a strong state in central Greece to act as a curb on Athenian ambitions. The Spartans favored the proposal; in fact, it seems probable that they had had such a plan in mind when they began their expedition. The purpose of their march to the southeast corner of Boeotia, then, was to intimidate Tanagra, in the interests of Thebes, and also to have a base suitable for an invasion of Attica in case the encouragements from the Athenian oligarchs proved promising.

If the Spartan campaign into central Greece had been motivated partly by the desire to revive the Boeotian League under the aegis of Thebes as a check on Athenian aggressiveness, the return of the Spartans to the Peloponnesus after their victory at Tanagra jeopardized this policy, for two months later the Athenians achieved their success at Oenophyta over the Boeotians alone. The lack of further Spartan interference can be explained in part by the difficulty of proceeding through Megara, then controlled by the Athenians. Athenian policy in this period also raises puzzling questions. The presence of a large Spartan army at Tanagra and the suspicion that oligarchic malcontents in Athens were in communication with it caused such alarm that it explains why Athenian hoplites marched out against the formidable Spartan infantry. Only a year or two earlier, because of the troops engaged in Egypt and Aegina, Athens had had to rely on a levy of the oldest and the youngest, but now, although those two undertakings were still in progress, Athens sent to Tanagra 14,000 men, including 1,000 Argives and contingents from other allies. Since the emergency at Tanagra seemingly developed rapidly, one is almost forced to the conclusion that the Athenians had long been preparing for some venture.

One possible venture should be mentioned to emphasize the influence of the Delphic Amphictiony. A fragmentary inscription (*Supplementum Epigraphicum Graecum,* XIII, 3), which by its letter forms can be dated to the middle of the fifth century, records that Athens had made an alliance with the Delphic Amphictiony, or rather with those Amphictions who had a share in the sanctuary. As Athens possessed one of the Ionian votes and hence was a member of the Amphictionic Council, why was there a need for this alliance? Since the alliance was only with those Amphictions who had a share in the sanctuary, the phraseology suggests that there was a schism in the Amphictiony. It would be idle to speculate here on the significance of this schism—according to one scholar causing a Sacred War of the "loyal" Amphictions against the schismatic ones[22]—for not enough evidence is available to form a coherent picture of the confused situation in central Greece at this time, but even though one cannot explain the confusion, it is clear that problems concerning things Delphic were very prominent in the middle of the fifth century. To illustrate this one need only mention the following events: in 457 the Spartans liberated the Delphians from the Phocians; about this time there was some sort of schism among the Amphictions; after its victory at Oenophyta Athens apparently put the sanctuary under the control of the Phocians again, while some years later, ca. 449, Sparta in the Sacred War restored the sanctuary to the Delphians, an action soon followed by the Athenians returning it to the Phocians (Thucydides, 1.112.5).

After his brief mention of Oenophyta and its results, Thucydides states that the Athenians completed their long walls, and "after this" (the year 457/6?) the Aeginetans surrendered to the Athenians. The old rivals of the victor were thoroughly humiliated, being forced to destroy their walls, give up their ships, and agree to pay tribute (*phoros*) in the future. The next event listed is Tolmides' circumnavigation of the Peloponnesus with an Athenian fleet, in the course of which the Spartan dock yards (at Gythium) were burned. This episode provides one of the rare absolute dates in this period, for, as mentioned above, the scholiast to Aeschines (2.75) assigns Tolmides' exploit to the archonship of Callias (456/5).

Thucydides then returns to Egypt and completes his account of the expedition of the Athenians and their allies. When an attempt to bribe Sparta to invade Attica had failed, King Artaxerxes sent a large army to Egypt. The Persians defeated the Egyptians and their allies, drove the Greeks out of Memphis, and then blockaded them in an island named Prosopitis. After a siege of eighteen months the Persians, by diverting the waters, managed to march onto the island and capture it. Thucydides (1.110) remarks that the Greek expedition collapsed then, after six years of fighting, and that only a few of the Greeks succeeded in escaping. The Egyptians once again fell under Persian domination, except for Amyrtaeus, "the king of the marshes," and his followers. Inaros, the leader of the revolt, was betrayed and subsequently crucified. A relief squadron of 50 ships from Athens and the allies, unaware of the defeat of the main force, was overwhelmed by the Persians and the Phoenician fleet and almost totally destroyed. Thus, says Thucydides, "ended the great expedition of the Athenians and their allies to Egypt." A literal reading of his account implies that the original 200 ships and the subsequent 50, with a total force of some 50,000 men, were almost entirely wiped out. This can hardly be true, for it is most unlikely that the original 200 ships all remained continuously in Egypt to carry on the siege of the "White Castle." As with so many matters in these years a definitive answer cannot be given, but the fact that Athens was not crippled suggests that, although Athens and its allies, in unknown respective proportions, suffered a severe and costly defeat, the disaster was not as catastrophic as Thucydides' wording seems to imply.

After ending his account of the Egyptian expedition Thucydides relates briefly the failure of the Athenians, accompanied by the Boeotians and Phocians, to restore an exiled king(?) of the Thessalians to Pharsalus. Possibly this king had been expelled by the factions of the Thessalians who had deserted at Tanagra, and the Athenians were hoping through him to renew their alliance with the Thessalians who, besides their efficiency as cavalry, controlled, with their *perioeci*, half of the votes of the Delphic Amphictiony. Next in order Thucydides lists Pericles' activity with an Athenian fleet in the Corinthian Gulf, which led to an alliance with the Achaean cities on the south coast of the gulf, a further blow to Corinthian western trade.

Several matters not included in Thucydides' sketch of the Pentecontaetia should be mentioned at this point. It was in the year 454/3 that the treasury of the Delian League was moved from Delos to Athens. Although several literary sources (for example, Plutarch, *Aristides,* 25; *Pericles,* 12; Diodorus, 12.38) refer to this significant step, it is epigraphic evidence which provides the date. A series of very important inscriptions known as the tribute-quota lists, many fragments of which have been found especially on the Athenian Acropolis, furnish invaluable information on various aspects, particularly financial, of the Delian League/Athenian empire.[23] These inscriptions, all dating from the period after the transfer of the treasury to Athens, record not the annual tribute paid by each tributary ally, but the one-sixtieth of each payment, turned over by the hellenotamiai to the goddess Athena as first fruits (*aparchai*). These tribute-quota lists, containing the names of every state which made a payment, with the quota recorded opposite the name, were inscribed each year on stone, for the first fifteen years on a large block of Pentelic marble, for the next eight years on a smaller block, and thereafter on separate stelai for each year. Since almost every list contains a serial number and since list number 34 also records the archon (Aristion, 421/0), it is clear that the first of these lists recorded in Athens belongs to the year 454/3.

If the Egyptian expedition collapsed in 454, as is likely, then the removal of the league treasury to Athens can surely be associated with that defeat. Some members of the Delian League may have been genuinely alarmed that Persia might take advantage of the discomfiture of the league forces in Egypt to launch an offensive in the Aegean. Imperialistically-minded Athenians would not have been slow to capitalize on these apprehensions, which provided them with a cogent argument for transferring the treasury from exposed Delos to well-protected Athens. The Athenians would also have been influenced by a realization, as reflected in irregularities in payments of tribute, that discontent was becoming more and more prevalent among their allies in the league. Reasons for this general discontent can be traced, as both Thucydides and Plutarch remark, to the increasing harshness of Athenian leadership. A fragmentary inscription and a passage in Pausanias (5.10.4) disclose that at the battle of Tanagra Ionians, as well as Argives, were fighting on the Athenian side. It would hardly be surprising if members of the Delian League had little enthusiasm for fighting against fellow Greeks in what was a purely Athenian struggle, and many allies may well have objected to the long campaign in distant Egypt.

In the case of two Ionian cities, in particular, the scattered and fragmentary evidence reveals how their discontent displayed itself. The tribute-quota lists provide the information that Erythrae paid no tribute in 454/3 and 453/2, but was paying again by 450/49 at the latest. The inference is clear that the city had revolted in 454/3 or earlier. The text of a mutilated inscription (M&L, no. 40), preserved only in a copy made by a nineteenth-century traveler and to be dated probably in 453/2, discloses that Persian-supported tyrants had been in control of Erythrae and that on their expulsion the Athenians had established a democracy and installed a garrison. A similar situation existed in Miletus, for the tribute-quota lists reveal that Miletus was in revolt from at least 454/3 until 452/1, and certain fragmentary inscriptions suggest that there also Persian-backed tyrants had wielded power until driven out by the Athenians. Revolts like these, which could have provided important bases for the Persian fleet, may have been as influential as the failure of the Egyptian expedition in motivating the transfer of the treasury of the Delian League to Athens.

The course of events in Greece in the years following Pericles' campaign in the Corinthian Gulf (454?) is very obscure. Thucydides (1.112) merely says, "And later, after an interval of three years, a five years' truce was made between the Peloponnesians and the Athenians." He then proceeds to mention Cimon's expedition to Cyprus with 200 Athenian and allied ships, a campaign which probably should be dated to 450 or 451. The establishment of the truce almost certainly belongs to the year 451, for hostilities between Athens and Sparta broke out again in 446, presumably at the expiration of the truce. It would seem logical to believe that Cimon negotiated this agreement on returning from his ostracism in 451. There is a tradition, however, that the Athenians recalled him after their defeat at Tanagra in 457 (Plutarch, *Cimon,* 17.6–18.1; *Pericles,* 10) or, according to Theopompus (fragment 88), when the war with the Lacedaemonians had not yet lasted five years. A recall of Cimon after the Athenian disasters at Tangara and three years later in Egypt might seem reasonable, but, if he returned then to arrange a truce with the Peloponnesians, he apparently did not achieve that goal until 451.

Following the defeat of the Athenians and their allies in Egypt, it is likely that the Persians had been strengthening their bases in Cyprus. Because of the discontent among the Ionian members of the Delian League and the Persian interference in cities like Erythrae and Miletus, it is possible that Persia was contemplating an offensive in the Aegean. The reason for Cimon's expedition into eastern waters, therefore, seems clear. Of the 200 ships, 60 were sent to assist Amyrtaeus, the king in the marshes of the Nile Delta, who was still in revolt against the Persians. The rest of the squadron besieged Citium on the southeast coast of Cyprus, the chief Phoenician city on the island. The death of Cimon and difficulties about supplies necessitated the abandonment of the siege, but the fleet then sailed to Salamis on the east coast and there defeated the Phoenicians, Cyprians, and Cilicians both at sea and on land. Despite this victory, the loss of Cimon and possibly the nearness of the end of the sailing season caused the Greek fleet, including the detachment which had sailed to Egypt, to return home. The departure of the fleet may have had some connection with what is known as the Peace of Callias.

The Peace of Callias is one of the most puzzling problems of fifth-century Greek history, and for generations scholars have argued the question of its authenticity. Since the Delian League had been organized in 478/7 to carry on offensive and defensive war against Persia, one would expect that the conclusion of this war after almost a generation would have loomed as one of the decisive facts in the century. Nevertheless, although the cessation of hostilities with Persia would have raised fundamental questions about the continued existence of the Delian

League and, in particular, about the payment of tribute (*phoros*), specifically imposed "against the barbarian" (1.96.1), Thucydides in his sketch of the Pentecontaetia, included in his first book largely to explain the growth of Athenian power as league evolved into empire, fails to mention the peace. In fact, no fifth-century sources clearly mention the peace, although Herodotus (7.151) makes a passing reference to an embassy of Callias and other Athenians to Susa on unspecified business; but since Argive envoys were also present, the most logical date for these embassies would seem to have been ca. 461, when the Argives, having outraged Sparta by making an alliance with Athens, may have been seeking assurances of Persian friendship. Certain passages in book 8 (for example, 56.4) of Thucydides, however, can best be interpreted as alluding to the peace. In the fourth century, beginning with Isocrates' *Panegyric Oration* of 380, Attic orators several times refer to the peace, and from then on references to it are common. It was often mentioned by way of shining contrast with the humiliating Peace of Antalcidas (King's Peace) which the Greeks made with Persia in 387/6 and thus lent itself to patriotic exaggeration of the "good old days." Scholars who question the existence of the peace cite the negative attitudes of two fourth-century historians, Callisthenes and Theopompus. Callisthenes, however, denied the formation of a peace following Cimon's victory at Eurymedon in 466(?) (Plutarch, *Cimon*, 13.5), and Theopompus, in some badly preserved fragments, states that the peace with Darius II (in 423) is falsified.[24]

The fullest treatment of the peace is provided by Diodorus (12.4). The reliability of Diodorus, of course, depends on what authority he was following. In this case the source was certainly Ephorus, a fourth-century historian whose universal history acquired great popularity in the ancient world. Ephorus could easily have been influenced by the prevailing propaganda—he had been a pupil of Isocrates—but it seems arbitrary skepticism to reject totally his account of the peace, which Diodorus summarizes as follows: "The Athenians and their allies concluded with the Persians a treaty of peace, the principal terms of which were the following: All the Greek cities of Asia are to be autonomous, the satraps of the Persians are not to come nearer to the sea than a three days' journey and no Persian warship is to sail inside [west] of Phaselis [in Lycia] or the Cyanean Rocks [apparently at the eastern end of the Bosporus]; and if these terms are observed by the king and his generals, the Athenians are not to campaign in the territory over which the king rules."

In this book, therefore, the idea of a Peace of Callias is accepted, since a cessation of hostilities seems to make the subsequent history more intelligible. The reader should be warned, however, that this acceptance is accompanied by doubts, for some of the matters soon to be discussed are themselves questionable, and scholars may have interpreted them incorrectly to support the notion of a peace. It should also be noted that in the revolt of Samos (440/39), which will be mentioned below, the Persians seemingly were violating the terms of the peace.

Diodorus is probably correct in ascribing the initiative in the peace negotiations to Artaxerxes, but it was Pericles who was responsible for persuading the Athenians to respond favorably to the proposal. There is no reason to believe that he had previously been opposed to the war against Persia, for the Egyptian expedition, although possibly planned by Cimon, had been carried out during his ostracism, and Pericles may well have approved the eastern expedition in 450 (or 451), thinking that a display of Athenian power in the east was necessary to quell the dangerous discontent in Ionia. Nevertheless, the death of Cimon removed the strongest advocate of continuing the war with Persia and of attempting to maintain good relations with Sparta. Pericles' sway over the Athenian assembly was now greatly increased, for Cimon's "successor," Thucydides, the son of Melesias, did not become a serious rival for several years. Pericles was an ardent imperialist, and in his thinking the two most important objectives in Athenian foreign policy were to retain control of the maritime allies and to increase Athenian prestige in Greece proper. He realized that the five years' truce was a precarious agreement and that war was likely to follow its expiration, for true peace was impossible with the Peloponnesians, above all with the Corinthians, unless Athens surrendered Megara, Achaea, and Naupactus, through control of which it was encroaching on Corinthian westward trade. Athenian resources, however, especially in manpower, were limited, and there had been a terrific drain on them in the past generation. Ever since the aftermath of Salamis and Mycale Athens had been engaged in offensive warfare with Persia, and since 461/0 it had become involved in the "First Peloponnesian War." Some of the campaigns, such as the Egyptian expedition and the battle of Tanagra, had been extremely costly in human lives. Pericles, therefore, decided that to promote his two priorities—maritime empire and Athenian influence in Greece—curtailment of Athenian activities and husbanding of human resources were necessary. And so, Athens and its allies in the Delian League became partners to the Peace of Callias, ending a state of war which one could say had really begun with the Persian conquest of the Asiatic Greeks in the middle of the sixth century.

The peace was a victory for the Greeks—and thus in the fourth century quite properly could be praised in contrast to the Peace of Antalcidas, which recognized Persian rule over the Asiatic Greeks—but it was not a triumph. Cyprus with its many Greek inhabitants was surrendered to the Persians, and for the rest of the century the Phoenicians were dominant in that island. The Asia Minor Greeks, whose liberation from Persia had been one of the chief purposes of the Delian League, were freed politically from Persian rule, but there is reason to question how much they profited from that liberation. The Aeolian and especially the Ionian cities had attained great prosperity and a brilliant civilization in the sixth century, which declined in the latter half of that century and in the first decade of the following one as a result of the Persian conquest and of the suppression of the Ionian revolt. This decline continued throughout the fifth century despite the achievements of the Delian League and the Peace of Callias. Archaeological work in the region has been limited, but the few results, in the opinion of some archaeologists, seem to demonstrate that the whole area was a depressed one and that some of the cities were in fact little more than straggling villages. The tribute payments to Athens were often surprisingly low for cities that had once been so flourishing.

The failure of the Asiatic Greeks to recover their prosperity is strange, and in the absence of adequate evidence cannot be satisfactorily explained. The suggestion which has been made several times, however, that although the cities were freed politically from Persia, some of the good land in the adjacent plains remained under Persian control, may deserve consideration. If one works backwards from the more abundant fourth-century evidence, one derives the impression that much of the land belonged in the category of King's land, granted in fiefs, large or small, to Persians or to Greeks, either exiles or persons friendly to Persia. If this impression is correct, then the inference would be that the rents from these lands were paid to the King. This hypothesis, therefore, postulates an unhealthy dichotomy among the Ionian and Aeolian Greeks—oligarchic landowners paying rent to Persia and on the whole friendly to Persia, and city dwellers, mostly artisans and laborers, paying tribute to, and oriented towards, Athens. Many scholars reject this hypothesis, and it is mentioned here primarily to emphasize the dearth of evidence.[25] The hypothesis, however, does make one think of Herodotus' description (6.42) of Artaphernes' settlement of Ionia after the suppression of the revolt in 493: "Having measured their lands by parasangs, the name which the Persians give to thirty stades, having measured by these, he assigned tributes (*phoroi*) to each which continue to be in force from that time continuously down to my time as they were assessed by Artaphernes."

Diodorus (12.4) dates the Peace of Callias under the Athenian archon Pedieus (449/8), but the preceding year fits better with the admittedly ambiguous evidence. Cimon died in 450 (or 451), and the negotiations for peace probably started soon thereafter. These negotiations could explain the withdrawal of the Greek fleet from Cyprus and Egypt, despite the recent victory at Cyprian Salamis.

THE TRIBUTE-QUOTA list for 450/49 is proof that the allies in the early spring of 449 made their payments as usual to Athens, but the existence of many partial payments suggests that by the time the tribute was due at the City Dionysia in March, word about the impending peace was circulating in the Aegean world. The news must have caused great excitement among the members of the Delian League and also given rise to much speculation about the future of the league. Since the tribute (*phoros*) was to be used "against the barbarian," many cities probably assumed that with the establishment of peace they would be rid of that burden. The very existence of the league was at stake, for the memory of the ceremony of casting lumps of metal into the sea performed in 478/7 to symbolize the permanence of the new organization had by now presumably grown dim. Athens realized that the question of tribute was uppermost in the minds of the allies and that skillful diplomacy was necessary. Scholars who have worked on the restoration of the great marble block that recorded the first fifteen tribute-quota lists think that there was one year without a tribute-quota list, although there is opposition to this assumption. If there was one year in which no tribute-quota list was recorded, the generally accepted interpretation is that, in view of the emotions stimulated by the establishment of peace, tribute was not collected in 449/8. Since tribute is recorded thereafter, some scholars argue that it would have been psychologically foolish to suspend tribute only to renew it the next year. They make the interesting suggestion that in 449/8 all the tribute was allotted to the building of a temple of Athena Nike; a temple was under discussion at this time, although it was not erected until the 420s (*M&L,* no. 44). In such a situation no tribute-quota list would have been inscribed.

Athens, obviously, was facing a serious crisis. Its position as a great power depended almost exclusively on the fleet, and for years that fleet had been maintained chiefly by the payments of tribute. Curtailment of the fleet, therefore, would have led not only to curtailment of Athenian hegemony but also to the dangerous problems of unemployment that are the usual concomitants of large-scale demobilization. Pericles, as an imperialist and a statesman probably already imbued with the belief in Athens' "manifest destiny" which he advocated so eloquently later, must have foreseen these problems when he decided on the necessity of peace. He was determined that some sort of organization of the Greeks should be maintained, and he could justify his conviction by the sound argument that unless the Greeks remained united and retained a strong fleet, Persia could easily encroach on Ionia and the Aegean again, and piracy would become rampant.

In the study of this critical period for all the Greeks, but especially for Athens and its leaders, of whom Pericles clearly was dominant, the most significant information, beyond the suspension for a year of the tribute-quota lists already mentioned, seems to be furnished by two partially preserved decrees, the Congress Decree and the Papyrus Decree, both sponsored by Pericles. The interpretation of these documents adopted here is the one generally accepted, but the reader should be warned that no matter how logical this interpretation may appear it is based on tantalizingly inadequate data.

Pericles' first action in this tense period was to try to convoke at Athens a congress of delegates of Greeks from both Europe and Asia to discuss some of the problems created by the new international situation. His attempt is mentioned only by Plutarch (*Pericles,* 17), who, as so often, assigns no date, but the need for some such action was so pressing that some scholars have no hesitation in placing it shortly after the ratification of the peace, and still in the spring of 449. Of the agenda outlined for the congress in the decree that Pericles proposed, usually called the Congress Decree by modern scholars, Plutarch mentions merely the following items: the delegates were "to deliberate concerning the Hellenic sanctuaries which the barbarians had burned down, concerning the sacrifices which were due to the gods in the name of Hellas in fulfillment of vows made when they were fighting against the barbarians, and concerning the sea, that all might sail it fearlessly and keep the peace."[26]

The historian would give much to know more about these proposals and about others which were presumably made at the same time, and also about the reaction of the Greeks in general to them, but Plutarch merely says that nothing came of Pericles' plan because of the opposition of the Spartans. Spartan opposition was so certain that one wonders whether it was only a propaganda move on Pericles' part, with no expectation that the congress would actually assemble. As propaganda it was a supremely clever move. By taking the initiative, Pericles cast Athens in the role of leader of the Greeks in an irreproachable desire to give the gods their due and to preserve order on the sea. From the evidence of the second decree to be discussed, it seems possible that Pericles may have been planning to raise the question of the proper employment of 5,000 talents, no longer needed against Persia, which had accumulated in the treasury of the Delian League. Nothing apparently was openly said about the fact that it was at Athens especially that temples had been destroyed and hence needed to be rebuilt—although this was forbidden by one version of the Oath of Plataea—and that the command of any fleet would surely fall to Athens. If the Spartans had attended the congress, that in itself would have been tantamount to recognizing Athenian leadership in matters of religion, and they also would probably have been called upon to make eventual contributions to the maintenance of a fleet dominated by Athens, for 5,000 talents would not have met the costs of temple building and fleet maintenance indefinitely. In fact, if Sparta had participated in the congress, it would have had either to recognize Athenian hegemony in matters both religious and secular or to appear publicly as impious, uncooperative, and jealous. Its reaction to Pericles' propaganda, so far as the chronology can be reconstructed, was to march into central Greece in a Sacred War and to return the control of Delphi, held by the Phocians who were allied with Athens, to the Delphians. This was certainly an attempt to counteract the prestige which Athens had gained from Pericles' proposal and to prevent Athens from capitalizing on the religious influence of Apollo. Athens retaliated, probably later in 449, by restoring Delphi to the Phocians (Thucydides, 1.112.5).

When Pericles was frustrated, as he may have expected, in his plan to hold a Panhellenic congress at Athens, he apparently did not attempt to discuss matters with members of the Delian League who were particularly concerned, but decided that Athens should act for itself alone. He succeeded in carrying through the assembly another decree authorizing, among other things, that the 5,000 talents be transferred from the public treasury to that of Athena. Evidence for this important and drastic step, except what can be inferred from later developments, is provided by a fragmentary papyrus of about 100 A.D. known as the Strasbourg Papyrus or the *Anonymous Argentinensis*. This papyrus contains a commentary on the twenty-second oration of Demosthenes, *Against Androtion*. The portion relevant to the problem under consideration here concerns the statement in section 13 of the speech that the Athenians built the Propylaea and the Parthenon. A new edition of this badly damaged papyrus appeared in 1957, but one should be warned that over half of the beginning of each line is restoration.[27] This document states that the Athenians began to build the Propylaea and the Parthenon on the motion of Pericles in the archonship of Euthydemus from the 5,000 talents deposited in the public treasury according to the assessment of Aristides.

Some scholars have wished to identify the archon mentioned in the papyrus with the Euthydemus known to have been archon in 431/0. There is evidence, however, that the Euthynus attested by an inscription as the archon for 450/49 was recorded in literature (Diodorus, 12.3.1), for reasons unknown, as Euthydemus. The information provided by the restored papyrus and the subsequent history of Athens make it as certain as anything can be, when evidence is meagre, that this decree of Pericles was carried in the eventful year 450/49. Since it clearly was passed after the Congress Decree, which presupposes the Peace of Callias, the relative chronology of events in this period can be presented thus: death of Cimon, summer 450 (or 451); negotiations for peace, winter 450/49; Peace of Callias, early spring 449; Congress Decree, late spring 449; Papyrus Decree, probably June 449, almost at the end of Euthydemus' term of office.

Information furnished by two important financial decrees (*M&L*, no. 58) of the year 434/3 (decrees of Callias, "the financier") renders it likely that the 3,000 talents (part of the restoration of a line of the Papyrus Decree) were taken up to the Acropolis to the treasury of Athena in annual installments of 200 talents. The full significance of Pericles' drastic—or one may prefer the word ruthless—policy as propounded in the Papyrus Decree now becomes clear. Athens not only appropriated for its own purposes the 5,000 talents, accumulated in ways not properly understood, which by law belonged to the members of the Delian League as a whole, but also, whatever explanation is accepted for the anomaly of 449/8, decided to revert to collecting tribute, for the installments of 200 talents were to be taken from the annual tribute. Building accounts which have been preserved reveal that the Athenians were constructing the Parthenon from 447/6 through 433/2; that Phidias' huge chryselephantine statue of Athena, the cult image of the Parthenon, was completed in 438/7; and that work on the Propylaea began in 437/6.

The Delian League, from shortly after its establishment, had steadily fallen more and more under Athenian control. The Papyrus Decree, if correctly interpreted, can be considered as marking the end of the evolution, for now all pretense was stripped away and Athens acted openly as an imperial city. One can suspect that the fleet was active in these years enforcing Athenian will, and it was in this period especially that Athens founded various colonies and *cleruchies* (citizen colonies) which, among other purposes, could serve as military outposts to keep the "allies" obedient.[28] In 448/7 the tribute-quota list recorded a small payment, presumably revealing the resentment of the allies. In response to these unsatisfactory returns the Athenians passed a decree (*M&L*, no. 46), probably in the spring of 447, on the motion of Cleinias, perhaps the father of the notorious Alcibiades, which set forth new and stringent regulations for the collection of tribute. The much larger collection in the following year, 447/6, and the heavy payment of arrears demonstrate that these regulations were enforced successfully.

It was apparently in the period 449-447 that the Athenians passed what is known as the Currency or Monetary Decree, or the Decree of Clearchus, after the name of its proposer (*M&L,* no. 45). This measure stipulated that every city in the Delian League was to bring its silver coinage to the mint at Athens for conversion into Athenian silver coinage, and that thereafter only Athenian silver coinage, weights, and measures were to be used by the league cities. Copies of this decree were to be set up in the agora of each city, and if a city refused to do this, then the Athenians themselves were to erect the stele. Several fragments of this document have been found on the sites of various ancient cities, and from them scholars have succeeded in establishing a composite text, still fragmentary, but sufficiently complete to provide some idea on how the proposal was to be carried out and on the punishments threatened for disobedience.

Scholarly opinion formerly assigned this decree to the 420s or later and saw in it a measure associated with the needs of the Peloponnesian War. This late dating seemed confirmed by Aristophanes' humorous lines (1040-41) in the *Birds* (produced in 414), where a decree-seller tries to sell to two Athenians, who are building a new city (Nephelococcygia) in the air, a decree reading: "The Nephelococcygians are to use the same measures and weights and coinage as the Olophysians." In 1938, however, a new fragment of the decree, found in Cos, a Doric island belonging to the Delian League, was published. The inscription was written in Attic, which presumably meant that the Athenians had inscribed it and set it up when the Coans refused. Epigraphic specialists, by a careful study of the development of the letter forms, are able to date fifth-century Athenian inscriptions with remarkable accuracy. This particular Coan fragment, among other qualities, has what is known as the three-barred sigma, which, according to present evidence, disappeared from Athenian use before the four-barred form (similar to the modern Greek capital sigma) by 446. This observation combined with other characteristics too technical to be mentioned here has convinced most scholars, although some are in vehement opposition, that the monetary decree should be dated ca. 449–447, and must be interpreted as another imperialistic measure advocated by Pericles after the Peace of Callias and the failure of the Congress Decree. The decree was certainly intended to aid commerce, hampered by the variety of currencies, weights, and measures in the Aegean world, but it was also an effective blow against the autonomous spirit of Greek city-states to deprive them of their distinctive coinages.

While Athens in the years following the Peace of Callias was rapidly and successfully consolidating its imperial control over the maritime allies, trouble was brewing in the land empire in central Greece which it had started to establish after the victory at Oenophyta in 457. The cities in Boeotia, Phocis, and Locris had not been incorporated into the Delian League but had become allies of Athens, owing military service rather than tribute. Athens had tried to assure their loyalty by the establishment of democracies and the expulsion of oligarchic factions. It was probably in the winter of 447/6 that Boeotian exiles managed to seize Orchomenus, Chaeronea, and other places in western Boeotia. In the spring of 446 the Athenians under the command of Tolmides, not realizing the seriousness of the trouble, marched out with an inadequate force, captured Chaeronea, enslaved the inhabitants (only the oligarchs?) and installed a garrison. As they were returning to Athens, they were attacked at Coronea by Boeotian, Locrian, and Euboean exiles and badly defeated, Tolmides himself falling in the battle. To recover those who had been taken prisoner, the Athenians had to agree to evacuate Boeotia. The loss of Phocis and Locris, where the oligarchs gained the ascendancy, followed in quick order. Thus the Athenian "land empire" in central Greece collapsed after some eleven years of existence (Thucydides, 1.113).

Shortly afterwards a dangerous revolt broke out on the large and important island of Euboea. The reasons for the uprising are nowhere specifically mentioned, but Athenian policies since the Peace of Callias and the establishment of *cleruchies,* apparently in 450, at Carystus and on the islands of Andros and Naxos must have been contributing factors.[29] As mentioned above, Euboean exiles fought against the Athenians at Coronea. On hearing of the revolt, Pericles immediately crossed to the island but had to return hurriedly when word reached him that Megara had revolted, assisted by the Corinthians and other Peloponnesians, and that the Peloponnesians were on the point of invading Attica. Presumably the Five Years' Truce had expired. The Peloponnesian forces under the Spartan king Pleistoanax, son of Pausanias, marched through the Megarid into Attica and, ravaging the countryside, advanced as far as the Thriasian plain east of Eleusis. They then returned home. Possibly their intentions had been merely to aid the rebelling Euboeans by diverting the Athenians, but Plutarch (*Pericles,* 22) is more likely to have been correct in his statement that Pericles succeeded in bribing Pleistoanax and his chief adviser, Cleandridas. In any case the Spartans exiled their king, while Cleandridas, the father of the Gylippus who so greatly helped the Syracusans against the Athenians in 414 and 413, they condemned to death *in absentia*. After the departure of the Peloponnesians, Pericles once more crossed over to Euboea and subdued the whole island. Some of the territory of Chalcis and probably of Eretria in the Lelantine plain was consecrated to Athena and subsequently leased to tenants. Plutarch (*Pericles*, 23.2) states that the Hippobatae (the wealthy class) of Chalcis were banished, but despite the common modern view, there is no clear evidence that their land was assigned to Athenian *cleruchs*.[30] The Histiaeans at the north end of the island were expelled from their city, and the Athenians colonized the place under the name of Oreos. Plutarch remarks that the Histiaeans were treated thus harshly because, having captured an Athenian ship, they had slain the crew (Thucydides, 1.114).

Soon after their return from Euboea the Athenians made a peace with the Spartans and their allies for thirty years. This pact can be dated securely in the year 446/5, probably in the winter, because Thucydides (2.2.1), when describing the outbreak of the Peloponnesian War which he places in the spring of 431, states that the Thirty Years' Peace then was in its fifteenth year. By the terms of the peace Athens had to relinquish Megara with the two ports, Nisaea and Pagae, Achaea, and Troezen, but was permitted to retain Aegina and Naupactus. Aegina was declared autonomous, which presumably meant that although Athens was entitled to the receipt of tribute, it was not to interfere in the local affairs of the island. Any Greek state not listed in the treaty as an ally of Athens or of Sparta was to be free, if it so desired, to become an ally of either. If disputes arose, Athens and Sparta and its allies agreed that they should be submitted to arbitration (Thucydides, 1.115.1).

The peace was a rather humiliating one for the Athenians, who accepted it probably because of the consternation caused by the dangerous revolt of Euboea and by the Peloponnesian invasion of Attica. As tangible results of the grandiose idea, possibly promoted chiefly by men like Myronides and Tolmides, to build an Athenian hegemony in Greece proper, a policy carried out since 460 at great cost in lives and wealth, there were only Aegina and Naupactus—and the bitter hatred of Corinth. Nevertheless, there was one valuable gain. The fact that Sparta and its allies permitted Athens to sign for itself and its maritime allies constituted a public recognition on the part of the Peloponnesians of the Athenian empire and of Athens' right to it. In the following years Periclean policy placed great emphasis on strengthening that empire and the fleet which held it together, for a Greece divided into two hostile camps did not augur well for a lasting peace.

Little information is available about the relations of Athens with the members of its empire for five years after the signing of the Thirty Years' Peace, except for what can be inferred from the variations in certain tribute payments, but in the sixth year serious trouble broke out. Miletus and Samos had gone to war over possession of the territory of

Priene, and when Miletus was defeated, the democratic government which the Athenians had recently established there appealed to Athens for help. In this appeal they were joined by some Samians who wished to overthrow the oligarchy in their homeland. The Athenians ordered the Samians to submit the dispute to arbitration, but Samos, one of the three members of the "League" (along with Chios and Lesbos) still supplying ships and hence theoretically rating as an equal ally, refused. The Athenians promptly sailed with forty ships to the island, deposed the oligarchy, set up a democracy and, leaving a garrison, returned home. Samian oligarchs, however, with assistance from the Persian satrap of Sardis, possibly acting independently of the king, seized control of Samos again and openly revolted from Athens, a revolt in which Byzantium, possibly influenced by its mother city of Megara, joined.

The situation was clearly critical, for there was danger of a general revolt in the east from Athens. The Athenians realized that Byzantium could try to close the important route to the Black Sea, and, despite the Peace of Callias, they were worried that the Phoenician fleet might sail to the aid of Samos. The seriousness of the situation can be inferred from Thucydides' brief account (1.115–117), from which it seems that the whole board of Athenian generals, including Pericles and, according to other sources, the tragic poet Sophocles, and 160 Athenian ships and 55 from Chios and Lesbos were involved in the war. After some indecisive fighting the Samians were brought under a siege, which they endured for nine months—until the spring or early summer of 439—before they capitulated. By the terms of the peace the Samians had to raze their walls, surrender their ships, furnish hostages, and, instead of becoming tributary, agree to pay a war indemnity of 1,300 or 1,400 talents payable in annual installments of 50 talents each. It is clear also that a democracy was established.

Thucydides ends his account of the revolt and suppression of Samos with the bare statement that Byzantium agreed to become subject again to Athens, and with that remark he brings to a close his sketch of the Pentecontaetia. Elsewhere in his history (4.102.3) he mentions the important undertaking of the Athenians in founding Amphipolis, on the site of Ennea Hodoi, in 437/6. This colony was established on the Strymon at a point where the river could be bridged and thus could profit from the east-west and west-east trade as well as that coming down the river from the interior. The settlement, consisting partly of Athenians but largely of local allies, soon became a powerful city because of the grain, minerals, and timber in the general area. Amphipolis was not only important to Athens as a center from which essential raw materials could be imported; it also could serve to keep watch on the kingdom of the Macedonians to the west and on the recently organized kingdom of the Thracian Odrysians to the north and east. About three miles to the south, at the mouth of the Strymon, was the fortress of Eion, taken from the Persians by Cimon in 477/6, and now a market and probably a fortified naval base for the Athenians.

It may have been about the same time as the founding of Amphipolis that Pericles' expedition into the Black Sea, mentioned by Plutarch (*Pericles,* 20), occurred, although some scholars prefer to place it earlier, possibly in 450, thus making it simultaneous with Cimon's campaign in Cyprus. It was seemingly a demonstration in considerable force, with the aim of showing Athenian power and establishing good relations with both Greeks and barbarians resident on the coasts, and presumably above all with the dynasty ruling in the Crimea, which controlled the export of grain grown in the interior. If the expedition did take place in the 430s it may have been a violation of the Peace of Callias, but in view of the many unknowns connected with that mysterious peace, it would be rash to insist that it debarred Athens from all activity in the Black Sea area. One should note that the help provided by the Persian satrap to the Samian oligarchs in 440 had already constituted a breach of that peace. If one accepts the opinion commonly held that the Black Sea expedition should be dated ca. 437, then one of its motives may have been the recent disturbing revolt of Byzantium.

B Y THE 430s—and, in fact, well before then—it was evident to all the Greeks that the Delian League had been transformed into an Athenian empire. As one considers the course of fifth-century history from 480 on, one can argue with considerable justice that force of circumstances caused Athens to become imperialistic. The fleet which Themistocles had built saved Greece at Salamis and almost overnight revealed Athens as the greatest sea power among the Greeks. When many Ionian Greeks revolted from Persia in the wake of the battle of Mycale, the need to protect them and to liberate those Asiatic Greeks still under Persia inaugurated a new phase of the war against the Persians, a phase which would require naval forces. For such an undertaking Athens, with its newly won prestige, was the natural leader, and it capitalized on the unpopularity of Pausanias and its supposed kinship to the Ionians to acquire that leadership. When the Delian League was formed in 478/7, the Greeks in the enthusiasm of the moment may have thought that they were establishing an organization of free and autonomous states, but the hegemony gave Athens a controlling influence which was furthered by the system that each member had an equal vote, for Athens could easily sway and intimidate the smaller states. As Thucydides emphasizes, the reluctance soon exhibited by many states to endure the hardships of campaigning and their preference to buy protection by paying tribute (*phoros*) played into Athenian hands, since the league fleet more and more became an Athenian fleet. When attempts to secede from the league occurred, beginning with Naxos ca. 467, it was presumably the assembly of the Delian League, with Athens in the chair, that decided that secession could not be tolerated, for it would jeopardize the existence of the league and render it unable to carry out its purpose of continuing the war with Persia. The task of suppressing the seceding or revolting states and forcing them to return to the league fell primarily, or entirely, to Athens as the strongest member and the hegemon. Suppression invariably resulted in loss of full autonomy for the defeated states and in some kind of dependence on Athens. It is well to remember that, in these early years when the seeds of empire were being sown, Cimon was the leading Athenian statesman and general, and thus, despite his so-called aristocratic and conservative point of view, he was really launching Athens on an imperial career.

In 454, apparently as a result of the collapse of the Egyptian expedition, the league treasury was moved from Delos to Athens. The evidence is insufficient to determine whether the threat of Persian interference in the Aegean justified this transfer, but there is little doubt that it strengthened Athenian control over the affairs of the league. It is certain that by the outbreak of the Peloponnesian War, the assembly of delegates from the allies had ceased to function. The demise of this assembly may have occurred when, with the transfer of the treasury, Athens became the "capital" of the league in place of Delos. The crisis raised by the Peace of Callias and the Athenian answer to that crisis hastened the trend from league to empire, a trend which had its beginning in the early days of the league. The Peace of Callias endangered the very survival of the league and of its fleet—now mostly Athenian—which was dependent for its maintenance on the tribute payments. Pericles, realizing that Athenian political, social, and economic life was inextricably interwoven with the maintenance of a fleet, was able to argue on wider and less nationalistic grounds that organization and fleet were essential to prevent disunited Asiatic Greeks from falling prey to the Persians again. He tried to achieve some sort of Panhellenic organization, with Athens to be recognized as hegemon rather than Sparta, through the somewhat disingenuous propaganda of the "Congress Decree." When this proposal miscarried, Pericles, inspired by his vision of making Athens the true capital of the Greek world, but also yielding to political, social, and economic realities, consummated the growth of league into empire by the enactment of such measures as the "Papyrus Decree" and the Monetary Decree, and by enforcing the tribute obligation.

The character of the Athenian people as a whole was conducive to the growth of imperialism. In the fifth century in particular they were noted for their restless energy, a quality expressed by the adjective *poly-pragmon*,[31] which when used by their enemies had the derogatory connotation of "meddlesomeness." In several speeches Pericles used the word with the diametrically opposite meaning, *apragmon*, to characterize—scornfully—spiritless and unambitious states and persons as mere drones. The best description of this Athenian characteristic can be found in a speech which Thucydides puts into the mouth of a bitter enemy of Athens—a Corinthian delegate who at a meeting of the Peloponnesian League in 432 was trying to arouse the Spartans to the danger inherent in Athenian aggressiveness by contrasting the unbounded energy and venturesomeness of the Athenians with the conservative caution and apathy of the Spartans. This speech is so remarkable and so perspicacious that it will be illuminating to quote a few passages from it (1.70): "The Athenians are addicted to innovation, and their designs are characterized by swiftness alike in conception and execution . . . They are adventurous beyond their power, and daring beyond their judgment, and in danger they are sanguine . . . Their only idea of a holiday is to do what the occasion demands, and to them laborious occupation is less of a misfortune than the peace of a quiet life (*apragmon*). To describe their character in a word, one might truly say that they were born into the world to take no rest themselves and to give none to others."

Economic motives also contributed to the growth of an imperialistic spirit at Athens, but these were closely linked with political motives—the passion to rule over others. The revolt and subsequent subjection of Thasos were caused by Athens' desire to control certain markets and a mine on the neighboring Thracian coast. Aegina, an old and hated political and economic rival—the "eyesore of the Piraeus"—was defeated and made tributary. When Megara came over to Athens in 460, the Athenians were not slow to begin exploiting the two harbors, Nisaea and Pagae, particularly the latter which, combined with influence in Achaea and control of Naupactus, enabled Athens to present a serious threat to Corinthian western trade. Even as early as the second quarter of the sixth century, Attic black-figure pottery had largely replaced Corinthian wares in Etruria, and this trend increased with the emergence of the red-figure technique in the latter part of that century.

It was not until after the Athenian acquisition of Megara, however, that, so far as is known, Athens first entered into political relations with a city in the area of the western Greeks. A fragmentary inscription (*M&L,* no. 37) probably to be dated in 458/7 reveals that Athens contracted an alliance with Segesta, the Elymian city in northwestern Sicily, a city which some forty years later was partly responsible for influencing Athens to undertake the ill-fated Sicilian expedition. It is startling to find Athens making this alliance at a time when it was involved in the Egyptian expedition and in the "First Peloponnesian War." Athens, with its wars so far progressing well, may have been interested in the grain fields of the west and also in the opportunity to spread its influence in Sicily, while Segesta may have hoped that Athens' reputation would help it against its chief enemy, Selinus, the Dorian city on the southwest coast of Sicily. Some years later, apparently in the period of the Five Years' Truce (451–446), Athens made alliances with Rhegium in the toe of Italy on the important straits of Messina and with the Ionian city Leontini in eastern Sicily, the constant enemy of Dorian Syracuse, the loyal colony and friend of Corinth (*M&L,* nos. 63, 64). It is unlikely that these alliances and the one with Segesta obligated Athens to furnish military assistance. From the Athenian point of view they may have opened up economic possibilities, and they certainly were intended to be a means of extending Athenian influence.

Another undertaking of Athens in the west in this period was the founding of Thurii in the instep of southern Italy near the site of the ancient city of Sybaris. Sybaris had been destroyed towards the end of the sixth century by Croton, lying to the south. About the middle of the following century the survivors of the Sybarites and their descendants, who had been living in neighboring cities, tried to refound Sybaris, but once again were driven out by the men of Croton. Thereupon the Sybarites invited the Athenians and Spartans to cooperate with them in founding a new city. Sparta declined, but some Athenians and allies went out as colonists about the same time as the establishment of alliances with Rhegium and Leontini. These colonists soon quarreled with the Sybarites, who claimed a privileged position for themselves; they then expelled the Sybarites and appealed to Athens for more settlers. The Athenian response was interesting. In 444/3 they invited all the Greek states in old Greece and the east to send settlers to share in founding a Panhellenic colony. The colony, called Thurii, was laid out according to the plans of the famous town-planner Hippodamus of Miletus, and its law code was drawn up by the sophist Protagoras. The official leaders or founders were two Athenians, and among the settlers, whether at the beginning or later is unknown, was the historian Herodotus of Halicarnassus. The population of Thurii was divided into ten tribes, whose names bear witness to the diversity of origin of the colonists. It is probable that Pericles, as he had in the case of the Congress Decree, envisaged a Panhellenic undertaking which would redound to the credit of Athens and serve as a center of Athenian influence among the western Greeks. If these were his hopes, they did not materialize, for within a decade the Attic element ceased to be predominant in Thurii.[32]

If the term "economic imperialism" has too many modern overtones to be applied appropriately to Athens, it would, nevertheless, be misleading to minimize matters of economic concern which influenced Athenian policy. Athens, with its growing population, had to import many raw materials, particularly grain and timber, and it also needed markets for the excess of its olive oil and for the products of its numerous artisans. When one bears in mind the regions which occupied much of its attention and energy in the Pentecontaetia—Egypt, Thrace, Sicily, Italy, and the Black Sea, all grain-producing, and Thrace, important for timber also—it is obvious that economic, as well as military and political, motives played a role in many of Athens' undertakings in the fifth century.

The wealth that empire brought to Athens from the annual tribute, from the appropriation of the 5,000 talents which had accumulated in the Delian League treasury, and from the fact that Athens with its harbor, Piraeus, became the commercial center of the Greek world benefited the Athenians in so many ways that their imperial fervor grew correspondingly. Among these advantages it will be sufficient to mention the great public works program inaugurated by Pericles in 449 which, according to Plutarch (*Pericles,* 12), gave employment to "carpenters, moulders, bronze-smiths, stone-cutters, dyers, workers in gold and ivory, painters, embroiderers, embossers, to say nothing of the forwarders and furnishers of the material, such as factors, sailors and pilots by sea, and, by land, wagon-makers, trainers of yoked beasts, and drivers . . . also rope-makers, weavers, leather-workers, road-builders and miners"; the maintenance of a large fleet; the sending out for eight months each year, according to Plutarch's probably exaggerated statement (*Pericles,* 11.4), of sixty triremes manned by citizens who received pay while learning seamanship; the founding of many colonies and *cleruchies* which, while serving imperial interests, removed the unemployed from Athens and gave them a better position in life; and the creation of many salaried jobs required by the administration of the empire.

Indissolubly linked with all these materialistic incentives to the imperialistic movement were Pericles' advocacy and justification of Athenian imperialism—an attitude similar to what the nineteenth century termed "manifest destiny." Convinced of the need of unity and organization among the Greeks to protect them against the Persians and against themselves, he believed that the Athenians, because of their rest-less energy and unlimited daring, their remarkable versatility, their en-lightened form of government, and their native intelligence and quick wit, were uniquely qualified for the role of ruler. Athens, as Pericles ex-pressed it later in the funeral oration of 431 (Thucydides, 2.41.1), should become the school of Hellas, a city which would inspire the passionate devotion of its citizens and a sense of awe and admiration, mingled with fear, among the other Greeks. To achieve his aim of making Athens a city worthy of its high imperial role and its far-reaching influence, he began, immediately after the failure of the Congress Decree, the great building program which in the course of a generation produced such su-preme works as the Parthenon, the Propylaea, the Hephaisteion, the Temple of Poseidon at Sunium, and the Telesterion at Eleusis, not to mention many constructions of more utilitarian nature, thereby creating a congenial atmosphere for that fascinating intellectual life which is as-sociated with the "Golden Age of Pericles." So glorious were these works of architecture and sculpture, "no less towering in their grandeur than inimitable in the grace of their outlines" (Plutarch, *Pericles*, 13.1), that mankind down through the ages has tried—and usually successfully—to forget that the initial payments for these constructions came from the 5,-000 talents cynically appropriated from the allies of the Delian League in 449, and that subsequently recourse was had at times to the tribute annually extorted from often unwilling subjects.

An excellent summary of the imperialistic motives discussed above is provided by a speech which Thucydides assigns to an Athenian envoy addressing the Spartan assembly in 432. Among his arguments explain-ing and justifying Athens' empire, he states (1.76): "It follows that it was not a very wonderful action, or contrary to the common practice of mankind, if we did accept an empire that was offered to us, and refused to give it up under the pressure of three of the strongest motives, fear, honor, and self-interest." Fear was experienced first for the Persians and subsequently for their rebellious allies and the hostile Peloponnesians. "Honor" certainly refers to the pride which Athenians felt in being citi-zens of the greatest city in the Greek world and one that was the "school of Hellas." And "self-interest" alludes to all the benefits, political, social, and economic, which accrued to Athens from its empire.

Aristophanes in the *Wasps* (1.707), produced in 422, says that a thousand cities paid tribute to Athens, but that figure, of course, is comic exaggeration. The sober evidence of the tribute-quota lists proves that the number was between two and three hundred. Over the years Athens resorted to many means for holding these cities within the em-pire, often varying the technique from city to city. The following discussion will be concerned only with methods that were applied generally in the period of the fully developed empire after the Peace of Callias, although it should be noted that some of these devices had also been employed earlier when Athens theoretically was no more than the hegemon of the Delian League.

The most important means of maintaining the empire, obviously, was the powerful Athenian fleet which Pericles had insisted on retaining in the critical years of 449 and 448 despite the peace with Persia. Fear of the rapid striking power of this fleet kept many a subject state obedient, no matter how disgruntled. One can well imagine that the officers of the triremes, sent out annually for training purposes, had instructions to cruise in areas where disaffection was suspected. The fleet was financed in large measure by the system of tribute, which the Athenians organized with extreme care. After the treasury of the Delian League was moved to Athens in 454, the Athenian Council of Five Hundred (Boulē) was assigned the responsibility of making the assessments. Assessments were ordinarily made at four-year intervals on the occasion of the Great Panathenaea in July. Tributary cities were notified in advance so that they could send envoys to participate in the festival and, after learning their assessment, initiate an appeal if the figure seemed unreasonably high. Payments were due in March before the celebration of the City Dionysia. The money was counted out in the presence of the council and delivered to the *hellenotamiai*, who, checked by auditors, removed a sixtieth (Athena's quota) from each payment and gave it to the treasurers of the goddess. The amounts of these quotas, recorded on stone, were the tribute-quota lists mentioned earlier in this chapter, whose extensively preserved fragments are a fundamental source for the study of Athenian imperialism. After the Dionysia an assembly was held at which the *hellenotamiai* enumerated to the people the cities which had paid their tribute in full and those which were delinquent. Thereafter Athenian envoys were dispatched to furnish receipts to the cities which had met their obligations and to demand money from defaulters. In the early years of the Peloponnesian War, when financial problems were increasing, Athens passed a decree (426/5; *M&L,* no. 68) directing that in every city of the empire local collectors of tribute be appointed who should themselves be responsible for the collection of the proper amount of tribute and its transmission to Athens.

Athens was able to exercise a powerful economic control over cities both within and outside of the empire, for, since most Greek states were dependent on imports and exports for their very existence, the imperial city with its great fleet could enforce obedience to its wishes. The economic importance of sea power for maintaining empire is one of the basic themes of an interesting pamphlet called in the mediaeval manuscripts *The Constitution of the Athenians* of Xenophon, which fortunately has been preserved. A Xenophon may have written it, but certainly not the well-known man of that name, the young friend of Socrates and the author of the *Anabasis* and the *Hellenica*. The writer of this little tract has been aptly dubbed the "Old Oligarch," because he clearly was an oligarch and seemingly a man of mature years, contemptuous of, but wryly resigned to, the vagaries of democracy. He admits that if Athens is so perverse as to want a democracy, the machinery of government has been worked out very logically, and if Athens must have an empire, then it is only reasonable that the common people should control the state since they are the ones who man the fleet which holds the empire together. If one keeps in mind the Old Oligarch's prejudices and his weakness for exaggeration, his brief essay, written probably in the 420s, is a fascinating source on Athenian democracy and imperialism and the intimate connection between the two. On the question of Athenian employment of economic pressures as a means of controlling the empire, it will suffice to quote one passage from the Old Oligarch (2.11): "Wealth they alone of the Greeks and non-Greeks are capable of possessing. If some city is rich in ship-timber, where will it distribute it without the consent of the rulers of the sea? Again if some city is rich in iron, copper, or flax, where will it distribute without the consent of the rulers of the sea?"

Since Athens became increasingly democratic after 462/1, and the cleavage between the democrats and the conservatives or oligarchs became constantly more pronounced, especially after the death of Cimon in 450, it was natural that Athens, convinced that democracies were more likely to be loyal to the empire, favored this type of government among the tributary cities. Athens was not doctrinaire in its policy, however, and certain cities within the empire retained full autonomy in their political life, which generally was oligarchic in character. Since revolts in the cities were usually, if not always, oligarch-inspired, Athens, after suppressing the rebellions, almost invariably established democracies, although at Miletus, where special circumstances were involved, an oligarchic constitution, accepted in the settlement of 450/49, prevailed briefly. The Old Oligarch, in his typically prejudiced language where "the best citizens" are equated with the upper classes and "the worst" with the lower, comments as follows on Athenian policy (3.10): "Also in the following point the Athenians seem to me to act ill-advisedly: in cities embroiled in civil strife they take the side of the lower class. This they do deliberately; for if they preferred the upper class, they would prefer those who are contrary-minded to themselves. In no city is the superior element well disposed to the populace, but in each city it is the worst part which is well disposed to the populace. For like is well disposed to like. Accordingly the Athenians prefer those sympathetic to themselves."

The Athenian system of colonization played an important role in imperial policy. From the beginning of the Delian League Athens had at times settled, or tried to settle, strategic sites which it had just conquered or which it wished to protect, as, for example, Eion and Scyrus in 476/5 and Ennea Hodoi on the Strymon in 465. Sometimes the settlers were entirely Athenian, but at times, as in the cases of Ennea Hodoi, Thurii, and Amphipolis, allies were also included and even Greeks from outside the league or empire. It was particularly in the critical period from 450 to 443, when league was disappearing into empire, that the largest number of settlements were made. The foundations were of two kinds, colonies (*apoikiai*) and *cleruchies*. The colonies were similar to the usual type of Greek colony; the settlers ceased to be Athenians politically (or members of whatever other state they had come from) and became citizens of the new city-state that was being founded. These colonies were usually established in uninhabited territory or on sites from which the original inhabitants had been expelled, as when the Athenian colony Oreos was located on the site of Euboean Hestiaea after the expulsion of the Hestiaeans in 446/5. *Cleruchies,* on the other hand, were always established in the territory of some existing city—usually one that had aroused Athenian anger or suspicion—and the settlers (*cleruchs*) were always Athenians and continued to be Athenian citizens. These settlements, therefore, did not create new city-states, but were, so to speak, extensions of Attic territory. Neither the colonies (if founded after 478/7) nor the *cleruchies* paid tribute. So far as one can judge from the tribute-quota lists, when Athens appropriated land for a *cleruchy* (and also for a colony if the land was in the territory of some city), the tribute of the state losing the land was reduced. There is no way to know—although one may doubt—whether the tribute reduction was adequate compensation for the land lost. By means of these two types of settlements, Athens in effect established garrisons to keep watch over troublesome cities and also to protect areas important for strategic and economic reasons, such as the Thracian Chersonese. In addition, these settlements served the useful social and economic purpose of removing the poor and unemployed from Athens and giving them a new start in life. The decree concerning the foundation of the colony Brea in Thrace ca. 445, which has been preserved on an inscription (*M&L,* no. 49), specifically directs that the colonists should come from the *thetes* and the *zeugitai,* the two lowest economic classes.

In an examination of Athenian imperial methods, the problem of the extent, in the administration of justice, to which Athens interfered in the jurisdiction of the cities of the empire is clearly fundamental. The subject is a difficult one because of the nature of the scanty evidence, and can probably best be studied, as a scholar has successfully argued, by viewing it under three headings.[33] One category, referred to in a notoriously ambiguous passage of Thucydides (1.77.1), includes the large number of suits arising from a variety of business and personal relationships between an Athenian and a man from an allied city. These cases were tried according to the terms of the treaties which Athens had with all or most of its allies. In this type of litigation the plaintiff could bring suit in the city of his choice, which almost invariably was the home of the defendant, for only there, where the defendant's property was, could the plaintiff, if he won his suit, hope to collect the damages awarded to him by the court. In suits of this sort, governed by treaty regulations, the growth of the Athenian empire brought few, if any, changes, and many an Athenian, to collect the damages to which he thought he was entitled, must have brought suit in the courts of allied cities.

The second category, concerned with imperial administration, comprised cases which by their very nature had to be tried at Athens. Many decrees passed by the Athenian assembly on matters affecting the empire, for example the monetary decree and the decree of Cleinias regulating the methods of tribute collection and delivery, contained clauses stipulating that violations of the terms of the decree should be prosecuted at Athens. Also, naturally, if a city wished to appeal its tribute assessment, the suit was heard in Athens. In such trials Athenian verdicts may have been harsh and prejudiced, but they were not instances of Athens appropriating jurisdiction that had formerly belonged to the cities of the empire.

The third category embraces cases where Athens definitely interfered in the jurisdiction of the allied cities. A good example, probably typical, is furnished by the settlement which Athens made with Chalcis after the suppression of the latter's revolt in 446/5.[34] Among the regulations, fortunately preserved on an inscription (*M&L*, no. 52), is the following statement: "The punishments for Chalcidians against themselves to be in Chalcis just as at Athens for the Athenians, except in matters of exile, and [putting to] death, and disfranchisement; concerning them there is to be appeal in Athens to the court of the *thesmothetai.*"[35] The Old Oligarch contains a sentence which provides a good commentary on the reasons for Athenian interference in these "capital" cases (1.16): "If the allies were each to hold trials locally, they would, in view of their annoyance with the Athenians, ruin those of their citizens who were the leading friends of the Athenian people." It was undoubtedly true that in most cities of the empire, even in those that were democracies, the upper classes, hostile to Athens, controlled the courts because of their wealth and prestige. Consequently Athens considered it necessary to protect its friends in the cities, when serious charges were brought against them, by insisting that those convicted had the right to appeal to an Athenian court. Athens also interfered in allied jurisdiction by demanding that certain privileged persons friendly to Athens among the citizens of allied cities, for whom special decrees had been passed, were to have one or both of the following rights: (1) to be immune from punishment except by Athens, and (2) if injured by an Athenian or ally, to be allowed to bring suit at Athens in the court of the polemarch.

Various other means by which Athens maintained control over the empire, although important and effective, are sufficiently self-explanatory that they do not require much comment. The Athenians often installed garrisons in cities, particularly after suppression of revolts. The terms of the Peace of Callias may have debarred Athens from placing garrisons in the cities of Asia Minor, but it remained free to establish *cleruchies* and colonies anywhere as its interests dictated. The sources, both literary and epigraphic, contain many references to Athenian officials, inspectors (*episcopoi*) and *archontes,* who supervised Athenian interests in allied cities, while being supported by those cities.[36] Aristotle (*Ath. Const.,* 24.3) says that these officials numbered about 700, a figure which many scholars now are inclined to accept. One particularly useful practice for Athens was the custom, common among the Greeks, of one state appointing a citizen of another state to represent its interests in that state. These representatives were known as *proxenoi.* Probably in every city of the empire Athens appointed a pro-Athenian local citizen as *proxenos,* and often more than one. These *proxenoi* received special privileges, including the preferred treatment in matters of litigation mentioned above. Among other services for the Athenians, they reported, when necessary, on anti-Athenian movements in their cities, thereby often becoming objects of hatred among many of their fellow citizens.

And finally, many Athenians, with Pericles as their leader and spokesman, hoped to instill among the cities a feeling of loyalty towards the empire—or, at least, of acquiescence in their lot—by arousing emotions of awe for the greatness and grandeur of Athens. The building program, which was to win for Athens the admiration of the ages, was begun in 449. The Great Panathenaea, the festival honoring Athena and Athens, became in many ways an imperial festival. Delegates from the allies and colonists were required to participate in the pageantry, and each city was obligated to contribute a cow and a panoply of arms as offerings. Representatives of the allies were present at the celebrations of the City Dionysia in March, when tribute payments were due, and accordingly were in the audience at the performances of the dramas of the great masters of tragedy and comedy. The ancient cult of Demeter and Korē (Persephone) at Eleusis was encouraged, and its fame spread abroad. The rebuilding of the Telesterion, the temple of Demeter at Eleusis destroyed by the Persians, was part of Pericles' building program. Efforts were made to attract Greeks from far and wide to be initiated into the Eleusinian Mysteries, which, beyond the religious consolation they provided, emphasized the theme of Athens as the mother of civilization. A decree (M&L, no. 73), passed probably in the 420s, ordered all Athenians and allies to send the first fruits of barley and wheat to the goddesses in accordance with ancestral customs and the oracle from Delphi, and urged all other Greeks to join in this homage to Demeter and Korē. Athens, through its preeminence in piety to the gods, in all fields of cultural and intellectual endeavor, in the democratic way of life, and in military and economic power, was to reveal itself as worthy of empire and of hegemony throughout the Greek world.

10
The Development of Athenian Democracy

WHILE THE DELIAN League was developing into the Athenian empire, Athens was simultaneously undergoing political, social, and economic changes which culminated in the fully developed democracy of the second half of the fifth century. The interplay of these two forces—imperialism and democracy—was so great that it is impossible at times to be sure of the cause and effect relationship, for, if imperialism influenced the growth of democracy, it is equally true that democracy fostered imperialism.

Cleisthenes in 508/7 and the following years had provided Athens with the framework of its future democracy by substituting ten tribes based on *demes* as the fundamental units for the four old Ionian tribes based on phratries and *genē*. Despite Cleisthenes' reforms, however, the Athenian government remained essentially aristocratic and plutocratic for some fifty years. The four census classes continued to serve as criteria for the assignment of privileges and duties, and the higher magistrates were chosen only from the two upper classes—the *pentacosiomedimni* and the *hippeis*. There was no pay for governmental service, a fact which in itself effectively barred the poor from much participation in the political activities of the state. The Areopagus, a highly conservative body, retained considerable, if ill-defined, influence. This persisting conservatism in the nature of the governmental machinery is understandable if one remembers that democracy was a new idea, still in its formative stage, and that the people were slow to realize that sovereign power really belonged to them when meeting in assembly. In keeping with this state of mind, the tradition remained strong of following the leadership of men connected with powerful and wealthy families. Plutarch (*Cimon,* 15) makes a telling comment on the character of the government in these years when he remarks that Cimon, after Ephialtes' assault on the Areopagus in 462/1, tried to restore the aristocracy of Cleisthenes' times.

In order to conform with Cleisthenes' new ten-tribe system, the board of nine archons was enlarged by attaching an annual secretary to the six *thesmothetai*. It is probable that since the time of Solon, the two upper classes had been eligible for the archonship, although some scholars think that the *hippeis* were excluded until a change was introduced in the method of appointment in the year 487/6. In the *Constitution of the Athenians* (22.5) Aristotle describes this change as follows: "They appointed the nine archons by lot, tribe by tribe, from the five hundred candidates previously elected by the demesmen, then first after the tyranny; all the previous archons were elected." Since Aristotle in an earlier part of this work (8.1) says that Solon instituted the system of appointing archons by lot from a group previously elected, the passage just quoted presumably implies that Solon's method fell into abeyance under the Pisistratids, who abolished lot, and was restored only in 487/6. Since many scholars, probably correctly, reject the introduction of sortition by Solon, it seems better to assume that lot was not employed in the appointment of archons until some time after the expulsion of the tyrants. Aristotle's statement that five hundred candidates were chosen in a preliminary election also raises a problem, for that number would have represented about a third or a fourth of the eligible members of the two upper classes, some of whom may have been unwilling to devote a year to such public service. Either the figure is incorrect—some scholars have suggested one hundred[1]—or one must assume that approximately the same men, minus those on whom the lot fell each year and with the addition of new men who had reached the age of thirty, were elected again and again in the preliminary election (*prokrisis*).

It has generally been claimed that this new method of appointing archons resulted in a serious loss of prestige for that office. Several studies,[2] however, have demonstrated that that magistracy in the late sixth and early fifth centuries was not the important post for which Aristotle (*Ath. Const.*, 13.2) says men fought vigorously in Solon's time. Probably the manipulation of the archonship by the Pisistratids had reduced the significance of the office. In the confused years following the expulsion of Hippias, the archonship may have temporarily become a key magistracy again. As archon in 508/7, Isagoras, with the support of Cleomenes of Sparta, banished many of his opponents, but the exiles soon returned and the reforms of Cleisthenes began to be implemented. Since one of the purposes of the new ten-tribe system was to reduce factional struggles between powerful families, it is quite possible, although not mentioned in the sources, that Cleisthenes was the one who changed the method of choosing archons from election to appointment by lot, hoping that this new system would lessen the bitter rivalries always aggravated by elections. This suggestion is confirmed by the statement of Herodotus (6.109) that Callimachus, the polemarch at Marathon in 490, had obtained his position by lot. It is probable, therefore, that the electoral reform of 487/6, mentioned only by Aristotle, would have been merely a refinement of the method previously introduced by Cleisthenes. The picture is not clear, but it is reasonable to assume that from the one hundred (?) men selected in the preliminary election the assignment to the particular archonships and the secretaryship was determined by lot.

Since the minimum age for eligibility to the archonship was apparently thirty, it is likely that the holding of an archonship was a way for a young man to launch himself into governmental activity. One important advantage of holding this office was that the incumbent, after completing his term, passed automatically into the Council of the Areopagus. Office holding, however, was not the regular path to prominence in Athenian public life as the *cursus honorum* was to the Romans, although increasing warfare in the fifth century added to the prestige of successful military commanders. Men became conspicuous in Athenian political life through the reputation of their families and the social circles to which they belonged, from their association with and influence on members of the Council of Five Hundred, and from their ability to win favor in the assembly.[3]

There presumably had been a board of four generals (*strategoi*) when Athens was organized on the basis of the four Ionian tribes. After the reforms of Cleisthenes, quite naturally, a board of ten was established. Since Herodotus (6.104) says that in 490 Miltiades was elected by the people (assembly), it seems necessary to interpret Aristotle (*Ath. Const.*, 22.2) as meaning not that each tribe elected one of its members as general but that "they [the people] elected the generals on a tribal basis at one from each tribe."[4] At Marathon (Herodotus, 6.110) each general commanded the contingent of his own tribe, but by rotation became general of the whole army for one day. The polemarch (Callimachus) was also present, but he did not seem to be acting as commander in chief, which had been the original function of the polemarch. Possibly that magistracy had been unable to regain its pre-Pisistratid status. In the campaigns of 480 and 479 the generals were definitely the highest military officers. There is no reference to the polemarch, who presumably no longer served as an officer in the field.

Since the generals commanded the navy as well as the army and thus became involved in foreign and financial policies, it was only natural that these men, elected for their ability and eligible for reelection year after year, soon became the most important officials in the government. It is important to remember, however, that the Athenians, harboring an instinctive fear of officialdom and of placing too much power in the hands of one man, insisted that the generals in the college should all be of equal authority. As state officials, they had responsibilities other than commanding their own tribal regiments, for a general assigned to a particular campaign might have under him contingents from all the tribes. The task of commanding the tribal regiments fell to officers known as *taxiarchs,* who also were elected by the assembly.

Besides the archons and the generals, and various other boards of magistrates, the chief organs of government were the assembly (*ecclesia*), a primary body which all citizens, including the landless *thetes,* could attend; the Council of Five Hundred (Boulē), consisting of 500 new members each year from the top three census classes, possibly appointed by lot following a preliminary election; and the Areopagus. Little is known about the assembly and the council in this period.

Even less is known about the Areopagus. It is significant, however, that in the fourth century Ephialtes' attack on that council was commonly believed to have marked the beginning of radical democracy. Before the time of Solon, the Areopagus, a development from an old Council of Elders, was clearly an important, probably the dominant, body in the aristocratic state. If Solon established a Council of Four Hundred, an assumption which is generally accepted, the role assigned to the Areopagus in his "constitutional" arrangements is difficult to fathom. It certainly served as a court for homicide cases and other matters relating to religion, but the fourth-century notion that, as guardian of the laws, it had wide jurisdiction and also broad censorial powers is open to suspicion. Under the Pisistratids its influence and reputation presumably declined because of subservience to the tyrants. The meager evidence concerning Cleisthenes' reorganization of the state contains not a word about the Areopagus, but, since its membership consisted of ex-archons who, after their annual term of office, passed into the Areopagus for life, its prestige must have increased as the new members gradually came to outnumber the older ones, tainted because of their association with the tyrants. The introduction of lot for the appointment of archons in 487/6, or probably as early as 507, by making it possible for a large number of the first two classes to become members of the college of archons, if they felt inclined to devote a year to state service, probably caused the Areopagus to contain fewer "distinguished" men than in the pre-Pisistratid years. Nevertheless the old council, hallowed by tradition and consisting of well-to-do-men, many of whom were elderly, was, as the only permanent body in the government, still an important force in the state; but to progressive leaders and to the thousands of sailors becoming increasingly conscious of their potential political power, it must have seemed reactionary and anachronistic.

According to Aristotle (*Ath. Const.,* 25) the opposition to the Areopagus, led by Ephialtes, reached its peak in 462/1. To understand better the motives of Ephialtes, whom Aristotle depicts only as a radical doctrinaire, it is important to keep in mind what little is known of the political events and rivalries of the period, including the anti-Spartanism that had been characteristic of Themistocles. The prosecution of Cimon for accepting bribes in 463 was part of this political struggle. After the subjection of Thasos and the occupation of Thasian holdings in Thrace, Cimon was accused of failure to appropriate certain Macedonian territory because of bribes received from Alexander, king of the Macedonians. Pericles participated in the prosecution (Plutarch, *Cimon*, 14–15). Cimon, owing to his general popularity, was acquitted, but the trial seems to show that, although he was enhancing the influence of the common people by his emphasis on sea power and although he was noted for his demagogue-like liberality to the poor, his position was vulnerable because in domestic affairs he favored the conservative, usually pro-Spartan, forces in the state.

This was the period of the helot revolt against Sparta following the great earthquake and Cimon's two expeditions to aid the Spartans. Ephialtes had argued in favor of letting haughty Sparta be trampled underfoot, but Cimon had swayed the assembly by pleading that Athens be not robbed of its yokefellow (Plutarch, *Cimon*, 16.8). The first expedition apparently saved Sparta itself, but later, in 462/1, the Spartans appealed again to Athens and others to assist them in the siege of the helots at Ithome. When Cimon returned to Athens after the Spartans had insultingly dismissed him and his hoplites, he found that Ephialtes, supported by Pericles, was carrying, or had carried, various measures through the assembly against the Areopagus. Cimon tried to restore this conservative council, many of whose members, like him, may have been favorably disposed towards Sparta, to its former position, but the failure of his pro-Spartan policy had been so dismal that he was ostracized in the spring of 461.

The fullest account of Ephialtes' attack on the Areopagus preserved in the extant sources is provided by Aristotle in the *Constitution of the Athenians*, 25.1–2, which reads as follows:

> For seventeen years following the Persian Wars, the political order remained essentially the same under the supervision of the Areopagus, although it was slowly degenerating. But as the common people grew in strength, Ephialtes, the son of Sophonides, who had a reputation for incorruptibility and loyalty to the constitution, became leader of the people and made an attack upon that Council [the Areopagus]. First he eliminated many of its members by bringing suits against them on the ground of administrative misconduct. Then, in the archonship of Conon, he deprived the Council of all its added [recently acquired?] powers [prerogatives?] through which it was the guardian of the state, and gave them

[back?], some to the Council of Five Hundred, some to the people [assembly], and some to the law courts.

This passage is notoriously difficult, if not impossible, to explain satisfactorily. The seventeen-year supremacy of the Areopagus, which gradually declined, is mentioned by no other ancient source. It is possible, of course, that in the confused period of Xerxes' invasion and the immediately following years the Areopagus, as a distinguished, permanent body, did assume various responsibilities which did not properly belong to it. Aristotle, then, in a desire to explain the motivation of Ephialtes' actions, which he considered revolutionary, characterized these years as a period of Areopagite supremacy. Ephialtes' elimination of various members of the Areopagus for "administrative misconduct," therefore, may refer to preliminary attacks on men performing duties to which they had no claim in law, although it is difficult to visualize how individuals, rather than the corporate body, would have been implicated. Ephialtes' taking away from the Areopagus in 462/1 the added (recently acquired?) powers and giving or restoring them to the Council of Five Hundred, the assembly, and the courts may also refer in part to those quietly assumed responsibilities.

In essence, then, Aristotle is describing the overthrow of a moderate Areopagite government—although how such a government was possible after the reforms of Cleisthenes is not explained—and the establishment of a radical democracy. It is this picture, associated with the great name of Aristotle, which has often led to the characterization of Ephialtes as a radical, ideological reformer. In his insistence on ideology, a concept which seems somewhat out of place as early as 462/1, Aristotle never suggests that one of the major motives of Ephialtes and his followers may have been their anger at the favorable attitude of Cimon and probably of many Areopagites to Sparta. If Ephialtes had been a revolutionary doctrinaire, it is hard to understand why no ancient source of the fifth or first half of the fourth century even bothered to mention him. It was not until about 356, the date of Isocrates' *Areopagiticus* and the subsequent work of his pupil, the Atthidographer Androtion, a source used by Aristotle, that the picture began to take shape of a benevolent ancestral Areopagus whose influence in guarding the laws and supervising morals was destroyed by revolutionary radicals.

Two other statements in the *Constitution of the Athenians* seem to confirm Aristotle's judgment on the revolutionary nature of Ephialtes' work in 462/1. The chapter (25) on the destruction of the power of the Areopagus ends with the remark that not long afterwards Ephialtes was craftily murdered—surely with the approval of outraged Areopagites. Then in chapter 35 Aristotle says that the Thirty Tyrants, after their seizure of power in 404, pretending that they were adopting the ancestral constitution, "took down from the Areopagus the laws of Ephialtes and Archestratus about the Areopagites." At first glance it seems logical that the Thirty would have wished to revive that conservative body. On reflection, however, one wonders if they, whose position had been achieved and was maintained by wholesale murder, would have been anxious to strengthen the Areopagus, one of whose main tasks had always been to conduct homicide cases. This remark linking the Areopagus with the Thirty, made by Aristotle alone of the ancient sources, hardly agrees with the decree of Teisamenos which, after the restoration of democracy in 403, stated: "When the laws have been ratified, they shall be placed under the guardianship of the Council of the Areopagus to the end that only such laws as have been ratified may be applied by magistrates" (Andocides, 1.84). Lysias also (6.14; 12.69), a violent opponent of the Thirty, speaks well of the Areopagus in this revolutionary period. Certainly neither Teisamenos nor Lysias would have used such favorable language about the Areopagus if it had cooperated with the Thirty.[5]

It seems clear that Aristotle's discussion of Ephialtes is too ideological and inaccurate to inspire much confidence. What attitude, then, should a modern historian take? In view of the sorry state of the evidence, one has to admit that it is futile to try to spell out in detail the exact measures which Ephialtes carried through the assembly. It will probably be best to work from the known to the unknown—that is, by observing Athenian practices in the later fifth century to try to infer from them what were the general trends of Ephialtes' work.

First, in the second half of the fifth century the magistrates presiding over courts no longer had the right to give verdicts, and the dikastic courts, which had developed out of the Heliaea, were courts of first instance and not merely courts of appeal as formerly. It is quite possible that these changes owed much to Ephialtes' legislation; certainly the popular courts came to be considered the heart of the radical democracy. Since the jurisdiction of the Areopagus in this period was limited to homicide cases and various matters pertaining to religion and sacred property, any opportunity it may have had formerly to influence magistrates—particularly the archons, who expected to enter the Areopagus on completion of their term of office—would have been eliminated.

Second, in the fully developed democracy, magistrates at the end of their terms of office had to submit to thorough examinations of their conduct in office—called *euthynai*—before a committee of the Five Hundred and the dikastic courts. If the Areopagus had retained, or appropriated, similar duties in the early fifth century, which it presumably had had in the seventh century, then the Aristotelian statement that Ephialtes had eliminated many Areopagites for their "administrative misconduct" could refer to their corruption in approving unworthy magistrates and convicting worthy ones.

Third, certainly by 415 and probably considerably earlier, the Athenians were employing a legal action known as the *graphē para-nomōn*—an indictment for proposing measures contrary to the laws (it could be directed also against proposals which had already become decrees by vote of the assembly). This was a public action and, therefore, could be brought by any citizen. Thus the duty of protecting and interpreting the laws fell on the individual citizens themselves. This was complete democracy and reveals clearly that in the eyes of the Athenians the task of running and maintaining the democracy was the responsibility of every citizen. The very fact that it was deemed necessary to introduce the *graphē paranomōn* can be taken as evidence that the Areopagus had had some power of surveillance over the laws and that, when it lost that power, the Athenians subsequently realized that some substitute was essential to prevent life and government from becoming completely unsettled through the irresponsible passage of revolutionary and contradictory decrees by the assembly.

Finally, it is pertinent to recall that just four years after Ephialtes' legislation Aeschylus produced his famous *Oresteia*. In the third play of the trilogy—the *Eumenides*—Athena establishes on the Hill of Ares (Areopagus) a court of Athenian citizens to try Orestes, son of Agamemnon, for the slaying of his mother Clytemnestra. In explaining her action the goddess says (lines 483–484), "I will appoint judges of homicide bound by oath and establish a tribunal, a tribunal to endure for all time." It seems legitimate to believe that in this play, produced in 458 while passions in Athens were still inflamed over Ephilates' measures, Aeschylus, by altering the old and sacred legend that Orestes had been tried on the Areopagus to the extent that he represented this trial as the cause of the establishment of the court, was deliberately attempting to emphasize that the original divine purpose of the Areopagus was to be a court for cases of homicide.

Any discussion of the legislation of Ephialtes is bound to be unsatisfactory because of the lack of adequate evidence. It seems reasonable, however, to suggest that his measures were a logical consequence of previous acts and trends in fifth-century Athens—the change in the method of appointing archons, the growing power and political consciousness of the naval crowd, the increasing hostility towards Sparta, the failure of Cimon's pro-Spartan policy and his subsequent ostracism. To interpret Ephialtes in terms of fourth-century ideological polemics as a radical doctrinaire would be to isolate his career from contemporary Athenian and Spartan history. In the framework of that history the "revolution" of Ephialtes can be seen as a natural culmination of previous tendencies and not as an ideological revolution. Whatever the "added powers" of the Areopagus had been, there is no doubt that by removing them Ephialtes weakened the old council. The murder of Ephialtes—certainly at the instigation of violent oligarchs—shortly after his proposals had been voted into decrees is vivid evidence for the bitterness and seriousness with which many contemporary conservatives regarded his attack on the Areopagus. The weakening of an old traditional body consisting of well-to-do men holding office for life—the only permanent body in the government—could not fail to stimulate Athenian "progressives." It was certainly not just by chance that the great strides in the growth of democracy and the conscious emergence of the idea of the sovereignty of the people followed so soon on Ephialtes' successful campaign against the political influence of the Areopagus.

AFTER THE death of Ephialtes, the leadership of the more liberal Athenians soon, if not immediately, fell upon Pericles. Plutarch (*Pericles*, 16.2) speaks of Pericles as preeminent for forty years (469–429 B.C.), but this is clearly an exaggeration, for in 469 he was too young to have become prominent in political life. For some years he was only one among the democratic leaders, but because of his later fame, the others gradually lost their place in the tradition, with the result that the various steps promoting democracy came to be considered Periclean. Cimon's ostracism in 461 and his death in 450 removed an important rival and opponent—in domestic affairs, at least—and after the ostracism in 443 of Cimon's "successor," Thucydides, the son of Melesias, Pericles remained dominant until his death. As the historian Thucydides (2.65.9) expresses it, "There was in word a democracy, but in fact government by the first citizen." In this chapter, accordingly, the growth of democracy in Athens after the death of Ephialtes will be considered the outcome of Pericles' policies, whether or not certain measures are specifically assigned to him by the ancient sources.

In 457/6 the third census class, the *zeugitai*, also became eligible for the archonship (Aristotle, *Ath. Const.*, 26.2). Since the *zeugitai* formed the bulk of the hoplites, who had been doing much of the fighting in recent years, particularly at Tanagra and Oenophyta in 457, it was only common justice that they should be granted the opportunity for greater participation in the government. In actual fact this measure was of no particular value to them until a system of pay for the holding of office was introduced. Aristotle (*Ath. Cont.*, 7.4) says that the disability of the *thetes* to hold office was never removed, but implies that various ways were found to circumvent this legal disqualification. At some subsequent time, apparently still in Pericles' lifetime, the preliminary election of candidates from whom the proper number were selected by lot was abandoned for the archons and for any other bodies to which that system may have applied. From then on only two methods of selection to office were employed—direct election, as in the case of the generals, and lot. For the archons, however, a double system of lot was used (*Ath. Const.,* 8.1): ten candidates were appointed by lot from each of the ten tribes, and from these one hundred, the nine archons and the secretary to the *thesmothetai* were chosen by a second drawing of lots. The reason for eliminating the preliminary election (*prokrisis*) presumably was that the large landowners had been able to influence this election in the *demes.*

No measure was more important for the promotion of democratic government at Athens than the introduction of pay for government service. Its significance cannot be overemphasized. For the first time in the history of the world, so far as is known, a system was adopted which enabled the poor to participate actively in the work of government—in fact, not just in theory. As Pericles said in the funeral oration for the Athenians fallen in war in 431 (Thucydides, 2.37.1), "In regard to poverty, if a man is able to benefit the city, he is not debarred because of the obscurity of his position." This statement obviously presents a somewhat idealized picture, for, since the rate of pay was low, the wealthy, as usual, had the advantage. Nevertheless, after the adoption and expansion of the system, many a poor man who previously had been able to participate in the business of government only by occasionally attending meetings of the assembly now could afford to abandon his job for a year so as to serve in some official capacity—on a board of magistrates, in the Council of Five Hundred, or in the law courts. Pay was first provided for the jurors (*dikasts*) in the law courts. At some time between the reforms of Cleisthenes and the death of Ephialtes the Heliaea had ceased to be the assembly sitting as a court of appeal, and in its place there had been established various courts (*dikasteria*) of first and last instance. They will be discussed fully later in this chapter. Aristotle (*Ath. Const.,* 27.2–4) and Plutarch (*Pericles,* 9.2–4), relying on oligarchic sources, do not provide a specific date for the introduction of pay, but they emphasize that it was Pericles' proposal, and state that he resorted to it so that by currying favor with the people through the spending of public money he might offset Cimon's popularity acquired through the liberal spending of his private wealth. Plutarch also adds that Pericles employed this "demagogic" method to win support for his attack on the Areopagus. Since, however, it seems certain that Ephialtes was the leader of the campaign against the Areopagus and since no ancient source attributes the important innovation of pay to him, it is more reasonable to assume that Pericles, soon after his predecessor's death, took this revolutionary step as a means of meeting the new situation caused by Ephialtes' legislation.

Although there is little specific information about the scope of Ephialtes' work, it is probable that the Areopagus was deprived of most of its jurisdiction and magistrates, of the right to give judgments. If this is true, other courts were clearly essential to handle the litigation which previously had been in the province of the Areopagus and the magistrates. It is also important to bear in mind that the growth of Athens and the Piraeus and the problems arising from the Delian League must have augmented tremendously the volume of legal business. Although certainty is impossible, it is likely that the weakening of the Areopagus necessitated the creation—or the expansion—of popular courts (*dikasteria*). An obvious purpose of Ephialtes and Pericles was to remove jurisdiction from the control of the conservatives, but the popular courts which were to be the means of achieving this aim could fulfill their function only if the providing of pay enabled the poor to serve as jurors along with those of a better financial status. Jurors were appointed by lot annually, and they could be reappointed indefinitely. It is known from Aristophanes' *Wasps* (l. 662), produced in 422, that by that date the jurors numbered 6,000, but if the development of the *dikasteria* was gradual, then presumably that figure would have been smaller ca. 461 when the system of pay was introduced. The rate of pay was low at first, apparently two obols a day, a figure which was increased to three obols by 425—probably on the motion of Cleon.[6] Three obols (half a drachma) represented in the second half of the fifth century the equivalent of half a day's wages. Low as this rate of pay was, it was sufficient to ensure that a large number of men in the lower economic brackets submitted their names when the lots were drawn annually.

The system of pay was soon extended to many other branches of the government. Precise dates are not available, but the ancient sources are practically unanimous in attributing to Pericles the establishment of the practice of payment for service (*misthophoria*). Soldiers and sailors on active duty received probably three obols a day as maintenance pay, the rate being increased if the expedition was a lengthy and distant one.[7] Originally an Athenian gave military service as part of his obligation as a citizen. Evidence is confused or lacking about the question of pay to sailors in the large fleet active at the time of Salamis and in the many expeditions in the early years of the Delian League. Plutarch (*Pericles*, 11.4) remarks that in the Periclean period pay was also given to crews who received training on the sixty triremes sent out each year for eight months. There is evidence that by 411 (and probably much earlier) the 500 councillors and the archons were recipients of pay (Thucydides, 8.69.4; Aristotle, *Ath. Const.*, 29.5); to judge from data available for the fourth century, the councillors received five obols a day and those serving as *prytaneis*, a drachma (six obols), the archons, only four obols (*Ath. Const.*, 62.2). One can safely assume that the numerous other boards of magistrates were also on the state payroll. There is a problem about the generals and other high military officers who were elected rather than appointed by lot. Certain passages in the ancient authors imply that they did receive pay, but a sentence in the Old Oligarch (1.3), written probably in the 420s, which states that the *demos* was glad to have the upper classes hold the important and responsible military offices but was anxious to hold those offices which brought pay and profit, strongly suggests the reverse. Members of the Areopagus seemingly did not receive pay, while payment for attendance at meetings of the assembly was not introduced until the fourth century.

In 451/0 the assembly passed a law on the motion of Pericles restricting citizenship only to those, both of whose parents were Athenian. Previously it had been necessary only for the father to be a citizen. Aristotle (*Ath. Const.*, 26.3) specifically says that the reason for the law was the great number of citizens. Since Aristotle in his political thinking associated radical democracy with an increase in the number of citizens, particularly among the lower classes, the implication is that Pericles' measure was undemocratic. Many scholars, however, have interpreted the law as demagogic. By 450, with the rapid growth of Athenian power and with the recent introduction of pay for government service, citizenship was a source of great pride and many privileges to the Athenians. Pericles' aim was to strengthen the position of the existing citizens by preventing their privileges from being diluted by an increase in numbers. But how was Pericles' law to control the number of citizens? Presumably, if Athenian men could not marry foreign women, they would have married Athenian women, and there would have been no change in the number of offspring. As one scholar has remarked, the chief beneficiaries of this law would seem to have been Athenian women, whose chances of marriage were enhanced.[8]

If the law, however, had retroactive force, then obviously the number of citizens would have been reduced, for all those born from an Athenian father and a non-Athenian mother would have been struck from the citizen-lists. It seems incredible, however, that the law could have been made retroactive, for the resulting injustices would have been too outrageous. Those Athenians who prior to 451/0 had, in good faith, married foreign women would suddenly have found their children barred from citizenship. Men of adult age whose mothers had not been Athenians would have lost their civic status and their real property, since only citizens were allowed to own land. To emphasize the preposterous nature of this suggestion, it is necessary only to recall that men like Cimon would have been disfranchised because their mothers were non-Athenians.[9]

If Pericles' law was not made retroactive and hence had no bearing on restricting the size of the citizen body, what was its purpose? Since a definitive answer may be impossible, one can only resort to speculation. Marriages between Athenians and foreigners may have been reasonably common, especially among the poor living in crowded sections of Athens and Piraeus where many transients and metics resided. Some of these aliens were not Greeks, but Thracians, Anatolians, Syrians, and so forth. As Juvenal centuries later complained that Syrian Orontes was flowing into the Tiber, some Athenians, and probably particularly the proud aristocrats, may well have been disturbed by what was happening, or might happen in the future, to the Athenian stock. This suggestion disregards the fact that Athenian aristocrats, like all Greek aristocrats, were usually Panhellenic in their social attitudes. It is hard to imagine them voting for this measure unless they were seriously worried by what was happening to the "masses." In the last analysis, therefore, one may have to consider this law, proposed by the aristocrat Pericles, as an example of the arrogance of Athenian imperialism, for it raised a barrier between proud Athens and the rest of the world, including some 200 or more cities belonging to the empire.

By the middle of the fifth century, except for elaboration in detail and the carrying of certain trends to their logical conclusions, the Athenian government had acquired the character of a "radical democracy," which, with only two short interruptions, it was to retain until late in the fourth century. The main organs of this democratic government were the magistracies, Council of Five Hundred, assembly, and law courts. One fact which must always be kept in mind is that, no matter how powerful certain magistracies or the Council seemed to be, ultimate control lay with the people in the assembly and the law courts.

The magistrates, usually forming boards or colleges of ten, one from each tribe, were appointed either by election through show of hands or by lot. In most cases property requirements for the holding of office were abolished or disregarded, although if, as is probable, the military offices were not paid, the poor were effectively excluded from aspiring to them. Election was reserved for those magistracies where professional knowledge was necessary: military offices like those of the *strategoi* and taxiarchs, probably the *hellenotamiai* in the fifth century, various commissions for special purposes such as public works, where architects and supervising commisioners had to be appointed, embassies, religious missions, and the like. These special commissions did not always consist of ten members, and in place of the usual annual appointment the term of office was often for the duration of the task assigned.[10]

By far the most important and influential of these elected magistrates were the generals. They and other high military officials were elected in the assembly by show of hands in the first *prytany* after the sixth in which the omens were favorable (Aristotle, *Ath. Const.*, 44.4). Normally, therefore, the elections (*archairesiai*) took place in the seventh *prytany* (February-March), and could not be delayed beyond the ninth, because time was needed for checking the qualifications of the newly elected officers before they entered upon their duties on the first of Hekatombaion (ca. July). Some scholars have argued that the generals began their annual term shortly after the election, thereby avoiding the complications arising from a change of command in the middle of a campaigning season, but, logical as this would have been, the evidence points to the beginning of the Athenian year (1 Hekatombaion) as the date for the assumption of office.[11]

Aristotle (*Ath. Const.*, 61.1) states that the Athenians elected ten *strategoi*, formerly one from each tribe, but now "from all," to five of whom specific responsibilities were assigned—command of the hoplites, defense of the Piraeus, and the like. Some scholars argue that the words "but now" signify that the change to electing *strategoi* "from all" must have occurred in Aristotle's time, while others maintain that it could have happened any time after the original system of electing one *strategos* from each tribe. Opposing the first point of view is the fact that from 441/0 on, and possibly earlier, inscriptions show that on occasions two *strategoi* were elected from the same tribe. Since the tribe Akamantis sometimes provided Pericles and another as *strategoi,* the theory has been advanced that because Pericles was elected *strategos* year after year he was at times elected "from all" so that another man from his tribe also could hold that office. In 1971 a scholar argued rather persuasively that one of Ephialtes' reforms in 462/1 established the procedure that all the ten *strategoi* should be elected "from all," thus eliminating the requirement of each tribe furnishing a *strategos*.[12] Within a year this suggestion was questioned.[13] It would be futile to enter the controversy here, for the evidence now available is inadequate to settle the problem definitively. It is enough to say that literary and epigraphic sources show that over the years, whatever the method of election, the board of *strategoi* usually came from ten different tribes.

The Athenians believed strongly in the principle of collegiality and in the equal responsibility of all magistrates in a college. The assembly, when voting on a campaign, did not appoint one man as commander in chief. When Nicias, Alcibiades, and Lamachus were placed in charge of the Sicilian expedition in 415, the assembly conferred full powers upon each (Thucydides, 6.8). The supremacy which Pericles enjoyed for years rested probably not on any special powers voted to him, but on his ability, experience, and prestige.[14] The first certain case of the voting of supreme powers to a *strategos* belongs to the year 407/6. In that critical period the assembly, which had elected Alcibiades *strategos,* subsequently voted that he should be commander in chief (*autocrator*) (Xenophon, *Hellenica,* 1.4.20). It is true that some late sources (for example, Plutarch) characterize both Themistocles in 480 and Aristides in 479 as *autocrator,* but the use of the term is probably anachronistic, for in Hellenistic and Roman times the idea of individual authority had become common.

The duties of the generals, who, like the other magistrates, probably had to be thirty years of age before they were eligible for office, were manifold. As the highest military officers in the state they were responsible for commanding both the army and the navy, and individually or in groups were dispatched on campaigns in accordance with the vote of the assembly. They worked in close association with the Council of Five Hundred, possibly being *ex officio* members of that body, and through that contact and the knowledge they acquired from their military experience they were in a position to influence foreign policy. They could compel the council to call special meetings of the assembly, and although it was the province of the council to prepare the agenda for meetings of the assembly, it seems clear that the generals could have their proposals included in the agenda for both ordinary and extraordinary meetings of the people. Their familiarity with the necessary military expenses gave them an important role in formulating the financial policies of the state. In fact, in the fifth century, a general who had the confidence of the people and hence was elected to office year after year was in a position to dominate both the foreign and domestic policy of Athens, as is shown by the careers of Cimon and Pericles.

The prominence of such men, however, raises a problem which is too often glossed over. Since the ancient sources almost invariably emphasize the key figure and speak, for example, of Cimon doing this and Pericles that, one is likely to forget that each general had nine colleagues. Although these ten men may have included bitter enemies and rivals, little or no information is available on the dissensions which must have existed among them. One can guess that Pericles, if he was a general in 446, was overridden by his colleague Tolmides, who, against his advice, marched to Coronea and defeat (Plutarch, *Pericles,* 18); and Thucydides (6.9–23) emphasizes that in 415 the generals Nicias and Alcibiades had views almost diametrically opposed. Most commonly, however, the particular aims and aspirations of the various members of the board are not mentioned, with the result that an interesting and personal aspect of Athenian history is largely hidden from view. One thing, nevertheless, can be accepted as certain. Once the assembly had voted a specific policy, a general, no matter how much he was in opposition, was unlikely to try to sabotage it for two very basic reasons—his love of Athens and his fear of being called to account by the people.

The great majority of the magistrates, usually consisting of boards of ten and serving for a year, were appointed by lot. As the radical democracy took deeper and deeper root, the powers of these magistrates were reduced, partly by the creation of many new boards, which had the effect of leaving only a limited sphere of responsibility to each board, and partly by the increasing role played by the council, the assembly, and the law courts in exercising control over the magistrates. The curtailment in the powers of magistrates can best be seen in the case of the archons. The manipulation of the archonship by the Pisistratids and the subsequent introduction in 507 or 487 of lot as the means of selecting these officials prevented them from regaining the prestige they had had in Solon's time. After the reforms of Ephialtes the archons apparently no longer could give judgments in cases brought before them. Their judicial jurisdiction was limited to taking care of certain routine preliminaries before a trial, but in the trials themselves they merely presided over the dikastic courts without having any role in influencing the verdict. It is impossible to trace step by step their loss of power, but from Aristotles' account of their activities in his time (*Ath. Const.,* 56–59) it is clear that by then—and surely since the last half of the fifth century—they were limited to routine duties. The archon (eponymous) after whom the year was named had various responsibilities in connection with supervising the Dionysia and other festivals and in appointing men to provide and train the necessary choruses, and he presided over litigation pertaining to the family—ill-usage of parents, orphans, heiresses, guardianships, and the like. The king archon (*basileus*) had duties in connection with the celebration of the Eleusinian Mysteries, and, for conservative religious reasons, he directed almost all the ancestral sacrifices. His judicial jurisdiction included presiding over suits concerned with impiety and over the various courts dealing with different types of homicide. The polemarch also conducted sacrifices, among others, to Enyalius (an epithet of Ares) and to Harmodius and Aristogiton, and he was in charge of the funeral games held in honor of those who had been killed in war. In litigation, he presided over cases in which metics and *proxenoi* were involved. The six *thesmothetai*, because they had been established after the other three archons, conducted no religious rites of significance but had a wide variety of juridical duties, including presiding over a great number of suits. They also were responsible for drawing up the court calendar, and they assigned the courts to the various magistrates.

Aristotle lists (*Ath. Const.,* 47–54), and characterizes the duties of, a large number of boards of officials, appointed by lot, which were active in his day. A few are mentioned here to illustrate the role they played in carrying on the secular and religious business of the state. These boards acted chiefly in a supervisory capacity, and they were helped in their work by public slaves.[15] Some of the boards may not have been established until late in the fifth century or in the fourth century, but the first three listed below were in existence at least as early as the time of Solon, although presumably it was only after the reforms of Cleisthenes that the membership was raised to ten.

The treasurers (of the sacred property) of Athena were still appointed from the *pentacosiomedimni* as in the time of Solon, but, because of the steady inflation in the fifth and fourth centuries, membership in that class was no longer a sign of wealth. These officials, in addition to guarding the treasure of the goddess housed in the Parthenon and making inventories, which were periodically checked by auditors, appointed by lot, also made loans at interest to the state. The *pōletai* (vendors) farmed out to the highest bidders the right to work the mines and to collect certain taxes, let out numerous public contracts, and sold at auction property confiscated by the state. Many fragments have been found of the inscriptions (*M&L,* no. 79) recording the sale of the property confiscated from Alcibiades and others who had been convicted in the notorious case concerning the mutilation of the herms and the profanation of the Eleusinian Mysteries in 415. The Eleven (ten members and a secretary) were in charge of the prison and, through their slaves, were responsible for the execution of those condemned to death by the courts; the hemlock which Socrates drank was brought to him by one of these slaves. A board of ten men was responsible for the necessary repairs to temples, and one of five members, for keeping the roads in proper condition. Ten city commissioners (*astynomoi*), five for Athens and five for Piraeus, had supervision over female entertainers, and saw to it that houses were not built so as to encroach on streets and that dung collectors dumped their loads at least 6,000 feet from the city wall. Market superintendents (*agoranomoi*), five for Athens and five for Piraeus, were charged with preventing the sale of impure and adulterated goods and with keeping the markets clean. According to a late lexicon, *Suda,* they also supervised the *hetairai* (courtesans) and imposed the appropriate tax on each. Grain wardens (*sitophylakes*), originally five for the city and five for Piraeus, but by Aristotle's time increased to twenty and fifteen, respectively, checked to see that unground grain was sold at a fair price and that millers and bakers sold their products at prices consonant with the cost of barley and wheat.

These boards and many others were the executive agencies responsible for carrying out most of the administrative tasks assumed by the state. Since they were so numerous and each year consisted of new personnel, some means of coordinating and controlling their activities and seeing that each performed its particular duties without encroaching on the province of another department was essential. This unifying and supervisory role fell to the Council of Five Hundred, which, after the reforms of Ephialtes, was known as the Council (Boulē).[16]

So little is known about this council in the decades immediately following its establishment by Cleisthenes that one cannot even be certain how or from what financial classes the members were selected. From the end of the fifth century, except during the oligarchic interludes of 411 and 404/3, appointment by lot from the whole citizen body always prevailed. Since the Athenians ca. 453 in their regulations for Erythrae insisted on a council selected by lot (*M&L,* no. 40), it is logical to assume that they were introducing there their own system. The inference from this statement is that, whatever method or methods of appointment had existed at first, the employment of lot in selecting councillors was the standard procedure at Athens at least since the reforms of Ephialtes in 462/1. Every year fifty men, thirty years of age or older, were appointed by lot from each tribe, within which an attempt was made to have the *demes* represented in accordance with their population. Substitutes (*epilachontes*) were selected by lot to replace councillors who might fall sick or die, but in view of the limited citizen population it seems unlikely, as some lexica and scholia state, that the number of substitutes equaled that of the councillors who had been selected. Reappointment to the Boulē was possible, but only once and, apparently, not for consecutive terms. The suspension of the general rule against the reappointment of officials suggests that there may have been some difficulty in obtaining the required number of candidates each year. Until pay was introduced, probably shortly after 461, the poor could not undertake the demanding role of councillor, for the Boulē, in the fourth century at least, met daily except holidays, and the steering committee (*prytaneis*), every day. The rate of pay in the fifth century is unknown, but when Aristotle was writing the *Constitution of the Athenians* (in the late 330s), it was five obols for a councillor and six obols (a drachma; at this time, the equivalent of half a day's wages for a laborer) for the *prytaneis* (62.2). The consensus of most scholars is that the poor seldom served as members of the Boulē.

Since 500 men were too numerous to keep in permanent session, the fifty councillors from each tribe served as a steering committee for one-tenth of the year—a *prytany*. These *prytaneis* met daily in a circular building on the west side of the agora, called the Tholos, and one-third of them, selected in a way that is rather obscure, were on constant duty. Towards the end of each *prytany*, the tribe which was to provide the *prytaneis* for the next one-tenth of the year was selected by lot. Every day a new foreman (*epistatēs*) was appointed by lot from the fifty *prytaneis*, and for twenty-four hours this man was what might be called President of the Republic. He had in his possession the keys to the temples where the treasures and archives were kept, and he also presided over sessions of the Boulē and assembly if they met in that period. Since a man could be *epistatēs* of the *prytaneis* only once, the result was that each year more than two-thirds of the councillors held this important post. In the fourth century this foreman, before every meeting of the Boulē or assembly, appointed by lot each day nine chairmen (*proedroi*) from the non-prytanizing tribes and from them another *epistatēs* to preside over any meeting which had been summoned. The purpose of this measure probably was to distribute the burden of work more fairly among the councillors.[17]

The powers and duties of the Boulē were so wide and varied that it is difficult to classify them, but in general, they can be described as deliberative, administrative, and judicial. As a deliberative body it had the important responsibility of preparing the agenda to be submitted to the sovereign assembly. Only matters which had previously been discussed by the Council and formulated as proposals (*probouleumata*) could be brought before the assembly. In its *probouleutic* capacity the Boulē sometimes acted alone, but more often after consultation with the generals who, as stated earlier, may have been *ex officio* members of that body. Other officials and also private citizens, if they were granted access to the Council, could discuss problems with the councillors and suggest items to be brought before the assembly. Since the Boulē received foreign envoys and consulted with them before introducing them to the assembly, the results of these negotiations would be included in the agenda. All such matters, after being formulated into proposals (*probouleumata*), were presented to the assembly by the *prytaneis* and their foreman for the day—the *epistatēs*. These various steps are partly revealed in the standard wording of the preambles of decrees passed by the assembly which have been preserved on inscriptions. The preambles of the financial decrees of Callias (434/3 B.C.), for example, run as follows (*M&L*, no.

58): "Resolved by the Boulē and the *demos;* Kekropis was the prytanizing tribe, Mnesitheos was secretary, Eupeithes was *epistatēs.* Callias proposed ..." It is not certain, but probable, that the proposer always was a councillor.

The Boulē was the most important administrative body in the state. It was responsible for seeing that the decrees passed by the assembly were properly carried out. Aristotle (*Ath. Const.,* 49.4) states that in administrative matters the Boulē cooperated with most of the boards of officials. Its role was usually supervisory; for example, the farming out of the taxes, the leasing of the mines, and the letting of contracts for the construction of public buildings by the *pōletai,* the leasing of sacred lands by the king archon, and the payments stipulated by the contracts all took place in the presence of the Council. Since administration was in the hands of so many boards, there would have been chaos—especially in the field of finance—had it not been for the overall control exercised by the councillors.[18] The Boulē had general supervision over public buildings, both religious and secular, over the assessment of the tribute owed by members of the Athenian empire, and over the warships and dockyards. When the assembly voted that new triremes be built, the Boulē appointed a board of ten from its own members who, as *triēropoioi,* saw to the construction of the ships in cooperation with naval architects elected by the people. There were many other administrative tasks undertaken by the Boulē—far too many to list here—but the few that have been mentioned should be sufficient to emphasize that the successful administration of the Athenian government was largely dependent on the Council of Five Hundred.

In pursuance of its duties, the Boulē had various police and judicial powers. It checked the *deme* registers and fined the responsible demesmen if any youths under eighteen were enrolled. It also checked the rolls of the knights and imposed fines if the horses were not kept in good condition. As will be seen later, it investigated the qualifications of candidates for office and played a role in the periodic examinations to which magistrates were exposed.

Aristotle (*Ath. Const.,* 45.1) says that formerly the Council had authority to fine, imprison, and impose the death penalty. This surprising statement about the earlier judicial powers of the Boulē has naturally been associated with a badly damaged inscription (*Inscriptiones Graecae,* I², 114) recording a decree or a law, which seems to have listed various matters, such as the declaration of war and the imposing of fines, imprisonment, and the death penalty, on which the Council could not take action without the approval of the "full" assembly. The inscription, by its letter forms, can be dated to the last decade of the fifth century, but be-

cause of the presence of certain archaic words and expressions, it is believed to be a copy of an earlier document dating from the first half of
the fifth century or even earlier. Since the inscription contains certain
phrases from the *bouleutic* oath, introduced according to Aristotle (*Ath.
Const.,* 22.2) apparently in 501/0, one scholar, at least, has dated the
prototype of this fragmentary document to that year.[19] On this assumption, and arguing that the document lists powers which the Boulē had
lost, he maintains that in the years immediately following Cleisthenes'
reforms (508/7) the Boulē had such large powers that it is almost proper
to speak of representative government in Athens at that time. Although
one can argue that this would have been a possible stage in the evolution from aristocracy and tyranny to democracy, one can only wonder
why such drastic changes were made in the powers of the Boulē some
six or seven years after its establishment. The *bouleutic oath* was not introduced until 501/0 probably because it took several years for the new and
elaborate arrangements of the Council of Five Hundred to be implemented.

Another scholar suggested in 1972 that the restrictions on the Boulē
listed in the fragmentary inscription should be considered a consequence
of the reforms of Ephialtes in 462/1.[20] Ephialtes had succeeded in taking
away from the Areopagus various "added" powers, including judicial
ones, which he then assigned to the Boulē, the assembly, and the popular
courts. Wishing to ensure that the democratic Council of Five Hundred,
while receiving new powers, would not have a chance to expand them
into "added" prerogatives, as he claimed the Areopagus had done,
Ephialtes carried through the assembly a decree to guarantee that matters such as those referred to in Aristotle (*Ath. Const.,* 45.1), and certainly
also the right to declare war, should always be under the control of the
assembly and of the popular courts. These suggestions and others that
could be mentioned are included here only to emphasize the importance
of problems which remain obscure because of lack of adequate evidence.
All that can definitely be said is that apparently in most of the fifth, as
well as in the fourth century, the Boulē could not imprison a man except
in very special circumstances, could not inflict the death penalty—although it could initiate suits which led to those penalties—and could
impose fines only up to the sum of 500 drachmas (Demosthenes, 47.43).
Ultimately, it seems, even those fines could be appealed to the law
courts.

To the modern mind the practice of appointing officials and councillors by lot may seem absurd, but the Athenians, whom one would call
absurd at his peril, not only cheerfully adopted sortition but also fostered their "folly" by steadily increasing the number of boards ap-

pointed by lot and insisting that tenure of office be annual with reappointment to the same magistracy forbidden, thereby assuring a greater rotation of personnel in office. In the case of the Boulē alone, two nonconsecutive terms were permitted. Aristotle in the *Politics* (6.1.8–9) emphasizes that lot and rotation were characteristics of radical democracy. They also could be adapted to the needs of aristocracy and oligarchy, rotation ensuring that the few full citizens all had an equal chance at office holding, and sortition deciding the order in which the candidates should hold office. In aristocracies and oligarchies rotation in office was especially necessary to prevent any magistrate, by means of continuing tenure, from becoming too powerful in opposition to the collective nobles or oligarchs gathered together in the council. Certainly Athens adopted the practice of rotation in office from early in the seventh century, when the disintegrating kingship was supplanted by annually appointed archons.

The introduction of lot as a political device at Athens cannot be dated precisely. Aristotle, beliving that Solon was the founder of Athenian democracy, attributed the step to him, but it is more probable that it was connected with Cleisthenes' reforms or was a consequence of them. In 487/6, or some twenty years earlier, the Athenians adopted a system for the appointment of archons which consisted of a preliminary election in the *demes* of candidates from whom the appropriate number was selected by lot. It is reasonable to assume that simultaneously the same method was applied to other magistrates and also to the Council. Under the radical democracy the preliminary election (*prokrisis*) was abolished, and the Council and the magistrates, except those few boards which were always directly elected, were appointed exclusively by lot.

The aim of the democrats was that the people—the *demos*—should be sovereign, and to the Athenians, and to the Greeks in general, the people meant the assembly (*ecclesia*), which all citizens could attend.[21] Through this primary assembly the people could rule directly in a way which is impossible in a modern state, where, because of the size of the territory and the population, citizens can exert little influence except periodically at elections. Since the Athenian assembly met frequently—at least forty times a year and as many other times as was necessary—it could and did rule directly. This sovereign body, of course, had to delegate authority, but it wanted officials who would carry out its wishes, not men who, because of ability and ambition, might become dangerously powerful and independent. The people had to acquiesce in election for the generals and other magistrates whose duties required special and technical knowledge, but they managed to control such officials by a strict system of surveillance. For the great mass of administrative tasks, however, the people furthered their democratic aspirations by insisting on lot as a means of appointment to office and on the principle of rotation in office. Innumerable boards of magistrates were appointed by lot. Since each board usually consisted of ten men and the task assigned to it was specific, there was little opportunity for any member to become too prominent; moreover, the board could not expand its activities into related areas, for those areas were the bailiwicks of other boards. Because of the limited duties assigned to each board, the average man was qualified to perform the work, and even if some members of a board were incompetent, the others could carry on despite them. This practice, therefore, permitted great numbers of citizens—including the poor, since pay was provided—to take part in the work of government, and the collegiate principle, the annual term, and the prohibition against being reappointed to the same magistracy prevented any man from becoming too influential. The fear of the power to be gained from holding some office too long was so strong that Lysias (30.29) says the same undersecretary could not serve the same magistracy twice.

This insistence on rotation in office had a very significant effect on the nature of the Boulē. Since this basic body in the machinery of government consisted of new personnel each year, there was no chance for the development of the corporate feeling which was so characteristic of the Roman Senate and is so prevalent in modern parliaments. The councillors may have been amateurs, although, like many boards of magistrates, they were assisted by the "civil service" (consisting of clerks, attendants, and numerous public slaves), but because every year the membership consisted of 500 newly appointed men, there was a total lack of practices detrimental to the best interests of the people, such as senatorial courtesy and seniority rules.

By means of lot, rotation, collegiality, and pay for service, the Athenians achieved what they considered essential for the existence of true democracy—the participation of a large number of citizens, beyond their role in the assembly and the law courts, in the active work of the magistracies and the Boulē. Critics, both ancient and modern, have attacked and ridiculed a system whereby men, no matter how humble their social and economic position, had through the vagaries of sortition an equal opportunity to share in many aspects of administering the state with the classes more favored by birth and wealth. The incredible achievements of Athens in the fifth and fourth centuries, made possible by the free and open society which was created and fostered by its liberal governmental institutions, furnish the most effective rebuttal to these criticisms. It should be emphasized also that many of these critics, including the Athenian Socrates, distort the picture when they state or imply that the direction of the state was entrusted to men appointed by lot. Magistrates whose duties required experience, knowledge, and technical skill were always elected, and the highly important generals could be reelected indefinitely if they demonstrated ability.

All magistrates also, whether elected or appointed by lot, had to submit to an examination, called *dokimasia,* before assuming office (Aristotle, *Ath. Const.,* 55). In the fourth century the outgoing councillors checked the qualifications of the newly selected councillors and of the archons, but there was an appeal from their judgment to the law courts. All other magistrates, apparently, were checked only by the law courts. Aristotle lists the questions which in his time were put to each archon at this scrutiny; they were aimed at ascertaining whether his parents were citizens, whether he belonged to a phratry and had family tombs, whether he treated his parents well, paid his taxes, and had performed military service. These questions, some of which have an archaic ring, were clearly designed to ensure that the prospective magistrate was a citizen and had met all the obligations of citizenship. Certain magistracies had special requirements: for example, the king archon had to be married to an Athenian woman who had not previously been married (Demosthenes, 59.75), and the *strategos* had to have legitimate children and to own land in Attica (Dinarchus, 1.71). In the early fourth century, when the citizens of the restored democracy, despite the amnesty, harbored suspicion and hatred of the oligarchs and those who had collaborated with them, the *dokimasia* apparently was sometimes used as a political weapon in an effort to exclude oligarchs and their fellow-travelers from office. In general, however, it seems that the *dokimasia* was a rather routine investigation, but, nevertheless, sufficiently searching to discourage a man with a shady past from entering his name for the drawing of lots or from running for election. Many a man also, reflecting on the tremendous responsibilities which fell on the *epistatēs,* even if for only twenty-four hours, may have hesitated to place his name among those from whom the 500 councillors were drawn.

The *dokimasia,* then, provided some check on the qualifications of magistrates and councillors before they assumed office. If this examination ordinarily may have been somewhat perfunctory, the supervision exercised over officials during their term of office and the investigation into their official conduct at the end of their tenure were anything but perfunctory, and revealed clearly that the ultimate power lay with the people, who, although by the nature of things, having to delegate authority, nevertheless watched jealously the men to whom powers had been delegated. In each *prytany,* ten auditors (*logistai*), chosen by lot from the Council, examined the accounts of those magistrates who had access to public funds, and also in each *prytany* the assembly proceeded to a vote of confidence—or lack of confidence—on the officials. A magistrate, or apparently, at times, the entire board, whose transactions had aroused suspicion was deposed and sent before the appropriate court. Acquittal brought immediate restoration to office (Aristotle, *Ath. Const.*, 43.4; 48.3; 61.2). Usually magistrates remained in office until the end of their terms, but then they had to submit to a thorough investigation into their official conduct, both financial and administrative. Auditors, appointed by lot from the people, examined their accounts and, if they found evidence of dishonesty, sent the magistrates to a law court for trial (*Ath. Const.*, 54.2).

This financial accounting was followed by an administrative accounting. Ten investigators (*euthynoi*), each with two assistants, were appointed by lot from the Boulē to receive any complaints which citizens might bring against the administrative actions of the magistrates during their term of office. If the *euthynoi* considered the complaints legitimate, then the accused were sent to the proper tribunal for trial (*Ath. Const.*, 48.4–5). The councillors, who were classified as magistrates, also were subject to supervision (Aeschines, 3.20). The Council could depose one of its own members if he was deemed guilty of wrongdoing. If the deposed man appealed the action, then the Boulē held a formal trial. At the end of its term of office, the Council as a whole had to render account of its administration to the assembly. If the accounting was accepted, the assembly would vote that a golden crown be presented to the Council for dedication in some shrine. If the assembly was displeased with the record of the Boulē—especially if it had not seen to the construction of the authorized number of triremes—then the crown was not granted (*Ath. Const.*, 46). Individual councillors with whom the assembly found fault were sent to one of the courts for trial.[22]

I N THE FULLY developed democracy of the last half of the fifth and of the fourth centuries, and intermittently thereafter, the will of the people as expressed in the assembly (*ecclesia*) and the popular courts was supreme. As with all Greek democracies, the assembly was a primary, not a representative, body, and hence all citizens were entitled to attend its meetings.[23] After Pericles' citizenship law of 451, the requirement for citizenship for those born subsequent to that date was that both parents be Athenians. As had been the practice since Cleisthenes' reforms, a boy on becoming eighteen was enrolled in the *deme* of his father. This enrollment automatically assigned him to the tribe to which the *deme* belonged and signified that he had attained citizen status. Sons of Athenian parents not legally married were also enrolled in *demes* and thus were recognized as citizens, but as illegitimate children (*nothoi*) they were debarred from membership in a phratry, an exclusion which limited their rights of inheritance and prevented their holding the archonship and certain priesthoods.[24]

Adult male Athenians only could attend meetings of the assembly, for women, metics (resident aliens), and slaves did not possess citizenship and hence played no political role. It is important to remember that Athenian democracy, the democracy *par excellence* in the Greek world, was a restricted affair in which the majority of the population was denied the privilege of sharing in the government. It has been estimated that in the Age of Pericles the adult males who monopolized this privilege numbered some 40,000 to 50,000.[25] There is no accurate information on how many Athenians ordinarily attended meetings of the assembly. Since certain sessions, for example, those dealing with ostracism and with conferring citizenship on a foreigner (Demosthenes, 59.89) required a quorum of 6,000, the inference is that at other sessions fewer members were usually present.[26] Many citizens were too busy with their farms or businesses, or with military campaigns on which they had been dispatched, to be regular attendants, and the youngest men, those recently enrolled in the *demes,* had to devote so much of their nineteenth and twentieth years to military training and guard and patrol duty in Attica that they rarely, if ever, engaged in political activity. Nevertheless, in the last half of the fifth century, at least, it is probable that several thousand were on hand for most meetings.

The usual meeting place for the assembly, probably from the time of Cleisthenes, was the hill of the Pnyx, a short distance west of the Acropolis and southwest of the Areopagus. Early in the fifth century the assembly met probably once each *prytany,* but with the increase of citizen participation in the governing of Athens and with the growth of empire, it became necessary to have four regular meetings each *prytany*—thus forty a year—and as many extraordinary meetings as circumstances dictated (Aristotle, *Ath. Const.,* 43.3–5). In eacy *prytany* one session was designated as the principal assembly (*kyria ecclesia*) in which it was obligatory that the following matters, among others, be taken up: a vote of confidence (or lack of confidence) on the magistrates in office, and a consideration of the state of the food supply and of the defense of the county; in the sixth *prytany* it was also necessary to determine whether or not an ostracism should be held.

Sessions began early in the morning. Citizens from the outlying districts of Attica, for whom no lodgings were available in Athens, had to trudge to the city during the preceding night. Meetings could not continue after the coming of darkness. Unfinished business was postponed until the next regular meeting, or if it was of a pressing nature, an extraordinary session would be scheduled. Since meetings were held under the open sky, unfavorable omens such as thunder, lightning, rain, an eclipse, or an earthquake necessitated adjournment. The task of maintaining order fell to the current *prytaneis,* who sat on the first row of benches just below the speaker's platform. Their chairman (*epistatēs*), appointed by lot for a day, had the demanding responsibility of presiding over the meeting.

The meeting commenced with a sacrifice of purification, which was followed by the herald's proclamation of a curse against those who might try to deceive the people, the curse which Aristophanes parodied in the *Thesmophoriazusae* (ll. 295–371). After these preliminaries the secretary of the people inaugurated the real business of the assembly by reading aloud, at the order of the chairman, the *probouleuma*—the agenda which had been prepared by the Boulē. A law stipulated that no matters should be brought before the assembly which had not previously been considered by the Boulē and been posted publicly five days (according to the lexicographers) before each meeting of the assembly (Aristotle, *Ath. Const.,* 45.4). Since the agenda contained various items that required action, it is probable that after the reading of each item the chairman would call for a show of hands to ascertain whether the Council's proposal would be accepted as it stood or whether the people wished to proceed to a debate. If the verdict was approval, then, apparently, the second item on the agenda would be read, to be followed by the same procedure. Except for minor and more or less stereotyped matters, the assembly would demand a debate, which began when the herald pronounced the formula "Who wishes to speak?" The speaker would then advance to the tribune and, after placing a myrtle wreath on his head, address the assembly. This was the setting in which the great debates recorded by Thucydides and Xenophon occurred and in which Demosthenes delivered his famous *Philippics.* The discussion was practically unlimited, except that supposedly it was restricted to the matters included in the *probouleuma.*

Since the *probouleuma* was prepared and introduced to the assembly by the Boulē, does this *probouleutic* function of the Council mean that the individual Athenian citizen had no right of initiative? A study of the relevant evidence—the speeches contained in Thucydides and Xenophon, the works of the Attic orators, especially Demosthenes, and, above all, the decrees of the assembly, some of which, inscribed on stone, have been preserved complete or in part—demonstrates that the answer to this question should be in the negative. Initiative from the assembly could arise in ways such as the following. In the first place, in the discussion which took place in the assembly on some particular item in the *probouleuma*, anyone could arise and suggest an amendment. If, after hearing the arguments in favor of the amendment, the assembly voted approval, then it was appended to the original motion of the Boulē contained in the *probouleuma*. Many inscriptions provide evidence for this procedure; after the main body of the decree, representing the proposal of the Boulē, there follows a rider beginning with some such formula as "Y proposed: the other matters just as X proposed (X presumably being the councillor who gave his name to the motion), or as seemed best to the Boulē," and then continuing with the wording of the amendment or amendments. Often also, the *probouleuma* prepared by the Boulē was deliberately couched in very general terms so that the details and specific proposals had to be worked out in the assembly.

Thucydides' account of Athenian treatment of the Mytileneans in 427 after the collapse of their revolt from Athens is revealing. Cleon carried through the proposal that all adult male Mytileneans be put to death and that the women and children be sold as slaves. Since Cleon was a councillor in 428/7 or 427/6, this harsh sentence may have been advocated in the *probouleuma*. On the other hand, the *probouleuma* may have only included an entry like "Mytilenean affairs," without any recommendation as to action, and Cleon's proposal may have emerged from the debate in the assembly. On the following day many Athenians, repenting this brutal decree, persuaded those in office (the *prytaneis?*) to reconvene the assembly for further debate on the issue. It may not have been illegal, although it certainly was unusual, for a decree of the assembly to be challenged so promptly. In the second assembly, after many opinions had been voiced, the famous debate between Cleon and Diodotus occurred which Thucydides records (3.37–49). This time the milder proposal of Diodotus prevailed by a slight majority. Whether Diodotus' proposal was part of the original *probouleuma* or a case of initiative from the floor cannot be determined. The whole episode, however, illustrates the active role of the assembly, if aroused by influential leaders, in the initiation of policy.

It was also possible for a matter to be initiated in the assembly which had no bearing—or immediate bearing—on the *probouleuma* under discussion. A man could arise and propose some measure. If the assembly, impressed by the supporting arguments, voted approval, then the proposal was referred to the Boulē, which was instructed to consider the matter and to include it in the *probouleuma* to be presented to the next meeting of the assembly.

In Athens, therefore, in contrast to Republican Rome, the individual was not denied the right of initiative, and the assembly was not lim-

ited to voting aye or nay on measures that it had no share in formulating. It is true that most proposals took shape in the Boulē, often suggested by the *strategoi* who were *ex officio* members of that body or by
other magistrates and politicians who had friends among the councillors. Individual citizens in the assembly, however, if they could influence
and persuade a sufficient number of their fellows, were in a position to
exert control over state policy through offering amendments, implementing *probouleumata* of a general type, and, on occasions, by proposing
entirely new measures.

Theoretically any citizen could take such steps, but in reality, one
can be sure that only citizens having some political stature and, therefore, followers would be able to win the necessary approval of the assembly—or even recognition. Thus one can say that, although provisions of a *probouleuma* could be circumvented, the *probouleuma* was the
basic method of initiative and played also an important role in discouraging ill-considered proposals. The *prytaneis,* whose task it was to put
matters to the vote, were well aware that they were accountable if they
submitted an illegal motion to the vote (Aristotle, *Ath. Const.,* 29.4).

Athenian democracy was based on the principle of the sovereignty
of the people. Since the people met in the assembly, the final authority
lay in that body and in the popular courts. The evidence offered by authors such as Thucydides and Xenophon and by the inscriptions reveals
the assembly exercising this authority through its decrees in numerous
aspects of foreign and domestic affairs. The assembly decided on matters
of war, peace, and alliances; it appointed envoys to, and received them
from, foreign states. It controlled military affairs by determining the
number and character of the forces to be employed, by authorizing the
campaigns, and by appointing the generals and hearing their reports. It
dispatched colonies and *cleruchies,* and had the ultimate authority in the
administration of the empire. It was responsible for the building of temples and other public buildings, for the introduction of new cults, and
for supervision over state finances and problems of the food supply. It
passed decrees honoring citizens and foreigners and controlled the machinery of ostracism and of granting citizenship to deserving aliens. It is
true that all these matters ordinarily were first introduced to the assembly in the form of specific or general *probouleumata,* but, as mentioned
above, the assembly, in addition to its right to accept or reject, also had
powers to amend, implement, and initiate. It may be well to emphasize
here that relations between Boulē and *ecclesia* normally were good.[27] The
people realized that a body like the assembly could not prepare the
agenda and were satisfied that a council, appointed by lot, to which
many of them had belonged or would belong, should prepare the busi

ness for the people. To judge by the speeches of orators such as Demosthenes and Aeschines, it seems clear that on occasions certain groups of politicians in the Boulē could manipulate matters in questionable ways, but in general it is correct to say that the assembly approved the working of the Boulē, which it could consider its committee.

Since the sovereign assembly was so active, it is easy to visualize democratic Athens as a state rendered unstable by the constant passage of new and possibly contradictory decrees rather than one kept stable by obedience to the laws. Aristotle's judgment is interesting. In the *Politics* (4.4.3–4), with fourth-century—and also late fifth-century—Athens in mind, he wrote, "A fifth variety of democracy . . . here the people, and not the law, is the final sovereign. This is what happens when popular decrees are sovereign instead of the law; and that is a result which is brought about by leaders of the demagogue type. In democracies which obey the law there are no demagogues; it is the better class of citizens who preside over affairs. Demagogues arise in states where the laws are not sovereign. The people then becomes an autocrat—a single composite autocrat made up of many members, with the many playing the sovereign, not as individuals, but collectively" (Barker translation).

A good Athenian democrat could have answered this aristocratic and conservative criticism by quoting a law adduced by Andocides (1.87) in 399: "No decree, whether of the Boulē or of the *demos* [people] is to have more authority than a law." The distinction between decree (*psephisma*) and law (*nomos*) is not an easy one to make, and the Athenians of the fifth century were not as aware of the problem as those of the fourth century. To an Athenian of the Periclean Age the laws were primarily those of Solon, and also of Draco and Cleisthenes. These laws were regarded with reverence, but, as liberals, the Athenians were not inclined, like the Spartans, to allow their state to become fossilized through blind adherence to the past. Despite their respect for the laws of Solon and Cleisthenes they managed to alter governmental procedure several times in the fifth century, as has been described above. In those cases there is no satisfactory information on the method and reasoning used to disregard or annul previous laws. There is plenty of evidence, however, that the Athenians, when contemplating measures of general or permanent significance, such as settling the affairs of a city belonging to the empire, establishing a constitution for a new colony, or laying down regulations for the offering of first fruits to the deities at Eleusis, proceeded in a very careful and orderly manner.[28] Commissioners (*syngrapheis*) were elected by the assembly to study the particular problem. After they had prepared their proposals, they reported to the Boulē which, in turn, presented the report in a *probouleuma* to the assembly, where a full discussion took place before the final vote enacted the proposals into a decree.

It sometimes happened also that for the welfare of the state a reform was needed which was forbidden by some law or previous decree. In such a situation the man who wished to propose something "illegal" had to appear before a plenary assembly (that is, at least 6,000 present) and request that he be granted *adeia* (immunity; literally, freedom from fear) so that he could make his proposal with impunity at the next meeting of the assembly. Further, and conclusive, evidence that the Athenians were aware of the danger that could arise from thoughtless passing of contradictory and possibly dangerous decrees lies in the institution of the *graphē paranomōn* mentioned earlier in this chapter, and in the oath taken by the members of the Boulē not to put to the vote any motion contrary to the laws (Aristotle, *Ath. Const.*, 29.4), an oath whose enforcement was the responsibility of the *prytaneis* and especially of the *epistatēs*.

Any citizen could initiate a *graphē paranomōn* when a measure was being proposed either in the Boulē or in the assembly, or at any time subsequent to its enactment.[29] The illegality that was attacked sometimes concerned a matter of form—for example, the measure had not been included in a *probouleuma* presented to the assembly—but most commonly it lay in the contents. The proposer of the measure in question was free from prosecution one year after he had offered his motion, but the motion, if it had been enacted into a decree, could be attacked at any time. The trial took place before one of the popular courts with a jury of at least 1,000 *dikasts,* presided over by the *thesmothetai.* The importance which the Athenians assigned to this suit is revealed by the size of the jury and by the severity of the punishment in case of conviction— usually a heavy fine, but occasionally death. In the fourth century the *graphē paranomōn* degenerated at times into a means of attacking a political enemy, for three convictions on this charge caused a man to suffer partial disfranchisement by not being permitted to address the assembly. In an effort to discourage the irresponsible bringing of these suits, a measure was passed stipulating that the prosecutor who did not receive one-fifth of the votes of the jurors should be fined and denied the right to institute such a charge thereafter. In the fifth century at least, however, the *graphē paranomōn* served the democracy well, as is proved by the fact that in the revolution of 411 the oligarchs abolished the suit and also that part of the *bouleutic* oath which forbade putting to the vote any motion contrary to the laws (Aristotle, *Ath. Const.,* 29.4).

The assembly also had a share in the administration of justice, but the importance of this role diminished in the fifth century in direct proportion to the increase in the activity of the popular courts. It was Solon who, according to a seemingly sound tradition, first caused the assembly to participate in the administration of justice by permitting every citizen to appeal to it from the verdicts of magistrates. Nothing more is known for certain about the juridicial activity of the assembly, apparently called the Heliaea when sitting as a court of appeal, until the first decades of the fifth century, although it is probable that its competence was curtailed during the tyranny of the Pisistratids. In the year 489, however, Miltiades, after the failure of his expedition against Paros, was brought to trial before the assembly for having deceived the people, as Herodotus (6.136) explicitly says. This is the earliest definite evidence which has been preserved for the assembly acting as a court of first instance, but it is probable that Miltiades' trial in 493 for "tyranny in the Chersonese" also took place before the assembly (6.104). Evidence for the assembly in this role can be pushed back as far as 506 if one accepts the statement of the scholiast on line 273 of Aristophanes' *Lysistrata* that the Athenians condemned to death *in absentia* Isagoras and his partisans, who in conjunction with Cleomenes of Sparta had seized Eleusis.

These trials were concerned with offenses against the state and hence should be classified under the process known as *eisangelia,* which, as defined in the fourth century, covered such crimes as an attempt to overthrow the government, the betrayal of military forces, and an orator's intent to mislead the people as a result of receiving bribes. Since the trial took place before, or at least was introduced in, a political body, the appropriate word to translate *eisangelia* (literally, an information) is impeachment. Solon was said to have made a law dealing with *eisangelia* which stipulated that the suit should fall under the jurisdiction of the Areopagus. Since the cases mentioned in the preceding paragraph were tried before the assembly, the inference is that Cleisthenes added the assembly as another body competent to hear impeachments. After the reforms of Ephialtes such actions were always introduced in the assembly or the Boulē. The procedure in the assembly,[30] which alone need be considered here, was as follows: the people, after hearing the plaintiff and the response of the defendant, decided by vote whether the accusation merited investigation. If the decision was in the affirmative, then the Boulē was instructed to consider the matter and to include in a *probouleuma* a recommendation that the case be tried before the assembly or before a popular court. If the assembly judged the case (the more common procedure in the fifth century), it could, in case of conviction, impose any penalty it saw fit. If the suit was assigned to one of the courts—usually a court of 1,000 jurors presided over by the *thesmothetai*—then the assembly stated what penalty should be inflicted in case the accused was found guilty. Punishments were often very severe—death, disfranchisement, or heavy fines.

Another way in which the assembly participated in the judicial aspects of government was through the *probole*—a presentment or preliminary charge.[31] Any citizen could introduce a *probole* in the assembly against a man whose actions, he claimed, were detrimental to the best interests of the state. The assembly, after hearing the arguments of the accuser and the rebuttal of the accused and his friends, revealed, by show of hands, whether it approved or disapproved the charges. If the vote was in favor of the accuser, he could institute the appropriate action before a regular law court, with his chance of success enhanced by the favorable verdict of the assembly. Often, however, it seems that the accuser remained satisfied with the moral victory over the accused—sometimes a personal enemy—represented by the assembly's vote, which in itself did not necessitate further legal steps. The most famous case of a *probole* known from antiquity was Demosthenes' procedure against the wealthy and unscrupulous Meidias. Demosthenes won a favorable reaction from the assembly but did not carry the matter to a regular court because of various political complications and the receipt of a sum of money.

This discussion of the assembly, limited as it is, should make it clear that the ultimate power in democratic Athens lay with the people in assembly. That power is perhaps best revealed in the control that the assembly exercised over the magistrates. The assembly not only elected those who were not appointed by lot, but also maintained a close supervision over all magistrates during their term of office and took part in the investigation of their official conduct when that term was over. Generals could be deposed at any time, as happened in the case of Pericles (Plutarch, *Pericles*, 35.4). Supervision over magistrates is a necessary safeguard against the fallibility of man, especially when entrusted with power, but the assembly, jealous of the powers it perforce had to delegate, sometimes was too zealous, particularly in its suspicion of the generals. The result was that many a magistrate, from fear of the assembly, failed to act with sufficient independence. Any reader of books 6 and 7 of Thucydides will find that Nicias, the Athenian commander in the Sicilian expedition, was a tragic victim of this paralyzing dread, which crushed the little initiative with which nature had endowed him.

THE ADMINISTRATION of justice is of central importance to any government, and in a democratic state like Athens of the fifth and fourth centuries it is hardly surprising that it came under the control of the people. Solon, in the early sixth century, had started the process by granting every citizen the right of appeal from the verdicts of magistrates to his peers in the assembly. To judge from the two trials of Miltiades before and after Marathon, the assembly by that time could act in important cases as a court of first and final instance. In the following years the authority of magistrates to decide legal cases independently came to be considered an unwarranted interference with the rights of the people. The last specific evidence for a magistrate acting thus independently is an inscription (*M&L,* no. 31) recording a judicial treaty between Athens and Phaselis, dated almost surely in the 460s, in which the polemarch is expected to pronounce judgment. Largely through the work of Ephialtes and Pericles, popular courts (*dikasteria*) began to develop in which the members (*dikasts*), appointed by lot, determined the verdict, while the magistrate's competence was limited to taking care of certain preliminaries and then presiding at the trial. These courts grew in size and importance until by the last third of the fifth century 6,000 *dikasts* were appointed annually to be allocated to different panels. Like the assembly, they represented the people, and they will be discussed in some detail as conclusion to various comments on Athenian administration of justice.

The machinery of government in democratic Athens included nothing equivalent to a modern department of justice. Prosecution of public offenders was left largely to citizen volunteers (Solon's "he who wishes"). Nevertheless, when they thought the situation required it, the Athenians did not hesitate to appoint state prosecutors.[32] For example, in the attempt to impeach Cimon in 463, the assembly appointed Pericles to be one of the prosecutors, and over a century later Hyperides was chosen to prosecute Demosthenes on the charge of having accepted bribes from Harpalus, the absconding treasurer of Alexander the Great. Every year, also, the accounts of retiring magistrates were officially examined, as was mentioned above.

Suits were primarily divided into two general categories, private ones (*dikai*) and public ones (*graphai*). In the *dikai* the interests of individuals were chiefly at stake, and these suits could be initiated only by the parties concerned or by their legal representatives. In the *graphai*, on the other hand, the interests of the state were mainly or at least partly involved. This type of action, whose origin was attributed to Solon, could be initiated by any citizen. Since there was no regular department of justice, the state was largely dependent on these volunteer prosecutors to bring malefactors to account. The man who did not assume his share of this responsibility was frowned upon as a poor, if not worthless, citizen—a do-nothing (*apragmon*). A common way for a man with political ambitions to become favorably known was to bring charges against retiring officials on the occasion of the examination into their financial and administrative acts. The state encouraged these volunteer prosecutors by granting to them in certain cases, if successful, a share of the fine imposed or of the property confiscated.

This volunteer method was effective in inducing citizens to take an active part in the functioning of government and in the stamping out of corruption, but the dangers in the system rapidly became evident. The literary sources, especially Aristophanes and the fourth-century Attic orators, are full of reference to an ugly breed which emerged in Athens known as *sycophants*, or professional and unscrupulous accusers. These men, sometimes acting on their own, sometimes acting for the enemy of a prominent politician, made a career out of bringing prosecutions, based often on trumped-up charges, but ones that would appeal to the prejudices of the jurors. The sycophants also carried on a prosperous business by subjecting to blackmail well-known persons about whom they had discovered something questionable or capable of being presented as questionable. It would be a mistake, certainly, to believe that all the men branded in Athenian literature as sycophants were malicious, for it was an effective term of abuse for defendants to use against their accusers. It is clear, however, that sycophancy was recognized as a menace, for two laws were directed especially at prosecutors of this type. One stipulated that an accuser who abandoned a suit after it had been launched should be fined 1,000 drachmas and be debarred from ever instituting a similar action again, while the other provided similar penalties for the plaintiff if he did not receive more than one-fifth of the votes of the *dikasts*.[33]

To a modern person one of the strangest consequences of the lack of a regular department of justice in Athens lies in the area of homicide.[34] Athenian procedure in homicide cases provides a vivid illustration of the continuing power and influence of tradition. Because of the persistence of the old clan spirit, with its inherent notion of self-help and of the enduring force of religious conservatism, homicide cases were classified as *dikai,* and since they were private suits, only members of the family of the victim ordinarily could institute proceedings. As in the epics of Homer, vengeance was due the victim, but if before his death he forgave his slayer, then no prosecution was possible. The practice frequently mentioned in Homer whereby the killer could be freed from the danger of punishment on payment of a blood price (*poinē, wergeld*), however, apparently lapsed. The reason for the decline or disappearance of the custom was the belief that the shedding of human blood caused pollution which required religious purification, an idea not recognized in the aristocratic society depicted by Homer, but which became widespread in the Dark Age and thereafter. In historical Athens there was a clear overlapping of religious and legal procedures which it is often impossible to unravel. On occasions the kin or friends of the slain man, in doubt about the proper procedure, would consult the *exegētai*, three expounders elected by the people, who as authorities on religious tradition and especially on rites of purification would, while hesitating to give legal advice, provide the appropriate religious answers.

In the launching of a homicide prosecution the first stage was of a religious rather than a legal nature. The relatives of the slain man assembled for the funeral and carried a spear to the tomb. The spear obviously symbolized that vengeance would be sought. The next stage is most fully described in Draco's law concerning homicide, which, reinscribed on stone in 409/8, is still partly extant. The lines preserved deal with unintentional homicide, but in the initial steps of the process, before the king archon had ruled on the question of classification, the procedure was presumably the same in all types of homicide. The pertinent lines of the law are: "A proclamation is to be made against the killer in the agora by relatives as far as the degree of cousin's son and cousin. The prosecution is to be shared by cousins, sons of cousins, sons-in-law, fathers-in-law, and members of the phratry."[35] The third stage in the preliminaries leading to a homicide trial was the proclamation made by the king archon after he had received a formal charge from the relatives of the dead man. This proclamation, like the previous one of the victim's kin, named the killer, if known, and ordered him to stay away from "the legal things," which, as can be gleaned from various sources, included things like "holy water, libations, bowls of wine, holy places, and the agora" (Demosthenes, 20.158).

The king archon next had the responsibility of holding three pretrials (*prodikasiai*) at intervals of a month in which, by consulting with the parties concerned, he decided on the character of the homicide and hence on the proper court to try the case. Then in the fourth month he introduced the case before the appropriate court, over which he himself presided (Aristotle, *Ath. Const.*, 57.2–4). Cases classified as premeditated homicide went before the Areopagus, those as unpremeditated and justifiable homicide before a body of fifty-one *ephetai* sitting at the Palladion and Delphinion, respectively. The *ephetai* were selected by lot, possibly from the Areopagus. In the trials held at the Palladion and the Delphinion, if the *ephetai* were not convinced that the homicides were unpremeditated and justifiable as the king archon's assignment to those courts suggested, the accused presumably were sentenced as men guilty of premeditated homicide, for which the penalty was death and confiscation of property. If the accused were convicted of the less serious types of homicide, the penalty was exile, from which they could return if the victim's kin granted pardon unanimously—a clear survival of the old concept of the solidarity of the family.

In the trials themselves each litigant spoke twice, in the order plaintiff, defendant, plaintiff, defendant.[36] After his first speech, the defendant could leave Attica unharmed and go into exile. The dilemma he faced was horrible: if he gambled on acquittal and remained for the whole trial, then, if his gamble failed, the death sentence automatically followed; on the other hand, if he chose exile after his first speech, the very fact of his choice would influence the court to find him guilty. Many an exile must have been tortured for the rest of his days by the nagging thought, "Supposing I had seen the trial through, what then?"

Of the two other regular homicide courts, only one need be mentioned here as an example of the preservation of archaic ritual. Cases in which the killer was unknown or in which death had been caused by an animal or an inanimate object were tried at the Prytaneion by the king archon and the four *phylobasileis*. Although Cleisthenes at the close of the sixth century had effectively discarded the four old Ionian tribes as a political factor, the "tribal kings" still were perpetuated to participate in ceremonies such as those which took place in the court at the Prytaneion. This court, in order to cleanse the land of pollution, pronounced exile against the unknown killer, cast beyond the borders of Attica the object which had caused death, and possibly killed and cast beyond the frontiers the animal which had been responsible for human death.

The suits brought before the special homicide courts were all classified as *dikai* (private suits) because only relatives of the slain person could institute proceedings. There were ways, however, by which any citizen ("he who wished") could take action against homicides. When an accused homicide was found in one of the places (agora, temples, and so forth) from which he had been debarred by proclamation, or when an exiled homicide had returned without permission to Attica, any citizen by a process known as *apagoge* (dragging away)[37] could take the suspected man in the former case to "the Eleven," the officials in charge of the prison, and in the latter case to the *thesmothetai*. These officials then were responsible for bringing the accused before a dikastic court. By the same process malefactors (*kakourgoi*)—robbers, kidnappers, and the like—were brought before the Eleven, who, if the prisoners confessed, put them to death, apparently even if no killing had occurred. If the accused denied their guilt, they were tried before a dikastic court.

Since the death penalty was inflicted on those found guilty of premeditated homicide, treason, temple robbery, crimes like robbery and kidnapping, and in various other cases when the assembly or the *dikasts* saw fit, it is appropriate to comment briefly on the methods of execution employed.[38] In early times throughout Greece, as is clear from Homer and later sources, the stoning to death of the person deemed dangerous to the community was a common form of community self-help. As mentioned in an earlier chapter, an example of this occurred in Athens as late as 479, when a councillor, who had suggested that the proposals of the Persian Mardonius should be submitted to the assembly for consideration, was stoned to death by his fellow councillors. Among the Athenians, although not necessarily among all the Greeks, this method of inflicting death seems always to have been a form of "lynch law" rather than one officially decreed. Until the end of the fifth century a common form of execution at Athens was the hurling of the victim from a precipice into a rocky chasm called *barathron*, into which spikes and hooks had been driven.

A different type of execution, possibly beginning as early as the custom of throwing the criminal into the *barathron* and lasting until late in Athenian history, was named *apotympanismos*. It was formerly thought that this word referred to cudgeling a person to death with a club. A book published in 1923, however, based on excavations at ancient Phaleron, has rudely changed this conception.[39] In a common grave seventeen skeletons were discovered, each having an iron collar around the neck and cramp irons about the wrists and ankles. Most scholars now agree that these men had been executed by *apotympanismos*, which is explained as follows: the criminal was fastened by means of five cramp irons to a wooden plank which was then set upright in the ground. It is uncertain whether the victim was left to die in agony after possibly days of exposure, or whether death was hastened by gradually tightening the iron collar. A witty, but gruesome, parody in Aristophanes' *Thesmophoriazusae* (ll. 930 ff.) might lead one to accept the second alternative. Whichever interpretation is correct, this hideous method of inflicting death rates high among the endless examples of man's inhumanity to man.

From the end of the fifth century the drinking of a poison made from the seeds of the hemlock plant (*kōneion*) became the usual means of carrying out capital punishment. Famous men like Theramenes, Socrates, and Phocion were executed in this way. The first definite mentions of the use of hemlock as a method of execution refer to the period of the Thirty Tyrants (404/3), but a joke about hemlock as a chilling way to get to Hades in Aristophanes' *Frogs* (ll. 123–126), produced in 405, suggests that its official employment in putting people to death was well known at that time. One would like to think that hemlock completely superseded other forms of capital punishment, but the evidence shows that *apotympanismos* continued in use—possibly for those considered guilty of particularly heinous offenses.

This discussion of the Athenian laws concerning homicide should make it clear that from the time of Draco, at least, the state, in order to abolish the custom of family self-help and the ruinous feuds to which it gave rise, had taken under its control the procedure in cases of homicide. The old idea of family solidarity, however, still persisted in the law that only members of the family of the victim could initiate proceedings in one of the special homicide courts. Another concession to the hatred engendered by the strong family feelings is revealed by Demosthenes' statement (23.69) that "the prosecutor is permitted to see him [the victim] suffering the penalty awarded by law, and that is all." Another passage, if it is properly interpreted as referring to the prosecutor watching the execution of the accused, shows that the prosecutor had this "privilege" in any case which involved the death penalty. In 343 Aeschines, fighting for his life against a charge of treason brought by Demosthenes, uttered these harrowing words in his peroration to the jurors (2.181–182), "For it is not death that men dread, but a dishonored end. Is he not indeed to be pitied who must look into the sneering face of an enemy and hear with his ears his insults?"

The great majority of public cases and also of private ones, except for the special category of homicide, belonged in theory to the jurisdiction of the popular courts, but in practice, means were found to relieve the *dikasts* of some of the tremendous volume of litigation. Pisistratus had established a group of district judges who went on circuit throughout Attica with the aim of settling locally as many disputes as possible. These district judges apparently did not survive the fall of the Pisistratids, but they were revived in 453/2 (Aristotle, *Ath. Const.*, 26.3) to the number of thirty, presumably because the increased litigation, resulting from the growth of the city of Athens and from the problems concerning empire, was overtaxing the capabilities of the new popular courts. Shortly after the fall of the Thirty Tyrants in 403, the number of these "judges" was increased to forty, and it is about these officials that most of the information is available. Although their activity fell almost entirely in the fourth century, it seems best to include them in the present discussion of the administration of justice, which almost necessarily bridges the fifth and fourth centuries.

The Forty, as they were usually called, were appointed annually by lot, four from each tribe (*Ath. Const.*, 53). Many private suits were initiated before them in their quarters in Athens, and they had the authority to settle petty cases involving less than ten drachmas. Suits in which a larger sum was at stake were assigned to a body of public arbitrators (*diaitētai*). This institution of public arbitration provides further evidence for the Athenian democratic ideal that citizens owed active service to the state. It was probably established almost simultaneously with the Forty in an effort to lighten the congested dockets of the dikastic courts. Each year men who were in their forty-second year of military service (that is, in their sixtieth year), except those who were holding office or had some other legitimate excuse, were required to be available as arbitrators for that year. An inscription (*Inscriptiones Graecae*, II², 1926) which lists all the arbitrators of the year 325/4 contains 103 names. Although the number is surprisingly small, it probably does not justify the hypothesis that the *thetes* were excused from this service. These arbitrators were divided into ten groups, apparently with no reference to tribal affiliation, but each group was assigned to a tribe and had a regular meeting place in Athens. When a case came before the four members of the Forty acting for the tribe of the defendant, they would select an arbitrator from the group assigned to that tribe.[40] Aristotle's account (*Ath. Const.*, 53.2–3) of the procedure which was followed is worth quoting:

> These [the arbitrators] take over the cases, and if they are unable to effect a compromise, they give judgments, and if both parties are satisfied with their judgment and abide by it, that ends the suit. But if one of the two parties appeals to the *dikasterion*, they put the witnesses' evidence and the challenges and the laws concerned into deed-boxes, those of the plaintiff and those of the defendant separately, and seal them, and attach to them a copy of the arbitrator's verdict written on a tablet, and hand them over to the four judges taking the cases of the defendant's tribe. When these have received them they bring them before the *dikasterion*, claims within 1,000 drachmas before a court of 201 dikasts, and claims above that amount before one of 401 dikasts. The litigants are not permitted to put in laws or challenges or evidence other than those passed on by the arbitrator, that have been put into the deed-boxes.

It is interesting to note that all the evidence had to be in writing, a requirement that may have been associated with the establishment of the public arbitrators in or shortly after 403, and that no new evidence could be introduced before the *dikasterion* hearing the appeal. Thus, although the majority of the arbitral judgments were apparently appealed, the system did help to expedite the business of the dikastic courts because all the tedious preliminaries were attended to before the suit went to the *dikasts,* and the trial itself had to be based on the written evidence gathered by the arbitrator. The use of written evidence proved so successful that the requirement was subsequently—possibly in

378/7—adopted for all private and public cases tried before the popular courts.[41]

The popular courts, as was stated above, presumably came into existence largely or entirely as a result of Ephialtes' reforms of 462/1. Aristophanes in the *Wasps* (l. 662), produced in 422, and Andocides (1.17) in a speech referring to the year 415 provide the information that these courts were made up from 6,000 *dikasts*. Every Athenian citizen in good standing on reaching the age of thirty was eligible to be a *dikast*. Each tribe furnished annually 600 of these jurors, selected by lot from those who had submitted their names. Since citizens were liable for military service through their sixtieth year (in the fourth century they had to be available as public arbitrators in their sixtieth year), it is obvious that men of military age could serve as *dikasts* only through some official dispensation.

The common criticism, both ancient and modern, against these popular courts is that the uneducated masses were the ones who primarily submitted their names for the lot. This blanket denunciation can be accepted only with considerable skepticism. Since dikastic pay was originally merely two obols a day, and from 425 three obols, half the daily wage for a laborer, it is unreasonable to assume that the average worker could have afforded to give up his better-paying employment for a year. In various periods of the long Peloponnesian War, when Athens and the Piraeus were crowded with refugees from the country, it is quite probable that many of this expanding urban crowd, if jobless and not conscripted into military service, welcomed the chance of earning something by trying to become a *dikast,* a position which was available year after year if the lot was favorable. Aristophanes in the *Wasps* gives a vivid picture of old countrymen trudging through the night so as to be present in Athens for jury duty by sunrise. One may doubt if many old men trudged night after night from the country to the city, but it is logical to assume that many men over sixty, living in the city complex rather than on farms, were glad to add three obols a day, as the equivalent of an old age pension, for the needs of their families. Besides the money, service as *dikasts* offered a sense of power by enabling men to participate in the important decisions and scandals of the time. In the fourth century, however, when the employment of mercenaries became increasingly common, younger men may have served more often if the small pay was not too discouraging. The speeches of Demosthenes, in particular, give the impression that the juries contained a considerable number of representatives from the middle classes. Since important current issues frequently were argued in the courts, it is quite possible that some politicians urged their "followers" to submit their names at the time of the annual drawing of lots for the *dikasts*.

The number 6,000, as in the case of the plenary assembly, was assumed to represent or rather to be the people. By a convenient legal fiction this concept was extended to the personnel of each dikastic court. Since, therefore, the *dikasts* were the people, they were not held accountable at the end of the year, and also there was no appeal from their verdicts. How could one appeal from the people? If there was a scrutiny of their qualifications (*dokimasia*) before they assumed office, it probably consisted merely of a check on age and citizen status. The one requirement, as lexicographers state, was that at the beginning of the year before entering upon their duties the assembled *dikasts* had to take the dikastic oath, which emphasized the seriousness and responsibilities of the function upon which they were embarking.

The *dikasts* were divided into sections or panels in which each tribe was supposed to have equal representation. It is clear from Aristophanes' *Wasps* that in the fifth century certain sections, at least, were assigned to a particular court for the year and, hence, to the magistrate who presided over that court. Since, then, the litigants could know in advance before what jurors they would appear, it might seem that bribery would have been possible (Aristotle, *Ath. Const.*, 27.5). The large size of the panels—apparently a minimum of 200 for private suits and 500 for public ones—however, made bribery difficult. Nevertheless, several notorious cases prompted certain changes in procedure at the end of the fifth and in the fourth century, such as the allotting of the panel of jurors and of the presiding magistrate to a court only on the morning of the trial.[42] In the fifth century the courts met every day except festival days—on some 300 days a year according to the possibly exaggerated estimate of Aristophanes; in the fourth century they also did not meet on days when assemblies were held. Since sessions began early in the morning it would seem that the majority of the *dikasts* must have been residents of Athens, Piraeus, or the immediate environs. Obviously all 6,000 *dikasts* did not apear each court day. There is no certain information on what happened if those present were either too many or too few. Possibly the answer is that, despite the general regulations about the size of panels, the number of *dikasts* in certain cases varied depending on how many jurors were available at any given time.

The first step in the institution of a suit, whether private or public, was the summons of the defendant by the plaintiff, who was usually accompanied by two witnesses. The plaintiff then submitted his complaint in writing to the magistrate whose jurisdiction seemed to cover the charge in question. Many private cases, as mentioned above, were brought before the Forty, who, in the fourth century, turned them over to the public arbitrators. In regard to other cases, except those of homicide, the magistrate, if he accepted them, set a day for a preliminary hearing. This hearing (*anakrisis*) was a survival from the earlier type of trial in which a magistrate had had full powers to render a verdict. For such trials, obviously, all the evidence had to be produced. At the *anakrisis*, however, only enough evidence was furnished to enable the magistrate to decide such matters as whether the case was admissable and the indictment properly drawn, what form of action should be followed, and the eligibility of the litigants to appear in court. Some of the speeches delivered at the actual trials, which have been preserved, reveal that sometimes a litigant was startled by the subsequent introduction of unexpected evidence—in one case, at least, by the appearance of a person supposedly dead.[43] After completing the preliminary hearing, the magistrate communicated with the *thesmothetai*, whose responsibility it was to set a day for the trial and to determine the size of the panel of *dikasts*. On many occasions, of course, the *thesmothetai* themselves had been conducting the *anakrisis*. The number of jurors depended in a private suit on the amount of the claim and in a public one on the seriousness of the charge.[44]

At the trial itself, which was often long delayed because of the crowded dockets of the courts, the magistrate who had received the case was the presiding officer. His role was to preserve order and to see that all pertinent regulations were followed, but he could not interfere in the actual proceedings like a modern judge, nor at the end did he summarize the case and instruct the jurors. All litigants had to speak for themselves except women and children, who were represented by their legal guardians, and metics and slaves, usually by their patrons (*prostatai*) and masters, respectively. Nevertheless, the litigants, if they made the request, were usually permitted to have the assistance of more experienced and articulate friends. One of the chief functions of the oligarchic clubs was to provide this type of legal aid to fellow members entangled with the law.

From the end of the fifth century the great volume of litigation gave rise to a new profession, that of professional speech writers (ghostwriters). A man involved in litigation, not trusting his own abilities, would secretly hire the services of such a professional. The speech writer, after learning all the facts of a case, would compose an appropriate speech which the litigant would then memorize. Some Athenian citizens, like Antiphon, Isocrates (in his youth), and Demosthenes, besides their other activities, wrote such speeches, and metics like Lysias and Isaeus (probably a metic from Chalcis) became professionals in this field of endeavor.

Lysias was particularly noted for adapting the tone of his speeches to the personality of his clients, while Isaeus became a specialist in inheritance cases. His twelve extant speeches, despite all the ambiguities introduced by an advocate, are one of the main sources for a study of many aspects of Athenian private law.

Litigants were allowed only a certain period for speaking, the length depending on the importance of the case. The passage of time was marked by a water clock (*klepsydra*), to which there are various references in the extant forensic speeches. Sometimes several private suits were handled in one day, but for important public actions the whole day was allotted. No trial could last more than one day. After the litigants had finished speaking, then the *dikasts,* without any discussion or instructions from the presiding magistrate, proceeded to record their verdicts.

In the fifth century two urns were set up in the court, one for the plaintiff and one for the defendant. The *dikast* dropped the single pebble with which he had been provided into one of the two urns. Since this method did not sufficiently ensure secrecy, another procedure was adopted in the fourth century. Each *dikast* recived two ballots made of bronze, looking like small discs with a short peg running through the middle. The only difference between them was that in one the peg was hollow, in the other solid. Just before the voting the herald of the court proclaimed, "The one with the hole for the first speaker (that is, the plaintiff), the solid one for the second speaker (that is, the defendant)" (Aristotle, *Ath. Const.,* 68). The *dikast,* then, holding a ballot in each hand with his fingers covering both ends of the pegs so that no one could tell which ballot had the hollow or the solid peg, walked to that part of the court where two urns were placed, one of bronze and one of wood. He put the ballot which represented his vote in the bronze urn and the disc which he was discarding in the wooden one. After all the jurors had cast their votes, the court attendants emptied the contents of the bronze urn and separated and counted the two kinds of ballots.[45] The litigant who received the most votes was declared the winner in the suit. A tie in the votes was counted in favor of the defendant. In many private suits the prosecutor, if he did not receive a fifth of the ballots, had to pay the defendant the *epōbelia,* that is, one-sixth of the sum in dispute (an obol for each drachma). In public suits the plaintiff who did not receive a fifth of the votes was fined 1,000 drachmas and lost the privilege of instituting such an action again.

The acquittal of the defendant ended the case except for the application of the penalty, when relevant, against the accuser who had not received one-fifth of the ballots. If the prosecutor won his suit, however, punishment was often awarded in one of the following two ways. Suits, in general, belonged in one of two categories. In one category (*agones atimetoi*) the *dikasts* could not assess the penalty, for it already was fixed by law or decree; in the other type (*agones timetoi*) the awarding of punishment rested with the litigants and the *dikasts*. After the accused had been found guilty, each litigant was allowed a brief period in which to propose and justify a penalty. Then the jury voted again. The *dikasts* themselves had no powers to propose a penalty; all they could do was to vote in favor of one of the two suggestions which had been made. The most famous case belonging in this category was the trial of Socrates in 399. After the jurors had voted against him by a small margin (thirty votes), his prosecutors recommended the death sentence. Socrates, as Plato tells the story, exasperated the *dikasts* by suggesting that as a public benefactor, he deserved maintenance in the Prytaneion (town hall). Finally he jestingly proposed the absurdly low fine of one *mina* (100 drachmas), which at the urging of his friends he then raised to thirty *minai*. The *dikasts,* in response to this arrogant insult to the popular courts, which in conjunction with the assembly they considered the core of their beloved democracy, felt obligated to vote for the death penalty. Plato's account of this trial in the *Apology* is a masterpiece of literature, but it should not be taken as literal reporting, as so often is done. Certainly there was no place in Athenian juridical procedure for the lecture, magnificent as it was, which Socrates delivered to the *dikasts* after the verdict of death had been reached.

At the termination of a trial, if the case had been a public one, officials of the state were responsible for carrying out the sentence.[46] In private suits the state interfered in the execution of the verdict only to the extent that its interests were involved in some way, as, for example, if it were entitled to a share in the fine. For the rest, the plaintiff himself had the task of enforcing the court's sentence. If within the time limit assigned by the court the defendant failed to satisfy him, he had the right of distraint (*enechurasia*) upon the defendant's property.

In ending this discussion of the Athenian government, a few general observations are appropriate. One should never forget that the assembly, the ultimate power in the state, was a primary body which all adult male Athenian citizens could attend. The numbers present at each meeting probably were several thousand, but the nature of the personnel could vary considerably depending on circumstances such as the time of the year or the existence of a military expedition. It cannot be emphasized too often that in Athens there were no political parties in the modern sense of the term. Various groups may have tended to vote somewhat as units—the poor, the rich, the young, the old, the admirers and friends of a particular leader—but this was far different from adherence to a definite party line. Each time an ambitious politician addressed the assembly, he faced an audience whose components might vary considerably from those of a previous meeting or of some future gathering. Since there were no recognized parties, each leader or aspiring leader had to be an effective speaker, capable of swaying an audience which changed with every meeting. In view of this fact, any man who could influence the assembly and lead the people was a demagogue, whether a Pericles or a Cleon, and it is clearly improper to use the word in a pejorative sense only when referring to a Cleon.

Because of the brilliance and prejudice of antidemocrats like Thucydides and Plato, it is customary to speak of the government of Athens in the second half of the fifth century and in the fourth century as a "radical" democracy. This is an unfortunate and deceptive term, for it suggests a great industrial proletariat which did not exist in Athens. Such men, and particularly Plato, when referring to the members of the assembly, the dikastic courts, and the innumerable boards appointed by lot, create the impression of a stupid, ignorant mob. The picture is arrogantly misleading unless one subscribes to the aristocratic doctrine that only *kalokagathoi* (gentlemen) were intelligent and educated. The thousands of unpretentious Athenians—the small farmers, the artisans, the sailors—by their continuous participation in meetings of the assembly, in the dikastic courts, in the innumerable boards of magistrates, in frequent tours of military duty, and in the daily give and take of a "face-to-face" society became too familiar with the processes of government and the nature of current problems to be written off as an ignorant rabble.

The large popular courts, which in essence were sections of the people fulfilling a judicial function rather than the legislative and electoral ones of the assembly, have been ridiculed and denounced as "about the worst legal system ever invented" and also approved as possessing on an enlarged scale the virtues and vices of a modern jury. The evidence, chiefly from the extant fourth-century forensic speeches, can be interpreted in varying ways. There seems little doubt that at times the *dikasts* were moved by the "sob tactics" of the defendants, and it is possible that on occasions, when state finances were low, they may have convicted a rich man so that his property could be confiscated. There is no convincing evidence, however, that the verdicts of the juries were not in accord with their sense of justice. The most telling retort to critics of "radical" democracy, whether ancient or modern, is that in both the fifth and fourth centuries Athens was the most enlightened and successful state in the Greek world, suffering only twice from oligarchic revolution (*stasis*), until, like the other Greeks, it was overwhelmed by the might and genius of Philip and Alexander of Macedonia.[47]

T HIS CHAPTER has treated in some detail the nature and functioning of the constitution which the Athenians developed in the fifth century, a constitution which, with only minor changes, remained in force throughout the following century until the Macedonian conquest in 322. Little has been said, however, except for passing remarks, about the social and economic characteristics of the people living in Athens. It seems fitting here to try to give a brief demographic sketch of the Athenian population when the Golden Age of Pericles was at its height, for the horrors and bitterness of the Peloponnesian War, with all its accompanying disillusionments, led to many changes in the points of view of the Greeks.

No census figures are available for the population of the city-state of Athens on the eve of the Peloponnesian War. Scholars have valiantly tried to make estimates, using as evidence such treacherous figures as military numbers and amount of grain consumed. In view of these attempts, the following round numbers do not pretend to be accurate, but they are probably close enough to reality so as not to give a fanciful picture: 175,000 Athenians, of whom approximately 45,000 were adult males, 30,000 metics or resident aliens, and some 100,000 slaves. Although these three elements mingled constantly, it will be best, so far as is possible, to treat them separately.

Thucydides (2.14; 16.1) states that at the beginning of the war, when Pericles urged the people to come to Athens and seek protection within the long walls, the majority of the Athenians still lived in the country. This comment is evidence that, populous as Athens and Piraeus had become, the Athenians, like most Greeks, were still an agricultural people. These country people included both the old wealthy families to which men like Pericles and Cimon belonged, who had houses in the city and also estates in the country managed, at least in the case of Pericles, by a slave supervisor, and worked by labor, mostly slaves; and also the large number of peasants whose holdings, although small, obviously varied in size. These peasants, whom Aristophanes loved to depict, worked their fields themselves with the help of members of the family and probably one or more slaves. In rush seasons such as harvest time it seems clear that they could hire temporary labor, both free and servile. Since their lots were often on rough and hilly ground, the land was largely assigned to vineyards and to olive and fig trees. The grain, chiefly barley, grown between rows of trees was primarily for home consumption, thereby contributing to the countryman's unattainable ideal of self-sufficiency (*autarkeia*). The peasants' activity naturally varied depending on the location and the quality of their land. Those living at Acharnae, where timber was still available, devoted their energies particularly to producing charcoal, and those whose little lots were adjacent to the urban areas were commonly market gardeners. These latter may have lived in Athens, going out to their gardens in the morning and returning in the evening. It is likely that some of these workers and also some of the other peasants, although ordinarily residing in the city, lived during certain seasons in temporary shacks on their property.

As Athens became a great imperial city, its population and that of Piraeus grew steadily. Some members of wealthy families, despite their ancestral estates in the country, probably lived more or less permanently in the city because of their political interests. When sophists arrived in Athens or Socrates talked in the agora, the ancient sources give the impression that many wealthy men, particularly the young, were always available. Although the aristocratic clubs (*hetaireiai*) became more prominent in the course of the Peloponnesian War, they surely existed earlier, and their very existence suggests a membership with a largely urban residence. The continuing wealth of these aristocrats is difficult to explain satisfactorily, although revenues from their estates were certainly the basis of their affluence. Since the generals (*strategoi*) were elected from such families, the distribution of booty after a successful campaign must have swelled their coffers. Marriages, with large dowries, between prominent families had both political and financial significance. Also, although capitalistic investments in any modern sense did not exist, there is little reason to doubt that some aristocrats, perhaps through agents, profited from loans at interest and particularly from bottomry loans.

Besides the wealthy old families, the Athenians in the urban region, where numbers naturally increased with the exodus from the country to the city at the beginning of the war, ranged from the prosperous to the very poor. In their occupations these Athenians were often indistinguishable from the metics, and the Old Oligarch even remarks sourly that it was dangerous to strike a slave in the streets for fear that he might actually be a citizen. These citizens worked as artisans, as traders, and as laborers. Industry was centered in workshops (*ergasteria*) located in individual homes or in adjacent quarters. In these shops the owner, his wife and children, and often one or more slaves produced commodities of various types—metal goods, pottery, textiles, and the like. These products were sometimes sold at the workshop and sometimes hawked in the markets. Although most of these enterprises were small, a few expanded sufficiently to become really profitable; for example, Cleon inherited a successful tannery from his father, Isocrates' father fared well economically from his slaves who made flutes, and in the fourth century Demosthenes' father had two *ergasteria,* one in which thirty-two or thirty-three slaves produced swords and one in which twenty slaves manufactured furniture. From the middle of the fifth century, Athens, under the leadership of Pericles, was engaged in a large building program, a project which, as Plutarch (*Pericles,* 12) emphasizes, gave employment to a wide variety of craftsmen and laborers. Athenians, whose passion for independence abhorred the condition of being permanently under the restraint of another, worked intermittently on many of these enterprises as contractors, artisans and laborers, and in these undertakings they toiled side by side with metics and slaves. The fleet which had become the foundation of Athenian power provided thousands of jobs, for the *thetes* more than any other group served as rowers. The dockyards were in constant need of labor, skilled and unskilled, and here again many citizens, taking temporary jobs, worked in conjunction with metics and slaves.

One could continue listing more and more types of work in which the Athenians participated, including their activity in many governmental posts, but enough has been mentioned to show the absurdity of the charge that the Athenians as a whole were idlers living on the profits of empire and the sweat of their slaves. In fact, so many Athenians were workers and laborers, often in dirty and difficult jobs, that many aristocrats, and especially fourth-century philosophers like Plato and Aristotle, acquired a contempt for those working at mechanical and manual tasks (the *banausoi*), whose bodies became misshapen from the nature of their toil and whose minds had no leisure to devote to lofty subjects—a prejudice, hallowed by the distinction of its proponents, from which society still suffers.

The Athenian democracy which Pericles idealized in the funeral oration of 431, before the evil effects of twenty-seven years of war had taken their sorry toll, was a remarkable human achievement. Some incorrigible reactionaries, like the Old Oligarch, could sneer at the control and privileges enjoyed by the common people, but if one takes Athens as a whole, there was a mutual tolerance between rich and poor. Since only citizens could possess land, and the majority did, they had the proud feeling of ownership, a feeling that was strengthened by the absence of any regular property tax. The landless citizens in the city found occupation as artisans, traders, and laborers, and apparently suffered no disturbing competition from the metics and slaves. For any who were unemployed there was often an opportunity to enroll in a *cleruchy*, when one was sent out, and thereby to raise themselves to the *zeugitai* class if they had been *thetes*.

The maintenance of the "radical" democracy, in which the common people did not want to be at a disadvantage because of poverty, placed heavy financial burdens on the state. Money had to be allocated as salaries to a large number of officials and members of government bodies—the magistrates, except for a few special cases like the *strategoi;* the numerous administrative boards, usually consisting of ten men each; the 500 members of the Boulē; and those of the 6,000 *dikasts* whose panels were in session. From the beginning of the fourth century pay was also granted to a certain number of those arriving early at meetings of the assembly. The stipends were moderate, but they enabled many to have the satisfaction of feeling that they really were sharing in the running of the state. There was a police force and an unknown number of public slaves, who had to be maintained and replaced when necessary. Since the time of Pisistratus, at least, the government had been generous in providing for disabled veterans and for the orphans of those killed in war until on reaching their majority at eighteeen they were enrolled in their *demes*. In the fifth century, helped by the steady flow of tribute, the government was active in the erecting of public buildings. This activity was curtailed in the first part of the fourth century, but obviously some building and repairing were always necessary. In Athens and elsewhere—and always—war and preparation for war consumed the greatest share of the revenues. The government had to build and restore triremes, pay for the rowers and the rest of the crew when on duty or in training, and subsidize the land forces when on service.

Athens was noted for the number of festivals it celebrated. Although the wealthy, through the liturgy system, shouldered some of the expenses, many costs fell to the state, including the supplying of thousands of victims for sacrifice. The animals roasted on these occasions provided many of the poor with the only meat in their diet. Of these festivities, those in honor of Dionysus included choral and dramatic performances for which a small admission fee was charged. To encourage the poor to attend these presentations, Pericles, according to one tradition, introduced the custom of supplying the needy with the necessary admission money. This festival or theatre fund may have been the ancestor or the inspiration of the Theoric Fund of the fourth century, which will be discussed in a later chapter. These donations, if they were initiated by Pericles, in addition to their demagogic aspect would have had an important cultural and educational purpose. Since Athens had no public school system, the poor, when children, had had little or no chance for formal schooling, but the theatre fund would have permitted them to attend the dramatic performances for which Athens was justly famous. The state's concern for the poor revealed in the ways mentioned above can be considered an acknowledgment of its obligation to those who, by rowing, suffering, and dying on the ships, gave Athens its power.

It is natural to assume that it was the empire and the annual tribute paid by the "allies" which enabled Athens to meet these expenditures. The fact, however, that in the fourth century, when empire was gone, Athens still had a fleet and continued to increase its "welfare" measures is definite evidence that sources of revenue other than the profits of empire alone enabled the "radical" democracy to prosper. As was probably true of all Greek states, the Athenian state owned sections of the land, including forests, quarries, and mines. Very little is known of the manner in which these holdings were exploited except in the case of the silver mines at Laurium, which were leased to individual contractors. Various types of indirect taxes existed, such as import and export duties at Piraeus and different kinds of sales taxes. The law courts always produced some revenue through court fees, fines, and particularly, when it occurred, the confiscation of the property of some unfortunate defendant. Direct taxes the citizens hated to impose on themselves, but they felt no qualms about exacting them from non-citizens; metics had to pay an annual head tax, and transient foreigners (*xenoi*) were taxed in some way, as also were prostitutes.

One device which enabled the average Athenian to avoid the payment of direct taxes was the institution of liturgies, which succeeded in extracting much money and also the display of civic spirit from the wealthy. Except for the trierarchy, almost all these liturgies or public services were associated with the religious, or better, the festival life of Athens. Originally these services were probably entirely voluntary, but in course of time they became obligatory responsibilities of the wealthy. Men were selected by the appropriate government agency to provide and train the choruses for the tragedy and comedy performances at the festivals of Dionysus and for the men's and boys' choruses which played a part in many other festivals. Since these performances were always of a competitive nature in which the winning of a prize brought prestige to the *choregus,* the expense involved in procuring competent training, satisfactory costumes, and skilled musicians could be considerable. Many men used these occasions as a means of winning favor with the people, and it became customary for a wealthy man on trial for some misdemeanor to emphasize to the *dikasts* how much he had spent in liturgies for the benefit of the people. These liturgies, which were very numerous, occurred on tribal and *deme* as well as on state levels. They inevitably led to much litigation in which men claimed that they had been unfairly selected to perform such a service, but they played an important role in making the rich, rather than hoarding their wealth, take an active share in a fundamental part of the social and religious life of the community, thereby reducing the ill will which the poor are likely to feel instinctively for those in more fortunate financial circumstances.

By far the most costly of the liturgies was the trierarchy. Each year the generals selected from the wealthiest citizens the necessary number of trierarchs to command the triremes whose employment was anticipated. The state provided the hull and rigging of a trireme and supposedly the sum of money for the maintenance of the crew, but all the other expenses, sometimes amouting to a talent (6,000 drachmas), fell upon the individual trierarch. Since each trireme had a trierarch, the number of men performing this service was very large, and their burdens were heavy, for in addition to having to collect crews and serve on the ships themselves they were responsible for all sorts of expenses and repairs. The enthusiasm and pride that strengthened the system are emphasized by Thucydides (6.31.3) on the occasion of the departure of the great Athenian expedition against Sicily in 415, but later in the Peloponnesian War financial conditions became so bad that it was necessary to appoint two trierarchs to be responsible for one ship.

The liturgy system, by appealing to, and in fact compelling, the patriotism of the wealthy, relieved the state of many expenses. At times, however, a national emergency made a regular direct tax imperative. This impost, called *eisphora,* was a tax on capital and could be resorted to only after a formal and rather elaborate legislative procedure. Since its occurrence was much more frequent in the fourth than in the fifth century, comment on it will be postponed to a later chapter.

The metics—the resident aliens—contributed greatly to the economic and intellectual life of fifth- and fourth-century Athens. Foreigners (*xenoi*) had migrated to Athens in considerable numbers earlier under Solon and probably under the Pisistratids, but it is impossible to describe their status satisfactorily. Through the reforms of Cleisthenes some, or many, of them acquired citizenship in the new constitution based on the ten tribes and the *demes*. It was the growth of the Athenian empire and the emergence of Athens as the leading state in the Greek world that led to such an influx of foreigners that official steps had to be taken to handle this immigration. The transient foreign merchants presented no difficulties, for, after paying the appropriate customs duties and transacting their business, they departed again. The problem lay with the many Greeks, and subsequently some "barbarians," who, because of dissatisfaction with their own cities and interest in the economic and cultural potentialities of Athens, wished to remain in Attica either permanently or for a long time. Such a foreigner, desiring to become a metic, had to persuade an Athenian to be his sponsor (*prostates*). The sponsor was then responsible for having the aspiring metic registered in his *deme*. Presumably at this time the metic took the equivalent of an oath of loyalty, swearing to abide by the laws of Athens. Since most metics were artisans, traders, or intellectuals, their sponsors were usually citizens belonging to the urban *demes* or ones in the neighborhood of Athens and Piraeus. These *demes*, then, must have kept registers of metics as well as of citizens. The evidence about the role of the *prostates* is confusing, but it seems safe to say that until the middle of the fourth century, at least, when a metic was involved in litigation his sponsor had to take part in the preliminaries to the trial, the *anakrisis*.

Resident aliens were present in many Greek cities, but since they were more numerous and more prominent in Athens, the metics there are the only ones about whom considerable information is available. Since they were not citizens, they had no political rights and were debarred from owning land or a house, but as privileged foreigners, they were liable to all the duties of citizenship. In addition to paying an annual head tax of twelve drachmas for a man and six for an independent woman, they paid the ordinary citizen taxes, contributed to the regular liturgies, except the trierarchy, and, depending on their wealth, performed military service as hoplites, light armed troops, or rowers in the fleet. The fact that the metics were willing to accept the obligations without the privileges of citizenship is clear evidence of how many more economic and cultural advantages Athens offered to them than their native cities.

The metics neglected none of these opportunities. In the public building programs they participated, along with citizens and slaves, as laborers, artisans, and contractors. In "industry" their workshops ran all the way from tiny *ergasteria* in their homes producing pottery, textiles, metalwork, and the like to the largest known "factory," the *ergasterion* of Cephalus and later his son, Lysias, which employed 120 slaves in making shields. In trade the activities of the metics ran the gamut from the noisy hucksters in the streets to those largely responsible for importing such necessities as grain. As some of these metics became wealthy, they also assumed the role of "bankers" (*trapezitai*), in which capacity they received deposits, served as money changers, and negotiated loans at interest. In the fourth century, as is known from the speeches of Demosthenes, the two best known bankers at Athens were Pasion and then Phormion, both of whom became metics after having been manumitted from slavery.

As craftsmen and traders and as men willing to devote their energies and talents to countless types of work, the metics contributed greatly to the economic welfare of Athens. Coming from all parts of the Greek world and certainly by the fourth century including "barbarians" from Thrace, Phrygia, Syria, Egypt, and elsewhere, they added a cosmopolitan flavor to Athenian life. Some of these "barbarians" may originally have been slaves who, becoming freedmen after manumission, fell into the metic class. These non-Greeks on various occasions beginning with the end of the fifth century received permission from the state to introduce the cult of their own native divinities, sometimes acquiring the privilege to own property on which to erect an appropriate temple. Thus the cults of the Thracian goddess Bendis, of the Anatolian Cybele, of Adonis from Syria and Cyprus, and of Isis from Egypt were introduced into Athens, and in the course of time many Athenians joined in the ecstatic worship of these divinities.

The metics influenced the Athenians in many other ways than through religion. Beginning with the Golden Age of Pericles, Athens became the intellectual center of the Mediterranean world for several centuries, but one should remember that metics as well as Athenian citizens contributed to that glory. Names, such as the following, of aliens living in Athens for long periods, whether or not the ancient sources officially call them metics, confirm that statement:[48] Anaxagoras from Clazomenae on the coast of Asia Minor, a philosopher who had great influence on Pericles; Hippodamus of Miletus, among other things an architect and town-planner who designed the Periclean colony of Thurii in Italy and remodelled Piraeus on a rectangular pattern; Protagoras of Abdera in Thrace, the greatest of the sophists, and all the other sophists; Polygnotus of Thasos, the most famous of the fifth-century painters, later made an Athenian citizen; Aristotle of Stagira in Chalcidice, the founder of the peripatetic school of philosophy, and his successor Theophrastus, from Eresos in Lesbos; in the late fourth and the first half of the third century, Zeno from Citium in Cyprus, probably a Semite, the founder of Stoicism.

The metics were an important part of the population of Athens, and they presumably were satisfied with their lot or the majority would not have continued living there. There is no evidence that they suffered from social discrimination. The artisans and laborers seemingly mingled naturally with their Athenian counterparts, and the wealthy and intellectual metics associated freely with comparable Athenians. One should remember that the house of the metic Cephalus in Piraeus was the scene of the discussions that form Plato's *Republic*. To a modern person it may seem strange that more of these talented and industrious metics were not granted citizenship. For an ancient Athenian (and for Greeks in general), however, his passionate nationalism and his personal pride in the privileges attached to citizenship made him reluctant to share that precious possession with others. Occasionally a distinguished metic who had performed a great service for the state was rewarded with citizenship, but the reward to such a person was more commonly the voting of certain honors of which the granting of *isoteleia,* equality with citizens in matters of taxation, was the most frequent one. This city-state parochialism did not begin to wane until the Hellenistic period.

The third chief element in the population of Athens consisted of slaves. The earliest extant Greek literary works, those of Homer and Hesiod, reveal that as far back in time as satisfactory evidence exists the Greeks were familiar with the custom of slavery. As commerce and industry increased in the archaic period in the wake of colonization, it seems certain that Greeks began to employ more and more slaves as their economy ceased to be almost entirely agricultural. Exceptions to this trend naturally existed in states exploiting a conquered population, such as Sparta with its helots and Thessaly with its *penestai.* The literary evidence, especially Aristophanes and the Attic orators, and the preserved inscriptions disclose an Athens of the fifth and fourth centuries and a Greek world in general in which the presence of slaves was a common feature of social and economic life.

Slavery was so omnipresent that it is not surprising that the charge has often been made that Greek civilization was based on slave labor. Substantiation of such a charge obviously should be based on population statistics rather than on impressions, but, as so often, statistics are lacking in Greek history. Some startling figures are offered by Athenaeus of Naucratis, writing toward the end of the second century A.D. In his *Deipnosophists,* 6.103, he says that a census taken in Athens in the time of Demetrius of Phaleron (ca. 310 B.C.) recorded 21,000 citizens, 10,000 metics, and 400,000 slaves. The figures for the citizens and metics at that period of Athenian history seem reasonable, but the number of slaves as listed in the manuscript is almost universally rejected as fantastic. In the same chapter Athenaeus states that there were 460,000 slaves at Corinth and 470,000 at Aegina. It is hard to imagine how in such a small area, 1,330,000 slaves could have been fed and prevented from annihilating the citizens. Scholars have made various attempts to estimate the size of the slave population in Athens on the eve of the Peloponnesian War, but they all have to admit that their conclusions are only approximations. For the purpose of this and subsequent chapters it seems reasonable to select from these studies the round number of 100,000, a number large enough to emphasize the importance of slavery to the Athenians but not so large as to make one wonder why Athens was not overwhelmed by its slaves.

The chief source of slaves was war. Prisoners who were not ransomed were turned over to the ubiquitous slave dealers, who transported them to various cities and sold them in the markets. According to the tradition Cimon, after his victory at the Eurymedon River, flooded the slave markets with 20,000 prisoners. Wars between "barbarian" tribes, piracy, and slave dealers making kidnapping raids, usually in remote regions, also constantly supplied the slave markets with human merchandise. To judge from slave names known at Athens it is clear that the majority of slaves there were "barbarians." The prevalence of "barbarian" slaves gave rise to the notion that there was something slavish about "barbarians"—that, compared to Greeks, they were created by nature to be slaves. Aristotle tried to develop this idea in his *Politics,* but, as he realized, slavery was too universal to be explained by any general theory. In the fifth century, at least, the Greeks did not hesitate to enslave fellow Greeks. One need only remember Thucydides' accounts of how the Syracusans enslaved the Athenians and their allies after the collapse of the Athenian Sicilian expedition, and of how the Athenians, after taking Scione and Melos, slaughtered the men and sold the women and children.

The Athenians employed slaves in every type of occupation. In the country the peasants worked their small lots with the help of members of their families, but it is likely that many a household had at least one slave to perform various domestic functions. Wealthy men like Pericles had large estates whose management was usually entrusted to a slave. The regular work force may have been largely servile, for Greek pride rebelled against working permanently under the control of another, but it is possible that sections of the land were leased to free tenant farmers. Hired free labor was often employed in rush agricultural seasons, since such tasks, being temporary, were acceptable to the Greek passion for independence. In Athens and Piraeus thousands of slaves worked at a great variety of tasks. In the little *ergasteria* of the free craftsmen, the owners and their families often had a few metics and slaves sharing in the work. Some *ergasteria* were considerably larger; as mentioned above, 120 slaves were employed in the shield factory of Cephalus and his son Lysias. Citizen families and also metics, unless very poor, usually possessed a female slave to perform domestic duties such as weaving and caring for the children. Wealthier families naturally could enjoy the services of several slaves. Since the market price of slaves ordinarily was rather cheap, many men bought them as an investment. Xenophon in his *Poroi* (4.14), says that the general Nicias leased out 1,000 slaves to contractors at the silver mines of Laurium, receiving an obol a day for the use of each slave. Such enterprises on a more moderate scale were common. Many of the slaves working in *ergasteria,* serving on trading ships, and assisting in agricultural rush seasons were probably leased by their owners for these particular jobs.

In their desire to derive greater profit from their investment in slaves and also probably as a reward to faithful workers, citizens would often allow their slaves to work independently, possibly assisting them in setting up a shop. These slaves, known as "those who live apart," did not have to live in their master's household but owed him a certain percentage of their earnings. In appearance these slaves were indistinguishable from citizens and metics, and they formed part of the craftsman class in the city. If such slaves needed additional labor for their undertakings or, in a slack season, wished to take on some temporary job for which they were qualified, they would go to a particular district in Athens known as Colonos Misthios where, as at a labor market, workers—free, metic, and slave, skilled and unskilled—could be hired.[49] It is probable that the varied types of workers needed for some of the great building projects were hired there by contractors.

In addition to the wide use of slaves by citizens and metics, the state also took advantage of this cheap and useful form of labor. Slaves were widely employed in the government-owned quarries, in the making and repairing of roads, and in the cleaning of streets, but these workers, rather than being owned by the state, were frequently, if not always, a labor force provided by various contractors, whether citizen or metic. It is known that at times 20,000 to 30,000 slaves worked in the state-controlled silver mines of Laurium, but these unfortunates were probably entirely the chattels of contractors who had bid for the privilege of exploiting certain sections of the mining regions. The famous police force, the Scythian archers, were definitely slaves purchased and cared for by the state. It is interesting to observe that these slaves, possibly some 300 in number, could on occasion compel obedience from the proud citizens. From the point of view of the functioning of the government, the most important state slaves were the large numbers selected for their intelligence who served as governmental clerks of various sorts. These underlings formed what one can call the civil service at Athens, and because of their intelligence and experience they were of tremendous service to the frequently inexperienced citizens appointed by lot to serve in governmental posts previously largely unfamiliar to them.

There is no evidence that the large number of slaves was a threat in this noncapitalistic world to the job possibilities of the poorer citizens, but it is obvious that the easy availability of slaves made life simpler and pleasanter for Athenians of moderate and affluent circumstances. Without the presence of slaves and probably of temporarily hired free "servants," average Athenians could not have allotted so much time to participation in the government and intellectuals could not have devoted themselves so unreservedly to the realms of thought. A scholar has characterized the situation aptly by remarking, "One aspect of Greek history, in short, is the advance, hand in hand, of freedom *and* slavery."[50] The attitude of the Athenians towards slavery was unreflective. They accepted the institution as a fact of life, as their ancestors also had done. A few lines have been preserved from poets and sophists revealing that they at least realized the cruelty and injustice of slavery, but no reformers appeared to challenge the institution. People subconsciously knew that their prized way of life would collapse if slavery were abolished. To them slaves were chattels, but the fact that they were human chattels raised ethical and emotional questions. The subject is too technical to be discussed here, but Athenian law did take cognizance of the problems raised by the presence of thousands of human chattels throughout the land. Defenders of Athens naturally tend to soften the unpleasant fact that slavery was a basic part of that remarkable civilization, and often emphasize the humane treatment of slaves. The orators, in particular, give many insights into the treatment of Athenian slaves, both brutal and kindly, but not enough is known of the plight of slaves elsewhere to make an informed comparison possible.

The attitude of the slaves themselves is only too evident. Manumission was a constant hope. Those slaves "living apart" always tried to save enough money from the jobs at which they worked to buy their freedom. Slaves were sometimes rewarded with freedom in return for some great service, and manumission was frequently stipulated in the master's will. The manumitted slave acquired the status of a metic, but his freedom of action was usually hampered by obligations that he still owed to the master's family. A slave naturally thought of the possibilities of escape from the land of his slavery. Before the outbreak of the Peloponnesian War Pericles complained of the encouragement the Megarians offered to runaway Athenian slaves. Thucydides (7.27.5) discloses the passion of slaves to escape when he remarks that in the years following the Spartan occupation of Decelea in 413, more than 20,000 slaves, a great part of them artisans, escaped. Many of these probably also fled from the hell of the Laurium mines. Escape from the land of their bondage was no easy task for slaves far away from the lands of their origin. Since a historian (*Hellenica Oxyrhynchia,* 12.4) reports that following the Peloponnesian War the Thebans were unusually prosperous, the natural inference is that most of these escaping slaves succeeded only in exchanging Athenian slavery for Theban slavery.

11

The Peloponnesian War

THE PELOPONNESIAN War broke out in 431 and dominated Greek history for twenty-seven years until the capitulation of Athens in 404. Since the chief source for this devastating conflict is Thucydides, generally recognized as one of the world's great historians, a few comments are necessary as introduction to this man and his work. The scholarly literature on Thucydides and his philosophy of history is enormous and extremely varied in points of view. At the beginning of this brief discussion it will be well to emphasize the obvious, but not always realized, fact that in the last analysis the interpretation of the war and of the motives of the belligerents which has prevailed since antiquity is almost entirely based on his judgments. It can be said of Thucydides more than of most historians that, through his criteria for the inclusion or exclusion of material, by his organization of subject matter, and by his choice of what to emphasize or not to emphasize, he "created" the history of the period about which he wrote. It should be a sobering thought to all, and especially to those who will tolerate no criticism of Thucydides, that if his history had been lost and in its place there had been preserved the work of an equally gifted and dramatic writer, but one with a totally different political, social, and intellectual outlook, the picture of Greece in the Periclean and post-Periclean ages might diverge greatly from the one made canonical by Thucydides.

Little information is available about the career of Thucydides, his social and political attitudes, or his intellectual growth beyond what can be gleaned from his writings.[1] He was born about 460 into a family which seemingly had kinship ties with both Cimon and Thucydides, son of Melesias, the two great conservative opponents of Pericles. Despite this heritage, it is clear from the first two books of his history that he rebelled against the conservative tradition and fell under the charismatic spell of Pericles. Thucydides reached manhood when Pericles was at the height of his powers and Athens was in its so-called Golden Age—the period in which Athenian hegemony was changing to empire; in which the city, with its harbor, Piraeus, was becoming the economic and intellectual center of the Greek world; in which wonders of architecture and sculpture were being erected on the Acropolis; and in which Sophocles, Euripides, and the forerunners of Aristophanes were producing their dramatic works at the festivals. To this city, renowned for its political, economic, and intellectual prestige, men from all over the Greek world were constantly flocking, impelled sometimes by political necessity and sometimes by the economic or intellectual opportunities. Of these visitors to Athens by far the most interesting were the men called sophists, those skilled in teaching. The impression made by these sophists on the intellectual life of the times was profound. Endless discussion has been and still should be devoted to these teachers, but here only a few remarks can be made to emphasize their influence on Thucydides.

It is hard to form a clear picture of the sophists, both because their writings are extant only in miserable fragments and also because Plato, believing with religious fervor in absolutes, found their relativist teachings insidious and demoralizing. The sophists produced a revolutionary change in Greek thinking, one which is often compared with the enlightenment of the eighteenth century. The ideas they introduced resulted primarily from the changing conditions in the Greek world. Of these changes the most important was the current wide prevalence of democracy, not only in Athens but in Syracuse and elsewhere in the west and in various parts of the Aegean world. To participate actively in the democratic process, a man had to learn to be an effective speaker in the council, assembly and law courts. The sophists, no matter what their individual differences, were all interested in rhetoric, the art of persuasion, and in their instruction they tried to prepare men to play a meaningful role in the affairs of state by teaching them "to think, to speak, to act."

The sophists came from many parts of the Greek world; as itinerant teachers they traveled widely, although Athens, because of its glamor and wealth, was a favorite destination. As intelligent, well-traveled men, they naturally were cosmopolitan in their thinking, an outlook quite different from the parochialism of the individual states. Familiar with the diverse customs of many places, they were impressed by the varieties of the man-made customs and laws which they encountered, and they developed the idea of the contrast between the variable man-made pronouncements, the *nomoi,* and the characteristics which seemed inherent in nature, *physis.* A partial quotation from the sophist Antiphon illustrates the point vividly: "The edicts of the laws are imposed artificially, but those of nature are compulsory. And the edicts of the laws are arrived at by consent, not by natural growth, whereas those of nature are not a matter of consent. So, if the man who transgresses the legal code evades those who have agreed to these edicts, he avoids both disgrace and penalty; otherwise not. But if a man violates against possibility any of the laws which are implanted in nature, even if he evades all men's detection, the ill is no less, and even if all see, it is no greater.

For he is not hurt on account of an opinion, but because of truth."[2]

It is hardly strange that such men were skeptical of accepted absolutes, particularly in the field of religion—the Inherited Conglomerate, as it has brilliantly been termed,[3] that is, the congeries of beliefs and superstitions of different ages which, despite their contradictions and irrationalities, have been welded into sacred conventions. Protagoras, the greatest of the sophists, openly expressed his agnosticism by saying: "About the gods, I am not able to know whether they exist or do not exist, nor what they are like in form; for the factors preventing knowledge are many: the obscurity of the subject and the shortness of human life." Another fragment of Protagoras, hard to interpret because of lack of context, is "Man is the measure of all things," which certainly signifies the liberation of man from the bonds of arbitrary dogmas. Ideas such as these, undoubtedly propounded with fitting eloquence, impressed many men, including Pericles, Thucydides, and Euripides, but they outraged the conventional conservatives, who were dismayed that their sons, seduced from family influences and the old conception of education based on physical training and music (the whole domain of the Muses), were being exposed to such seemingly insidious and immoral notions.[4]

In their efforts to teach their pupils to speak persuasively, the sophists trained them to analyze the evidence about a particular problem and to learn how to argue effectively both sides of a case. This method of presenting *antilogies* led the enemies of the new type of instruction to claim that the goal of the sophists was to teach how to make the worse cause better,[5] an accusation which has lingered down through the ages despite the obvious fact that the method employed was essential to any intelligent debate. In their instruction the sophists placed much emphasis on arguments based on notions of probability and on the opposition between the claims of conventional law and custom (*nomos*) and the law of nature (*physis*). It is probable that in their thinking about *physis* they were applying to human conduct the concept of fixed natural law which the earlier Ionian philosophers and physicists had associated with the universe. With the arguments based on probability the sophists, following the generic way of thinking of the Greeks, concluded that, just as an individual's actions can often be predicted, so also can the reactions of a particular class of people.[6]

Notions such as these combined with the argument from expediency, which seems to be endemic in governments at all times despite frequent appeals to standards of justice and honor, became part of Thucydides' historical thinking, as is evident from his work as a whole but especially in the speeches, usually grouped in pairs. In these speeches the argument from expediency and the argument that it is the law of nature for the strong to dominate the weak appear frequently. In such passages Thucydides accepts the instinct of the strong to increase their power as a universally acknowledged fact. As has been well said, he apparently assumed that relations between states were governed by no conceptions of justice as conditions within a state were supposed to be, an assumption which is responsible for what has been called his "moral bleakness."[7]

Another strong influence on Thucydides, in addition to the sophists and his daily observation of a powerful government in operation, was the current development of scientific writing, particularly what is called the "Hippocratic" literature. These medical writings fostered his probably innate passion to assemble and sift evidence as thoroughly as possible in the search for truth and to find, when possible, a cause and effect relationship. These intellectual influences, all tending to release man from subjection to the "Inherited Conglomerates," led Thucydides to believe that the universe operates on rational principles. Inexplicable phenomena, like the plague, whose occurrence frustrates man's rational plans he attributes to fortune—*tyche*. *Tyche* is not divine, for there is no hint of divine intervention in the pages of his work, but rather a concept to account for the occasional presence of the unpredictable in a world otherwise rationally predictable.

In his first chapter Thucydides states that he began writing the history of the war between the Peloponnesians and the Athenians from its initial outbreak, because he foresaw that it would have a momentous effect on the Greeks. The first phase of this war ended in 421 with the Peace of Nicias. The peace, however, was only an uneasy truce, and before long full-scale war was resumed. In a second preface (5.26), inserted in the history after his account of the Peace of Nicias and the alliance made between Athens and Sparta, Thucydides argues that the ten years' war, the treacherous truce, and the subsequent fighting all formed part of one war, lasting for twenty-seven years until the fall of Athens. Since he mentions the capitulation of Athens, it is obvious that this preface was not written before 404. He remarks in this passage that the same Thucydides *also* wrote the history of the period following the Peace of Nicias. This statement implies that by the time he began to write of the events subsequent to 421 he had already composed a history of the ten years' war, often called the Archidamian War from the name of the Spartan king. These observations should suffice to call attention to some of the problems concerning the period or the periods during which Thucydides composed his work. If he had written an account—or only a rough draft—of the Archidamian War before he had decided that the period 431–404 embraced just one war, it is obvious that some of his ideas about the ten years' war must have changed after he had reached the conclusion that it was not a separate entity, but part of a larger whole. In addition, if one remembers that there is a reference to the year 404 in book 2 and also in the second preface and that, probably because of death, Thucydides did not carry his history beyond 411, it should not require much imagination to sense the existence of many problems concerning the dates at which the various parts of the history were written. These are largely matters of historiography, but, since Thucydides is the chief source for the period, they also affect history. Clearly his views and judgments must have changed as he grew older and as a result of the memorable events in the period of 431 to 399, at which date he apparently was still alive. Any reader of Thucydides—and a student of Greek history in particular—must constantly bear in mind that it makes a great difference for the understanding of the historian and of the history of the fifth century whether a particular passage reflects the judgment of the younger or the older Thucydides.

Two biographical facts about Thucydides deserve emphasis. In 424 he was one of the ten *strategoi* and for reasons which are obscure he failed to prevent Amphipolis from falling to the Spartan Brasidas. Regarding this episode he writes (5.26): "It was also my fate to be an exile from my country for twenty years after my command at Amphipolis; and being present with both parties, and more especially with the Peloponnesians by reason of my exile, I had leisure to observe affairs somewhat particularly." Twenty years of exile, which were spent partly among the enemies of Athens and partly, probably, on his estates in Thrace, certainly contributed to the detached and objective attitude for which his history is noted. The second point to emphasize is that Thucydides, like many a Greek aristocrat, had contempt for the lower classes. He could idealize Athenian democracy as it existed under Pericles when "what was nominally a democracy was becoming in his [Pericles'] hands government by the first citizen," but once Pericles was dead and the so-called excesses of democracy began to occur, the conservative, if not oligarchic, sympathies of Thucydides show through his famed objectivity. This fact, although minimized by many scholars, obviously has a bearing on Thucydides' attitude to the Athenian empire and to "low-class" leaders like Cleon. Objective as he tried to be, he could not completely emancipate himself from being influenced, at least subconsciously, by the prejudices of those of his social circle.[8]

Before turning to Thucydides' account of the causes of the Peloponnesian War, it is necessary to speak briefly about his method of work. He had a passion for factual accuracy and scorn for those who accepted uncritically the easy and popular account of events. His own words are (1.22): "With reference to the narrative of events, far from permitting myself to derive it from the first source that came to hand, I did not even trust my own impressions, but it rests partly on what I saw myself, partly on what others saw for me, the accuracy of the report being always tried by the most severe and detailed tests possible. My conclusions have cost me some labor from the want of coincidence between accounts of the same occurrences by different eye-witnesses, arising sometimes from imperfect memory, sometimes from undue partiality for one side or the other."

Even more interesting are Thucydides' statements about his policy with regard to the speeches included in his history. "With references to the speeches in this history, some were delivered before the war began, others while it was going on; some I heard myself, others I got from various quarters; it was in all cases difficult to carry them word for word in one's memory, so my habit has been to make the speakers say what was in my opinion demanded of them by the various occasions, of course adhering as closely as possible to the general sense (or main thesis) of what they really said." Needless to say, Thucydides' remarks about the speeches have been interpreted in widely different ways, from the traditionalist view that the speeches were largely verbatim reports of what was actually said to the skeptical view that they were free inventions of the historian. On the whole it seems reasonable to assume that speeches such as the three of Pericles and also others delivered at Athens prior to the war and in its early years reflect at least the sense of the words actually spoken, as interpreted by Thucydides. With speeches delivered elsewhere than in Athens or in Athens after Thucydides' banishment, skepticism is certainly permissible, and probably desirable. One can be certain, however, that Thucydides put into the mouth of each speaker what he thought the occasion called for. Thus, even though the speeches may reproduce badly what was really said, they represent what an astute student of politics thought should have been said on the two sides of the debate. It is quite probable, then, that Thucydides provides a more penetrating analysis of the issues at stake than the actual words of the speakers, presumably not as profound students as the historian, would have furnished. It is necessary to remember, therefore, that the points of view expressed may reflect the ideas and prejudices of Thucydides more than those of the historical speakers.

A DISCUSSION of the causes of the Peloponnesian War will best begin with a quotation from the end of Thucydides' introduction (1.23.4–6): "The Athenians and the Peloponnesians began it [the war] by breaking the thirty years' truce which had been established after the conquest of Euboea. As to why they broke it I have set forth first the complaints and disagreements [*aitiai* and *diaphorai*] so that no one may ever have to seek why so great a war arose for the Hellenes. For the truest cause [*prophasis,* an often ambiguous word which can mean the real or the alleged cause], but least publicized, I consider to be the fact that the Athenians, becoming great and alarming the Lacedaemonians, forced them into war. But the complaints openly expressed on both sides, as a result of which they broke the truce and began the war, were these."

Thucydides treats two examples of complaints and disagreements, both of which involved Corinth, at some length. Corinth's colony Corcyra towards the end of the seventh century had established a colony, Epidamnus (the later Roman Dyrrachium), on the Illyrian coast. Following ancient practice the actual founder (*ktistēs*) came from the original mother city, Corinth. Like so many Greek cities, Epidamnus was plagued with hostility between the few and the many. In 435 this struggle resulted in the expulsion of the few, who promptly joined with the neighboring barbarians in plundering the inhabitants of the city by land and sea. The latter, hard pressed, appealed for help to Corcyra, but without success, and then to Corinth. Corinth, which had long resented what it considered the insolent attitude of its colony Corcyra, agreed to send help, but the fleet which it dispatched was badly defeated by the Corcyrean navy. Corinth, now worried that its influence along the western coast of Greece was being undermined, spent the years 434 and 433 in preparing a powerful fleet with which to humble its intransigent colony. This alarmed the Corcyreans, who realized that, because of their previous policy of avoiding entangling alliances, they had no one to support them in the face of the threatening danger. Accordingly—probably in June 433—they sent envoys to Athens to try to negotiate an alliance. The Corinthians, on hearing of this, also sent ambassadors to Athens in the hope of preventing the alliance.

Thucydides presents the arguments of the respective envoys in the first speeches included in his history. The Corcyrean stressed the imminence of war between the Peloponnesians and Athens and argued that Athens should secure for itself the Corcyrean fleet and an ally situated strategically on the route to Italy and Sicily. The Corinthian, while not denying the danger of war, maintained that the threat could be lessened if Athens did not act too provocatively by interfering in what was strictly a Corinthian-Corcyrean quarrel. After the envoys had retired, the Athenian assembly opened debate on the issue. At first the inclination was to accept the Corinthian advice, but at a second meeting of the assembly—presumably an extraordinary one—the Corcyrean arguments prevailed, and particularly the conviction that war with a naval power like Corinth was a strong probability. In this immediate context Thucydides does not mention the feverish shipbuilding activity of the Corinthians and some of their allies in the two years since their humiliating defeat by the Corcyreans, but this knowledge must have been a determining factor in the Athenian decision. Although Pericles is not mentioned by name at this point in the sources, it is reasonable to assume that he carried the assembly with him at the second meeting and was responsible for the forming of a defensive alliance with Corcyra.

The defensive aspect of the alliance was clearly a subterfuge, as is evident from Thucydides' wording (1.44.1): "They made a defensive alliance to go to the aid of one another's territory, if anyone should go against Corcyra or Athens or their respective allies." Since the Athenians were aware that the Corinthians were on the point of launching a large expedition with the aim of overpowering Corcyra, they were using the defensive alliance to try to shield themselves from the charge of violating the Thirty Years' Truce. The tactics remind one of a favorite device employed by Rome of allying itself with a state which it knew an enemy, against which it was seeking justification for going to war, was about to attack.

The Athenians at first dispatched only ten ships with instructions not to go into action unless the Corinthians should attempt a landing on Corcyra. In the big naval engagement which occurred in August or September 433 off the Sybota islands near the southeastern tip of Corcyra, however, these ships were ultimately drawn into the fighting and, to quote Thucydides (1.49.7), "it came to this point of necessity that the Corinthians and Athenians laid their hands on each other." The arrival of twenty more Athenian ships frustrated the advantage which the Corinthians had gained in the battle. Consequently the Corinthians sailed for home, not surprisingly convinced that the Athenians had violated the terms of the peace of 446/5.

The Corcyra episode was followed almost immediately by trouble in Chalcidice. The city of Potidaea on the northern end of the promontory of Pallene was a Corinthian colony but also a subject ally of Athens. The Athenians, fearing that Corinth might try to sow the seeds of revolt in the Chalcidic region in retaliation for the Athenian interference on behalf of Corcyra, ordered the Potidaeans to destroy the southern section of their wall, to furnish hostages, to dismiss the Corinthian magistrates, and to receive no more in the future. In this year, 432, the tribute of Potidaea, which had been only six talents, is recorded as fifteen talents. Whether this large increase was first imposed in this year or on the occasion of the assessment of 434 is unknown, but the figure gives further evidence for the tension between Potidaea and Athens. This tension may have been increased by the possibility that it was through Potidaea that Corinth was obtaining the necessary Macedonian timber for its shipbuilding. The situation was complicated by the activities of Perdiccas, the king of the Macedonians. He had been an ally of Athens, but Athenian support to his brother and cousin, who were rivals to his throne, naturally turned him into an enemy, and he exerted every effort to foment rebellion against Athens among the cities of Chalcidice. The Potidaeans at first tried to placate the Athenians, but failing in this, they sought help from Corinth and Sparta. Thucydides (1.58.1) states that the "authorities" of the Spartans promised to invade Attica if the Athenians attacked Potidaea. Since the promise was not fulfilled, one wonders whether by "authorities" Thucydides was referring only to those magistrates who belonged to the Spartan "war party." The Corinthian response was to send troops to assist in the defense of Potidaea. Before the end of the year 432 most of the Chalcidic communities had revolted from Athens, and an Athenian army, including Socrates and the young Alcibiades, was besieging Potidaea, among whose defenders were Corinthian troops.

By the autumn of 432, Corinth, thoroughly exasperated by Athenian interference in behalf of Corcyra and the investment of its colony Potidaea, summoned representatives of the Peloponnesian League to Sparta and bitterly denounced Athenian aggression before the Spartan assembly. The speech which Thucydides (1.68–71) assigns to the Corinthian envoy is a brilliant example of inflammatory rhetoric and contains a masterly contrast of the differing national characteristics of the Athenian and the Spartan—the one restless, aggressive, tireless, always attempting some new project; the other slow to act, overly cautious, reactionary, and unimaginative. Some Athenian ambassadors who happened to be in Sparta on other business, when they heard the outcry against Athens, received permission to address the assembly. The speech of their spokesman did not attempt to answer any of the specific charges, but restricted itself to an explanation and justification of the growth of the Athenian empire and to a warning to the Peloponnesians not to embark upon war hastily and heedlessly. After the Athenian had finished his remarks, the Spartans dismissed all foreigners and proceeded to consider the issue among themselves. The elderly king Archidamus advised caution and emphasized that the Peloponnesians needed an interval of two or three years for making the necessary preparations to undertake war with an imperial and naval power like Athens. His speech was followed by a brief and belligerent harangue delivered by one of the ephors. After his talk, the ephor (Sthenelaidas) put the matter to the vote of the assembly, but stating that he could not decide which was the louder acclamation (the Spartan method of deciding an issue was by acclamation rather than by vote) he ordered all those who felt that Athens had broken the treaty to go to one place and those of contrary opinion to another. This device, obviously intended to shame the Spartans into voting for war, led to a verdict by a large majority that Athens had been guilty of breaking the treaty of 446/5. The Spartans thereupon made arrangements for the convening of delegates from all the members of the Peloponnesian League so that war should be undertaken, if this seemed the best policy, only after all the allies had participated in the deliberations.

As this summary of the complaints and disagreements leading to the war demonstrates, Thucydides' emphasis on the paramount role of Corinth in protesting Athenian aggression does not seem to harmonize with his statement that the "truest cause" of the war was Sparta's alarm at the growth of Athenian power. If one keeps in mind, however, that the Corinthians were members of the Peloponnesian League and that Sparta's power was based on its hegemony of this league, the apparent inconsistency in Thucydides' narrative largely fades away. In the episodes involving the Corinthians, the Athenians, through their success, had increased their power and frustrated a member of the Peloponnesian League. In their complaints to the Spartan assembly the Corinthians had threatened that, unless Sparta took action, they might be forced to seek alliance elsewhere. Was this a threat of possible alliance with Argos, or even with Athens? Since Spartan power and prestige depended on the proper functioning of its league, the discontent of Corinth and of the non-Peloponnesian ally, Megara, which will be discussed below, could have led to a serious breach in the effectiveness of the Peloponnesian League. The prevailing forces in the Spartan government, therefore, despite contrary feelings of some Spartans, considered it essential to appease exasperated allies in order to preserve the solidarity of the league, for any weakening of Spartan hegemony would have merely contributed to the continually growing influence of the enemy Athens. In conclusion to his account of the speeches before the Spartan assembly, Thucydides (1.88) states the Spartan position very clearly: "The Lacedaemonians voted that the treaty had been broken and that war must be declared, not so much because they were persuaded by the arguments of their allies, as because they feared the growth of the power of the Athenians, seeing most of Hellas already subject to them." And then he proceeds to give his valuable account of Athenian activity in the

Pentecontaetia, adducing as one of his reasons for including this digression (1.97.2) that "the history of these events contains an explanation of the growth of the Athenian empire."

Admiration for the glories of Periclean Athens, brilliantly idealized in the funeral oration delivered by Pericles in 431 as reported by Thucydides, has so dominated man's thinking throughout the centuries that there has been a general tendency to minimize any Athenian responsibility for the disastrous and futile Peloponnesian War. This attitude is revealed in the very name assigned to the war, a name, incidentally, never employed by Thucydides himself. From the point of view of the Peloponnesians, obviously, the war should have been called the Attic or the Athenian War. If one reasons in Thucydidean terms, thinking of the "law of nature" according to which the stronger always tries to dominate the weaker, one will probably be reluctant to brand any *one* state with the guilt of starting the war. Athenian power had been growing since the days of the Persian Wars and, despite certain reverses, was still imbued with this instinct for expansion in the 430s. Spartan hegemony had been widely recognized at the time of the Persian invasions but, largely through the evils of its social system and the aggressive energy of Athens, had been reduced by the 430s to the hegemony of the Peloponnesian League, a leadership now threatened unless Sparta took action to satisfy the bitter enmity of its allies Corinth and Megara to Athens.

It will be useful to list here, even at the cost of some repetition, the foreign activity, whether aggressive or not, of the two great powers in the years following the Thirty Years' Peace of 446/5. Certain factions in Sparta and in the Peloponnesian League were frustrated by the terms of that peace, thinking that a favorable opportunity to humiliate Athens had been lost—an attitude which led to the exile of King Pleistoanax. Some scholars think that within five or six years of the peace Sparta was planning aggressive action against Athens by assisting the Samians in their revolt from the Athenians.[9] No information is available concerning the type of aid Sparta was advocating—dispatch of a fleet to Samos, which seems unlikely, or an invasion of Attica? The only specific reference to this Spartan plan is contained in Thucydides' rendering of the speech of the Corinthians directed against the Corcyreans at Athens in 433, in which they claim that they caused the Peloponnesians to refuse to support the Samians (1.40.5). It is characteristic of the unwavering faith placed in Thucydides that this statement, found in a speech in which the Corinthians were using every method to influence the Athenians in their favor, is accepted without question as a fact.

There are several strange aspects about this proposed plan of the Spartans. No certain reference to it exists in any other extant source, not even in Thucydides' relatively full treatment of the revolt of Samos in his sketch of the history of the Pentecontaetia. Also Sparta, as hegemon, was careful not to call a meeting of the delegates from the Peloponnesian League unless it was convinced that its proposal would be supported by a majority. On this occasion, if the account is factual, it would have suffered the humiliation of being outvoted by its allies. Two other possible allusions to the Spartan plan do not carry much weight. In the inscription (M&L, no. 56) recording the Athenian treaty with Samos in 439/8, the first fourteen lines, although hopelessly damaged, may contain part of the word "Peloponnesians." It would take considerable ingenuity to explain why the Peloponnesians, who did not participate in the war, should be listed in this treaty between Athens and Samos. The other possible allusion is contained in Pericles' speech to the Athenians in the fall of 432 in which he makes the general statement that the Lacedaemonians both formerly and now plot against them. This charge against the Spartans is a natural one to find in a speech delivered on the eve of war, but it cannot be proved that there is an allusion to Spartan support for Samos. At the risk of being heretical, one seems to have some reason to question the statement made by the Corinthians in their speech. Other cases of Peloponnesian and Spartan aggression have been included in the discussion just given of the complaints and disagreements leading to the war and of the unfulfilled promise of the Spartan "authorities" to aid Potidaea.

The foreign activity of the Athenians in this period was, as might be expected, more extensive than that of the Spartans. When the necessity of accepting the Thirty Years' Peace in 446/5 had frustrated whatever plans Athens had had for an Athenian hegemony in central Greece, thereafter Pericles concentrated on strengthening the maritime empire. Samos was crushed in 439, and in 437 Athens strengthened its position in the north by founding the colony of Amphipolis. Thucydides reveals that sometime before 432 Athens had been trying to expand its influence in the northern area by supporting the rivals of Perdiccas, the king of the Macedonians. Pericles' Black Sea expedition, usually dated about 437, added to Athenian prestige in that important region and probably had the additional aim of putting the alliance with Byzantium on a firmer basis. Certainly by the beginning of the Peloponnesian War, Athenian dominance was almost complete in the Aegean and Black Sea areas. Athens' activities had also been directed westward. In the 450s and early 440s Athens had made alliances with Segesta and Leontini in Sicily and with Rhegium on the toe of Italy, and about 443 it established the "Panhellenic" colony of Thurii on the instep of Italy. Naupactus, guarding the western entrance and exit of the Corinthian Gulf, Athens had been allowed to keep by the terms of the Thirty Years' Peace. At an unknown date, probably in the early 430s (although some scholars advocate the year 432), the Athenians, through their general Phormio, by aiding the Amphilochians and Acarnanians on the west coast of Greece against some Ambraciots, formerly from Ambracia, a Corinthian colony, had acquired the Acarnanians as allies (2.68). In 433, by forming an alliance with Corcyra, Athens had frustrated Corinth's efforts against that island. Athenian control of or influence in Naupactus, Acarnania, and Corcyra, and its alliances in Sicily and Italy, two of which—those with Rhegium and Leontini—were renewed in 433/2 (M&L, nos. 63, 64), must have caused the Corinthians to wonder if they would not ultimately be pushed out of western waters as they had been from the Aegean.

In any discussion of Athenian foreign activity in this period, the Megarian decree requires more consideration than apparently Thucydides thought, and some modern scholars believe, it merits. Thucydides mentions the problem several times. The first possible (or probable) allusion to the subject is in the speech of the Corinthians at Athens in June or July 433 in reply to the Corcyreans (1.42.2), although the reference to the suspicion existing because of Athenian behavior to Megara is rendered ambiguous by the presence of the word "formerly." Thucydides' first specific reference to the decree occurs in his account of the gathering, at the urging of Corinth, of delegates from various allies at Sparta in the fall of 432 (1.67). At the meeting of the Spartan assembly many allies brought complaints against Athens, among them the Megarians who mentioned many other disagreements and in particular that by an Athenian decree they were debarred from the harbors in the Athenian empire and from the Attic agora. Thucydides (1.139) refers to the decree again when, after the delegates of the Peloponnesian League had voted for war, he mentions a Spartan embassy to Athens which stated, among other things, that war could be prevented if the Megarian decree were revoked. The Athenians, in rejecting this proposal, accused the Megarians of cultivating the sacred and undefined land (between Eleusis and Megara) and of harboring their escaping slaves. This Spartan deputation was followed by another which merely stated that there could be peace if the Athenians would leave the Hellenes autonomous. The Athenians thereupon held an assembly in the hope of reaching a decision on the issues facing them. Some argued that war was necessary, while others maintained that the Megarian decree should not be permitted to stand in the way of peace. At this point Thucydides introduces Pericles and reports his speech (1.140–144), the gist of which was that there should be no concessions to the Peloponnesians. Concerning the

Megarian problem, Pericles predicted that if the Athenians yielded on that issue they would immediately be presented with some greater demand. He recommended that the Spartan envoys be dismissed with the reply that "we will allow the Megarians to use agora and harbors if the Lacedaemonians suspend their alien acts (*xenelasia*) in favor of us and our allies."

Thucydides' treatment of the Megarian issue is strange. He does not develop it in a continuous narrative as he does the circumstances involving Corcyra and Potidaea. Nevertheless after reporting Pericles' speech, in which there are several references to the Megarian decree, he writes, "These were the complaints and disagreements existing between the rival powers before the war, arising immediately from the affair at Epidamnus and Corcyra," thus implying that the problems concerning Corcyra, Potidaea, and Megara all belonged in the same category. By citing the Spartan statement that war could be avoided if the Megarian decree were revoked, he shows that he realized the importance of the dispute. His comments, however, are disjointed, and if Plutarch (*Pericles*, 29–32) is correct in mentioning more than one decree, as scholars generally agree, it is clear that Thucydides for some reason has compressed and omitted data concerning the Megarian situation.

The earliest extant references to the Megarian decree are in two comedies of Aristophanes, the *Acharnians,* produced in 425, lines 509–539, and the *Peace,* produced in 421, lines 603–624. To try to extract history from the brilliant fantasies of Aristophanes is a perilous task, and the account in the *Peace* that Pericles started the Peloponnesian War to divert the people from prosecuting him as they had his friend Pheidias is best ignored. Most scholars, however, would probably agree that the passage in the *Acharnians* depicts a steady progression of episodes—sycophants denouncing Megarian products in Attica, the stealing of a Megarian whore followed by the retaliatory stealing of two of Aspasia's whores, Pericles thundering out the Megarian decree, the Megarians gradually suffering from hunger, the Spartans, at Megarian request, asking for a revocation of the decree, the repeated Athenian refusals, and then the clattering of arms. The exact date for the Megarian decree—or decrees—is unknown, although it is usually assigned to 433 or 432. There is no satisfactory explanation for the trouble the Megarians had in disposing of their products; it could have been nothing more than continuous attempts to avoid the payment of customs duties.

In the Greek world, as the years passed by, the picture presented by Aristophanic humor and the known fact that Pericles had refused to rescind the Megarian decree fostered the belief among some that it had been the decree itself which was responsible for the war. In 390 Andocides (3.8) states that it was the Megarians who caused Athens to go to war, and the same tradition is reflected in the fourth-century historian Ephorus and centuries later in Plutarch's *Life of Pericles*. Modern scholars, in their efforts to analyze the causes of the war, influenced at least subconsciously in their thinking by these lines of the *Acharnians*, usually admit that the Megarian decree by excluding the Megarians from trade with Athens and its empire would have caused great economic hardships for them. The recent lengthy argument that the motive of the decree was religious in order to punish the Megarians for encroaching on land sacred to the goddesses of Eleusis[10] is too fanciful to be considered seriously. In fact, the true reasons for the Megarian decree remain a mystery. Thucydides obviously knew the answer, but his succinct remarks yield no explanation. His brevity may have been his way of showing contempt for the vicious rumors which were circulating, but, since his account reveals that the issue was important, the suspicion lingers that he may have deliberately minimized Pericles' responsibility.

In the speech delivered to the Athenians following the last embassy of the Spartans, Pericles showed his intransigence when he said that Athens would revoke the Megarian decree if the Spartans would not enforce their expulsion of foreigners (*xenelasia*) against the Athenians and their allies. Even the hastiest glance at the situation in the Peloponnesus in 432 would reveal how utterly unconciliatory this proposal was. The iron curtain policy of the Spartans was deplorable, but it was a long-standing custom, considered essential for the maintenance of their closed society and their oppressive social system. To throw open Sparta and Messenia to the Athenians and their allies when war was in the air would have been a betrayal of the system under which Spartans had lived for generations and an open invitation to violent internal disturbances abetted by enemy agents. Pericles' implication that there was an analogy between the recent Athenian exclusion of Megarians and the old Spartan custom of *xenelasia* may have been clever demagoguery in Athens, but it was a sneering proposal which any Spartiate would have considered an offensive and officious insult to the Spartan state. The speech was defiant and breathed the pride and self-confidence so characteristic of Periclean Athens. The Athenians voted as Pericles recommended and told the Spartans that they would do nothing on dictation, but were ready to submit all complaints to arbitration. This willingness to arbitrate gave Athens a moral advantage, which the Spartans later realized (Thucydides, 7.18.2).

Despite Thucydides' extensive discussion of the causes of the war, many unknowns remain. For instance, although the Megarian decree is mentioned, nothing is said about the many other "disagreements" with Athens which the Megarians reported to the Spartan assembly. One matter on which Thucydides is surprisingly silent is the problem of Aegina. When, at the urging of the Corinthians, allies came to Sparta in the fall of 432 to lodge their complaints against Athens, Thucydides (1.67.2) writes, "The Aeginetans, formally unrepresented from fear of Athens, in secret proved not the least urgent of the advocates for war, asserting that they had not the autonomy guaranteed to them by the treaty." The Spartan embassy to Athens, after the Peloponnesian League had voted for war, in addition to stating that the war might be prevented if the Athenians would rescind the Megarian decree, ordered the Athenians to raise the siege of Potidaea and to let Aegina be autonomous (1.139.1). Since Aegina had been recognized in the treaty of 446/5 as tributary to Athens, this complaint presumably meant that Athens had been interfering in the internal affairs of the island. Nothing further is said about Aegina until the first year of the war (431). Thucydides writes (2.27): "During the summer the Athenians also expelled the Aeginetans with their wives and children from Aegina, charging that they not least were responsible for the war." For strategic reasons Athens decided to settle the island with its own colonists. One would like to know why the Aeginetans were "not least responsible for the war," but Thucydides gives no such information on this "eyesore of the Piraeus."

Some influential Peloponnesians, such as King Archidamus, were clearly trying at least to postpone war. One finds the strange situation that, even after Sparta and its allies had voted for war, Spartan envoys continued to go to Athens, trying to persuade or intimidate the Athenians to yield on certain points, and above all on the Megarian decree. Hence the Megarian decree did loom large and became almost a symbolic test case. Why did Pericles propose the decree, whatever its true nature was, and insist so stubbornly on its maintenance? It was obviously a provocative act at a time when talk of war was widespread. The Athenians had not forgotten how valuable Megara had been to their strategy in the fourteen-year period from 460 to 446 by providing a harbor on the Corinthian Gulf and forming a barrier against any Peloponnesian advance into central Greece. They surely knew that Megarian defection from the Spartan alliance in 460 had initiated the First Peloponnesian War, and they certainly realized that, since Megara's return to the Spartan fold in 446, Sparta was obligated to support its errant ally. Whatever motivated the decree against Megara, a hostile state since 446, if Pericles could argue that concessions to the Peloponnesians would lead to "slavery," the Peloponnesians presumably felt that acqui-

458

The Ancient Greeks

escence in the Megarian decree on their part would lead to "slavery" for them, and that the time had come when Athenian aggression must be stopped or soon it might be too late.

In this period of increasing tension, Pericles had devoted much attention to the development of Athenian financial and military resources. In 434/3, as the financial decrees of Callias (*M&L*, no. 58), best dated then, demonstrate, expenditures on the great building program on the Acropolis were curtailed—presumably in anticipation of an outbreak of war. By the spring of 431, when the Peloponnesian War formally began, Athens was fully prepared for hostilities. Pericles (Thucydides, 2.13) reported to the people that, in addition to other sources of revenue, 600 talents came in annually, mostly from the tribute of the allies; that there were 6,000 talents of coined silver in the Acropolis; and that large amounts of wealth, in the form of spoils, dedications, and the like, accumulated in the temples, could be utilized in the form of loans, if necessary. As for military forces, there were 13,000 hoplites, and also 16,000 more, from the oldest and youngest and from the metics, available for defensive duty. The cavalry numbered 1,200, including mounted archers, and the foot archers, 1,600. And, most important of all, there were 300 triremes fit for service. This thorough preparedness of the Athenians, when contrasted with the lack of preparedness on the part of the Peloponnesians emphasized by Thucydides (1.125), is clearly relevant to the question of responsibility for the war—although the Athenians would have declared that these preparations were an essential defense against hostile aggression. Thucydides, a fervent admirer of Periclean Athens, reveals that in his judgment the aggressive attitude of Athens was the ultimate cause of the war. His words could not be more explicit (2.8.4–5): "The good wishes of men made greatly for the Lacedaemonians, especially as they proclaimed themselves the liberators of Hellas . . . So general was the indignation felt against Athens, whether by those who wished to escape from its empire, or were apprehensive of being absorbed by it."

W AR BEGAN in the spring of 431, and it was precipitated by the actions of allies of Sparta and Athens rather than by those of the protagonists themselves. Thebes had long resented the refusal of Plataea to join the Boeotian League like other Boeotian communities and its insistence on remaining loyal to the alliance struck as early as 519 with Athens. A group of oligarchs in Plataea, however, who wished to increase their power by bringing Plataea into the league entered into negotiations with Thebes, which resulted in a force of a little over 300 Thebans being admitted secretly into Plataea on a dark night in the spring of 431. The

Thebans, rejecting the proposal of the oligarchs to butcher the leaders of their political enemies, issued a proclamation through a herald urging the Plataeans to join the Boeotian League. The Plataeans, terrified by the presence of the Theban soldiers, felt compelled to accept the proposal, but later in the night when they discovered how few the occupying troops were, they seized arms and in a scene of wild confusion killed or captured all the Thebans. In the morning another Theban force arrived in Plataean territory and, on learning what had happened in the town, made plans to round up the many Plataeans who, engaged in agricultural work, were living in the fields, so as to be able to exchange them against the Thebans who had been captured during the night. The Plataeans sent word to the invaders that unless they returned home immediately, without laying hands on man or beast, the Theban captives would be killed. When the Thebans had retired, the Plataeans brought in their citizens and stock from the fields and then slaughtered the prisoners, 180 in number. In the meantime the Athenians, informed of the events of the night, had sent word to the Plataeans bidding them not to execute their prisoners without instructions from Athens, but the messenger arrived after the deed had been done. The Athenians then marched to Plataea, left a garrison in the town, and took away the women, children, and least serviceable men (Thucydides, 2.1–6).

Thus a small event, possibly initiated by Thebes to eliminate any chance of a compromise between Athens and Sparta, and replete with the brutality and treachery which were to characterize the war throughout its long and sordid course, launched the great Peloponnesian War. In the Theban-Plataean episode the hatred felt by city-state for city-state blazed forth, but *stasis*—civil dissension—also played its sinister role, as it had at Epidamnus in 435 and two generations earlier at Naxos, where the spark was ignited which led to the Ionian revolt.

At the beginning of the war the Spartan allies included all the Peloponnesians except the Argives and the Achaeans, who were neutral. Actually one Achaean city, Pellene, joined Sparta at the start, and the others followed suit before long. Beyond the Peloponnesus the alliance embraced Megara on the Isthmus, the Boeotians, Phocians, and Locrians in central Greece, and along the western coast the Ambraciots, the Anactorians, and the islanders, the Leucadians, the last three being colonists of Corinth. Of these allies, only Corinth was a considerable sea power. On the Athenian side, the alliance included some 200 tributary members of the Athenian empire and also the islands of Chios and Lesbos, which still provided ships and maintained a precarious independence. In Greece proper the allies were limited to the Plataeans, the Messenians in Naupactus, most of the Acarnanians, the Thessalians on occasions, and the islanders off the west coast, the Zacynthians and the Corcyraeans (Thucydides, 2.9). Ultimately, in one way or another, a large part of the population of the ancient world played some role in the war, the Greeks and Carthaginians in the west, the Macedonians and Thracians in the north, and the Persians in the east. In view of the number of participants and of the shattering effects of the war, it is quite natural to speak of the struggle as the World War of antiquity.

After the Theban attack on Plataea, the Spartans sent word to each of their allies to send two-thirds of its military contingent to the Isthmus by a specified date in anticipation of an invasion of Attica. When the troops had assembled, Archidamus dispatched one last envoy to Athens in the hope that the realization that the Peloponnesians were already on the march might cause the city to be more inclined to yield. The Athenians, however, on the proposal of Pericles, had passed a motion to receive no embassy from the Spartans once they had marched out. The envoy, consequently, was dismissed without a hearing, and he was escorted to the frontier to prevent his entering into communication with anyone. On hearing of the failure of this mission, Archidamus led his army through the Megarid, and entering Attica from Boeotia began to attack the border fortress of Oenoe.

Meanwhile Pericles had expounded to the Athenian assembly the policy which he advocated. This was to place confidence in the fleet, keeping a tight control on their tributary allies on whose contributions the welfare of the fleet depended, and not to risk a land battle with the Peloponnesians, but to come into the city with their families and guard it. The Athenians followed his advice and began to move their property into Athens, while possessions like cattle and pack animals were transported to Euboea and other adjacent islands. Thucydides (2.16–17) emphasizes how reluctantly they abandoned their old homes, the hereditary temples, and all the rural associations, for, despite the growth of the city of Athens and of Piraeus, the majority of Athenians had always lived in the country. The problem of finding shelter for this enormous influx was obviously very great. Many took up residence in temples and shrines, and ultimately they were assigned plots between the long walls extending to Piraeus.

While the Athenians were moving from the open country to the protection of the city walls, the Peloponnesian army wasted valuable time in a futile assault on Oenoe. Archidamus' lingering at the Isthmus and the delay at Oenoe aroused considerable indignation in his army, for it was felt, probably correctly, that a prompt invasion of Attica would have found many Athenians and their property still in the fields. The Spartan king clearly was loath to push the war; presumably he hoped that the threat of a Peloponnesian invasion would cause the Athenians to be more inclined to negotiate. When no envoy was forthcoming from Athens, however, Archidamus led his troops south to Eleusis and the Thriasian Plain and then, after ravaging the region, eastward to Acharnae, the largest of the Attic *demes*, some seven miles north of Athens. Here the Peloponnesians encamped and proceeded to pillage the countryside. The sight of the enemy so near to Athens provoked anger and consternation among the citizens. Many men, particularly the young and the Acharnians, clamored that the Athenian army should march out and stop the depredations. Pericles managed to restrain them, realizing that a pitched battle with the seasoned Peloponnesian infantry would be disastrous. By means that are obscure he even prevented the assembly from meeting, for he feared that the excited citizens might vote dangerously rash proposals. He attempted to satisfy the need felt for action by frequently sending out detachments of cavalry to break up enemy raiding parties. Later he dispatched 100 ships with hoplites and archers aboard with orders to sail around the Peloponnesus and make whatever damaging descents along the coast were possible.

The Peloponnesians, because of their naval weakness, had to attack the enemy on land, and their fields of action were limited to Attica, Plataea, and later the Thracian region. Pericles' policy was to avoid confrontation with the superior enemy infantry. This meant the sacrifice of Attica, which he considered expendable because Athens could import all necessary supplies. Offensively Athens was to try to wear the enemy down by constant coastal raids. Historians have generally assumed that his policy would ultimately have been successful, but one may well question whether it would have led to anything more than a stalemate. An answer would be easier if there were more information on how dependent the Peloponnesians were on imported foodstuffs. It seems unlikely that the Athenian hit-and-run attacks could have seriously damaged the homegrown grain, since most of the cornland was not near the coast.

It is erroneous to think that Pericles advocated only a defensive policy and that it was his successors who disrupted his strategy by their passion for aggression. On the assumption, which seems legitimate, that Athenian policy was largely Periclean in 431, in 430 except for his brief suspension from office, and in 429 until he fell victim to the plague in the autumn, Athenian activity in these years, except for the ban on fighting the Peloponnesians in Attica, was definitely aggressive. In the summer of 431 a hundred ships sailed from Athens, soon to be joined by fifty Corcyrean vessels. This detachment, after raiding and circumnavigating the Peloponnesus, sailed past the entrance to the Corinthian Gulf and strengthened the Athenian-allied Acarnanians against Corinthian pressures. Its most important achievement was to win over to the Athenian alliance the large island of Cephallenia, which, in conjunction with the already allied island of Zacynthus, lay in a strategic position in relation to the Gulf of Corinth. In roughly the same period thirty other Athenian ships, with the aim of protecting Euboea and the important waterway between Euboea and the mainland from Locrian pirates, captured the town of Thronium and later fortified the desert island of Atalanta.

In the course of the same summer the Athenians expelled the Aeginetans—men, women, and children—from their island, charging that they had had large responsibility in bringing on the war (Thucydides, 2.27). For generations the Athenians had feared and hated the Aeginetans, and it is very probable that they had found the islanders reluctant tributary allies since their forced incorporation in the Delian League in 457. From a military point of view Aegina, which was soon occupied by Athenian settlers, could furnish a useful base against the Peloponnesians, but more important, probably, in Athenian thinking was the desire to keep it from falling into the control of the Peloponnesians. The banished Aeginetans were received by the Spartans, who settled them in Thyrea, a border district between the Argolid and Laconia. Here the exiles lived until their survivors were restored to their homeland by the Spartan Lysander at the end of the war.

Towards the end of this summer Pericles invaded the Megarid at the head of a very large army consisting, according to Thucydides (2.31), of 10,000 citizen and 3,000 metic hoplites, and of a great number of light armed troops. These were joined by the 100 ships which had just returned from their pillaging voyage around the Peloponnesus. The Athenians thoroughly ravaged the territory and then returned home. Thereafter, as both Thucydides (4.66) and Plutarch (*Pericles*, 30) state, the Athenians despoiled the Megarid twice a year until they captured the harbor, Nisaea, in 424. The strategic location of Megara is obvious, but the intensity and ferocity of the attacks on the Megarid suggest strongly that the motives behind the Megarian decree had been deep and passionate.

At some point in the winter of 431/0 the Athenians, following a custom which Thucydides calls ancestral but which may have been established in 465/4, held a public funeral in the Ceramicus of those who had fallen in the war. Part of the ceremony was the pronouncement over the dead of a panegyric spoken by a distinguished citizen chosen by the council and the assembly. On this occasion Pericles was selected. The speech which Thucydides (2.35–46) reports is one of the greatest documents surviving from Greek antiquity. As is the case with all the other speeches included in Thucydides' history, there is the problem here of whether the speech reflects the particular speaker or Thucydides himself. Some scholars have argued that this speech was composed by Thucydides after the fall of Athens in 404 as an epitaph on Periclean Athens. It seems more reasonable, however, to accept it as an attempt to reproduce what Pericles himself said in 431/0. Pericles was trying to emphasize to his fellow citizens at the beginning of the ordeal of the war the true greatness of Athens and, consequently, how much was at stake in the struggle. To judge from other specimens of funeral orations which have been preserved, the convention was to elaborate on the glories of Athens' past, both mythical and historical, and then to eulogize in general terms the heroism of those who were being buried on the particular occasion. Pericles, however, after a brief bow to the convention turns to the subject of the greatness of Athens, the form of government and the national habits which had produced such a phenomenon. There follows a stirring description of the democracy, the freedom of the government and the freedom enjoyed in daily life, the absence of any pressure to produce conformity, the military prowess achieved without the stultifying lifelong training imposed on the Spartans, the versatility of the Athenians capable of mastering any situation, and the civilized and cultured atmosphere which had made Athens the school of Hellas. The Athens depicted is an idealized Athens, of course, but the ideals of a nation are as important as the reality. The whole speech is suffused with a fierce pride, an ardent nationalism—the glory and bane of the city-state—and a glorified imperialism. After reading it one can understand Pericles' lofty dictum—"no concessions to the Peloponnesians"—but one can also understand why Sparta and its allies felt that an Athens so great, so tireless, and so boundlessly ambitious had to be humbled if their own identities were not to be submerged in the relentless growth of Athenian power.

Early in the summer of 430 (probably in May), the Peloponnesians with two-thirds of their forces under Archidamus invaded Attica again and began to ravage the countryside. Shortly after their arrival the plague made its first appearance in Athens. Apparently originating in Ethiopia, this pestilence spread into Egypt, Libya, and various parts of the Persian Empire in Asia, and then broke out in Piraeus whence it passed with growing intensity to Athens itself. Thucydides, a victim and survivor of the sickness, vividly describes its symptoms and course in language that clearly reveals his familiarity with the current medical writings. Despite his detailed description, imitated by later authors such as Lucretius, Vergil, Ovid, and Procopius, scholars and medical historians have been unable to identify the disease positively, partly because various epidemic fevers have numerous symptoms in common and also vary from one visitation to another, and partly because the first manifestation of a disease among people with no immunity to it is characterized by symptoms much more drastic than those prevalent among people who have become somewhat immunized. The chief suggestions have been ergotism, a severe poisoning caused by a fungus on rye—an unlikely candidate because rye was not ordinarily used for bread in classical Greece—measles, appearing for the first time and consequently devastating in its effects, bubonic plague, and typhus, perhaps the most likely.

The plague raged in Athens throughout the years 430 and 429, and then, after an abatement, recrudesced in the winter of 427/6 for another year. Thucydides states that some 4,400 from the hoplite ranks and about 300 members of the cavalry perished from the sickness in addition to an unascertainable number from the rest of the population—the young and the old, the women, metics, and slaves. It seems reasonable to assume that a quarter or even a third of the population died in agony of body and spirit amid scenes of incredible horror, aggravated by the overcrowding created by the influx of refugees within the protection of the walls. The effects of these horrors and of the feelings of blank despair on the morality of the Athenians were far-reaching and should be kept constantly in mind when one is confronted with the so-called collapse of Athenian morality, commonly ascribed to causes such as the "new breed of demagogues" and to the influence of the sophists. Thucydides (2.53–54) summarizes these effects in a memorable passage, part of which runs as follows: "Fear of gods or law of man there was none to restrain them. As for the first, they judged it to be just the same whether they worshipped them or not, as they saw all alike perishing; and for the last, no one expected to live to be brought to trial for his offenses, but each felt that a far severer sentence had been already passed upon them all and hung over their heads, and before this fell it was only reasonable to enjoy life a little. Such was the nature of the calamity, and heavily did it weigh on the Athenians; death raging within the city and devastation without."

The Peloponnesians, after ravaging Attica for about forty days, returned home. Meanwhile a hundred Athenian ships under Pericles, joined by fifty from Chios and Lesbos, sailed to the coast of the Argolid, where they raided the territory of Epidaurus but failed to take the town. Then after ravaging the land of Troezen, Halieis, and Hermione, and destroying Prasiai on the eastern coast of Laconia, they returned to the Piraeus. Somewhat later in the summer two of Pericles' fellow generals took over the command of the fleet and proceeded to Chalcidice, where they joined in the siege of Potidaea. The only significant result of this expedition was that the Athenian reinforcements spread the plague among their fellow citizens who were already investing the city.

As the summer of 430 drew to a close, the Athenians, who by then had experienced two Peloponnesian raids and the terrors of the pestilence, became so despondent that they sent envoys to Sparta concerning the possibilities of peace. One would like to know who sponsored these peace feelers, but Thucydides maintains a stony silence. When nothing came of the embassy, the people vented their anger and frustrations on Pericles as the cause of all their tribulations. Pericles, realizing that their morale had to be restored and that the plague, an unforeseen act of *tyche*, had contributed more than anything else to their depression, had an assembly convened. Thucydides (2.60–64) records the speech which he made on that occasion, the so-called last speech of Pericles. Despite the difficulty of the task, his brilliant eloquence succeeded in reviving the people's sagging spirits. To achieve this aim, however, Pericles had to resort to chauvinistic methods and appeals which, if employed by a leader like Cleon, critics both ancient and modern would not have hesitated to call demagogic. The speech should be read in its entirety, for it reveals Pericles the realist as opposed to the idealist of the funeral oration. Here there is space only to illustrate the dangerous nature of his appeal, and to emphasize that Pericles, although termed a moderate by Thucydides, put ideas—if Thucydides is representing them faithfully— into the minds of his audience which easily could be (and were) taken as suggestions for imperial conduct that was anything but moderate.

Pericles stated emphatically that submission would mean "slavery," an oversimplification of the issues at stake based on the demagogic device of depicting all things as either black or white. Then, to encourage the Athenians and make them fully aware of their power and proud of their militant achievements in the past, he uttered such provocative exhortations as the following:

> You perhaps think that your empire extends only over your allies; I will declare to you the truth. The visible field of action has two parts, land and sea. In the whole of one of these you are completely supreme, not merely as far as you use it at present, but also to what further extent you may think fit: in fine, your naval resources are such that your vessels may go where they please, without the king or any other nation on earth being able to stop them ... You should remember also that what you are fighting against is not merely slavery as an exchange for independence, but also loss of empire and danger from the animosities incurred in its exercise.

Besides, to recede is no longer possible, if indeed any of you in the alarm of the moment has become enamoured of the honesty of such an unambitious part. For what you hold is, to speak somewhat plainly, a tyranny; to take it perhaps was wrong, but to let it go is unsafe . . . Remember, too, that if your country has the greatest name in all the world, it is because she never bent before disaster; because she has expended more life and effort in war than any other city, and has won for herself a power greater than any hitherto known, the memory of which will descend to the latest posterity; even if now, in obedience to the general law of decay, we should ever be forced to yield, still it will be remembered that we held rule over more Hellenes than any other Hellenic state, that we sustained the greatest wars against their united or separate powers, and inhabited a city unrivaled by any other in resources or magnitude.

Pericles' eloquence succeeded in dissuading the Athenians from attempting further negotiations with Sparta, but failed to assuage the rancor felt against him personally. Thucydides (2.65.1–4) reports that he was fined, but soon, as is the way of a crowd (*homilos*), he was elected general. This statement, beyond revealing Thucydides' low opinion of the "people," illustrates the common habit of ancient historians of avoiding technical language when dealing with procedures currently familiar. Presumably Pericles did not receive a vote of confidence in the vote held each *prytany* by the assembly and consequently was deposed. He was tried on a charge not specified in the sources and fined a sum ranging in the different accounts from fifteen to the highly improbable eighty talents. It is reasonable to assume that shortly after the payment of the fine he was restored to office, and that in the seventh *prytany* (ca. February 429) he was elected *strategos* for the year 429/8.

In these early years of the war, although one's attention naturally centers on Athens and its difficulties with the annual invasions of Attica and with the plague, many important phases of the struggle were occurring elsewhere. Athenian alliances with Acarnania and with the great islands off the west coast of Greece—Corcyra, on the regular route to and from southern Italy and Sicily, and Cephallenia and Zacynthus, both near the entrance to the Corinthian Gulf—were a threat to what had been the Corinthian sphere of influence and also to the arrival of materials from the western Greeks. In the summer of 430 the Spartans and their allies sailed with a hundred ships against Zacynthus, but the expedition succeeded only in ravaging the island's territory. In order to support their allies and to strengthen their control over this vital area, the Athenians in the following winter sent out twenty ships under Phormio who, after circling the Peloponnesus, established his base at Naupactus. From this strategic location, peopled by the exiled Messenians, loyal allies of Athens, Phormio could interfere, when necessary, with anyone entering or leaving the Corinthian Gulf. The importance to both warring parties of control of the approaches to the Corinthian Gulf was vividly illustrated by their activities in the summer of 429. The Peloponnesians, particularly the Corinthians, and their allies in western Greece including the Ambraciots and the Leucadian islanders made a serious effort to detach Acarnania from the Athenians and to conquer Zacynthus, Cephallenia, and, if possible, Naupactus. Thucydides (2.80–92) describes the campaign in considerable detail. Here it is sufficient to say that the invasion of Acarnania miscarried and that Phormio, before the arrival of supporting ships from Athens, achieved two remarkable naval victories with his twenty ships over contingents double or treble that size.

Besides maintaining influence in western Greece, Athens also directed its interests to the north, where many Chalcidic cities had revolted and Potidaea had been under siege since 432. In the first year of the war, through the agency of Athens' *proxenos* in Abdera, a Greek city on the coast of Thrace tributary to Athens, an alliance was made with Sitalces, the powerful king of Thrace whose father, Teres, had established the Odrysian kingdom, which embraced most of the tribes dwelling from the Nestos River eastward to the Black Sea and northward to the Danube and also, westward, some tribes living between the Nestos and Strymon rivers.

Through the same agency Perdiccas, king of the Macedonians, although usually suspicious of the Athenians, was also persuaded to make an alliance with them after they had restored to his jurisdiction Therma, a city at the head of the Thermaic Gulf. The understanding was that the two monarchs should assist Athens against the insubordinate Chalcidians (Thucydides, 2.29). In the following year (430) Sitalces' son, Sadocus, who had been granted Athenian citizenship, proved to be of great value to the Athenians. Some Peloponnesian envoys, the Corinthian Aristeus who had been instrumental in the revolt of Potidaea and several others, including three Spartans, while proceeding through Thrace on their way to Asia to try to obtain financial and military assistance from Persia, attempted to induce Sitalces to abandon the alliance with Athens. Two Athenian ambassadors who were with Sadocus induced him to turn the Peloponnesians over to them. They were sent to Athens where, without even a hearing, they were immediately executed. Since such callous brutality is commonly associated with the Athens of the "demagogues," it should be noted that this grim episode occurred while Pericles was still alive, although it may have taken place in the period in which he had been deposed from office. Thucydides (2.67) remarks that the Athenians thought themselves "justified in using in retaliation the same mode of warfare which the Lacedaemonians had begun, when they slew and cast into pits all the Athenian and allied traders whom they caught on board the merchantmen around the Peloponnesus. Indeed, at the outset of the war, the Lacedaemonians butchered as enemies all whom they took on the sea, whether allies of Athens or neutrals."

In the winter of 430/29 the Potidaeans, reduced almost to starvation by the two years' blockade, entered into negotiations concerning surrender with the besieging army. The Athenian generals on the scene, aware that their own troops were suffering from the stormy weather and that 2,000 talents had already been spent on the siege, accepted the surrender and permitted the Potidaeans, men, women, and children, taking with them a small amount of clothing and money, to depart to wherever they could find asylum. The Athenians at home, however, criticized the generals for this leniency, presumably thinking that a surrender at discretion would have enabled them to make an example of the Potidaeans to any allies who might be contemplating revolt. Somewhat later some Athenians were sent out to colonize the deserted city (Thucydides, 2.70).

Early in the summer of 429 the Peloponnesians and their allies under the command of Archidamus, instead of invading Attica, marched against Plataea. In a parley with the Spartan king the Plataeans appealed to their heroic role during the great Persian invasion and to Pausanias' pledge that their city should remain autonomous. Archidamus replied that they had invalidated any pledge through their alliance with Athens, the aggressor against Hellenic liberty, but stated that he would leave them unharmed if they would assume the status of neutrals. The Plataeans then received permission to send envoys to Athens, where they received assurance that the Athenians would not abandon them. If Pericles was responsible for this promise—he did not die until autumn of this year—one wonders how he intended to honor it, since his fixed policy was to risk no land engagement with the enemy. The Plataeans, accordingly, decided to remain loyal to Athens. When Archidamus was informed of their decision he immediately began an attack on the town, but every type of assault attempted was met successfully by countermeasures on the part of the Plataeans. Thwarted in their efforts to take Plataea by storm, the Peloponnesians proceeded to surround it with a wall and then, leaving an adequate force to maintain the siege, returned home. Since two years earlier the Plataeans had sent to Athens their wives, children, and least serviceable men, there were within the beleaguered city only 400 Plataeans, 80 Athenians, and 110 women, presumably slaves, to prepare their food (Thucydides, 2.71–78).

At the beginning of the winter of 429/8 there was great confusion and consternation in the northern regions. Sitalces, king of the Thracians, led a great expedition against Perdiccas, king of the Macedonians, with whom he had had disagreements. Accompanying Sitalces were Perdiccas' nephew, whom he planned to establish as king of the Macedonians, and some Athenian envoys, since he was apparently planning to subdue the rebellious Chalcidians as had been proposed at the formation of his alliance with Athens in 431. Arriving in Macedonia with an army of 150,000 men, according to Thucydides, he pillaged the country without meeting much resistance since the Macedonians, unable to face such a horde, sought refuge in whatever fortresses were available. After coming to an understanding with Perdiccas, Sitalces moved into Chalcidice and ravaged the territory of the cities. Then, realizing that he was not achieving his aims, whatever they really were, and that his troops were suffering from the winter weather, he retired quickly into Thrace.

Thucydides, because of his familiarity with Thrace, devotes some five pages (2.95–101) to a description of this episode, but his account leaves much that is obscure. The Athenians did not arrive with their fleet as Sitalces apparently had expected. Had the Athenians assumed that Sitalces would support them at the time of their futile attack on the Chalcidians in the preceding summer (2.79)? Communication between the two powers was obviously faulty. One can imagine that there was considerable confusion at Athens because of the sickness and death of Pericles in the autumn. Thucydides mentions the not surprising rumors that the Greeks north of Thermopylae feared lest the Thracians would advance against them and that talk even circulated among the enemies of Athens that Sitalces, urged on by his ally, would march against them.

In the autumn of 429 Pericles died, a victim of the plague. Thucydides' eulogy of him (2.65.5–13), composed, in part at least, not before 404, is another illustration of how thoroughly the historian's views have colored subsequent judgments. He describes Pericles as a moderate whose wise policies were abandoned by later leaders, which led to the capitulation of Athens. Thucydides states that under Pericles what was nominally a democracy became, in fact, a government by the first citizen, a condition greatly changed by his successors who ended by committing even the conduct of state affairs to the people. Few words reveal more vividly Thucydides' attitude towards democracy, an attitude, one should remember, shared by a majority of Athenian—and Greek—historians.

THE FOURTH year of the war (428) opened with another Peloponnesian invasion of Attica at the time when the grain was ripening. Almost simultaneously four of the five cities on the large island of Lesbos, under the leadership of Mytilene, revolted from Athens, Methymna on the north coast alone remaining loyal to the imperial city. The Athenians were forewarned of the impending revolt, which the Spartans and Boeotians were said to be fomenting, by their *proxenoi* in Mytilene and by various enemies of that city. At first they were incredulous, for Lesbos, along with Chios, was one of the two remaining so-called autonomous members of the empire, each providing ships rather than tribute. Once convinced of the seriousness of the situation, they ordered the Mytileneans to surrender their ships and demolish their walls, and when the order was ignored, they began a siege of the city which continued until the following year. In the meantime the Mytileneans had managed to dispatch envoys to Sparta. On arriving they were instructed to proceed to Olympia so that they could also address Sparta's allies, who would be assembled for the festival. Thucydides (3.9–14) records the speech of the spokesman of the envoys, which contained charges against Athens probably similar to those made by many another state which by then had fallen into subject status: "Between ourselves and the Athenians alliance began when you [Sparta and its allies] withdrew from the Median war and they remained to finish the business. But we did not become allies of the Athenians for the subjugation of the Hellenes, but allies of the Hellenes for their liberation from the Mede; and as long as the Athenians led us fairly we followed them loyally; but when we saw them relax their hostility to the Mede, to try to compass the subjection of the allies, then our apprehensions began." The envoy also emphasized that "it is not in Attica that the war will be decided, as some imagine, but in the countries by which Attica is supported," a lesson that the Spartans were slow to learn. On hearing the plea of the Mytileneans the Spartans and their allies took them into alliance and agreed, at their request, to invade Attica a second time that summer. This project, however, was not realized because of the inertia of all members of the Peloponnesian League except Sparta. Consequently, Mytilene received no aid in the course of that year, although towards the end of winter a Spartan named Salaethus managed to make his way into Mytilene and assured the discouraged inhabitants that Attica would be invaded and that a Peloponnesian fleet would come to their aid.

At the beginning of the summer of 427 the Peloponnesians did undertake an unusually destructive invasion of Attica, but the fleet of forty-two ships under the command of the Spartan admiral Alcidas loitered so long on the voyage that it failed in its mission to relieve Mytilene. Meanwhile in the beleaguered city shortage of provisions produced a crisis. The Spartan Salaethus, with the intention of launching an attack upon the Athenians, equipped the "commoners" as hoplites. Once in possession of arms, the people demanded that the ruling class should distribute food to all or else they would come to terms with the Athenians and surrender the city. This action of the commoners on receiving arms is sometimes taken as evidence that the "people" in Mytilene and elsewhere in the empire were favorable to the Athenians.[11] Although this may be true, it should be noted that in this particular case the question at issue was the distribution of food to people approaching starvation. The oligarchic rulers of the city, realizing that the situation was now out of their control, surrendered to the Athenian commander Paches on the understanding that they should be allowed to send an embassy to Athens and that no drastic action should be taken against the Mytileneans until its return.

The Peloponnesian fleet under Alcidas, after its failure to assist Mytilene, sailed to the coast of Asia Minor where, if properly led, it could have fomented trouble among the Athenian allies. When Paches received this information, realizing the danger inherent in the presence of enemy ships in the Ionian area, he hurriedly went in pursuit, but Alcidas had already set out for home. Paches then, after interfering in a treacherous and bloody manner in the *stasis* at Notion, the port of Colophon, returned to Lesbos where he sent off to Athens the Spartan Salaethus and those Mytileneans whom he considered most responsible for the revolt. The Athenians immediately put the Spartan to death, although he made the improbable promise to bring about a cessation of the siege of Plataea. The assembly then met to decide the fate of the prisoners, and in fury at the revolt of an "autonomous" ally and in alarm over the fact that a Peloponnesian fleet had dared to sail into Ionian waters, voted to put to death all adult male Mytileneans and to sell the women and children as slaves. A trireme bearing this order was dispatched to Paches. By the next day, however, many Athenians were feeling remorse over this brutal decree, and accordingly, an extraordinary meeting of the assembly was convoked to debate the issue once again.

It is at this point that Thucydides (3.36.6) first introduces Cleon into his history, and the words that he employs merit attention. "An assembly was therefore at once called, and after much expression of opinion upon both sides, Cleon, son of Cleaenetus, the same who had carried the former motion of putting the Mytileneans to death, the most violent man at Athens, and at that time by far the most powerful with the commons, came forward again and spoke as follows." These lines prepare the reader to expect a violent outburst, and he is not disappointed. Those familiar with the historian Tacitus may remember the viciously effective beginning of his account of the reign of Tiberius: "The first crime of the new reign was the murder of Agrippa Postumus." Thucydides' reputation for objectivity, however, is so strong that generations of scholars, despite his blatant bias against Cleon, have clung instinctively to the notion that he wrote *sine ira et studio*.

Cleon represented a different social class from the one which previously had provided leadership in Athens. As far as can be inferred from the inadequate source material, the men who held prominent office in Athens throughout the sixth and fifth centuries down to the death of Pericles had all, with the possible exception of Ephialtes, been members of old "aristocratic" families whose position and wealth were based on inherited land. Immediately following the death of Pericles, however, and largely as a natural consequence of his emphasis on the city, as distinct from the countryside, and on the empire, some merchants and manufacturers gained prominence. Eucrates, a dealer in hemp, was briefly recognized as "leader of the people," and after him Lysicles, a dealer in sheep, who, as general in 428/7, was killed when trying to collect money—tribute or special contributions?—from the allies in the Carian district. In the same year Cleon, sneeringly called "the leatherseller" by Aristophanes, was a member of the Council of Five Hundred. Since his father, Cleaenetus, was rich enough in 460/59 to serve as *choregus* for his tribe Pandionis, it is probable that Cleon inherited from him a profitable tannery. Plutarch (*Pericles, 33.6–7;35.4*) relates that in the first year of the war Cleon was one of the most vociferous critics of Pericles' military strategy and that in the following year, according to one tradition, he was the prosecutor of Pericles.

The chief extant sources concerning Cleon—his contemporaries Thucydides and Aristophanes, and the later authors influenced by them, Aristotle in the *Constitution of the Athenians* and Plutarch, especially in his *Life of Nicias*—were all bitterly hostile to him. Thucydides was thoroughly convinced that all Athenian leaders in the war after the death of Pericles were woefully inferior to him, and as an aristocrat he had an instinctive contempt for the "vulgarity" of Cleon. The fact that his banishment in 424 for failing to save Amphipolis from the Spartan Brasidas may have resulted from a prosecution instituted by Cleon would not have contributed to his liking of the man. Aristophanes, usually representing the point of view of the Attic farmer, and conscious of the follies of war, depicts Cleon, especially in the *Knights* (424) and the *Wasps* (422), as a venal, corrupt bully, and a demagogue in the most pejorative sense of that term. The comic poet also had felt the wrath of Cleon, who had brought some sort of suit against him for ridiculing Athens and its leaders in the *Babylonians,* produced at the City Dionysia in the spring of 426, at a time when many representatives of the "allies" were present in Athens. The Aristophanic picture, largely because of the overwhelming influence of Thucydides' judgment, has to a remarkable extent been accepted. Although scholars reject—and rightly—Aristophanes' portraits of Socrates and Euripides as absurdly distorted and falsified delineations, there is a tendency to minimize the comic element in the poet's characterization of Cleon and to recognize a figure more or less true to life. It cannot be emphasized too often that Athenian authors, and Greek authors in general, who wrote history or discussed historical persons were almost exclusively oligarchic, aristocratic, or, at least, conservative. In the final analysis it is necessary to admit that an accurate characterization of Cleon will never be possible, but at least the historian should be constantly alert to the violently biased nature of the ancient traditions about him.[12]

Cleon was an unabashed imperialist, as was Pericles, and in realistic language he reminded the people in the assembly that their empire was a "tyranny" and that their subjects were disaffected conspirators. For subjects who suffered under the rigors of Athenian imperialism he might have understanding, but not for the Mytileneans, who had enjoyed a privileged position. The welfare of the empire demanded that extreme punishment of the Mytileneans serve as a terrifying warning to Athenian subjects. "For if the Mytileneans were right in rebelling, you must be wrong in ruling. However, if, right or wrong, you determine to rule, you must carry out your principle and punish the Mytileneans as your interest requires; or else you must give up your empire and cultivate honesty without danger." The similarities between some of the phrases in this speech and those in the "last" speech of Pericles are remarkable, although, naturally, Cleon's language has a coarser tone. Was Cleon in 427 deliberately imitating the Pericles of 430, or are the similarities to be attributed to Thucydides' literary artistry?

Thucydides assigns the speech in rebuttal of Cleon to an otherwise unknown Diodotus who, according to the historian, had spoken against putting the Mytileneans to death at the first assembly. Diodotus argued strongly for a more moderate treatment of the Mytileneans, but he carefully confined his plea to notions of expediency. He reminded the Athenians that "we are not in a court of justice, but in a political assembly; and the question is not justice, but how to make the Mytileneans useful to Athens." Few politicians or statesmen have ever admitted so honestly that in national policy expediency, not morality, is the determining factor. The most effective part of Diodotus' argument rested on his claim that throughout the empire the "people" were friendly to Athens. If the Athenians should put to death all Mytilenean men, commoners as well as oligarchs, the inevitable result would be the loss, throughout all the subject cities, of the goodwill of the "people" towards Athens. This passage, incidentally, provides a strong argument against Thucydides' assertion that the Athenian empire was universally hated.[13]

When the Athenian assembly voted on the proposals of Cleon and Diodotus and of others, the motion of Diodotus was victorious, although only by a slight majority. A ship, immediately sent out to countermand the execution orders which had been dispatched the previous day, arrived just in time to prevent the general slaughter. On the motion of Cleon, executions were carried out against those Mytileneans whom Paches had sent to Athens as chiefly responsible for the revolt. If the text of Thucydides is accepted, slightly more than a thousand rebels were put to death. As for Lesbos itself, the Athenians destroyed the walls of the Mytileneans and appropriated their ships, and then divided the land of the island, except that of Methymna, into 3,000 lots. These lots, excluding 300 reserved for the gods, were assigned to Athenian *cleruchs* who were sent to the island. Since the Lesbians cultivated the land themselves, on agreement to pay annually two minas (200 drachmas) for each lot, it is probable that the role of the Athenian *cleruchs* was to perform garrison duty (Thucydides, 3.2–18; 25–50).

The year 427 witnessed two other events which in cynical brutality surpassed the reduced brutality of the fate that befell the Mytileneans. The first episode was the destruction of Plataea and of its surviving defenders. The Spartans and their allies had been besieging Plataea since 429. In the summer of 427 the Plataeans, weakened and almost starving, capitulated on the understanding that their destiny would be decided by legal process. The Spartans, under the influence of their valuable allies, the Thebans, reduced the legal procedure to asking the Plataeans one question only: "Had they done the Lacedaemonians and allies any service in the war then raging?" The Plataeans, against the wishes of the Thebans who hated them because of their long anti-Boeotian alliance with Athens, obtained permission to speak, and Thucydides (3.52–68) records their speech and also the rebuttal of the Thebans. The Plataeans, in addition to a plea for mercy and morality, placed chief emphasis on their heroic role in the years of the Persian invasions. The Thebans stressed particularly the unnatural anti-Boeotian attitude of the Plataeans and the evil of their Atticizing, which led them to assist the Athenians in their assaults on the Hellenes. Unmoved by the desperation of the Plataeans, the Spartans repeated their previous question and, on receiving a negative answer, executed the pathetic prisoners, some 200 in number, and also 25 Athenians who had surrendered in accordance with the original agreement. The small number of Plataeans involved is to be explained partly by the smallness of Plataea itself and partly because both in 429 and in 428 a considerable number of Plataeans had been moved to Athens.

Beyond Thucydides' account of the murderous brutality of the Thebans and the immoral callousness of the Spartans, his final words on the tragedy, "such was the end of Plataea in the ninety-third year after she became the ally of Athens," emphasize the ignominious role of Athens. When the siege began in 429 the Athenians, by fine promises, had encouraged the Plataeans to resist. Two years later, because their military might was almost exclusively naval, they had to watch helplessly while the Plataeans, their close neighbors and old friends, paid the ultimate price for trust in Athenian promises.

The second hideous event was the explosion of civil war (*stasis*) in Corcyra, the ally of Athens since 433. The trouble began with the return from Corinth of the Corcyrean prisoners who had been captured in the struggles ignited by the Epidamnian affair. Corinth hoped that these repatriated men might be able to persuade Corcyra to abandon the Athenian alliance for a Corinthian one. Conflict quickly arose between these returned prisoners and the pro-Athenian democratic faction. The failure of the former to convict the Athenian *proxenos*, the leader of the "people," led to his accusation of several of the richest of his opponents on a charge of some religious violation, which carried a heavy financial punishment. The sequel was an armed attack by the oligarchs on the Boulē, which resulted in the murder of the Athenian *proxenos* and of sixty of his followers. Thus full-scale *stasis* broke out, whose potentiality for evil was aggravated by the arrival of both Peloponnesian and Athenian ships.

Thucydides describes this revolution in detail and ends his treatment with two famous chapters (3.82–83) devoted to an analysis of the revolutionary trend which, beginning in Corcyra, ultimately engulfed the Hellenic world. Since this general phenomenon did not become endemic until the years following 413, it is clear that part of Thucydides' discussion, at least, was composed well after the outbreak of the Corcyrean revolution in 427. The opposition between the many and the few, based on the hatred felt by the poor for the wealthy and on the ill-concealed contempt for the masses shared by many of the upper classes, was a common characteristic of the Greek world, but Thucydides reveals vividly how this dangerous cleavage, normally kept under control by the requirements of civilized life, was fanned by the war, for, under such unstable conditions, the poor felt they could bank on Athenian help and the rich looked to the Peloponnesians for support. These two chapters provide a grim analysis of how war-induced fears, emotions, and sufferings devastate the foundations of society and shatter hard-won morality. Especially telling is Thucydides' insistence that in such conditions the extremists flourish while the moderates, considered to be futile and spiritless, are trampled underfoot by the true believers in both militant camps. In the particular case of Corcyra, the many, because of the easy availability of the Athenian fleet, were able to dominate the situation by butchering those who thought themselves socially and economically superior.

LATE IN THE summer of 427 circumstances aroused Athenian interests in the problems of the western Greeks. Envoys, including the famous rhetorician Gorgias, from their allies Leontini (threatened by Syracuse) and Rhegium (on the toe of Italy) appealed to Athens, on the basis of alliance and Ionian kinship, for help against Syracusan aggression. The Athenians, motivated, according to Thucydides (3.86), primarily by the desire "to prevent the exportation of Sicilian corn to the Peloponnesus and to test the possibility of bringing Sicily into subjection," responded by sending twenty ships westward under Laches. This force, subsequently somewhat augmented, remained intermittently active in western affairs until its withdrawal in 424, as will be mentioned below.

Despite the recrudescence of the plague in the winter of 427/6, the Athenians were active in the following summer on various fronts. The military manoeuvres are described in considerable detail by Thucydides in the closing pages of book 3. It will be sufficient here merely to emphasize the importance of central Greece to both warring parties. Thirty Athenian ships under Demosthenes, a general, not to be confused with the famous later orator, sailed around the Peloponnesus and, joining with contingents from Acarnania, Zacynthus, Cephallenia, and Corcyra, ravaged the territory of the island of Leucas. Rather than besieging the town and thus acquiring control of the last of these large islands lying off the coast, Demosthenes approved the suggestion of the Messenians from Naupactus to invade their constant enemies, the Aetolians. Subjection of the Aetolians would induce the Phocians to defect to the Athenians, their former friends, and then Athens could attack Boeotia from the west. In this same summer, incidentally, Athenian naval and land forces ravaged the territory of Tanagra in eastern Boeotia. The Aetolians, however, were a mountain people, living in scattered villages, and their light armed soldiers, trained in guerrilla tactics, proved more than a match for the Athenian hoplites, who suffered a serious defeat.

At approximately this time the Spartans, at the request of the Trachinians and the Dorians of the metropolis, both enduring damaging raids from a mountain tribe, founded a colony called Heraclea in Trachis a short distance to the west of Thermopylae. The hope was that this establishment, in addition to being a strong point on the route to Thrace, would also be a base from which ships could ravage adjacent Euboea. Later in the summer troops from Heraclea assisted in a Peloponnesian attack on Naupactus urged by the Aetolians. This venture, beyond a plundering of the countryside, failed because Demosthenes with a contingent of Acarnanians was able to protect the city.

Hostilities continued into the winter. As the Spartan commander retired from the territory of Naupactus, the Ambraciots persuaded him to employ his Peloponnesian army in an attempt to subdue Amphilochia and Acarnania, a conquest which would bring the whole area, including the Ambracian Gulf, into Spartan control. The plan miscarried when Demosthenes with the Acarnanians badly defeated the Peloponnesians and Ambraciots at Olpae at the eastern end of the gulf. Demosthenes then succeeded in tarnishing the reputation of the Peloponnesians by permitting some of them to retreat secretly in small groups. A reserve force of Ambraciots was almost annihilated on its arrival at Idomene, somewhat to the north. Thucydides (3.113) states that the losses suffered by the Ambraciots were incredible. Demosthenes wanted the Acarnanians and Amphilochians to capture Ambracia, which would have been a simple task at that time, but they refused, thinking that Ambracia, under Athenian dominance, would be detrimental to them. The shattered Ambracia was later strengthened by a garrison of 300 Corinthians.

Also in this winter (426/5) the Athenians purified Delos as Pisistratus had done over a century earlier. The motive was probably thanksgiving for the ending of the plague and the desire to glorify Apollo of Delos, since Apollo of Delphi seemed entirely allied with Peloponnesians and Dorians. A new quinquennial festival was established— the Delian Games—the only international festival under Ionian control.

In the spring of 425 the Athenians sent out forty ships to Sicily under the generals Eurymedon and Sophocles, who had received instructions to stop on their route at Corcyra whither sixty Peloponnesian ships had been dispatched to help the exiled oligarchs. Demosthenes accompanied the Athenian detachment; he had received permission, presumably from the assembly and with the backing of Cleon, to employ the fleet on the Peloponnesian coast if a satisfactory opportunity presented itself. Off the west coast of Messenia Demosthenes, aided by adverse weather, persuaded the generals to put in at Pylos. Pylos was a high promontory facing south which, with the neighboring narrow island of Sphacteria, largely enclosed a body of water now known as the bay of Navarino. Demosthenes figured that this was an excellent site on which to establish a fort in enemy territory and thus to provide an asylum for escaping helots. For six days the Athenians made what fortifications they could on the promontory, and then the fleet resumed its voyage to Corcyra and Sicily, while Demosthenes was left behind with five ships to garrison Pylos.

In the meantime, the Spartans received word of Athenian activity on the Messenian coast. Sensing the potential danger, they recalled the Peloponnesian army which was ravaging the Attic countryside and dispatched a considerable force to Pylos. The sixty ships at Corcyra also received orders to hurry to the endangered spot. For fear that Sphacteria might fall into the hands of the Athenians, the Spartans put 420 of their hoplites on the island; they then attacked Demosthenes and his small contingent by land and sea. Because of the difficulty of the terrain the Athenians succeeded in resisting the assaults for two days. The fleet under Eurymedon and Sophocles, with the addition of more ships from Naupactus, hurried to Pylos as soon as news of the battle reached them. They sailed through the inlets north and south of Sphacteria into the harbor and decisively defeated the Peloponnesian ships. A consequence of this defeat was that the Spartan hoplites on Sphacteria were completely isolated, for the victorious Athenian ships now could methodically patrol the island. The emergency was so acute that officials who were sent from Sparta realized that an armistice was necessary, while envoys went to Athens to try to obtain some solution for the difficulty in which the Spartans found themselves. By the terms of the armistice, the Spartans agreed to turn over temporarily to the Athenians at Pylos all their warships which were either in the harbor or anywhere in Laconia, and the Athenians granted permission that a limited amount of food be sent to the marooned hoplites.

The Spartan envoys at Athens had an almost hopeless case to make, as is evident from the words which Thucydides (4.17–20) assigns to them. The gist of their plea was that the Athenians would be wise not to try to push their present good fortune too far, and that they now had the chance to make a lasting peace with the Spartans and to win much goodwill among the Greeks as a whole. These proposals were little more than rhetoric and certainly had no bearing on the basic causes of the war. It was clear that the Spartans in their eagerness to recover the 420 Spartan hoplites were seeking a peace which totally disregarded the interests of their allies. It is not strange, therefore, that the Athenians, on the advice of Cleon, replied that peace would be possible only on the following terms: "First, the men in the island must surrender themselves and their arms and be brought to Athens. Next the Lacedaemonians must restore Nisaea, Pagae [the harbors of Megara], Troezen, and Achaia, all places acquired not by arms, but by the previous convention"—that is, the peace of 446/5, made at a time when Athens itself was in trouble. If these terms were met, then the 420 Spartans would be returned. The failure of these negotiations naturally led to the end of the armistice at Pylos. The Spartans, according to the agreement, asked that their ships be returned, but the Athenians refused to comply, alleging that the Spartans had violated the armistice by attacking their fortifications.

Hostilities, accordingly, began again at Pylos and continued for a long time, because the Spartans found various devices for providing food to their men on Sphacteria. At Athens the citizens became restless and apprehensive, and criticism began to be directed against Cleon. He maintained that another expedition should be sent to Pylos and suggested that Nicias, an enemy of his, should conduct it. Nicias replied that he was perfectly willing to resign his generalship to Cleon. Cleon at first tried to quash this unusual proposal, but the more he tried to decline the suggestion, the more, according to Thucydides, the people clamored for him to undertake the mission. He finally accepted, and stated that, with some non-Athenian light armed troops that he would take, he and the soldiers at Pylos would either kill the Lacedaemonians or bring them back alive within twenty days. Thucydides says that amid laughter the assembly voted him the command—some sort of special commission, for he was not a general—and he then set out to join forces with Demosthenes. The two men worked well together, and their task was made somewhat easier by the fact that recently a fire had burned down all the undergrowth on the island. Nevertheless, hard fighting was necessary, but finally the Lacedaemonians on Sphacteria agreed to surrender rather than to face annihilation. Of the 420 hoplites who had crossed to the island, 128 had been killed, but the rest, including about 120 Spartiates, were taken prisoner. Thus, "crazy as Cleon's promise was, he fulfilled it, by bringing back the men to Athens within the twenty days as he had pledged himself to do" (Thucydides, 4.39.3).

The Athenians put the captives in prison and let it be known that, if the Peloponnesians invaded their country, the prisoners would be put to death. The decision of the Spartans to capitulate rather than die at their posts caused much surprise throughout the Greek world, but it emphasizes vividly what the preservation of 120 Spartiates signified to the dwindling number of dominant "equals." As for Pylos, some Messenians from Naupactus took possession of it and from there made various raids into Laconia, which, because of the frequent desertions of the helots, caused the Spartans great anxiety.

After the surrender of the Spartans at Pylos, the Athenian fleet under Eurymedon and Sophocles resumed its original plan of sailing to Sicily. On its way it stopped at Corcyra, and the Athenians helped the Corcyraean democrats dislodge the oligarchs, who had established themselves on Mount Istone. The outcome, aided by duplicity, was so horrible that the *stasis* came to an end, "for of one party there was practically nothing left" (Thucydides, 4.48.5).

In the winter of 425/4 the Athenian assembly passed a decree providing for a new and greatly increased assessment of the tribute. Thucydides, although well aware of the inevitable connection between war and finances, for some strange reason makes no reference to it. Forty-three fragments of a marble stele recording the document, however, although representing less than half of the original inscription, have enabled scholars to achieve a restoration revealing the main provisions of the measure (*M&L,* no. 69). From the contents of the decree, which are rather complicated, it is sufficient to mention here only the following: Representatives from all the cities are to appear in Athens in Maimakterion (November–December), and their appeals are to be decided by a court of 1,000 jurors (sitting in panels?) by the end of Posideion (January–February). Since the tribute has become too little, no assessment is to be reduced except in case of special hardship. Below the decree the cities with their assessments were listed under the heading: "Tribute was assessed upon the cities as follows by the Council . . . in the archonship of Stratocles" (425/4). Despite the shattered condition of the inscription it is clear that the names of some 400 cities were recorded, a number in sharp contrast to the approximately 180 which seems to be the maximum figure for any one year on the fragmentary tribute-quota lists of cities that actually paid. Included in these 400 cities were places in the Black Sea area not previously listed, places on the southern coast of Asia Minor east of Phaselis which had not paid for years, and places like the island of Melos which had refused to become tributary. The sum total assessed was somewhat over 1,460 talents.

This decree is often termed disparagingly "the assessment of Cleon." Since Cleon's reputation after his success at Pylos was high, it is very probable that he was the force behind the motion. The official proposer of the decree, an otherwise unknown Thoudippos, may very well have been a supporter of Cleon. Since in the early fourth century there is a reference to a Cleon, son of Thoudippos, it has been suggested that Thoudippos became the son-in-law of Cleon. The assessment of 425/4 was aggressively imperialistic, but it would be misleading to consider it as an isolated example of Athenian harshness.[14] Plutarch in a passage idealizing the original assessment of Aristides (*Aristides*, 24.3) speaks of the gradual increase of the tribute, which he ascribes not so much to the needs of the war as to the desire of the demagogues to curry favor with the people.

Pericles and Cleon, in their different ways, were realists and understood the vital importance of money for successfully carrying on war. The campaign and siege of Potidaea in 432–430 alone had cost 2,000 talents (Thucydides, 2.70.2). In 428 the Athenians, for the first time in the war, had recourse to a capital tax (*eisphora*) on themselves and their metics, which produced 200 talents, and they also dispatched twelve money-collecting ships to the allies. The fact that the general, Lysicles, and some of his troops were killed by the Carians suggests that the purpose of this expedition was to make a special levy rather than to collect arrears of tribute. In this same year the Athenians issued a new assessment decree, which scholars estimate may have raised the tribute requirement considerably. Two years later, in an effort to guarantee that the full amount of tribute be collected, the Athenians issued a stern decree (*M&L*, no. 68) insisting that in each city of the empire collectors of tribute should be appointed who, like the *curiales* or *decuriones* of the late Roman Empire, would be personally responsible for the tribute due. Since Pericles died in the autumn of 429, it is quite possible that the influence of Cleon should be suspected in all these measures just mentioned, even though his name is officially attached to none of them. They are all actions characteristic of a harsh military power embroiled in a ruthless war. The tribute aspirations in the assessment of 425/4 may have been too grasping to be effectively carried out, but it is interesting to note that in the assessment of 422/1 the tribute demanded seemingly was scaled down only to about 1,000 talents.[15]

The year 424 began well for the Athenians. The Spartans, who had regularly invaded and ravaged Attica every spring since 431, except for two, abandoned that strategy because of fear for the Spartiates who were prisoners in Athens. The Athenians, however, continued to be active. In view of the *stasis* existing in Megara, they hoped to get control of the city whose territory they had plundered every spring and fall since the beginning of the war. The timely interference of an energetic Spartan, Brasidas, thwarted the Athenian designs on the city, in which a narrow oligarchy was established, but the Athenians did succeed in seizing and garrisoning Nisaea, the Megarian harbor on the Saronic Gulf. About the same time the Athenian general Nicias attacked Cythera, the island slightly south of Laconia, and forced the Spartan *perioeci*, the chief inhabitants, to capitulate. This loss, and the previous one of Pylos, increased Spartan worries about enemy influence among the helots (Thucydides, 4.66–74; 53–55).

These initial successes for the Athenians in 424 were soon overshadowed by unexpected disappointments and dangers. In Sicily the various Sicilian cities met in a congress at Gela at which the Syracusan Hermocrates convinced the delegates that the Athenians had come to the island not so much to help their allies as to make preparations for the conquest of all Sicily. On a slogan of "Sicily for the Sicilians" the cities made peace with one another, a phenomenon which left the Athenian fleet no option except to return home. The Athenian assembly, which had begun to dream of the conquest of all Sicily, accused the generals of having taken bribes when they should have carried on the war, and banished two of the commanders and fined the other (Thucydides, 4.58–65). In the autumn the Athenians, encouraged by their military successes in Greece and hoping to capitalize on democratic unrest in various Boeotian cities, launched a three-pronged assault on their northern neighbor. Secrecy and exact timing were prerequisites for the plan's success, but both were lacking. The Boeotians, sufficiently alerted, forestalled the anticipated uprising at Chaeronea in the west, prevented Demosthenes from landing on the southern coast, and badly defeated a large Athenian army, including Socrates and Alcibiades, at Delium on the east coast of Boeotia. The Athenian general, Hippocrates, about a thousand hoplites, and many light armed troops were killed, a grim reminder of Pericles' warning to avoid land conflict with the enemy (Thucydides, 4.76–77; 89–101,1–2).

While the Athenians were planning their campaign against Boeotia, a threat to their empire in the north was emerging. This threat and its consequences, discussed below, became the dominant theme in the Peloponnesian War until the Peace of Nicias in 421; Thucydides treats the subject fully at the end of book 4 and the beginning of book 5.

Unrest and revolt in Chalcidice had continued despite the Athenian capture of Potidaea in the winter of 430/29, and this discontent had been aggravated, at least among the wealthier classes, by the increased tribute assessment of 425/4. Some of these communities, fearing that Athens' recent successes might cause it to turn its attentions northward again, appealed to Sparta for military aid. In this appeal they were joined by Perdiccas, king of the Macedonians, who, because of Athenian control of Methone and attempts against Pydna and Therma, distrusted the Athenians as much as they distrusted him. The Spartans, dismayed by the Athenian seizure of Pylos and Cythera and terrified at the possibility of a helot uprising, responded favorably to a proposal which would divert Athenian activity from the Peloponnesus. To emphasize this terror of the helots, Thucydides (4.80) tells the sordid story of the Spartan promise of freedom to those helots selected by their fellows as bravest against the enemy and of the mysterious disappearance of the 2,000 so designated. The Spartans appointed Brasidas, whom the Chalcidians had requested, to command the expedition and, because of the lack of Spartan manpower, assigned to him 700 helots trained as hoplites, thereby removing a possible source of trouble; Brasidas was also given money, presumably supplied by Sparta's new allies, to hire 1,000 mercenaries in the Peloponnesus.

Brasidas, whose bravery, resourcefulness, and intelligence Thucydides repeatedly emphasizes, achieved the difficult task of leading his 1,700 men through a supposedly pro-Athenian Thessaly by means of great speed and the assistance of certain local oligarchs. On arriving in southern Macedonia, he was immediately confronted with the complexity of his assignment. As a Spartan commander his chief goal was the capture of the important Athenian colony of Amphipolis, but Perdiccas and the Chalcidians, who were providing the support for his army, had their own aspirations and were worried lest a Spartan domination might replace the Athenian. Brasidas, after first outraging Perdiccas by coming to terms with, rather than fighting, a rebellious prince of the Lyncestian Macedonians, marched with the Chalcidians against Acanthus, a city tributary to Athens, at the continental end of the most easterly of the three promontories of Chalcidice. The Acanthians, worried for their unharvested vineyards, allowed Brasidas to enter the city alone to address their assembly. He, "no incapable speaker for a Lacedaemonian," told the people that the Spartans had undertaken the war to liberate Hellas, that they had no desire to introduce Spartan governors to interfere with a city's internal affairs, and that Acanthus should set the example of escaping from the tyranny of Athenian imperialism. His eloquence and their fear for their crops persuaded the Acanthians to revolt, a step quickly followed by neighboring Stagirus, also an Andrian colony and likewise influenced by the pledge of no Spartan interference, a pledge that was soon violated.

Brasidas moved against Amphipolis in the winter of 424/3. The Athenians had founded Amphipolis with mixed settlers in 437. Many of the settlers had come from another Andrian colony, Argilus, about ten miles west of the Strymon River, a community whose welfare had been stunted by the increasing prosperity of Amphipolis. Argilus came over to Brasidas, and its settlers in Amphipolis were active in fomenting discontent in the Athenian colony. It has been suggested that these three Andrian colonies may have reflected the anger of their mother city, on which Athens had imposed a *cleruchy* about 450.[16] Brasidas advanced on Amphipolis at night and easily routed the inadequate guard posted at the bridge over the Strymon. By daytime he had become master of the territory surrounding the city. Capitalizing on the disagreements existing among the varied population of Amphipolis and offering unusually generous terms, Brasidas brought about the surrender of the city in the course of the day. The Athenian general, Eucles, stationed in Amphipolis, at dawn had summoned his colleague in the area, the historian Thucydides, who sailed rapidly with his seven ships from Thasos but arrived too late to save Amphipolis, although he did succeed in securing the adjacent port of Eion.

It is customary to defend Thucydides, but the lack of preparation of the Athenians, although they knew that the energetic Brasidas was in the area, was inexcusable, and the responsibility certainly lay with the generals. Nothing is known of the fate of Eucles, but the Athenian assembly, probably on the motion of Cleon, banished Thucydides. He did not return to Athens until the end of the war in 404. The twenty years of exile, although it ruined his life as a citizen, enabled him to concentrate fully on historical research and to communicate at will with the foes of Athens. It is not surprising that the Athenians were angered at the loss of Amphipolis, following so soon after their costly defeat at Delium. Amphipolis had given them access to the abundant timber resources of Thrace and also to the Pangaean gold and silver mines. The Athenians also feared that Brasidas might push eastward through Thrace and reach the Hellespont and Bosporus by the land route. Whatever ultimate plans Brasidas may have had, the Spartans refused at the time to send him reinforcements, partly because of the jealousy he inspired among some of their leading men, and partly because, in their desire to recover their prisoners, they were hoping to capitalize on his current successes to secure a favorable peace. Brasidas, therefore, devoted the winter to winning over many of the communities on the most easterly Chalcidian promontory and then, with the help of anti-Athenian groups, gained control of Torone on the central peninsula.

In the spring of 423 the peace elements in both Sparta and Athens established an armistice for a year, based on the status quo principle, with the obvious hope that this temporary cessation of hostilities might lead to a permanent peace. The truce seemingly was honorably maintained everywhere except in Chalcidice. When envoys from Athens and Sparta sailed northward to announce the armistice, Scione on the western promontory had already revolted from the Athenians. The Athenian emissary claimed that the revolt had occurred after the signing of the agreement on 14 Elaphebolion (March–April), but Brasidas insisted that Scione had come over to him before the signing. The revolt may well have occurred during the envoys' voyage, when Scione was unaware of the armistice. Thucydides apparently accepted the Athenian version, but it is interesting to note that when Spartan envoys at Athens suggested settling the matter by arbitration, the Athenians, although shortly before they had agreed to the principle of arbitration stipulated in the armistice, now rejected the proposal (4.118.8; 122.5). Cleon carried through the assembly a motion to prepare a force to sail to Chalcidice with the object of overpowering and slaying the Scionaeans. The situation was soon further complicated by the revolt of Mende, Scione's neighbor to the west. Brasidas, who was about to leave on another expedition with Perdiccas, left some troops with the two cities and removed their women and children to Olynthus.

This second campaign of Perdiccas and Brasidas against the Lyncestian Macedonians ended in a complete break between the two leaders. Perdiccas, disillusioned with the Spartans, sought relations again with Athens and, to guarantee his good faith, agreed to persuade the Thessalians to permit no Spartan reinforcements to proceed through their territory. A few Spartans, however, did manage to reach Chalcidice, whom, on order from the Spartan authorities, Brasidas placed in charge of the cities which had come over to him. On his return from his expedition with Perdiccas, he had found that an Athenian force under Nicias had already taken Mende and allowed the pro-Athenian citizens to pass judgment on those supposedly responsible for the revolt. Unable to help the cities which he had encouraged to rebel, Brasidas remained temporarily in Torone while the Athenians began the siege of Scione.

The much-battered armistice ended in the spring of 422, and shortly thereafter Cleon with a considerable force sailed to Chalcidice. He succeeded in capturing Torone on the central peninsula before Brasidas could arrive to aid the city. Then, sending word to Perdiccas to join him, he proceeded, by sailing around Mt. Athos to Eion, to prepare for his attack on Amphipolis. Dissatisfaction among his troops caused him to advance on Amphipolis without awaiting the arrival of Perdiccas and his Macedonians. In the ensuing battle as described by Thucydides, Brasidas and his men by a sudden charge from the city caught Cleon off guard and badly defeated the Athenians. Cleon was killed in the general flight. In view of Thucydides' contempt for Cleon and of his unexplained insight into Cleon's thoughts, some scholars have questioned the validity of the historian's account.[17] Brasidas also fell in the engagement. The Amphipolitans buried him with honors and subsequently paid homage to him as their founder, destroying all memorials of the Athenian Hagnon who had been their original founder in 437 (Thucydides, 5.11).

THE DEATHS of Cleon and Brasidas, the pestle and mortar of the war as Aristophanes called them, stimulated the peace parties, led by Nicias at Athens and King Pleistoanax in Sparta, to greater activity. Sparta's need for peace seems to have been genuine. The desire to recover the prisoners taken at Sphacteria was very urgent, and the establishment of enemy garrisons at Pylos and Cythera, with their constant encouragement to the helots to revolt, was causing great concern. The fact that the thirty years' peace with its ancient enemy Argos was about to expire also increased Sparta's worries. As for Athens, the defeat at Delium and the loss of Amphipolis were severe blows, and the impulse to revolt exhibited by its Thracian allies was ominous. If either Cleon or Pericles had been alive, an effort to rectify the Thracian situation would have been a prerequisite to any peace negotiations, but Nicias was thinking of the immediate present. Peace, which in Athenian tradition was called the Peace of Nicias, was signed in the spring of 421 after a series of conferences in the preceding winter, but since some of Sparta's most important allies, the Boeotians, Corinthians, Eleans, and Megarians, refused to sign it, it really was an agreement between Sparta and Athens alone. The peace was to be for fifty years. Included in the various stipulations were Sparta's promise to relinquish Amphipolis, Athens' to abandon Pylos (the promonotory of Coryphasium) and Cythera, and the release of all prisoners of war. Thucydides (5.16–18) records the agreement in full. The longest clause is concerned with Chalcidice, and the somewhat obscure language seems to reflect a Spartan effort at face saving and an Athenian desire to prevent any merging of small communities in the area. The difficulty of wording this section was obviously complicated by the fact that certain cities (for example, Olynthus) had revolted from Athens before the beginning of the war. Cities then controlled by Sparta were to be restored to Athens, but the inhabitants were free to go elsewhere, taking their property with them. The cities were to be autonomous, paying only the tribute of Aristides—thus being freed from the increased assessment of 425/4. They would rate as allies of Athens only if they so wished. Cities which Athens controlled or had recovered the Athenians could treat as they pleased.[18]

Ten years of war and constant bloodshed thus ended in a peace so unsatisfactory to many of the combatants that none of the issues which had launched the Greek world into hostilities was really settled. Sparta in its desire for peace had disregarded the claims of its allies and could not persuade them to accept the agreement. Corinth was angry that the Athenian empire was still largely intact and that it did not recover from Athens two communities on the west coast of Greece, Anactorium and Sollium; Athens gave up its claim to Plataea but was allowed to retain Nisaea, which outraged the Megarians; the Boeotians refused to relinquish the border fortress of Panactum, which it had recently taken from Athens. In fact, the temper of its allies was so belligerent and Argos so unwilling to renew the treaty that Sparta, to protect itself, made a fifty years' alliance with Athens. This alliance naturally aroused suspicion among all the Greeks and also was of uncertain value to the two allies, for Sparta could not persuade Amphipolis to return to Athens, and Athens, in retaliation, retained Pylos. Thucydides remarks that for six years and ten months the Athenians and Spartans did not invade each other's territory, but their diplomacy was constantly hostile. It is at this point (5.26) that he inserts his second introduction in which he explains that the Peace of Nicias did not mark an end of the war and that in fact the Peloponnesian War was a continuous struggle which lasted for twenty-seven years.

The next few years provided an appalling picture of the instability of the political life of the Greek city-states. Thucydides (5.25–83) describes the manoeuvres and countermanoeuvres, both diplomatic and military, in considerable detail, but even he could not make order out of the chaos. Of this confusion, which temporarily endangered Spartan hegemony in the Peloponnesus, only a few items need be mentioned here. The Corinthians, disgusted with the dangerous possibilities of the Spartan-Athenian alliance, told the Argives that this was their chance to assume leadership in the Peloponnesus and in other parts of the Greek world. In short order Corinth, Elis, Mantinea in Arcadia, and the Thracian Chalcidians joined in alliance with Argos. These developments naturally worried the Spartans, and under a new board of ephors they proceeded secretly to make an alliance with the Boeotians, although this step was contrary to their agreement with Athens. By means of this alliance the Spartans persuaded the Boeotians to restore Panactum and their Athenian prisoners to Athens—steps which the Spartans hoped would cause the Athenians to abandon Pylos. Unfortunately for their plans the Boeotians first destroyed Panactum, which so infuriated the Athenians that they would not consider relinquishing Pylos. Argos, aware of this diplomatic manoeuvring and apprehensive of falling victim to Spartans, Boeotians, and Athenians all united as allies, started to take steps to make what sort of treaty it could with Sparta. At this point a change in policy at Athens created new confusion.

Since the death of Cleon the leading statesman in Athens had been

Nicias. Nicias, a wealthy and conservative man, was a strong advocate of peace, and the peace that bears his name reflects his belief that the most satisfactory solution of the problems of the Greek world lay in the general acceptance of a leadership divided between Athens and Sparta, as Cimon had advocated over a generation earlier. In the years following 421 Nicias' task was the difficult one of trying to make the two states abide by the terms of the peace and alliance. This policy was constantly opposed by the warlike and imperialist faction in Athens, the group commonly known as the radical democrats. Their leader was Hyperbolus, a demagogue presumably similar to Cleon in his views, who was ignored with aristocratic disdain, except for a passing remark to his death, by Thucydides (8.73.3) and a favorite target for the shafts of Aristophanes.

A more serious threat to the ideas of Nicias was embodied in a new figure in Athenian political life, Alcibiades, who held the office of *strategos* for the first time in 420. From that date until the end of the Peloponnesian War Alcibiades, for better or for worse, played a dominant role in Greek history.[19] By birth and marriage he was connected with the old families and *genē* of Attica,[20] through his father with the Salaminioi, through his mother with the Alcmaeonids, and through his wife with the Kerykes of Eleusis. His father, Cleinias, had been killed in the battle of Coronea in 447, and thereafter Alcibiades, who at his father's death was only about three years old, was reared in the household of his kinsman Pericles. Through all his youth, therefore, he was a close witness of Pericles in the period of his greatest influence, and he was closely associated with all the intellectual developments encouraged by Pericles. Because of his beauty, his intelligence, his courage, and his high birth he was allowed to lead a rather undisciplined life. His favorite teacher was Socrates, to whom Alcibiades was drawn partly by the man's charismatic nature and partly by his dialectical skill, which seemed unencumbered by current traditions. Alcibiades was closely associated with Socrates in both the Potidaea and Delium campaigns. The tremendous power and influence exercised by Pericles made an indelible impression on the young man, and he became obsessed with the ambition to become the dominant leader in Athens. The lack of any serious restraint on his youthful impulses, the lowered morality engendered by the horrors of the war and the plague, and the excitement caused by the many "sophistic" ideas in circulation, especially the notion of the conflict between natural law and customary law with the resulting scorn that could be heaped on conventional morality, encouraged his passionate nature, convinced of its superiority, to pay slight heed to the restraints under which Pericles had normally worked. Alcibiades' one aim became self-aggrandizement, and from his totally amoral point of view any means were legitimate which contributed to the growth of that aim. To him, as he said later, democracy was an absurdity (Thucydides, 6.89.6), but he was willing to pay lip service to it as long as it conformed with his purposes.

Alcibiades had been humiliated because in the negotiations for the peace of 421 the Spartans had worked in collaboration with Nicias. He felt that, since his grandfather had been a *proxenos* of Sparta and since he had been trying to revive the position by paying considerable attention to the Sphacterian prisoners, the Spartans should have made use of his services. After the conclusion of the peace he maintained that the Spartan intention was to crush Argos and then, liberated from that worry, to attack Athens. The confusion in 420, resulting from Athenian anger at Sparta because of the alliance with Boeotia and from the efforts of Argos to reach an agreement with Sparta, gave Alcibiades his opportunity. He sent messengers to the Argives urging them along with the Mantineans and Eleans to dispatch envoys as soon as possible to Athens to discuss the possibility of an alliance. These envoys arrived and almost simultaneously ambassadors from Sparta, endowed with plenipotentiary powers to try to settle the matters in dispute with the Athenians. By promising to bring about the restoration of Pylos to the Spartans, Alcibiades persuaded their envoys not to mention to the asembly the full powers of which they had spoken to the Boulē. When they followed his instructions in speaking to the assembly, Alcibiades was the first to accuse them of duplicity, with the result that the assembly, in exasperation, passed a decree setting forth the terms of a hundred years' alliance with Argos, Mantinea, and Elis (Thucydides, 5.43–47).

Despite this new quadruple alliance, the treaty between Athens and Sparta theoretically remained in effect, but the activity of Alcibiades was directed towards the outbreak of war. The Athenian people ultimately became so uneasy that Alcibiades was not reelected *strategos* for 418. His absence undoubtedly weakened the strength of the anti-Spartan coalition of Argives, Mantineans, and Athenians when they faced the Spartans and their allies at Mantinea in that year. King Agis won a decisive victory—so decisive that Sparta regained its military prestige, which had been on the wane since its defeat at Pylos. Almost immediately the oligarchic faction seized power in Argos, which, abandoning the quadruple alliance, entered into a fifty-year treaty with Sparta. A year later the democratic faction overthrew the oligarchs and once again Argos joined Athens. Friction between Argos and Sparta continued until finally in 414 it led to open hostilities between Athens and Sparta.

The role of Athens at Mantinea had not been effective, partly because of the absence of Alcibiades and the violent political disagreements between him and Nicias. Since the two "parties" were thwarting each other, it was an obvious occasion on which to hold an ostracism, and Hyperbolus used his influence to have the ostracism carried out. Alcibiades, however, sensed the danger, and he and Nicias instructed their followers to write the name Hyperbolus on the potsherds. The outcome was that—in 417 probably—the "demagogue" was the man ostracized. This was the last occasion on which the institution was employed; the Athenians apparently felt that its usefulness was over now that a method had been discovered to circumvent it. The cleavage between factions remained at Athens, for Nicias and Alcibiades were both elected *strategoi* for 417/16 (Plutarch, *Nicias*, 11; *Alcibiades*, 13).

The year 416 was marked by an event which Thucydides' account has made eternally notorious. The Athenians, who had been rather frustrated in the Peloponnesus and the Thracian region since the Peace of Nicias, were now concentrating on their naval empire in the fervid belief, which had become almost a religious dogma, that the Aegean Sea was theirs. The little island of Melos in the southwestern Cyclades, a former Spartan colony, was, apparently, the only exception in that sea to Athenian maritime control. According to Thucydides Melos assumed a role of neutrality in the Peloponnesian War, but a mutilated inscription which has been preserved reveals that it contributed to the financial support of the Spartan fleet, probably in 427 (*M & L,* no. 67). In 426 Nicias made an unsuccessful attempt on the island, and in the following year, in the decree which approximately tripled the imperial tribute, the Athenians listed Melos as a tributary member of the empire. In 416, following a measure sponsored by Alcibiades, the Athenians again attacked the island, and when Melos fell all the adult males were put to death and the women and children were sold as slaves. Subsequently the Athenians sent out 500 colonists to the island.

Thucydides' account is remarkable and memorable. At the end of book 5, prior to his description of the fall of Melos, he includes what is usually called the Melian Dialogue, a debate between the Athenian generals and the Melian magistrates prior to the actual beginning of hostilities. The Athenian argument is a cold and ruthless presentation of the "moral bleakness" which Thucydides seems to accept as axiomatic in interstate relations. Two sentences starkly assert the "might makes right" doctrine. "Since you [Melians] know as well as we do that right, as the world goes, is only in question between equals in power, while the strong do what they can and the weak suffer what they must ... Of the gods we believe, and of men we know, that by a necessary law of their nature they rule wherever they can." This dialogue, even more than many of the speeches, raises the question of how Thucydides could have obtained an accurate report of what was actually said. There is the further problem of why Thucydides at this point chose the format of a dialogue rather than the customary one of set speeches. Various explanations have been suggested, but whatever their varying nuances, the general conclusion is difficult to avoid that Thucydides, influenced at least subconsciously by the dramatic and tragic sense so prevalent in Athenian (and Greek) culture, used this occasion to emphasize, in language that hardly could have been employed in an actual diplomatic meeting, the hideous extent to which *hybris*—the arrogance of power— had corrupted Athenian sanity on the eve of the great Sicilian expedition which was to be the Athenian *nemesis*.[21] In the very next year Euripides' devastating antiwar tragedy, *The Trojan Women*, was produced. It is worth noting that, when Thucydides recounts the equally brutal punishment which the Athenians inflicted on Scione in 421, he is satisfied with one matter-of-fact sentence.

THE ATHENIAN expedition to Sicily is described so fully, so brilliantly, and so dramatically by Thucydides that any attempt to retell the tale can be little more than a pale reflection of the words of the great historian. Since anyone interested in Greek history or in great literature should read Thucydides' account as given in books 6 and 7 of his work, only a brief summary of this Athenian venture will be presented here.

Since the Congress of Gela and the withdrawal of the Athenian fleet from Sicily in 424, Athens had paid little attention to the island, although it can be assumed that dreams of conquests in the west were still favorite topics of conversation and discussion among the aggressive imperialistic group. In the winter of 416/15, however, envoys from Segesta in western Sicily, a city with which Athens had made an alliance about 457, renewed in 427, arrived with a plea for help against the neighboring city of Selinus, strongly supported by Syracuse. The Segestans argued that Athenian interference in Sicily was necessary to prevent the island from falling under the total domination of Syracuse, a contingency which augured benefits for the Peloponnesians and dangers for the Athenians. They also promised that they could provide the necessary military funds, a promise which time proved illusory. The Athenians sent envoys to Segesta to investigate the situation and, on their return in the spring with a favorable, albeit misinformed, report, voted to send an expedition under the joint command of Nicias, Alcibiades, and Lamachus. In a second assembly held five days later to decide various matters concerning the project, Nicias, who had been chosen against his will as one of the commanders, tried to dissuade the Athenians from the undertaking. He argued that Athens, with the uncertain conditions in Greece and with the Chalcidic region still in chaos, was in no position to attempt distant conquests which it probably would be unable to control. Alcibiades, however, foreseeing an opportunity for his own aggrandizement, took the aggressive line, emphasizing the disorganized nature of the Sicilian cities, stressing the great rewards that would fall to Athens, and insisting that an empire which did not constantly keep expanding was doomed to decline. The assembly, with little real knowledge of the situation in Sicily but excited by all the glamorous prospects, abided by its original decision that the expedition should be undertaken under the command of the three generals who had been designated (Thucydides, 6.9–26).

While the extensive preparations for the enterprise were in process, a scandal occurred which severely shook Athenian society. On one night practically all the stone herms, the square figures which were placed in the doorways of many temples and private houses, were mutilated. Excitement in the city was intense, for the episode was interpreted as a bad omen for the coming expedition, and also there was a feeling that it might be a precursor of some antidemocratic political action. Rewards were offered to any who could provide information about the herms, or about other acts of an impious nature. Some slaves and metics furnished evidence, not concerning the herms but about other statues which had been desecrated by some drunken youths and about the burlesquing of the Eleusinian Mysteries in various private homes, in which Alcibiades had participated. Alcibiades denied such charges and begged that he be allowed to stand trial before the departure of the Sicilian expedition. His enemies, however, feeling that in the presence of the army he would probably win acquittal, urged that the departure should not be delayed, and that his trial should be postponed until his return. Their plan was to have him recalled so that they could prosecute him at a time when his supporters would be absent. The assembly voted that Alcibiades should sail.

In June 415 the expedition was ready to depart. Thucydides (6.30–32.2) describes the magnificence of the preparation and the rivalry for perfection which existed among the various branches of the service. His picture of the descent of practically the total population of Attica, civilian and foreign, to the Piraeus on the day of departure, of the mixed emotions of the spectators, of the solemn prayers and libations before putting out to sea, and of the subsequent racing of the ships as far as Aegina is masterly and deeply moving.

The Athenian fleet sailed to Corcyra, where the various allied contingents had already assembled. From there the great armada, with its complement of about 30,000 men, crossed to the Iapygian promontory and then, meeting with generally unfriendly receptions, followed the Italian coast to Rhegium. Even this old ally presented an aloof attitude but did allow the Athenians to pitch camp near the city and provided them with the facilities of a market. Here, apparently for the first time, the generals met and prepared what action they thought should be taken. In brief, the plan of Nicias was to sail immediately to Selinus and to settle the war between it and Segesta, and then, after displaying the power of Athens, to sail home unless some unusual opportunity presented itself; that of Alcibiades was to send heralds to all the cities except Selinus and Syracuse and then, knowing who their allies were, to attack those two cities; that of Lamachus was to attack Syracuse immediately while the Syracusans were still in a state of terror and disorder, for a victory over Syracuse would open the rest of Sicily to them. When Lamachus' realistic proposal was not accepted, he threw his support to Alcibiades. Shortly thereafter the Athenians sailed down the east coast of Sicily and, after ousting the Syracusan party from Catana, built their camp there.

About the same time the official Athenian dispatch-ship, the *Salaminia,* arrived with orders that Alcibiades and some of the soldiers should return to Athens to stand trial for their alleged participation in the scandals concerning the herms and the Mysteries. Ever since the first publicity about these matters, Athens had been victimized by vicious witch-hunts which were only partially alleviated by the future orator Andocides turning state's witness. Many men were executed or fled into exile, and Alcibiades' enemies were confident that they could procure his execution if he stood trial in Athens. The *Salaminia* was instructed not to arrest Alcibiades openly, from fear of the damage that might be done to the morale of the army, but to have him follow the dispatch-ship in his own vessel. Alcibiades proceeded in this fashion as far as Thurii in Italy, but then he and the other accused soldiers disappeared. As soon as possible he made his way to the Peloponnesus and to Sparta, while the Athenians passed sentence of death by default upon him and his companions.

The departure of Alcibiades, the great advocate of the expedition, left the Athenian forces somewhat disorganized and unmotivated. They sailed to Segesta in a futile attempt to win allies in the north of Sicily and, subsequently sailing into the great harbor of Syracuse, landed and fought an indecisive battle with the Syracusans. Then, with the year 415 an almost total loss from the point of view of the expedition, the Athenians went into winter quarters in their camp at Catana. The Syracusans, relieved by the lethargy of the Athenians, appointed Hermocrates as one of the three commanding generals and devoted considerable time to building or strengthening fortifications around the city and the harbor.

In the winter of 415/14 envoys from Syracuse and Corinth reached Sparta and pleaded for the sending of aid to Sicily. Alcibiades, who had recently arrived there, urgently supported their plea in the speech which he delivered to the Spartan assembly. In this speech, as reported by Thucydides (6.89–92), Alcibiades revealed what were the purposes of the Sicilian expedition, at least in the minds of the aggressive imperialists among the Athenians: the conquest of Sicily and Italy, an assault on Carthage, and then with all the resources, both human and material, thus gained, a naval blockade of the Peloponneseus and a land attack on its cities. The ultimate aim was to bring all Hellenes under the rule of Athens. In view of the seriousness of the situation he advised the Spartans to send troops to help the Syracusans or at least a Spartan general to take charge of the Syracusan resistance. He also strongly urged the Spartans to weaken and dismay the Athenians by taking and fortifying Decelea in central Attica, a step which would deprive the Athenians of the profits from the silver mines of Laurium, disorganize their agriculture, and encourage the allies to be less prompt and thorough in the payment of tribute. The Spartans were alarmed by his words. For the present they merely took note of the Decelea proposal, but they immediately appointed one of their officers, Gylippus, to the command of the Syracusans and ordered him to take the necessary steps.

In the spring of 414 the Athenians in Sicily finally began an effective offensive. By means of a pass known as Euryalus they succeeded in climbing and occupying a plateau named Epipolae which lay directly to the west of Syracuse. They immediately began to build a wall across the plateau from north to south with the aim of starting a blockade of the city. The Syracusans, aware of the danger, tried to erect a counter-wall which would frustrate the intentions of the enemy. This competitive building led to various skirmishes, and in one of them the Athenian general Lamachus was killed. Thus the Athenian forces were left in the sole charge of Nicias, the man who had vigorously opposed the undertaking of the expedition. Nevertheless, for a while Nicias demonstrated commendable activity. The Athenian fleet was brought into the Great Harbor, at the western end of which an Athenian camp was established. The aim now was to extend the besieging wall from Epipolae down the cliffs to the northern end of the harbor, thus, with the assistance of the fleet, establishing a complete blockade of Syracuse. In the meantime, however, Gylippus, conveyed by Corinthian ships, had arrived in southern Italy and from there had crossed to Himera on the north central coast of Sicily. Collecting reinforcements from Himera, Selinus, and other allies, he marched towards Syracuse and on approaching the city was met by a large contingent of Syracusans. He climbed Epipolae by the pass Euryalus, which the Athenians had incredibly left unguarded, and then, through the section of the wall which the Athenian had not completed, proceeded into the city. For the next few weeks the opponents engaged in frantic wall building, with the result that the Syracusan counter-wall successfully ruined the Athenian hope to blockade Syracuse by land.

The situation for the Athenians had become so bad by the end of the summer that Nicias wrote a long letter to the assembly, of which the main points were the following: the besieger, from the land side at least, had really become the besieged; additional anti-Athenian forces were expected from the Peloponnesus and Sicily; the Athenian fleet, both ships and men, because of the impossibility of making repairs and lack of training, was in danger from the Syracusan fleet; either the present expedition should be withdrawn or an equally large fleet and army should be sent in support; and a successor was needed for Nicias, who was suffering from a disease of the kidneys. Despite the realism and pessimism of the report, the proud and aggressive democracy would not even consider the idea of withdrawal. Plans were promptly made for organizing the necessary reinforcements, and Demosthenes and Eurymedon were appointed as colleagues for Nicias.

In the spring of 413 Sparta and its Peloponnesian allies resumed their raids on Attica, which had been in abeyance since 425. The Spartans, because of their lack of success in the Archidamian War, had been suffering from superstitious fears that their misfortunes had resulted from their unwillingness to submit to arbitration in 432 and 431 and from the fact that the Theban attack on Plataea had initiated the war. But now Athenian aggression in Sicily, Athenian attacks on Spartan territory from Pylos and from Argos on Epidaurus, and their unwillingness even to consider arbitration, convinced the Spartans that this time the Athenians were clearly the aggressors. The Peloponnesians ravaged parts of Attica and then, following the suggestion of Alcibiades, moved to Decelea which they took and fortified, leaving a permanent garrison there. The occupation of Decelea, about fifteen miles north of Athens and a key position for surveying Attica, enabled the Spartans successfully to carry out the actions which Alcibiades had suggested. Despite these difficulties at home Athens dispatched its second armada to Sicily, and in July Demosthenes and Eurymedon sailed into the harbor of Syracuse with seventy-three triremes and a total force of from 15,000 to 20,000. The arrival naturally brought dismay to the Syracusans but considerable cheer to the Athenians who, in addition to their numerous former woes, had recently suffered a reverse from the Syracusan fleet in the harbor.

Demosthenes was determined to attack the Syracusans while they were still disheartened by the arrival of the new Athenian contingent, thus avoiding the mistake which Nicias had made two years before when, by his procrastination in taking action, he had allowed the Syracusans to regain their courage and make necessary preparations. Convinced that it was essential to gain control of Epipolae and the Syracusan wall and fortifications there, he undertook a secret night expedition. The ascent of Euryalus was made successfully, but then in the confusion of the darkness the Athenians were badly defeated by the Syracusan forces on the plateau. After this failure Demosthenes insisted that the whole Athenian fleet should return to Greece where it could be of great use, or at least should sail to another part of Sicily where its activity would not be confined and jeopardized as it was in the harbor of Syracuse. Nicias, however, refused to move without specific instructions from the Athenian assembly; he also argued that the Syracusans were in a bad plight and that a party in the city wished to betray Syracuse to the Athenians. In the meantime Gylippus, who had been traveling throughout Sicily collecting allies, arrived with a large number of Sicilian troops and also of Peloponnesians who had been sent to the aid of Syracuse. This was enough to convince Nicias that something had to be done, and with his consent the Athenians planned to sail secretly out of the harbor. Just as they were embarking an eclipse of the moon occurred which terrified many of the soldiers, and Nicias refused even to consider departure until thrice nine days had passed.

The Syracusans, on learning what the Athenians had been planning, launched a naval attack on the Athenian fleet in which they succeeded in driving many of the Athenian ships ashore and causing considerable damage. Then, with their confidence increasing rapidly, they proceeded to block the exit from the harbor as effectively as they could, for they wished to prevent the Athenians from escaping and establishing a base somewhere else in Sicily. The Athenians were now in a desperate situation, and their generals decided that a great effort must be made to break out of the harbor and sail to Catana; if this proved impossible they must burn their ships and proceed by land to the nearest friendly community, Hellenic or barbarian. Thucydides' description of this last battle in the harbor is wonderfully dramatic and emotional and should be read in his pages. The Athenians, despite mighty efforts, were overwhelmed and driven back to the shore. Demosthenes still thought they should make one more attempt the following morning, but the sailors were too weary and discouraged to entertain the idea. Thus departure by land became necessary, a withdrawal which had to begin with the abandonment of the sick and wounded in camp. This flight of about 40,000 men, which continued for some days, was a hideous nightmare, for the Syracusans, thirsting for vengeance, hounded the retreating men at every step. In the confusion Demosthenes and Nicias became separated; each ultimately, to stop the carnage, surrendered. Against the wishes of Gylippus both Nicias and Demosthenes were butchered. The number of captured fugitives who fell to the state was comparatively small, for thousands had been slaughtered and many were secretly taken off into private slavery. The captives, to the number of 7,000, were thrown into the quarries where for many days they suffered from the confined quarters, from the heat by day and cold by night, from inadequate food and water, and from the stench of decaying corpses. After seventy days all except the Athenians and any Sicilians or Italians who had joined with them were removed and sold as slaves. The Athenians had to endure the ordeal for another six months.

It is a tremendous tribute to Thucydides as artist and dramatist that the reading of book 7, and particularly its final pages, overwhelms one with pity for the tragedy which befell the Athenians in Sicily. This almost universal reaction to Thucydides' account is also a striking example of the prejudices inherent in the writing and reading of history. A more rational emotion would seem to be a feeling of rejoicing, tinged with pity for the defeated, for the victory of the Syracusans who, through great effort and much suffering and blood, had frustrated the attempt of a grasping imperialistic state to reduce them to a humiliating subject status. It is worth recalling that Thucydides in his estimate of Pericles, when he speaks of the blunders committed by his successors, includes the Sicilian expedition, imputing its collapse primarily to the failure of the Athenians to support sufficiently the original expeditionary force, a criticism flatly contradicted by the pages of book 7. The Syracusans, however, knew what they had escaped, and they celebrated their achievement in a festival called Assinaria, named after the river Assinaros where Nicias made his last grisly stand, and in connection with this festival and the associated games they issued some of the most beautiful coins that have survived from the ancient world.

WHEN NEWS OF the Sicilian catastrophe reached Athens in the autumn of 413, at first there was incredulity and then, when the horror of the reality was finally grasped, there was overwhelming grief among the innumerable families affected by the casualties, and a crushing apprehension for the future of Athens.[22] For a while there was terror that the victorious Syracusans would immediately sail to the support of the Peloponnesians and that these latter would intensify their efforts, and there was a well-founded dread concerning the effect that Athens' humbling would have on the loyalty of its allies, particularly those in the east whose tribute was so essential to the financial welfare of the state. The financial situation, which had been previously weakened by the loss of Amphipolis and the mines of Mt. Pangaeus, was naturally shattered by the tremendous, and wasted, expenditure of money on Sicily and by the loss of hundreds of ships. The permanent Spartan army located in Decelea, as Alcibiades had predicted, was already inflicting damage, destroying crops and flocks in the plains and the hills, making it impossible to transport supplies from Euboea via Oropus to Athens but necessitating the long and expensive haul around Sunium, and blocking effective exploitation of the silver of Laurium. Thucydides says that ultimately 20,000 slaves deserted, and many of these must have been from the cruelly exploited workers in the mines. Money was desperately needed, and the upper classes, who supplied most of the funds through the liturgies and the capital tax (*esiphora*), were the very ones particularly harmed by the garrison at Decelea. A strong feeling spread among the Athenians that some sort of curb was necessary on the assembly and Boulē which had endorsed the Sicilian expedition, and a magistracy of ten elderly *probouloi,* including the poet Sophocles and Hagnon, the founder of Amphipolis, was elected to assume many of the advisory duties of the council. Some months earlier the Athenians had replaced the usual tribute system by a tax of 5 percent on all maritime exports and imports from or to the harbors in the empire (Thucydides, 7.28.4). How successful this method was is unknown; in any case, it was replaced as soon as possible by the previous system.

In the winter of 413/12 the revolt of allies, so much feared by Athens, began to become a reality. Envoys from Euboea and Lesbos made their way to King Agis in Decelea, and envoys from Chios and Erythrae proceeded directly to Sparta. The latter were accompanied by an ambassador from Tissaphernes, the Persian satrap of the maritime regions (Lydia, Ionia, Caria). Somewhat later there arrived envoys from Pharnabazus, the satrap ruling from Dascylium in Hellespontine Phrygia. The interference in Greek affairs of Persia, with which Athens had had little concern since the Peace of Callias except at the time of the revolt of Samos and in the probable renewal of the peace with Darius II in 424/3, marked the beginning of a sinister role which Persia was to play in Greek history until the conquests of Alexander the Great some eighty years later. Since the formation of the Delian League the Persians had been debarred from collecting tribute from the Greek cities of Asia

Minor, but now the king, Darius II, felt that the time had come to reassert his authority, and he was demanding the payment of the tribute from the satraps of the regions in which the Greeks lived. Both satraps felt that the most logical solution of their problem was to employ Spartan ships and land forces against the Asiatic Greeks, thus encouraging them to revolt from Athens, and they offered to meet the military expenses. The Spartans believed that their interests would best be served by replying to the appeals of the Chians, and in this decision they were strongly supported by Alcibiades, who had been living in Sparta since the end of 415. The choice fell on Chios because as the last "free" and "independent" member of the Athenian empire, its defection would probably have important repercussions. Moreover, Chios had a fleet of some sixty ships, and an oligarchic group there was ready to expedite the revolt (Thucydides, 8.5–6).

In the summer of 412 a few Spartan ships and Alcibiades succeeded in sailing to Chios and with the aid of local oligarchs effected the revolt of the island. This achievement was rapidly followed by the revolt of Erythrae and Clazomenae. When the news of the defection of Chios reached Athens, the Athenians, realizing the danger to their empire, voted to make use of the 1,000 talents which since the beginning of the war had been set aside as a reserve (2.24.2), to man as many ships as possible, and to send the few that were available immediately to Ionia. These ships made their headquarters at Samos (8.15). In the meantime Alcibiades and the Spartans, again with the assistance of an oligarchic faction, brought about the revolt of Miletus. It was then that, through the agency of Tissaphernes, the first "alliance" was struck between the Persians and the Spartans. The agreement specifically stated that "whatever country or cities the king has, or the king's ancestors had, shall be the king's," and emphasized that the war upon the Athenians was a joint enterprise of the king and the Lacedaemonians and their allies (Thucydides, 8.18.1). Nothing was said about financial obligations, presumably because Tissaphernes had previously promised to subsidize the Spartans. Since oligarchic groups were cooperating with the Spartans in various places, it is not surprising that the Athenians gave their blessing to a proletarian revolution in Samos. In that island the "many" put to death some 200 of the upper classes, banished 400, and confiscated their land and houses. In reward for this example of fidelity the Athenians decreed autonomy for the Samians (Thucydides, 8.21).

Fighting continued through the summer of 412, with more revolts, and attempted recoveries, sometimes successful, by the Athenians. The Spartans did achieve two important victories, however, in causing both

Cnidos and Rhodes to revolt. The "treaty" of Miletus was renewed, this time with the added clause that "the expenses of all troops in the king's country, sent for by the king, shall be borne by the king." Subsequently a commission of eleven Spartans held a conference with Tissaphernes to clarify certain matters in the agreements, and one of them, Lichas, made the point that it was outrageous for the king now to lay claim to all land formerly ruled by himself or by his ancestors; such a statement supported a Persian claim to recover the islands, Thessaly, Locris, and everything as far as Boeotia, and "made the Lacedaemonians give to the Hellenes instead of liberty a Median master." This statement so outraged Tissaphernes that he broke up the conference (Thucydides, 8.37; 43).

In the winter of 412/11 the role of Alcibiades once again became prominent. During his sojourn in Sparta he had made many enemies and in particular had outraged Agis, whose wife he was reputed to have seduced. A letter now came to the Spartan admiral from Sparta with instructions to put Alcibiades to death. Warned of his danger, Alcibiades fled immediately to Tissaphernes, and now began a duel of wits between two brilliant and unscrupulous men whose diplomatic aims were to exploit one another to the maximum. With the desire of hurting the Spartans, Alcibiades advised the satrap to be chary with his expenditure of military funds, of which the Spartan fleet was in great need. He also tried to persuade Tissaphernes that the best Persian policy was to let the two Greek sides wear each other out—a policy that in the years to come became typically Persian—and he added that at present Sparta was more a danger than Athens, for the Spartans did not want to liberate Greek cities from Athens only to surrender them to Persia.

Alcibiades, of course, now that Sparta was debarred to him, was trying to devise ways for his return to Athens. Partly through his contrivances, his influence with Tissaphernes became known to some of the Athenian officers and trierarchs at Samos, who dispatched a group to consult with him. Alcibiades explained to them that he could persuade Tissaphernes and the king to become friends of Athens, if Athens would become more trustworthy in their eyes by establishing an oligarchy. These men, on returning to Samos, organized a clique of those opposed to democracy and then told the army that the king of Persia would become their friend and provide them with money if Alcibiades should be restored and the democracy at Athens abolished. The soldiers as a whole naturally resented this suggestion about the democracy, but the arguments of the oligarchic conspirators and the welcome prospect of receiving the much-needed money kept them quiet. In a subsequent discussion among the plotters the general Phrynichus, a former democrat now turned oligarch, warned them that Alcibiades cared no more for oligarchy than democracy, that he was interested only in securing his restoration to Athens, and that it was illogical to think that the king would abandon his new allies, the Peloponnesians, to aid his old enemies, the Athenians. He was outvoted, however, and an embassy headed by Pisander was sent to Athens to argue for the restoration of Alcibiades and the abolition of democracy, and thus to prepare the way for friendship with Tissaphernes and the Persians (Thucydides, 8.45–49).

On arriving in Athens, the embassy appeared before the assembly and made its report. As was to be expected, the first reaction of the Athenians was one of heated opposition, the majority being indignant at the threat to the democracy, and the enemies of Alcibiades, in particular the priests of Eleusis, expressing horror at the thought of the restoration of the profaner of the Mysteries. Pisander, by enumerating the dangers confronting Athens—the number of the Peloponnesian ships, the revolting allies, the Persian supply of money available to the Peloponnesians—finally convinced the people that their only hope of salvation lay in the recall of Alcibiades, who alone was in a position to win the Persians as allies. The assembly, accordingly, in the belief that they could subsequently change the government again, voted that Pisander and ten others should sail and make the best possible arrangements with Tissaphernes and Alcibiades. Pisander, before leaving Athens, visited all the oligarchic clubs that existed in the city, primarily for providing help in lawsuits and elections, and urged them to combine their efforts for the overthrow of the democracy (Thucydides, 8.53–54).

In Asia Minor, the Athenian envoys had several conferences with Tissaphernes and Alcibiades, described by Thucydides in a confusing passage (8.56). In these interviews Tissaphernes did not want to alienate Alcibiades, who was useful to him, but he was worried about the Spartans and also, as a Persian, he wished to exact a price from the Athenians. Alcibiades, feeling unsure about Tissaphernes but anxious that the envoys should not underestimate his influence with the Persians, sought to place the responsibility for failure to reach a satisfactory agreement on the Athenians by steadily increasing the Persian demands: first, the cession of all Ionia, then the adjacent islands, and finally, when these demands were accepted, "the right of the king to build ships and sail along his own coast wherever and with as many as he pleased." The threat of a Persian domination in the Aegean was too much for the Athenians, and the conference broke up in an atmosphere of angry frustration. Tissaphernes, then, realizing that pay was necessary to hold the Peloponnesian fleet together, arranged, apparently in the spring of 411, a third treaty with the Spartans.[23] In this it was stated specifically that

Tissaphernes would pay for the ships now present until the arrival of the king's vessels (the Phoenician fleet); thereafter the Spartans must pay for their own ships. This Phoenician fleet, which, in fact, never "arrived," and possibly had never been released for such action by the central government of the king, provided a convenient argument for Tissaphernes whenever the Peloponnesians, angered by lack of pay, demanded more activity from the Persians.

Pisander and his colleagues, after leaving Tissaphernes and Alcibiades, returned to Samos where they did what they could to arouse oligarchic interests in the Athenian soldiers and the Samians. Then Pisander and half of the envoys returned to Athens with the intention of fostering the oligarchic movement there. In their absence various antidemocratic steps had been taken. A group of young men from the oligarchic clubs had assassinated Androcles, a "demagogue" largely responsible for the banishment of Alcibiades. At the time the thought was that the elimination of Androcles would be a measure to win the favor of Alcibiades and Tissaphernes. Talk was spread abroad that citizenship should be restricted to 5,000 men capable of serving the state without pay. Various people who protested the current trends were quickly put to death. The result was that the people as a whole were cowed, for no one was sure who the conspirators were and who the loyal democrats were. It was into such an Athens that Pisander arrived. An assembly was held in which it was voted to elect twenty men who, in conjunction with the ten *probouloi* (Aristotle, *Ath. Const.*, 29.2), should prepare suggestions for the common good, to be presented to the people on the 14th of Thargelion (April–May, 411). When that day arrived, the assembly was held in the precincts of the temple of Poseidon at Colonus, about a mile and a quarter beyond the walls of Athens. This location ensured that the session would be attended primarily by hoplites and cavalry who could be spared from military duty, and not by the unarmed city population who would have been dangerously exposed to the Spartans patrolling the countryside from Decelea. The first proposal of the thirty commissioners was to abolish the *graphē paranomōn*, thus making it possible to suggest any measure no matter how "unconstitutional." Then measures were passed eliminating pay for government service, in view of the desperate financial situation, electing a body of Four Hundred who should serve as a council, and establishing a rather obscure system for enrolling the Five Thousand.

A few days later, Thargelion 22, the Four Hundred, possibly on receipt of information unfavorable to them from Samos, took a revolutionary step. Because of the proximity of the Spartans, the Athenians went armed in the daytime whether they were serving on the walls or elsewhere. On this particular day, when most people went home at sun-down, certain men in the conspiracy remained available near their posts. With this support in the background, the Four Hundred, each with a concealed dagger and accompanied by 120 young men who had proved their usefulness when violence was needed, entered the Bouleuterion and dismissed the councillors, emphasizing that their term of office was over by paying each one the balance of his annual salary. Thereafter the Four Hundred, acting as councillors and ruling in despotic fashion, put to death some men whom they considered dangerous and imprisoned or banished others. They also sent envoys to Agis and later to Sparta to try to negotiate a treaty of peace.

In Thucydides' account of this extremely confusing period, which seems more historical than Aristotle's in chapters 29–33 of the *Constitution of the Athenians* where the emphasis is on a constitutional reform rather than a coup d'état, Pisander is the man mentioned most frequently in this establishment of the Oligarchy of the Four Hundred. Thucydides remarks, however, that the real leader behind the scenes was the orator Antiphon. Antiphon, whose ability, at least, Thucydides clearly admired, seldom appeared in the assembly because of his well-known contempt for the masses but devoted his energies to the aristocratic clubs, serving as an advocate in defense of oligarchs in legal or political trouble and as a strategist in formulating revolutionary policy. Thucydides also comments at some length on Phrynichus, who, once he felt confident that Alcibiades would not be recalled, forgot his plebeian background and worked zealously for the oligarchs, and on Theramenes, the son of the *proboulos* Hagnon, about whom more will be said later (Thucydides, 8.64–70).

Shortly after they had seized arbitrary power, the Four Hundred, fearing a hostile reaction among the Athenian sailors at Samos, dispatched envoys to defend the steps they had taken. Samos had been experiencing a revolutionary period more or less simultaneously with Athens. Of the Samians who recently, with the blessing of the Athenians, had established a democratic government, some 300, influenced by the propaganda of Pisander, began to plan an oligarchic coup. They murdered Hyperbolus, the Athenian "demagogue" who was spending his ostracism in Samos, and made plans to attack the Samian people. Word of this conspiracy reached some loyally democratic Athenians, including the trierarch Thrasybulus and the hoplite Thrasyllus, who organized resistance so effectively that the assault of the 300, when it came, was crushed and the democracy at Samos was more firmly established. The victorious democrats then sent messengers to Athens to report their success, not knowing that the Four Hundred had already seized power.

These envoys were immediately arrested, but one managed to escape and, returning to Samos, told a vivid, even if somewhat exaggerated, story of the horrors that were being perpetrated in Athens. The first reaction of the army in its fury was to plan to sail to Athens and expel the oligarchs, but Thrasybulus and Thrasyllus, showing remarkable foresight and restraint in this emotional period, succeeded in calming the soldiers and persuading the whole population of Samos, native as well as Athenian, to take an oath of loyalty to the democracy and enmity to the Four Hundred and the Spartans. The Athenians on the island came to think of themselves as the real government of Athens rather than the oligarchic usurpers there, and they deposed the old generals and appointed new ones, including Thrasybulus and Thrasyllus (Thucydides, 8.72–77).

As the summer of 411 progressed, some Spartan ships, invited and promised pay by the Hellespontine satrap, Pharnabazus, sailed through the Hellespont and caused the revolt of Byzantium. Since Abydos had revolted some months earlier, the danger to Athens' Black Sea grain trade was obviously great. Thrasybulus, probably partly in response to this threat, felt that the best solution for Athenian troubles was to recall Alcibiades in the hope that then Tissaphernes would swing his support from the Spartans to the Athenians. Thrasybulus succeeded in persuading the Athenian assembly at Samos to vote for the recall and amnesty of Alcibiades. Soon after Alcibiades had arrived on the island, he was elected general together with the former ones. In the meantime the envoys dispatched previously by the Four Hundred, after hiding in fear at Delos during the civil strife in Samos, put in their appearance there. They addressed a bitterly hostile assembly and tried to explain that the oligarchy at Athens was resisting the Spartans and that the Five Thousand would have a proper share in the government. The reaction of the Athenian soldiers was to revile them and to advocate sailing immediately to the Piraeus. At this point Alcibiades, with some difficulty, dissuaded them from a course of action which would surely have led to the Hellespont and Ionia falling to the enemy. He then dismissed the envoys with the statement "that he did not object to the government of the Five Thousand but insisted that the Four Hundred should be deposed and the Council of Five Hundred reinstated in power" (Thucydides, 8.86.6).

The envoys returned to Athens and reported what Alcibiades had said and his hopes for a reconciliation between the Samian and the Athenian factions. These proposals were encouraging to the majority of the Four Hundred, many of whom were dissatisfied with the performance of their group, and some of whom, like Theramenes, apparently wanted a moderate oligarchy or a limited democracy in which the Five Thousand, existing in fact and not only in name, would have legitimate citizenship rights. The extreme oligarchs, on the other hand, were greatly disturbed, Phrynichus, because of his fear and hatred of Alcibiades, and the others from terror of losing their power and of the punishment that would fall upon them if any sort of democracy were established. Antiphon, Phrynichus, and ten others set out for Sparta to try to arrange some possible terms of peace, or complete surrender if necessary. In the meantime the remaining extremists continued more energetically their fortifying of Eetionia, a mole forming the western side of the great harbor at Piraeus. This fortification Theramenes and his followers declared was intended more to welcome a Spartan fleet than to try to resist the Athenian ships from Samos. Theramenes' charge seemed more real to the Athenians when it was learned that forty-two Peloponnesian, Sicilian, and Italian ships were assembling at Las in southern Laconia. Emotions became so intense that, when Phrynichus returned from his mission to Sparta, he was assassinated in the marketplace.

Excitement became still more violent when a few days later it was reported that the Peloponnesian fleet had overrun Aegina. Theramenes, as general, went down to the Piraeus, and with his encouragement the hoplites, who were stationed at Eetionia, began, with the help of various people in Piraeus, to demolish the fortifications. A few days later word arrived that the Peloponnesian ships had left Megara and were sailing along the coast of Salamis. The Athenians, now convinced that Theramenes' report was correct, rushed down to the Piraeus intending to oppose the enemy in any way possible. The Peloponnesian ships, however, sailed on around Sunium and then headed for Oropus, seized by the Boeotians in the winter of 412/11 to aid the Euboeans in their desire to revolt. The Athenians, terrified at the thought of losing Euboea, manned what few ships they had and sailed to Eretria. In the ensuing battle, the disorganized Athenians were badly beaten and all Euboea, except the Athenian *cleruchy* at Hestiaea-Oreus, revolted.

When news of this defeat reached Athens, a panic, worse even than the one caused by the Sicilian fiasco, seized the people. Since Attica, because of Spartan occupation of Decelea, was largely out of their control, the people had been dependent on Euboea for many vital supplies. Few ships were left in the Piraeus, and the fleet at Samos was hostile to the oligarchy in Athens. The Athenian democrats were terrified that the Peloponnesian fleet on its return from Eretria might assault the Piraeus. In fact, the Spartans had an ideal opportunity to exhibit some imaginative strategy. A joint attack on land by Agis from Decelea and by the fleet against Piraeus would have put the politically divided Athenians into a desperate position. If the fleet at Samos had sailed to the defense of the motherland, the whole Athenian empire—Ionia, the Hellespont, and the islands—might have collapsed. The Spartans, however, did not take advantage of the opportunity, "but here," as Thucydides (8.96.5) says, "as on so many other occasions the Lacedaemonians proved the most convenient people in the world for the Athenians to be at war with."

While still in doubt about Spartan plans, the Athenians called an assembly, as under the democracy, on the Pnyx. They first deposed the Four Hundred, who had been in power for four months, and then voted to turn the government over to the Five Thousand, who were identified with those able to furnish hoplite equipment. Since this hoplite franchise included roughly the members of Solon's first three census classes, the number of those entitled to the full rights of citizenship was well over 5,000—probably about 9,000 (see Pseudo-Lysias, 20, *For Polystratus,* 13). Subsequently many other assemblies were held in which the details of the government of the "Five Thousand" were worked out—the type of government which apparently Theramenes had visualized from the beginning of the oligarchic revolution. Thucydides (8.97.2), with his dislike of radical democracy, remarks that "it was during the first period of this constitution that the Athenians appear to have enjoyed the best government that they ever did, at least in my time." Some scholars have argued that in this "intermediate constitution" the right to hold office was limited to those of hoplite status while the *thetes* were permitted to participate in the assembly and the dikastic courts, but it seems preferable to believe that all rights of citizenship were restricted only to the "Five Thousand" of hoplite status, men who could discharge public office without receiving pay.[24] This "intermediate constitution" lasted for about eight months (September 411 to April 410) and then was abandoned for the fundamental reason that it excluded from citizenship the majority of the Athenians, the very ones responsible for the maintenance of the Athenian fleet.

Immediately after the deposition of the Four Hundred, most of the extreme oligarchs fled to the Spartans at Decelea. One escaped to Oenoe on the Boeotian frontier and by trickery succeeded in betraying this fortress to the Boeotians. Antiphon remained in Athens and was brought to trial for treason. Despite what Thucydides terms the brilliance of his defense, he was found guilty of treason and executed (Thucydides, 8.80–98).

WARFARE continued as usual off the coast of Asia Minor. The Spartan admiral, Mindarus, disgusted with the impossibility of extracting any pay from Tissaphernes, decided to accept the invitation of the Hellespontine satrap, Pharnabazus, to come to the Hellespont region and cause the revolt of the cities there which were under Athenian control. Mindarus sailed quietly and quickly from Miletus, hoping to be unobserved by the Athenians at Samos, but before long the Athenians followed him. A battle ultimately took place off Cape Cynossema in the Thracian Chersonese at the narrowest part of the Hellespont, and under Thrasyllus and Thrasybulus the Athenians won an impressive victory. Word was immediately sent to Athens, and the arrival of the good news, after the loss of Euboea and the revolutionary trouble which they had been having, revived somewhat the sagging spirits of the population. The Athenian ships next sailed into the Propontis and recovered Cyzicus, which had revolted. Then, hearing that the Peloponnesian fleet was causing trouble behind them, they returned to the Hellespont. It is at this point, with some remarks on Alcibiades and Tissaphernes, that Thucydides' history ends. Since it is known that he lived at least until the year 399, it is probable that death prevented him from completing his task. Subsequently Xenophon, who was born about 430, wrote his *Hellenica,* which began with the year 411 and carried the course of events down to 362 B.C.

The successes which the Athenians had achieved in the Hellespont-Propontis region continued, with extensions to the Bosporus, for several years. In the autumn of 411 the arrival of Alcibiades, with much money exacted from Halicarnassus, enabled the Athenian fleet to defeat the Spartans off Abydos. In the following spring the Spartans, who were besieging Cyzicus, were attacked by the Athenians under Alcibiades, Theramenes, and Thrasybulus, and in a sea and land battle the Spartan admiral Mindarus was killed and his ships either sunk or captured. Subsequently the Athenians erected a fortress at Chrysopolis, slightly to the north of Chalcedon, where Theramenes was left with a squadron to exact a 10 percent toll on all cargoes sailing out of the Black Sea. Then in 408 Chalcedon became tributary again, and Byzantium, guarded by a Spartan *harmost* (governor), Clearchus, a leading figure in the first two books of Xenophon's *Anabasis,* capitulated to a besieging Athenian force under Alcibiades, because a group of Byzantines was indignant that the Peloponnesian troops monopolized all the supplies.

The continuing successes of the Athenians finally convinced the Persian king that his interests were being frustrated by the lack of cooperation between Tissaphernes and Pharnabazus. He also realized that the treaties negotiated through Tissaphernes had become meaningless because of Spartan objections, as expressed chiefly by Lichas, to the implication that the Asiatic Greeks should fall under Persia. In the spring of 407, as Xenophon remarks briefly (*Hellenica,* 1.4.2), a Spartan embassy under Boeotius, which had been sent to the Persian court, returned with the claim that the Spartans had gained from the King all they wanted. A scholar had recently suggested astutely that this "Treaty of Boeotius" regulated the problem of pay to the Spartan ships and also clarified the status of the Asiatic Greeks by stipulating that they should be autonomous provided they rendered the old tribute to the King.[25] In order to enforce this new agreement Darius sent down to the coast in the same spring his younger son Cyrus as lord (*karanos*) of all the maritime regions in Asia Minor, with orders to give unlimited support to the Spartans. Cyrus established his headquarters in Sardis and then disregarded Tissaphernes' advice that it was not to Persian advantage to allow any one Greek state to become too powerful. Cyrus had several interviews with the new Spartan admiral, Lysander, who appeared in the area, and, impressed by his ability and his financial honesty, promised him unlimited support in carrying on the naval war against the Athenians.

The victories in the Hellespontine area won by the Athenian fleet, the democratic military arm, had great repercussions in Athens. Shortly after the success at Cyzicus in the spring of 410 the government of the Five Thousand came to an end, and the full democracy, uniting the separate Athenian state at Samos with Athens, was reestablished. All the details of the change are not known, but it is clear that the assembly was opened again to all adult Athenian males, regardless of financial status, that pay for government service was resumed, and that the Council of Five Hundred was appointed by lot. With the naval personnel dominating the assembly and with the hope of Athens regaining its naval supremacy seeming to be a possibility, the old imperialistic spirit recrudesced. This spirit was certainly fanned by the dispatch to Sparta from Mindarus' vice-admiral, which fell into Athenian hands after the battle of Cyzicus (*Hellenica,* 1.1.23): "The ships are gone. Mindarus is dead. The men are starving. We know not what to do."

The Spartans, discouraged by the loss of most of their fleet, sent an embassy to Athens to discuss the possibility of peace. The suggestion was based on the idea of the status quo, except that Decelea should be restored to Athens and Pylos to Sparta. Such a proposal would have required Athenian acquiescence in the loss of Euboea, parts of Thrace, Byzantium, most of Ionia, and many of the islands, and the assembly, under the leadership of Cleophon, emphatically rejected it. The Athenians have been criticized both in ancient and modern times for rejecting this offer. If one remembers that Athens had just recently been liberated from an oligarchy only too ready to submit to Sparta and that acceptance of these proposals would have meant surrendering to a temporarily weakened Sparta most of its disintegrating empire precisely when the chance of recovering its possessions seemed favorable, the so-called folly of the Athenians is easily understandable. It is worth noting that the evidence for this peace attempt is limited to Diodorus (13.52) and fragment 139 of the Atthidographer Philochorus as quoted by a scholiast to Euripides' *Orestes*. The peace offer is puzzling. The Spartan envoy was Endius, the guest-friend of Alcibiades (Thucydides, 8.6.3), who had been active in 412 in bringing about a Spartan-Persian alliance. In 410 was Endius really representing the policy of the Spartan government? One wonders what the attitude of Spartan allies and especially of Persia would have been if the peace had been achieved.

Cleophon maintained his position as leader of the people until his death in 404. As a "demagogue" and a tradesman—he was a lyre maker—he was hated by the aristocrats and treated with contempt by the ancient aristocratic historians. Different as he obviously was from Pericles in social position, culture, and education, he was a strong advocate of some of Pericles' basic political ideas as expounded some twenty years earlier—maintenance of the empire and a strong fleet, no concessions to the Peloponnesians, and measures to supply employment or support for the poorer classes. In 410 the old system of demanding tribute from the allies was restored. In the same year Cleophon established the *diobelia*, or two-obol payment per day to citizens. Precise knowledge about the *diobelia* is lacking, but it almost certainly was a means, in view of the economic difficulties caused by the Spartan occupation of Decelea, to take care of indigent citizens who were not recipients of pay for performing governmental or military duties. In the following year work was resumed on the Erechtheum, begun in 421 but discontinued during the Sicilian expedition. Building inscriptions, still extant (*Inscriptiones, Graecae*, I^2, 372–374), provide interesting information on the work and wages of citizens, metics, and slaves employed on that temple, which was to house the hero Erechtheus and the ancient wooden statue of the goddess Athena.

It was not easy for the radical democrats, restored to power in 410, to forget that in the preceding year the wealthy and the middle class had tyrannized over them and excluded them from the franchise. Since the Four Hundred had violated and destroyed many aspects of the democratic constitution, there was a general conviction that the laws, going back to those of Draco and Solon and including all subsequent additions, should be codified, revised, and inscribed on stelai placed in front of the Royal Stoa so that they would be available for all concerned. The Five Thousand, by appointing *nomothetai* (law-makers) (Thucydides,

8.97), may have initiated the project, but the work was carried out by a board of commissioners under the democracy in the period 410–404. One survival from this codification is the republication of Draco's law on homicide in the year 409/8 (*M&L*, no. 86).

Work on the codifying and publishing of the laws was an important step, but in view of the apprehension of the people that the oligarchs might attempt another coup, the Boulē and the assembly, on the motion of one of the commissioners, Demophantos, passed a decree which gave total police powers in certain situations to the individual citizens. The decree, dated to the first *prytany* of the year 410/9, reads as follows (Andocides, 1.96–98): "If anyone overthrows the democracy at Athens, or holds any office when the democracy has been overthrown, he shall be an enemy of the Athenians and shall be killed with impunity, and his property shall be confiscated and a tenth part of it devoted to the Goddess; and he who kills or helps to plan the killing of such a man shall be pure and free from guilt. All Athenians shall swear over unblemished sacrifices by tribes and by *demes* to kill such a man. The oath shall be as follows . . ." (against attempts to subvert the democracy and to establish a tyranny). The language reflects Draco's law on tyranny and the official outlawing of the Pisistratids.[26] In the following year a decree was passed honoring the assassins of the oligarch Phrynichus (*M & L*, no. 85).

A decree such as that of Demophantos according to which the citizens swore to slay, if they could, anyone subverting the democracy obviously contributed to a deadly atmosphere of suspicion, although no assassinations under this proclamation are recorded. If one remembers that under the Athenian system of administration of justice prosecution was usually left to the individual citizen and that the courts consisted of large numbers of *dikasts*, primarily men from the lower financial classes, it is not surprising that many suits were inaugurated, some undoubtedly justifiable, but others in which the prosecutor was motivated by hatred of the defendant and by the desire to acquire money, either through blackmail or by sharing in the fines, and that the *dikasts* were influenced, in part at least, by the knowledge that the property of the defendant, if convicted, would be confiscated to the benefit of the sadly impoverished state finances. The situation was vicious, and the suspicions and vindictive spirit caused many moderate oligarchs to become extremists. It was not until after the fall of Athens and the horrors of the rule of the Thirty in 404/3 that the democrats could rise to the idea of amnesty.

The period of the restored democracy following the victory at Cyzicus and the deposing of the Five Thousand was one seething with political passions which are inadequately revealed in the extant source material. One of the most perplexing problems is the question of the leadership of the naval contingents.[27] During the period of the oligarchy of the Four Hundred and of the Five Thousand there were two boards of generals, one elected at Athens and one appointed by the army at Samos. At the battle of Cyzicus Theramenes, elected at Athens, cooperated with Alcibiades and Thrasybulus, appointed at Samos. With the restoration of democracy in the spring of 410, the system of two boards of generals was abandoned. Under the resurgent democrats led chiefly by Cleophon, despite the great victory of Cyzicus, the relations of the government with Alcibiades, who had advocated suppression of the democracy, with Thrasybulus, apparently a moderate democrat who had been responsible for the recall of Alcibiades to Samos, and with Theramenes, a strong advocate for the government of the Five Thousand, were strained and opportunistic. For a period of two or three years these three men apparently held their military commands in some irregular way, supporting their crews by exactions and booty, and not as generals elected by the Athenians. Thrasybulus devoted his energies to the regaining of Thrace, Theramenes remained with a squadron guarding Chrysopolis, and Alcibiades, with inadequate forces, manoeuvred in the Hellespontine region. Thrasyllus, who had returned to Athens with news of the victory at Cynossema late in 411, lingered in the city and presumably was active in the restoration of democracy. In 409, as general, he was dispatched with the blessing of the democrats, not to cooperate with Alcibiades in the Hellespont but to try to recover Ionia. After suffering a defeat at Ephesus, he joined Alcibiades late in the year, but for a while there was ill feeling between the crews of the respective leaders (Xenophon, *Hellenica*, 1.2.15). In the following year the continued successes of Alcibiades, culminating in the betrayal to him of Byzantium, which contrasted vividly with Thrasyllus' failure in Ionia, finally convinced the Athenian democrats that Alcibiades was the man to lead their offensive, and they elected him general for 407/6.

Alcibiades, in anticipation of returning to Athens, had collected 100 talents from the Carian region. On learning of his election as general he sailed into the Piraeus, but disembarked only after recognizing many of his friends in the crowd which had gathered to meet him. By a decree of the assembly he was appointed commander-in-chief (*hegemon autocrator*) of the war in the east, and he was also freed from the curse which had hung over him as a profaner of the Eleusinian Mysteries (Xenophon, *Hellenica*, 1.4.20). Before leaving for military operations he participated in an important pageant. Part of the ceremony of the Eleusinian festival in September was a procession from Athens by the Sacred Way to the temple at Eleusis. Ever since the Spartan occupation of Decelea in 413 this ritual, for reasons of safety, had been conducted by sea. Now,

under the protection of Alcibiades' troops, the procession was able to re-
sume its customary route. After this festival Alcibiades with some 100
triremes sailed to Samos to keep watch on the Spartan admiral Lysander, who had his headquarters and fleet at Ephesus.

In the early spring of 406 Alcibiades moved his fleet to Notion, from
where he could block any attempt of the Peloponnesian ships to move
out of the bay of Ephesus. Lysander, however, refused to be budged, and
Alcibiades, feeling that his reputation required action, sailed off with a
few ships and his hoplites to assist Thrasybulus, who was blockading
Phocaea to the north. Before leaving he entrusted the fleet at Notion to
his pilot, giving him strict orders not to engage in battle with Lysander.
The pilot, disregarding the orders, sailed into the harbor with two ships
to investigate the situation. When he had to flee before advancing Spartan ships other Athenian ships came to his support, and in the battle
that ensued the Athenians were defeated with the loss of fifteen ships.
When Alcibiades heard the news, he quickly returned and, reassembling
his fleet, tried to force Lysander into a battle. Lysander wisely refused,
and Alcibiades was compelled to retire to Samos. By this time word of
the defeat at Notion had reached Athens. Alcibiades' enemies, of whom
there were many, and those who feared that his real aim was to establish
a tyranny at Athens immediately spread abroad the report that the defeat at Notion had been caused by his inefficiency, carelessness, and de-
bauchery. The slander was sufficient to condemn a man whom all Athenians feared, and in the ensuing election Alcibiades was not included
among the ten generals who were chosen. Realizing that it would be
suicide to return to Athens at such a time, Alcibiades sailed off to the
Chersonese where he had previously erected a "castle" to serve as a refuge in case of need—and now, being considered an enemy by Athenians,
Spartans, and Persians, his need was critical (*Hellenica*, 1.5.10–17).

About this time Lysander's appointment as admiral expired, and
since the Spartan government did not allow reappointment, a successor,
named Callicratidas, arrived at Ephesus. Lysander, who was as egotisti-
cal as he was able and ambitious, encouraged resentment among his
friends against his replacement and returned whatever Persian money
he had to Cyrus. Callicratidas tried to obtain funds from the Persian
prince, but met only with rebuffs. He then moved his headquarters to
Miletus and, by appealing to various Spartan allies among the Greek
cities of the east, managed to collect considerable money and a fleet of
170 ships. With this impressive armada he sailed to Lesbos and succeeded in taking Methymna by storm. When this news reached the
Athenian fleet at Samos, Conon, the general in charge there, sailed rapidly with 70 triremes, all that he was able to man, to the defense of

Lesbos. In an engagement with the much larger Spartan fleet he lost 30 ships, and with the remaining 40 was blockaded in the harbor of Mytilene. Despite the blockade, one of his ships succeeded in making its way by a circuitous route to Athens and delivered the news of the perilous position facing Athenian power in the east.

In this desperate situation Athens did not falter for a minute. Money was provided by coining silver and gold dedications from the temples, and a token copper coinage was struck. The 110 triremes that were in Piraeus were manned with any able-bodied men who were available, rich and poor, metics and slaves. After thirty days they sailed to Samos and then, adding 40 ships from their allies, proceeded to the Arginusae islands which lay between Mytilene and the coast of Asia Minor. It was here that in August 406 the battle occurred in which more Greek ships faced one another than ever had happened before. The Athenians were superior in numbers, for the Spartans had to assign 50 of their 170 ships to maintain the blockade of Conon in the harbor of Mytilene. The Athenian fleet won a decisive victory. The Spartan admiral, Callicratidas, was killed, and some 70 Spartan and allied ships were sunk or captured. The Athenians lost 25 vessels. A bad storm with high seas that arose prevented the Athenians from exploiting their triumph to the full, for they were unable to rescue their shipwrecked crews and to sail against the 50 ships which were blockading Conon. These ships consequently escaped. Conon thereupon sailed out from Mytilene and, in conjunction with the Athenian fleet, proceeded to Samos (*Hellenica*, 1.6.1–38).

The triumph at Arginusae was followed immediately by one of the grimmest episodes in the annals of Athenian democracy—the trial and execution of the victorious generals. Most historians accept the rather full account which Xenophon gives in *Hellenica* (1.7.1–35), but recently a scholar has argued persuasively that certain aspects of this version are questionable.[28] The gist of Xenophon's account is as follows. He begins, without stating the charge, by saying that the Athenians deposed all the generals who had served in the Arginusae area except Conon. Of these eight generals, two did not return home. The others appeared before the assembly where they were accused, especially by Theramenes, of not having recovered the shipwrecked. The defense of the generals was that they had planned to sail against the enemy and had assigned the recovery of the shipwrecked crews to trierarchs like Theramenes and Thrasybulus, but that the violence of the storm had made all such activities impossible. This explanation made a favorable impression, but before a vote could be taken the assembly was disbanded because of the arrival of darkness. The Boulē accordingly was instructed to prepare a *probouleuma* for the next meeting of the assembly, setting forth how the men should be tried. Before this meeting was held, the emotions of the people were aroused by the celebration of the festival known as the Apaturia, a gathering associated with the phratries at which kinsmen were wont to meet. On this occasion the relatives of those who had been lost at Arginusae appeared clad in black garments and with shaved heads. Theramenes and his friends encouraged these men to appear in this garb at the assembly, and they also persuaded a certain Callixeinos, apparently a councillor, to denounce the generals in the Boulē.

When the assembly convened, the Boulē produced a proposal prepared by Callixeinos that the people, who had heard the evidence at the previous meeting, should now vote whether the generals were or were not guilty of having failed to pick up the victorious sailors from the sunken ships, and that if they were found guilty they should be executed. Euryptolemos, a friend of several of the generals, and some associates thereupon tried to bring a *graphē paranomōn* against Callixeinos because it was illegal to try a group of men *en bloc*. This proposal was withdrawn when its advocates were threatened with being judged by the same votes which were to be cast concerning the generals. Then some of the *prytaneis* refused to put the question to vote, but when they were threatened with the same proposal that had been made against Euryptolemos, they capitulated and all, except Socrates alone, agreed to put the issue to the vote. After another effort of Euryptolemos to persuade the people that each general should be tried separately, the assembly, voting according to the *probouleuma* of Callixeinos, passed sentence of death on the six generals. Among the generals executed were Pericles, the son of the great Pericles by Aspasia, and Diomedon and Thrasyllus, who had done valiant service for the democracy, particularly in the days when the Athenians at Samos were holding out against the Four Hundred at Athens. Xenophon relates that not long afterwards the Athenians repented their action and held those who had misled the people in utter contempt.

Xenophon's account is graphic, but it has puzzling aspects: the strange beginning without mention of the charge, Theramenes' exploiting of the mourners from the Apaturia festival—one wonders if this tactic might not have boomeranged on him—and the assigning of the full odium to Theramenes. Despite this ugly role assigned to Theramenes and the statement that the Athenians soon regretted their action and scorned those who had misled the people, there is no evidence that Theramenes was pilloried for his conduct. Even the orator Lysias, with his bitter hatred of Theramenes, never associates him with the execution of the generals. It may be better, therefore, to accept Diodorus' version (13.101–103) of this episode. Diodorus presumably was following

Ephorus, as was his wont for this period, but it is likely that Ephorus was basing his account of the trial on the author of the *Hellenica Oxyrhynchia,* a man who, starting where Thucydides stopped, wrote a detailed and pragmatic history of the period from 411 to probably 394. Papyri discovered in 1906 and 1934 at Oxyrhynchus in Egypt have preserved some 1,000 lines of this work. According to Diodorus, the Athenians were angry that the dead from Arginusae had not been recovered for burial. Since Theramenes and Thrasybulus had returned to Athens soon after the battle, the generals, believing that these two men were their accusers, wrote to Athens that the trierarchs had been ordered to pick up the dead. When this letter was read to the assembly, the Athenians at first were enraged at Theramenes and Thrasybulus, but these men in their defense succeeded in appeasing the assembly which promptly ordered the generals to return for trial, a trial which had the same outcome as the one described by Xenophon. In this version, then, the trial and its tragic ending were the result of an unfortunate and fatal misunderstanding between the generals and the trierarchs, men who in the poisonous political atmosphere were naturally mistrustful of one another. This account does not depict Theramenes as an unscrupulous villain. It is strange that in the pages of both Xenophon and Diodorus, the trierarch Thrasybulus, who, if the trierarchs were negligent, shared the guilt with Theramenes, is almost forgotten in the narrative.

This notorious trial has been treated at some length here because in both ancient and modern writers it is constantly cited as a lurid example of the pernicious nature of extreme (or radical) democracy. There is no doubt that the trial was a terrifying case of the perversion of justice and that the performance of the assembly presented a hideous picture of the evils of mob psychology, aggravated by the excessive tensions under which the people had been living for years. The fact remains, however, that between 4,000 and 5,000 Athenians drowned at a time when the state desperately needed men, and the suspicion is reasonable that the tragedy could at least have been lessened. Certainly part of the confusion arose from the presence of eight generals of equal power at a time when the emergency clearly called for a decisive order from one commander. The extant evidence is insufficient to demonstrate whether in the final analysis the generals or the trierarchs were chiefly culpable. One would like to be able to make a confident judgment on Theramenes, who played such an important role in Athenian history from 411 until his death in 404/3. His part in the trial of the generals was almost surely not as sordid as depicted by Xenophon, but it is obvious that as an oligarch, albeit a moderate one, he must have found life in the restored democracy a precarious and dangerous adventure.

The defeat at Arginusae was a severe blow to Sparta. For six years it had been receiving subsidies—sometimes in a galling manner—from Persia, but Athens still was dominant at sea. In the autumn of 406 Sparta once again tried to negotiate a peace with Athens on the basis of a status quo, except that it offered to evacuate Decelea. Cleophon, who apparently had taken no part in the trial of the generals, persuaded the assembly to reject the proposal unless Sparta would agree to return the various cities of the Athenian empire which it had occupied (Aristotle, *Ath. Const.*, 34.1). Since the Spartans would not consider such a suggestion, they turned to Persia again. Cyrus, however, made it clear that his support would be dependent on the assignment of Lysander as commander, and various allies of Sparta in the east expressed the same request. The Spartan law against reappointing the same man admiral was circumvented by naming Lysander vice-admiral, although in fact full military authority was given him. Lysander resumed his friendly relations with Cyrus and received generous financial help. In the spring of 405, when the prince went to Media where his father was in his final illness, the revenues of Cyrus' provinces were made available to the Spartan. Lysander assembled a large fleet at Ephesus and then, after some subsidiary campaigns, sailed to the Hellespont and seized Lampsacus, which he made his base. This threat to the free passage of the grain ships from the Black Sea caused the Athenians to hurry to the area, and they took up their position at Aegospotami in the Chersonese, roughly across the straits from Lampsacus. During the preceding winter and spring, by using every resource, the Athenians had assembled a fleet of 180 triremes. To try to deter their former allies and the Greeks in general from serving on Lysander's well-financed ships, the assembly had passed a decree permitting their generals to amputate the right hand of every captured seaman.

The Athenians were anxious to draw Lysander into battle, and each day they sailed across to Lampsacus with this intention. When no action occurred they returned to Aegospotami, beached their ships, and went in search of provisions. Alcibiades, who was living in a neighboring "castle," realized that their position was very vulnerable and urged the Athenians to move their fleet to the good harbor and market of Sestos slightly to the southwest. His suggestions were greeted with contempt. On the fifth day—about September 1, 405—Lysander, who had kept his ships in readiness, waited until the Athenians had disbanded at Aegospotami and then launched a swift attack. There was no regular sea battle, for the great majority of the Athenian ships were unmanned. They fell without a struggle into the hands of Lysander. Twenty ships which were prepared, but too few to offer resistance, escaped and with them the general Conon. He sent some of the ships to Athens to bear the ghastly news and then, having no desire to face the fury of the people at home, sailed to Cyprus where he took service with Evagoras, the king of Salamis. At Aegospotami Lysander rounded up all the prisoners, and segregating the Athenians, to the number of about 3,000, had them all executed. One Athenian general, Adeimantus, was spared; the explanation was that he had opposed the vote of the assembly to amputate the right hands of all captives. There was also a tradition that, bribed by Lysander, he had turned traitor. Treason on the part of Adeimantus and possibly others cannot be proved, but in view of the stupidity of Athenian conduct at Aegospotami and the completeness of the disaster, the democrats can hardly be blamed for suspecting oligarchic machinations (*Hellenica,* 2.16–32).

The description of the consternation at Athens when the *Paralus,* the dispatch ship, arrived is related vividly by Xenophon (*Hellenica,* 2.2.3): "It was at night that the Paralus arrived at Athens with tidings of the disaster, and a sound of wailing ran from Piraeus through the long walls to the city, one man passing on the news to another; and during that night no one slept, all mourning, not for the lost alone, but far more for their own selves, thinking that they would suffer such treatment as they had visited upon the Melians, colonists of the Lacedaemonians, after reducing them by siege, and upon the Histiaeans and Scionaeans and Toronoeans and Aeginetans and many other Greek peoples," whom the Athenians had punished with varying degrees of brutality. On the following day the assembly decided that, since the fleet was gone, the city must ready itself for a siege. In the meantime Lysander took control of Byzantium and Chalcedon, and one of his generals secured the various posts in the Thracian region. In fact, after the news of the Athenian collapse at Aegospotami had spread abroad, all the remaining members of the empire abandoned their allegiance to Athens except the Samians, who tried to hold out against the Spartans. This act of loyalty was rewarded by the gift of Athenian citizenship (*M&L,* no. 94). As Lysander and his fleet proceeded from place to place, all Athenians encountered—colonists, *cleruchs,* garrisons, or individuals—were ordered to return immediately to Athens or suffer the fate meted out to the Athenians at Aegospotami. Since Lysander realized that Athens would have to be starved into submission, he wanted to increase the number of consumers for Athens' dwindling food supplies.

The siege of Athens was both by sea and land, for Lysander sailed into the Piraeus with 150 triremes, and the Spartan kings, Agis and Pausanias, were in Attica with armies. As conditions grew worse the Athenians tried to make an alliance with the Spartans on the condition that they should retain their land and also their walls. The Spartan response was that large sections of the long walls would have to be destroyed, a proposal which the assembly on the advice of Cleophon rejected. Early in the winter, as deaths by starvation were becoming a reality, Theramenes received permission to go to Lysander to try to reach some acceptable terms. He was absent for three months, detained by the Spartan, as he claimed later. In the interim, because of the appalling conditions, the Athenian tendency to split into oligarchic and democratic factions, with many gradations in each group, was aggravated. The oligarchs became powerful enough to bring Cleophon to trial on a flimsy charge and to have him executed (Lysias, 13.12; 30.10–12). When Theramenes returned in the fourth month, reporting that Lysander had said that only the ephors had authority in matters relating to peace, he, with nine associates, was sent to Sparta to work out a peace on almost any terms.

The Spartan demands were that Athens must destroy the long walls and those of the Piraeus, give up all claims to the cities of its empire, surrender its triremes except twelve, permit its exiles to return, and become a Spartan ally. Various allies of Sparta, particularly Corinth and Thebes, argued that Athens should be destroyed, which meant presumably that the adult males should be killed and the women and children sold as slaves. Sparta held out against such demands, emphasizing that no city which had been so heroic at the time of the Persian invasions should be destroyed, and also doubtless dreading the prospect of the Boeotians overrunning Attica and of the Corinthians aspiring to naval supremacy. The Athenian envoys returned with the Spartan terms, and although some diehards spoke in opposition, the assembly, because of the hideous suffering in the city, voted to accept them. In the month of Munychion (April) 404, therefore, "Lysander sailed into Piraeus, the exiles returned, and the Peloponnesians with great enthusiasm began to tear down the walls to the music of flute-girls, thinking that that day was the beginning of freedom of Greece" (Xenophon, Hellenica, 2.2.1–23).

THE DESTRUCTION of the Athenian empire, of course, did not inaugurate the beginning of freedom for Greece. For Athens itself, the collapse of its power ushered in one of the most hidious episodes, fortunately brief, in its history. Athenian imperialism, symbolized in the closing years of the war by Cleophon, had long been opposed by oligarchs, both extreme and moderate, who realized that imperialism signified the dominance of the navy crowd. As mentioned above, the Athenian disaster at Aegospotami may have been partly caused by oligarchic desire to submit to Sparta. In the grim months of the siege of Athens,

September 405 to April 404, this oligarchic discontent increased, fanned by Lysander's policy of driving back to Athens all Athenians living anywhere abroad, among whom some political exiles were certainly numbered. The oligarchic clubs appointed five "ephors" to coordinate revolutionary efforts (Lysias, 12.43), won over many despairing moderates, and gained influence in the Boulē. Oligarchic manoeuvres were responsible, by means that are rather obscure, for bringing Cleophon to trial on a charge that he did not go to the military camp to sleep and for intimidating the *dikasts,* by having councillors sit with them, to condemn him to death. Theramenes and his fellow envoys who obtained terms from Sparta must have assured the Spartans that a more moderate type of government would be established in Athens. When the Athenians capitulated in April 404, one of the clauses of the peace treaty stipulated that exiles should be allowed to return.

Evidence for the next few months is very scanty, but it is clear that the oligarchs were busily at work, and it is probable that a Spartan garrison was left in Piraeus to ensure the proper dismantling of the walls. Lysander himself sailed to Samos where, after a siege, he allowed the people—the democrats—to depart and turned the city over to the former citizens—the oligarchs—under the control of a body of ten (*Hellenica,* 2.3.6–7). Apparently in July Lysander, at the summons of the Athenian oligarchs who now were ready to act, returned to Athens with some of his fleet. An assembly was held at which an oligarch named Dracontides proposed a decree that thirty men be elected to establish a constitution on the basis of the ancestral laws. When the people, realizing that ancestral laws would be oligarchic, objected, Theramenes insisted that the decree be passed (according to Diodorus, 14.3.6, opposing it until silenced by Lysander), and then Lysander spoke. He emphasized that the Athenians had broken the treaty by not demolishing the walls according to the time schedule and that, unless they approved the decree, they would have to pay the consequences. The assembly, helpless in the presence of Spartan troops, reluctantly succumbed and, according to instructions, voted—those who bothered to vote—for the ten men nominated by Theramenes, the ten nominated by the "ephors," and ten from their own ranks. The fact that the men elected were all antidemocratic shows how carefully the "ephors" and oligarchs had laid their plans in the preceding months. Among these thirty were Theramenes, Dracontides, and also Critias. This Critias was an unscrupulous aristocratic intellectual, an associate of Socrates and the sophists, a member of the Four Hundred, subsequently banished by Cleophon, and one of the exiles thirsting for revenge who returned to Athens either after Aegospotami or the peace of April 404. These constitutional commissioners immediately began to establish the necessary governing bodies, for it seems that because of the domestic confusion the officials of 405/4 had continued in office. The Thirty appointed: a new council of Five Hundred with membership satisfactory to them; a new archon, Pythodorus; a new board of the Eleven, guardians of the prison; 300 whip-bearers; and a board of Ten to watch over the Piraeus, whose population was customarily radical.

The Thirty acted with some moderation at first, pretending that they were establishing the proposed constitution. They removed from the Areopagus the laws of Ephialtes and canceled the sovereignty of the popular courts, the *dikasteria*. Their executions, presumably ratified by the Boulē, were primarily concerned with notorious informers of the last years of the democracy, and consequently did not arouse much protest. Their official status, however, was precarious, their commission supposedly being a temporary one, for after their appointment in July the Spartans probably left Attic soil. In the early fall they appealed to Lysander and received from him 700 troops and Callibius as governor (*harmost*). With this support, which obviously cost money, the leaders of the Thirty began to eliminate various citizens whose opposition might be dangerous. When Theramenes protested and insisted that an oligarchy, to survive, must have a broader base, Critias and the other extremists agreed to the establishment of a list of Three Thousand who should be considered citizens and be entitled to trial before the Boulē. Subsequently at a military muster of all the Athenians the Thirty and their supporters, with the assistance of the Spartan garrison, succeeded, by a trick, in confiscating the arms of all except the Three Thousand. At this point, feeling secure, the Thirty started a bloodbath whose victims were personal enemies, wealthy citizens, and also metics, who, having no political rights, were obviously put to death so that their property could be confiscated (Xenophon, *Hellenica*, 2.3.11–21; Aristotle, *Ath. Const.*, 34.2–36).

Against this shameless reign of terror, which counted ultimately for 1,500 lives, Theramenes protested so vehemently that the extremists became afraid he might arouse a dangerous resistance. A meeting of the Boulē was arranged at which a group of young ruffians, presumably sons of oligarchs and carrying concealed daggers, were posted in the background. As reported by Xenophon, in a passage where the speeches seem essentially authentic (*Hellenica*, 2.3.24–56),[29] Critias denounced Theramenes as a traitor—as one who, having betrayed the oligarchy of Four Hundred, was now threatening the present regime, a turncoat shifting sides to feather his own nest, like the *cothurnus* (a boot worn by tragic actors) which could fit either foot. Theramenes, in a moving defense which excoriated the atrocities perpetrated by men like Critias, insisted that he was remaining loyal to his ideal of a moderate type of government lying between the two extremes of narrow oligarchy and radical democracy. When Critias saw that the councillors were affected by Theramenes' words, he first consulted with the Thirty and then, ordering the young assassins to be ready for action if necessary, he struck Theramenes' name from the roll of the Three Thousand, thereby denying him the right of a trial before the Boulē. The Eleven, led by the bloodthirsty Satyros, then entered, dragged Theramenes from the altar where he had taken refuge, carried him to prison, and made him drink the hemlock. His last words became famous, for, as if he were toasting a beloved at a banquet, he threw out the dregs of the hemlock with the comment, "To my beloved Critias."

Because he met his death by defying a tyrant, it is easy to idealize Theramenes. Actually the extant evidence is insufficient to form an objective judgment on the man. Like many a person following a middle course, he was hated by both political extremes. His role among the Four Hundred Oligarchs, at the trial of the generals after the battle of Arginusae, with Lysander and the Spartans in the peace negotiations of 404, and among the Thirty will always be subject to diverse interpretations.

Freed from fear of Theramenes, the Thirty increased their madness. They forbade those not included among the Three Thousand to enter Athens and confiscated the farms of many of these people now completely without rights. Those evicted fled to Piraeus and many from there to Megara and Thebes, although the Spartans had issued orders that their allies should not receive Athenian exiles (Diodorus, 14.6). Dissatisfaction with the Spartan handling of the peace and sympathy for the victims of the Spartan-backed Athenian government rendered such a command ineffectual. It was from Thebes that the exiles' attempt to regain control of Athens began. Thrasybulus and about seventy men succeeded in seizing Phyle, a strong place on Mt. Parnes not far from the Boeotian-Attic boundary. The effort of the Thirty to attack and besiege them was frustrated by a heavy snowstorm. Subsequently the Thirty dispatched most of the Spartan garrison and two contingents of cavalry to a neighboring spot to protect the countryside from raids by the enemy, but Thrasybulus and his followers, now about 700 strong, attacked them early one morning and won an impressive victory. The Thirty now became worried and decided to prepare Eleusis as a place of refuge if the need should arise. A large number of Eleusinian men were treacherously seized and transported to the Eleven in Athens. On the next day Critias, wishing to strengthen his position by associating his followers in crime, persuaded the Three Thousand in the presence of the Spartan garrison to condemn the Eleusinians to death (Xenophon, *Hellenica*, 2.4.1–10).

A few days after his success against the oligarchs, Thrasybulus, with the backing of about a thousand exiles, marched to Piraeus by night. Since they were too few to hold the whole town, they took up their position on the hill of Munychia. The Thirty with their forces immediately came against them, but in attempting to storm the hill they were defeated. Two of their leaders were killed, Critias and Charmides, one of the ten supervisors of Piraeus. The oligarchic forces returned to Athens, and on the following day the Three Thousand voted to depose the Thirty, who thereupon sought refuge in Eleusis. Their place was taken by a new board of Ten who tried to organize defense against the constantly increasing number of exiles in the Piraeus. Ultimately the Ten and the Thirty from Eleusis appealed to Sparta for aid on the grounds that the people of Piraeus were in revolt from the terms of the peace. Lysander persuaded the Spartans to lend the Athenian oligarchs 100 talents and to send him out as *harmost* and his brother, as admiral, to blockade the Piraeus. Lysander was soon followed by King Pausanias, who, worried by the power and ambition of Lysander, obtained permission from three of the ephors to lead an army into Attica. Fighting continued for some time, but Pausanias, taking advantage of the desire for reconciliation among many of the Athenians, succeeded in having envoys from both the Piraeus and the city go to Sparta. After the Spartans had heard these ambassadors, they dispatched fifteen commissioners to Athens who, in conjunction with Pausanias and some Athenian statesmen, worked out an agreement between the warring factions. Eleusis was recognized as a separate state and, like Athens, was bound by an alliance with Sparta. The most remarkable aspect of the agreement was the declaration of a general amnesty from which were excluded only the chief perpetrators of the recent horrors—the Thirty, the Ten, the Eleven (guardians of the prison), and the ten governors of the Piraeus. Even these groups had the chance to be included if they were willing to submit to a regular investigation of their conduct in office.

Following this reconciliation the men from Piraeus proceeded under arms to the Acropolis, and made sacrifice to Athena. When they had descended, a general assembly was held in which Thrasybulus rebuked, but in conciliatory terms, the men of the city. It was apparently at this assembly that a commission of twenty men, presumably ten from the city and ten from the Piraeus, was elected to supervise the affairs of Athens until the democratic government could be restored. Agreement was reached that the Athenians should be governed under the laws of

Draco and Solon until the codification which had been erected in the
Royal Stoa in the period 410–404, some of which had been destroyed or
possibly changed by the Thirty, could be checked, repaired, and altered
by additions, when necessary, by a special board of commissioners. The
assembly made arrangements that a new Council of Five Hundred be
appointed by lot and that the appropriate magistrates be elected or appointed. Among the new magistrates was the archon Eucleides. Although he did not take office until October, his year, 403/2, was recognized as the one for dating the signing of the amnesty and the
restoration of the democracy. Two years later when it was learned that
the oligarchs at Eleusis were hiring mercenaries, the Athenians, by
means of force and treachery, captured and executed their generals and
incorporated Eleusis once again in the Athenian state (Xenophon, *Hellenica*, 2.4.11–43; Aristotle, *Ath. Const.*, 37–40; Andocides, 1.80–82).

The amnesty and the restoration of the democracy, following immediately upon the vicious and brutal period of oligarchic domination,
constitute one of the most inspiring and amazing phases of the history of
Athens. The intelligence and self-restraint of the people as a whole and
of the returned exiles in particular were remarkable. The wisdom of the
Spartans as represented by Pausanias and his followers, even though
motivated by jealousy and fear of the ambitions of Lysander and possibly by the hope that hostility between Eleusis and Athens could serve
sometime as a pretext for interference, contributed tremendously to the
revival of Athens. If Lysander had been allowed to act unhampered, the
agony of Athens would have been prolonged indefinitely.

In the years immediately following the restoration of the democracy, a little-known statesman, Archinus, who had marched with the
exiles from Phyle to Piraeus, became more influential than Thrasybulus,
the leader of the returning exiles (Demosthenes, 24.135). In the terms of
the reconciliation a statement had been included that any Athenians
who wished to migrate to Eleusis must register for this permission by a
certain date. Many members of the Three Thousand, apprehensive
about the return of the exiles and the reestablishment of the democracy,
were planning to leave Athens but kept postponing entering their names
on the register. Archinus, wishing to prevent these men from joining the
malcontents in Eleusis, declared the period of registration over earlier
than had been expected and thus forced these people to remain in
Athens. There was probably consternation at the time, but as the weeks
passed the move proved to be a contribution to the unification of the
Athenians.

At one of the first assemblies, Thrasybulus, honoring promises he
had made to his followers in Piraeus, proposed that citizenship be

awarded to all who had fought for the restoration of the democracy; certainly the proposal was intended to include the metics, and possibly the slaves as well. This proposition was passed by the assembly, but Archinus immediately and successfully attacked the decree under the *graphē paranomōn*. The illegality lay in the fact that the proposal had not come to the assembly in the form of a *probouleuma* from the Boulē. Possibly the Boulē had not yet been reestablished. Archinus' motives are not stated, but he may have felt that in this critical period the uniting of the citizens would have been jeopardized by the admission of too many new citizens, the majority of whom would be in the category of the "masses." Thrasybulus' motion and Archinus' attack on it raise an interesting question about one of the most important documents dealing with this troubled period, Lysias' speech *Against Eratosthenes*. Lysias was a metic whose brother had been killed by the Thirty, one of whom was Eratosthenes. This speech apparently was part of the attack on Eratosthenes when he was submitting his claim to be included in the amnesty. The speech, which has been preserved, was delivered at the trial by Lysias himself, a right ordinarily limited to citizens. Did Lysias temporarily become a citizen because of Thrasybulus' decree, or in this confused period—probably the end of 403—were special privileges given to those who had just cause to challenge members of the Thirty who chose to submit their account (Aristotle, *Ath. Const.*, 40.1–2)?

In the early days after the reconciliation, when passions still were high, there must have been many, motivated by hatred or grief, who hoped to disregard the amnesty. One such case is known. A returned exile, in violation of the amnesty, brought a prosecution. Archinus immediately had the man brought before the Boulē and persuaded the councillors to condemn him to death. This action was probably unconstitutional, for the Boulē ordinarily did not have such powers, but, according to Aristotle, this extreme example was effective in preventing further violations of the amnesty. Aristotle, who in the *Constitution* usually reveals an oligarchic point of view, speaks with the highest praise of the Athenians' willingness and ability to abide by the amnesty, and he adds that the restored democracy even repaid to the Spartans the money which the Thirty had borrowed (Aristotle, *Ath. Const.*, 40.2–3).

In the same period a dangerous attack on the extreme democracy was made by a man named Phormisios, who had returned with the exiles. He proposed that citizenship should be limited to those who possessed land. Since an ancient commentator[30] remarks that the proposal, if enacted, would have deprived 5,000 men of the franchise, the original proposition may also have included those who owned a house. This measure, if approved, would have stripped of citizenship many craftsmen, laborers, and sailors, and, true to their liberal tradition, the majority of the Athenians rejected it.

One last matter concerned with the period of reconstruction should be mentioned. A fragmentary inscription, to be dated in the year 401/0, contains a decree, almost surely proposed by Archinus, granting various honors to the metics who had assisted in the restoration of the democracy. If this decree is subsequent to the reincorporation of Eleusis, Archinus may have felt that the situation at Athens was now sufficiently stabilized to justify the granting of certain privileges which he had opposed when Thrasybulus made his proposal some three years earlier. As far as can be made out from the badly damaged stone, the metics who joined in the march from Phyle to Piraeus were rewarded with the grant of full Athenian citizenship, while those who joined the exiles at Munychia received the privileged status of *isoteleia* (equality in taxation with citizens). On the back of the stone there is preserved a partial list of those who received the gift of citizenship. The total number can only be guessed, but it was probably under 200. Opposite the names the men's professions or trades were recorded, a list which sheds interesting light on the role of metics in the Athenian economy: "farmhands, cook, carpenter, muleteer, builder, gardener, donkey-man, oil-seller, walnutseller, tub-maker, baker, fuller, hired laborer, statue-maker" (Tod, no. 100).[31]

12

The Fourth Century

I N APRIL 404 with the capitulation of Athens the hideous Peloponnesian War, after twenty-seven years filled with intermittent shedding
of blood and destruction of property, came to an end. Xenophon
(2.2.23) describes the enthusiasm of the victors as they began to demolish Athenian fortifications. The joy to which Xenophon refers, however,
was one in which innumerable Greeks could not share. Although the
empire had been aggressive long before the influence of the so-called
demagogues—even Pericles had called it a tyranny—it had performed
an important service in the fragmented Greek world. Some 200 cities,
many of which might have fallen under Persia or wasted their strength
in mutual struggles, had been united under Athenian authority, and the
example of and pressure from Athenian democratic institutions had
strengthened the position of the masses in city after city. It would be an
exaggeration to claim that the people throughout the empire preferred
subordination to Athens and the privileges of democracy to national independence and a humble role under local oligarchs, but the evidence
seems to show that the serious objection to the empire was an oligarchic
phenomenon—the point of view represented by Thucydides.

The collapse of the Athenian empire, beyond being a blow to democratic forces and a boon to oligarchic hopes throughout the Greek world,
also had a significant international consequence. In the fifth century
Athens with its empire and Sparta with its Peloponnesian League had
acquired such prestige that they formed a balance of power. Even states
that were not officially attached to either power were inclined to be
either pro-Athenian or pro-Spartan. In fact, the increasing strength of
Athens, which seemed to jeopardize the balance of power, was the chief
cause that persuaded the Spartans to undertake the Peloponnesian War.
The humiliation of Athens in 404, by destroying that balance, left
Sparta supreme in the Greek world. The future of that world for some
years was to be dependent on what use Sparta would make of its dominant position.

The history of the early years of the fourth century is notoriously
bewildering. In writing the history of the Peloponnesian War and its
causes, Thucydides was able to focus his interests on the rivalry and hos-

tility between Athens and its empire and Sparta and the Peloponnesian League. The early decades of the fourth century, however, had no such unifying theme. Consequently, the reader finds that his attention is constantly shifting from Athens and its numerous alliances to Sparta and its ambitions and its troubles in the Peloponnesian League, to Thebes, the Olynthian League, the Arcardian League, Messenia, Thessaly, Macedonia, the Asiatic Greeks, Persia, and Egypt, to mention only some of the centers of significant activity.

The chief contemporary source for these years is Xenophon, whose *Hellenica* covers the period from 411, where Thucydides stopped, through the battle of Mantinea in 362. Xenophon's account is disappointing—one wonders if even a Thucydides could have composed a coherent history of those chaotic decades—and his partiality for Sparta and King Agesilaus caused him to omit, misrepresent, or gloss over fundamental matters. He also wrote the remarkable *Anabasis,* which will be discussed shortly, and several useful, but specialized, monographs. Other contemporary sources are the last two preserved comedies of Aristophanes, the *Ecclesiazusae* and the *Plutus;* some of the Attic orators, particularly Lysias, Andocides, Isaeus, Isocrates, and Demosthenes; and an anonymous work called the *Hellenica Oxyrhynchia* because some papyri containing parts of this seemingly well-informed history, which apparently was intended to be a continuation of Thucydides, were discovered at Oxyrhynchus in Egypt. Unfortunately, only the papyri dealing with the years 397–395, and a few concerned with the latter part of the Peloponnesian War, are extant. Contemporary inscriptions, although often fragmentary, are rather numerous. Of later sources, two in particular should be emphasized. Diodorus in books 14, 15, and 16 of his Universal History gives a continuous narrative of the period, based largely on the fourth-century historian Ephorus. Despite the well-known inadequacies of Diodorus, his account is very useful because of its continuity and its different point of view from that of Xenophon. Plutarch's lives of Lysander, Agesilaus, Pelopidas, Phocion, and Artaxerxes II, despite their usual moralizing, are valuable. Other sources of importance are the voluminous writings of Plato and Aristotle, and the fragments of various historians which have been preserved.

Before beginning an account of the political history of the first half of the fourth century, it will be useful to make some general observations on certain aspects of social and economic conditions in Athens and Sparta, conditions which were largely the natural consequences of the long and demoralizing Peloponnesian War.

In 403, with the expulsion of the Thirty Tyrants, the declaration of the amnesty, and the restoration of the democracy, Athens faced the task of trying to recover from the ravages of war. The political situation was humiliating. The once proud imperial city was now without empire, without fleet, and reduced to the status of inferior ally to victorious Sparta. Social and economic traditions and customs had been seriously buffeted by twenty-seven years of war. The population of adult male citizens had dropped from about 45,000 in 431 to an estimated 22,000,[1] which should surprise no one who recalls the plague, the Sicilian disaster, the losses at Arginusae, Lysander's execution of some 3,000 sailors after Aegospotami, and the victims of the Thirty. Of more enduring effect on the Athenians than those sadly wasted lives were the changes brought about in their way of life. Before the Peloponnesian War, according to Thucydides, the majority of the Athenians lived in country districts. When war began, Pericles, confident that the might of the fleet would enable Athenians to exist for the duration of hostilities on imported necessities, decided to sacrifice the land, as expendable, to enemy attacks, and ordered all the rural people to come within the safety of the long walls of Athens and Piraeus. The first period of confinement (discounting the possible return of some to their farms after each annual Spartan invasion) lasted for ten years and was rendered hideous by the ravages of the plague. Although information is lacking, some or many of these refugees from the country may have returned to their farms after the Peace of Nicias in 421, or even as early as 425, but the Spartan garrisoning of Decelea in 413 and the constant raids thereafter throughout Attica forced the rural population to migrate again to Athens and Piraeus, where they lived under increasingly difficult circumstances until the peace of 404.

What was the reaction of the former peasants, now long citified, when the countryside once again became available to them? On this problem, important for an understanding of social and economic conditions in the fourth century, scholars disagree considerably in their interpretation of the inadequate and often ambiguous evidence. One key passage in this polemic is a section from Xenophon's *Oeconomicus* (20.22–29) in which Socrates is questioning Ischomachus, a gentleman farmer. Ischomachus describes his father's industrious and rewarding habit of buying neglected farms, improving them, and then, instead of adding them to his own property, selling them at a profit. Although the consensus of critics is that this little work was written between 380 and 360 B.C., about a generation after the execution of Socrates in 399, it is generally agreed that the enterprises of Ischomachus' father began in the immediate postwar period. Scholars who argue that the peasants were a declining group in the fourth century see this passage as typical evidence for the failure of the small farmers who tried to return to the land. Other scholars who do not accept the decline of the peasant at this time emphasize that Ischomachus' description is only an isolated item of evidence and that he and his father, as "gentlemen," were not thinking of peasants. They also point out correctly that the mortgage stones (*horoi*) which became common in the fourth century were associated primarily not with desperate peasants but with economically sound men who were mortgaging some of their property to acquire immediately needed cash or to serve as security for dowries.[2]

In view of the nature of the evidence, it is, and probably always will be, impossible to present a satisfactory picture of the rural population in fourth-century Attica. Depending on what items one selects for his argument, it is possible to reach a variety of conclusions. The result is that one's interpretation of this aspect of Athenian life is almost inevitably somewhat subjective. The few remarks made below will begin with the plight in which the Athenians found themselves in 403.

A city that had experienced and suffered what Athens had since 431 cannot emerge unscathed. Athens succeeded in reviving its democratic form of government, but some social and economic conditions and traditions could hardly be restored. The city was crowded with the displaced peasantry, whose numbers were increased by the *cleruchs* whom Lysander had driven home. Many of these peasants undoubtedly returned to their own plots of land. What they found must often have been disheartening—houses burned, vineyards destroyed, olive and fig trees cut down. Some may have struggled, successfully or unsuccessfully, to recapture their old way of living, but many probably drifted gradually into the categories of tenants, hired laborers, or rural proletariat, or returned to the city where they had learned to exist as artisans, petty traders, laborers, or as recipients of some type of subsidy from the state. Some peasants may never have returned to the land, since they had become reconciled to the different, and sometimes hard, but often more interesting life in the city.

Conditions such as these must have raised numerous problems about the status and ownership of land. In the years before the Peloponnesian War family land may have been alienable, but attachment to one's own share of the native soil, with all its family and religious associations, rendered the thought of disposing of it almost sacrilegious. From the beginning of the fourth century, however, buying, selling, and mortgaging land were becoming common procedures. It seems reasonable to assume that the uprooting of the peasants in the war, the elimination of whole families by the plague, the long separation from the land, the constant plundering of the enemy, and the cynical attitudes acquired in the struggle to survive may have released many Athenians from the old traditional concept of the sacred obligation to preserve family land. A new idea was emerging that land was just another commodity.[3]

For the fifth century, largely from the comedies of Aristophanes, one derives the impression of a strong peasant class that was proud of being as self-sufficient as possible. For the fourth century the self-sufficiency (*autarkeia*) of the peasant does not seem to have been so prominent, although one can argue that this impression can be attributed to the different types of sources available. There were still peasants, of course, but there is no evidence for their numbers. In the speeches of the Attic orators written for clients involved in litigation, however, one reads more about well-to-do landowners, slave managers, tenants, both citizens and metics or freedmen, and poor citizens working unwillingly as laborers. There is no evidence for the growth of large estates, but it is known that a man might own several farms located in different areas, and often managed by slaves. Newly enriched citizens brought farms, for ownership of land was still a social asset. When one reflects on the wide acceptance of the concept of land as a commodity, one is drawn more and more to the conclusion that Pericles' uprooting of the peasants and the long, demoralizing war produced conditions which contributed to the weakening of the sturdy self-sufficiency of the fifth-century peasant and of the tradition linking landowning citizens with the obligation of military service.

It is as hard to visualize social and economic trends in Athens and Piraeus as in rural Attica. The urban areas had been very congested in the final years of the war and immediately thereafter. The ancient sources provide no general picture of conditions, which must have been grim and discouraging until Persian money in 393 made shipbuilding and naval activity possible again. In the eyes of the poor the restoration of democracy was all-important. In the fifth century under the "radical" democracy, pay for government service had been widespread and various perquisites of empire had been available, including the *cleruchy* system. Now, although empire was gone and state finances were in chaos, the people, who were the state, expected pay for service and liturgies from the wealthy. About 393 the awarding of three obols to each of those arriving early at meetings of the assembly was introduced.[4] Since Athenians, with their passion for independence, were reluctant, except briefly, to work at the behest of another individual, it is likely that many jobs fell to metics and slaves. This competition did not disturb the poorer Athenians, for they, as citizens, assumed that the state would be concerned with their welfare.

Financial difficulties, aggravated by the endless wars which kept recurring, plagued the Athenians throughout the fourth century. The

Athenians found it necessary to have a regular direct tax when a national emergency called for it. This impost was a tax on capital and could be employed only after a formal and rather elaborate legislative procedure. When an urgent need for money arose, the assembly would vote that an *eisphora,* as the levy was called, for a particular sum be executed. Thucydides (3.19) remarks that in 428 at the time of the revolt of Lesbos the Athenians collected an *eisphora* of 200 talents for the first time (meaning, presumably, for the first time in the Peloponnesian War).

A change in the rather obscure nature of this tax was introduced in 378/7, the year in which the second Athenian League was formally established. The property liable to the tax was evaluated then and, according to Polybius (2.62.6), was found to amount to 5,750 talents. The amount is so surprisingly small that it is probably safe to conclude from it that the poorer people were not included in the estimate and that of the richer only a certain proportion of their property was considered liable to the tax. The taxable citizens were divided into 100 groups (*symmories*), which were responsible for contributing their share to the *eisphora* that had been voted. The evidence is vague on how it was decided in the different groups what each individual citizen should pay, but since declaration of wealth was a personal matter, based on oath, it is easy to understand why concealment of wealth became a common practice and why litigation flourished. Since it was essential to the government to receive the tax money promptly, a system was devised (*proeisphora*) by which the 300 richest men in the *symmories* paid the stipulated amount at the specified time and then tried to collect the appropriate shares from the members of their groups. Metics also were liable to this tax, being responsible apparently for one-sixth of the total sum demanded. Since metics were not allowed to own real property, the amount which they owed was based on a proportion of the movable wealth they possessed. They apparently were organized in their own *symmories.*[5]

The ideal set forth by Pericles in his funeral oration and by Aristotle in the late fourth century, that it was against the best interests of the state for citizens to let personal profit interfere with their political and social roles in the city, still persisted, but the evidence and particularly the passionately chauvinistic speeches of Demosthenes suggest that increasing numbers of Athenians were becoming more concerned with their own comfort than with opportunities to benefit the city. Metics and slaves, who could not participate in political life and its privileges, were more and more becoming responsible for much of the economic life of the city. One phenomenon that emphasized the declining sense of duty towards the state was the increasing use of mercenaries rather than of citizen soldiers—an innovation which aggravated the constant financial difficulties of the city.

The employment of mercenaries, of course, was not restricted to Athens alone. Throughout the Greek world, as a result of economic depression fostered by the Peloponnesian War and the following endless wars, and by the frequent civil struggles in which one party, if not massacred, was exiled, thousands of men were wandering about, homeless and desperate. These men, who like all Greeks had had military training, were only too glad to hire themselves out as mercenaries, for the pay was satisfactory and the chances of booty were good. In state after state the old civilian armies were often buttressed by detachments of mercenaries. Even militaristic Sparta made use of them. The Persian king and revolting satraps were always eager to hire Greek mercenaries, with the result, as Isocrates (4.168) pointed out, that in many battles launched by the Persians, Greeks were fighting against Greeks.

Athens in the fourth century did not suffer from *stasis* and hence did not contribute greatly to the breeding of mercenaries, although some of its generals like Iphicrates, Chabrias, and Chares took service under Persian, Thracian, and Egyptian kings to earn rewards for themselves and pay for their troops. The availability of mercenaries, however, affected the military attitudes of many Athenians. The poor were usually ready to serve as rowers in the ships, for the wages were important to them, but many Athenians who ordinarily would have served as hoplites or *peltasts* (lighter-armed foot soldiers) were glad to have the state employ mercenaries rather than call them to the colors. Part of the reason was that military tactics were becoming more complicated, and professional mercenaries knew the new skills better than men who ordinarily were civilians. It is also probable that some Athenians were acquiring a rather skeptical attitude about the never-ending wars. If they felt that Athens was in danger, then the old patriotism blazed out, but for many of the wars in which the leaders embroiled the state, and in which the people had little interest, a common sentiment was to leave the fighting and dying to mercenaries.

The growing complexity of life led to more professionalism in both military and civil matters. The gifted amateur of the fifth century was disappearing. While the economy was largely falling into the hands of non-citizens, the unhealthy cleavage between the "haves" and the "have-nots" was increasing. State finances were unsound, but the poor insisted on pay for governmental service, on the liturgies, and on various distributions. These demands drained money from the rich, and it seems likely that certain confiscations of property were carried out to replenish the treasury. These benefits to the poor, nevertheless, prevented any explosion of social revolution. The point of view of the fortunate "haves" and their failure to understand or sympathize with the plight of the "have-nots" are well summed up in the exaggerated rhetoric of the old and wealthy orator Isocrates, who in 353 included the following sentences in his composition known as *Antidosis* (159–160):

> It occurs to me as I am speaking what a change has come over Athens; people nowadays do not look at things in the same way as those who lived in the city in former times. For, when I was a boy, wealth was regarded as a thing so secure as well as admirable that almost everyone affected to own more property than he actually possessed, because he wanted to enjoy the standing which it gave. Now, on the other hand, a man has to be ready to defend himself against being rich as if it were the worst of crimes, and to keep on the alert if he is to avoid disaster; for it has become far more dangerous to be suspected of being well off than to be detected in a crime; for criminals are pardoned or let off with slight penalties, while the rich are ruined utterly, and it will be found that the number of men who have been spoiled of their property is greater than those who have been punished for their misdeeds.

If the long years of the Peloponnesian War brought in their train many changes in the social and economic life of defeated Athens,[6] they were responsible for even more fundamental upheavals in victorious Sparta. In any attempt to understand the situation in Sparta on the threshold of the fourth century, it is essential to bear in mind the characteristics of the "Lycurgan" constitution. Spartan citizenship was dependent on possession of a *kleros* of public land and the payment from its produce of fixed contributions to the public messes—the *pheiditia*. The citizens, the Spartiates, supported by the labor of helots and *perioeci*, devoted their energies exclusively to the welfare of the state. Since the purpose of life was service to the state, all gainful occupations were forbidden to the citizens. Throughout the fifth century, for reasons on which scholars disagree, there was a steady decline in the number of Spartiates, the equals. This decline was reflected clearly in the Spartan anxiety to recover the 120 Spartiates captured on Sphacteria in 425.

The long duration of the Peloponnesian War created new financial problems for Sparta. Previously Spartan soldiers and those of the Peloponnesian allies had served without pay and provided their own food, supplemented, of course, by the seizing of booty. The long campaigns in the Peloponnesian War necessitated different methods. In 424 Brasidas was sent to Thrace with 700 helots and 1,000 mercenaries levied in the Peloponnesus. The financing of these mercenaries was undertaken by the Chalcidians and Perdiccas of Macedonia, who had requested Spartan help (Thucydides, 4.80). In the final phase of the war, the Spartan fleet in its effort to destroy the Athenian empire in the east was financed by Persia. This arrangement was confused and ineffective until 407 when Cyrus, the younger son of the Persian king, arrived as governor of all western Asia Minor and Lysander appeared as admiral of the Spartan fleet. The Spartan officers who disbursed the funds, whatever their previous inexperience may have been, became fully aware of the power of money as men flocked to Lysander's headquarters to join the crews because the pay was higher than the Athenians could offer.

After the surrender of Athens in 404, Lysander entrusted to Gylippus, the Spartan commander of the Syracusan victory over the Athenians, the transportation of some of his acquired riches to Sparta. While the city was still excited over the discovery that Gyllipus had stolen a substantial amount of this wealth, Lysander himself returned home with various spoils and also 470 talents of silver, the balance of the money he had received from Cyrus for the prosecution of the war. A heated debate arose concerning what should be done with these treasures, some arguing that all gold and silver, as incentives to corruption, should be removed from the city, while others, including the friends of Lysander, insisted on their retention. The solution reached for this dilemma was a compromise: such wealth should be used for the needs of the state, but the possession of it by a private person should be a capital offense. The compromise proved to be unworkable, for citizens seeing wealth honored officially naturally tried to acquire it secretly. The comment of the moralizing Plutarch (*Agis*, 5) was that the Spartans could date the beginning of their corruption from the flow of gold and silver into their city following the crushing of the Athenian empire (Plutarch, *Lysander*, 16–17; Xenophon, *Hellenica*, 2.3.8).

The corruption of the Spartans, of course, did not have a formal beginning in 404, for there is adequate evidence that in the fifth century some Spartans succumbed to bribery, but there is little doubt that in a Sparta which had almost overnight passed from being hegemon of the Peloponnesian League to becoming hegemon of a large part of the Greek world, all sorts of accepted customs and values were being questioned and undermined. Plutarch (*Agis*, 5) states that an ephor named Epitadeus, whom he does not date, wrecked the Lycurgan land system by making it possible to alienate one's *kleros*. Once that break in tradition came about, the wealthy by purchase or by foreclosing on mortgages could become owners of the land of less fortunate Spartiates, thereby causing them to lose their citizenship rights and fall into the category of inferiors. Epitadeus surely can be placed either in the period following the defeat of Athens, when wealth began to pour into Sparta, or in the years immediately subsequent to Sparta's loss of Messenia in 369. In the course of the generation between these two suggested dates, the Lycurgan organization with its careful distinctions between the three castes, Spartiates, *perioeci*, and helots, was beginning to disintegrate. The most telling proof of this situation is an event which Xenophon assigns to the year 398.

In the *Hellenica* (3.3.4–11) Xenophon tells of an abortive attempt to stage a revolution against the established order in Sparta. The account centers around a young inferior named Cinadon. In an effort to win a recruit, Cinadon explains to him the status of the men in the marketplace; Spartiates—king, ephors, senators, and about forty others, all enemies; the rest, about 4,000 in number—helots, *neodamodeis* (helots freed because of bravery in war), inferiors, and *perioeci*, all allies. The proportions throughout the rest of Spartan territory would be about the same. Weapons, Cinadon points out, would be available, for those inferiors who are in the army have their own arms, while all the other potential rebels, filled with hate, would find the iron market full of knives, swords, spits, axes, hatchets, and sickles. Unfortunately for the success of the revolt, the prospective recruit turned out not to be a revolutionary, for he reported the whole episode to the ephors. They succeeded in arresting Cinadon and extracting from him the names of his confederates. These dangerous activists were then put to death after they had been scourged throughout the city. This episode is important for the vivid insight it furnishes into the deplorable social conditions prevalent in the most powerful state in the Greek world. Nowhere is there any suggestion, however, that the Spartan ruling oligarchy was thinking of some type of social reform.[7]

THE END OF THE long war, the abolition of an empire that had embraced several hundred cities, and the tremendous prestige of Sparta offered an opportunity for some constructive steps to be taken in the fundamental problem of Greek political history—the mutual relationship of countless city-states. The opportunity was there, but if Athens with all its brilliance and love of experiment had been able to produce nothing more satisfactory than a domination which could be called a tyranny, it is hardly surprising if conservative, unimaginative Sparta produced no new ideas. Sparta, also, was trapped by its own actions and propaganda. It had entered the Peloponnesian War, as Thucydides records, as the protector of Greek liberty and autonomy against the aggressiveness of the Athenians. The exigencies of war, however, made this a difficult slogan to honor without jeopardizing the aim to crush the might of Athens. The attempt to destroy the Athenian empire in the east soon illustrated the dilemma. When, following the Athenian collapse in Sicily, Sparta sent forces to Asia Minor in 412 in response to appeals from various Greek cities planning revolt from Athens and to offers of financial aid from Persian satraps, it immediately discovered that governors (*harmosts*) and garrisons were essential to protect the revolting oligarchs from democratic factions and from Athenian attacks. Since a fleet was necessary to achieve the disintegration of the Athenian empire, Sparta entered into an agreement with the Persians in 412/11, amended in 407, that in return for subsidizing the Spartan ships, the Greek cities, when liberated from Athens, should be autonomous provided they paid the old tribute to the King. Lysander, with generous subsidies from Cyrus, established oligarchies in the cities won from Athens and then in September 405 annihilated the Athenian fleet at Aegospotami.

Immediately after this victory Lysander, in order to ensure the complete destruction of the Athenian empire, took control of Sestos on the Hellespont and Byzantium and Chalcedon on the Bosporus, where he installed a *harmost* and garrison (Diodorus, 13.106.8; Xenophon, *Hellenica*, 2.2.1–2). With the route to Athens' chief source of grain thus blocked, he and his officers sailed to the coast of Thrace and throughout the Aegean islands, receiving the usually voluntary submission of the former Athenian allies. Since the democrats in these cities were anti-Spartan, Lysander established oligarchies, supported by garrisons, in these communities to guarantee their allegiance. Athens, after a prolonged siege, capitulated in April 404. By the peace terms, in which Sparta disregarded the arguments of its allies and failed to consult Persia, the abolition of the Athenian empire was officially recognized.

The Peloponnesian War was no exception to the generalization that the results of a war do not conform to the rhetorical pronouncements that attend its inception. For the Greek cities of Asia Minor the promise of liberty and autonomy which would follow release from Athenian domination became a tribute-paying obligation to Persia. The Spartan garrisons and *harmosts* which had been installed were removed, presumably because of the agreement with Persia and the tremendous assistance provided by Cyrus, although the pro-Spartan oligarchies which Lysander had established in many communities remained. It is impossible to say whether in his activities in 405 and 404 Lysander was executing official Spartan policy or concentrating on the increase of his own personal power. His influence was so great at this time that the Spartan government apparently gave him a more or less free hand. By 403, however, the old Spartan fear of entrusting too much power to any one man began to crystallize, as can be seen in the actions of King Pausanias and certain ephors in the spring of that year to curtail Lysander's efforts to aid the Thirty Tyrants, then ensconced in Eleusis. Nevertheless, it seems correct to attribute to Lysander the organization of the Spartan empire which began to take shape in late 405 and in 404.

The methods of establishing empire were similar to those which Lysander and his predecessors had been employing in Asia Minor, when they could, since 412. In the months after the battle of Aegospotami Lysander was very active in bringing under Spartan control the non-Asiatic Greek cities belonging to the Athenian empire. These cities, realizing that the Athenian fleet had been destroyed, usually capitulated without a struggle. Lysander established oligarchies in these communities, achieving this aim often by the slaughter of many of the common people. The governing oligarchy was frequently only a decarchy, a group of ten natives approved by Lysander. Each decarchy was supported by a garrison of mercenaries commanded by a Spartan officer (*harmost*). Even in Athens itself in 404–403 the Thirty can be considered as an expanded decarchy, and Callibius was the *harmost* in command of the garrison.

Although the decarchies and garrisons were probably defended as necessary measures to control the turbulent and often pro-Athenian democrats, it soon became clear that the earlier promise to grant liberty to those freed from Athenian domination was being transformed into the reality of a Spartan empire. In Asia Minor, with the end of Athenian control, the Persians now collected tribute from the Greek cities and no longer were obligated to subsidize the Spartans. In order to pay the mercenaries in the garrisons and to maintain a fleet, therefore, Sparta had to impose tribute on the cities freed from Athens. The Athenian tribute had been hated, but at least originally it had been collected from willing allies to continue the war against the Persians; the tribute paid to Sparta, from which the oligarchs in power presumably were exempt, had no justification beyond the desire to keep Sparta strong. The only ancient source (Diodorus, 14.10.2) that provides a figure on this subject states that the Spartans received in tribute annually more than a thousand talents, a sum which often is dismissed as grossly exaggerated but which, if one takes into consideration the money required for maintaining garrisons, ships, and crews, may be approximately correct.

Although the empire which Lysander organized in 405 and 404 did not include the Greek cities of Asia Minor, with the possible exception of Chalcedon, the activities of Cyrus, with whom Lysander had been so closely associated, soon led to further Spartan involvement in Asia. In the spring of 405 Cyrus had been recalled to Susa for the stated reason that his father was ill, but primarily because of his arbitrary execution of two prominent Persian nobles (*Hellenica*, 2.1.8–9). When Darius died early in 404, the succession fell to Artaxerxes, the older of his two sons by Parysatis, despite her vigorous efforts on behalf of her younger son, Cyrus. In the suspicious atmosphere at the royal court Cyrus was accused, by Tissaphernes among others, of plotting to assassinate his brother, and arrested on a capital charge. His mother's influence secured his release and, strangely enough, his reassignment to his command in Asia Minor (Plutarch, *Artaxerxes*, 3).

The statements in the ancient sources about the position of the Ionian cities in this period are confusing and confused. Apparently during Cyrus' two-year sojourn in Susa (405–403) they fell under the control of Tissaphernes, who was possibly thinking in terms of the treaties of 412–411, despite the fact that he himself was in Susa for much of that time. In Miletus, which Lysander had seized early in 405 by a bloody stratagem resulting in the establishment of an oligarchy and the expulsion of many democrats (Plutarch, *Lysander*, 8), Tissaphernes succeeded in restoring the democrats, who had fled to him and in driving out the oligarchs. According to Xenophon (*Anabasis*, 1.1.6–8), when Cyrus returned to the coast in 403, all the Greek cities except Miletus revolted to him and received garrisons, undoubtedly as protection against democratic factions. It seems clear that, since Cyrus was following Lysander's policy of favoring the oligarchs, Tissaphernes, with his suspicion of both Lysander and Cyrus, was supporting the democrats.

By the time of his return to Asia Minor Cyrus had resolved on a revolt against his brother. In the years 403 and 402 he made secret arrangements for the collection of troops. In order to restore the Milesian oligarchic exiles, who had sought refuge with him, and thus make Miletus secure for him, he besieged the city by land and sea. Since Cyrus sent to the King the tribute from the Ionian cities which he had taken from Tissaphernes, Artaxerxes, through the suggestions of Parysatis, was lulled into the belief that the situation at Miletus was merely a customary struggle between satraps. Cyrus' circulation of the rumor that he was planning an expedition against the Pisidians, a troublesome people living in the mountains to the south, gave him the excuse to assemble a considerable "barbarian" army. He was particularly anxious, however, to recruit as many Greeks as possible, for since 407, when he began to cooperate with Lysander, he had acquired a high respect for the efficiency of Greek infantry. The end of the Peloponnesian War and the numerous ensuing civil disturbances with the resulting exiles caused many Greek fighting men to be available. Cyrus gave money to various Greek officers whom he knew and urged them to hire mercenaries. By the spring of 401 when Cyrus was ready to begin his expedition, some 13,000 Greeks had been assembled. The man who became their chief officer was an exiled Spartan, Clearchus, who had been a *harmost* at Byzantium until the Spartans banished him for trying to become a tyrant. Cyrus also sent messengers to Sparta requesting help in return for all the assistance he had previously given them. The ephors responded by ordering their admiral to give full cooperation (*Hellenica*, 3.1.1). The Spartan ships, in conjunction with a Persian squadron, sailed from Ephesus to Issus, the most easterly city in Cilicia, where, with the help of 700 hoplites commanded by a Spartan, they were able to prevent the Cilician dynast from trying, if he had any such intentions, to resist Cyrus.

The tale of Cyrus' expedition and its immediate sequel is told in one of the great adventure stories which have been preserved from antiquity, Xenophon's *Anabasis* ("the going up inland"). Xenophon was an Athenian, in 401 about thirty years old, a friend and pupil of Socrates, who on the invitation of one of the Greek officers joined in this campaign unofficially as an observer. His account is wonderfully vivid and natural and should be read by all those interested in Greek and Near Eastern history. Here only the briefest synopsis can be given.

Cyrus and his army left Sardis early in the spring of 401. Apparently none of the Greeks except Clearchus knew the real purpose and destination of the expedition. Consequently as the march continued eastward, Cyrus and Clearchus had to suggest new destinations and resort to various stratagems to persuade the Greeks to continue. Raises in pay became necessary. The army proceeded through the Cilician Gates and then through the Syrian Gates into Syria. The Euphrates was crossed at Thapsacus; at this point Cyrus had to admit that Babylon was the goal and to promise a substantial bonus to each Greek at the end of the campaign. Then the march continued down the Euphrates to the village of Cunaxa, about forty-five miles north of Babylon, where Artaxerxes, who had been warned by Tissaphernes and had been waiting for the arrival of reinforcements, was drawn up with his army. In the battle which ensued, probably in September, Cyrus with his cavalry held the center opposite his brother Artaxerxes, also surrounded by horsemen. On the left were Cyrus' oriental troops and on the right, next to the Euphrates, Clearchus and the Greeks had their stand. Cyrus had hoped that the Greeks would incline to the left and join in the attack on Artaxerxes' forces, but Clearchus, unwilling to leave his flank exposed, charged straight against his opponents, commanded by Tissaphernes, and thoroughly routed them. In the meantime Cyrus attacked the enemy's center, and, spotting his hated brother, rode hard against him, but he himself was killed in the melee.

When the Greeks returned triumphantly from their pursuit, they discovered that the rest of the army had been defeated and their own camp ravaged, and on the next day they learned to their consternation that Cyrus had been killed. Their position, in the midst of a hostile land and about 1,500 miles from their starting point, was desperate, for with the death of Cyrus the whole purpose of the expedition had collapsed. Their victory over their opponents, however, had increased their confidence and they refused to surrender to Artaxerxes. Since it was important to the King to remove these unwanted Greeks from the heart of the Persian Empire, an arrangement was made that Tissaphernes would guide them home by a route different from the one through the Mesopotamian desert. They proceeded up the east bank of the Tigris for some time, but there was constant friction between the Greeks and Tissaphernes' troops. At Tissaphernes' suggestion Clearchus rashly agreed that the Greek leaders should hold a conference with the Persian. At this interview some of the lesser Greek officers were killed while the five generals, including Clearchus, were bound and shipped off to Susa, where they were executed.

Tissaphernes probably thought that the Greeks, deprived of their leaders, would have to capitulate, but they revealed in a remarkable way the value of Greek military and political training. They held an assembly and in the best manner of a democratic city-state elected new generals, including the Athenian Xenophon. They proceeded northward until they reached the mountainous region of the Carduchi where Tissaphernes, who had been harrying them, gave up the chase, for the Carduchi were not under Persian control. The Greek march through the narrow defiles of this rugged land, constantly threatened by the warlike natives, and their subsequent winter struggle through the mountains of Armenia in which they suffered severely from the snow and the cold, form an epic tale which is vividly described by Xenophon in the *Anabasis* (more accurately now, a *Katabasis*). Finally one day in the early months of 400, Xenophon, whose post was in the rear, heard a great shout arising from those in front who were reaching the summit of a mountain. Imagining that some danger was threatening, he galloped forward and soon realized that the soldiers were shouting "the sea, the sea." A few days later they reached the shore of the Black Sea and the Greek colony of Trapezus. The suffering of their long trek from Cunaxa was over, but many difficulties still remained. The arrival of some 10,000 soldiers, owing no loyalty to anyone except themselves, must have been an unnerving experience to Trapezus and other Greek colonies. Ultimately by sea and by land the Ten Thousand made their way to Chalcedon, where the satrap Pharnabazus succeeded in shipping them to Europe. Then most of them, after various troubles with Spartan officers now in control of the European Hellespontine region, took service under a Thracian prince who defrauded them of their pay. Finally in 399 some 6,000 crossed over to Lampsacus in Asia Minor and took part in the campaign that the Spartans were beginning against the Persians.

The expedition of Cyrus and the remarkable return of the Ten Thousand made a deep impression on the Greeks. The superiority of the Greek soldiers and the internal weakness of the Persians had been clearly demonstrated. Within a few years the Spartan king Agesilaus was undertaking campaigns against the Persians in Asia Minor, and from 380 on the Athenian orator and pamphleteer Isocrates was advocating a Panhellenic expedition against the Persians, the ancestral enemies of the Greeks. And looking further into the future, it can be said that the exploits of the Ten Thousand were a harbinger of the epoch-making expedition which Alexander of Macedonia inaugurated in 334 B.C.

In the year following the death of Cyrus, Tissaphernes, who had proved his loyalty to Artaxerxes, returned to Asia Minor as governor over the region which Cyrus had formerly controlled. Since the Greek cities, governed by oligarchs approved by Cyrus, were now apparently taking advantage of the confusion within the Persian Empire to try to recover their independence, Tissaphernes' first responsibility was to restore Persian authority. His siege of Cyme (Diodorus, 14.35) provided evidence to the other cities that their turn would come next. They, therefore, appealed for aid to Sparta, now universally recognized as the strongest power in the Greek world. This appeal confronted the Spartans with an embarrassing problem, and one would give much to know how they debated the issue. After the fall of Athens Lysander had abandoned Asia Minor, where, according to the Treaty of Boeotus, if properly interpreted, the Greek cities were to be autonomous provided they paid the ancient tribute to the King. What was the situation, however, after the failure of Cyrus' expedition, which the Spartans, possibly not fully understanding its real purpose, had supported because of their obligation to the young prince? Sparta's worry about having committed a belligerent act against the reigning King and its efforts to be conciliatory towards Persia through the medium of the satrap Pharnabazus can be traced in the last two books of the *Anabasis*, where Xenophon records the harshness with which the *harmost* of Byzantium and the Spartan admiral in the Hellespontine region treated the returning Ten Thousand. Was the Treaty of Boeotus made with Darius II still valid under Artaxerxes, or was Tissaphernes acting according to the disreputable agreements reached in 412 and 411?

Diplomatically Sparta was in an awkward situation, but its position as "leader" of the Greeks and its claim to be the champion of Greek autonomy theoretically carried the responsibility to aid the endangered cities of Asia Minor. The argument for meeting this responsibility was strengthened by knowledge of the prowess of the Greeks at Cunaxa and of the internal weakness of the Persian Empire revealed by the successful return of the Ten Thousand, and also by the hope that a Spartan arrival as defender of the Greeks would obscure whatever memories of the "Treaty of Miletus" still lingered.

In the winter of 400/399 the Spartans, after having sent envoys to tell Tissaphernes not to attack the Ionians, a warning naturally disregarded (Diodorus, 14.35.6), dispatched a force to Asia Minor. They began this new venture cautiously, as if feeling their way. The command was assigned to a Spartan officer, Thibron, who was given the rank of *harmost.* Since Spartan citizens (Spartiates) were too few in number to be risked in an overseas expedition, Thibron's contingent consisted of 1,000 *neodamodeis* (freed helots) and 4,000 Peloponnesians, presumably mercenaries. Three hundred horsemen were supplied by democratic Athens, glad to ship out suspected oligarchs who had served as cavalry under the Thirty. In Asia Minor Thibron levied more troops from the Greek cities, and he also enrolled some 5,000 to 6,000 veterans, including Xenophon, from the Ten Thousand who had crossed from Thrace to the Asiatic mainland. Since Thibron achieved very little and the Greek cities complained about the lack of discipline of his army, the ephors by the end of the summer replaced him with Dercyllidas, whose annual appointment was renewed twice.

The pattern of fighting was strange. Neither satrap—Tissaphernes, whose base was in Caria, or Pharnabazus in Hellespontine Phrygia— was willing, despite their superiority in cavalry, to join battle with the Greek infantry, and they resorted to numerous truces in the hope that additional forces would arrive from the Great King. The Spartan commander plundered much of the barbarian countryside and gained control of various Greek cities, some by agreement and others by force, but in all these cities the masses remained hostile to the Spartans, who always supported oligarchic governments. In these years the Persians gradually came to the realization that their most effective way to stop Spartan intrusions into Asia Minor was to prepare a fleet strong enough to deprive Sparta of its supremacy by sea. From the somewhat conflicting evidence in the sources it is clear that there were several advocates of this policy—the satrap Pharnabazus and two prominent men in Cyprus, Evagoras, the king of Cyprian Salamis, and the Athenian Conon, who had sought refuge with him after the disaster at Aegospotami.

Cyprus had been under the control of Persia since the time of Cyrus the Great, despite attempts of the Greeks in the fifth century to gain possession of this strategically located island. The various cities were ruled by Greek or Phoenician dynasts who paid tribute to Persia. According to tradition Evagoras belonged to the Teucridae family, descendants of the Homeric Teucer, who had long reigned as kings in Salamis.[8] Shortly after 450 a Phoenician seized power in the city, a rule which was replaced by another Phoenician dynasty about 415. Evagoras, who was born about 435, returned from exile in Cilicia and, driving out the Phoenician dynast, Abdemon, became king in Salamis, certainly by 410. A fragmentary Athenian inscription (*Inscriptiones Graecae,* I^2, 113), dated to 410 or 409, discloses that in return for benefits to the city, Evagoras had been granted citizenship. From the little evidence available and particularly from Isocrates' encomium (9) it is clear that Evagoras encouraged Hellenic migration to Salamis, and that around 407 he and the exiled Athenian Andocides arranged a convoy of grainships from Cyprus to Athens. Then from the autumn of 405 Evagoras gave hospitable asylum to Conon.

In the years 398 and 397 Pharnabazus, Evagoras, and Conon, with the assistance of Ctesias, the Greek physician at the Persian court, convinced Artaxerxes by correspondence and interviews of the wisdom of attacking Sparta by sea and of putting Conon, an experienced sea fighter anxious to humiliate the Spartans, in command of the fleet in conjunction with Pharnabazus. Orders were immediately dispatched that the Cyprian cities and also the dockyards in Phoenicia should concentrate on building warships. The eagerness of Conon to accept this command is easy to understand—the desire for vengeance on Sparta and the chance, if victorious, to return with honor to Athens. The motive of Evagoras is harder to grasp. Since this plan, if successful, would strengthen Persia, it is unlikely that at this time he was planning revolt from the Persians. Perhaps he was hoping that in return for his good services to the Great King he might be rewarded with more power in Cyprus, possibly even be appointed satrap of the island. As later events disclosed this was an unrealistic hope, since the King could hardly allow any man to acquire too much power in an island so important to the Persian navy.

When news of this Persian naval activity reached the Spartans, they, in considerable consternation, convoked delegates of their allies in the Peloponnesian League. It seems certain, therefore, that the campaigns which followed were approved by the league (*Hellenica,* 3.4.1–2). On the proposal of Lysander the decision was made to entrust the war in Asia Minor to the new Spartan king, Agesilaus. This man, who was to dominate Greek history for over a quarter of a century, had succeeded to the kingship in 399 under unusual circumstances. When Agis died in that year he left a son, Leotychides, who by normal procedure would have been his successor. A strong belief was current, however, that the young man was the son not of Agis, but of Alcibiades. A faction, led by Lysander, maintained, consequently, that the kingship should fall on Agis' brother, Agesilaus, a man who, although somewhat lame in one leg, had proved himself a staunch believer in the "Lycurgan" way of life. Defenders of Leotychides produced an oracle which predicted the evils that would fall upon Sparta from a lame kingship. Lysander argued that the oracle was really giving warning against the dangers of an impure kingship that would result from the appointment of a man half Athenian and half Spartan. Because of Lysander's prestige and the strong suspicions about Leotychides' paternity, this interpretation was accepted (*Hellenica*, 3.3.1–4).

Lysander had previously schemed to introduce a reform into the Spartan constitution which would have made all Spartiates and not just members of the Agiad and Eurypontid families eligible for the kingship. When this plan for securing the kingship for himself had collapsed because of inadequate support from the Greek oracles, Lysander threw all his support behind Agesilaus whom, because of his apparent modesty, he thought he would be able to dominate. Lysander also hoped that by attending Agesilaus on the Asia Minor expedition he would be able to increase his influence among his former associates in the Greek cities. As Xenophon puts it (*Hellenica*, 3.4.2), he wanted to reestablish the decarchies which he had set up, but which the ephors had suppressed when they ordered that ancestral constitutions be restored to the cities.

The question of the date of the suppression of the decarchies has exercised the ingenuity of many scholars. Probably most have argued for the period 403 and 402, when Lysander's fame was somewhat in eclipse. These dates seem unlikely when one remembers that the Spartans had had no authority in Asia Minor from the time of the fall of Athens until Thibron was sent there in 399. When Agesilaus arrived at Ephesus in 396 he found the cities in a state of confusion, having neither democracies as under Athens nor decarchies as under Lysander (*Hellenica*, 3.4.7). Plutarch's account (*Agesilaus*, 6) of Lysander's eagerness to go to Asia with Agesilaus contains the same picture of confusion—the friends whom Lysander had left in control of the cities, because of their evil and violent management of affairs, *were* being driven out and slain. It may be more reasonable, therefore, to question Xenophon's statement about the ephors' suppression of the decarchies, in Asia Minor at least, and to suspect that the decarchies, whether those established by Lysander or by Cyrus, had been under continuous attack from Tissaphernes and the citizens in general and that the cities still were in confusion in 397/396, as both Plutarch and Xenophon state.

Since internal conditions in Sparta were too dangerous to risk the sending of a citizen detachment abroad—the attempted rebellion of Cinadon had been crushed only two years previously—the forces allotted to Agesilaus were thirty Spartiates as an advisory council, including Lysander, 2,000 *neodamodeis,* and 6,000 Peloponnesian allies, a contingent which, when joined with the approximately 10,000 troops already in Asia Minor, was formidable enough to be effective. Of the league allies Corinth refused to take part in the enterprise, and beyond the Peloponnesus Thebes was recalcitrant and also Athens, now aware of Conon's activity with the Persian fleet (Pausanias, 3.9.2–3). Agesilaus, who took his command very seriously, first sailed to Aulis in Boeotia to perform a sacrifice after the manner of Agamemnon when he was departing for the Trojan expedition. This romantic idea was frustrated by the arrival of some Boeotian horsemen who drove Agesilaus away when he was in the midst of the sacrifice. Harboring an anger against the Boeotians which he never was to forget, Agesilaus joined his forces and sailed to Ephesus (*Hellenica,* 3.4.2–4).

In Asia Minor he immediately showed that he had no intention of being merely a tool of Lysander. When various delegates from the Greek cities tried to renew their relationships with Lysander and to obtain certain favors, Agesilaus invariably rejected the requests. Finally, in order to avoid humiliation, Lysander asked and received permission to go on a mission to the Hellespont. In his association with the Greek cities, however, Agesilaus followed in essence the policy which Lysander had established some years before. He suppressed the confusion existing in the cities by establishing *harmosts* and garrisons and by entrusting the government to limited numbers of oligarchs devoted to his interests.

In military matters Agesilaus proved himself a brave soldier, but neither he nor the Spartan government seemed to have any coherent strategic plan. From Xenophon and other sources it is not clear whether Agesilaus was thinking primarily of the "liberation" of the Greek cities or of conquest of Persian territory. In the summer of 395 he advanced victoriously through Lydia as far as Sardis. This success against the troops of Tissaphernes contributed to the downfall of that satrap, always the victim of the hatred of the queen mother Parysatis, who now persuaded Artaxerxes that a change of command was necessary. The new commander, Tithraustes, after executing Tissaphernes, reported to Agesilaus in an interview that now, since the man who had caused trouble for both Spartans and Persians was dead, the King thought that Agesilaus should sail home and that the Greek cities of Asia, being autonomous, should pay the ancient tribute to him. This seems like a reference to the Treaty of Boeotus. Agesilaus replied that this was a matter for the Spartan government to decide. No general truce was established, however, for Tithraustes encouraged Agesilaus to go north into the province of Pharnabazus, where the Spartans, after much plundering, spent the winter of 395/4 (*Hellenica*, 3.4.25–26).

While Dercyllidas and Agesilaus were conducting their raids in Asia Minor, the Persian fleet, consisting of Phoenician, Cilician, and Cyprian elements, was gradually being organized under the command of Conon. Although information that the Persians were assembling naval forces had induced the Spartans to entrust the Asia Minor campaign to Agesilaus and to make an alliance with Egypt, now in revolt from Persia, so as to ensure supplies for the Spartan fleet in the east, there is no evidence that Agesilaus, at least, appreciated the potential danger to Spartan supremacy of the Persian navy, to which even the Athenians were unofficially sending crews and arms. Conon's first significant achievement was concerned with the important island of Rhodes. Rhodes had revolted from Athens in 411 and under an oligarchy had been useful to Sparta in the last phase of the Peloponnesian War. The evidence for the years following 405 is scanty, but the Rhodians, probably exasperated by the character of Spartan imperialism, allowed Conon and his fleet, apparently in 396, to enter the harbor of the city Rhodes, formed by the *synoecism* of the three independent communities of the island in 408/7 (Diodorus, 13.75.1). It may have been in this year 396 that Spartan ships, convoying grain from Egypt and unaware of the recent defection of Rhodes, fell into the hands of Conon. In the following year the Rhodian democrats rose against the oligarchy dominated by the Diagorids, a family famous throughout Greece for its athletic prowess in the Panhellenic games (Pausanias, 6.7.1–7), and took control of the government (Diodorus, 14.79.4–8; *Hellenica Oxyrhynchia*, XV or X).

The loss of Rhodes and the establishment of a hostile democracy there finally aroused the Spartans to the dangers threatening their position in the east. Word was sent to Agesilaus to assume authority by sea in addition to his command by land and to take all necessary steps. Agesilaus ordered the cities on the coast and on the islands to make ready as many triremes as possible, and before long he was supplied with 120 ships over which, in conjunction with the formerly existing Spartan fleet, he placed his inexperienced brother-in-law Peisander as admiral (*Hellenica,* 3.4.27–29). The critical battle came in the summer of 394. Conon and Pharnabazus enticed Peisander into action off the peninsula of Cnidos, and in that one conflict, with loss of fleet and admiral, the Spartan domination in the Aegean collapsed. The victors immediately sailed along the coast of Asia Minor and, expelling Spartan *harmosts* and garrisons from the cities, promised autonomy. Many communities came over to them voluntarily. It was evident that, despite Xenophon's attempt to glorify him, Agesilaus' organization of the eastern Greek cities on the basis of government by cronies, supported by garrisons, had outraged the majority of the inhabitants (Diodorus, 14.83.4–7, 84.3–4). Agesilaus himself was not present to witness the foundering of his system, for, early in 394, conditions had become so dangerous in Greece proper that the Spartans had had to recall their king from the Asiatic conquests about which he was dreaming (*Hellenica*, 4.2.1–8).

THE DANGERS facing Sparta in Greece were both internal and external. The internal difficulties, of which other Greek states were only partially aware and before which the Spartans themselves were largely helpless, unless they were willing to alter drastically their social traditions, were the ones mentioned briefly earlier in this chapter—the unsettling effects on the Lycurgan system of the increasing amount of movable wealth, the steady decline in the numbers of the privileged Spartiates, and the ever-present threat of social revolution, illustrated vividly in 398 by the abortive attempt of Cinadon.

The external dangers lay in the resentment of various allies, both Peloponnesians and others, which developed in and after the Peloponnesian War. A few of these grievances should be listed here. In the confused years following the Archidamian War, the Peloponnesian League was threatened with disintegration, and it was only by its decisive victory in the battle of Mantinea in 418 that Sparta regained its former prestige. Elis, which had left the league shortly after the Peace of Nicias, outraged Sparta by not allowing it to compete in the Olympic Games of 420 on the ground that it had violated the sacred truce (Thucydides, 5.49–50), and later in the course of the Decelean War by forbidding King Agis to offer a sacrifice at Olympia, punitive measures which the Eleans as guardians of the sanctuary were entitled to exercise. Following the end of the Peloponnesian War Sparta antagonized several allies, in particular Corinth and Thebes, by the peace terms which it arranged with Athens and by its subsequent actions. All the spoils which Lysander collected in 405 and 404 were dispatched to Sparta alone, and when Sparta, forgetting its heralded role as liberator of Hellas, took over the management of the former Athenian empire, it was the sole beneficiary of the tribute collected. Corinth, Elis, Thebes, and Megara exhibited their anger by offering hospitality to Athenian exiles from the Thirty despite Spartan orders against furnishing any refuge.

By the year 402, apparently, the Spartans, feeling that it was necessary to organize affairs in the Peloponnesus more satisfactorily, vented their anger against the Eleans by ordering them to grant autonomy to their perioecic communities and—an item that raises unanswerable questions—to pay their share of the war expenses against Athens. When the Eleans refused, the Spartans, presumably after summoning a meeting of the delegates of the Peloponnesian League, declared war on Elis, a war in which the Peloponnesian ally Corinth and the non-Peloponnesian Thebes refused to participate, but to which Athens, probably from fear, sent a contingent. When the war was concluded in 400 the Eleans, after granting autonomy to their perioecic communities and surrendering their triremes to Sparta, had to rejoin the Peloponnesian League as a much weakened state. They were allowed, however, to retain their guardianship of the sanctuary at Olympia. Four years later, when Agesilaus set out on his "crusade" against Persia, the Corinthians, Thebans, and Athenians refused to contribute contingents to the expedition (Xenophon, 3.2.21–31; Diodorus, 14.17.4–12,34.1).

The resentment which various Greek states felt against Spartan policy since 404 needed only a small stimulus to be transformed into open hostility, and Persia, disturbed by the activity of Agesilaus and his predecessors in Asia Minor, played the part of catalyst. A Persian official dispatched an agent, the Rhodian Timocrates, to Greece with instructions to supply money to those leaders who would be effective in launching a war against Sparta. The mission was successful in Thebes, Corinth, and Argos, but Athens, because of lack of fleet and fortifications at Piraeus, probably was unresponsive. The ancient sources disagree on the date they assign to the sending of the Persian agent. Xenophon (3.5.1) and Pausanias (3.9.8) say that Tithraustes dispatched Timocrates, but since Tithraustes did not arrive in Asia Minor until the summer of 395 after the war had begun, the *Hellenica Oxyrhynchia* seems more logical in attributing the initiative to Pharnabazus in 397 or 396.[9]

The hostilities against Sparta began in 395 in a rather circuitous way, necessitated presumably because of the opposing factions in most cities. The Thebans persuaded the Locrians, whether western or eastern is uncertain, to make a raid on some land in dispute between them and the Phocians, whereupon the Phocians, as expected, raided Locris. The Thebans, consequently, were obligated to aid the Locrians by attacking Phocis, and, again as expected, the Phocians appealed to Sparta for assistance. The Spartans, thinking that they had grievances against the Thebans and feeling confident because of Agesilaus' successes in Asia Minor, decided to undertake a major campaign against the Boeotians. Lysander was ordered to invade Boeotia from the north through Phocis, while King Pausanias was to advance from the south. They were to meet on an assigned day and assault Haliartus, a city in the western part of Boeotia. As soon as the Thebans heard of the Spartan plans they appealed to the Athenians for aid, saying that this was the time for them to start regaining their former power. The Athenians, grateful for the Theban hospitality to their exiles in 404 and exasperated by Spartan arrogance, voted, probably on the motion of Thrasybulus, to send assistance to the Thebans. Two fragments of an inscription are still extant recording the alliance for all time of the Boeotians and the Athenians (Tod, no. 101).

The Spartan plan of a double attack on Haliartus failed miserably. Lysander arrived on schedule, accompanied by men from Orchomenus, which he had caused to revolt from the Theban-dominated Boeotian League. Without waiting for the other Spartan army, he started an attack but was killed by Thebans who had come to the support of Haliartus. A day or so later Pausanias arrived, and the day after that the Athenian contingent. Since the Peloponnesian troops were serving unwillingly—the Corinthians had refused to join in the expedition—Pausanias and his advisers decided it was advisable to make a truce in order to recover the bodies of Lysander and those slain with him. The Thebans declared that they would grant the truce only on condition that the Spartans depart from Boeotia. Pausanias accordingly returned to Sparta where he was immediately brought to trial, presumably by the Lysander faction, on a variety of charges. Realizing that under the circumstances he would be condemned to death, he retired into voluntary exile in Arcadian Tegea, where he subsequently died (*Hellenica,* 3.5.3–25).

The war which began with the battle of Haliartus in 395 and ended its futile, bloody course in 387/6 is usually called the Corinthian War because much of the military action occurred in or near the Isthmus. Fighting was resumed in 394 when the Athenians and the Thebans, now supported by two more allies, the Corinthians and the Argives, assembled near Corinth and, although defeated in a battle near the Nemean River, prevented the Spartans with contingents from the Peloponnesian League from entering central Greece through the Isthmus. Later in the summer Agesilaus, who had returned from Asia by marching through Thrace, Macedonia, and Thessaly, arrived in Boeotia. Reinforced by hoplites from Orchomenus and Phocis and by a detachment of Lacedaemonians who had sailed across the Corinthian Gulf, he faced the Thebans, Athenians, Corinthians, and Argives at Coronea. According to Xenophon, who probably was fighting in the Spartan ranks, news of the defeat of the Spartan fleet at Cnidos reached Agesilaus just before the beginning of hostilities. The battle was technically a victory for the Spartans, but Agesilaus, because of the heavy losses and his own wounds, returned to the Peloponnesus with his troops by sailing across the gulf (*Hellenica,* 4.3.10–23).

The fighting around the Isthmus continued for some five years. Only a few of the confused and badly dated events need be mentioned. The aim of the quadruple alliance to confine the Spartans to the Peloponnesus was partly frustrated when some Corinthian oligarchs enabled the Spartans to gain possession of Lechaeum, the Corinthian harbor on the Gulf of Corinth. Subsequently, near the walls of Corinth, the Athenian Iphicrates made a contribution to Greek military history when his light armed troops, *peltasts*, because of their superior speed and manoeuvrability, practically destroyed a company of 600 Lacedaemonian hoplites (Diodorus, 14.91.2–3). An interesting experiment in the relations between two city-states was a political unification of Argos and Corinth.[10] Unfortunately there is no satisfactory evidence on the details of the arrangement, which seemingly granted equality of civil rights (*isopoliteia*), and the experiment was abrogated by the terms of the peace of 387/6.

While the struggles around the Isthmus continued year after year, naval activity was also in progress. After defeating the Spartan fleet off Cnidos, Pharnabazus and Conon had sailed along the west coast of Asia Minor, driving out the Spartan *harmosts* and, at Conon's urging, promising autonomy to the Greek cities. They ran into resistance, however, at the Hellespont where Abydos on the Asiatic side and Sestos on the European side remained loyal to Sparta under the leadership of Dercyllidas, Agesilaus' predecessor in Asia Minor, strengthened by the support of many expelled *harmosts*. Failing to win over these cities, Pharnabazus and Conon in the following year, 393, sailed to Greece, raided various parts of the coast of Laconia, and took possession of the island of Cythera, which the Spartans always dreaded might fall to an enemy, where they left a garrison and an Athenian as *harmost*. They then went to the Isthmus of Corinth, where Pharnabazus gave money to members of the quadruple alliance and urged them, "remaining faithful to the King," to carry on the war.

Before he returned to Asia, Pharnabazus granted permission and money to Conon to sail to Athens and join in the rebuilding of the long walls and the fortifications of Piraeus, the achievement of which Conon declared would be a bitter blow to the Spartans. Conon sailed into the Piraeus with eighty triremes, and with the help of his crews and money the work of restoration was carried on. The Athenians also participated in the operation, and assistance came from Boeotia and other states. An extant inscription (Tod, no. 107) reveals that work on the walls had begun at least as early as June 394. Thus, although Conon was responsible for concentrated work on the task, it is clear that the formation of the quadruple alliance and the reports of Conon's activity with the Persian fleet had encouraged the Athenians to start surmounting their humiliation of 404 even before they received news of the Spartan disaster at Cnidos, probably in August 394. Persian money, therefore, was largely responsible for both the destruction and the subsequent restoration of these walls (*Hellenica*, 4.8.1–10).

With the rebuilding of the fortifications and the construction of triremes Athens was now ready to think in terms of foreign policy, a luxury which had been denied for a decade. It quickly took possession of the islands Scyrus, Imbros, and Lemnos, which it had controlled in the fifth century, and established *cleruchies* on them. Undoubtedly there was hope of exerting influence on the Asia Minor cities which Conon and Pharnabazus had liberated from the Spartans. This Athenian activity, in conjunction with the dangers from the other members of the quadruple alliance and with their concern about the consolidation of Argos and Corinth, convinced the Spartans that it was necessary to seek a reconciliation with the Persians by alerting them to the menace of the increasing Athenian naval power.

They sent an envoy, Antalcidas, early in 392 to discuss the situation with Tiribazus, the satrap governing from Sardis. Word of this intention spread abroad, with the result that when the conference was held at Sardis there were present, besides Tiribazus and Antalcidas, also Conon, representing the Athenians, and delegates from Thebes, Corinth, and Argos. Antalcidas argued for peace between Sparta and the King on the understanding that the Greek cities in Asia Minor should belong to the Persians and that all other Greek cities should be free and autonomous. The other conferees disagreed violently with this proposal, the Athenians fearing that they would lose Scyrus, Imbros, and Lemnos, the Thebans, that the Boeotian League would be dissolved, and the Argives, that they would lose their dominant influence over Corinth. The interview, accordingly, ended with no decisions reached. Tiribazus, however, convinced that Conon was using Persian money for purely Athenian purposes, arrested him; he soon escaped, but died shortly afterwards. To Antalcidas, Tiribazus secretly gave money to strengthen the Spartan fleet against the aggression of Athens and its allies. When the results of the conference were reported to Artaxerxes, he, still influenced by an anti-Spartan policy, sent down another man to take charge of the coastal area with instructions to favor the Athenians. The reaction of Sparta was to dispatch Thibron to Asia Minor, who immediately began to ravage Persian territory and to try to win over the Greek cities.

Xenophon's account (*Hellenica*, 4.8.12–17) of the abortive peace negotiations, given above, is obviously unsatisfactory. Persia naturally would have welcomed the surrender of the Asiatic Greeks and the proposal that all the states of the Aegean islands and of the Greek mainland should be autonomous, thereby making less probable the formation of a coalition against the King, but Sparta alone, without commitments from the Greeks in general, could not guarantee the fulfillment of these proposals. Antalcidas may have intended only to have a secret exploratory discussion with Tiribazus, a hope that was thwarted by the arrival of the delegates from Sparta's enemies. It is also baffling that Xenophon said not a word about the objection of the Athenians and their allies to the abandonment of the Asiatic Greeks. Further data on this peace attempt not mentioned by Xenophon, and considerable confusion, are provided by other ancient sources, Andocides' third oration, *On the Peace with Sparta*, fragment 149 of the Atthidographer Philochorus, and a puzzling passage in Plato's *Menexenus* (245). Of the two latter it need only be said here that both state that the peace proposal was indignantly rejected by the Athenians because it included the surrender of the Ionian Greeks to Persia.

Andocides' speech, long considered spurious, is now generally recognized as his report to the Athenian assembly concerning a Greek peace conference held at Sparta in 392/1, to which he had been sent as a delegate. Some scholars have argued that this conference preceded the one held at Sardis, but the most reasonable interpretation of the ambiguous extant evidence seems to be that on this occasion Sparta was trying to work out a solution to the difficulties which had wrecked the previous meeting. Since, according to Xenophon, the conference at Sardis had collapsed because of the refusal of Athens and its allies to accept the notion of the autonomy of the cities of the Aegean islands and of Greece proper, Sparta now, in an effort to disrupt the quadruple alliance, made the proposal of autonomy more palatable by accepting Theban supremacy in the Boeotian League, except in the case of Orchomenus, and by acquiescing in Athenian rebuilding of its walls and construction of triremes as well as in its control of Scyrus, Imbros, and Lemnos. These concessions were also made to reduce Athenian and Theban objections to the breakup of the merger of Argos and Corinth, on which Sparta was determined. In Andocides' report to the Athenian assembly he avoided mention of the emotional subject of the abandonment of the Asiatic Greeks, but the proposal surely was no secret. Since Callistratus, a strong advocate for revival of Athenian imperialism, proposed the decree for the exile of Andocides and his fellow delegates, it is probable that Athenian rejection of the peace was motivated not only by sentiment for the Greeks of Asia but also by fear of what the autonomy principle would do to its imperialistic ambitions as well as by distrust of Spartan aims against Argos and Corinth.

Andocides' speech, although full of obscurities, is particularly interesting because it contains in section 17 the first reference in extant sources to a Common Peace (*Koinē Eirēnē*), a concept which became increasingly current in Greek political language. In earlier Greek history, since peace was seemingly considered only a lull in the more normal condition of war, treaties were always bilateral and usually limited to specified periods of time. The horrors and follies of the Peloponnesian and Corinthian wars, however, induced some elements in the Greek population to wonder why peace should not be the normal state rather than war. As support for this antibellicose sentiment, ideas developed that peace treaties, rather than being contracts for a fixed number of years between two dominant parties, should become multilateral and without time limit, common to all who wished to be included, whether or not they had been participants in the war. As protection against encroachment from prevailing powers, states signing such agreements should be assured of autonomy and liberty. Many characteristics of a Common Peace are obscure to the modern student, as they were to the ancients themselves,[11] but it seems reasonable to conclude that the concept was intended to promote general peace among the Greeks and to recognize the rights of the small community in its relations with the more powerful. Great states found it expedient to pay lip service to the ideal, but on the excuse of national security they, in their greed, did not hesitate to twist the concept to their own advantage.

Following the collapse of Sparta's peace attempts the Corinthian War dragged on for four or five more years. The various details need not be discussed here, but the recrudescence of Athenian imperialism deserves mention. In the period 389–388 Thrasybulus sailed out with forty triremes and won as allies Thasos, Samothrace, the Thracian Chersonese, Byzantium, Chalcedon, most of Lesbos, and various other places. Finances always were a problem. Since subsidies no longer were coming from Persia, the building and maintenance of the ships necessitated unpopular property taxes. At Byzantium Thrasybulus reestablished the 10 percent duty on ships sailing from the Black Sea (*Hellenica*, 4.8.27). An inscription (Tod, no. 114) discloses that he reimposed on the allies the tax of 5 percent, resorted to briefly in the Peloponnesian War, on all maritime imports and exports. From many cities he had to request or demand contributions. One such occasion caused his death, for after the people of Aspendus, on the southern coast of Asia Minor, had contributed money, the Athenian sailors proceeded to raid the fields, in retaliation for which the Aspendians murdered Thrasybulus in his tent. The Athenians thus lost their most distinguished leader. Thrasybulus had served as a general at Samos in the period of the Four Hundred and in the closing years of the Peloponnesian War, and he had been the hero of the exiles in their return to Piraeus, which led to the overthrow of the Thirty. Under the restored democracy he apparently followed a moderate course, but he was a strong advocate of joining the quadruple alliance, and when Athens began to acquire a fleet, he, like many other Athenians, became a sponsor of a revived imperialism (*Hellenica,* 4.8.25–30).

Although in 392 Tiribazus had been unable to convince Artaxerxes that Athens now represented a greater threat to Persian interests than Sparta, events of the following years strengthened his arguments. In Cyprus Evagoras, the king of Salamis, who had been influential in persuading Artaxerxes to place the Persian fleet under the command of Conon in an effort to stop Spartan aggression in Asia Minor, was steadily acquiring control of various Cyprian cities by diplomacy or conquest. About 391 three island cities, Amathus, Soli, and Citium, appealed to the Persian king for help in resisting the ambitions of Evagoras. Evagoras officially was a loyal subject, but Artaxerxes, realizing that that strategic island could become potentially dangerous if too much power were centered in one man, ordered some of his satraps to undertake an expedition to Cyprus. Information is lacking on their activity, which was probably minimal (Diodorus, 14,98), but Evagoras in alarm appealed in 390(?) to Athens for assistance. In this general period he made an alliance, as Athens also did, with Akoris, king of Egypt, then in revolt from Persia.[12] Athens, because of close relations with Evagoras on whom it had conferred citizenship some twenty years earlier, felt obligated to send aid although knowing that this would jeopardize relations with Persia, nominally an ally since the outbreak of the Corinthian War. Ten triremes were dispatched, but they were captured by a Spartan fleet in the vicinity of Rhodes. Xenophon (*Hellenica,* 4.8.24) remarks on the anomaly of the situation: Athens, the friend of Persia, helping Evagoras now at war with Persia, and Sparta, at war with Persia, capturing ships that were sent to assist a rebel from Persia.

Evagoras' activity in Cyprus, Athenian willingness to support him, and the fact that both Evagoras and Athens were allied with the rebellious Akoris of Egypt raised the alarming possibility that a unified Cyprus might become a naval base dangerous to Persian security. Thrasybulus' energetic campaigning in eastern waters in 389 and 388 demonstrated clearly that the Athenians were thinking again in imperialistic terms. These discouraging prospects led the Persians to suspect that their earlier policy of supporting Sparta's enemies so as to reduce or end Agesilaus' enterprises in Asia Minor had outlived its usefulness, and that the time had come to change their role in the interminable Greek struggles.

Tiribazus, who had mistrusted Conon at the Sardis conference in 392 and had cooperated with Antalcidas, was reassigned to his former satrapy of Lydia, apparently in 388. It can hardly be a mere coincidence that Antalcidas appeared in Asia Minor as Spartan admiral (*nauarch*) for 388/7. He immediately went to Sardis for a conference, and then he and Tiribazus proceeded to Susa. The terms agreed upon there were almost identical with those proposed in 392. The Spartan diplomat acquiesced again in the surrender of the Asiatic Greeks to the Great King, and both parties, for somewhat similar reasons, insisted on the clause that all other Greek states should be autonomous. Since Athens would submit to these terms only under compulsion, measures were quickly taken to apply the necessary force. Soon Antalcidas with a fleet of eighty ships, provided by the Spartans, the Persian satraps, and Dionysius, tyrant of Syracuse, blocked the Hellespont completely. With no grain ships coming from the Black Sea region and with Spartan ships from Aegina raiding the Attic coast and deflecting cargo vessels, Athens, still haunted by memories of 405/4, consented to a peace conference, and its allies, of necessity, followed suit. When summonses were circulated by Tiribazus, therefore, that all who wished to hear the peace sent down by the King should be present at Sardis, delegates from Athens, Thebes, Argos, and Corinth duly made their appearance, to whom Tiribazus, after removing the royal seal, read the following document, which Xenophon (*Hellenica,* 5.1.31) has preserved: "King Artaxerxes thinks it just that the cities in Asia should belong to him, as well as Clazomenae and Cyprus among the islands, and that the other Greek cities, both small and great, should be left autonomous, except Lemnos, Imbros, and Scyros; and these should belong, as of old, to the Athenians. But whichever of the two parties does not accept this peace, upon them I shall make war, in company with those who desire this arrangement, both by land and by sea, with ships and with money."

At the conclusion of the audience the delegates returned home to report the will of the King to their respective governments. The situation was unparalleled and, because of propaganda, probably not completely clear to many of the contemporaries. The modern historian is hampered in his understanding of the issues largely because Xenophon, the chief ancient source, deliberately concealed aspects of the insidious role played by Sparta. The document read aloud by Tiribazus was in the form of an edict, and its contents surely represent the gist of the agreements reached between Artaxerxes and Antalcidas at Susa. The clauses about the abandonment of the Asiatic Greeks to Persia and the autonomy of all other Greeks, despite Artaxerxes' threat to enforce them, had little more chance of acceptance than the similar proposals of 392, unless ratification of them by all the Greeks could be obtained.

Sparta, the chief proponent of these diplomatic manoeuvres and backed by Persian power, alone was in a position to obtain this general ratification. Consequently, in the winter of 387/6 the Spartans convened a general conference at Sparta with the aim of achieving a Common Peace on the basis of the autonomy of all the Greeks. On this occasion the Thebans naturally insisted on the integrity of the Boeotian League, and the Argives, on their unification with Corinth. Agesilaus, who apparently was presiding over the meeting, told them that such policies contravened the stipulation of the King's edict that all Greek cities, both great and small, should be autonomous. When Thebes, Argos, and Corinth proved recalcitrant, Agesilaus, exploiting the questionable assumption that all members of the Peloponnesian League were autonomous, forced them to accept the King's provisions by threatening military invasions of their territories. Thebes, accordingly, acquiesced in the autonomy of all the cities of Boeotia, while in Corinth the Argive garrison was removed, the more violent democrats went into exile, and the previously banished oligarchs returned. Athens, by the terms of the King's edict, lost all the fruits of Thrasybulus' recent campaigns, but, weary of the war, frightened by the threat to its Black Sea source of grain, and bribed by the recognition of its right to Scyrus, Imbros, and Lemnos, consented to the agreement (*Hellenica,* 5.1.32–34).

Thus, probably with the enthusiastic approval of little states excited by the promise of autonomy, the first Common Peace (*Koinē Eirēnē*) in Greek history was ratified. As scholars have properly pointed out, the King's Peace, or the Peace of Antalcidas, was merely the edict pronouncing the will of the King and making him guardian of the peace. It was the peace convocation of Greeks at Sparta that gave birth to the Common Peace. This Common Peace, then, signed by all Greeks who wished, or were forced, to guarantee the autonomy of the Greeks, should be thought of as an adjunct to the King's edict.[13] The long, futile Corinthian War was now ended.

T HE KING's Peace is the more fitting term for the settlement reached in 387/6, since it emphasizes the influence that Persia was exerting on Greek affairs. Sparta had won the Peloponnesian War because of financial help from Persia. In subsequent years when the Spartans, who had been associated with Cyrus' campaign against Artaxerxes, saw the opportunity to make amends for their previous collaboration with the Persians by liberating the Greek cities of Asia Minor and attacking the territory of the King, Persia responded by such measures as the mission of Timocrates and the support of Conon, which enabled him to crush the Spartan fleet in the battle of Cnidos and to restore the fortifications of Athens. Then the continued aggressiveness of the Athenians caused the Persians to reconsider their policy, and, persuaded by the diplomacy of Antalcidas, their renewed support of Sparta led to the King's Peace of 387/6, a peace which was to influence Greek political life throughout the ensuing half century.

Since the peace, besides its benefits for Persia, was a triumph for Sparta and Agesilaus, Xenophon, with his idealization of Agesilaus, describes it in approving terms. Neither in his discussion of Antalcidas' proposals of 392 nor of the actual peace of 387/6 does he mention the consequences of this peace to the Greek cities of Asia Minor. Agesilaus' dreams of 396 and 395 were conveniently forgotten. The question of the fate of the Asiatic cities, however, was conspicuous in Greek thought in the fourth century. In particular, the Athenian orator and pamphleteer Isocrates emphasized the shame and humiliation which Greece had experienced at the hand of Persia, and contrasted the subservient role of Greece under the King's Peace with the glorious situation, suitably exaggerated, represented by the Peace of Callias. Undoubtedly it was a blow to Greek pride to surrender the eastern Greeks to Persia, but, as various scholars have suggested, the Asiatic cities after their disillusioning experiences under the aegis of Athens and Sparta may have found some solace in the comparative peace and economic prosperity provided by Persian sovereignty.

The peace of 387/6 was welcome to the King of Persia, for the departure of Athenians and Spartans from Asia Minor enabled him to turn his attention to matters vital for the welfare of his empire. Since the Greek cities in Asia were recognized as belonging to Artaxerxes, they had to be included in the Persian administrative machinery. Unfortunately, evidence is too scanty and scattered to provide a satisfactory comprehensive picture of the Greek Asiatic cities in this period. Much naturally depended on the character of the satraps under whose jurisdiction they fell. In general, it can be said that these cities were obligated to pay tribute and to furnish military aid, chiefly naval, to their Persian masters. Internally some cities seem to have remained autonomous, but others had to submit to oligarchic governments and Persian garrisons. Political life naturally became apathetic, but commerce, especially with the interior, thrived.

Beyond Asia Minor Persia had to try to reassert control over Cyprus, a claim emphasized in the terms of the peace. Evagoras in his effort to gain mastery of the whole island had been aided by the Athenian soldier Chabrias and by the Egyptian king, Akoris. Persia first attacked Egypt, but a campaign of three years (385–383) accomplished nothing, largely because the Egyptians were then aided by the military skill of Chabrias, whom the Athenians had recalled from Cyprus in conformity with the King's Peace. Evagoras took advantage of Persian involvement in Egypt to continue his work in Cyprus and to encourage revolts in Cilicia and Phoenicia. Artaxerxes, therefore, organized a great expedition to settle the Cyprus problem. In the years 381 and 380 Evagoras lost a naval battle off Citium and was besieged in his city of Salamis. Subsequently he had to accept terms of peace by which he evacuated all Cyprus except Salamis, where he remained as a tributary king to Persia (Diodorus, 15.2–11).

The departure of Athenian and Spartan forces from Asia was a valuable gain to Persia, but the autonomy clause of the peace was even more valuable to Sparta. Xenophon (*Hellenica*, 5.1.36) speaks of the Spartans as guardians (*prostatai*) of the peace. Whether this role was formally assigned by the Persians is unknown, although Spartan complicity with Persia in the formation of the peace is obvious, but, officially granted or self-assumed, the Spartans, under the leadership of Agesilaus, played the part to the hilt with total cynicism. To achieve the peace Agesilaus had coerced Thebes, Corinth, and Argos to accept the autonomy dictum much against their will. Thebes, with the dismantling of the Boeotian League, was left isolated, a situation the Spartans had long desired, and Corinth, deprived of union with Argos, had to rejoin the Peloponnesian League as an oligarchic city. After the peace requirements had been carried out to Spartan satisfaction, the Spartans, who alleged that the automony clause did not concern the Peloponnesian League since each member was an independent state, decided to discipline those members who had not been sufficiently loyal in the recent past. In 385 Mantinea, considered guilty of recent lack of cooperation and whose brief alliance with Argos in 420–418 had not been forgotten, was ordered to tear down its city wall. When the Mantineans refused, a siege was established which was expedited by damming the river which flowed through the town at the point where it emerged under the wall. The rising water undermined the sunbaked bricks of the wall so completely that surrender became necessary. Mantinea now ceased to be the city which had been established by the *synoecism* of four villages around the village of Mantinea and relapsed into its original status of five separate hamlets. Democracy was annulled, and each of the villages received an oligarchic government with an obligation to furnish military help to Sparta when needed (*Hellenica*, 5.2.1–7).

Soon thereafter Sparta became entangled in the affairs of Phlius, a strategic town in the northwestern part of the Argolid belonging to the Peloponnesian League. A group of Phliasian oligarchic exiles convinced the Spartans that the town would be far more loyal if they were allowed to return. When the democratic leaders of Phlius received an order from the Spartan ephors on this subject, they, having witnessed the recent fate of Mantinea, agreed that the state would meet the expenses involved in the restoration of property to the returning exiles. Several years later the exiles again complained to Sparta, claiming, probably correctly, that their property was not honestly being restored to them. Agesilaus marched out and demanded that the acropolis of Phlius be turned over to him. When the Phliasians refused, they were subjected to a siege which after twenty months forced them to capitulate. According to Xenophon (*Hellenica,* 5.3.25) Agesilaus in settling the affairs of Phlius decided "that fifty men from the restored exiles and fifty from the people at home [of whom some were oligarchic sympathizers] should, in the first place, make inquiry to determine who ought justly to be left alive in the city and who ought to be put to death, and, secondly, should draw up a constitution under which to conduct the government." Since Agesilaus left behind a garrison for six months, it can be assumed that the government became oligarchic and that the democrats were the victims of the executions.

In 383/2 Spartan attention was attracted to developments in the Chalcidic peninsula. Fifty years earlier, at the time when many Chalcidic communities were revolting from Athens on the eve of the Peloponnesian War, a rather remarkable league began to develop in that area with its capital at Olynthus, whose population, at the suggestion of Perdiccas of Macedonia, was greatly increased by the inhabitants of various coastal towns abandoned from fear of Athenian reprisals. This league, called the Chalcidians, or the *koinon* of the Chalcidians, revealed many aspects of a federal state. The few remarks included in this paragraph apply definitely to the league when it was revived in the early fourth century, as the slightly more abundant evidence confirms, but somewhat similar characteristics presumably can be attributed to the organization in the final decades of the preceding century. There was a federal citizenship and coinage, and a federal government about which, unfortunately, very little is known. Each constituent city retained its own citizenship and managed its internal affairs. Cities shared rights of intermarriage with each other, and a citizen of one town could acquire landed property in any town belonging to the league. The same laws prevailed throughout the whole confederacy. As in every league each constitutent city-state had to sacrifice some of its independence, especially in the field of foreign policy, and there was always the danger that the most powerful member would begin to dominate the affairs of the league. The frequent use of the term "Olynthians" rather than "Chalcidians" suggests that this trend was in operation in the fourth century.[14]

The history of the Chalcidian League in the years of the Peloponnesian War cannot be reported satisfactorily, for the information provided by Thucydides is rather sketchy and often it is impossible to be sure whether a particular city was independent or a member of the league. The incipient league, which had revolted from Athens in 432 and had later been the scene of the campaigns of Brasidas and Cleon, was thoroughly dissatisfied with the Peace of Nicias in 421, for by that treaty the league was to be broken up and the individual cities to become tributary to Athens again. The unsuccessful attempts to enforce the terms of that peace in the Thracian region need not be discussed here. It is sufficient to remember that at the end of the war, with the evacuation of Athenians from all their foreign possessions, the league, which seemingly had been confined to the general area of Olynthus, was free to think of expansion once again. The supremacy and imperialism of Sparta, however, called for caution. When various Greek states rose against Sparta in 395 and formed the quadruple alliance, the Chalcidians joined that alliance, although there is no evidence of their actual participation in the Corinthian War. Agesilaus' recall from Asia in 394 and his subsequent troubles in the Peloponnesus encouraged the Chalcidians to become more active. The first specific evidence about them in this period is the alliance they made with King Amyntas III of Macedonia. Since Macedonia from this time on played an increasingly important role in the affairs of the Chalcidians and of the Greeks in general, it will be useful to examine the relations of the Chalcidians with Amyntas rather fully.

Amyntas came to the throne apparently in 393, and probably in that same year he made the alliance, hoping to have support against a threatened Illyrian invasion. A partially preserved inscription (Tod. no. 111) on which the alliance was recorded discloses that the Chalcidians received permission to import pitch and constructional and shipbuilding timber from Macedonia, and that they and Amyntas agreed not to establish friendship, unless by common agreement, with Amphipolis, Acanthus, Mende, and the Bottiaeans, a Greek tribe just to the north of Olynthus. These four communities, located from the western part of the Chalcidic peninsula eastward to the Strymon River, obviously were not members of the Chalcidian League at the time. The importation of timber for shipbuilding and the extraction of a promise from Amyntas not to enter unilaterally into friendship with these cities suggest strongly that the league had in mind the possible incorporation of these areas. Shortly after the formation of the alliance the Illyrians invaded Macedonia and drove Amyntas out of his kingdom. The Chalcidians sent him no help, possibly because the raid was too rapid. Diodorus (14.92.3-4) states, however, that Amyntas, despairing of his kingdom, presented the Olynthians with some land adjacent to their territory. Nowhere is it stated in the ancient sources whether the gift was a final or a provisional one.

Before long, but at an undetermined time, Amyntas was restored to his kingdom by the Thessalians. Diodorus reports that there was a tradition that a pretender, Argaeus, ruled in Macedonia for two years, an occurrence which some scholars, suspecting the manipulation of Olynthus, date to 384-382.[15] In another passage (15.19.2-3) Diodorus says that Amyntas asked for the return of the land he had granted to the Olynthians. When they refused, he made an alliance with the Spartans and persuaded them to campaign against the Olynthians. This statement seems confirmed by the fact that in the ensuing war Amyntas worked closely with the Spartans.

Xenophon's account (*Hellenica*, 5.2.12-20) of the Spartan decision to undertake an expedition against the Olynthians is associated with the speech which envoys from Acanthus and Apollonia, cities in the Chalcidic region, made to the Spartan assembly and to delegates from the allies of the Peloponnesian League. The chief points in the speech were the following: the Olynthians had gathered into their league many cities in Chalcidice and had won over cities in Macedonia as far as Pella, with the result that Amyntas had almost been driven from his kingdom; Acanthus and Apollonia had been ordered to join the league or to face the consequences; ambassadors from the Athenians and Boeotians were at Olynthus, and envoys from Olynthus were expected to travel to those cities to consummate an alliance; the Olynthians were negotiating with the Thracians, and if an alliance should be established, the way would lie open to the gold mines of Mt. Pangaeus.

For the Spartans, who since 386 had been dreaming of a hegemony over all Greece, this report of a rapidly growing power in northern Greece seemed a direct threat to their aspirations. They also presumably reasoned that the actions of the Olynthians were a clear violation of the autonomy clause of the King's Peace. They and their probably cowed allies, accordingly, voted that a major expedition should be launched against Olynthus.

Xenophon's picture of the beginning of this war is very revealing of Greek prejudices. Although in his account of the hostilities he emphasizes the important roles played by Amyntas and his ally, the Elimaean prince, Derdas, he attributes Sparta's decision to act entirely to the envoys from two Greek cities in the Chalcidic area, Acanthus and Apollonia, which did not wish to lose their individuality by joining the Chalcidian League. From Xenophon's point of view he could depict Sparta in a better role as the defender of two Greek cities than as the protector of a "barbarian" king struggling against a Greek league.

The campaign was a hard one and dragged on from 382 to 379. The Spartans received valuable help from Amyntas and his ally, the Elimaean Derdas. Finally Olynthus was starved into surrender. By the terms of peace Amyntas regained his full kingdom and the Chalcidian League was supposedly disbanded. Each city of the confederation became an ally of Sparta, obligated to furnish military service when needed (*Hellenica,* 5.3.26). Thus Sparta, in its professed championship of the autonomy clause, tried to destroy a promising experiment in uniting various Greek cities along federal lines. The meagre source material is sufficient, however, to reveal that Olynthus in its zeal for expansion had been undiplomatically aggressive. A generation later the Greek world was to regret that there was not a more powerful Olynthus to withstand an emerging Macedonia.

In the same year, 382, in which Sparta launched its campaign against the Chalcidian League, it demonstrated to the Greek world, by its actions against Thebes, that any policy was acceptable which contributed to the growth of its power. Xenophon (*Hellenica,* 5.2.25–36) assigns the responsibility for the episode to an individual Spartan, but his account of subsequent events and also a statement in Diodorus (15.20.2) show that the desire to humble and weaken Thebes was basic to the strategy of the Spartan government and especially of Agesilaus. A Spartan general named Phoebidas, leading reinforcements for the war in Chalcidice, encamped en route near Thebes. He was visited there by Leontiadas, an oligarchic member of the Theban board of magistrates, who proposed a plan for seizing the acropolis, the Cadmea. Phoebidas gladly accepted the suggestion, which was easily carried out since the day chosen for the undertaking was the occasion of the festival of the Thesmophoria when women celebrants alone were occupying the Cadmea. After the coup the oligarchic faction arrested the democratic leader, Ismenias, whose followers to the number of about 300 fled to Athens.

The first Spartan reaction to the undertaking, publicly at least, was anger at Phoebidas for having acted independently, but when Agesilaus argued that the essential point was whether the action was expedient for Sparta, and Leontiadas, arriving, explained that Thebes now would be loyal to Sparta, the decision was reached to retain the Cadmea and let Phoebidas off with a fine. A commission consisting of Spartans and their allies was established to pass judgment on Ismenias. Since he was found guilty of being anti-Spartan, of having received money from Persia to engage in the Corinthian War, of favoring an alliance with the Olynthians, and of responsibility for a proclamation forbidding Thebans to participate in the campaign against the Olynthians, he was put to death as a medizer—a rather ironic sentence to come from a Spartan-dominated court.

The Spartan control of Thebes, where Leontiadas and a garrison of 1,500 men protected its interests, enabled Sparta to dominate all Boeotia. It was apparently at this time, or possibly immediately after the King's Peace, that Sparta restored Plataea, destroyed in 427, thus insulting Thebes and increasing the likelihood of dissension between that city and Athens. Sparta also installed a garrison in Thespiae and succeeded in having narrow oligarchies established in most of the Boeotian cities. The Theban exiles in Athens, however, were determined to liberate Thebes, and they knew that many of their fellow countrymen were eager to oust the Spartans. The story of the liberation of the city in the winter of 379/8 varies from one ancient source to another, but the chief credit apparently belonged to seven exiles led by Melon and Pelopidas, although Xenophon, with his prejudice against famous anti-Spartan Thebans, fails to mention the latter. These seven men crept into Boeotia and managed to enter Thebes unnoticed in the evening when laborers were returning from the fields. That night they spent at the house of a friend, and the following evening they became the chief actors in a plot arranged by a fellow conspirator who was a secretary to one of the magistrates. The officials were holding a party, and the secretary had promised that he would bring to them some of the most beautiful women in Thebes. When the conspirators, disguised as women, were introduced, they easily killed the surprised and drunken magistrates. They next went to the house of Leontiadas and killed him, and then to the jail where they released the political prisoners. In the morning the conspirators were joined by many Theban citizens and also by two Athenian generals and their regiments, who came probably as volunteers. An attack on the Cadmea followed which caused the Spartan *harmost*, despite his garrison of 1,500 men, to lose his nerve. At his request the Thebans allowed him and his troops to leave the city unharmed, but on reaching Sparta he was immediately executed for cowardice.

The Spartans then levied an army and entrusted the task of punishing the Thebans to the young king, Cleombrotus. Since the Athenian general Chabrias was guarding the road to Thebes, which ran through Eleutherae, Cleombrotus took the mountainous route to Plataea through Megara, which was guarded by a detachment of Thebans. He accordingly was delayed in reaching Boeotia and in his brief stay there accomplished nothing of significance. When he returned to Sparta, however, he left a Spartan named Sphodrias as *harmost* with a considerable number of troops at Thespiae. Although Cleombrotus' expedition was ineffectual, the marshalling of the Spartans and their allies worried the Athenians so greatly that they brought to trial the two generals who had aided the Thebans on the morrow of their liberation, executing one and exiling the other, who did not appear for the trial.

This account of the liberation of Thebes is based on Xenophon (*Hellenica*, 5.4.1–19). One puzzling aspect of it is the role of Chabrias. Although he was only "protecting" the Attic border, he was clearly aiding the Thebans by delaying Cleombrotus' progress. Since Chabrias presumably was acting on official instructions, the punishment of the two generals who assisted in the assault on the Cadmea can only be explained by assuming that the Athenian assembly, terrified by the size of the Spartan levy, offered them as scapegoats. Diodorus' story (15.25–27), supported by the late fourth century orator Dinarchus (1.38–39), is somewhat different and is important for throwing light on the confused political relations of the period. In this version the Thebans, at the beginning of the assault on the Cadmea, requested aid from the Athenians, reminding them of Theban assistance at the time of the Thirty Tyrants. The Athenians immediately voted to provide help and dispatched a force which joined in the assaults on and the siege of the Cadmea. The Spartan garrison, consisting largely of their allies, when no relief came from Sparta, capitulated as starvation became a reality. This account, with its clear statement of Athenian support for Thebes, would emphasize the anti-Spartan role of Chabrias and strengthen the conviction that the two generals, whose punishment Xenophon mentions, were merely scapegoats.

In the early spring of 378 when Athens, according to Diodorus, had broken with Sparta by actively helping Thebes and, according to Xenophon, was trying to disclaim its involvement in the Theban situation, an event occurred which is usually considered decisive for the development of the confused political history of the period (*Hellenica*, 5.4.20–33). The Spartan *harmost* Sphodrias set out one night with his army from Thespiae with the intention of seizing Piraeus in the early hours of the morning. He badly miscalculated the length of his march, however, with the result that when day dawned he was still in the Thriasian plain near

Eleusis. Since the element of surprise was no longer possible, he retraced his steps to Boeotia, ravaging property as he proceeded. The ancient sources suggest that either the Spartans or the Thebans (in the hope of arousing the Athenians against the Spartans) encouraged him to undertake this task, but it may be that he himself dreamed of presenting Piraeus to Sparta as Phoebidas had Thebes. The Athenians naturally were infuriated at the attempt and immediately seized some Spartan envoys who were in Athens, but when they insisted that they knew nothing of the plan and that the Spartans would execute Sphodrias for his deed, they were released. There were many Spartans who were outraged at Sphodrias' behavior, but Agesilaus' influence saved him from punishment. Sphodrias' son was a favorite of Agesilaus' son, Archidamus, and, as usual, Agesilaus followed his policy of government by crony. According to Xenophon (*Hellenica,* 5.4.32), he is supposed to have said: "It is impossible that Sphodrias is not guilty of wrongdoing; but when, as child, boy, and young man, one has continually performed all the duties of a Spartan, it is a hard thing to put such a man to death; for Sparta has need of such soldiers."

This behavior of the Spartans drove the Athenians further into the arms of the Thebans. An alliance was formed, and in the next three years Athenian soldiers fought side by side with Thebans in opposition to Spartan invasions. Agesilaus led a campaign late in 378, for he was afraid that Thebes would now try to reconstitute the Boeotian League, a contingency that all Spartans dreaded. In preparing for his expedition Agesilaus established or reorganized, for the arrangement may have been coincident with the Olynthian campaign, the military potential of the Spartan empire by dividing it into ten parts. The parts, according to Diodorus (15.31), were: (1) the Lacedaemonians, (2) and (3) the Arcadians, (4) the Eleans, (5) the Achaeans, (6) the Corinthians and Megarians, (7) the Sicyonians, Phliasians, and the inhabitants of the promontory of Akte (Epidaurians, Methonians, Troezenians), (8) the Acarnanians, (9) the Phocians and Locrians, (10) the Olynthians and the allies living in Thrace. Each district was responsible for providing an army group or, if it preferred, money in place of men. The money the Spartans employed in hiring mercenaries, who, even for the Spartans, were becoming an increasingly important factor in Greek warfare. Agesilaus marched into Boeotia with an army of some 1,500 horsemen and 18,000 hoplites, but since the Thebans and Athenians refused to meet him on level land, he had to satisfy himself with plundering the countryside. Similar destructive, but futile, expeditions were made in 377 and 376. Thereafter the Spartans ceased invading Boeotia, and the Thebans gradually were able to drive the Spartan garrisons out of the Boeotian cities, in which democracies were established. By 374 Orchomenus alone remained as a Spartan ally.

SPARTA'S POLICY towards Thebes and Athens, rendered more flagrant by Agesilaus' acquiescence in the actions of Phoebidas and Sphodrias, not only was responsible for the alliance between Thebes and Athens but also contributed to two developments which hastened Sparta's downfall—the revival of the Boeotian League under Thebes and the establishment of the Second Athenian Confederacy. Ever since Conon, with Persian resources, had made it possible for Athens to restore its fortifications and to begin rebuilding its fleet, many Athenians had started to dream of a revival of their maritime supremacy. The King's Peace moderated, but did not destroy, such dreams. In 380 the Athenian orator Isocrates eloquently supported Athens' right to regain its hegemony in his *Panegyricus,* a speech written as if to be delivered at the Olympic Festival. Although not delivered on that occasion, at least by Isocrates, copies of the speech presumably circulated widely in the Greek world. The oration presents a moving, if rhetorical, tribute to Athens' contributions to the Greeks and to the advancement of civilization, a denunciation of the evils of the King's Peace, and a comparison between the mildness of the former Athenian hegemony and the viciousness of the current Spartan domination. Isocrates' thesis was that the Greeks should cease their endless wars with one another, unite in concord (*homonoia*) under a tested leader—Athens—and conduct a national war or crusade against the ancestral enemy, Persia. Sparta was too powerful in 380 for any state to wrest the hegemony from it, and the appeal for Greek unity against the Persians, although preached earlier by the orators Gorgias and Lysias, was quixotic, but Isocrates' words may well have encouraged many to hope that Athens might provide a release from the oppressive Spartan hegemony.

The world in which the Second Athenian Confederacy emerged was one subject to the dictates of the King's Peace and the Common Peace which had been forced upon it in 387/6 by the combined efforts of Artaxerxes and the Spartans. The insistence on the autonomy of all non-Asiatic Greeks, a condition which every Greek state longed to possess for itself, although motivated by Persian desire for a disunited and hence powerless Greece and by Spartan realization of its advantages for attainment of hegemony, outwardly, at least, seemed aimed at reducing or eliminating the endless jealousies and wars of the innumerable Greek city-states. In view of the belligerence of the Greeks, their local pride, their ambitions, and their constant struggles to ensure themselves an adequate food supply, sanctions were necessary to forestall the age-old habit of one state infringing on the autonomy of another. The King, by threatening in his edict to make war on those violating the terms of the peace, represented a sanction, but a sanction dependent on a threat from a "barbarian" might produce fear, but hardly obedience, among the Greeks. It seems clear that in the King's eyes the sanctioning power, in fact, was Sparta. The preceding pages have shown how Sparta, as *prostates* of the peace—whatever technical meaning the term had in that context—exploited this role to enforce autonomy on its enemies and to promote its hegemony over Greece. It could be argued that in Phoebidas' seizure of the Cadmea Sparta was employing the sanctioning power, since Thebes had refused to cooperate in the Olynthus campaign whose professed purpose was to compel Olynthus to leave the Thracian cities autonomous. Thebes also was eager to rebuild its league, a desire which in itself was a threat to the autonomy of the other Boeotian cities.

When did Athens begin to form its new league? An important inscription, the decree of Aristoteles (Tod, no. 123), dated to February–March 377, is often erroneously called the charter of the league. This decree will be discussed below, but an examination of the extant evidence, some fragmentary inscriptions, the valuable although rather disjoined comments of Diodorus (15.28–29), and some relevant remarks in the orations of Isocrates show that the decree of Aristoteles was actually an extension and confirmation of earlier developments. An interesting insight into the Sparta-oriented nature of Xenophon's history is revealed by his failure to mention the formation of this confederacy, presumably because its stated purpose was anti-Spartan, a confederacy known to the Greeks as the Athenians and their allies.

In the years following the King's Peace in 387/6 Athens was on good terms, and probably allied, with cities such as Byzantium, Mytilene, and Rhodes, for there was no prohibition against establishing defensive alliances with cities not under Persian control. In 384 Athens renewed the alliance which it had made with Chios after Conon's victory at Cnidos in 394. The fragmentary inscription which survives (Tod, no. 118) emphasizes the great care that was taken to spell out that this treaty, which was "for all time," did not violate the peace to which the King, the Athenians, the Lacedaemonians, and the other Greeks had sworn. Such alliances—and there is no way to tell exactly how many were formed in this period—and Athenian friendliness to the Theban exiles naturally worried Sparta. It has even been suggested that Sphodrias' attempt on Piraeus was basically a protest against the incipient league rising around Athens. This suggestion seems unlikely, but it is interesting to note that at the time of Sphodrias' exploit Spartan envoys were at Athens, presumably trying to turn Athens away from Thebes and to reach some understanding on the autonomy problem raised by the new alliances.

It seems certain that following Sphodrias' acquittal by the Spartans, if not slightly earlier, Athens, believing that the Spartans had violated the King's Peace, began to take steps towards the creation of a league. It apparently sent envoys to its allies suggesting that these alliances should be consolidated in a league. In the year 378 new alliances were struck with Chios, Byzantium, Mytilene, and Rhodes. In the inscription recording the alliance with Byzantium (Tod, no. 121) it is specifically stated that "Byzantium is to be an ally of Athens and the other allies on the same terms as the Chians." These words can hardly mean anything else than that these states were joining in some type of organization and that Chios, since it served as a model, must have been the first to sign the new agreements. These five states, then, Athens, Chios, Byzantium, Mytilene, and Rhodes, spelled out the charter of the new league—the same principles which were expressed in the decree of Aristoteles in February–March 377. Methymna and Thebes joined the organization just before the publication of Aristoteles' decree. It seems that the response to the Athenian appeal of early 378 had been somewhat disappointing, probably because of fear of Sparta and apprehension about Athens. In the decree proposed by Aristoteles, therefore, the Athenians, in order to encourage more recruits to the new league, bound themselves by various promises of forbearance.[16]

This decree was passed in the seventh *prytany* of the year of the archon Nausinicus (378/7), hence exactly a century after the formation of the Delian League. Although the inscription which records the decree is restored from twenty fragments, the reconstruction of the document is generally secure except possibly for the restoration of a reference to the King's Peace (Common Peace) in the preamble. A few quotations or paraphrases will demonstrate the significance of this document. The purpose of the decree is clearly stated in the preamble: "In order that the Lacedaemonians may allow the Hellenes to live in peace, free and autonomous, having all their territory secure, and [that the Common Peace which the Hellenes?] and the King swore according to the covenants may continue valid for ever, the assembly has voted as follows." Next comes the invitation for new members of the alliance: "If anyone of the Hellenes or of the 'Barbarians' living on the continent or of the islanders, as many as are not under the King, wishes to be an ally of the Athenians and of their allies, let it be possible for him, being free and autonomous, enjoying the form of government which he wishes, neither admitting a garrison nor enduring a magistrate nor paying tribute (*phoros*), but on the same terms which apply to the Chians and Thebans and the other allies." The Athenians then promise to relinquish any land held privately or publicly in the territory of the states joining the alliance and to eradicate unfavorable records at Athens, if any, applying to those states. The prohibition for Athenians to acquire real property, whether house or land, in the territory of an ally in the future is then specifically stated, a prohibition strengthened by the right of any ally to denounce the offender to the *synedrion* (council) of the allies. The *synedroi* then are to sell the property and give half of its value to the accuser and the rest to the common treasury of the allies. A pledge of military support to any ally attacked by land or sea follows, and also a promise of punishment by death or exile, after a trial before the Athenians and the allies, for anyone who proposes a measure contrary to the wording of this decree. The secretary of the Boulē is then instructed to have the decree engraved on a stone stele and erected beside the statue of Zeus Eleutherios. On this stele the names of the cities now allies are to be engraved, and also whatever city shall subsequently become an ally.

The names of the cities that joined the alliance were inscribed in two columns below the decree and also, because of lack of space, on the left side of the stone. The cities with which Athens already had an alliance, the charter members, were recorded first in the same "hand" that inscribed the decree—Chios, Thebes, Mytilene, Methymna, Rhodes, and Byzantium. In the following few years as new states joined the confederacy, their names were also recorded in several different "hands." The total number ultimately was probably between sixty and seventy, and the area represented extended from Byzantium on the Bosporus to islands and countries in the western part of Greece. Cities in the Thracian region, the Aegean islands, and Euboea were well represented. Some thirty-five of the cities had formerly been members of the Delian League. Interesting entries, illustrating the civil discord so common among the Greeks, were the "demos" of the Corcyreans and the "demos" of the Zacynthians.

On the basis of the information provided by this decree and by various literary sources, a few general observations about the Second Athenian Confederacy can be made. The first lines of the document show that the motive which led to the formation of the league was the desire and need to establish an organization to curtail the autocratic activity of the Spartans. In this connection it was essential to make clear that no encroachment on the King's Peace was intended, for any infringement of that peace could easily have led to renewed Persian support of Sparta. This concern may explain the decision, mentioned towards the end of the decree, to send envoys to the Thebans to try to persuade them "of whatever good they can"—presumably an effort to discourage Theban revival of the Boeotian League at the expense of the autonomy principle. The insistence on the anti-Spartan nature of the alliance, although necessary at the time, was unfortunate, for in view of the rapidly shifting nature of Greek political alignments, there was no guarantee that Sparta would remain *the* enemy. In the case of Athens it was not long before Thebes became more of a menace than Sparta, and consequently, in trying to hold the alliance together, Athens faced a problem analogous to the one in the Delian League when, after 449, hostilities with Persia practically ceased.

In the planning of the new organization the Athenians revealed that they were well aware of the practices which had aroused hostility to their fifth-century hegemony. The decree of Aristoteles specifically stated that Athenians would not acquire landed property in the territory of the allies, interfere with local governments, dispatch garrisons or Athenian officials, or impose tribute (*phoros*). These stipulations both disavowed fifth-century policies and also condemned recent Spartan imperialistic devices. Since the decree used the word *enktemata* (property held in a foreign country), Athenian relinquishing of such property and the prohibition on acquiring any in the future must refer to acquisitions already made in allied territory prior to 377 as well as to the notorious *cleruchy* system. This measure, then, although passed by the people, eradicated the hope of many landless poor Athenians to acquire land abroad.

The policy of the new league was controlled by two theoretically equal and distinct bodies, the Athenian assembly and the *synedrion* of the allies, permanently resident in Athens. No proposal could be ratified unless it was approved by both bodies. The Athenian Boulē served as intermediary between these two assemblies. If agreement could not be reached, the proposal presumably was dropped. In the *synedrion* of the allies each city had one vote and apparently only one delegate (*synedros*). Proportional representation on the basis of the size of the population of each city would have been better, for under the existing system Athens probably was able to intimidate smaller members. Judicial problems which arose were to be handled, in a way sometimes obscure to the modern scholar, by the two assemblies.

Executive power and the responsibility of commanding military expeditions remained with the Athenians. Considering the strength and prestige of Athens and the circumstances in which the league developed, no other arrangement probably was possible, but the system obviously was dangerous. The league began as a defensive one, but situations constantly occurred in which Athenian generals could turn defensive operations into offensive ones advantageous to Athens. As hegemon, Athens was responsible for seeing that financial resources were adequate for the necessary activity of the league. Because of bad memories from the fifth century the custom of annual *phoros* was not renewed. A system of contributions, *syntaxeis*, was introduced, about which unfortunately there is little information. The evidence shows, however, that Athens was constantly short of money and that the allies often did not pay their contributions in full and were delinquent in furnishing ships and troops. Athenian generals had to resort to various forms of compulsion to keep their fleets operative. In the course of time the defensive purpose of the league was forgotten, and it more and more became a tool of Athenian imperialism. Despite the promises of the decree of Aristoteles, Athens did interfere in the government of some of its allies, impose garrisons, and establish *cleruchies*. It is not surprising, therefore, that twenty years after the founding of the league Athens was confronted with the revolt of some of its most important allies.

The formation of the Second Athenian Confederacy, with its anti-Spartan propaganda clearly heralded and with its potential of developing into an Athenian hegemony, could not be ignored by the Spartans. Consequently in 376, after repeated failures in their efforts against Thebes, they concentrated their energies on naval strategy against Athens. Their fleet, navigating in the waters between Aegina and Andros, succeeded in preventing a detachment of grain ships bound for Piraeus from proceeding beyond the southern tip of Euboea. Threatened by a shortage of grain, the Athenians launched their fleet. The admiral, Chabrias, joined battle with the Spartans off Naxos and won a distinguished victory. The whole Spartan fleet might have been destroyed if Chabrias, remembering the fate of the Athenian generals after the battle of Arginusae, had not concentrated on saving the Athenians from their disabled ships rather than pursuing the enemy (Diodorus, 15.34–35).

The success at Naxos was particularly gratifying to the Athenians, for it was their first naval victory since the ill-fated battle of Arginusae in 406. The battle of Cnidos in 394 had been tremendously important for them, but it had been won by an Athenian general, Conon, commanding Persian ships and crews. The Athenians, inspired by their victory at Naxos, increased their naval activity in the following year. One fleet under Chabrias, operating in the Aegean and the Thracian region, won over many islands and cities to the Athenian alliance. As early as 390/89 Athens had regained control of Delos, which it had lost by the peace of 404. An inscription (Tod, no. 125) recording the activity of the Athenian Amphictions of the Delian temple-properties for the period 377–373 suggests resentment of the Athenian presence, since it lists the fines and perpetual exile imposed on eight Delians who had dragged the Amphictions from the temple and beaten them. A second fleet led by Timotheus, in response to a Theban request to distract Sparta from another invasion of Boeotia, sailed around the Peloponnesus and brought Corcyra, Acarnania, and the island of Cephallenia into the Athenian confederacy (*Hellenica*, 5.4.60–66).

While the Athenian fleets were achieving successes in eastern and western waters, Sparta, since its victory over Olynthus in 379, had experienced nothing but humiliations—the liberation of Thebes and the gradual expulsion of Spartan garrisons from Boeotian cities, the formation and growth of the Second Athenian Confederacy, and the loss of Spartan influence in western Greece and the adjoining islands. In 375 Sparta suffered further frustration. In that year (although some scholars argue for the date 371) Polydamas, the ruler of Pharsalus, the last Thessalian city to hold out against the ambition of Jason of Pherae to unite all Thessaly, came to Sparta seeking extensive military aid. To Sparta, still dreaming of a hegemony in Greece, the prospect of a powerful united Thessaly, allied with the hated Thebans, was dismaying, but conditions in the Peloponnesian League, the dangers of its own social problems, worry about the rapid expansion of the Athenian League, and concern about the situation in central Greece compelled it to reject the Pharsalian request, although that city held a strategic position on the route to the north. Consequently Pharsalus submitted to Jason, who thereafter consummated the temporary union of Thessaly and received the old title of *tagos* (dictator of Thessaly), under which abundant military resources were available to him. Sparta had to restrict itself to dispatching an army to Phocis to forestall any possible Theban aggression (*Hellenica*, 6.1.2–19).

In this same year, 375, a Common Peace, modeled on the King's Peace of eleven years earlier, was established. Xenophon (*Hellenica*, 6.2.1) speaks only of a peace between Athens and Sparta and says that Athens, angry that Thebes was not contributing to the navy (a charge refuted by other sources), weary of paying war taxes, and distracted by Spartan piratical raids from Aegina, was the initiator. Diodorus (15.38.1–2) seems to be nearer the truth when he writes that the Great King, preparing for an expedition against Egypt and wishing Greece to be at peace so that mercenaries would be available, sent envoys to the Greeks to try to bring about a reconciliation. At Sparta a Common Peace, declaring that all states should be autonomous and ungarrisoned, was accepted by a war-weary Greece, but beyond Sparta, Athens, and Thebes, presumably as a member of the Athenian League, it is not known how many cities signed the document. The fact that this Common Peace was achieved voluntarily by the Greeks and not at the dictates of the Great King must have created special enthusiasm for the pact. Athens was particularly happy, for now its league was officially recognized, as the Peloponnesian League had been by the King's Peace. To commemorate the occasion it erected an altar to Peace and established an annual festival in her honor. The sculptor, Cephisodotus, made a statue of the goddess holding the infant Plutus (Wealth) in her arms, of which a Roman copy has been preserved (Nepos, *Timotheus, 2*). Statues were also erected to Chabrias and Timotheus, whose victories had been chiefly responsible for the growth of the Athenian League (Aeschines, 3.243). Those who were capable of hard thinking amidst the emotional excitement, however, must have realized that the dogma of the autonomy of cities was bound to lead to a confrontation with Thebes, and that the passion for hegemony which gripped Athens and Sparta and tempted Thebes and Jason of Pherae was totally antithetical to the ideal of autonomy embedded in the basic concept of a common peace.

In conformity with the terms of the peace, Sparta apparently withdrew its army from Phocis and removed whatever garrisons it still may have had in Boeotia. The Athenians sent orders to Timotheus to return, since peace had been declared. On his voyage home in the autumn of 375 he disembarked on the island of Zacynthus a group of exiled democrats. When the ruling oligarchs there reported this to the Spartans, they, according to Xenophon (6.2.2–4), maintaining that the Athenians had violated the peace, dispatched a fleet manned by themselves and their allies with instructions to recitfy the situation in the western area and in particular to launch an attack on Corcyra.

Xenophon's account is unsatisfactory. Beyond the question of whether Timotheus' action was a violation of the peace, Isocrates' *Plataicus,* published in the late summer of 373, demonstrates that at that date Sparta and Athens were still at peace. Since hostilities were not resumed until after that date, it is obvious that Xenophon's account (6.2.4–39) of warfare in and around the western islands is misleading, at least chronologically. From Diodorus (15.45–47) and Pseudo-Demosthenes (49, *Against Timotheus*), especially, the history of the badly documented years 375–372 has been reconstructed somewhat as follows, although the events of 374 remain almost a blank.[17] In the spring of 373 Timotheus sailed out of Piraeus with a fleet of sixty triremes on an unspecified mission. Since the government, as often, had failed to provide adequate funds, he spent the summer in trying to extract contributions and crew members from the communities on the Aegean islands and the coast of Thrace. By autumn, when word apparently reached Athens that a Spartan fleet was operating around Corcyra, Timotheus still had not properly equipped his ships. His enemies succeeded in having the assembly depose him from his command, which was then assigned to Iphicrates, and Timotheus himself was brought to trial. This trial aroused great excitement in Athens, for the prosecutors were the statesman Callistratus and the general Iphicrates, both rivals of Timotheus, and the most distinguished defense witnesses were Alcetas, king of the Molossians in Epirus, and Jason of Pherae, whom Timotheus on the occasion of his western campaign in 375 had persuaded to become allies of Athens. Because of the prestige of these witnesses and of Timotheus himself as the wealthy son of the famous Conon, he was acquitted, but his generalship was not restored. In the spring of 372 Iphicrates, who must have received more help from the state than Timotheus had, sailed to western waters where, finding that the Spartan general had been slain and that the fleet was disorganized, he was able to achieve considerable success.

This war, in which Sparta was achieving nothing and in which Athens was exhausting its finances and antagonizing many of its allies by trying to exact money and men from them, proved of benefit to the Thebans alone. While Athens and Sparta were otherwise occupied, they took the opportunity to strengthen the Boeotian League.[18] Plataea, which resisted incorporation into the league, they destroyed in the summer of 373. The Plataeans who escaped sought refuge in Athens as their ancestors had in 427. The increasing power and aggressiveness of Thebes worried the Athenians, particularly since Jason of Pherae, who remained on good terms with the Thebans, apparently no longer was in alliance with Athens. The problem of the relations between Jason and the Athenians is confused, but it should be mentioned here. Among the names of members of the Second Athenian Confederacy inscribed on the decree of Aristoteles was a group, added about 375, including Alcetas and his son Neoptolemos, dynasts of the Molossians in Epirus, followed by a name which had been deliberately erased. The final letter of this name could be n (Greek nu), and most scholars have accepted the restoration "Jason" on the assumption that he joined the league as a result of Timotheus' successful campaign in western waters in 375. As mentioned above, Jason and Alcetas appeared as witnesses for Timotheus at his trial in November 373. The elimination of his name (if his name was indeed recorded on the inscription) might have happened in 372 or 371 when his consolidation of control in Thessaly may have seemed contrary to the slogan of autonomy.

In this distracted Greek world, another attempt to achieve a Common Peace was made in the summer of 371. To judge from Xenophon (6.3.2), the initiative came from the Athenians, who, after urging the Thebans to follow, sent envoys to Sparta. If one takes into account other sources, however, especially Dionysius of Halicarnassus, *Lysias* (12), and even a speech Xenophon assigns to one of the Athenian delegates (6.3.12), it is probable that Diodorus (15.50.4), although repeating some of the language he used in reference to the peace of 375, was correct in saying that the Great King used his influence to promote this Common Peace. The conference, which was held at Sparta, must have been a memorable one. Present were delegates from Athens and Sparta and their respective allies, from many other Greek states, from Artaxerxes, and possibly from Dionysius, tyrant of Syracuse, and Amyntas III, king of the Macedonians. On such an occasion oratory surely flourished, although Xenophon merely paraphrases the speeches of three Athenian envoys. Other sources, such as Plutarch (*Agesilaus*, 27–28), Pausanias (9.13.2), and Nepos (*Epaminondas*, 6.4), however, emphasize that the drama of the convention centered in the speech of Epaminondas of Thebes, who, in support of the Boeotian League, denounced Spartan aggressiveness and hypocrisy and, in response to Agesilaus' demand that the Boeotian cities be autonomous, argued that the perioecic cities of Laconia also should be autonomous. Although Xenophon's account of the conference is the most detailed one, it is obvious that because of his omissions—he does not even mention Epaminondas—he presents only a prejudiced view of the negotiations. In these transactions it was agreed that fleets and armies should be disbanded and that the cities should be left autonomous and ungarrisoned. The provision was also added that "if any state should act in violation of this agreement, it was provided that any which so desired might aid the injured cities, but that any which did not so desire was not under oath to be the ally of those who were injured." One wonders if the Athenians were behind this resolution, hoping thereby to be released from any future obligation to Thebes.

When the time came for swearing to the peace, the Spartans signed for themselves and their allies, while the Athenians and their allies signed separately, city by city. Concerning the Thebans Xenophon says (6.3.19): "The Thebans also signed their names among the cities which had sworn, but on the following day their ambassadors came in again and demanded that the writing be changed to read that 'the Boeotians' instead of 'the Thebans' had sworn." Agesilaus, the chairman of the conference, refused, and when the Thebans insisted, struck their name off the list. Many attempts have been made to interpret this passage of Xenophon. Why, since Epaminondas was representing the Boeotians, did the original wording read "Thebans" rather than "Boeotians"? One interpretation—and probably the best—of this enigma, offered in 1972,[19] is that on the first day Epaminondas was overruled by his fellow envoys, who succumbed to their fear of Sparta, but that by the following day he had prevailed over their timidity and insisted on a reading which would confirm the unification of the Boeotian cities in a league. Because of his hatred of Thebes and his admiration for Agesilaus, Xenophon could not, or would not, discuss the issues fully. All that can be said with certainty is that this peace, often called the Peace of Callias from the name of one of the Athenian envoys, immediately became a meaningless document since the clash between Thebes and Sparta ignited a renewal of hostilities. Xenophon ends his description of this scene with the sordid comment that the Athenians now had hope that Thebes would be totally destroyed.

In conformity with the terms of the peace the Athenians recalled their armies and garrisons, and the Spartans did likewise except for an army under King Cleombrotus which they had recently dispatched to Phocis. Despite their oaths and the advice of a lone figure, Prothous, in an address to their assembly, the Spartans ordered Cleombrotus to march immediately against the Thebans unless they granted autonomy to the Boeotian cities (Xenophon, 6.4.1–3). The Thebans for their part made preparations to resist the invasion. Cleombrotus did not enter Boeotia from the west because he learned that the Thebans were waiting for him in various narrow passes, but marching south to the sea and then turning eastward, he came to Leuctra at the western end of the Theban plain. Here he, with about 10,000 troops, was confronted by the Boeotians, numbering probably about 6,000. The Thebans, who had been undergoing intensive military training in recent years, were led by their two remarkable leaders, Epaminondas and Pelopidas, whom Xenophon does not deign to mention. Epaminondas, who as one of the seven Boeotarchs was in chief command after having convinced some doubting colleagues that battle and victory were essential now, placed his Theban hoplites in a solid formation fifty shields deep on his left wing. This phalanx, whose rear lines could be used as reserves, faced the strongest part of the Spartan army where Cleombrotus was stationed.

The battle began with a cavalry skirmish in which the Thebans so routed their opponents that the Spartan infantry was somewhat disorganized by the retreating horsemen. At just this moment the Theban phalanx advanced, and its heavy, disciplined attack was too much even for the Spartans who, disconcerted by their fleeing cavalry, were also assailed as they attempted to outflank the Theban left by a brilliant charge of the Sacred Band of 300 elite hoplites under Pelopidas. After losing their king and 400 of the 700 Spartiates who were present, the Spartans retreated to their camp on a neighboring hill. News of the disaster, following the conclusion of the peace conference by only twenty days, was sent to Sparta, which received the tidings with studied calm. The two remaining regiments were immediately levied and placed under the command of Agesilaus' son, Archidamus. As they marched northward they were joined by contingents from various members of the Peloponnesian League. The report of the victory was carried to Athens by a garlanded messenger from the Theban army, who called on the Athenians to join in taking vengeance on the Spartans. The Athenians, however, although only six years earlier they had established their league to check Spartan aggressiveness, were now so frightened by this evidence of Theban power that the messenger, after receiving no official hospitality, returned to Leuctra with the clear knowledge that the alliance between the Athenians and the Thebans was now a thing of the past (*Hellenica*, 6.4.4–20; Diodorus, 15.52–56).

The Thebans also sent word of their victory to their ally Jason of Pherae. When he arrived rapidly with his troops, the Thebans proposed that he and they should make a joint attack on the Spartan camp. Jason, however, who probably did not want the Thebans to acquire any greater power, succeeded in establishing a truce under which the Spartans began their retreat. In Megara, after falling in with Archidamus and his reserve army, the Spartans reached the decision to dismiss their allies and to return to Sparta. Jason himself returned to Thessaly. On his march he destroyed the Spartan-controlled town and fortress of Heracleia near Thermopylae, thereby ensuring for himself unimpeded access into central Greece in the future. This man, about whom so little is known, now clearly revealed that he wanted to employ his military and financial resources as *tagos* of Thessaly to acquire a dominant role in the Greek world. He planned to exploit the Pythian Games at Delphi in 370 as a means of advertising his power and of increasing his influence. He ordered the Thessalian cities to provide a large number of animals for a great sacrifice at the games, and with his military backing he apparently was hoping to preside at the festival. The rumor circulated that he intended to propose a united Greek expedition under his leadership against the Persians. Whatever his dreams were, they were cut short by assassination. One day, while he was holding an audience at Pherae, seven young men approached him, as if they wanted an answer to some quarrel, and murdered him. Two of the assassins were immediately killed, but the others escaped and, according to Xenophon (6.4.32), were held in honor among most of the cities to which they went. The Greek world was plainly apprehensive of the power and ambition of Jason. If he had lived he might very well have tried to do what Philip II of Macedonia did a generation later.

LEUCTRA, although not a great battle in terms of the numbers of the opposing forces, marked an important transition in the development of Greek political history. The fifth century had been characterized by a division of power between Athens and Sparta. The Peloponnesian War ended this dualism, and for the following generation, 404–371, Spartan hegemony, despite frequent opposition, dominated the lives of the Greeks. This leadership, despite its brutality, contributed a certain amount of unity to the chaotic Greek world, for the Greeks could at least agree on acquiescence in, or resistance to, Spartan supremacy. Leuctra stunned the Greek world, and once the realization had spread that the Spartan hoplite was no longer invincible, individual states began to think of their own aspirations. The Peloponnesian League, which for two centuries had been a stabilizing influence in Greek politics, began to disintegrate, although oligarchic factions tried to rally to the support of Sparta. New aspirants to hegemony emerged, first Jason of Pherae, then the Thebans, and then the Athenians again. The period was one of such confusion that the account left by the contemporary Xenophon is far too limited and prejudiced to provide a satisfactory guide to the issues involved.

In the autumn of 371 or the winter of 371/0 the Athenians, wishing to capitalize on Sparta's weakened condition and to strengthen their position against a victorious Thebes, summoned to Athens envoys from all the cities which wished to share the King's Peace. Unfortunately Xenophon (6.5.1–3) does not list the cities that accepted the invitation, but subsequent events make it clear that Sparta and most of the Peloponnesian cities were present. Thebes, which had been excluded from the Peace of Callias in 371—really a reaffirmation of the King's Peace—apparently was not invited. The delegates agreed to abide by the King's Peace "and by the decrees of the Athenians and their allies." The significance of this last clause, which Xenophon does not explain, has never been satisfactorily interpreted. Since the Peloponnesian cities certainly did not become members of the Athenian confederacy, the purpose of the words may have been to emphasize that the Athenian league professed the autonomy principle and that Athens, rather than Sparta, was now the defender of the King's Peace. The oath which was taken also included a guarantee of the autonomy of individual cities and a pledge to go to the support of any city which had sworn the oath if it were attacked. This compulsory guarantee may have put teeth in the Common

Peace, but there is no evidence that any proper machinery was established to decide in any given case who the aggressor was. In the case of Athens, this particular clause caused it to become involved in various disputes of questionable value to the city. All the cities represented at this conference took the oath except the Eleans, who claimed that it was not right for certain cities which the Spartans had taken from them in 399 to be classified as autonomous.

In the Peloponnesus, so long dominated by Sparta, it was only natural that the Spartan defeat at Leuctra and the subsequent conference at Athens confirming the principle of autonomy encouraged aspirations for independence. In the spring of 370 Mantinea, the Arcadian city which had been dissolved into its constituent villages by the Spartans in 386, began, on the urging of democratic forces frustrated by the control of landed aristocrats, to reassemble as a city once again. The attempt of Agesilaus to discourage the project had no success. More important than the rebuilding of Mantinea for the future of the Peloponnesus and for the weakening of Sparta was the determination of many Arcadian communities to strengthen themselves against internal wars and foreign aggression by uniting in a league. The chief advocate for the Arcadian League was the Mantinean Lycomedes, but some of the earliest difficulties in effecting the league occurred in Tegea. In that city the oligarchs, loyal as usual to Sparta, resisted the idea of federation, but they were overcome by the democratic faction aided by troops from Mantinea. Many of the oligarchs fled to Sparta. Tegea, located near the northern border of Laconia, had long been a cooperative member of the Peloponnesian League, and the prospect of its becoming a member of a hostile Arcadian federation filled the Spartans with apprehension. Interpreting the autonomy clause of the conference at Athens to suit themselves, they dispatched Agesilaus with an army to restore the exiled oligarchs. The campaign was futile, and the Arcadians continued with their work of uniting their cities (Xenophon, 6.5.3–22).

One of the first tasks was to establish a capital for the new league. Since the selection of an already existing Arcadian city as capital would have led to jealousy among the other communities, it was decided to build a new city. The site chosen was in the plain to the west of Tegea, and the nucleus of the city was formed by persuading the inhabitants of neighboring communities to leave their villages and become the citizens of the new foundation. The capital received the name of Megalopolis— Great City—a title deserved by the double wall with a circuit of five and a half miles which surrounded it. The city had a twofold character,[20] for the northern section housed the citizens of the city-state Megalopolis, while south of the Helisson River the capital of the Arcadian League was built, provided with federal buildings and barracks for the permanent army. The construction of the city probably should be assigned to the years 370–367. This large, strongly fortified capital located near the northwestern boundary of Laconia was obviously intended to be a barrier against the Spartans, a fact which presumably explains why Xenophon does not mention its founding.

From the literary sources and an inscription (Tod, no. 132), dated in the 360s, a little information can be gleaned about the constitution of the Arcadian League. The inscription records a resolution of "the Boulē of the Arcadians and of the Ten Thousand (Myrioi)." The Boulē, whose size is unknown, consisted of representatives from the constituent cities; its duties presumably were chiefly deliberative and administrative. The Ten Thousand were clearly a primary assembly. If the word *myrioi* means Ten Thousand in this context, and if the figure is taken as a round number, then the franchise apparently was restricted to men of hoplite status. It is also possible, but less probable, that the word *myrioi* here has its other meaning, in which it denotes an undefined large number. The inscription, after stating its business, then contains the entry "the following were *damiourgoi*," after which a list of names, arranged by cities, is recorded. Since ten cities are listed, the logical conclusion is that at that time they were the constituent members of the league. Scholars generally believe that the *damiourgoi* were a working committee of the Boulē, like the *prytaneis* at Athens. Of the ten cities listed, seven furnished five *damiourgoi* each, apparently the normal delegation, but Megalopolis provided ten, while two cities sent three and two men, respectively. It seems clear, therefore, that the number of *damiourgoi,* and presumably of the members of the Boulē, was selected from each community on the basis of the size of its population. The chief executive of the league and also the commander of the federal army was the annual *strategos,* or possibly a board of *strategoi.* Lycomedes of Mantinea, who was so influential in creating the confederacy, is recorded as holding this position.[21]

While the Arcadians were planning the organization of their league in 370, the Spartans, under the leadership of Agesilaus, continued to be a threat to their activity. Feeling that outside help was essential to the achievement of their purpose, the Arcadians, associating Argives and Eleans with themselves, sent envoys to Athens. Since the Spartans were clearly interfering with the autonomy of the Arcadians, the Athenians were obligated by the terms of their recent conference to assist the Arcadians in the prevention of aggression. But the Athenians, worried by the Thebans, had no desire to jeopardize their relations with Sparta. When the Arcadian envoys received no encouragement from the Athenians, they continued their journey to Thebes, where their request was soon honored (Diodorus, 15.62).

Since Leuctra, Thebes had been reaping the fruits of its victory. It rounded out the Boeotian League by including Orchomenus near the northwest border, thus following the advice of Epaminondas rather than the first impulse to destroy the city. In 371 or 370 it won or received as allies most of the peoples of central Greece—the Phocians, probably the Aetolians, the Acarnanians, the Locrians, both eastern and western, several communities bordering on the Malian Gulf, and the cities of Euboea (Xenophon, 6.5.23). Its alliances accordingly stretched from the Ionian to the Aegean sea. The death of Jason of Pherae freed Thebes from an embarrassing ally and a possible future menace. The chance to strike a blow against Sparta naturally appealed to the Thebans, and, although winter was approaching, they dispatched Epaminondas and Pelopidas with a considerable Boeotian and allied force. At Mantinea they were joined by Arcadian, Argive, and Elean contingents so that the total army reached a number of between 50,000 and 70,000 men. Since Spartan troops had already left Arcadia, Epaminondas was persuaded by his Peloponnesian allies and by assurances that many Spartan perioecic communities would revolt to undertake an invasion of Laconia.

The invading army, keeping the Eurotas on its right, and plundering and burning as it advanced, proceeded southward until only the river separated it from Sparta. The Spartans, in recorded history, had never faced such a situation. The women, schooled to bear stoically the loss in battle of husbands and sons, became hysterical at the thought that they now might be cast in the pathetic role of the captured (*Hellenica*, 6.5.28). The panic spread also among some of the men, for Plutarch (*Agesilaus*, 32) speaks of two conspiracies, one involving Spartiates, which Agesilaus and the ephors suppressed by methods of martial law. The enrollment of about 6,000 helots as soldiers, with promise of freedom, also added to the worries and uncertainties. Nevertheless, the depleted Spartan manpower presented so formidable a resistance that Epaminondas decided not to try to force his way across the bridge. He moved his army a few miles south to a point opposite Amyclae, where a ford made it possible to cross the river, swollen by rains. By the time the army was ready for action after the crossing, the Spartans had received reinforcements from various members of the Peloponnesian League. Despite the fact that Sparta was unwalled, Epaminondas decided against the bloodshed which an attempt to seize the city would have caused, for he knew that Agesilaus would never yield. Having had the satisfaction of seeing once imperial Sparta in terror, he continued the raiding expedition to the sea where he attacked, but failed to take, the naval yard of Gytheum. Then he returned to Arcadia with his allies, in particular the Arcadians, Argives, and Eleans, heavy with booty (Xenophon, 6.5.27–32).

From Arcadia Epaminondas led his army southward into Messenia and with the aid of thousands of enthusiastic helots laid out on the slopes of Mt. Ithome the foundations of a new city, Messene. This community, whose fortifications were impressively strong, became the center of a new city-state; for all Messenia, except for the perioecic towns on the coast, shook off its subjection to Sparta. Exiled Messenians were encouraged to return from abroad to lend strength to the growing state. By this act Epaminondas not only righted a wrong over two centuries old, but he also struck a crippling blow at Spartan power by enforcing the principle of autonomy. By the loss of Messenia the Spartans were deprived of a third of their territory and of at least half of their helots, on whom their social and economic system was based. The ensuing chaos was so great that the measure of Epitadeus by which a Spartiate was permitted to alienate his ancestral *kleros* may possibly belong in this period rather than in the early years of the Spartan hegemony. The problem of the discontented "inferiors" had faced Sparta earlier, as the attempted revolt of Cinadon in 398 revealed, but the loss of Messenia and the measure of Epitadeus, whenever dated, significantly accelerated the dual evils of concentration of land in the hands of a few and the increase in the number of the "inferiors." Epaminondas may not have been able to capture Sparta, but he contributed greatly to its decline. Hereafter, in addition to internal difficulties, Sparta was always faced with a hostile state to the west; and to the north the new Arcadian League with its capital, Megalopolis, near the Spartan border, which Epaminondas had made possible by his weakening of Sparta, presented a constant threat. Thebes fully had its revenge, a fact so repugnant to the Spartan-enamored Xenophon that he failed to mention the liberation of Messenia in his history; in fact, he did not even acknowledge the presence of Epaminondas and Pelopidas in the campaign of the winter of 370/69 (Diodorus, 15.66; Pausanias, 4.26–27).

While the Thebans were still in the Peloponnesus, envoys from Sparta and some of its allies appeared in Athens to beg for help. Some months before the Athenians had refused the Arcadian request for assistance against the aggressions of the Spartans, but now worry about the potential danger represented by a victorious and ambitious Thebes drove the Athenians to action in defense of the old balance of power. They dispatched Iphicrates with a considerable force to the Peloponnesus, but either from inefficiency or lack of opportunity he failed to prevent Epaminondas and his army from returning to Boeotia in the spring of 369.[22] At this point Spartan envoys went to Athens to settle the terms of an alliance. The result was the rather surprising agreement that in wartime the chief command should alternate between them every five days. The Spartans and the Athenians, accordingly, tried to prevent Epaminondas from entering the Peloponnesus when he returned in the summer, but without success. Little is known about this campaign, except that it was apparently opposed by political opponents in Thebes who had brought Epaminondas and Pelopidas to trial in the spring of 369 for having remained in the Peloponnesus beyond the terminal date of their command as Boeotarchs. In view of their remarkable achievements, the accused were naturally acquitted. In the second Peloponnesian expedition Epaminondas, although joined by his allies, the Arcadians, the Argives, and the Eleans, accomplished little and, after meeting stiff resistance in the plain of Corinth from Spartan allies and Celtic and Iberian mercenaries dispatched by Dionysius, tyrant of Syracuse, he returned home. Once again he was brought to trial and once again was acquitted, but his enemies were influential enough to prevent his election as Boeotarch for 368 (Xenophon, 6.5.33–52; 7.1.1–22).[23]

The Theban defeat of Sparta at Leuctra and Epaminondas' expeditions into the Peloponnesus in 370 and 369 had created conditions favorable to the formation and development of the Arcadian League. In 368 when the Thebans, because of other activities, were unable to campaign in the south, the Arcadians took the opportunity to free themselves from any Theban supervision. Lycomedes, one of the main founders of the league, attempted successfully to awaken a feeling of patriotic nationalism among the Arcadians. He reminded them that they were the only autochthonous people in the Peloponnesus (they were pre-Dorian), and that they were recognized as the strongest and best soldiers among the Greeks. Since by following the Spartans they had made the Spartans great, they should avoid this mistake in the case of the Thebans. Aroused by such suggestions, the Arcadians became very active; they defeated the Athenians and Corinthians in the Argolid and then, marching into Messenia, overcame the Spartan garrison at the perioecic town of Asine and plundered the suburbs. They outraged their allies, the Eleans, by incorporating into their league the Triphylians whom, now liberated from Sparta, the Eleans claimed. Later in the summer, however, the Spartans, strengthened by a second detachment of troops from Dionysius of Syracuse, penetrated into southern Arcadia and, under their leader Archidamus, annihilated a contingent of Arcadians in a ravine. This victory in which, as reported, no Lacedaemonians were killed came to be known as the "tearless battle." News of the success brought great joy to Sparta, but, according to Xenophon, the Thebans and Eleans, in their annoyance at the "presumption" of the Arcadians, were almost equally pleased (Xenophon, 7.1.23–32). It was this defeat which caused the Arcadians to complete the construction of Megalopolis as a barrier against further Spartan incursions.

Since the first Common Peace of 386 and the various subsequent attempts, always enmeshed in power politics, to revive it, the Greek states had been almost constantly at war. The devasting disasters which Epaminondas had inflicted on Sparta and the increasing fear of Thebes felt by Athens led to further efforts to capitalize on Persian influence as a peacemaking force. One such attempt occurred in 368 when a Persian emissary, Philiscus of Abydos, presumably following suggestions of either Sparta or Athens, or both, came to Greece to negotiate a Common Peace for the Greeks assembled at Delphi. The endeavor collapsed when the Thebans, quite naturally, refused to consider the proposal that Messenia should again be subjected to Sparta. Before returning to Abydos Philiscus employed his abundant funds to hire a mercenary force for the Spartans, thereby revealing where his, and presumably Persia's, sympathies lay at the time (Xenophon, 7.1.27).

Thebes' shattering of the established order in Greece and the worries thus engendered caused Athens in these years to belie its pious declarations about the liberty of the Greeks. Not only, as an ally of the Spartans, did it support their passion to enslave Messenia again, but it also made alliances with figures who ignored the very concept of freedom. Wishing to gain the favor of Dionysius, the tyrant of Syracuse, as the Spartans already had, the Athenians in the summer of 368 voted honors for him and his sons and conferred citizenship upon them (Tod, no. 133). Early in the following year Dionysius won first place in the contest for tragedies at the Lenaea in Athens, a triumph which was shortly followed by the establishment of an alliance between Athens and Dionysius and his sons (Tod, no. 136). The death of the tyrant occurring soon thereafter, however, prevented this agreement from yielding any results. It was in this same period that Athens allied itself with a bitter enemy of Thebes, Alexander, tyrant of Thessalian Pherae.

In the autumn of 367 the Spartans, encouraged by the support they had received from Philiscus, sent envoys to Susa with the hope of obtaining further favors from the Great King. When the other Greek states heard of the Spartan mission, they quickly dispatched their own emissaries. The conferences with Artaxerxes and his advisers mirror luridly the degraded condition of contemporary Greek political life, as envoys from the Spartans, Athenians, Arcadians, Argives, Eleans, Thebans, and probably many others attempted to twist Persian policy to their own advantage. In view of Spartan weakness and the potential threat of the Athenian fleet it was only natural that Pelopidas, because of his personal distinction and because of the current renown of Thebes and its historic pro-Persian record, won the approval of Artaxerxes. In the peace which the King proposed, Theban influence was conspicuous in the clauses that Messenia was to be independent, that the Athenians should dock their ships, and, reflecting the current exasperation of the Thebans with the Arcadians, that Triphylia should be assigned to the Eleans. This new peace proposal revealed that now the Thebans were to be the King's agents, as the Spartans had been after 387/6 and the Athenians had hoped to be since 371. The opposition to these negotiations was so violent in Greece that the Athenians executed one of their envoys, and the story, probably apocryphal, arose that Antalcidas had been one of the Spartan ambassadors and that, fearing to return home, he had committed suicide. Early in 366 the Thebans tried to obtain confirmation of this peace by summoning representatives of the Greek states to Thebes, but this conference and the ensuing dispatch of Theban envoys to the various cities merely emphasized Greek rejection of this King's Peace. The Spartans would not acquiesce in the loss of Messenia, the Athenians had no intention of dismantling their fleet, and the Arcadians were more determined than ever not to yield to Theban dictation (Xenophon, 7.1,-33–40; Plutarch, *Pelopidas,* 30).

The belligerent independence of the Arcadians convinced the Thebans that their influence in the Peloponnesus, necessary to prevent the revival of Sparta, was in jeopardy. Consequently, in the spring of 366 Epaminondas, intending to make the Achaeans his allies and thus provide a check on the Arcadians and a means of entering the Peloponnesus by sea, forced his way, with the help of the Argives, through the Isthmus supposedly blocked by the Spartans and the Athenians. He achieved an alliance with the Achaeans without much difficulty, for he did not attempt to disrupt their traditional aristocratic governments. When he returned home, however, the Achaean democrats and some Arcadians brought charges against him that his arrangements, by strengthening the aristocrats, had actually been a benefit to the Spartans. In response to these complaints his opponents in the Theban government sent *harmosts* and garrisons to the Achaean cities and, driving out the aristocrats, established democracies. These exiles banded together and before long recovered the cities, whose garrisons presumably were small. To protect themselves against further Theban interference, these aristocratically controlled cities now became firm allies of the Spartans (Xenophon, 7.1.41–43).[24]

In the summer of 366 the Athenians lost control of the town of

Oropus, a loss which contributed to significant changes in Athenian domestic and foreign policies. Oropus, geographically a part of Boeotia, lay on the northeastern boundary between Attica and Boeotia. It was apparently in 507 following the reforms of Cleisthenes that the Athenians, when fighting against the Boeotians and the Chalcidians, had taken control of this Boeotian town. Its status under Athens is rather obscure, but it became important as the primary center for receiving supplies from Euboea. In 411 at the time of the Four Hundred the Athenians, to their great distress, lost the town to the Thebans, a loss which, again under obscure circumstances, was redeemed in the early 370s. In 366 Themison, tyrant of Eretria in Euboea, presumably at the suggestion of the Thebans, seized the town, which in the seventh and early sixth century had belonged to Eretria. The Athenians, enraged at the loss, for economically Oropus was important to them, sent a considerable force to recover it. When Themison then yielded Oropus to Thebes, the Athenians found themselves confronted with the danger of a major war. They appealed to their Peloponnesian allies for help, but the only response they received was a recommendation that the problem should be submitted to arbitration.

In view of this increased hostility between Athens and Thebes, Lycomedes persuaded the Arcadian Ten Thousand to let him try to form an alliance with Athens. The Athenians at first hesitated to become allies of enemies of the Spartans, but they ultimately agreed, feeling that this alliance would make the Arcadians less dependent on the Thebans. Interstate relationships among the Greeks now became more involved than ever, for Athens was allied to both the Spartans and Arcadians, who were at war with one another, while the Arcadians were allied to the Thebans and Athenians, who also were at war. On his return from Athens Lycomedes was murdered by some Arcadian exiles. The Arcadians thus lost their most effective leader, the man who had been chiefly responsible for establishing the Arcadian League (Xenophon, 7.4.1–3).[25]

As allies of the Arcadians, the Athenians decided that it was necessary to have unimpeded access into the Peloponnesus. The plan they devised was to seize Corinth, although that meant action against a city which was an ally of their ally Sparta. Since the project was discussed in the assembly, it was not long before it came to the attention of the Corinthians. When the Athenian general Chares with a fleet arrived off Cenchreae, saying that he had come to protect Corinth against possible danger, the Corinthians refused to admit him to the harbor and sent him home along with the various Athenian troops who had been doing guard duty on the Isthmus. This episode convinced the Corinthians of the jeopardy of their situation. With Spartan permission, for Sparta was unable to give them military assistance, they and several other small communities in the neighborhood made peace with Thebes, but they refused to enter into an alliance (Xenophon, 7.4.4–11).

The loss of Oropus and the reluctance of the Peloponnesian allies, from their fear of Thebes, to respond to the Athenian desire to recover it caused the Athenians to become dissatisfied with their foreign policy. The leading statesman since the formation of the Second Athenian League in 378/7 had been the eloquent orator Callistratus, whose policy was based largely on maintaining good relations with Sparta and Persia. Since the Theban victory at Leuctra, however, the league had suffered the defection of Arcarnania and the Euboean and Chalcidic cities. In Athens a preliminary to a change of policy was often the prosecution of former leaders. In conformity with this pattern Callistratus and his close associate, the general Chabrias, were brought to trial in 366 on a charge of treason that their negligence had been responsible for the loss of Oropus. The accusation apparently far exceeded the evidence, and both defendants were acquitted. The trial was a famous one. Plutarch (*Demosthenes*, 5) records that it was when the eighteen-year-old Demosthenes witnessed the eloquent Callistratus at these proceedings that he decided to prepare himself for a career in oratory, and particularly political oratory. Following the trial Callistratus' influence waned, and new policies and methods were exploited. Timotheus, who had played no part in public life since he had been prosecuted by Callistratus and Iphicrates in 373, was elected general for 366/5 and immediately launched a different foreign policy. Athens now became much more aggressive and imperialistic, and the idea gained favor that empire should become a paying proposition, thereby relieving the financial burden on wealthy Athenians.

WHILE ATHENS and the Peloponnesian states were gropingly adjusting themselves to the shattering effects of Leuctra, northern Greece was the scene of much confusion, which foreshadowed the problems soon to arise between Philip II of Macedonia and the Greek states, in particular Thessaly, Thebes, and Athens. Thessaly had acquired considerable unity and power under the leadership of its remarkable *tagos*, Jason of Pherae, but his aspirations for achieving a Thessalian hegemony of the Greek world perished with his assassination in 370. He was succeeded by his two brothers, Polydorus and Polyphron, the first of whom was soon killed by the second, who, in turn, was murdered by Polydorus' son. The new ruler, Alexander of Pherae, who assumed power in the summer of 369, tried by ruthless means to retain the various Thessalian cities within the framework of a united Thessaly (Xenophon,

6.4.33–37). He immediately found himself faced with an invasion of Macedonians who, under their king, Alexander II, had accepted the request of the Aleuadae of Larissa to liberate Thessaly from the domination of Pherae. The Macedonian king, overcoming the resistance from Alexander of Pherae, took control of Larissa and Crannon and then, instead of liberating them, held them by his own garrisons.

The Thessalians, threatened with the prospect of being subject to a second Alexander, appealed to the Thebans for assistance. Thebes, which had already won over Jason's former allies in central Greece, accepted the proposal, for the resources and potentialities of Thessaly were important to it. Pelopidas was dispatched with a limited force, since Epaminondas had already set out on his second expedition to the Peloponnesus. The freeing of the Thessalian cities from the Macedonians was easily accomplished, since Alexander II at the time was occupied with a pretender to his throne. The fighting and negotiations with Alexander of Pherae are not well documented in the sources but clearly were inconclusive. Pelopidas was then called into Macedonia to try to settle the controversy between Alexander II and his rival, Ptolemy of Alorus (a Macedonian community). All that can be said of this mission is that Pelopidas decided in favor of Alexander (Diodorus, 15.67.3–4; Plutarch, *Pelopidas,* 26).[26]

It was apparently during Pelopidas' stay in Thessaly, and under his influence, that the League of the Thessalians was somewhat reorganized. Since the successors of Jason had not been elected to the office of *tagos,* it seems probable that various cities refused to recognize their authority. In an effort to defend themselves against Alexander of Pherae, the Aleuadae of Larissa had even invited the interference of the Macedonians. Such independent and potentially dangerous actions on the part of individual cities Pelopidas tried to prevent by establishing concord among them (Plutarch, *Pelopidas,* 26.3). Since an extant inscription recording an alliance between the *koinon* of the Thessalians and the Athenians (Tod, no. 147; 361/0 B.C.), while Alexander of Pherae was still alive, names as chief Thessalian magistrate the archon Agelaus, probably a Pharsalian, it may be that the chief purpose of the reorganization of the league was to achieve the election of a new *tagos,* now called archon. This long-term or lifelong office was the position which subsequently Philip II and Alexander III of Macedonia held among the Thessalians. As a strong, united Thessaly could have been a threat to the Boeotian League, one wonders why the Boeotians were contributing to that end unless they were thinking primarily of a barrier to Macedonian intrusions. It is possible, of course, that the policy was entirely that of Pelopidas, who envisaged that an alliance between a powerful Boeotia and Thessaly could control a revived Delphic Amphictiony and thereby form a basis, almost Panhellenic, for a hegemony over Greece. In the inscription just mentioned it is interesting to note that among the officials who swore to the alliance with Athens were included the *hieromnemones*, presumably the Thessalian representatives on the Amphictionic Council.

The negotiations which Pelopidas had carried out in 369 in Thessaly and Macedonia had become ineffective by the following year, for Alexander of Pherae was again attacking the Thessalian cities, and Ptolemy the Alorite had murdered Alexander II. When requests for aid came to Thebes both from the Thessalian cities and from the friends of the murdered Macedonian king, the Theban government, seemingly wishing to avoid military involvements, sent out Pelopidas merely as an envoy with instructions to try to settle the pressing problems by diplomacy. In Thessaly Pelopidas learned that Ptolemy, threatened by a new pretender, Pausanias, had requested help from Iphicrates, who, with a small Athenian fleet, was operating around Amphipolis. Iphicrates succeeded in expelling Pausanias and then began to arrange matters in Macedonia in the interests of Athens. Since Athens, now allied with Sparta, was a threat to Thebes, Pelopidas went immediately to Macedonia. The evidence is unsatisfactory, but somehow Pelopidas diverted Ptolemy from the Athenians and made an alliance with him, by which the Macedonian was to be regent for Perdiccas and Philip, the younger brothers of Alexander, the dead king; Philip was surrendered to Thebes as a hostage.[27] Then, returning to Thessaly, Pelopidas tried to continue negotiations with Alexander of Pherae, but his efforts resulted in his imprisonment. The Thebans thereupon dispatched an army to rescue their envoy. Meanwhile, however, Alexander had fashioned an alliance with the Athenians, who, excited by the prospect of causing trouble for Thebes, erected a bronze statue of him and quickly dispatched thirty ships and a thousand soldiers to assist him. The result was that the Theban expedition failed to win the release of Pelopidas, but in the next year, 367, Epaminondas, now Boeotarch again, rescued Pelopidas, although he may have had to make concessions to Alexander since Thebes apparently did not interfere in Thessaly for several years (Plutarch, *Pelopidas*, 27; 24; 31.4).

In the autumn of 367 Pelopidas traveled to Susa where, as discussed above, Artaxerxes proposed to the assembled Greeks a peace which favored the interests of the Thebans. The stipulation that the Athenians were to beach their ships naturally aroused violent indignation in Athens, and the conviction that Persian power was waning strengthened the determination of the Athenians to employ their sea power as they wished. In the following year the Theban seizure of Oropus, the refusal of Athens' Peloponnesian allies to assist in its recovery, the trials of Callistratus and Chabrias, and the return of Timotheus to a prominent position all contributed to the growth of a militant Athenian attitude. The revolt of Ariobarzanes, the satrap of Hellespontine Phrygia, from Artaxerxes in 366 seemed a propitious time for activity. Timotheus was sent to Asia with thirty triremes and 8,000 mercenaries with instructions not to violate the King's Peace. He first sailed to Samos which, in violation of the King's Peace, the Persians were holding with a garrison. After a siege of ten months Timotheus took the island in the summer of 365, and subsequently, after the expulsion of Samian oligarchs, the Athenians dispatched there 2,000 *cleruchs*. Since Samos had not belonged to the Second Athenian League, this action did not violate the *letter* of the clause in the decree of Aristoteles, but the violation of the *spirit* was recognized by all Greeks. Timotheus then sailed to the Hellespont where, in conjunction with Agesilaus, now commanding the satrap's mercenaries, he performed various services for Ariobarzanes, in reward for which the satrap granted him Sestos and Crithote in the Thracian Chersonese. Possession of a foothold on the Chersonese raised pleasant expectations in the Athenians, and in the ensuing years they expended great effort in trying to increase their control. In 364 Timotheus was recalled from the Hellespont and ordered to take over the task of attempting to capture Amphipolis, whose loss in 424 the Athenians had never ceased to regret.[28]

Iphicrates had been patrolling the sea around Amphipolis with an Athenian fleet since 368, but his hopes of gaining possession of the city by force or by persuasion were unsuccessful. In the peace conference at Sparta in 371, if the Attic orators are to be trusted (Demosthenes, 19.253; Aeschines, 2.32), the Athenians had persuaded the assembled Greeks and also apparently representatives of the Great King and of Amyntas, king of the Macedonians, to recognize their claim to Amphipolis. This concession would have been canceled by the peace of 367/6 favoring Thebes, but after Timotheus' capture of Samos in 365, the grant, this time including the Chersonese, was apparently made again by an alarmed Artaxerxes (Demosthenes, 9.16; 19.137). Amphipolis, however, unwilling to be a pawn of the bickering Greek states, was determined to remain independent. Olynthus and the revived Chalcidian League, some members of which, although once belonging to the Second Athenian League, had withdrawn after the battle of Leuctra, were also anxious to prevent Athenian aggression from expanding in Thrace.

When Timotheus arrived in the area in 364 he found the situation somewhat more favorable for Athens than it had been under Iphicrates' command, when the Macedonian regent Ptolemy was allied with Thebes. In 365 Perdiccas had assumed the throne after slaying the regent, and he soon found it useful to cooperate with the Athenians since the death of Pelopidas in 364 presaged an end of Theban interference in Macedonia. Little is known of Timotheus' activity in these years, but he did take Methone and Pydna, Greek cities on the west coast of the Thermaic Gulf which probably had been under Macedonian influence, and forced them to join the Athenian League. In his operations in Chalcidice Timotheus received the active help of Perdiccas who, as son of Amyntas, was well aware of the aggressive policy of Olynthus some twenty years earlier. Attacks against Olynthus were fruitless, but Timotheus did succeed in taking Torone and Potidaea from the Chalcidian League. Soon thereafter Athenian *cleruchs* were sent to Potidaea (Tod, no. 146; 361 B.C.). The revival of Athenian imperialistic spirit as exemplified by Timotheus is illustrated by a later orator (Deinarchus, 1.14), who writes that "he took Samos, Methone, Pydna, Potidaea, and twenty other cities in addition." The attempts of Timotheus and his successors on Amphipolis, however, were no more successful than those of Iphicrates had been, for the city was aided by the Olynthians and ultimately by the Macedonians.

Diodorus (15.78.4–79.1), under the year 364/3, gives the surprising information that Epaminondas convinced the assembly that Thebes should attempt to gain mastery of the sea. Scattered references in other sources suggest that the proposal belonged to the year 365 and the maritime expedition itself to 364. It is likely, then, that Epaminondas was influenced by the aggressive naval policy of Timotheus which had begun in 366. The dispatch of *cleruchs* to Samos in the following year would have convinced many Greeks that Athens was now thinking in terms of its fifth-century imperialism, and Epaminondas may have hoped that Athenian power could be weakened by exploiting the apprehension prevalent among members of the Athenian League. Diodorus says that the assembly voted the construction of 100 triremes, probably at Larymna in Locris on the Euboeic Gulf, which Pausanias (9.23.7), speaking of its fine harbor, says came over to Thebes in the period of its great power. Since a Boeotian inscription from this period honors a Carthaginian,[29] it is often argued that this man from a famed seafaring city was in charge of the shipbuilding.

With whatever ships were available Epaminondas sailed forth in 364. Data concerning this expedition are confused, but, although no battle was fought, it is clear that anti-Athenian feelings were fanned in such important members of the Athenian League as Byzantium, Chios, and Rhodes, and that the little island of Ceos, despite its proximity to

Attica, tried to revolt (Tod, no. 142). This favorable response to the Theban expedition should have warned the Athenians that their new aggressive imperialism was fomenting disillusionment in the league. The Theban naval activity did not persist beyond this one year, because Pelopidas' death in 364 and the increasing confusion in the Peloponnesus, which required Theban attention and resulted in 362 in the death of Epaminondas, prevented its continuation. What long-range plans, if any, Epaminondas had are unknown, for Plutarch's life of him is not extant. Like leaders in Sparta and Athens he presumably wanted his state to achieve hegemony, and that would have required curtailing Athens' maritime empire. The Athenians, at least, thought that he meant to supplant Athens, for some twenty years later Aeschines (2.105) stated, possibly with his own embellishments, that Epaminondas had told the Thebans that "they must remove the Propylaea of the Acropolis of Athens to the entrance of the Cadmea."[30]

Since the release of Pelopidas in the spring of 367 from his captivity in Pherae, the Thebans had seemingly refrained from interfering in Thessaly, a respite which Alexander of Pherae exploited for further aggression against the Thessalian cities. In 364 these cities, probably as members of the *koinon* of the Thessalians, appealed to Thebes for assistance. The Theban authorities voted to dispatch Pelopidas with an army, but before he could depart an eclipse of the sun (13 July 364) gave rise to many superstitious fears. It is possible that the Boeotian officials welcomed the fright produced by the eclipse as an excuse to countermand, or to curtail the size of, the proposed expedition, for they may well have thought that a Thessaly weakened by internal struggles would be a less troublesome neighbor. Plutarch (*Pelopidas*, 31–32) reports that Pelopidas set out with only 300 volunteer horsemen, and that when he arrived at Pharsalus, Thessalian troops joined him. In the hills near Cynoscephalae he met Alexander, and it was only his death in battle that prevented a complete victory. The Theban magistrates, whatever their earlier plans had been, were now compelled to send an army to avenge the death of a national hero. By the beginning of 363 Alexander had to admit defeat, withdraw from all the places he had acquired, remain confined to the territory of Pherae, and agree to serve with the Theban army when needed (Diodorus, 15.80–81; Plutarch, *Pelopidas*, 35.1–2).

In chapters 33 and 34 of his *Life of Pelopidas* Plutarch gives a moving account of the overwhelming grief of the Thessalians at the death of Pelopidas and of the heroic burial which they persuaded the Thebans to allow them to give him. Pelopidas had aided them against the aggressions of Alexander of Pherae and had contributed to the reorganization of the Thessalian League, having in mind probably, among other things, the potentialities of the Delphic Amphictiony in which the Thessalians and their *perioeci*, when all were present, controlled half the votes in the council.

This old Amphictiony based on the archaic structure of tribes became less effective in a world dominated by city-states, with their perpetual ambitions and quarrels. Nevertheless, powerful states, because of the fame of the sanctuary and the oracle, tried to influence the disintegrating Amphictiony for their political purposes. In the year 380, to judge from the Athenian fragmentary copy of an inscription that is extant, an Amphictionic law was passed at Delphi whose aim was to rejuvenate and refashion the Amphictiony and to impel it to carry out its duties concerning the maintenance of the sanctuary, the guarding of the treasure, and the prosecution of states or individuals guilty of impiety against Apollo's holy precinct. Since Thessaly and its *perioeci* were probably not sufficiently influential at this time to reorganize the Amphictiony, it is usually argued that Sparta, actively trying to establish a hegemony of Greece under the cloak of the King's Peace, had encouraged and promoted this law for its own propagandistic purposes.[31] Spartan aims, however, were soon frustrated by the liberation of Thebes in 379 and its subsequent growth in power and by the establishment of the Second Athenian Confederacy.

In 373 the temple of Apollo at Delphi was destroyed by fire, a destruction that may have been part of the disasters caused by an earthquake and tidal wave which obliterated Helice and Bura, Achaean cities on or near the southern coast of the Gulf of Corinth (Diodorus, 15.48–49). As had happened when an earlier temple burned down in 548, contributions from all parts of the Greek world were necessary to finance the rebuilding of the structure. The assembling of these funds at Delphi and the problem of guarding and managing them properly provided an opportunity for various states to try to increase their influence over the Amphictiony. A passage in Xenophon (6.4.2) suggests that the question of contributions to Delphi was part of the agenda of the peace conference held at Sparta in 371 before the battle of Leuctra, but the chief evidence for the problems of financing and reconstructing the temple, with their innumerable ramifications, is to be found in the large number of inscriptions, many of them fragmentary, found at Delphi. From these inscriptions it is clear that an international board of *naopoioi* was established to guard the contributions and to expedite the building process (for example, Tod, No. 140). Although their records for many years are preserved, scholars still dispute whether the board began to function in 371 or not until 366; in the latter case it would be logical to detect the guiding hand of Pelopidas.

In the months following the battle of Leuctra, when the Greek world was adjusting itself to the reduced influence of Sparta, many eyes were turned nervously to the north. In the late 370s Jason had been elected *tagos* of Thessaly, which signified that he had under his control a united Thessaly including the various perioecic tribes. For the Pythian festival at Delphi in 370 he had planned an elaborate sacrifice and an impressive display of his military might. He presumably was thinking of presiding over the Pythian Games and then of exploiting the Amphictiony, the majority of whose votes he could control, as his base for aspiring to a hegemony of Greece, to which Sparta had now lost all claim. His grandiose proposals aroused great concern in some Greek states, and the fact that his assassins in their flight were welcomed by many Greeks suggests that the two states, Sparta and Athens, who had most to lose by diminution of their influence at Delphi, may have been cognizant of the scheme to eliminate Jason. The situation at Delphi, as in all Greece, remained confused, but it seems reasonable to believe that Pelopidas' frequent assistance to the Thessalians and the reorganization of their league had the aim of continuing Jason's work, with the difference that now Thebes, with Thessalian support, would be dominant at Delphi.[32]

The Amphictionic Council and the holy city of Delphi more than ever in these years became the center of frictions and intrigues. This confusing situation was aggravated by the fact that Delphi was a polis, entitled to the autonomy promised by the King's Peace and its subsequent versions, but as the meeting place of the Amphictiony it was also subject to the machinations of the Amphictionic states and of the Greek cities trying to exert pressure or receive privileges in the sacred area. An extant Athenian inscription reveals how bitter the passions could be. It contains a decree, passed in the late summer of 363, in which the Athenians honored and granted privileges to a Delphian, Astykratas, and his associates who had been exiled and deprived of their property by a decree of the Amphictionic Council presided over by a Thessalian. The Athenians claimed that the exile was contrary to the laws of the Amphictions and of the Delphians. In their eyes Astykratas and his companions were Delphic citizens who were favorable to the Phocians, supported by the Athenians and Spartans and hated by the Thessalians, Thebans, and their Delphian partisans. A preserved Delphic inscription records that shortly thereafter the Delphians granted *promanteia* (priority in consulting the oracle) to the Thebans first after the Delphians. The conclusion seems inescapable that the Thebans had contributed to the suppression of *stasis* in the holy city by assisting in the expulsion of the pro-Phocian Delphians.[33]

It was apparently shortly after the death of Pelopidas, when emotions were greatly aroused, that Thebes carried out the type of atrocity so tragically common among the Greeks. The city of Orchomenus, famous as the Minyan center in the Heroic Age, had been forced to join the Boeotian League shortly after Leuctra. Enmity had existed between Orchomenus and Thebes for generations, or rather centuries, and now a suspicion arose that the former city, located near the Phocian border, might revolt or try to overthrow the democracy in Thebes. Three hundred Orchomenian cavalary who were present at Thebes for a military review were seized and condemned to death by the assembly. Then the Thebans marched against Orchomenus, took the city, slew all the adult males, and sold the women and children into slavery (Diodorus, 15.79). The tradition was preserved among the Greeks that Epaminondas, who was absent with the fleet, deplored the action.

Since early 366 Thebes, because of its activities elsewhere, had neglected the Peloponnesus, and the states there had taken advantage of that neglect. The chief trouble broke out in Elis, which after Leuctra had joined Thebes and Arcadia, thus abandoning its position in the Peloponnesian League in anger over the territory which Sparta had detached from it in 401 and 400. The most important part of this territory, the district of Triphylia, the Arcadians appropriated after driving out the Spartans in 368, and they refused to relinquish it even though the peace proposed at Susa in 367 ruled in favor of Elis. By 365 the Eleans, in exasperation, began to take military action, and they renewed their former alliance with Sparta. In the warfare that ensued the Arcadians were victorious, and by 364 they were in control of the sanctuary at Olympia. To humiliate the Eleans they decided that the Olympic festival, which fell due that summer, should be supervised by the neighboring Pisatans, who centuries before had controlled the sanctuary. The games were held on schedule, although the celebration was marred by an unsuccessful attempt of the Eleans to drive out their enemies.

The Arcadians, as masters of Olympia, were in control of the temples, which over a long period of time had been enriched by Greek piety, and they yielded to the temptation to use this wealth to provide long overdue pay to their soldiers. This sacrilege and the impiety associated with disrupting the traditional handling of the Olympic festival brought to a breaking point the dissension which had been growing within the Arcadian League. At a session of the Ten Thousand the Mantineans, against the opposition of the contingents from Tegea and Megalopolis, succeeded in pushing through a resolution forbidding the use of the treasures of Olympia and offering peace to the Eleans. Early in 362 a peace was consummated by which the Arcadians restored to the Eleans all their conquests except Triphylia (Xenophon, 7.4.12–35).

Loss of access to the Olympic treasures presented a serious problem to the Arcadians, for they lacked money to pay their permanent military force (*eparitoi*) of some 5,000 men which, in view of their many enemies, it was necessary to maintain. Some of the wealthier Arcadians offered to serve without pay. When this proposal was reported to Thebes, Epaminondas feared that a wealthy military elite in Arcadia might easily bring about a reconciliation with Sparta. Theban influence in the Peloponnesus, however, was dependent on the continued hostility of Arcadia and Messenia to Sparta. Epaminondas decided, therefore, that his presence in the Peloponnesus was necessary, and in the early summer of 362 he marched southward with his allies from central Greece. After reaching Tegea, he was joined by contingents from Messenia, Argos, and Sicyon. The Arcadian League by this time had split over the question of cooperation with Thebes. Tegea and Megalopolis remained loyal to Epaminondas, but Mantinea, resenting Theban interference, renewed its old alliance with Sparta. Mantinea also made an alliance with Athens, Achaea, Elis, and Phlius (Tod, no. 144; Xenophon, 7.5.4–8).

While at Tegea, Epaminondas learned that Agesilaus had set out for Mantinea with the Spartan army. Thinking that this was a chance to seize an undefended Sparta, he hurriedly marched south. A Cretan runner, however, brought the information to Agesilaus, who immediately returned to the city. Epaminondas, consequently, found Sparta well protected, and rather than risking a bloody battle there he hurried back to Tegea. Suspecting that many of the troops stationed at Mantinea would have left to join in the defense of Sparta, he dispatched his cavalry to try to seize Mantinea, but just as they were approaching the city the Athenian cavalry arrived there. The ensuing battle caused this second attempt at a surprise attack to fail also. In view of these two failures and the difficulties of supplying his troops, Epaminondas realized that to restore Theban influence in the Peloponnesus he must attack the united army of the enemy.

The battle which followed in the plain of Mantinea was not only the largest one that had ever occurrred between Greek forces, but also one in which troops from practically every Greek state participated. On each side there were between 20,000 and 30,000 combatants. In the use of cavalry and in the bruising attack of the Boeotian hoplites led by Epaminondas himself against the strong right wing of the enemy, where the Spartans and Mantineans were posted, the tactics were similar to the ones employed at Leuctra. The Spartans finally yielded and victory seemed assured for Epaminondas, but as he was pursuing the retreating enemy, he was wounded mortally in the breast by a spear. The news of his fall spread rapidly, and there is probably no better proof of the charismatic quality of Epaminondas' leadership than that his victorious troops of many nationalities immediately stopped their pursuit. According to the story, Epaminondas, before he died, advised the Thebans to make peace with the enemy. Peace was made soon after the battle on the basis of the status quo. Since the autonomy of Messenia was recognized, the Spartans alone refused to sign the document (Xenophon, 7.5.9–27; Diodorus, 15.82–89; Plutarch, *Agesilaus,* 34–35).

It is with his account of the battle of Mantinea that Xenophon ends his *Hellenica,* an erratic and very pro-Spartan history of the Greeks since 411. A few lines from his conclusion are worth quoting to illustrate the depression of a contemporary at the sorry state of affairs in the Greek world in 362:

> For since well-nigh all the people of Greece had come together and formed themselves in opposing lines, there was no one who did not suppose that if a battle were fought, those who proved victorious would be the rulers and those who were defeated would be their subjects . . . While each party claimed to be victorious, neither was found to be any better off, as regards either additional territory, or city, or sway, than before the battle took place, but there was even more confusion and disorder in Greece after the battle than before. Thus far be it written by me; the events after these will perhaps be the concern of another.

The death of Epaminondas removed from the stage one of the towering figures of Greek history. It is a great loss to the understanding of the period and of the man that Plutarch's life of him has not survived, for this would surely have contained information of a personal nature and some account of his training under the Pythagorean Lysis, although it is probable that the good Boeotian from Chaeronea would have eulogized Epaminondas as he did his friend and associate, Pelopidas. Cicero's statement (*Tusculans,* 1.2), "princeps meo iudicio Graeciae," may be taken to embody the view of the man held in ancient times.

The career of Epaminondas is a sad chapter in Greek city-state history. He is usually considered to have been a destructive force who, by humiliating Sparta and wrecking the Peloponnesian League, facilitated the enterprises of Philip of Macedonia a generation later. To single him out alone as responsible is to forget that Sparta, Athens, and the city-state system itself bore even greater responsibility. The Greeks, despite their brilliance, never were able to devise a satisfactory and enduring pattern for interstate relations. The Peloponnesian War revealed their failure. Learning nothing from that dismal war, the Spartans, Athenians, and then the Thebans continued their struggles for hegemony and uncertain balances of power, tarnished by dependence on Persian support. Because of their past achievements Sparta and Athens were the leaders, and, despite their fundamental differences and hostility to each other, they became what can be called the "establishment." Isocrates in his *Archidamus,* written in 366, makes this point very clearly when he assigns to that young Spartan prince these words (6.62): "For I know, in the first place, that the Athenians, although they may not hold with us in everything, yet if our existence were at stake would go to any length to save us."

In fighting and humbling aggressive Sparta, which had sought to obliterate Thebes, Epaminondas was following the most human of instincts, but Sparta was part of the "establishment," and when that was endangered Athens and its allies, frightened by the rise of Thebes, went to its support. Mantinea was the indecisive result. It is hardly strange that thereafter various states were inclined to look elsewhere for protection against this overweening and often unprincipled "establishment."

Xenophon's pessimism at the end of the *Hellenica*, although aggravated in his case by his realization of the low estate into which Sparta had fallen, was—or should have been—shared by many Greeks. Mantinea had represented a tremendous, but fruitless, military effort. The chief consequence was the death of Epaminondas, but it may have taken some time for people to realize that the loss of one man was to mark the beginning of the rapid decline of Thebes. The fact that the Greeks—with the exception of the Spartans—almost immediately established a Common Peace suggests that many were thinking of some remedy against the evils represented by the hegemonies of powerful states. It is unfortunate that so little is known about this general peace. The chief information comes from a fragmentary inscription (Tod, no. 145), almost surely to be dated in 362/1, which records the answer of the Greeks to an envoy from the Persian satraps who were seeking Greek help in their revolt from the Persian king. Since the envoy had sought them out and since the Greeks replied as a unit, it seems that some sort of administrative machinery existed for the peace. In their response the Greeks stated that they had joined in a Common Peace and that they wished to remain at peace with the King provided he did not interfere with them. Although officially the Greeks refused to send aid to the satraps, unofficially Charidemus, a mercenary officer from Oreus in Euboea who had served under Timotheus against Amphipolis, went to the Troad, and the Athenians permitted their general Chabrias to seek service in Egypt. Sparta, bitter against Persia because of its support of Thebes and financially desperate, sent Agesilaus with 1,000 men to aid the Egyptian pharaoh, Tachos, in his revolt. Agesilaus switched his loyalty to a pretender named Nectanebo, and after some fighting sailed home well laden with treasure. In Cyrene the 84-year-old king died early in 360 (Demosthenes, 23.154, 171; Diodorus, 15.92–93; Plutarch, *Agesilaus*, 35–40).

IN THE YEARS following Mantinea, with Thebes weakened by the death of Epaminondas and with Sparta in decline, Athens became the leading Greek state. Although the general peace was presumably based on the principle of the autonomy of individual states, Athens' sea power and the existence of its confederation stimulated its old passion, which had never died, for hegemony. The attempt to recover Amphipolis, in which the Athenians had been actively engaged since 368, continued its fruitless course. Perdiccas, feeling more secure in his rule of Macedonia, abandoned his alliance with Athens and in 361 or 360 furnished some troops to aid Amphipolis.[34] Events in the Thracian Chersonese and in the important sea route from the Hellespont to the Bosporus became very complicated. In 362 Byzantium, which had entered into friendly relations with Epaminondas in the course of his naval expedition in 364, joined with Chalcedon and Cyzicus in deflecting Athenian grain ships, sailing from the Black Sea, to their own harbors. An Athenian fleet dispatched to remedy the situation and to protect Proconnesus, an allied island which was threatened by Cyzicus, accomplished little (Demosthenes, 50.4–6).

The Chersonese, where Timotheus had received Sestos and Crithote in 365 as reward for aiding the rebel satrap Ariobarzanes, was under constant attack from the Odrysian Thracian king, Cotys, who considered that region part of his kingdom. For a while Cotys was helped by his son-in-law, the Athenian Iphicrates, who resented having lost his command to Timotheus. In 360 the Athenians lost Sestos by a surprise attack, and a Thracian garrison was established there. In the meantime Iphicrates had returned to Athens, but his post with Cotys was soon filled by Charidemus, who left the Troad to accept service with the Thracian king. In 360 or 359 Cotys was murdered by two Greeks from the city of Ainos, a Greek colony and member of the Athenian League on the southern coast of Thrace, who were subsequently honored by the Athenians (Demosthenes, 23.119). The events of the following years were too involved to be described in any detail here. The Thracian kingdom was divided among three successors, with Cersobleptes, the son of Cotys, receiving the eastern section. Finally in 357, after much fighting and many conferences, Athens reached an agreement with the three Thracian rulers (Demosthenes, 23.170–171; Tod, no. 151). The Chersonese, with the exception of Cardia at its northern extremity, was assigned to Athens. The Thracian kings agreed to help Athens collect the *syntaxeis* from the cities in their realms belonging to the Athenian League, but they also retained the right to collect the ancestral Thracian tribute from those same cities.

While Athens was engaged in actions around Amphipolis and the Hellespont region, it also had troubles in Greece proper and the adjacent islands. Alexander of Pherae, with whom Athens had made an anti-Theban alliance in 368, had subsequently in 363 been forced to become an ally of Thebes. After the death of Epaminondas, Alexander, feeling free from restraint, launched various piratical attacks on the Aegean islands. One raid even succeeded in carrying off some loot from the Piraeus. Athens thereupon made an alliance with the Thessalian League (Tod, no. 147) according to which neither party was to cease war with Alexander without the consent of the other. The trouble with Pherae was ended temporarily in 358 when Alexander was murdered by his wife and her three brothers. In the same year (361/0) in which the Athenians made their alliance with the Thessalians they also sent Chares with a fleet to Corcyra, presumably on the request of the democrats there. Chares handled the situation badly, for, after much bloodshed, the oligarchs took control of the island and promptly severed their connections with the Athenian League. The influence of Athenian democracy in the west never recovered from this failure to defend the democratic cause (Diodorus, 15.95).[35]

Athenian difficulty with the adjacent little island of Ceos deserves fuller treatment, for the troubles which erupted there in the years 364–362 reveal much about conditions in the Athenian League. This small area contained four separate cities which in some matters acted as a group (Ceans) and in others as separate units. In the fifth century it belonged to the Delian League, but after 404 it was controlled by the Spartans. In the 370s the four cities joined the Second Athenian League; they are listed separately in the decree of Aristoteles. Dissatisfaction with the Athenian alliance, however, existed among certain elements of the population, for the appearance of the Theban fleet under Epaminondas in the Aegean caused the island to revolt from Athens in either 364 or 363. The Athenian general Chabrias regained control of the island and restored the exiles, but no sooner had the Athenian fleet left the scene than the party banished by Chabrias returned and drove out its opponents. Subsequently, since Thebes no longer was able to bring naval aid, the Athenians appeared and regulated the affairs of the island. Most of the information about these events is preserved in an inscription (Tod, no. 142) recording the arrangements which Athens in 363/2 made with

Iulis, one of the Cean cities. This valuable document provides a vivid picture of revolts and counterrevolts, executions, exiles, and confiscations of property. It also states that the people of Iulis owe the Athenians three talents (probably their share of the *syntaxeis*), which, if not paid by the specified time, Athenian commissioners aided by the generals of Iulis are to collect in whatever way they determine. The oath taken by all the cities of Ceos is also included, in which the Ceans swear loyalty to the Athenians and their allies and agree that all legal suits involving more than 100 drachmas in which Athenians are concerned shall be tried at Athens.

The disturbances just mentioned, involving the loss of lives, liberty, and property, refer only to Ceos, but there is sufficient evidence in the widely scattered sources, particularly in the Attic Orators, to suggest that discontent with the Second Athenian League was not restricted to just one little Aegean island. That league had been established in 378/7 as a defensive alliance against a threatening Sparta. Leuctra marked the end of Spartan hegemony, and Thebes, Athens' new enemy, faded into comparative insignificance after Mantinea. Even before that battle an aggressiveness, having little to do with defense, was becoming characteristic of Athens. The reaction of its allies to this aggression is usually hard to determine. If a project clearly concerned the allies, their *synedrion* in Athens presumably continued to deliberate and vote on it. There were certainly many matters, however, which were considered purely the business of the Athenian Boulē and assembly, although the consequences of these actions may have directly affected the allies. When Timotheus forced Methone, Pydna, Potidaea, and Torone to join the Athenian League in the 360s, the obligations to these new members became a responsibility of all the allies. Athenian activity in Chalcidice and around Amphipolis, and in the Chersonese, may not have required the allies to furnish ships or troops, but their financial contributions (*syntaxeis*) helped defray the military costs. This constant aggression of Athens, its temporary alliance with Perdiccas of Macedonia against the Chalcidian League and Amphipolis, and its alliance with the kings of Thrace made it obvious to everyone that Athens had become imperialistic again. Its reintroduction of the *cleruchy* system increased that conviction. In 365 Athens sent 2,000 *cleruchs* to Samos and additional ones in 361/0 and 352/1. *Cleruchs* were dispatched to Sestos in 364 and to Potidaea in 361. Since before their conquest these places had not been members of the Athenian League, Athens was theoretically not guilty of violating its promise in the decree of Aristoteles to refrain from sending *cleruchs* to its allies, but the actions provided an unhappy memory of the evils of Athenian fifth-century policy.

The rapid growth in the size of the Athenian navy also was a source of worry to many. In the 350s the fleet grew to about 350 triremes, an armament which was difficult to finance.[36] There is adequate evidence that frequently the generals did not have sufficient funds to carry out their campaigns and that impossible burdens were placed on the trierarchs. Contributions from the allies, accordingly, were very important, but since the collection of the *syntaxeis* often fell on the Athenian generals, it is hardly strange that high-handed methods and corruption became common. In many cases the allies must have considered these extortions of funds as sheer piracy and a violation of their autonomy. Further infringement of local autonomy also lay in the requirement to transfer certain legal cases to Athens. Discontent arising from such abuses of power by Athens caused some states to break away from the league and in 357 led to a serious revolt of some key allies. Before Athens became involved in this "War of the Allies," however, it achieved an important success in Euboea. The various cities of this strategically located island had joined the Athenian League in the 370s, but after Leuctra they had abandoned Athens to throw in their lot with Thebes. In the year 357 anti-Theban feeling was increasing in many of the Euboean cities. The Thebans sent over a force to try to settle the situation, but it was too weak to oppose an Athenian contingent which rapidly appeared on the scene. In a campaign which reportedly was completed in a month the Athenians were victorious, and all the Euboean cities were once again enrolled in the Athenian alliance (Diodorus, 16.7.2; Aeschines, 3.85; Tod, nos. 153, 154).

The War of the Allies, frequently called the Social War from the Latin word for ally, broke out in the autumn of 357. Growing dissatisfaction with the Athenian League in the 360s and the appearence of a Theban fleet in 364 had fostered the spirit of revolt. The decline of Theban activity after Mantinea removed an obvious support for the restlessness of the Athenian allies, but the necessary encouragement was soon provided by Mausolus, the satrap of Caria. This region, peopled by the native Carians and numerous Greeks, had obtained the status of a separate satrapy through the skillful diplomacy of Hecatomnos, a noble living in the inland city of Mylasa. His son, Mausolus, really ruled as an independent dynast, but he acknowledged the superiority of the King of Persia by paying tribute regularly. He was involved for a while in the Great Satraps' Revolt (362–361) but quickly resumed his loyalty when it seemed expedient. Either he or his father moved to Halicarnassus and made it the center of their government, but it was Mausolus who enlarged the city by joining six native communities to it and by extensive building activity, including his tomb, the famous Mausoleum, completed by his sister wife, Artemisia. Mausolus extended his power or influence to Miletus to the north and in the south to parts of Lycia. He was anxious to develop the maritime energies of the Carians, for which in past centuries they had been noted, but found opportunities blocked by the Athenian League. Cos, an ally of the Athenians, formed a barrier to the harbor of Halicarnassus, and an Athenian *cleruchy* was located at neighboring Samos. Mausolus was aware, however, that opposition was rising against Athenian leadership, particularly among oligarchic groups who were being oppressed by democratic regimes. By diplomatic means he fanned this opposition, with promises of assistance, and in the autumn of 357 saw his policy bear fruit when Rhodes, Cos, Chios, and Byzantium, soon to be followed by other states, severed their connection with the Second Athenian League.[37]

Although Athens had had sufficient warning about the discontent of the allies, the revolt was a serious blow, for it was still worried about the security of Euboea, and Philip of Macedonia was undermining its interests in the areas of Chalcidice and Amphipolis. Nevertheless, Athens dispatched a fleet under Chares and Chabrias to Chios, but in attempting to force his way into the harbor, Chabrias was killed (Diodorus, 16.7.3–4). Chares then had to retire to the Hellespont, while the rebel ships began to ravage Athenian holdings in Lemnos and Imbros and to besiege Samos. The Athenians felt it necessary to establish garrisons on the islands of Andros and Amorgos. In the following year they managed to send out more ships under Iphicrates and Timotheus. After various manoeuvres they joined with Chares and prepared to meet the hostile fleet off Embata, a little island between Chios and the Asiatic mainland. On the day planned for the battle Timotheus and Iphicrates felt that the weather was too stormy for safe action, but Chares entered battle by himself and suffered a considerable loss. He subsequently claimed that he had been betrayed, and his friends brought his fellow generals to trial for cowardice and treachery. Iphicrates and Timotheus may well have been correct in refusing battle under the existing conditions, but the Athenian people were frustrated by another military failure. In the years since Mantinea Athenian forces had suffered defeats around Amphipolis, in the Hellespont, at Corcyra, and against Alexander of Pherae. In this period general after general had been called to account, and many had been executed or fined heavily if they had not escaped to exile abroad. In this particular trial Iphicrates was acquitted, but Timotheus, who had many enemies, was fined the huge sum of 100 talents. Unable to pay it, he went into exile where soon afterwards he died (Diodorus, 16.21).

Chares now was left in charge of the war, but he had no money with which to pay his troops. Consequently late in 356 he went to Asia Minor, where he helped Artabazus, the revolting satrap of Hellespontine Phrygia, to win a decisive victory over the forces arrayed against him. In gratitude Artabazus supplied him with money to maintain his army. The new Persian king, Artaxerxes III (Ochus), who had succeeded Artaxerxes II in 358, was outraged by these activities in Asia Minor and sent an ultimatum to Athens to recall Chares or to expect war (Diodorus, 16.22). At the same time rumors spread that the Persians were organizing great fleets in Phoenicia and Cilicia. Some chauvinistic Athenians argued that this was the time to conduct a crusade against Persia, but soberer men, including the young Demosthenes (*Oration,* 14), carried the day against this emotional reaction. Athens was in no position, politically, militarily, or financially, to undertake a campaign against Persia, particularly when the empire was now led by a much more aggressive king. Talks about peace began to be held.

It was at this time that Isocrates wrote his remarkable political pamphlet *On the Peace* (355?). In 380 when he wrote the *Panegyricus* he had been indignant at the King's Peace and enthusiastic about a crusade of a united Greece against the ancestral enemy. Now, twenty-five years later, he was disillusioned about Athens and the folly of its aggressive policy. His oration is a magnificent denunciation of the evils of imperialism. He emphasizes the sinister effects that imperialism had had on Athenian character and reputation when the Delian League was changed into a domineering empire and the ruin that it had brought subsequently on Sparta. The present is not the time for such ventures, but a time when Athens should try for peace with everyone—a general peace such as the King's Peace should have been.

Late in 355 or early in 354 Athens agreed to peace. Chares was recalled from Asia Minor, and the independence of the revolting states, Byzantium, Chios, Cos, and Rhodes, was recognized. Before long Lesbos and other states broke away from Athens. The Athenian League continued to exist, but it now lacked its most important eastern members. The war had turned out as Mausolus hoped, and he helped establish oligarchies, backed by Carian garrisons, on the islands he had encouraged to revolt. He died soon afterwards—in 353—but his wife and successor, Artemisia, saw to it that the Mausoleum, on which the most famous Greek sculptors of the time, including Scopas, worked, was completed. The great statue of Mausolus, the hellenized Carian, that was in the tomb is now in the British Museum.

13
Macedonia and Greece

WHILE THE GREEKS in general were trying to adjust themselves to the increasingly confused situation brought about by the indecisive battle of Mantinea, and Athens in particular was drifting into the Social War, the new ruler of Macedonia was restoring his disorganized kingdom and strengthening it to resist the century-old passion of the Athenians to exert influence in the "Thraceward region." Since the achievements of Philip II ultimately marked a basic turning point in the course of Greek history, some background information is appropriate here on the Macedonians, the emergence of their kingdom, and the policies of their earlier kings, especially in their relations with the Greeks.

The origins of the Macedonians, as is the way of origins, are largely shrouded in darkness. In the centuries following the breakdown of Mycenaean civilization, tribes which Greeks later identified as primarily Dorian were living on both sides of the northern extension of the Pindus range. In the course of time those on the western slope migrated into Epirus, while some of those on the eastern side, designated as "Makednon" people (*ethnos*) by Herodotus (1.56; 8.43), began, probably early in the seventh century, to move eastward under the Argead clan in search of land. No record of the wanderings of these "Macedonians" is preserved, but Justin (7.1) states that they took possession of the Thracian stronghold, Edessa, located on what subsequently became the famous Egnatian Way of the Romans. Since Justin says they named the captured fortress Aegae, it was long thought that this was the early Macedonian capital. The remarkable archaeological discoveries at Vergina since 1976, however, where among many earlier and later remains the tomb of Philip II seems to have been found, suggests that the Macedonians first came into northern Pieria. Most scholars now believe that, after expelling the Illyrians, the Macedonians established a settlement called Aegae just east of the Haliacmon River and some fifteen miles west of the future Methone on the Thermaic Gulf, a location which appears to accord well with later literary evidence.[1]

From Aegae, which became the Macedonian capital and the burial place of the Argead kings, the Macedonians, overpowering or expelling Thracians, Illyrians, Paeonians, and other peoples, occupied the western and northern shores of the Thermaic Gulf, pushing inland as far as the Edessa mentioned by Justin, an area subsequently called Lower Macedonia. Thucydides (2.99), writing on the early years of the Peloponnesian War, speaks of the Macedonian kingdom which had been created by Alexander I and his ancestors and includes in it the Pierian plain west of the Thermaic Gulf, and the land north of the gulf extending eastward as far as the Strymon River. In the same passage Thucydides, referring to districts in Upper Macedonia such as Elimaea and Lyncestis, says that the tribes resident there, "though Macedonians by blood and allies and dependents of their kindred, still have their own separate governments." When these tribes became associated with the Argead Macedonians is not clear. There may have been some dependence when the Argeads began to migrate eastward in the seventh century, but this relationship could have lapsed in the ensuing generations. The Argead king Alexander I, when freed from the Persian burden in 479, devoted much time and energy to strengthening his kindgom in Lower Macedonia. In these years he may have marched west from Aegae against the Macedonian tribes dwelling on the eastern slopes of the Pindus range and forced them to acknowledge dependence, or to renew their dependence, on the Argead kingdom of Lower Macedonia.

This kingdom of Lower and Upper Macedonia had come into existence after many generations of migrations and conquests. Its position as a strong state with distinct boundaries was not achieved until the rule of Philip II. Prior to that time it had constantly faced the threat of disintegration from the ambitions of the princes of the districts in Upper Macedonia, from the marauding instincts of the barbarian Illyrians, Paeonians, and Thracians on their western, northern, and eastern boundaries, from Persian dreams of conquest, and from the steady encroachments of Greek states like Athens. The growth and survival of the state were largely the accomplishment of the royal family of the Argeads, of whom, according to Herodotus (8.139), Perdiccas was the progenitor. Since both Herodotus and Thucydides (2.100) seem to place the emergence of the Argeads in the seventh century, Perdiccas may well have been the king who first led some of the Makednian tribes in their migration eastward, which ended several generations later in their reaching the Thermaic Gulf.

Because of lack of evidence for the social and political customs and institutions of the Macedonians in these early years, one has to make use of the more abundant material of the fifth and particularly of the fourth century in any effort to visualize earlier Macedonian organization. The land conquered by the migrating Macedonians from Thracians, Illyrians, and possibly some unknown Greek tribes became the spear-won property of the kings. All Macedonian land seemingly belonged to the king, some of which was retained as royal domains, but much of which was granted to his loyal supporters as fiefs. These fief holders were the *hetairoi,* the companions, of the king. It is interesting to recall that Homer called the Myrmidons, the followers of Achilles, his *hetairoi.* The Macedonian *hetairoi,* in return for the grants of land, owed the king military service as horsemen. It is probable that holders of large fiefs were responsible for providing other horsemen in addition to themselves and their kinsmen. These horsemen, selected from those living on the fiefs, thus became part of the *hetairoi* cavalry, but presumably of a lower status than the families of the fief holders. As companions of the king, the *hetairoi* had free access to him at any time. Many served as his advisers and officials, a topic which will be discussed in the account of Philip's court.

Since the conquests of the migrating Macedonians paved the way for the formation of the kingdom, it is not surprising that the little extant information about the early state is exclusively concerned with wars in which the *hetairoi* cavalry demonstrated its military efficiency. A substantial part of the population, however, consisted of the commoners—the farmers, shepherds, and artisans. These people seemingly were free workers living on the royal domains and on the fiefs of the *hetairoi,* presumably paying some sort of tax to their landlords. Since the advancing Macedonians won their land by overpowering the natives, the question naturally arises about the fate of the earlier inhabitants. Certainly many were slain and many were driven into other areas, but some must have been absorbed. In view of the lack of evidence one can only hazard the guess that some blended with their conquerers while others, as captives, were employed in some type of bondage as workers in activities such as mining and road building, and possibly as "serfs" on the royal domains and the fiefs.

Since so little is known about the early Macedonians, it is hardly strange that in both ancient and modern times there has been much disagreement on their ethnic identity. The Greeks in general and Demosthenes in particular looked upon them as barbarians, that is, not Greek. Modern scholarship, after many generations of argument, now almost unanimously recognizes them as Greeks, a branch of the Dorians and "Northwest Greeks" who, after long residence in the north Pindus region, migrated eastward. The Macedonian language has not survived in any written text, but the names of individuals, places, gods, months, and the like suggest strongly that the language was a Greek dialect. Macedonian institutions, both secular and religious, had marked Hellenic characteristics, and legends identify or link the people with the Dorians. During their sojourn in the Pindus complex and the long struggle to found a kingdom, however, the Macedonians fought and mingled constantly with Illyrians, Thracians, Paeonians, and probably various Greek tribes. Their language naturally acquired many Illyrian and Thracian loanwords, and some of their customs were surely influenced by their neighbors.

To the civilized Greek of the fifth and fourth centuries, the Macedonian way of life must have seemed crude and primitive. This backwardness in culture was mainly the result of geographical factors. The Greeks, who had proceeded further south in the second millennium, were affected by the many civilizing influences of the Mediterranean world, and ultimately they developed that very civilizing institution, the polis. The Macedonians, on the other hand, remaining in the north and living for centuries in mountainous areas, fighting with Illyrians, Thracians, and among themselves as tribe fought tribe, developed a society that may be termed Homeric. The amenities of city-state life were unknown until they began to take root in Lower Macedonia from the end of the fifth century onward.

Greek colonization in the seventh century in Chalcidice and at Methone and Pydna on the west coast of the Thermaic Gulf naturally made the Greeks aware of the Macedonians, but there is no available evidence on the relations between the two peoples until the latter half of the sixth century. At that time Pisistratus, in his second exile, was active in the area of the Thermaic Gulf and of Mt. Pangaeus to the east. It is probable that he had some sort of negotiations with the Macedonians, a suggestion which is confirmed by the fact that the king of the Macedonians, Amyntas, offered the district of Anthemus to Hippias when he was expelled from Athens in 510 (Herodotus, 5.94). Since Anthemus lies to the north of Chalcidice, this episode proves that at that date the Macedonians already had moved eastward from the Axius River. Amyntas is the first Macedonian king about whom some historical statements can be safely made. The earlier kings, listed by Herodotus (8.139), are largely legendary figures, although there seems to be no serious reason to doubt that an early conqueror, Perdiccas, was the first of the Argead kings. Amyntas had to become a vassal of Darius the Great on the occasion of the first Persian expedition into Europe about 514. He was succeeded by his son Alexander I, and from his reign the Greeks became increasingly aware of the kingdom lying on their northern border.

As a Persian vassal Alexander had to cooperate with Xerxes in his invasion of Greece. According to Herodotus (8.136), however, he was a "*proxenos* and benefactor" of the Athenians; if Alexander did supply timber for Themistocles' fleet, the Athenians may have honored him in gratitude. In the war he secretly furnished advice to the Greeks when they had taken a position at Tempe and later before the battle of Plataea. When the Persians were retreating after their defeat at Plataea, Alexander attacked them as they were crossing the Strymon River, and from the spoils gained there he dedicated a golden statue to Apollo at Delphi. He then consolidated his kingdom in Lower Macedonia, which had been disrupted by the Persian presence. In this same period he apparently marched westward and forced the Makednian tribes on the eastern side of the northern range of the Pindus to become vassals, or to renew their status as vassals, to the Argead kings. The success of his reorganization of the kingdom is emphasized by the fact that he was the first Macedonian king to issue coins in his own name.[2]

This enterprising ruler was anxious to be recognized as a Greek, and on one occasion he appeared at the Olympic Games with the intention of competing. The other competitors tried to exclude him on the grounds that barbarians were debarred from entering the contests. Alexander, however, won the right to compete by convincing the managers of the festival that his family, the Argeads, were descended from the Temenids of Argos (Herodotus, 5.22; Thucydides, 2.99). The connection with the Argives is almost certainly a myth, but the decision made at Olympia was important, for from that time the Macedonian royal family—not the Macedonians as a whole—was recognized as Hellenic, although, of course, many opponents of Macedonia refused to accept the judgment.

One measure which probably should be ascribed to Alexander proved to be very significant in strengthening the army and assuring the loyalty of the Macedonians to the Argead kingship. A fragment from a fourth-century historian, Anaximenes of Lampsacus, is the key passage on this subject. Anaximenes (Jacoby, 72, fragment 4) states that Alexander "accustoming the most distinguished men to serve in the cavalry called them *hetairoi* [companions], and dividing the masses and infantry into companies ... called them *pezetairoi* [foot-companions] in order that each group by sharing in the royal *hetairia* [companionship] should continue to be most zealous." The available evidence reveals that the Macedonian army from the seventh century had consisted chiefly of cavalry furnished by the *hetairoi*, the members of the great families and clans. In relation to these *hetairoi*, Alexander's intention must have been to organize them more effectively. The mention of the *pezetairoi*, however, raises a problem. Thucydides' account (4.124–128) of the military operations of Perdiccas (the successor of Alexander) suggests little infantry action. Consequently many scholars, citing Thucydides' statement (2.100) that Archelaus (the successor of Perdiccas) was responsible for more military improvement than all the preceding eight kings, argue that in the Anaximenes fragment the name Archelaus should be substituted for that of Alexander. Needless to say, it is a hazardous procedure to rewrite an ancient source. Since Alexander II ruled too briefly (370–368) to merit serious consideration here and since the quoted passage appeared in the first book of the *Philippica,* in which Anaximenes was presumably discussing early Macedonian history, it seems logical to understand the Alexander as Alexander I.

The early implementation of this measure is unknown. Formerly the infantry seems to have been little more than an ill-armed crowd, the peasants and shepherds from the lands of the king and the nobles—a picture which is reminiscent of the Achaean army in Homer's *Iliad.* Alexander presumably found a way to organize these workers in military fashion, but from lack of funds the project could have been carried out only on a small scale. It was not until the time of Philip II that sufficient wealth was available to develop the peasants and shepherds into an effective infantry. The adoption of the term *pezetairoi* was clearly a stroke of genius, with political as well as military implications. As foot-companions of the king the infantry, however limited in numbers, became a national force rather than merely provincial dependents of great nobles. The title must have increased their morale and status, and as companions of the king and regular members of the army assembly, the infantry must have strengthened the kings in their frequent troubles with insubordinate nobles.[3]

Alexander was succeeded about 450 by his son, Perdiccas II. The expansion of the Athenian empire, which undoubtedly had worried Alexander, became a serious problem to his son, for Athens, through its allies and fleet, gained control of the Thermaic Gulf and the Chalcidic peninsula, and in 437 established the important colony Amphipolis near the mouth of the Strymon. Macedonia, which needed a seacoast if it was to play a role in the Greek world, must have found that the export of its chief products, timber and pitch, was largely dependent on whatever terms Athens felt like establishing. General statements about the relations between the Athenians and Perdiccas are very difficult to make. The Athenians looked upon him as faithless and unscrupulous; a fragment of a comic poet (Hermippus) listing Athenian imports adds the item "and lies by the ship-load from Perdiccas." If one regards the situation from Perdiccas' point of view, one will admit that he was shifty and an opportunist, but will also acknowledge that he maintained the independence of Macedonia against the greed and ruthlessness of others—particularly of Athens.

Perdiccas was succeeded in 413 by Archelaus, who ruled until 399, his death thus falling in the same year as the execution of Socrates. Plato in the *Gorgias* depicts Archelaus as the son of a slave woman who murdered his way to the throne, but this discussion of whether power can make a wicked man happy seems to have added lurid details to the story. Archelaus, apparently a bastard son of Perdiccas, was sufficiently influential to have been one of the signers of the alliance between Perdiccas and Athens in 422 (Bengston, no. 186). Later, appointed as guardian to Perdiccas' legitimate minor son, he seized the throne by the all too common method of eliminating a rival. However bloody his accession to power may have been, Archelaus proved himself to be an able and enlightened ruler. Since Athens had been weakened by the disaster in Sicily, Archelaus did not have the trouble with that imperial city which his predecessor had had. In 410 when Pydna had revolted from his control, possibly because he had taken away its right of coinage, the Athenian fleet gave Archelaus temporary help in besieging that city. A fragmentary inscription from the year 407/6 (*M&L*, no. 91) reveals that the Athenians honored him for his services and particularly for his granting of timber. Since the loss of Amphipolis in 424, the acquisition of timber for the fleet had been an urgent problem for Athens. In 400/399 Archelaus, in responses to an appeal from the oligarchs in Larissa, took possession of that Thessalian city. This interference of an outsider in Greek affairs seemed a threat to the Spartan desire to establish a hegemony throughout Greece. A possible struggle between Archelaus and the Spartans was prevented by the former's death and the ensuing confusion among the Macedonians, which led to their withdrawal from Larissa.[4]

The Macedonian kings were great admirers of Greek civilization and encouraged the hellenization of their kingdom. Alexander I, as mentioned above, had gained the privilege for the Argeads to compete in the Olympic Games. When the Argives destroyed ancient Mycenae about 470 he received half of the displaced population in his realm, and some years later, in 446, Perdiccas welcomed the refugees from Hestiaea in Euboea after the Athenians under Pericles had captured the city. Archelaus was particularly active in opening Macedonia to Hellenic influences. He moved the capital from Aegae, which continued to remain a holy city and the burial place of the royal family, to the more central Pella, which had access to the sea through the Loudias River, an act that foreshadowed the ever-increasing role that Macedonia was to play in the Aegean world. The famous painter Zeuxis was brought to Pella to paint the frescoes in the new palace. An effort to convince the Greeks of the hellenization of Macedonia was Archelaus' establishment of games, athletic, musical, and dramatic, at Dium at the foot of Mt. Olympus, in the region of Pieria sacred to the Muses. Among notable Greek artists whom he invited to his court were Timotheus, the dithyrambic poet from Miletus, and Agathon, the Athenian tragic poet. The most famous visitor, however, was Euripides, who, probably disillusioned with conditions at Athens, spent the last year or two of his life (408–406?) in Macedonia. Pella must have been much more than a barbarian city to attract the elderly poet. While in Macedonia, where he was honored as a *hetairos* of the king, he produced one of his greatest—some would say *the* greatest—tragedies, the *Bacchae.* The less sophisticated Macedonian life and Thracian influences may have given him a deeper insight into the nature of Dionysiac religion. Euripides also composed a drama in honor of his patron. The *Archelaus* is not extant, but it is known to have dealt with the establishment of the Macedonian kingdom. Archelaus, the son of Temenus and the grandson of Heracles, was depicted as the founder rather than the usually accepted Perdiccas. This fiction obviously strengthened the claim of the Argeads to be Hellenes, and in writing the play Euripides surely found the opportunity to allude to matters which concerned the living Archelaus.[5]

The period between the death of Archelaus in 400/399 and the accession of Amyntas III in 393/2 was a confused and bloody one in Macedonian history, marked by violent dynastic struggles, barbarian invasions over the frontiers, and the aggressive growth of the Chalcidian League to the east. Shortly after his accession, Amyntas, wishing to ensure peace on his eastern border while he concentrated his energies against the Illyrians to the west, made a defensive alliance with the Chalcidians (Tod, no. 111). When an Illyrian invasion forced him to evacuate Macedonia, he gave some of his eastern territory, presumably with the aim of protecting its inhabitants from the Illyrians, to the Chalcidians. He quickly regained control of his kingdom with Thessalian help, although he had to agree to pay tribute to the Illyrians, and then proceeded to organize and pacify the western Macedonian princedoms, always exposed to Illyrian interference. Around 385 he requested the Chalcidians to return the territory he had ceded to them, but the ambitious Olynthians refused and proceeded to overrun Macedonian land—apparently as far as Pella—and to support the claims of a pretender to the throne, Argaeus. The situation became so dangerous for Amyntas that he had to flee from his kingdom again, and from 384 to 382 Argaeus ruled as king. It was then that Amyntas appealed to Sparta for help, and the Spartans, unwilling to let the Chalcidians in the north become too powerful, began their campaign which in the years 382–379 broke up the Chalcidian League and forced its members to become their military allies. Amyntas regained his throne in 382 and for the duration of the war fought with the Spartans against the Chalcidians.

Through the Spartans Amyntas had recovered his kingdom and been freed from the menace of the Chalcidian League, but the increase of Spartan power soon confronted him with the same problem that Athenian ambitions had presented to the fifth-century Perdiccas. To protect Macedonia against possible Spartan aggressions and against dangers from a reviving Olynthus, he made an alliance with the Athenians, probably in the year 374/3 (Tod. no. 129). Athens had started the establishment of its second league in 378/7 and had proved its naval power in the defeat of the Spartan fleet off Naxos in 376. It may have seemed wise to join with an Athens that was emphasizing its nonimperialistic intentions. From the point of view of Athens, the alliance meant easier access to the valuable Macedonian timber. A year or so later Amyntas made an alliance with the ambitious Jason of Pherae (Diodorus, 15.60.2). With the recognition of these two rising powers, Macedonian prestige rose in the Greek world. At the important peace congress at Sparta in 371, a representative of Amyntas may have been present, and, if Aeschines' remarks (2.32) can be trusted, he supported the Athenian claim to Amphipolis. At the time Athenian control of Amphipolis may have seemed to be in the interests of Macedonia, but in ensuing years the problem would be viewed in a very different light.

Amyntas was succeeded in 370 by his eldest son, Alexander II, who in the following year tried to extend Macedonian influence in Thessaly. The death of Jason in 370 had been followed by a vicious struggle for the succession, in which Alexander of Pherae emerged victorious. His efforts to enforce his authority throughout Thessaly caused the Aleuadae of Larissa to appeal to Alexander of Macedonia for help. The young Macedonian king answered the appeal, but instead of restoring Larissa and Crannon to the Thessalian nobles he placed his own garrisons in these cities. When a revolt against his kingship necessitated his return to Macedonia, the Thessalians appealed to Thebes for assistance. Pelopidas answered the appeal in 369 and freed Larissa and Crannon from the Macedonian garrisons, although he failed then to come to an agreement with Alexander of Pherae. Then Pelopidas was called to Macedonia to try to arbitrate the dispute between Alexander and his brother-in-law, Ptolemaios, who was claiming the throne. Some sort of arrangement was made in favor of Alexander, but shortly after Pelopidas' departure Alexander was murdered by Ptolemaios. The person responsible for this crime apparently was Alexander's mother, Eurydice, who, through her lover Ptolemaios, saw the opportunity to rule as queen once again.

At the end of 369 or early in 368 Eurydice set her approval upon the cruel deed by marrying Ptolemaios. One wonders what happened to his former wife, the daughter (or possibly stepdaughter?) of Eurydice. The general horror of the situation at court caused a kinsman of the royal family, Pausanias, to attempt to seize the throne. Since he entered Macedonia from Chalcidice with a Greek force, it is probable that he received support from Olynthus, always anxious to profit from the difficulties of Macedonia. As more and more followers flocked to Pausanias, Eurydice, to save her position, appealed to Iphicrates, who was cruising around Amphipolis with an Athenian fleet. Aeschines (2.27-29) describes the scene in pathetic terms—the sorrowing mother placing her two little sons, Perdiccas and Philip, on Iphicrates' knees and begging him to preserve the dynasty. When one remembers that the younger son, Philip, was fourteen at the time, the pathos of the scene seems somewhat fraudulent. Iphicrates, seeing a chance to strengthen Athenian influence in Macedonia, responded to the mother's tears and drove Pausanias out of Macedonia, thus supporting the rule of Eurydice and Ptolemaios. Athenian plans, however, were thwarted by the Theban Pelopidas, who, in response to a call from the friends of the dead Alexander, arrived on the scene. The evidence is unsatisfactory, but Pelopidas somehow achieved an alliance between Ptolemaios and Thebes, and an arrangement that Ptolemaios' kingship should last only until the young Perdiccas should come of age. It was at this time that Perdiccas' younger brother, the future Philip II, was taken to Thebes as a hostage.

In 365 Perdiccas killed Ptolemaios and established himself as king. In the first year of his reign the Athenians sent Timotheus to replace Iphicrates in command of the "Thracian" area. Timotheus succeeded in capturing Methone and Pydna on the west coast of the Thermaic Gulf and adding them to the Athenian League. Since both these cities had apparently been under Macedonian control, this action of the Athenians was really an act of war against the Macedonians. Nevertheless a year or two later, after the death of Pelopidas in 364 had reduced Theban influence in the north, Perdiccas joined the Athenians in their attacks on the Chalcidian League and Amphipolis. It was then that Timotheus took possession of Potidaea and Torone. In 361, at the request of the pro-Athenian element, the Athenians sent a *cleruchy* to Potidaea. About this time Perdiccas withdrew his support from Athens. Feeling that he was safe in the east because of the mutual hostility between Athens, the Chalcidian League, and Amphipolis, he left troops to aid in the defense of the latter city and thereafter devoted himself to problems in the west. As mentioned earlier, the Illyrians had driven his father, Amyntas III, from Macedonia. Even after the recovery of his kingdom Amyntas had been obliged to pay tribute to the Illyrians, an obligation which fell also upon his son, Alexander. The evidence is confused, but it is probable that the Illyrians continued to exert some influence in the western princedoms or provinces of the Macedonian kingdom. In 359 Perdiccas decided that he was strong enough to free Macedonia from the dangers and threats represented by the Illyrians, and advanced with a large army against them. The circumstances of the battle are unknown, but the result was a great victory for the Illyrians in which Perdiccas and 4,000 Macedonians were slain (Diodorus, 16.2.4–5).[6]

The death of a Macedonian king was often followed by incursions from Illyrians, Paeonians, and Thracians eager to take advantage of the confusion sometimes attendant on the selection of the new king. On this occasion the confusion was aggravated by the fact that Perdiccas' son, the natural heir, was only a child. Consequently claimants to the throne arose, including Pausanias, the former opponent of the regent Ptolemaios, and Argaeus, who had ruled briefly (384–382) when the Chalcidians had forced Amyntas to flee from his kingdom. Acclamation of a new king or of a regent was the responsibility of the Macedonian army assembly. On this critical occasion Perdiccas' younger brother, Philip, was acclaimed, but whether as regent, as Justin (7.5.9–10) alone asserts, or as king is an open question. Whatever the proper answer is, soon he was ruling as king. Philip at this time was a young man of twenty-three or twenty-four. In 368 when Pelopidas arranged an alliance with Ptolemaios he had been sent to Thebes as a hostage, and he remained there probably until Perdiccas became king in 365. In those three years he had had an opportunity to learn many political and military lessons from Epaminondas and Pelopidas, to become imbued with the Greek culture represented by those two enlightened men, and to observe the chaotic condition of Greek political life. After returning to Macedonia he apparently was assigned a district to govern by his brother. Thus by 359 he had had the opportunity to acquire administrative experience and to become acquainted with many prominent Macedonians.

ON ASSUMING power, Philip wasted no time in grappling with the dangers facing him and the state. Gifts of money quieted the Paeonians temporarily and also caused the Thracians to abandon their support of Pausanias, who thereupon ceased to be an active pretender. Argaeus seemed at first a serious threat, for he was backed by the Athenians who assisted him by sending a fleet and 3,000 hoplites to their recently acquired Methone on the Thermaic Gulf. Philip, learning that Argaeus was encouraging the Athenians in their passion to acquire Amphipolis, withdrew the Macedonian troops which Perdiccas had assigned to that city. This move probably explains why the Athenian general at Methone did not accompany Argaeus on his march to Aegae. This expedition failed to arouse any enthusiasm for the pretender, and on his return to the coast he was completely defeated by Philip. The Athenians who were captured among Argaeus' troops Philip immediately released without ransom. Shortly thereafter he sent envoys to the Athenians, stating that he desired peace with them (Diodorus, 16.2.6–4.1).

In his first year as ruler Philip had removed the dangers from other claimants to the throne; in his second year (358) he concerned himself with problems arising beyond the confines of Macedonia. After defeating the Paeonians in the north he marched westward into Upper Macedonia, where the Illyrians, following their defeat of Perdiccas, had occupied various areas. It is hard to understand why the Illyrians had not invaded Macedonia immediately after their great victory.[7] Their own losses may have been heavy, and Philip may have delayed action through diplomacy. That was probably the time when he married the Illyrian princess Audata, and it is likely that he agreed to continue with payment of tribute. In the plain of Monastir, historians believe, he fought a major battle in which 7,000 Illyrians were slain. As a consequence of their defeat the Illyrians had to evacuate Macedonia and accept Lake Lychnitis (Ohrid) as the boundary between the two nations. Philip used this opportunity to incorporate more permanently into the Macedonian state the princedoms of Lyncestis, Orestis, and Elimaea, which previously, sometimes voluntarily and sometimes under compulsion, had cooperated with the Illyrians. His next activity was in Thessaly. Alexander of Pherae was murdered in 358, but his murderers and successors continued the same aggressive policy against other Thessalian cities. The Aleuadae of Larissa appealed to Philip for help, and he marched southward from his Illyrian campaign. He remained long enough in Thessaly to win much goodwill from the nobles in various cities by supporting them against the tyrants of Pherae (Diodorus, 16.4).

In 357, after two years of successfully establishing his rule and repelling invasions, Philip turned his attention to Amphipolis. Athens had never reconciled itself to the loss of this important trading center to Brasidas in 424, and in recent years had been making continuous efforts to recover it. Philip obviously was reluctant to have this city fall under the control of either Athens or the Chalcidian League, both of which had long disclosed their hostility to Macedonia. He also surely was aware that slightly east of Amphipolis lay the rich gold and silver mines of Mt. Pangaeus, a region of supreme importance to a ruler whose expenses had recently been so excessive.

Philip's assault on and capture of Amphipolis in the autumn or early winter of 357 are historical facts, but the diplomatic preliminaries are lost in a maze of propaganda. The Athenians always insisted that Philip had agreed that Amphipolis should belong to Athens. Since Amphipolis had been an independent city since 424, it is hard to see how it belonged to anyone except itself. The Athenian claim presumably rose from the fact that when Philip was threatened by Athenian support of the pretender Argaeus in 359 he, to conciliate the Athenians, recalled the troops which his predecessor, Perdiccas, had granted to the Amphipolitans. Possibly in later diplomatic exchanges Philip may have disclaimed interest in Amphipolis, but without necessarily suggesting that the autonomous city should fall to Athens.

The Athenian obsession that they had a right to Amphipolis is well illustrated in a passage in the *First Olynthiac Oration* (8), delivered in 349. Demosthenes states that in the summer of 357, after the Athenians had returned from their successful campaign in Euboea, two Amphipolitans, Hierax and Stratocles, worried about Philip's intentions, tried to persuade the Athenian assembly to take over Amphipolis. The passage gives the impression that the city would have voluntarily yielded to Athens. In view of the long hostility of Amphipolis to Athens, one can safely assume that these two "envoys" did not represent Amphipolis officially, as Demosthenes implies, but only an anti-Macedonian group.

The contemporary historian Theopompus gives a different version of the diplomatic manoeuvres which occurred before Philip's attack on Amphipolis. In fragment 30 he states that Athens sent envoys to Philip to discuss friendship, and that they, on arriving, tried to arrange a "deal" by which Athens should receive Amphipolis as recompense for granting him Pydna. When they returned to Athens the envoys, in order that Pydna should remain unaware of the project, did not report to the assembly but transacted this business secretly with the Boulē. Historians in general have accepted the notion that there was some sort of secret pact, which can only be dated vaguely in the period 359–357, but several scholars have argued that secret action by the Boulē was contrary to the functioning of the Athenian democracy.[8] In the confused history of Athens, however, there seem to have been a few cases where in an emergency the Boulē acted independently.[9] Relevant to this problem is a passage in the *Second Olynthiac Oration* (6) in which Demosthenes, listing various trickeries of Philip, says, "He won our simple hearts by promising to hand over Amphipolis to us and by negotiating that secret treaty once so much talked about." It has been argued that in this long complex sentence, of which only a part is translated here, the secret treaty need not refer to Amphipolis, but this is not the natural interpretation. With such ambiguous evidence a certain conclusion is impossible, but one is tempted to suspect that some sort of deal may have been discussed in the Boulē which subsequently was "leaked" by one or more of the 500 councillors. Such garbled information later appeared in different guises in Theopompus and Demosthenes, the former assigning the initiative to the Athenians, the latter to Philip.

Whatever the truth of these obscure negotiations, Amphipolis faced the assault of Philip alone, and it fell in the early winter of 357. An inscription found at Amphipolis (Tod, no. 150) reveals that the city continued to function as a democracy and that it banished forever Stratocles and a certain Philon, and their children, of whom the former was the one who had appealed to Athens. Later, at some time before 336, Amphipolis was incorporated into the territory of Macedonia.[10]

Athens declared war on Philip over the Amphipolis issue, but at the time this was a war in name only since Athenian military energies had to be concentrated on trouble in the Chersonese and on the revolt of Byzantium, Chios, Rhodes, and Cos from the league. Philip, free from any fear of Athenian interference, continued with his plans of gaining more access to the sea by capturing Pydna in the winter of 357/6. It is unfortunate that the information for this period is so slight, but one derives the impression that, whether or not there was a deal, the "barbarian" Philip had outsmarted the civilized Athens. The loss of its claim to Amphipolis, although deserved if Theopompus' statement is correct, was never accepted by Athens and became one of the main factors in its increasing suspicion and hatred of Philip.

In the winter of 357/6, after the Athenian declaration of war because of his capture of Amphipolis, Philip realized that the Chalcidian League under Olynthus could again become a serious threat to Macedonia. In the period 384–383 Olynthus had forced Amyntas III to flee from his kingdom and had helped establish the pretender Argaeus on the throne, the man whom the Athenians had supported in 359. Although Athens and Olynthus had long been hostile to one another because of their conflicting ambitions in the Thraceward region, there was always the chance that they might unite in an alliance to obstruct Philip's activities. Actually in 357/6, worried by the successes of Philip, Olynthus did turn to its old enemy for assistance (Demosthenes, 1.8; 2.6–7). The Athenians, however, were already embroiled with the revolt of various allies from their league, and before any agreement could be reached Philip succeeded in enmeshing Olynthus diplomatically. He offered to the city the district to its north, Anthemus, and also the territory of Potidaea. The Olynthians may have signed the alliance with Philip because in their alarm they saw no other alternative, but their fears did not prevent them from playing the unsavory role of joining in the attack on Potidaea, whose territory they had long coveted. The city was taken and destroyed, and the Olynthians were made happy with the acquisition of its land. Philip, to palliate the anger of the Athenians who had dispatched a fleet too late to help Potidaea (Demosthenes, 4.35), sent back to Athens all the *cleruchs* without ransom.

Two aspects about this alliance between Philip and the Chalcidians should be emphasized because of their significance for the future. Libanius in his hypothesis to the *First Olynthiac Oration* of Demosthenes states that in the treaty Philip and the Olynthians agreed to wage war in common against the Athenians and not to make peace unilaterally. A fragmentary inscription (Tod, no. 158) recording this alliance includes the statement that the god at Delphi (Apollo) declared to the Chalcidians and to Philip that it would be beneficial for them to be friends and allies as they had agreed. In 356, therefore, as in 363, the dominant faction at Delphi was hostile to Athens.

The year 356 was a particularly successful one for Philip. Four years before the Thasians had established a town called Crenides in the Pangaeus mining district. When it began to be threatened by the Thracians, it appealed to Philip for help. He responded immediately to the request, drove back the Thracians, and took control of the town, which he renamed Philippi. This is the first known instance in Greek history of a city being named after a ruler, a custom that became common under Alexander the Great and the Hellenistic monarchs. Philip developed the mining possibilities so effectively that before long he was receiving a thousand talents of gold annually from Pangaeus (Diodorus, 16.8.6). Philip's activity worried his warlike neighbors, who were accustomed to think of Macedonia as a place for them to plunder. Consequently the Thracians, Paeonians, and Illyrians (presumably a different tribe from those defeated in 358) banded together; a preserved Attic inscription (Tod, no. 157) records the alliance that Athens made with the kings of these three nations in July 356. The coalition proved to be ineffectual. The Athenians were probably too occupied with the Social War to send much, if any, assistance, and their new allies were completely defeated. Philip dispersed the Thracians, reduced the Paeonians to a state of vassalage, and his general Parmenio won a great victory over the Illyrians (Diodorus, 16.22.3).

It was possibly in this year, 356, that the Macedonian army assembly, in recognition of Philip's achievements, acclaimed him king, if one accepts the view that formerly he had been acting as regent. The accomplishments of Philip in these three of four years were remarkable. The borders of Macedonia became more fixed than they probably ever had been. Lake Lychnitis was recognized as a frontier by the Illyrians, who no longer made constant invasions and raids. In Epirus Philip acquired influence by marrying the princess Olympias. In the north Paeonia acquiesced in the status of a vassal kingdom, and to the east the

Thracians, because of Philip's advanced post at Philippi, were forced to think of the Nestus River as the line between them and the Macedonians. Southward Philip had entered into good relations with aristocrats in various Thessalian cities. The long and natural desire of the kings of Macedonia to control their coastline was becoming a reality. With the capture of Methone in 354 Philip cleared the Thermaic Gulf region of the Athenians, who for generations had thought of the Macedonians as barbarians whom they were entitled to exploit. Chalcidice with its valuable harbors and its powerful and ambitious league was a tempting and still unattainable target, but the Olynthians had manoeuvred themselves into a dangerous position. Eastward—to the fury of the Athenians—Philip now controlled Amphipolis with its rich trade and easy access to Mt. Pangaeus.

While engaged in these conquests and matters of foreign policy, Philip did not neglect the internal problems of Macedonia. He clearly devoted much time to the development of the army, building on the improvements which predecessors like Alexander I had made. The heavy armed infantry, the *pezetairoi,* now that money was available, he developed into the famous Macedonian phalanx. These infantrymen were probably responsible for providing their own equipment, but on campaign and in the periods of training necessary to master the use of the long thrusting spear (*sarissa*) and the intricacies of maintaining a formation often sixteen rows deep, they received regular wages. The effectiveness of the phalanx, which might consist of many thousands of men, was increased by the employment of *peltasts* and various types of light armed troops, and especially by the *hetairoi* cavalry who, in addition to their offensive duties, could guard the flanks and rear where the phalanx was particularly vulnerable. The *hetairoi,* consisting primarily of members of the aristocratic families and clans throughout Macedonia, continued, as formerly, to be the chief offensive weapon in the army. Many of these nobles acquired the habit of living regularly in Pella rather than in their country or mountain estates. Theopompus speaks of 800 of them as residing in the capital, and it was from them that Philip selected his most trusted advisers. As had probably been the custom previously, the sons of the nobility, for a certain period at least, lived at court serving as royal pages. In this capacity they received training for future military or administrative posts. This trend for many of the nobles and their sons to live in Pella must have contributed greatly to reducing the old separatist tendencies, particularly in Upper Macedonia, which had made it so difficult for Macedonia to become a united nation. Philip probably was responsible for considerable road building which, besides aiding the movement of armies and of objects of trade, contributed further to the unification of the nation. In later times, at least, the inhabitants of cities which Philip had captured were transferred to different areas so that these new settlements could serve both strategic and economic purposes.[11]

Economically and politically Philip aided his kingdom, once the gold and silver began to flow in from Pangaeus, by coining gold staters (Philippi) based on the Attic standard. These staters circulated widely and became as well known and popular as the old Persian darics. Since the amount of gold available reduced the price of gold in relation to silver from 12:1 to 10:1, Philip issued a new silver coinage, based on the Phoenician standard used by the Chalcidians, thus maintaining the Greek custom of equating twenty-four silver drachmas to one gold stater.[12]

In the field of government Philip probably made no changes since, like his predecessors, he was an army king. The nature of the kingship was similar to what had existed in all Greek states berfore the rise of the polis had made it possible for aristocracy to supplant monarchy. As king, Philip was chief general, judge, and priest. Since his power was almost absolute, he was not bound to seek advice, but he had a body of counselors with whom he consulted when he wished. This body was selected from the *hetairoi,* among whom some Greeks might be present, for Philip, and after him his son Alexander, granted that status to certain Greeks who performed loyal service for them. As *hetairoi* these Greeks were presumably granted estates from the king's land. As far as can be ascertained from the evidence, the Macedonian people in arms, the army assembly including both *hetairoi* and *pezetairoi,* had two basic rights in their relation with the king. First, the army assembly had the right to acclaim a new king from the Argead family; if the logical successor was a minor, it had the duty to appoint a regent. Second, any Macedonian belonging to the army assembly, if he was under a capital charge, which usually meant treason, had the right to be tried before his peers in the assembly. This body both passed the sentence and carried out the execution, if such was the verdict.[13]

Since PHILIP was soon to be engaged in a crucial diplomatic and military struggle with the Greek world, it is relevant to recall here Xenophon's statement that "there was even more confusion and disorder in Greece after the battle [of Mantinea] than before." A glance at the Greek mainland in the 350s corroborates this judgment. The Peloponnesus, in which the Peloponnesian League had long had a stabilizing influence, was now in turmoil, as Sparta struggled to surmount its humiliation and Argos, Megalopolis, and Messenia, in their different ways, tried to prevent any revival of Spartan domination. In central Greece Thebes was striving to retain the prestige and power which its great leaders, Pelopidas and Epaminondas, had acquired for the Boeotians. In Thessaly, after the death of Alexander of Pherae in 358, his successors were trying to maintain the tyranny against the resistance of the Thessalian League.

Athens, because of its aggressive actions in which it ignored the anti-imperialistic pledges of the decree of Aristoteles of 378/7, had been confronted in 357 with the revolt of some of its chief allies. By 355/4, partly from fear of Persian intervention, it had had to acquiesce in the independence of Byzantium, Chios, Cos, and Rhodes. Soon Lesbos and other states broke away from the league. In 354 Athenian prestige was at low ebb. Philip had driven the Athenians from the Thermaic Gulf region and had acquired Amphipolis, for which Athens had long and futilely struggled. The Athenian League was disintegrating, and although Athens still had a large fleet, it did not have the revenues to man it effectively. Dreams of imperialism were unrealistic, as Isocrates maintained in his oration *On the Peace.* A period of peace and economic recovery was needed, and a new type of statesman who could persuade divergent interests to compromise.

The statesman who tried to play this role in Athens for a few years following the War of the Allies was Eubulus, the man who apparently had proposed the necessary but humiliating peace (Scholiast to Demosthenes, *Olynthiac* III, 28). He and his supporters realized that financial conditions at Athens were so inadequate that military expeditions had to be avoided unless vital interests of the city were at stake. The contributions (*syntaxeis*) from the allies had never been large, and after the war they may have been almost nonexistent. Demosthenes in the *Fourth Philippic* (10.37) reports that the general revenues of the state had sunk to 130 talents annually. The official position that Eubulus held was membership on the board of Commissioners of the Theoric Fund. Aristotle (*Ath. Const.,* 43.1) says that this elected board held office from Panathenaea to Panathenaea; this reference is almost certainly to the annual festival rather than to the quinquennial Greater Panathenaea. Since the members of this annual board were elected, it is logical to assume that they could be reelected, as was true, for example, of the *strategoi.* What seems clear is that Eubulus remained a significant figure for at least a decade, whether as a continuing member of the board or as a distinguished citizen able to influence current members of the board and the assembly.

The ancient sources that mention the Theoric Fund, chiefly remarks in the orators and comments by late lexicographers and scholiasts, provide disappointingly little, and often distorted, information. This is particularly unfortunate, for, since one purpose of the fund was to grant distributions of money—a procedure at festival time initiated by Pericles, according to Plutarch (*Pericles*, 11.4)—it has been customary among authors, both ancient and modern, to depict the *theorika* as a ruinous dole to the poor which deprived Athens of resources desperately needed for other purposes, especially for defense against Philip of Macedonia. To discuss the puzzling problems concerning the *theorika* is impossible here, but according to an important article published in 1963, the following statements seem reasonably credible.[14]

The surplus, if any, from the annual budgets of the government at the end of the year was channeled into a fund which was usually spent on military matters. Eubulus, endeavoring to curtail needless warlike campaigns, succeeded in having a law passed that all the surplus should be assigned to the Theoric Fund. From this sum distributions were made to the citizens in the *demes* in which they were registered before some of the great festivals and possibly on other occasions. The sources on the whole suggest that these distributions were not large—an estimate of fifteen talents a year has been made[15]—while the rest of the fund was allotted to various work projects such as repairing roads and fortifications. The law that the Theoric Fund could not finance military expeditions was effective in preventing the assembly under the influence of militant leaders from authorizing ill-considered campaigns, but this attempt to preserve peace engendered its own financial problems, for the poor who received wages from military service, especially as rowers in the fleet, were left with no, or insufficient, employment. The Theoric Fund by providing distributions and work programs compensated largely for the lack of military wages, and thus helped reduce the friction between poor and rich by furnishing necessary assistance to the former and welcome relief from taxation to the latter.

Eubulus succeeded in bettering Athens' economic condition by checking corruption in the handling of money, by reducing the expenditures on the employment of mercenaries, by stimulating renewed work on the largely neglected silver mines of Laurium, by encouraging the increase in the number of metics through more favorable treatment, and by carrying out numerous utilitarian building projects. According to Demosthenes (10.38) the general revenues of the state rose from the low of 130 talents to 400 talents. The later orator Demades described the Theoric Fund as "the glue of the democracy." In the words of Eubulus' admirer Aeschines (3.25), almost the whole administration of the state was placed in the hands of the Commissioners of the Theoric Fund. Since Eubulus was, and is, often blamed for his pacifistic policy, it should be stressed that he worked for a Common Peace throughout Greece, that he did not oppose military operations when real peril threatened Athens, and that, to strengthen Athens to meet future dangers, he was responsible for the building of many triremes and for starting construction on the great naval arsenal (Philochorus, fragment 56a).

While Athens was unsuccessfully engaged in trying to curb the revolt of its allies, a war broke out in central Greece which in time was to provide Philip with an opportunity to interfere in the affairs of the Greek world as a whole rather than merely in Thessaly as his predecessors occasionally had done. The trouble began with controversies between the Thebans and the Phocians. After Leuctra Phocis had been included in the Theban alliance, but the Phocians' lack of enthusiasm was revealed by their refusal to serve under Epaminondas in the Peloponnesian campaign which ended with the battle of Mantinea. This refusal, based on the argument that the alliance was a defensive and not an offensive one, was followed in the years after 362 by the Phocian desire to sever all political relations with the Boeotians. The Thebans, anxious to retain their faltering hegemony and worried because of the proximity of the Phocians to the western Boeotian cities, always restive under Theban leadership, decided to strike at the Phocians through the medium of the Delphic Amphictiony. The council of this league, largely dominated by the Thessalians and their perioecic states, traditionally hostile to the Phocians, voted at the spring meeting of 356 a heavy fine upon the Phocians for some sacrilegious offense against Delphi. When the fine was not paid the council decreed that the land of the offending Phocians should be confiscated and consecrated to Apollo. At the same time, a large fine which had previously been declared against the Spartans for their seizure of the Theban Cadmea in 382 was confirmed and enlarged. A leading Phocian named Philomelus persuaded his countrymen not to yield to the Amphictionic decree and won their confidence sufficiently to be elected *strategos autocrator*. He then went to Sparta, where King Archidamus secretly gave him fifteen talents to help finance his resistance to the Amphictiony. With this money, increased by his own funds, Philomelus enrolled a thousand Phocians, hired mercenaries, and then seized the temple at Delphi in the early summer of 356 (Pausanias, 10.2.2–3).

Some Locrians from adjacent Amphissa, always hostile to the Phocians, tried to expel Philomelus from Delphi, but without success. Philomelus then sent envoys to Athens, Sparta, Thebes, and other Greek cities to explain that he had no designs on the treasures of Delphi but was merely asserting the ancestral claim of Phocis to control Delphi, a claim which was supported by the authority of Homer (*Iliad*, 2.517–519). The Athenians and Spartans, although neither was in condition to take part in an Amphictionic war, both made alliances with the Phocians. As mentioned earlier, Athens in 363 had honored with citizenship a pro-Phocian Delphian who, with his associates, had been banished from Delphi by a Theban-inspired Amphictionic decree. The Theban response to Philomelus' envoys was to persuade the Amphictionic council at the fall meeting of 356 to declare a sacred war against the "sacrilegious" Phocians. Thus a holy war, motivated by petty political grievances and ultimately entangling a large number of Greek states, began its sorry course. Diodorus (16.29.1) lists as the protectors of Apollo's temple the Boeotians, Locrians, Thessalians, Perrhaebians, Dorians (of the metropolis), Dolopians, Athamanians, Achaeans of Phthiotis, Magnesians, Aenianians, and others, and as allies of the Phocians the Athenians, the Spartans, and some other Peloponnesians.

This war, usually called the Third Sacred War, dragged on until 346, lasting for ten or eleven years depending on whether one assigns its beginning to 356 or 355. Its chronology is obscure at times, for Diodorus, whose account in book 16 is the only continuous one extant, seems at times to be confused and repetitive. The accounts of the Delphian *naopoioi*, the international temple builders for the reconstruction of the temple burned down in 373, provide, by the variations in their membership, potentially valuable information on the course of the war, if some certain method of interpreting the data could be discovered.[16]

After the declaration of war by the Amphictionic Council, Philomelus, anticipating a major offensive against him and the Phocians, erected a wall around the temple area and enrolled more mercenaries, whom he was able to pay by exacting money from certain wealthy Delphians. The fighting in 355 and 354 was chiefly in the area of the eastern Locrians, where Philomelus was trying to prevent a joining of the forces of the Thessalians and Boeotians. As the need for more mercenaries increased, Philomelus may have "borrowed" from the treasures in Apollo's temple at Delphi, although some scholars attribute this expropriation of sacred money only to his successors. At a place called Neon north of Mt. Parnassus, defeated in a battle against superior numbers and facing capture, Philomelus threw himself off a cliff. His colleague, Onomarchus, succeeded in bringing the defeated Phocian army back to Delphi.

The defeat and death of Philomelus caused some Phocians to think in terms of peace, but Onomarchus, who, according to Diodorus, was liable to a heavy fine imposed by the Amphictionic Council, succeeded in making the war spirit prevail. Once elected *strategos autocrator* he began to appropriate the treasures at Delphi, turning the bronze and iron dedications into weapons and the gold and silver into coinage. With the money thus obtained, which was increased by confiscation of the property of

Phocians opposed to him, he was able to attract even more mercenaries and also to bribe key politicians in various Greek states. He then campaigned successfully against both the eastern and western Locrians, in Doris, and even in western Boeotia.

Before the beginning of Onomarchus' campaign, the Thebans responded to an appeal for aid from the revolting satrap, Artabazus, who, after the Athenian recall of their general Chares in 355, found himself in difficulties. Since Theban policy usually was to maintain good relations with the Persian king, the decision to assist a rebel must have been influenced by their need for money and also by their belief that the death of Philomelus had reduced the danger from the Phocians. They dispatched the general Pammenes with 5,000 soldiers, presumably mercenaries, to Asia Minor. On his march through Thrace Pammenes had a meeting at Maronea with Philip who, when a hostage at Thebes, had lived in his house. What happened at this meeting is obscure, but some sort of agreement was arranged between Philip and one of the Thracian kings, Cersobleptes (Demosthenes, 23.183). Philip's presence is hard to explain. After a protracted siege, in which an arrow blinded one eye, he had taken Methone, the last of the Athenian holdings on the Thermaic Gulf, in the spring of 354. Since Philip was in Thessaly during the summer and fall of 353, he must have made this journey to Maronea by sea shortly after the capture of Methone. As for Pammenes, he won two victories for Artabazus, but then, falling under suspicion, he was dismissed. It might be mentioned here that a few years later (352?) Artabazus, after the failure of his revolt, sought refuge at Philip's court.

When Philip returned from his excursion into Thrace, the confused situation in Thessaly enabled him to interfere there again as he had in the year 358. Late in that year Alexander of Pherae had been murdered by the sons of Jason. The eldest of them, Tisiphonus, took over the reins of government and adopted a more conciliatory policy towards the cities of the Thessalian League. In the Sacred War which the Amphictionic Council declared on Phocis in the autumn of 356, the Thessalians, possibly including Pherae, at first took part, but after their defeat by Philomelus in the following year (Diodorus, 16.30.4) they neglected the war temporarily because of the recurrence of domestic problems. On the death of Tisiphonus late in 355 or early 354, his younger brothers, Lycophron and Peitholaus, took control in Pherae and almost immediately resumed the aggressive policy of Alexander against the cities of Thessaly. This course of action was encouraged by Onomarchus, who subsidized them with the money obtained from Delphi in the hope of fostering dissension in Thessaly and thereby weakening its participation in the Sacred War. Unable to cope with the threat from Pherae, the Thessalian cities, undoubtedly at the urging of the Aleuadae of Larissa, appealed to Philip for aid. He responded in 353 and marched directly against Pherae and its port Pagasae. Lycophron then requested assistance from Onomarchus, who sent his brother Phayllos with 7,000 troops to support the tyrants of Pherae. After Phayllos' defeat, Onomarchus himself with a large force hurried into Thessaly. He succeeded in overpowering the Macedonians and their Thessalian allies so thoroughly in two battles that Philip found it necessary to return to Macedonia, leaving the Phocians in possession of sections of Thessaly (Diodorus, 16.35.1–3).

Philip renewed his campaign against Pherae the following year. He now commanded, besides his Macedonians, a large contingent from the Thessalian League. Onomarchus, who had been fighting in western Boeotia, marched quickly at the head of 20,000 infantry and 500 horsemen to help his allies at Pherae. To prevent a junction between the armies of his enemies, Philip succeeded in forcing the Phocians into battle in the Crocos plain near the Pagasaean Gulf. Since his troops were still dispirited from the defeats of the preceding year, Philip had them garlanded with laurel wreaths to encourage them to believe they were defenders of Apollo against those who were desecrating his temple (Justin, 8.2.3). The Thessalian and Macedonian cavalry were chiefly responsible for routing their opponents and then the victors slaughtered 6,000 of the enemy, including Onomarchus, as they fled into the sea in the vain hope of reaching Athenian triremes which were sailing by. Subsequently, the body of Onomarchus was hanged or crucified and the innumerable dead of the foe were denied burial rites[17]—an interpretation which seems more probable than that 3,000 captives were hurled into the sea as temple robbers (Diodorus, 16.35.4–6). By this denial of the customary respect for the dead, an action quite in keeping with the spirit of this holy war, Philip assumed the role of champion of Apollo and leader of the "crusade" to subdue the sacrilegious Phocians. After the battle, Lycophron and Peitholaus, realizing that they could not hold Pherae against an assault from Philip, submitted to him on the understanding that they could depart with 2,000 of their mercenaries. They immediately joined forces with Phayllos, who had succeeded his brother as leader of the Phocians. The important port of Pagasae then fell to the Macedonians (Demosthenes, 1.12–13).

Philip, after arranging affairs in Thessaly, marched on Thermopylae in the summer of 352 with the intention of ousting the Phocians from Delphi. Athens, however, which had sent a fleet under Chares too late to help Onomarchus in his final battle, now became thoroughly aroused. It was one thing for Philip to take Amphipolis, Pydna, and Methone, but it was something quite different for the Macedonian king, under the guise of champion of Apollo, to take possession of the key pass into Greece. On the motion of Eubulus' party, Athens quickly dispatched by sea 5,000 foot soldiers and 400 cavalry to Thermopylae, and they were joined by 1,000 Spartans, 2,000 Achaeans, Lycophron and Peitholaus and their 2,000 mercenaries, and the Phocians under Phayllos. Philip, knowing that to break through such an army in the narrow pass would be a difficult, if not impossible, task, retired into Thessaly, where his fame now was very great, and then returned to Macedonia (Diodorus, 16.37–38.1–2).

Philip's reputation in Thessaly had a startling consequence. At some point in his career it is known that he became archon for life in Thessaly. His election to this position has usually been assigned to the period 344–342, but several scholars have convincingly associated it with the crushing victory over Onomarchus and the ending of the tyranny of Pherae.[18] The nobles in the various cities of the Thessalian League had long suffered from the aggression of the dominant family of Pherae, and their joy at its suppression was unbounded. When Philip campaigned against Pherae in 352 he was the supreme commander of the Thessalians as well as of his Macedonians. The statements in two ancient sources are particularly relevant to the prevailing Thessalian attitude towards Philip. Justin (8.2.1), referring to the war against Onomarchus, says that "the Thessalians elected as their leader (*dux*) not one of their own citizens, whose power in case of victory might have become oppressive, but Philip, king of Macedonia, spontaneously granting to a foreigner a domination which they feared to entrust to one of themselves." Isocrates (5.20), writing in 346, remarks, "Has not Philip converted the Thessalians, whose power formerly extended over Macedonia, into an attitude so friendly to him that every Thessalian has more confidence in him than in his own fellow-countrymen?" For a Greek state to grant supreme power over its welfare to a foreigner was an unprecedented act, but it seems that this position was awarded to Philip voluntarily and not under duress as Demosthenes claimed. The trust that the Thessalians felt in Philip suggests that he may have been able to benefit them more frequently than is recorded in the sources.

While the Sacred War was raging in central Greece, an explosive situation was also developing in the Peloponnesus. Sparta, unreconciled to the loss of Messenia and the presence of a hostile Megalopolis on its northern frontier, felt that the time for action had come since its bitter enemy, Thebes, was embroiled in an exhausting struggle with the Phocians. By the year 353 Sparta had won as allies Mantinea, Phlius, and Elis by proposing that lands lost in the 360s should be restored to their original owners. Either then or later, Sparta suggested that Oropus should be returned to Athens and that in Boeotia, Orchomenus, Plataea, and Thespiae should be rebuilt and made independent. As Spartan warlike activity increased, the Megalopolitans, realizing that an attack on them was imminent, sent envoys to Athens, who were immediately followed by Spartan ambassadors. Of the many speeches that were then delivered before the Athenian assembly, the one given by the young Demosthenes has been preserved. In this oration, 16, *For the Megalopolitans,* which is the chief extant source for the matters at issue, Demosthenes developed the balance of power theme. Since he was aware that the ultimate purpose of the Spartans was to invade and recover Messenia, which Athens was bound by a treaty to protect from invasion (Pausanias, 4.28.1–2), he argued that immediate help for Megalopolis would thwart Spartan plans. Athens fared best when both Sparta and Thebes were weak. If Athens did not assist Megalopolis now, Thebes would, thus gaining an important ally. Demosthenes' proposal was rejected, for Athens, under Eubulus' leadership, was trying to avoid unnecessary wars and certainly did not want to engage in hostilities with Sparta, its ally at the battle of Mantinea. In the desultory and indecisive fighting that ensued in the Peloponnesus, the Megalopolitans were assisted by the Argives, Sicyonians, Messenians, and, after Philip's victory over the Phocians, the Thebans, while Sparta received aid only from 3,000 Phocians and some cavalry under the exiled tyrants of Pherae, Lycophron and Peitholaus. Sparta's plans to regain some of its former hegemony thus failed. The wisdom of Demosthenes' rejected proposal is debatable, but obviously his prophecy was correct that Megalopolis would become a staunch ally of Thebes.

In central Greece the Sacred War continued its futile course. After the death of Onomarchus, his brother, Phayllos, took over the command of the Phocians, and with the help of the Athenians and other allies he frustrated Philip's attempt to pass through Thermopylae. Thereafter the war degenerated into a dreary series of battles and raids in east Locris, Phocis, and Boeotia. The Boeotians, finding themselves short of money, repented their policy of having sent Pammenes to aid the rebel Artabazus in 354 and appealed to Artaxerxes for financial aid. The sum of 300 talents was forthcoming, probably on the understanding that the Boeotians would supply Persia with troops for the projected expedition against Egypt in 351/0 (Diodorus, 16.40). In the meantime Phayllos fell sick and died, and the young son of Onomarchus, Phalaecus, took over the leadership of the Phocians. As long as the treasures of Delphi continued to be at his disposal, he could hold his own, but the treasures were not unlimited.

AFTER HIS repulse at Thermopylae in the summer of 352, Philip did not interfere in the problems of Greece and of the Sacred War for several years. In the autumn he marched eastward into Thrace where Cersobleptes, the king of the eastern section, was disregarding whatever agreements he had made with Philip at Maronea in 354. In 353 Athens had dispatched Chares with a fleet to the Chersonese. He first captured Sestos and then, in barbarous punishment of its defection from Athens in 360, presided over the execution of all the adult males and the selling as slaves of the women and children. Athenian *cleruchs* were quickly sent out to the denuded spot and to other places in the Chersonese (Diodorus, 16.34.3–4). Cersobleptes, receiving no aid from Philip who was fighting unsuccessfully with Onomarchus in Thessaly, was intimidated by Chares and assured the Athenians that he was abandoning his claims to the Chersonese except for Cardia at its northern end and that he would help them to win Amphipolis through his general Charidemus, the Euboean mercenary recently honored with Athenian citizenship. When Philip late in 352 arrived in the region north of the Propontis, which was the center of Cersobleptes' kingdom, he began to besiege the capital, Heraeon Teichos, an enterprise in which Byzantium, Perinthus, and another Thracian king, all having grievances against Cersobleptes, joined. The Athenians, who at first planned to send help to Cersobleptes, renounced the idea when they learned of Philip's allies. Philip consequently was able to return to Macedonia in 351 strengthened by the goodwill of Byzantium and Perinthus and a renewed alliance with Cersobleptes.[19]

Philip's campaign in the Propontis, his establishment of friendship with Byzantium and Perinthus, and his alliance with Cersobleptes, secured by taking that king's son as a hostage (Scholiast to Aeschines, 2.81), alarmed certain Athenians. In the summer of 351 Demosthenes delivered his *First Philippic,* the first of his many attacks on Philip. In this speech he expressed indignation that "a Macedonian is triumphing over Athenians and settling the destiny of Hellas." Athens had been humiliated too often by Philip's victories, made possible by its weakness or inertia. Demosthenes proposed that an army and navy, small but composed of citizens as well as mercenaries, should be dispatched to carry on a war of harassment against Philip and thus prevent him from further exploits abroad. Demosthenes' appeal at this time, because of Eubulus' policy of no unnecessary wars, had no effect on Athenian policy, but having decided that Philip was a threat to Athens and to Greece as a whole, he repeated this theme constantly until the bitter end.

The question of Philip's attitude towards the Greek world, and

Athens in particular, is difficult, if not unsolvable, since the chief source of information lies in the speeches of Demosthenes, the most brilliant and passionate orator of the ancient world. Philip, despite his obvious admiration for Greek culture, was a king of the Macedonians, and his first obligation was to strengthen his kingdom and protect it from encroachments, whether barbarian or Greek—a natural ambition which critics, both ancient and modern, deplore. The motives for Philip's campaign into the Propontis in 352 and 351 cannot be stated with assurance. If one wishes to believe, as Demosthenes did, that Philip was already dreaming of the domination of Greece, then possibly the expedition into eastern Thrace was part of a plan to humble Athens by interfering with the vital grain ships sailing out of the Black Sea. Philip's thinking in 352 was hardly that far-reaching, however. The southwestern part of Thrace Philip had already partly secured by the founding of Philippi in 356, but the region stretching from the Nestus River to the west coast of the Black Sea and northward to the Danube River was unpredictable and dangerous. This large area, after the murder of Cotys in 360 or 359, had been divided among three kings—Cersobleptes receiving the eastern section—each of whom was always trying to extend his realm at the expense of one of the others. Philip had good reason to be uneasy about the Thracians, for in the first year of his rule they had threatened to invade Macedonia, and in 356 they, together with the Illyrians and Paeonians, had entered into an alliance with Athens directed against him. Philip knew that Athens always tried to keep on good terms with at least one of the Thracian kings, who might be used at any moment in an attack on Amphipolis. His suspicion of the meddling inclination of Athens had been aroused in the first year of his reign when the Athenians backed Argaeus, a pretender to the throne, and by their alliance with the Illyrians, Thracians, and Paeonians in 356; and as a Macedonian, Philip was bound to remember with repugnance the former Athenian imperial outposts of Pydna and Methone.

In view of such considerations, one is probably justified in suspecting that Philip's chief motive in his campaign of 352 and 351 was to punish his unreliable "ally" Cersobleptes and to prevent that Thracian king from falling into the clutches of Athens. Needless to say, he was also interested in the manpower of Thrace and in its great resources in timber and grain, assets which he hoped would ultimately be at his disposal rather than that of the ever-threatening Athens.

As Philip's power and influence steadily grew, the position of the Chalcidian League became increasingly precarious. The Chalcidians must have realized that sooner or later he would want to include the peninsula in his realm. To many of them the inevitability of this step caused no apprehension. The Chalcidians were primarily a commercial people, and the trade with Macedonia, particularly since the treaty of 356, had been very extensive. Philip's change of Macedonian coinage to the Chalcidian standard obviously simplified and fostered these commercial relations. Since the Chalcidians, because of their federation, had long been accustomed to the absence of certain aspects of autonomy, they were immune to many of the passions of city-state particularism. To such men a peaceful and friendly inclusion into the Macedonian state was an idea, under current circumstances, which seemed attractive or even desirable. There was a party, however, which, believing strongly in the idea of national sovereignty, looked upon the menace from an expanding Macedonia with dread. This group gained political ascendancy, and probably in the autumn of 352 when Philip was absent in Thrace, it sent envoys to Athens to discuss the situation. Contrary to the alliance of 356 with Philip, these delegates arranged a peace with Athens and presumably talked about the possibility of an alliance. Later in the year as Philip returned from the Propontis—or early in the following spring, if the sickness incurred in Thrace necessitated delay—he led his army to the confines of the Chalcidian League where an embassy met him. Despite his anger at the breach of the treaty with him, Philip decided to maintain peace for the present. As a result of his restraint, the pro-Macedonian Chalcidian party, which numerically must have been about equal to its opponents, gained ascendancy, and its first act, seemingly, was to banish Apollonides, the leader of the nationalistic faction[20] (Demosthenes, 1.13; 9.56).

By 349 Philip decided that the time had come to end the ambiguities of the policies of the Chalcidian League. He demanded of the Olynthians that they surrender his two half-brothers who had fled from Macedonia either when Philip became ruler in 359 or later. It is quite possible that these two men were urging the Olynthians to place one of them on the Macedonian throne, as the Olynthians had formerly driven out Philip's father, Amyntas III, and established the pretender Argaeus. The Olynthians, reacting naturally to a command from a foreigner, rejected the demands although it seemed certain that this refusal would lead to war. Presumably the "nationalists" had acquired control again in the Chalcidian League. These anti-Macedonians sent envoys to Athens in the summer to beseech an alliance, which the Athenians, influenced in part by the eloquence of Demosthenes in his three Olynthiac orations, finally granted. A small force under Chares which had been operating in the north was sent to Chalcidice, but probably because of the usual lack of funds it seems to have accomplished nothing. In the meantime Philip had marched into the peninsula where various towns submitted to him, some voluntarily, others through fear.[21]

Philip's progress in Chalcidice in 349 was limited, presumably because he was sounding out the mood of the cities in the league and also because he had to make a hurried trip to Thessaly. In the first two Olynthiac orations Demosthenes speaks of the Thessalians' anger that Philip was holding Pagasae, planning to build fortifications in Magnesia, and using their market and harbor dues for his own purposes. He urges the Athenians to send envoys to exacerbate this discontent. In the third oration, however, like the first two delivered in the second half of the year 349, not a word is said about Thessaly. The logical inference is that by that time Philip had succeeded in allaying the disturbances. The chief grievance had been that Philip, as archon, was using the revenues not for the benefit of the Thessalians but for his campaigns in Thrace and Chalcidice, activities which were of no concern to the league. Philip pacified the Thessalians, although he did not relinquish control of Pagasae which was too valuable to him as a naval base and a commercial port. He must have assured them that he would soon return to the Sacred War, for what the Thessalians obviously wanted was that the Phocians be expelled from Delphi so that they could regain their dominance over the Amphictiony which had been interrupted by the Phocian occupation of the holy site.[22]

In 348, in addition to the confusion in Chalcidice, trouble broke out in Euboea. Plutarch in his life of Phocion (12–14.1) states that a leading citizen (and tyrant) of Eretria and a friend of Athens, also named Plutarch, urged the Athenians to send him help against the Macedonian troops who were infiltrating into Euboea. The Athenians, who were worried about the loyalty of the Euboean cities which they had recovered only in 357, sent over their leading general Phocion in February with a small force. A common interpretation of these events has been that Philip, in retaliation for the Athenian assistance sent to Olynthus in the preceding fall, was trying to deflect Athenian attention by stirring up trouble in the important island so adjacent to Attica. It is true that Aeschines (3.86–87), when referring to this period in his denunciation of Demosthenes in 330, says, according to the manuscript, that two brothers from Chalcis summoned forces from Philip and brought over Phocian mercenaries. Troops from Philip and troops from Phocis, however, are a strange combination since Philip had been, and would be again, fighting against the "sacrilegious" Phocians. Altering a manuscript reading is a perilous practice, but it does seem suggestive that the scholiast to this passage of Aeschines makes no reference to Philip but does mention Phalaecus, the leader of the Phocians. The speeches of Demosthenes are significant in trying to interpret the current situation in Euboea. In the three Olynthiac orations, delivered in the latter half of 349, he denounces Philip vehemently but makes no reference to his intrigues on the island, and in the speech *On the Peace* (5) spoken in 346 he claims that he alone argued against sending Athenian forces to Euboea. It is hard to believe that the violent opponent of Philip would have dared or wanted to try to prevent dispatching military aid to Euboea if it were generally known that Macedonian forces were on the island. These arguments do not deny that Philip may have been in correspondence with certain Euboeans hostile to Athens, but they suggest that the picture of Macedonian forces on the scene given by Plutarch and others may be a reflection of later activity of Philip.[23]

The Athenian campaign in Euboea cannot be satisfactorily described, for the evidence is too scanty. Phocion, faced by the revolt of Chalcis and probably other cities and tricked by the duplicity of Plutarch of Eretria, had great difficulty in saving his army. When he returned to Athens late in the spring, the garrison he had left behind fell into the hands of the enemy. To ransom these troops Athens had to pay a reported sum of 50 talents, a serious blow to its limited resources. By the peace which was made in June or July much of Euboea, except for Carystus at the southern tip, was lost to the Athenian League.

Despite the difficulties in Euboea, Athens responded to a second appeal from the Chalcidians by sending Charidemus to them in the spring with the contingent he had been commanding in the Hellespont. This expedition proved ineffectual. Meanwhile Philip became more active. He took the harbor town of Olynthus, defeated the Olynthians in two battles, and then succeeded in cutting off and capturing 500 of their best cavalry. Demosthenes believed and frequently charged that the debacle with the cavalry was the result of the treason of the two Olynthian commanders, Lasthenes and Euthycrates. Philip now began the siege of Olynthus, which appealed a third time to Athens for help, this time requesting not mercenaries but Athenians. Chares was sent out again, but hampered by the Etesian winds, he arrived in Chalcidice only after Olynthus had had to surrender late in the summer of 348.

In view of Olynthus' violation of the treaty with Macedonia it is not surprising that Philip decided to make an example of the city, although his treatment was not as ruthless as the one that Athens had inflicted on Sestos a few years before. Olynthus was leveled to the ground and the population, although presumably not the pro-Macedonian faction, was enslaved (Diodorus, 16.53); many men were carried off to forced labor on the king's estates or were settled in colonies in the remoter parts of Macedonian territory. Philip's two half-brothers, who had remained at Olynthus to the end, were executed (Justin, 8.3.10). The territory of Olynthus was distributed among Macedonian nobles. The account of the fate of the Chalcidian League that is usually remembered is the one which Demosthenes in 341 presented in the *Third Philippic* (26), where, in enumerating the evils which Philip had brought upon the Greek world, he says, "I pass over Olynthus and Methone and Apollonia and the two and thirty cities in or near Thrace, all of which Philip has destroyed so ruthlessly that a traveller would find it hard to say whether they had ever been inhabited." This picture of the fate of the cities in the Chalcidian League does not lack rhetorical exaggeration. Besides Olynthus, Philip undoubtedly destroyed some settlements in the campaigns of 349 and 348, but the great majority were incorporated into the Macedonian state. It is not known whether they were subjected to certain penalties or forced to accept various Macedonians as inhabitants, but whatever their actual status, it was not the grim one which Demosthenes presents.

Even before the fall of Olynthus some Athenians were thinking of the advisability of coming to terms with Philip, an idea which was encouraged by Euboean peace ambassadors, probably in June 348, who reported that Philip was anxious to reach an understanding with Athens. Philocrates thereupon carried a motion through the assembly that it be possible for Philip to send envoys to Athens to discuss peace (Aeschines, 2.12–13). Subsequently this motion was declared unconstitutional and a fine of 100 talents was proposed for Philocrates. This indictment can best be explained by the consternation which gripped the Athenians when the news of the fall of Olynthus reached them in August or September. Athens' efforts to assist Olynthus had only been desultory, but the realization that Philip now controlled the whole Chalcidic peninsula was a sobering and frightening thought. Eubulus, whose policy had been to deter Athens from unnecessary wars, believed that now the danger was sufficient to justify dispatching ambassadors to the Greek states urging them to send envoys to Athens to discuss the problem of a common war against Philip. Of these embassies, which traveled in the winter of 348/7, the only one on which specific information is preserved was Aeschines' mission to Megalopolis (Demosthenes, 19.10; 303–304), where he addressed the Ten Thousand. In view of Athens' alliance with Sparta and its refusal in 353 to aid Megalopolis when in distress, it is not strange that Aeschines had no success in recruiting the Megalopolitans or other Peloponnesians to a cause which seemed to them an entirely

Athenian problem, linked probably with the passion to recover Amphipolis. By the end of the summer of 347 it had become clear that the search for allies was a failure.

Meanwhile the Sacred War had degenerated into a series of destructive raids carried out by the Phocians and Boeotians. Since the treasures of Delphi were beginning to fail, a faction of the Phocians, believing that Phalaecus was embezzling the money for his own use, deposed him, probably in the early summer of 347, and appointed three other generals. These new generals, when they learned that the Boeotians, frustrated by their lack of success in the war, were appealing to Philip for assistance, feared that Macedonians and Thessalians might soon arrive; they sent envoys to Athens early in the winter, asking for help and offering to turn over to the Athenians the fortresses controlling Thermopylae. This proposal caused much excitement in Athens, for it seemed to provide the means to prevent Philip from marching into central and southern Greece. The assembly passed a decree that the Phocians should surrender these places to the general Proxenos and that the Athenians should man fifty triremes and levy all citizens up to the age of forty (Aeschines, 2.133). The Athenians were still anxious for a settlement with Philip, but one that would leave them in as strong a position as possible. Disappointed by the lack of response to Eubulus' appeal for allies in a joint war against Philip, they, as scattered and confused evidence reveals, had been campaigning in Thrace in the summer together with the shifty Cersobleptes to acquire some strong places in the Propontid region and on the Aegean coast. The purpose of these forts, which apparently were garrisoned by Cersobleptes, was obviously to strengthen Athenian control of the Chersonese and to provide a defense against any Macedonian attempts to advance eastward. The Phocian proposal to surrender Thermopylae to the Athenians seemed like a windfall, and the Athenians promptly dispatched new envoys throughout Greece urging the Greeks to send ambassadors to Athens to discuss whether a joint war or a common peace would be the better policy in relations with Philip (Aeschines, 2.57–60).

This optimism was short-lived, for by the time Proxenos arrived in the area of Thermopylae some internal and little understood trouble among the Phocians had enabled Phalaecus and his mercenaries to establish themselves in power again. Phalaecus had no intention of surrendering the key position to the Athenians, and he ordered Proxenos and the Spartan king Archidamus, who had also arrived, to depart. He then arrested the Phocian ambassadors who had made the proposals to Athens and, to emphasize his repudiation of any transactions with the Athenians, he refused to accept the sacred truce of the Mysteries which

Athenian heralds were announcing. The mention of the sacred truce is the only specific evidence for dating these events. Aeschines (2.133–134) provides the information that, when the Athenians were debating the delayed report of a traveling actor who announced that Philip was anxious for both peace and alliance with Athens, a letter arrived from Proxenos with word that the Phocians had rejected the sacred truce. Since it is known that the Athenians first sent an embassy to Philip to discuss the question of peace early in March 346, scholars have argued convincingly that the Mysteries mentioned were the Lesser Mysteries, for which the sacred truce ran from January into March.[24]

This assembly, in which the Athenians heard the report of Philip's friendship for them and of his desire for peace and alliance and then the chilling news that their hopes to occupy Thermopylae had been shattered, must have been an emotional scene. The Athenians, ignoring the fact that only recently they had sent out envoys to query the Greeks on the issue of a joint war against Philip or of a common peace, felt in their excitement that negotiations with Philip should not be delayed. When Philocrates, who through the efforts of Demosthenes had been acquitted of the indictment brought against him in 348 for advocating consultation with Philip, again proposed that a commission be sent to Macedonia to explore the possible terms of peace, the assembly promptly ratified the motion and elected ten ambassadors including Philocrates, his nominee, Demosthenes, and Aeschines, an orator who was becoming prominent as an adherent of Eubulus.

The negotiations leading to this peace and the peace itself—the Peace of Philocrates—are the core of the political history of this period. It is essential to keep constantly in mind the nature of the available sources. Since the narrative account of Diodorus disregards the basic issues and the attendant intrigues, the Attic Orators, and particularly Demosthenes and Aeschines, provide most of the relevant information. "Misinformation" or "propaganda" might be more appropriate words, for, since the two orators became bitter enemies in these tense years, their speeches are almost as much devoted to misrepresenting the actions and motives of one another as they are to a presentation of the facts. The passage of time fostered these tendencies. The two main debates were held in 343 and 330 respectively, and after that lapse of years the orators, realizing that their audience would have forgotten or become confused about various particulars, could take liberties with motives and chronological niceties in order to appeal to the current attitudes and prejudices of their listeners. Since the period ended with the victory of Philip over the Athenians and the Greeks, it is only natural that Demosthenes, the passionate opponent of Macedonia and the ardent defender of the glories of Athens as they had been in the fifth century, has usually been viewed with admiration, if not adulation, from ancient times to the present. Heroic he certainly was in his determination, energy, and courage, but the wisdom and morality of some of his policies so vehemently advocated should be examined impartially, if that characteristic is possible in a situation heavily charged with emotion. In fact, the relations between the Greek world and Macedonia, which assumed an entirely different character with Philip's steady increase in power and stature and continued in this vein for generations thereafter, present a situation where objective judgment on the part of the historian or reader is almost impossible to attain. Swept along by the fiery patriotism and magnificent rhetoric of Demosthenes, one often accepts too uncritically his denunciation that Philip was a crude barbarian lusting for power and that any Greek who did not share this conviction was beneath contempt.

The rapid rise of Philip to prominence, however, was causing many reasonable men to wonder if, rather than letting him grow stronger by exploiting Greek mutual animosities, it would not be more intelligent to try to reach some sort of agreement with him. In modern parlance, they were thinking in terms of coexistence. They may have been unrealistic in not realizing that coexistence with a more powerful state leads almost by a "law of nature" to dominance by that state, but they believed that voluntary coexistence was preferable to more endless fighting, suffering, sordid suspicions, and ultimate military defeat. In the eyes of Demosthenes such men, and Aeschines in particular, were scoundrels and traitors; but fanatical eloquence can be a deceptive guide.

The ten Athenian envoys proceeded to Pella, where Philip gave them a cordial reception. He made it clear that he was interested in a peace and alliance based on the understanding that each party would recognize the other's rights to territory controlled at the time when the agreement should be signed; he also promised not to attack the Chersonese during the peace negotiations. The ambassadors returned to Athens towards the end of March, where they were well received by the council and the assembly. Two meetings of the assembly were scheduled for the middle of April so that the people could reach a decision on these proposals after the arrival of the Macedonian envoys in the city.

In the interim the *synedrion* of the allies of the Athenian League met and voted the following decree, which is quoted by Aeschines (2.60): "Wheareas the people of the Athenians are deliberating with regard to peace with Philip, and whereas the ambassadors have not yet returned whom the people sent out into Hellas summoning the cities in behalf of the freedom of the Hellenes, be it decreed by the allies that as soon as the ambassadors return and make their report to the Athenians and their allies, the *prytaneis* shall call two meetings of the assembly of the people according to law, and that in these meetings the Athenians shall deliberate on the question of peace; and whatever the people shall decide, be it voted that this decision stand as the common vote of the allies." To this decree the following resolution was added: "that any Greek state that wished should be permitted within the space of three months to have its name inscribed with the Athenians on the same stone, and to share the oaths and agreements" (Aeschines, 3.70).

If Aeschines is not misquoting the decree, which is possible but unlikely, one gains the impression that the allies of the Athenian League were thinking in terms of a Common (*koinē*) Peace. If the notion of Common Peace was in the air, then it is obviously strange that so soon after the return of the ten ambassadors from Macedonia two meetings of the assembly to discuss the peace questions were proposed by Demosthenes for consecutive days, the eighteenth and nineteenth of Elaphebolion (Aeschines, 2.61). Because of the confused and misleading statements in the speeches of Aeschines and Demosthenes, it is probably impossible to obtain a satisfactory picture of the political manoeuvring in these years; but the evidence seems to suggest that some Athenians, at least, and the Athenian allies were thinking in terms of a peace to embrace all Greeks and not just the Athenian allies, as some scholars argue. Demosthenes, however, convinced that Athens needed a truce at once in which to prepare itself for subsequent war with Philip, was interested only in a bilateral peace with Macedonia, and feared that prolonged negotiations for a Common Peace might jeopardize the immediate necessity of reaching an agreement with Philip. Certainly limiting the debate on peace to two consecutive days in mid-April restricted the discussion to the matter of a bilateral understanding and eliminated the possibility of achieving a Common Peace.

At the first meeting of the Athenian assembly Philocrates, aware of Philip's terms, proposed that a peace and alliance should be made with Philip and that the Phocians should be excluded from the negotiations. Aeschines (3.71) opposed this proposal and urged the acceptance of the resolution of the council of the Athenian allies that any Greek state should be allowed to sign the peace within three months. Demosthenes (19.15) in his denunciation of Aeschines in 343 also says that he supported the resolution of the allies. Since Demosthenes was responsible for the two consecutive meetings of the assembly, and thereby the chance to secure a swift acceptance of the peace with Philip, it is hard to believe that he supported the three months' period of grace in which other Greeks could sign the document. When he spoke three years later in 343, however, it was important for him to try to create the impression that in his desire to aid the Phocians he had supported the notion of a Common Peace. The first meeting of the assembly, therefore, probably created the impression that a Common Peace would be made. In the ensuing night, presumably, the Macedonian envoys, Antipater and Parmenio, explained, what Philocrates (and surely Aeschines and Demosthenes also) apparently had already known, that Philip would not accept a peace which included the Phocians. Philip obviously could not risk outraging his allies, the Thessalians and the Boeotians, whose aim was to crush the Phocians. At the second meeting of the assembly Philocrates' motion was introduced again, but this time, instead of the specific exclusion of the Phocians, it apparently stated that Athens and its allies should make peace and alliance with Philip and his allies. It seems that the people started to protest, but they were silenced by Eubulus' statement that the only alternative was war, payment of a capital tax (eisphora), and assignment of the Theoric Fund to military purposes. Accordingly, the measure was passed (Demosthenes, 19.290–291).[25]

A few days later the Athenians and the representatives of the allies in the council of the league took the oath to this agreement in the presence of the Macedonian envoys. The Athenian people as a whole may have been vague as to just what the term "their allies" signified, but the politicians such as Demosthenes, Aeschines, Philocrates, and Eubulus knew that it embraced only the allies in the Athenian League and not allies such as the Phocians. They felt, however, that peace was essential and hence bowed to the will of Philip. A representative of Cersobleptes, whose relationship to both Athens and Philip was ambiguous, was rejected when he tried to sign Cersobleptes' name to the oath. Since this treaty was based on the idea of a territorial status quo, the Athenians by signing it acquiesced in Philip's control of Potidaea, Amphipolis, Pydna, and Methone.

The consummation of the treaty required the signature of Philip and his allies. The same ten envoys were instructed to obtain the oaths, but when there was some delay in their departure Demosthenes procured a decree of the Boulē, of which he was a member, stating that the envoys should proceed to the Athenian ships under Proxenos, now stationed just north of Euboea, and sail in them to wherever Philip was. Despite Demosthenes' haste, however, the ambassadors were slow in carrying out their assignment and, instead of searching for Philip, went straight to Pella. Demosthenes, who later interpreted the delay as treasonable, claimed that the embassy took twenty-three days to go from Athens to Pella and that they waited there for twenty-seven days before Philip returned to his capital. He maintained that, if they had obeyed their instructions promptly, they could have prevented Philip from making certain conquests in Thrace. The procrastination of the embassy may be hard to explain, but when one remembers that Philip was fighting against Cersobleptes, who had been faithless to him, and against fortresses garrisoned by the Thracian king, the idea that Athenian envoys could have stopped Philip from attending to his own business smacks of rhetoric rather than of truth.

The scene at Pella testified vividly to the impression, a mixture of fear and hope, which Philip had made on the Greek world. Word had spread abroad that Philip and Athens, and their respective allies, were about to conclude a bilateral peace and alliance. To many Greeks this must have been an alarming prospect. Just as in recent years, when Sparta and later Thebes sent ambassadors to the Persian king in the hope of acquiring his assistance in helping them settle affairs in Greece, envoys from other Greek states promptly arrived, so now, in addition to the Athenians, delegates from the Thebans, Thessalians, Spartans, Phocians, Euboeans, and probably others, each with their special hopes and worries, came to Pella to discuss their problems with the Macedonian king. The main duty of the Athenian ambassadors was to obtain the signatures of Philip and his allies to the bilateral peace, but they had also received vaguely expressed instructions from the assembly to arrange matters as well as they could for the interests of Athens. Aeschines, apparently representing the thinking of all the Athenian envoys except Demosthenes, and acting in conformity with the general Athenian hatred of Thebes and the desire to help their difficult allies, the Phocians, attempted to influence Philip towards a moderate policy to the Phocians, by which the leaders and not the people as a whole should be punished for the sacrilege through the medium of the Amphictionic Council. He also emphasized how Thebes had violated the principles of the Amphictiony by its destruction of various Boeotian cities. These suggestions, whose aim was to assist the Phocians, allies of Athens, and to weaken the ties between Philip and the Thebans, current Athenian enemies, seemed logical to those Athenians who were seeking a solution to the chaos of Greek affairs by achieving a genuine bilateral peace with Philip.

Demosthenes, however, convinced of the aggressive intentions of Philip against the Greeks in general and Athens in particular, was not thinking of an effective peace, which in his view would play into Philip's hands, but only of an armistice which would give Athens time to prepare itself militarily and to acquire more allies. Since he felt that Philip was merely waiting for the proper opportunity to launch a full-scale attack on Greece, it was all-important to improve relations between Athens and

Thebes, for those two states, if united in purpose, offered the only chance to thwart Macedonian ambitions. His ideas, farseeing if he was correct in his analysis of Philip's plans, had to be expressed very carefully, for they jeopardized the fate of the Phocians, Athenian allies, and also ran counter to the deep-seated hatred of Athens for Thebes.

Philip also had to employ great ingenuity in dealing with the conflicting purposes of the Athenian and other ambassadors at Pella. If, as Demosthenes believed, his intentions were to dominate the Greek world, it was important for him to prevent a coalition of Thebes and Athens. The Thebans and Thessalians were insistent that he end the Sacred War by destroying the Phocians, and he could not risk frustrating his allies. He also genuinely wanted peace and alliance with the Athenians, the majority of whom were well disposed towards the Phocians. One would like to have a recording of his conversations with the various embassies. In view of the suspicions and antagonisms that the Greeks harbored for one another and the explosive nature of their international life, Philip must have chosen his words with great discretion, but he did hint to the Athenians, and especially to Aeschines, that he held no serious hostility against the Phocians but was unhappy about the greed and aggressiveness of the Thebans.

Philip did not sign the peace and alliance with Athens and its allies until he had marched south with his army to Pherae. Demosthenes later used this fact as evidence of the duplicity of Philip and of the treason of Aeschines and Philocrates, but the procedure seems less strange if one remembers that it was known that Philip was allied to the Thessalians and Thebans and obligated to aid them in the Sacred-Amphictionic War against the Phocians. At Pherae he and his allies, including the city of Cardia at the continental end of the Chersonese just captured from Cersobleptes (Demosthenes, 5.25), took their oaths to the treaty. As Philip had insisted from the beginning, both the Phocians and Cersobleptes were excluded from the peace. The Athenian envoys then returned home, arriving in the city on Skirophorion 13 (about 6 July), while Philip in the meantime proceeded towards Thermopylae. The ambassadors reported immediately to the council, where Demosthenes excoriated his colleagues for their conduct on the embassy. Three days later the envoys gave their report to the assembly. Aeschines apparently was the chief speaker. He tried to persuade the people not to be worried over the Macedonian approach to Thermopylae, stating, as he probably believed, that Philip was well disposed to his new allies, the Athenians, and that the Sacred War would be settled in a way more detrimental to the Thebans than to the Phocians. Despite Demosthenes' attempted protests, the assembly was influenced by the language of Aeschines and his associates and passed a decree, proposed by Philocrates, thanking Philip for his cooperation, extending the peace and alliance to his descendants, and bidding the Phocians, under threat of Athenian military action, to surrender Delphi to the Amphictions (Demosthenes, 19.48–49).

About this time Philip sent two letters to the Athenians asking them, as his allies, to send troops to his army at Thermopylae so that they, as an Amphictionic state, could join in deciding the various problems facing the Amphictions. This invitation was rejected by the assembly on the advice of Demosthenes, who warned the people that Philip might seize some of the Athenians as hostages (Aeschines, 2.137–139). Demosthenes' real reason for opposition was not this rather melodramatic effort to arouse fear and suspicion, but his conviction that any Athenian attempt to encourage Philip towards leniency in the treatment of the Phocians would antagonize the Thebans and thus jeopardize the possibility of a future Athenian-Theban alliance.

Athenian envoys were dispatched to bear to Philip the wording of Philocrates' decree passed a few days before. They had only reached Chalcis in Euboea in their journey when they received word that the Phocian general, Phalaecus, and his mercenaries had surrendered themselves and Thermopylae to Philip. Since Phalaecus and his 8,000 mercenaries were allowed to retire unharmed to the Peloponnesus, it is clear that he, who had been quarreling continually with various Phocian leaders, had come to a previous agreement with Philip (Diodorus, 16.59). Thus by one act the Sacred War was ended, and the Phocians, because of Demosthenes' advice to the Athenians not to send a contingent to Philip at Thermopylae, were left to the mercy of the Macedonian king and those Amphiction allies who were with him, primarily the Thessalians and Thebans. The news of the fall of Phocis was received with great consternation at Athens, for the people had been led to believe at the assembly of 16 Skirophorion through the reports of Aeschines and Philocrates that their allies, the Phocians, stood in no serious danger. The fear now spread that Philip might march on Attica, and in response to this unrealistic rumor, since peace and alliance had just been established between the two parties, a decree was passed that women, children, and movable property should be brought within the walls of Athens and the Piraeus, and that all necessary steps for defense should be taken. The envoys who had returned from Chalcis were instructed to proceed to Philip and to negotiate as best they could concerning the unexpected situation. Neither Demosthenes nor Aeschines had participated in the previous embassy, Demosthenes having refused and Aeschines fearing what he might attempt if left unwatched, but on this occasion Aeschines undertook the task. Subsequently Demosthenes derided him for associating with Philip at a time of Athenian humiliation, but the truth was, as Phocian exiles later testified, that Aeschines used his influence to alleviate the fate of the Phocians (Aeschines, 2.142–143).

Since the Sacred War had been an Amphictionic one, Philip delegated the formulation of peace terms to the Amphictionic Council. An early proposal of one of the Amphictionic tribes, the Oetaeans, that all adult Phocian men should be hurled off a cliff was rejected (Aeschines, 2.142), but since the council was dominated by the Thebans and the Thessalians, who had been excluded from membership since 356, it was natural that the penalty inflicted on the Phocians was severe. They were expelled from the Amphictiony, and their two votes in the council were assigned to Philip and his descendants. Diodorus (16.60) records the peace terms in some detail: "All the cities of the Phocians were to be razed and the people moved to villages, no one of which should have more than fifty houses, and the villages were to be not less than 600 feet distance from one another; the Phocians were to possess their territory and to pay each year to the god a tribute of sixty talents until they should have paid back the sums entered in the registers at the time of the pillaging of the sanctuary . . . the Amphictions and Philip were to hurl the arms of the Phocians and of their mercenaries down the crags and burn what remained of them and to sell the horses." The Amphictions also voted that Philip should preside over the Pythian Games which were to be held in the fall of that year.

Demosthenes in his prosecution of Aeschines in 343 (19.64–66; 80–82) paints a pathetic picture of the fate of the Phocians and attributes the disaster to his fellow ambassadors in the peace negotiations, Aeschines and Philocrates. The accusation is particularly revolting when one remembers that Demosthenes himself, by his efforts, however statesmanlike in the long range, to lay the grounds for a future Athenian-Theban alliance, was primarily responsible for the abandonment of the Phocians to the vengeance of the Thebans and the Thessalians. Considering that the Phocians were the defeated party in a vicious Sacred War and that they exhausted Apollo's treasures at Delphi, one can argue that, because of the influence of Philip and Aeschines, their punishment, by Greek standards, was surprisingly mild. Subsequently Philip lightened their burden in the payment of amends. The vengeance which Thebes exacted on Coronea and Orchomenus, two Boeotian cities which had assisted the Phocians in the Sacred War, presents a glaring contrast, for these two communities were totally destroyed and their inhabitants sold into slavery (Demosthenes, 5.22; 6.13; 19.112, 141, 325).

The bilateral Peace of Philocrates was a triumph for Philip and a humiliation for Athens. Philip now had a foothold south of Thermopylae, membership in the purely Greek Amphictionic Council, the prestige of having defended Apollo by bringing the Sacred War to a close, and strengthened relations with the Thebans and Thessalians, who through his efforts had regained their former dominance in the Amphictiony. The Athenians, on the other hand, although they retained control of the Chersonese, had lost the diplomatic battle to Philip and to Thebes and realized that in the eyes of the world they looked, as they were, like betrayers of their allies, the Phocians. The peace immediately became intensely unpopular, which explains why envoys like Demosthenes and Aeschines tried hard to exonerate themselves of any responsibility for the policies which had turned out so badly. The first reaction of the Athenians was to reject Philip's appointment to the Amphictionic Council and to refuse to send their usual delegates to the Pythian Games, since they now were to be celebrated under the aegis of Philip (Demosthenes, 19.128). When a conciliatory letter from Philip, whose contents are garbled in the Demosthenic text (18.39–40) was disregarded by the Athenians, the Amphictions and Philip subsequently sent envoys to protest the attitude of the Athenians (Demosthenes, 19.111).

At this point Demosthenes, knowing in what an isolated position Athens stood, hated by the dominant Amphictionic people, the Thessalians and Thebans, and mistrusted by the Peloponnesians because of its alliance with Sparta, realized that too much recalcitrance on the part of Athens might precipitate an attack on it from many states joining under the leadership of Philip. In the autumn of 346, in his speech *On the Peace*, delivered at the meeting of the assembly convened to discuss the protests of the Amphictionic embassy, he succeeded in persuading the refractory people to accept temporarily the unpleasant realities, and "concerning the shadow in Delphi" not to risk having an Amphictionic war launched against them. There was a sneer in the reference to the "shadow in Delphi," the sneer of a leader in Greece's most civilized state directed against the ancient institution of the Amphictiony which, to Athenian consternation, had been revivified by Philip's skillful building on the foundations laid by Pelopidas and Epaminondas. That, despite the sneer, he appreciated the inherent danger emerged vividly in his prosecution of Aeschines three years later when, referring to Philip's success in the Sacred War, he said (19.64), "Nothing more awful or more momentous has befallen in Greece within living memory, nor, as I believe, in all the history of the past" than the domination of one man in Greece. The context makes it clear that the domination was rooted in the Delphic Amphictiony of which Philip, a single individual, was now a member possessed of two votes and able to exert almost complete control through his relations with the Thessalians and Thebans.

It is hard to grasp satisfactorily the political complexities of the year 346, because there were two separate peaces, the bilateral Peace of Philocrates consummated at Pherae, and the immediately following Amphictionic Peace negotiated at Delphi which terminated the ten-year Sacred War. Both ancient and modern writers frequently confuse the two peaces, which is hardly surprising in view of the fact that they were almost simultaneous and that Philip was a party to both, as was Athens to a certain degree through its association with the Phocians. Diodorus (16.60.3) ends his account of the terms of the Amphictionic Peace with the sentence, "In similar tenor the Amphictions laid down regulations for the custody of the oracle and all the other matters pertaining to due respect for the gods and common (koinē) peace and concord for the Hellenes." Because of his words "common peace," some scholars insist that the Amphictionic Peace was a common one, while others argue that Diodorus was merely using general language in following his sources, and that the peace was Amphictionic, not common.

Despite the constant outbreaks of war, many Greeks were clearly dreaming of a widespread peace, a peace which would have adequate sanctions to protect the autonomy of all states, great and small. Among these people, dismayed by the political, social, and economic havoc produced by the endless wars, the longing for general peace could have caused the notion of Common Peace, however vaguely the concept was understood, to become almost a shibboleth. The Athenians in the winter of 348/7 had attempted to arouse the Greeks to participation in a general war against Philip, but when their efforts were fruitless, they tried in the following winter to interest the Greeks in the idea of a Common Peace. Whatever prospects of success this proposal might have had were frustrated by the hurried consummation of the bilateral Peace of Philocrates. This was followed immediately by the Amphictionic Peace. Although this agreement was obviously to the advantage of Philip, the Thessalians, and the Thebans, the very fact that the Amphictiony, embracing twelve tribes, had the sanction to declare a sacred war against any member contravening the peace made an Amphictionic Peace strikingly similar in nature to the imperfectly understood concept of a Common Peace. Demosthenes, although sneering at the "shadow in Delphi," showed by his earnestness in persuading the Athenians to acquiesce in the demands of the Amphictions that he realized the potential or actual danger for an Amphictionic state like Athens to defy the will of the Amphictiony. The confused situation in Greece and the difficulty for both ancients and moderns to define satisfactorily the nature of a Common Peace suggest that there may be some sort of semantic difficulty, and that in the eyes of many Greeks, at least, an Amphictionic Peace may have signified a Common Peace.

During the peace negotiations between Athens and Philip, but before the collapse of the Phocians in July 346, the Athenian orator Isocrates, now ninety years old, published an open letter to Philip. Thirty-four years before in the *Panegyricus* Isocrates had urged that the Athenians (and Spartans) unite the Greeks in a crusade against their ancestral enemies, the Persians, thereby repudiating the shameful King's Peace and relieving the evil social, economic, and political conditions in Greece. The chaos and follies which had characterized Greek history throughout the intervening years, in which Spartan, Athenian, and Theban attempts at hegemony had failed miserably and Argos had been in the throes of social revolution (Diodorus, 15.58), had convinced Isocrates that no Greek state could unite the Greeks and prevent them from destroying themselves. He turned, therefore, to Philip who, as a descendant of Heracles, the mythical benefactor of the Greeks, was in the unique position to consider all Hellas his fatherland. He urged him to lead the Greeks in a campaign against Persia, for only such a crusade could unite the Greeks in a common cause, liberate their Ionian kinsmen, and save the homeland from the violence and depredations of the rootless mercenaries by enabling them to settle as colonists in Asia Minor. Isocrates was realistic in his analysis of the evil conditions in Greece, but he was assigning Philip the quixotic role of undertaking the expedition for the benefit of the Greeks. Philip may not have had the sinister designs on Greece which Demosthenes imagined, but as a national king his first concern was the welfare of Macedonia. It is impossible to know just when Philip began to think of a hegemony over the Greek world and an expedition against Persia, but this expression of confidence from the old orator must have been a welcome relief from the constant denunciations of fervid patriots like Demosthenes.

THE Amphictionic Peace, closely related to the immediately preceding Peace of Philocrates, ended the Sacred War which had kept the Greek world in turmoil for a decade. The violent opposition of the Athenians to the terms of the bilateral Peace of Philocrates, however, made the peace agreement precarious from the very beginning. These two peaces were so closely related that in discussing and reporting the historical events of the period it is often necessary to blend the two as a unit. The termination of the Sacred War, in which Athens had been in the awkward position of being in alliance with the Phocians who, whatever their justification in seizing Delphi in 355, by 346 were branded as temple robbers, confronted the Athenians with the sickening realization that they had abandoned their allies, the Phocians, that the hated Thebans had fared well, and that the enigmatic and frightening Philip had gained greatly in power and stature. When one reflects on these years, one is baffled by the illogical aspirations of the Athenians. By the beginning of 346 they were convinced that peace with Philip was a necessity, but since he was obligated to the Thessalians and Thebans to end the Sacred War to their satisfaction, it was obvious that, unless he betrayed his allies, the Phocians had to be expelled from Delphi and punished for their sacrilege. Philocrates and Aeschines may have sincerely believed that, because of his desire to win favor with Athens and because of his suspicion of Thebes, Philip would treat the Phocians as leniently as possible, but whatever Philip's ultimate aims might have been, it is hard to understand how Demosthenes, a firm advocate of the necessity of at least a temporary peace, could have believed that a victorious Philip would have accepted an agreement detrimental to his own interests.

In the months following the surrender of the Phocians, as Philip's success and Athenian humiliation became more and more apparent, the Athenian envoys found their position extremely difficult. In the autumn of 346, Demosthenes, impressed by the dangerous political situation in Greece, advised the assembly to accept Philip's status in the Amphictiony, but in his speech he disassociated himself as much as possible from any responsibility for the hateful turn of events. When Aeschines about this time appeared before the board of auditors (*logistai*) to give an account of his role as ambassador, Demosthenes and his friend Timarchus launched an attack on him. Whether Demosthenes had already worked out in detail his theory of Aeschines' guilt is uncertain, for the extant accusation is dated three years later, but it was clear to him that the more the responsibility for the unpopular peace could be attributed to Aeschines and Philocrates, the more innocuous his own role would appear. Aeschines realized the danger of standing trial on charges of inefficiency and treason at a time when the people, frustrated by the outcome of events, were looking for a scapegoat. To delay the proceedings, therefore, he struck at Timarchus who, although a political figure for some years, had led a youth notorious for its immorality. On the charge that a man who had prostituted himself was debarred by law from taking any part in political life, Aeschines won his suit early in 345, with the result that Timarchus was disfranchised. The case was sufficiently notorious to deter Demosthenes from continuing his attack on Aeschines until the year 343.

The years following the peace of 346 are difficult to assess satisfactorily because of the partiality of the evidence. With rare exceptions Demosthenes is the chief source, and he immediately took the line that the peace was a fraud, achieved by the duplicity of Philip and the venality and treason of the Athenian ambassadors. One would like to know the attitude of the seven other envoys as distinct from Demosthenes, Aeschines, and Philocrates. Demosthenes had believed in the need for peace, although he later claimed that the need was really Philip's, but when the outcome turned out to be advantageous for the opponents of Athens—a result that was logical in view of the situation—he became even more convinced that Philip's aim was the conquest or domination of Greece and the ruin of Athens in particular. In the uneasy period of peace, therefore, Demosthenes believed that he had a holy mission to arouse the Athenians to their danger, to increase their military strength, to frustrate Philip at every turn, and to persuade as many other Greeks as possible to join Athens in what he considered the inevitable confrontation with Macedonia. Because of his inexhaustible energy and the brilliance of his oratory, Demosthenes was a formidable figure. Patriotism, especially when degenerating into chauvinism, has a powerful effect on men's emotions. Demosthenes finally did win over many Greeks, and his impassioned arguments have largely colored the interpretation of this period of history to the present day. The continuation of the Peace of Philocrates rapidly became an impossibility, for an agreement cannot long endure when one party is constantly accused of the most flagrant dishonesty, treachery, and arrogance. Whether a settlement on the basis of coexistence, such as Philocrates, Aeschines, and Isocrates apparently wished, was a possibility must be left an unanswered question, for there is no accurate way to know Philip's intentions. The notion, however, that he early formulated the dream of conquering or dominating Greece is primarily based on the fulminations—or prophecies—of Demosthenes. It is equally clear that, whatever Philip's original aspirations may have been, Demosthenes' policies contributed substantially to Philip's ultimate achievement of exactly what the Athenian orator most dreaded.

After presiding over the Pythian Games in the fall of 346 Philip returned to Macedonia. For several years he devoted most of his efforts to regulating affairs in his own kingdom and in neighboring areas. In Macedonia, with the aim of spreading civilizing influences and strengthening borders against barbarian incursions, he established various colonies or settlements on troublesome frontiers, transferring to these new foundations both Macedonians and some of the Greeks from the cities in Chalcidice and Thrace which he had conquered. At some point in 345 a campaign against the Illyrians, in which Philip was severely wounded, solidified the western frontier of Macedonia. Then early in 344 he marched into Thessaly, where the cities, always struggling with one another for predominance, were jeopardizing Philip's influence. Since Thessaly was important to Philip for its cavalry and revenues, for its wide representation in the Amphictionic Council, and as the route to central Greece, he was determined to find a permanent solution to the Thessalian question.

Philip's procedure cannot be traced in detail because of the scanty and often hostile sources. Diodorus (16.69.8) reports that he won the goodwill of the Thessalians by driving out the tyrants. These "tyrants" most probably refer to the oligarchic cliques or families which ruled the various cities. Under such leadership the particularism of the cities flourished to the detriment of the proper functioning of the Thessalian League, which had been revivified by Pelopidas. City was jealous of city and, within the cities, factional strife was often vicious. Diodorus' statement suggests that Philip deposed some of the leading families from their seats of power, in some cases establishing temporary garrisons. When Demosthenes (6.22) says sneeringly that Philip established a *decadarchia* among the Thessalians, by this rare word he presumably means a system similar to the decarchies of Lysander, although some scholars think that the manuscript should read *tetrarchia*. To curtail the particularism of the often rebellious cities, Philip based the Thessalian League on the four old territorial divisions (*tetrads*), in each of which a tetrarch, elected by the league but certainly from supporters of Philip, had control over civil and military matters. In this reorganization work Philip was assisted by the city of Pharsalus, which for many years, according to Aristotle (*Politics*, 5.5.7), had lived under a responsible oligarchy. There is considerable evidence that several Pharsalians held important offices in the newly structured Thessaly. As archon, with the tetrarchs directly responsible to him and with the belligerent oligarchs in disfavor, Philip became the controlling figure in Thessaly. Demosthenes (18.43; 295) contemptuously refers to the Thessalians as slaves. On the other hand Isocrates, probably in 344 (*Letter* 2, *To Philip*, 1.20), remarks that "to many you appear to have been well advised because your treatment of the Thessalians has been just and advantageous to them, although they are a people not easy to handle, but high-spirited and seditious." The evidence is so slight and contradictory that one can only say that the Thessalians, whether from fear or satisfaction, remained loyal followers of Philip and his son Alexander. They were also soon freed from the constant attempts at exploitation by Spartans, Thebans, and Athenians.[26]

In Athens the peace, and chiefly dissatisfaction with it, continued to be the main issue. It was probably late in 346 that an envoy, Eucleides, was sent to Philip to argue that the Thracian towns taken by Philip before his signing of the peace should be returned to Cersobleptes and that he should be included in the peace (Demosthenes, 19.162). Since these requests were flatly contradictory to the terms of the agreement which the Athenians had signed, Philip naturally rejected them, but in his effort to improve his relations with them he offered—presumably at this time—to cut a canal through the neck of the Chersonese at his own expense (Demosthenes, 6.30). The channel might have provided a useful barrier for the Athenian settlers against Thracian raids, but the Athenians were in no mood to accept a favor—or a bribe—from Philip.[27]

An episode in the next year, 345, is particularly significant for the light it sheds on attitudes in the Greek world following the Amphictionic Peace. A faction of the Delians brought before the Delphic Amphictionic Council a complaint against the Athenian control of the temple of Apollo at Delos. Since there is no previous evidence that Delphic Apollo had any control over the affairs of Delian Apollo, why was the Delphic Amphictionic Council now acting as a court of arbitration? The answer surely lies in the fact that the peace established at Delphi was an Amphictionic one which, as suggested above, bore great similarity to, if not actual identity with, a Common (*koinē*) Peace. The Delians, who had long felt aggrieved, now seized their first opportunity, presumably at the spring Pylaea, to place their complaints before a "world" court. Since the Athenians, although sullenly hostile to the Amphictionic Peace, considered it dangerous to ignore a suit to be argued before *hieromnemones* largely from states under Philip's influences, the assembly elected Aeschines to defend the Athenian side of the case, a foolish choice because of Aeschines' former defense of the Phocians. Subsequently, the Areopagus rather mysteriously annulled Aeschines' appointment and selected in his place Hyperides, a staunch supporter of Demosthenes. Hyperides won the case, a result which suggests that Philip, anxious not to antagonize the Athenians, used his influence on the Amphictionic Council (Demosthenes, 18.134).

The interference of the Areopagus in ousting Aeschines and substituting Hyperides for him is an action hard to explain in terms of the normal functioning of the Athenian government, but it is clearly related to happenings of the preceding few months. In the summer of 346 the Athenians carried out a revision of the citizen lists (*diapsephisis*). One would like to know why this particular year was picked for a procedure which was bound to raise passions (Aeschines, 1.77; 86). A certain Anti-

phon was stripped of his civil rights. The sequel is told most luridly in
Demosthenes' defense of his career in 330 against the denunciations of
Aeschines (18.132–133):

> You all remember Antiphon, the man who was struck off the regis-
> ter, and came back to Athens after promising Philip that he would
> set fire to the dockyard. When I had caught him in hiding at
> Peiraeus, and brought him before the Assembly, this malignant
> fellow [Aeschines] raised a huge outcry about my scandalous and
> undemocratic conduct in assaulting citizens in distress and break-
> ing into houses without a warrant, and so procured his acquittal.
> Had not the Council of the Areopagus, becoming aware of the
> facts, and seeing that you had made a most inopportune blunder,
> started further inquiries, arrested the man, and brought him into
> court a second time, the vile traitor would have slipped out of your
> hands and eluded justice, being smuggled out of the city by our
> bombastic phrase-monger. As it was, you put him on the rack and
> then executed him, and you ought to have done the same to Aes-
> chines.

Demosthenes ends his account of this episode by adding that it was the
Areopagus' knowledge of the complicity of Aeschines which caused it to
reject him and to give Hyperides the commission to defend the Athenian
cause against Delos before the Delphic Amphictionic Council.

These remarks of Demosthenes about Antiphon and Aeschines, in
which he emphasizes his vigilant patriotism and the corruption and
treason of these men, present a sordid picture reminiscent of a state existing under martial law. What is particularly noteworthy is the role of
the Areopagus, apparently on the urging of Demosthenes, in overriding
the decisions of the popular assembly. One wonders also under what authority Demosthenes, no longer a councillor, acted so independently and
violently. It is hard to take seriously the charge against Antiphon. Philip
had just recently made peace and an alliance with Athens, and for the
next two years he tried, whether sincerely or not, to foster amicable relations with the city. Was it probable that he would jeopardize that aim
by hiring a man to engage in sabotage likely to be discovered and thus
frustrating his efforts? It is reasonable enough to believe that the resentful Antiphon, on his own and not as an agent of Philip, may have
planned to damage the city that had rejected him. About a quarter of a
century later, the orator Dinarchus in his speech against Demosthenes
(62–63) scathingly enumerates victims of Demosthenes' suspicions and
of the Areopagus' drastic interference. The gentle Plutarch (*Demosthenes*,
14.4) also condemns Demosthenes for such behavior. Demosthenes, the
brilliant orator and the passionate patriot, was also a master in the art of

character assassination when referring to those who opposed him. Since his fiery speeches are the chief source of information for these critical years, the task of the historian to acquire a rational understanding of the problems becomes well-nigh hopeless.

In the spring of 344, while Philip was stabilizing conditions in Thessaly, Demosthenes and other envoys were sent to the Peloponnesus to try to counteract the growing Macedonian influence among the Argives, Arcadians, and Messenians. In view of Athens' friendship with Sparta, which continued to threaten Megalopolis and Messenia, it is hardly surprising that the embassy bore no fruit. Soon after Demosthenes' return several embassies appeared in Athens. The information about these embassies is slight, but since one of them and the Athenian response contributed greatly to the worsening of relations between Athens and Philip, it is necessary to be familiar with the evidence.

Under the year 351/0, but actually referring to a later time, Diodorus (16.44) speaks of envoys sent by King Artaxerxes III (Ochus) to the greatest cities in Greece to seek mercenaries for his projected campaign to reconquer Egypt. Didymus in his commentary (8.7–32) on the *Fourth Philippic* of Demosthenes (341/0) mentions envoys from Philip and Artaxerxes; his quotation from Philochorus reveals that these envoys arrived early in the archonship of Lyciscus (344/3), hence presumably in July or August. This fixed date, very welcome in this confused period, would have been a logical time to search for mercenaries for a campaign that was to fall in 343/2. Demosthenes in the *Second Philippic,* delivered in the summer of 344, and Libanius in his hypothesis to this oration mention envoys from Philip and from the Argives and Messenians. The seventh oration of Demosthenes, *On Halonnesus* discloses that Python, a Byzantine, had been the spokesman for the delegates sent by Philip. Three embassies, then, from Artaxerxes, Philip, and Argos and Messenia, respectively, arrived in Athens in the summer of 344.

In answer to the request from Artaxerxes, Athens (and Sparta) refused to contribute mercenaries, although Thebes and Argos did; the Athenians, possibly influenced by the Panhellenic and anti-Persian argument with which Isocrates in 346 had tried to arouse Philip, merely said they would remain at peace with the King if he did not attack the Greeks. The speeches of Python and of the envoys from Argos and Messenia provoked Demosthenes into delivering the *Second Philippic* before the Athenian assembly. In vehement language he maintained that Philip was benefiting the Thebans, Argives, and Messenians only to gain strength for an ultimate attack on his real enemy, Athens. He also denounced Philip's abuse of the peace and the Athenian politicians who, through their dishonesty and greed, were playing into Macedonian hands. This attack, clearly directed against men like Philocrates and Aeschines, was preparing the way for the indictments which were made in the following year.

The *Second Philippic* was not the official reply to Philip's envoy and the other ambassadors, but an effort to minimize the favorable effect that the eloquence and conciliatory tone of Python had had on the assembly. Python, a former pupil of Isocrates, stated that Philip was willing to consider appropriate amendments to the peace and was distressed by the constant opposition to him of certain orators. A better understanding of Philip's proposals and of the polemics to which they gave rise might clarify some aspects of Philip's basic intentions, but unfortunately the chief evidence lies in a violently partisan speech, *On Halonnesus,* delivered in 342 by Hegesippus, one of Demosthenes' most fiery supporters. Philip might have been thinking of peace conditions in general, which would have been appropriate for the existing situation, in fact of a common peace which would have freed him for carrying out plans he may have been forming concerning Thrace and possibly Asia Minor. The Athenians, at least as represented by Hegesippus who was sent as an envoy to Philip, were interested in a revision of the Peace of Philocrates in particular. They wanted the original wording "each party to retain what it possessed" to be changed to "each party to retain what was its own." By this proposal, which would have been inflammatory in a country like Greece with its city-state jealousies and animosities, the Athenians were raising their old claims to places such as Amphipolis, Potidaea, and Pydna. They also wanted the Thracian places taken by Philip before he signed the Peace of Philocrates to be returned to Cersobleptes, and Cardia to be "restored" to them. These proposals, which would have annulled everything that Philip had gained by the peace of 346, were naturally rejected by the Macedonian king. He was outraged by the arrogance of Hegesippus, although he still offered to submit certain matters to the test of impartial arbitration, an offer which the Athenians scorned.

There is much about the embassy of Python and its sequel which is perplexing. The original proposals of Philip, which were favorably received by the Athenian assembly, were assigned, for unknown reasons but probably by some parliamentary manoeuvre, to the violent anti-Macedonians for negotiation. The effects of these negotiations on worsening the relations between the two states were obvious. The anti-Macedonians, by skillful and passionate rhetoric, attributing their humiliation in 346 and later to the duplicity of Philip, succeeded in causing many of the people to lose faith in the pro-Macedonians who had talked of the advantages of cooperating with the Macedonian king. As for Philip, whatever his original hopes and plans had been, he now decided that friendship with Athens by peaceful means was impossible and that methods other than negotiation were necessary.

Some scholars have thought that the diplomatic rebuff tendered by Athens to both Philip and Artaxerxes could have been responsible for the little-known alliance which may have been struck between Macedonia and Persia. The "friendship and alliance" pact between Philip and Artaxerxes is known only from a reported letter of King Darius III to Alexander after the battle of Issus in 333 (Arrian, *Anabasis*, 2.14.2). No date is assigned to this supposed agreement, but the international situation in the spring of 343 could be considered a logical time for its formation. Artaxerxes might have wanted assurance that Macedonia would not interfere in Asia Minor when he was engaged in his wars with Phoenicia and Egypt, while Philip, apparently already contemplating a campaign into Thrace, might have wished to be free from fear of Persian activity in that region or in the confused affairs of Greece. Those scholars, however, who reject the existence of such a pact are probably correct. Certainly the source is questionable, and the pact, if even suspected, would have been disastrous to Philip's and Artaxerxes' relations with the Greeks.[28]

In Athens, after the failure of Python's mission, the anti-Macedonians became more active. Their wrath first fell upon Philocrates, who was prosecuted by Hyperides, with the support of Demosthenes, on a charge of corruption and of giving bad advice to the people. Because of the intense unpopularity of the peace which bore his name, Philocrates, feeling that he had no chance of an impartial trial, left Athens, only to be condemned to death in his absence. He may have received bonuses from Philip, for Greek ambassadors were notoriously prone to accept gifts from states or men with whom they had cooperated, but there is no proof that he was guilty of treason. In their need for a scapegoat, however, the people branded him as a traitor; even Aeschines, in his trial which followed later in the summer of 343, assumed this attitude towards Philocrates.

Aeschines' trial, held before a court of 1,501 *dikasts* under the supervision of the auditors (*logistai*), was a revival of Demosthenes' original accusation, which had been postponed because of the attack on Timarchus. This trial is of more interest than that of Philocrates to the modern student for the simple reason that the actual speeches of the two distinguished orators, although subsequently somewhat edited, have been preserved. Demosthenes' prosecution is a devastating and vitriolic attack on Aeschines and the other ambassadors and an attempt to exonerate his own role in the ill-famed Peace of Philocrates. His distortion of the facts about the sorry fate of the Phocians, for which he was partly responsible, and his effort to throw all the blame on Aeschines who, in fact, had worked in behalf of the Phocians, are sickening examples of the depth to which self-righteous patriotism can descend. Aeschines' defense, although lacking Demosthenes' rhetorical brilliance, was a remarkable achievement. His task was not easy, for the peace which he had struggled to obtain and influence had become anathema to the average Athenian. He was ultimately acquitted by the close margin of thirty votes. He owed this acquittal to the fact that despite his deluge of words Demosthenes could not prove him guilty, to the testimony of Phocian exiles on his behalf, and to the presence of two distinguished Athenians as character witnesses, the statesman Eubulus and the general Phocion. The narrowness of his escape, however, is vivid evidence for the increasing influence of the anti-Macedonians since the year 346, an influence strengthened by the unwillingness of Philocrates to stand trial.

The activity of Philip in the year 343, except for his expedition into Epirus in the autumn, is almost unknown. From such passages of Demosthenes as 19.259–262 and 18.295, one could believe that he was busy then in backing his supporters with troops or with money in Euboea, Megara, and throughout the Peloponnesus, especially in Elis. The Argives, Arcadians, and Messenians continued to consider Philip favorably as a possible protector against the constant menace of the Spartans. A scholar who has studied these years carefully finds no trustworthy evidence for the interference of Philip, and hence no violation of the Peace of Philocrates, before the early summer of 342.[29] This may be true, but since *stasis* was common in the fourth-century Greek world and there is evidence for such disturbances in Euboea, Megara, and Elis, it is possible that the warring factions may have appealed to Philip, Thebes, or Athens for aid. Money which Philip supplied to his supporters could have been used by them to hire mercenaries to achieve their aims without involving the interference of Macedonian troops. Athens itself, probably at this time, interfered in the *stasis* in Megara according to a notice of Plutarch (*Phocion,* 15). The policies of regions as strategically close to Athens as Megara and Euboea were naturally of great concern to the Athenians. Developments in any state contrary to the aims of Demosthenes' policy for Athens, the orator does not hesitate to attribute to the machinations of Philip. Generations later Polybius (18.14), while granting much praise to Demosthenes, rebuked him severely for slandering many distinguished leaders in Greece and summarized his criticism by saying: "Measuring everything by the interests of his own city, thinking that the whole of Greece should have its eyes turned on Athens, and if people did not do so, calling them traitors, Demosthenes seems to me to have been very much mistaken and very far wide of the truth."

Late in 343 Philip marched into Epirus. He had married an Epirote princess, Olympias, and the immediate reason for his expedition was to support the interests of her brother, Alexander. This mountainous tribal state had usually been on the fringes of Greek history, although Alcetas, the king of the dominant Molossian tribe, and his son, Neoptolemos, had for a while been members of the Second Athenian League. Along with Jason of Pherae, Alcetas had been a character witness for Timotheus at his trial in 373. Neoptolemos succeeded his father as king and seemingly shared the rule with his younger brother, Arybbas. Among Neoptolemos' children were Olympias, whom Philip married, and her younger brother, Alexander. On the death of Neoptolemos Arybbas continued to rule, but probably with the understanding that he should act as regent for Alexander, the minor son of his older brother. When Alexander, who may have been residing at Pella, came of age, Philip proceeded into Epirus in order to place him upon the throne. There is no evidence that there was a struggle. Arybbas and his children went into exile and sought refuge in Athens. An extant inscription (Tod, no. 173) records that the Athenians conferred on Arybbas the citizenship which his father and grandfather had possessed. The final clause stipulates that the generals should see to it that Arybbas and his children recover their ancestral realm.

The close relations established by Philip with Epirus strengthened the defense both of that country and of Macedonia against Illyrian incursions. Philip also helped Alexander extend Epirus, or the Molossian holdings, southward to the Ambracian Gulf by compelling the Elean colonies of Cassopia to join the Molossian *koinon* (Demosthenes, 7.32). This acquisition, beyond its benefit to Epirus, offered Philip a route to the Corinthian Gulf and to the western regions of the Peloponnesus. These manoeuvres came at an awkward time for Philip, however, for in the winter of 343/2 he had sent envoys with a letter to Athens in the hope of reviving the proposals which Python had made in the summer of 344. Philip may also have promised to assist Alexander in taking control of Ambracia, but these plans had to be temporarily abandoned because of the rising opposition of many Greeks. Corinth, worried about its colonial interests in places like Ambracia and the island of Leucas and too weak to act alone, appealed to Athens. Acarnania also began to fear for its independence. Both these states made alliances with Athens, which promptly sent a military force to Acarnania. The Athenians then succeeded in acquiring as allies the Achaeans on the south coast of the

Corinthian Gulf, who were outraged when they heard that Philip had promised Naupactus, a port they were struggling to hold, as bait to win over the Aetolians.

This unusual activity of Athens on both military and diplomatic fronts is clear evidence that Demosthenes' influence in foreign policy was increasing. In early 342 he, Hegesippus, and others traveled as envoys throughout the Peloponnesus. By eloquently insisting on the dangers, real and potential, of Philip, they were successful in procuring pacts of some sort with the Argives, Messenians, and Arcadians, even including the Megalopolitans. To secure these agreements Athens, reversing its previous policy of friendship with Sparta, must have promised these states active help against Sparta if necessary. Argos, Arcadia, and Messenia, therefore, had alliances with both Athens and Philip. The sequel shows that they had really assigned themselves to a role of neutrality.[30]

Because of Athens' aggressiveness and the influence it was having on various Greek states, Philip abandoned whatever intentions he had had concerning Ambracia and Acarnania and returned to Macedonia by way of Thessaly. It was then, apparently, that he quieted some confusion in the area of Pherae caused by Demosthenes' agent, Aristodemus (Aeschines, 3.83). By this time Philip must have received a report on the letter and embassy he had sent in the winter to Athens in an attempt to revive the conciliatory proposals which Python had made two years before. Any hope that those proposals might lead to some sort of understanding had been frustrated, it will be remembered, by the irreconcilable attitude of Hegesippus, who had been sent by Athens to negotiate with Philip. Information about Philip's suggestions on this later occasion is preserved in "Demosthenes' " speech *On Halonnesus,* delivered in spring 342 by Hegesippus. The name of the speech is derived from a little island off the coast of Thessaly which had apparently belonged to Athens, or at least had been a member of its league. About the time of the Peace of Philocrates, a pirate named Sostratus had seized the island and engaged in plundering merchant vessels bound for Macedonia. Philip expelled the pirate and kept the island, a fact which aroused great indignation in Athens. In his present attempt to reach some agreement with the Athenians, Philip made the following offers and proposals: to give Halonnesus to Athens; to establish trade agreements; to join in common action against pirates; to expand the Peace of Philocrates into a Common Peace; to submit to impartial arbitration the question of the status of the places which he had taken in Thrace in 346 before he signed the peace, and the question of Cardia in the Chersonese. Hegesippus' speech, which presumably reflects the Athenian response to Philip, ridiculed all the proposals in insulting language. Since Halonnesus had belonged to Athens, Philip must restore, not give, the island—a quibble which lent itself to much literary mirth. Athens, the queen of the seas, did not need help—above all from a Macedonian—to suppress piracy; Philip's present actions showed the little respect he had for the idea of a Common Peace; arbitration about the Thracian places and Cardia was absurd, for they belonged to Athens and any judges would be bribed by Philip.

Philip's proposals interested the pro-Macedonian Athenians (Demosthenes, 7.45), but Demosthenes' party succeeded in having them laughed out of court. Philip probably was not surprised at the result. His suggestions may have been no more than propaganda. He knew that Artaxerxes III had succeeded in conquering Phoenicia and Egypt, and he feared that Persian influence might spread in Greece. He may have hoped that his proposals would have some effect in swaying public opinion throughout Greece in a war with Athens, which now seemed likely.

IN THE summer of 342 Philip began one of the most difficult undertakings of his career—the conquest of Thrace from the Nestus River eastward to the Black Sea. Philip probably had many motives in entering upon this task. Partly it was a campaign of pure conquest, for the various Thracian kings such as Cersobleptes were unpredictable, and the resources of Thrace, both in men and in products like timber, minerals and grain, were significant. Philip also surely had Athens in mind. Since the Peace of Philocrates he had failed again and again, although his intentions may have been more sincere than Demosthenes would grant, to reach some sort of agreement with that city. He must have realized that if he could push his conquests to the Bosporus he would be in a position to exert great pressure on the proud maritime city by threatening its supply of grain from the Black Sea area. Persia, likewise, must have been very much in Philip's thoughts. The Achaemenid kingdom under the energetic Artaxerxes III was beginning to play a prominent role again in international affairs. After his recovery of Phoenicia and Egypt in 343/2, Artaxerxes would probably attempt to settle the unrest in Asia Minor. Since the writing of Isocrates' open letter to Philip in 346, at least, rumors were circulating that Philip, encouraged by rebellious Persians living at his court, might undertake an expedition into Asia Minor. To frustrate this attempt it was possible that Artaxerxes might arrange an alliance with various Greek states, and particularly Athens, with the purpose of launching an attack on Philip. In such an enterprise Thrace would play a key role. The rumors about Philip's designs on Asia

Minor were based, in part at least, on fact, for it was known that the Macedonian king had entered into relations with at least one dynast there, Hermias, tyrant of Atarneus, on the Asiatic coast opposite Lesbos.

Hermias was a Greek, about whose earlier life little is recorded except gossip. Somehow he became ruler of various villages around Mt. Ida and, presumably through payment of money, received recognition from the Persian administration. He made his headquarters at Atarneus. Whether Hermias had ever been in Athens is uncertain, but his person and position became known to Plato. In his *Sixth Letter,* which scholars accept as authentic, Plato wrote to two of his former pupils, then living at Scepsis in the Troad and engaged in political reforms, to associate with Hermias, apparently in the belief that their theoretical ideas, when blended with the practical experience of Hermias, might change his tyranny into a more constitutional rule and enable him to extend his sway over much of northwestern Asia Minor. In recognition of their beneficial advice Hermias granted to the two Platonists the town of Assos, and it was there that Aristotle went when he left Athens on the death of Plato in 348/7. Aristotle spent several years there as a teacher in a "provincial" academy. He became closely associated with Hermias and married his niece and adopted daughter, Pythias. Aristotle remained at Assos and subsequently at Mytilene in Lesbos until the first half of the year 342, when he received an invitation from Philip to come to Pella to become the tutor of Philip's thirteen- or fourteen-year-old son, Alexander. Since Aristotle had not yet gained his later fame as a philosopher, it is largely anachronistic to think that Philip selected him as the foremost of Greek intellectuals. It is more likely that a political motive was involved and that Aristotle, whose father had been the personal physician of Philip's father, in addition to becoming a tutor, was also an emissary between Hermias and Philip. The details of negotiations between Philip and Hermias are unknown but presumably were concerned with an eventual Macedonian incursion into Asia Minor. Rumors circulated, for Demosthenes (10.32) reported in 341 that Philip's "agent" had been seized by the Persians. Later in that year Hermias was crucified. Aristotle honored his memory with a hymn (*paean*), and Aristotle's nephew, the future historian Callisthenes, wrote his eulogy.[31]

Philip's expedition into Thrace, beginning in the summer of 342, was a formidable undertaking and was not completed until the spring of 339. Most of the information available concerns his activities in the Chersonese, at Perinthus on the northern shore of the Propontis, and at Byzantium on the Bosporus. It is known, however, that he deposed kings like Cersobleptes and pushed on to the Black Sea, where he made alliances with Apollonia and probably other Greek colonies. In the north he entered into friendly relations with the Getae living between the Haemus mountains and the Danube, marrying the daughter of the king. To try to control the great area which he traversed, he occupied various existing communities, turning them into military colonies, and also established new settlements such as Philippopolis (modern Plovdiv) on the upper Hebrus. Hostile Greek and native tradition attached pejorative nicknames to some of these foundations, like "adulterer's city" (*moichopolis*) and "scoundrel city" (*poneropolis*), but these places were certainly not merely convict colonies. By means of these settlements Philip was able to exercise enough control over Thrace to be able to profit from its resources and also to draw on its military strength. At some point he established an official over the whole region called the general of Thrace, although the earliest mention of this officer comes from the first year of Alexander's rule (336/5). In many ways, seemingly, Thrace and its immediate commander were similar to a Persian satrapy and satrap.[32]

It was in the Thracian Chersonese, as might have been expected, that violent friction arose between Philip and Athens. This peninsula, so important for controlling the Hellespont, had been recognized as Athenian by the Peace of Philocrates except for the city of Cardia at its neck, which remained allied to Philip. Late in 343 Athens sent a detachment of *cleruchs* there under the general Diopeithes, the father of the future dramatist Menander, to aid in the defense of the region. To procure the money he needed for hiring mercenaries, Diopeithes employed a technique common among Athenian generals, according to Demosthenes (8.9; 24–25): he waylaid various merchantmen and forced their skippers to pay "benevolences," in return for which he protected them from other pirates on their voyages. In the winter of 343/2 Diopeithes settled many of the *cleruchs,* but he encountered resistance from the people of Cardia, who did not want Athenian *cleruchs* in their territory. In such cases boundary quarrels were inevitable; Philip's request for arbitration was disdained (Demosthenes, 7.39–45). When Diopeithes resorted to force, the Cardians appealed for help to Philip, who promptly sent a letter to Athens again asking for arbitration. On the rejection of this proposal, Philip sent military support to Cardia.

In the early spring of 341, when Philip was active in the interior of Thrace, Diopeithes invaded parts of Thrace then under Macedonian control and after thorough plundering returned to the Chersonese. Soon an envoy from Philip arrived to arrange ransom for the prisoners who had been taken, but Diopeithes imprisoned this man, Amphilochus, tortured him, and released him only after payment of a ransom of nine talents (Demosthenes, 12.3–4). Philip then sent a strong protest to

Athens, which caused the pro-Macedonians to demand the removal and punishment of Diopeithes, but Demosthenes in one of his most powerful speeches, *On the Chersonese,* won over the assembly by denouncing Philip's many breaches of the peace and his desire to destroy Athens, and by arguing that Diopeithes should be supported in his efforts to protect Athenian interests. Shortly thereafter, when Diopeithes appealed for reinforcements, Demosthenes delivered his most fiery and devastating speech, *The Third Philippic.* Contrasting Philip's actions with the periods of Spartan hegemony and of Athenian hegemony in the previous century, he said (9.25), "Yet all the faults committed by the Lacedaemonians in those thirty years, and by our ancestors in their seventy years of supremacy, are fewer, men of Athens, than the wrongs which Philip has done to the Greeks in the thirteen incomplete years in which he has been coming to the top—or rather, they are not a fraction of them." Again and again he referred to what he termed the crimes and treacheries of Philip, and ended by urging Athens to increase its military preparations and to call upon the rest of the Greeks and even the Great King of Persia to aid in the defense of Greece. A reading of these two speeches leaves little doubt that Demosthenes was now in control of Athenian foreign policy and that Diopeithes, whatever the character of his actions in the Chersonese, was carrying out the orator's orders.

While these events were taking place in the Chersonese, Euboea was also the scene of considerable activity. This island had revolted from the Athenian League early in 348. In the ensuing years the cities in Euboea were in a constantly unsettled condition because of mutual jealousies, social unrest, and hostility between pro-Athenian and pro-Macedonian factions. A precise account of the sequence of events on the island throughout the 340s is impossible, for the evidence has to be gleaned primarily from the contradictory and misleading statements of Demosthenes and Aeschines, but the general trend can be traced. A leading citizen of Chalcis, Callias, endeavored in the years following the Peace of Philocrates to establish a league of Euboean cities. He sought support from Macedonia, but Philip, still trying to obtain better relations with Athens, was unresponsive. Callias then began negotiations with Demosthenes in 342, which resulted ultimately in an alliance between Athens and Chalcis. To thwart development of friendly relations between the Euboean cities and Athens, a combination which would impede Philip's desire to exert influence in Greece in view of the Persian campaign he may already have been contemplating, Philip, before he set out on his Thracian expedition, dispatched his general Parmenio (and others) with mercenaries to places in southeastern Thessaly so that they could take appropriate action in Euboea if necessary. In response presumably to appeals from the anti-Athenian factions, the Macedonian generals succeeded in establishing "tyrants" favorable to Philip in Eretria and Oreos. Despite various accusations of Demosthenes, this was apparently the first time since the Sacred War that Philip had sent military forces into Greece proper, a change in policy caused by his anger at the success of Hegesippus and Demosthenes in frustrating and ridiculing the peace proposals he had sent to Athens through Python of Byzantium.

This interference in Greek cities, which might have been handled more skillfully if Philip had been there in person, caused the denunciations of Demosthenes to seem more credible, for many Greeks, previously deaf to his warnings, now became worried about the presence of Macedonian troops in an area as central and important as Euboea. In the next year the Athenians, alarmed by the presence of Macedonian-backed "tyrants" in nearby Euboea, sent out two expeditions in the summer (Didymus, 1.13–25) which, with the help of the Chalcidians, were successful in ousting the "tyrants" from Eretria and Oreos and restoring democracies in these two cities. It was approximately at this time that Callias, with the loan of Athenian ships manned by Chalcidians, made raids in the Pagasean Gulf, harried (the text is probably wrong to say "captured") various cities allied with Philip, and sold into slavery all merchants sailing to Macedonia (Demosthenes, 12.5).[33]

Demosthenes had concluded his passionate *Third Philippic*, delivered in May or June 341, by insisting that Athens must concentrate on military preparations and try to win as many allies as possible against the increasing menace of Philip. In the fall of that year Demosthenes went on an embassy to Byzantium. This great city and Perinthus on the Propontis had made alliances with Philip when he aided them against Cersobleptes in 351 (Aeschines, 2.81 and scholia), but the Macedonian's conquests in Thrace and his establishment of relations with Greek colonies on the western coast of the Black Sea encroached on what Byzantium considered its sphere of activity and also seemed a threat to the city itself. Byzantium had long been hostile to Athens, but on this occasion Demosthenes was able to secure some sort of alliance with it. At the same time Hyperides reached certain agreements with the islands of Chios and Rhodes. This was apparently the time when Athenian envoys also went to the Persian king. No regular alliance was formed, but it is known that Artaxerxes sent money to Diopeithes in the Chersonese (Aristotle, *Rhetoric*, 2.1386a), and there is a tradition that both Demosthenes and Hyperides received monetary gifts (Plutarch, *Ten Orators*, 847F and 848E). In the winter of 341/0 Demosthenes and the Chalcidian Callias toured the Peloponnesus and other regions in an effort to obtain allies against Philip. They had no success with the Argives, Arcadians, and Messenians, who as adherents of Philip remained neutral, but the responses from the Megarians, Achaeans, and Acarnanians were more favorable.

In reward for his achievements the Athenian assembly voted that Demosthenes be honored with a "golden crown" (Demosthenes, 18.83). Either on this occasion or slightly earlier, the assembly on the proposal of Demosthenes recognized that the Euboean cities united in some type of league, although remaining allies of Athens, should not be considered members of the Athenian League. Presumably this measure freed them from the obligation of paying *syntaxeis* and of participation in the *synedrion* at Athens. Callias was granted Athenian citizenship in recognition of his services. These measures concerning Euboea were subsequently attacked by Aeschines in 330 (3.100–101) and by Hyperides in his prosecution of Demosthenes in 323 (fragment 5), but if one remembers the critical situation and the danger that a hostile Euboea would have been to Athens, it is clear that Demosthenes was demonstrating sound statesmanship. If Athens had been equally enlightened towards its allies in the first and second leagues, the fate of those organizations and of the Greeks in general might have been happier.

In the spring of 340 Philip shifted his activities to the northern shore of the Propontis. Control of this area was essential to complete his conquest of Thrace, and also for whatever plans he may have been harboring with regard to Athens and Persia. Since the two chief cities, Perinthus and Byzantium, had abandoned their alliance with him to join in an agreement with Athens, they were his first objectives. In his siege of Perinthus Philip experimented with the latest developments in siege warfare, but they proved inadequate against the rocky location of the city and the heroic efforts of its defenders (Diodorus, 16.74–76). He then decided that blockade by sea was also necessary. Since his ships were in the Aegean they had to proceed through the Hellespont, a dangerous task in view of the hostility of the Athenian *cleruchs* in the Chersonese and of the presence of a naval squadron under Chares in the vicinity. To give his fleet adequate protection, Philip and the Macedonians marched along the coast of the peninsula. Once he had successfully achieved the passage of his ships he wrote a letter to Athens to rebut the demands for a declaration of war, which he knew many Athenians would be proposing.

This letter, which two manuscripts of Demosthenes' works include as the last (no. 12) of the "Philippic" orations, is now generally accepted as a genuine composition of Philip and his secretarial staff.[34] As a unique document presenting Philip's point of view, it should be read by all who are seriously concerned with the conflict between Macedonian and Athenian interests. In it Philip skillfully blends condemnation of Athens, self-justification, and propaganda. Since it was addressed to the Boulē and the *demos* of the Athenians, Philip knew that it would be read to the assembly. From there its propagandistic purpose would surely circulate throughout the Greek world. To illustrate the effectiveness of Philip's diplomacy, a paraphrase of the chief points emphasized in the letter will be useful.

Philip begins by stating that, since the Athenians have disregarded numerous embassies from him concerning the observance of the oaths and agreements, he has sent them a letter, necessarily a long one, listing the matters in which he thinks he has been wronged. The Athenians had seized a herald in Macedonian territory, kept him prisoner for ten months, and read to the assembly Philip's letters which he had been carrying. When the island of Thasos, an ally of Athens, opened its harbor to Byzantine triremes and to any pirates (surely preying on shipping bound for Macedonia), the Athenians ignored the piracy although it had been specifically outlawed in the peace treaty. The complaints against Diopeithes and his treatment of the Macedonian envoy, Amphilochus, and the plundering of the Pagasaean Gulf area by Callias of Chalcis have already been mentioned. Athens had sent an embassy to the King of Persia, urging him to make war on Philip. The people of the island Peparethos, allies of Athens, had seized Halonnesus and the Macedonian garrison there. When Philip recaptured the island, the Peparethians complained to the Athenians, who ordered their general to take action on their behalf. On this point, as on many others, Philip once again proposed impartial arbitration.

After having enumerated Athens' many violations of the spirit and the letter of the peace, Philip comes to the immediate motive for sending the letter, his march through the Chersonese which has been forced on him by the hostile attitude of the Athenians. In his conclusion he bitterly denounces the warmongering Athenian orators who always refuse proposals for arbitration and still have the gall to claim Amphipolis despite its recognition as his in the terms of peace. His final words, that with justice on his side and the gods as witnesses he will determine his policy towards Athens, clearly contain a threat.

The effect of this letter on Athens can probably be seen in the fact that the Athenians did not then declare war on Philip, nor did they send assistance to Perinthus. That city, however, received valuable aid from Byzantium and from the King of Persia, who ordered the satraps in northern Asia Minor to send money and mercenaries to the beleaguered city. These reinforcements combined with the frenzied resistance of the

Perinthians themselves rendered Philip's assault tactics ineffectual. Consequently, leaving part of his army to continue the siege, he hastened early in the autumn against Byzantium. In the course of the march he assigned a contingent the task of blockading Selymbria so as to prevent the lines of communication between Perinthus and Byzantium from being endangered. Soon after arriving at the Bosporus, Philip had a chance to deliver a devastating blow to Athens. The Athenian merchant fleet, laden with grain, was assembling off Hieron on the Asiatic side of the Bosporus, with the expectation that Chares would escort it to Greece under the protection of his triremes after all the grain ships had arrived. When Chares left the scene briefly to attend a conference with the Persian satraps, Philip struck suddenly with navy and infantry and captured the whole merchant fleet. Any ships not belonging to the Athenians he seemingly let go, but the Athenian vessels to the number of 180 he commandeered, thereby winning a large amount of grain and money. The timber of the ships themselves he used for his siege-works against Byzantium (Didymus, *On Demosthenes,* 11.10.45–62; 11.1–5).

Realizing that this action would cause the Athenians to declare war, he immediately sent a letter, an "ultimatum," to them. The evidence for this critical period is inadequate, but from the hypothesis introducing the scholia to the eleventh oration of Demosthenes (Dindorf, 8.209), the situation seems to have been the following. In his letter Philip claimed that he had seized the ships because he suspected that they were bringing grain and aid to Selymbria, a city not included in the peace treaty, which he was besieging. If this information is authentic, then clearly Philip was hoping that his ultimatum would serve the propagandistic purpose of causing Greek states allied to Athens to believe that he had struck against the Athenians only under provocation. The allies of Athens were obligated to provide aid only if it were attacked. This episode concerning Selymbria and Philip's letter is very obscure, if not apocryphal, but in support of its truth is the fact that no ally from the mainland of Greece assisted Athens in the ensuing fighting around Byzantium.[35]

The Athenian response to Philip's seizure of the grain ships and to his ultimatum was to vote that the marble stele on which the Peace of Philocrates was inscribed should be destroyed, and on the motion of Demosthenes that war should be officially declared (Demosthenes, 18.73; Philochorus, fragment 55). This was in October 340. Early in the spring of 339 a fleet under Phocion was dispatched to the Bosporus. This armament was enthusiastically welcomed by the Byzantines who, according to Plutarch (*Phocion,* 14), had distrusted Chares. Byzantium's former allies in the Social War—Chios, Rhodes, and Cos—also sent help. These reinforcements, combined with the valiant resistance of the Byzantines, proved superior to all the siege devices that Philip employed. Late in the spring of 339 he abandoned the sieges of Byzantium and Perinthus (and Selymbria) and, after extricating his fleet by a ruse from the Black Sea where it had been confined, he withdrew from the region in which he had suffered the most severe military defeats of his career.

Philip realized that his failures at Perinthus and Byzantium might jeopardize his control over Thrace. Consequently he immediately marched northward to the lower Danube, where some migrating Scythian tribes were causing trouble. He completely defeated the Scythians and acquired extensive booty, but on his return to Macedonia he was attacked by a Thracian tribe, the Triballi, as he was crossing the Haemus range. In the fighting the Macedonians lost most of their booty and Philip was severely wounded, but he succeeded in bringing his army back to Pella late in the summer.[36]

ALTHOUGH Philip had been absent from Greece proper since the summer of 342, the fact that Athens had declared war on him gave warning that trouble was imminent. Trouble did break out soon, and Delphi, once again, was the scene of its earliest manifestations. For the spring meeting of the Amphictionic Council in 339,[37] Athens as usual sent a *hieromnemon* to represent one of the Ionian votes, and also three *pylagori* (delegates), one of whom was Aeschines. In his prosecution of Demosthenes nine years later, Aeschines (3.115–131) provides the fullest account of the proceedings at this meeting.

On arrival at Delphi the Athenian commission was informed by "those wishing to show goodwill to the city" that the Locrians of Amphissa, dependents and flatterers of the Thebans, were planning to introduce a proposal that Athens be fined fifty talents for having dedicated in the new temple, before it had been consecrated, gilded shields inscribed with the words "The Athenians from the Medes and Thebans when they fought against the Hellenes." This was clearly a case of refurbishing dedications which had been erected after the battle of Plataea in 479. Aeschines was assigned the task of answering this charge. Before he could begin to speak to the council, a Locrian arose and castigated the Athenians for their alliance with the Phocians in the Sacred War. Aeschines, faced with this threat which could have led to an Amphictionic war against Athens, turned the tables by a brilliant condemnation of the Amphissans. Two and a half centuries earlier the Amphictions had destroyed the "accursed" city of Cirrha, consecrated its plain to Apollo, and sworn a solemn oath that it should remain uncultivated forever. On the present occasion Aeschines pointed out from where the council was sitting how the Amphissans had desecrated this old oath, for the plain was being cultivated and was covered with farmhouses and pottery works, and the harbor had been rebuilt where port-dues were collected. Aeschines' eloquence and the truth of his charges were so effective that the grievances against Athens were forgotten, and on the next day the Amphictions and the population of Delphi descended to the plain of Cirrha and began to burn and destroy the property. This happy exercise in destruction was soon stopped by the arrival of Amphissans under arms, who drove the despoilers back to Delphi. On the following day the Thessalian Kottyphus of Pharsalus, who presided over the council, called a meeting of an assembly of the Amphictions, including not only the *hieromnemones* and *pylagori* but also all those who were at Delphi to sacrifice to Apollo or to consult the oracle. At this session, after much abuse of the Amphissans and praise of the Athenians, it was decided that before the fall Pylaea a special meeting of the Amphictionic Council should be held to decide on the nature of the punishment to be inflicted on the Amphissans.

When the Athenian delegates to Delphi reported their mission at home, the Boulē and the assembly at first, according to Aeschines, were favorably impressed, but Demosthenes finally succeeded in carrying through a decree that the Athenians, while continuing to attend regular (ancestral) Pylaea, would have nothing to do with extraordinary meetings. Accordingly, when the special meeting was held, probably in the early summer, Athens was not represented, nor Thebes either, the patron of the Amphissans. The other delegates voted a Sacred War against Amphissa and appointed as general their chairman, Kottyphus of Pharsalus. In the campaign, which was not a very martial one, the Amphictionic army extracted a promise from the Amphissans to pay a fine, to banish those guilty of the sacrilege, and to restore those whose piety had resulted in their exile. By the time of the fall Pylaea, however, the Amphissans had fulfilled none of their promises. The Amphictionic Council, therefore, certainly over the opposition of the Theban representatives, voted to carry on the war and to appoint as general Philip, who had returned to Macedonia from his Scythian and Thracian expeditions.

The beginning of this Fourth Sacred War, which in the ensuing year was to lead to the battle of Chaeronea and what is often called the end of Greek liberty, is cloaked in mystery never satisfactorily explained by ancient authors or modern historians. The two chief ancient sources are Aeschines and Demosthenes in their famous speeches delivered in 330 concerning the "crown" proposed for Demosthenes, and their accounts are hopelessly contradictory, for the lapse of nine years enabled both to take liberties with the niceties of truth when it suited their interests. Aeschines was clearly proud of his oratorical triumph at Delphi and thought that by deflecting the anger of the Amphictions from Athens to Amphissa he had saved his country from the frightening prospect of an Amphictionic war. In his eyes a Sacred War against Amphissa and its hated supporter, Thebes, was a desirable end and could have been completed rapidly in 339 without an appeal to Philip if Demosthenes, the "evil genius" of Athens, had not prevented Athenian participation. This point of view obviously disregarded the essential fact that in the fall of 340 Athens had declared war on Philip. Demosthenes could not forget that war or his long-standing hatred and fear of Philip. When Aeschines was reporting his successful oratorical victory over the Amphissans to the Athenian assembly, Demosthenes cried out, "You are bringing war into Attica, Aeschines, an Amphictionic war." Actually, Aeschines was preventing such a war at the time, but Demosthenes was looking further into the future. In his discussion of this period in *On the Crown*, he interpreted everything as examples "of the supreme craftiness of Philip" and of the total depravity of Aeschines (18.143–150).

Philip in 339 had to confront the reality that Athens had declared war on him in the preceding October. At the time of the Peace of Philocrates he may well have been hoping to establish some type of coexistence with the Athenians, but the bitter hostility of Demosthenes and his associates had demonstrated that any such solution was chimerical. By seizing the Athenian grain ships at Hieron and forcing Athens to declare war, Philip ended the equivocal period in which both parties, while professing to be at peace with one another, were actually at war. Since he was besieging Byzantium then and did not return to Macedonia until the late summer of 339, the military aspects of this newly declared war were long delayed. In planning for the future struggle Philip realized the importance of trying to prevent the formation of an alliance between Athens and Thebes, for that combination might be too strong even for his well-trained army. His experience with the Delphic Amphictiony since 346, and earlier, had revealed how valuable a skillful manipulation of that organization could be in playing off one hostile state against another. Because of his close relations with the Thessalians, he was in a strong position to influence the decisions of the Amphictionic Council. Was Demosthenes correct, then, in stating that "the supreme craftiness of Philip" was responsible for the explosive Amphissan affair in 339?

When one remembers that from summer 342 until summer 339 Philip was campaigning, apparently continuously, in Thrace and against the Scythians, it seems obvious that he could not have interfered personally in the affairs of Greece in those years. One may suspect, however, although specific evidence is lacking, that his close associates in the administration of his kingdom, men like Antipater and Parmenio, knowing his general aspirations, were carrying out diplomatic manoeuvres. At the spring meeting of the Amphictionic Council in 339, according to Aeschines, "those wishing to show goodwill to Athens" informed him about the proposed Amphissan charge against Athens. These unidentified well-wishers, possibly Thessalian supporters of Philip, could have been instructed that Philip's aim was to prevent an alliance between Athens and Thebes and that an effective way to forestall that was to incite a Sacred War against the Amphissans which presumably would include Thebes, as defender of Amphissa, and Athens, in its desire to punish the sacrilege of the Amphissans, as an opponent of Thebes. A complex Sacred War could easily lead, with the connivance of the Thessalians, to an appeal to Philip to take charge, thus giving him the justification, as leader of the Amphictionic forces, to interfere in Greek affairs as he saw fit. Aeschines, as a man who had believed in coexistence with Philip and now worried by the declaration of war between his own city and Philip, apparently reasoned that an attack on the sacrilegious behavior of the Amphissans would prevent a Sacred War against Athens and substitute for it a Sacred War against Amphissa and its ally Thebes. An enterprise that might overpower hated Thebes and lead to another Amphictionic Peace without necessitating a dreaded war between Philip and Athens would have seemed praiseworthy to many Athenians.

Demosthenes in his assault on Aeschines' performance at the Amphictionic Council denied that the Amphissans had prepared any charge against the Athenians. This part of Demosthenes' argument was invalid, for his denial of the Amphissan charge was correct only in the sense that, because of Aeschines' successful counterattack, the charge was never officially placed before the council. From his point of view, however, Demosthenes was logical in preventing Athens from participating in the Sacred War against Amphissa. Since the Amphissans were closely associated with the Thebans, that war would largely be directed against Thebes, and for a long time Demosthenes' policy had been aimed at trying to bring that city and Athens into an alliance. Convinced as he was that Philip was scheming to dominate all Greece and to destroy Athens, Demosthenes saw the only hope of resistance in an alliance between Athens, strong at sea, and Thebes, the possessor of Greece's most powerful land army. Athens must do nothing to jeopardize this possible alliance. And Demosthenes had hopes that an agreement with Thebes might materialize. As *proxenos* of that city, he knew that there were divergences of opinion among the Thebans as there were in every city in Greece. The Thebans were discovering that their alliance with Philip was assigning them to a secondary place, and that peoples in the Peloponnesus like the Argives, Arcadians, and Messenians, who had formerly looked to them for support, were now favoring Philip. The Thebans, or at least one party of them, demonstrated their displeasure and their aspirations for more independence in the summer of 399 by expelling a Macedonian garrison from Nicaea when Philip was fighting the Scythians (Didymus, *On Demosthenes,* 11.11.44–49) and occupying this important fortified post slightly to the east of Thermopylae. These grievances of the Thebans, with which Demosthenes was familiar, meant nothing to Aeschines, who retained the usual Athenian hatred for that Boeotian city.

On receiving news of his appointment as commander of the Amphictionic forces in the Sacred War against Amphissa, Philip marched rapidly southward with his Macedonian and Thessalian troops. Realizing that the Theban occupation of Nicaea would make it difficult to emerge from the pass of Thermopylae, he took a more westerly route. Leaving some of his troops at Cytinium in Doris, he hurried on to Phocian Elatea which, destroyed in 346, he immediately fortified. From the first of these posts he was in a position to threaten Amphissa, from the second, Thebes, and beyond that, Athens. His sudden appearance in central Greece caused consternation among both the Thebans and Athenians, for they had assumed that the garrison at Nicaea would prevent his approach. When the news of his presence at Elatea reached Athens one evening, the city fell into a panic, for Demosthenes had been preaching for years that Philip's aim was the destruction of the city. Demosthenes' description of the Athenian dismay that night and of the meeting of the assembly the following morning, which he presented nine years later in his speech *On the Crown* (18.169–179), is probably the most vivid and famous passage from any of the Attic orators. According to his account, which there is no reason to doubt, he dominated the business at the assembly. He assured the people that at the moment it was Thebes that was in immediate danger. If Philip had been certain that Thebes was his obedient ally, the Athenians would have heard not that Philip was at Elatea, but that he and the Thebans were on the borders of Attica. Since there were anti-Macedonians among the Thebans, it was essential that Athens immediately order all men of military age to march out to Eleusis so as to give courage and support to the pro-Athenian Thebans, and also dispatch envoys to Thebes to achieve an alliance with that city.

Demosthenes' proposals were promptly approved, and he was the leader of the envoys sent to Thebes. When they arrived there, they found that ambassadors from Philip and his Amphictionic allies were already on the scene. At a meeting of the Theban assembly, Philip's envoys were first introduced. In their speech, after demanding that Nicaea be surrendered to the eastern Locrians (Didymus, *On Demosthenes,* 11.11.40–48), they recalled all the benefits which Philip had conferred upon them and emphasized the many Theban grievances against Athens. They urged the Thebans to give Philip a free passage through Boeotia or to join him in the invasion of Attica, in which case much booty would fall to them. If, on the other hand, the Thebans should support the Athenians, Boeotia would be ravaged in war.

After Philip's envoys had addressed the Theban assembly, the Athenians were given an opportunity to express their views. Demosthenes' actual words have not been preserved, but in view of his policy for the previous few years it is certain that he appealed to Theban patriotism and emphasized the necessity for Panhellenic resistance to the threat to Greek liberty represented by Macedonian might. He also made it clear that if Athens were destroyed, the Thebans would be at the mercy of Philip. He offered alliance on generous terms, including the stipulations that the command on land should fall to the Thebans while the command on sea should be shared equally by both cities, that Athens would assume two-thirds of the cost of the war, would support Thebes in its aim to control all Boeotian cities, and would resign its claim to Oropus. Athens thereby abandoned its long-standing policy of encouraging and aiding the Boeotian cities to achieve and maintain their independence. The choice before the Thebans was a difficult and frightening one. To accept the Athenian offer meant suppressing their old hatred and jealousy of Athens, deserting their faithful ally, Amphissa, and facing the fury of their former benefactor, Philip, who was now almost at their borders. Nevertheless they decided to throw in their lot with Athens, partly swayed by the eloquence and passion of Demosthenes and also realizing that, if Athens should fall, their own aspirations would be controlled and curbed by a victorious Philip. Even to them, although not fired by any Panhellenic fervor, the idea of a Macedonian hegemony was repellent.

Immediately after the formation of the alliance the Athenian and Theban armies took the field with the aim of preventing Philip's advance. To protect Boeotia from invasion, one contingent made its base at Parapotamii where the Cephisus River flows through a narrow gap from Phocis into the Boeotian plane. A body of 10,000 mercenaries, under Chares and a Boeotarch, was sent to guard Amphissa against a possible Macedonian attack from Cytinium. It was in this general period that Demosthenes carried through the assembly the motion that all surplus revenues be deflected from the Theoric Fund to military purposes, a motion that he had long advocated (Philochorus, fragment 56). In the winter, which was primarily a period of defensive strategy, both sides called on their allies. Athens and Thebes received favorable responses from Achaea, Corinth, Euboea, and Megara, and from the states to the west, Acarnania, Corcyra, and Leucas (Demosthenes, 18.237; Tod, no. 178), but Philip's allies in the Peloponnesus, Argos, Arcadia, and Messenia, also allied to the Thebans, resolved to remain neutral. In these months of comparative military inactivity Philip began to rebuild many of the Phocian cities and assured them that soon their league would be restored and their reparations to Delphi would be reduced to ten talents a year, promises that were honored.[38]

In the spring of 338 Philip, who probably had received reinforcements, went into action. He arranged that a letter stating that he had been recalled because of a revolt of the Thracians should fall into the hands of the mercenaries guarding Amphissa—a ruse similar to the one by means of which he had extracted his fleet from the Black Sea a year before—and suddenly striking this force of 10,000 men who were performing their duties rather carelessly, annihilated it. He then took Amphissa, the cause of the Sacred War, but fulfilled the Amphictionic complaint against it by merely destroying its walls and banishing those citizens guilty of the sacrilege. He next took possession of Delphi, from where some Macedonian detachments made raids into Boeotia, while others, in a rapid push westward, seized Naupactus, held by the Achaeans, and turned it over to the Aetolians as Philip had promised several years earlier. These successful forays made the Greeks realize that their position at Parapotamii was becoming ineffective, and they retired to the plain of Chaeronea in western Boeotia, where Philip quickly followed them. About this time or slightly earlier Philip sent envoys to both Thebes and Athens suggesting that he and they try to settle their disagreements by peaceful means. Some Thebans, realizing the desperate danger in which their city stood, and Phocion at Athens recommended that negotiations be attempted, but Demosthenes, acting according to Aeschines (3.148–151; Plutarch, *Phocion*, 16) as violently as Cleophon in the closing months of the Peloponnesian War, shamed both cities into deciding the issue on the field of battle.

The decisive struggle between Philip and the Greeks took place in the plain of Chaeronea early in August 338. Philip had with him some 30,000 infantry and about 2,000 cavalry, all trained veterans, while the Greeks, including the Athenians, Thebans, mercenaries, and the allies that Demosthenes had gained, were equally numerous, but of them only the mercenaries and Thebans could be called experienced soldiers. Little is known about the course of the battle except that the Theban Sacred Band fell to the last man before the devastating attack of the *hetairoi* cavalry led by Philip's eighteen-year-old son, Alexander. According to the account of Polyaenus (4.2.2), whose accuracy cannot be checked, the Athenians, mistaking the methodical retirement of the Macedonian phalanx for a retreat, pursued in such disorderly fashion that Philip easily routed them when he ordered the phalanx to advance. Elsewhere, before the relentless pressure of the Macedonians, the Greek forces broke into headlong flight. A thousand Athenians fell and two thousand were captured. Philip, seeing that his victory was total and thinking of the problem of making terms with the conquered Greeks, ordered his cavalry not to pursue the demoralized enemy.

On the morrow of the battle Philip turned his mind to the question of his relations with the various Greek states, for, although victorious, he knew that all opposition to him would not collapse. Thebes, which had suffered serious losses on the field of battle, immediately capitulated. Philip treated the city harshy, both because it had been faithless to him and because it was the center of Greece's most formidable land army. Thebes was deprived of its predominant place in the Boeotian League, and the cities which it had formerly destroyed, Orchomenus, Plataea, and Thespiae, were to be restored. The government was put under the control of 300 oligarchs, who promptly executed or banished many of the anti-Macedonian democrats. Of their prisoners of war, those who were not ransomed were sold as slaves. Recognizing the important role Thebes had long played in the affairs of central Greece, Philip placed a garrison in the Cadmea (Pausanias, 9.1.8).

The next and the key problem was Athens. Rumor first brought news to Athens of the disaster at Chaeronea, but the full significance of the defeat was not realized until the soldiers who had fled from the battle, including Demosthenes, straggled home. In the belief that Philip would soon arrive in Attica and besiege the city, Hyperides put through the assembly the necessary measures for defense: that the women and children be brought into the city from the country, that the older men be equipped with arms to do garrison duty, that citizen's rights be restored to those who had been disfranchised, and that citizenship be granted to those metics and freedom to those slaves who agreed to fight for Athens. These last three measures were subsequently revoked as unconstitutional. Charidemus, the former mercenary captain from Euboea, now an Athenian citizen and a bitter enemy of Philip, was "elected" commander-in-chief. When Demosthenes returned, he prepared various other defensive measures; then, on being appointed grain commissioner, he departed on a ship to try to procure money and grain from the allies (Demosthenes, 18.248; Lycurgus, 1.16; 39–54).

The first reaction of the Athenians to their defeat, therefore, was to carry on the struggle to the bitter end, but when Philip took no hostile steps and Demosthenes was absent on his mission, a calmer mood began to prevail. The Areopagus, acting on powers unknown, soon replaced Charidemus with Phocion, who had advocated peace talks before Chaeronea (Plutarch, *Phocion,* 16.3). Shortly after the battle Philip sent an envoy to Athens stating that he wanted to start negotiations. This emissary, an Athenian orator named Demades, had, according to the story, caught Philip's attention in the following way. After the battle Philip and some of his friends, thoroughly drunk, made a jeering tour of the captives. Demades, a prisoner, when Philip was close to him, cried out, "O King, when Fortune has cast you in the role of Agamemnon, are you not ashamed to act the part of Thersites?" Sobered by this remark, Philip praised Demades for his boldness, liberated him, and soon thereafter dispatched him to Athens (Diodorus, 16.87). The Athenians decided to send Phocion, Aeschines, and Demades to discuss the situation with Philip, and the conferences resulted in what is known as the Peace of Demades. The main terms of this agreement were: Philip promised not to invade Attica or to send warships into the Piraeus; Athens was to retain all its possessions on the mainland of Greece and also the islands of Delos, Imbros, Lemnos, Scyros, and Samos, but to renounce claim to the rest of its league. The Chersonese was to belong to Philip, but Oropus was to be restored to Athens. Relieved by the unexpected mildness of these terms, the Athenians ratified the peace and contracted an alliance with Philip. In the spirit of this reconciliation Philip then released all the Athenian prisoners without ransom and sent a distinguished military escort, led by Alexander and two of his chief generals, Antipater and Alcimachus, to convey the ashes of the dead to the city. Emotionally stirred by the events of these days, the assembly voted that citizenship be conferred on Philip and Alexander and that a statue of Philip be erected in the marketplace.[39]

THE OVERWHELMING victory at Chaeronea confronted Philip with the problem, on which he may long have been reflecting, of how to unite the disparate Greek states into some type of organization—acceptable to them, if possible, but workable, at least—an organization which would permit him to undertake a campaign in Asia Minor without jeopardizing his own kingdom. If he had offered harsh terms to Athens, he would have been faced with the necessity of a long and difficult siege, and his failures at Perinthus and Byzantium had shown him how frustrating and hazardous such operations could be. Such a siege would have required tremendous expenditures in manpower and money, and probably, through the influence of Demosthenes, would have led to the arrival of Persian ships and wealth to aid Athens, thus thwarting Philip's hopes of arousing Greek interest in an expedition against the Persians. There is no reason, moreover, to doubt Philip's sincere admiration for Greek culture, and he was loath to engage in a deadly struggle with the center of that culture. Philip knew that the Athenian navy and merchant fleet were important factors in Greek civilized life, and he wished them to continue those roles in the world which now lay so largely at his feet and to provide essential assistance to his projected expedition into Asia Minor. Philip had been eager to reach some sort of accord with Athens since the time of the negotiations for the Peace of Philocrates. He knew, however, that to achieve any cooperation from Athens was the most delicate problem confronting him, for, although the city now lay stunned, the fires of resistance and resentment were still burning fiercely, as became vividly clear in the funeral oration which Demosthenes, elected by the people, delivered in the fall or winter.

In contrast to the fury, grief, and repressed hopes of Demosthenes, Isocrates, then ninety-eight years old, welcomed the results of Chaeronea, thinking that the opportunity for a uniting of the Greeks in a campaign against the Persians, which he had advocated since composing his *Panegyricus* in 380, was at last at hand. He wrote a brief letter to Philip urging this course of action and stating that he was grateful to his old age for having permitted him to live until his dream was approaching fulfillment. If Philip should carry out that project successfully, nothing would be left for him except to become a god. That statement which Isocrates made a few weeks before he died, whether metaphorical or not, can be considered a harbinger of the ruler cult which, beginning with Alexander, persisted throughout the Hellenistic and later ages.

In the fall of 338 Philip proceeded southward. Megara and Corinth, which had fought against him at Chaeronea, with the pro-Macedonians now in power welcomed him, as did all the Peloponnesian states except Sparta.[40] He marched through Laconia, ravaging the land as far as Gytheum, but did not attack the city itself. Peripheral parts of the territory were assigned to the Argives, Arcadians, and Messenians, with the result that Sparta was left with its "original" confines. Then, returning to Corinth, Philip sent out word that all Greek states should send delegates there to discuss the current situation of the Greek world.

All the Greek states including the islands, with the exception of recalcitrant Sparta, sent delegates to Corinth in response to what they considered an obligatory summons. It is frustrating that no ancient account has been preserved of the ensuing meetings, which were unparalleled in Greek history. In daily consulation with these delegates, mostly hostile, Philip, by threats and persuasion, worked out the details of the new order he envisaged for the Greek world. Three sources provide considerable information on the organization—the Hellenic League—which emerged from these conferences: a fragmentary inscription (Tod, no. 177) from Athens which records the oath taken by the Athenians, as presumably by the other Greeks, to abide by the recognized peace and agreements; an oration, *On the Treaty with Alexander,* included as number 17 in the corpus of Demosthenes, but probably composed by Hegesippus in 335; a treaty that can safely be equated with the one of 338/7; and an inscription, with large fragments, from Epidaurus which records, so far as changed conditions permitted, the restoration of the Hellenic League of 338/7 by the early Hellenistic kings, Antigonus and his son Demetrius, in 302.[41]

The result of these negotiations was the establishment of what modern scholars call the League of Corinth or the Hellenic League. There is considerable disagreement, however, concerning the nature of this league. The chief suggestions are a treaty of Common Peace, a treaty of alliance between Philip and all the Greeks, a combined treaty of Common Peace and alliance, or two separate treaties, one of Common Peace and one of alliance. It is known that before the congress at Corinth Philip had made pacts with various states, but these were individual agreements whereas the Hellenic League was based on a comprehensive understanding. It is certain that a Common Peace was established. In the Athenian inscription the peace and the agreements (*synthēkai*) are mentioned several times; only in one place is it possible for the word alliance (*symmachia*) to be restored. The oration *On the Treaty with Alexander* frequently refers to the agreements and to those sharing in the peace. From these two sources one becomes aware of many of the specific agreements.

The most important of the agreements are as follows: The Greeks are to be free and autonomous and not to make war on those abiding by the oaths, nor to work against the kingdom of Philip and his descendants, nor to do anything against the agreements, nor to set up a tyrant in any state, nor to allow exiles to depart from a city sharing in the peace with hostile intent against a state included in the peace. The constitution of any state in existence at the time the oath was signed is not to be overthrown. "It is the responsibility of the members of the *synedrion* and those entrusted with the common protection [an ambiguous phrase probably referring to the commanders of the garrisons which had been established] to see that in the states that are parties to the peace there shall be no executions and banishments contrary to the laws existing in those states, no confiscations of property, no partition of lands, no cancelling of debts, and no emancipation of slaves for purposes of revolution" (Demosthenes, 17.15, a challenge to the program of social revolutionaries). The sea is to be free to those sharing the peace. If anyone acts in a way contrary to the agreements, the states are to bring aid as the injured party requests and to fight the one transgressing the Common Peace according to the resolutions of the common *synedrion* and the commands of the hegemon.

These and other regulations were discussed by the delegates at Corinth. It was then, presumably, that the decision was made that the *synedrion* should consist of representatives from the various cities or *ethnē*, the number of delegates elected depending on the size of the population and the military strength of the state concerned. After the congress had voted on these and similar proposals, the envoys returned to their respective cities, where they reported to their assemblies on the business which had been transacted at Corinth. So far as is known, all the states accepted the terms of the Hellenic League, although at some places there may have been heated arguments. It is likely that all states erected an inscription similar to the one found in fragmentary condition at Athens. Such inscriptions, when complete, recorded the state's acceptance of the league, its oath and also the oath of Philip, and a list of the members of the league with numerals opposite each name indicating, seemingly, how many votes in the *synedrion* each particular state controlled.

After the various states had elected the *synedroi* to which they were entitled, these representatives returned to Corinth to the first official meeting of the *synedrion,* apparently held in the summer of 337. On this occasion Philip introduced the idea on which he had been pondering for years, an idea which Isocrates had advocated in 346. He proposed that he and the Macedonians and contingents of the Hellenic League should undertake an expedition against Persia. In an effort to arouse enthusiasm among the Greeks, many of whom he knew were hostile to him, he apparently represented his proposal as a crusade to seek vengeance from the Persians for all the evils which Xerxes had inflicted upon the Greek world. Under the circumstances the delegates, who from the evidence of the Hellenic League of 302 were plenipotentiaries, could hardly reject an idea so closely entangled with the glorious memories of their tradition, one also which would lead to the liberation of the Ionian Greeks from barbarian rule. They voted for the war and elected Philip *strategos autocrator* for the campaign, a more absolute title than that of hegemon, which characterized his civil and military roles in the Greek territory of the league.

As mentioned above, it is difficult to know how to define properly the essence of this Hellenic League. There is no doubt that it was based on a Common Peace, but should it also be considered an alliance (*symmachia*)? In the sources dealing with Alexander the Great various Greek contingents are referred to as allies, but it is hard to prove whether they were actually the allies of the Hellenic League or merely his allies in the campaign against Persia. Philip certainly had alliances with many Greek states, for example, the Argives, Arcadians, Messenians, and Athenians (after the Peace of Demades, according to Diodorus, 16.87.3), but one cannot demonstrate, by citing chapter and verse, that every individual state was linked to Philip by ties of alliance. The effort to obtain a precise terminology to describe technically the legal basis of this league may be impossible, but one is inclined to sympathize with the observation of a well-known scholar: "If a league with obligations which may involve its members in war, with a hegemon or commander-in-chief of its armed forces, and with an assembly to determine its policies is not a *symmachy*, then what is?"[42]

When one tries to envisage this Hellenic League, even if one characterizes Chaeronea, like Milton, as "that dishonest victory, fatal to liberty," one is impressed by the statesmanship, the understanding of the Greek mentality, and the lack of vindictiveness exhibited by the "cunning barbarian" from the north. In any attempt to form a judicious opinion of the league it is only rational to look at conditions in the Greek world in Philip's time from his point of view also rather than, as is the usual practice, exclusively through the vituperative rhetoric of Demosthenes. It is impossible to say just when Philip began to dream of the hegemony of Greece. In the early years of his rule his chief tasks were to defend his kingdom from barbarian invasions and the persistent encroachments of imperialistic Greeks. He ousted the Athenians from their posts in the Thermaic Gulf and rejected their perpetual and almost paranoid claims to Amphipolis. He incorporated Chalcidice, valuable for the welfare of his country and also a center from which Olynthus, Athens, and others had long launched or planned hostile attacks on Macedonia. The Sacred War offered him the windfall of extending his influence southward among the Amphictionic states.

By the end of the Sacred War Philip had changed a weak and vulnerable Macedonia, an inviting prey to Greek exploiters, into an enlarged and powerful kingdom which was, or could be, a threat to the Greeks. In the Peace of Philocrates he may have been thinking only of some type of coexistence with Athens, for coexistence in Philip's eyes, especially if he was already thinking of a campaign to Asia Minor, could offer advantages to Macedonians and Greeks alike. Following the peace he seems—hypocritically, according to Demosthenes—to have aimed at good relations with the Greeks, but before long the truculence of Demosthenes and his party, which assumed that Athenians alone had the right to expand, convinced him of the impossibility of any peaceful coexistence with Athens. Certainly by the time of his Thracian expedition, beginning in 342, and of his subsequent attempts to capture Perinthus, Byzantium, and the Bosporus, Philip had decided that a military showdown with Athens was unavoidable. In this period his serious interest in Asia Minor was revealed by his negotiations with Hermias of Atarneus.

After Chaeronea some settlement of Greek affairs was essential, both for the sake of the Greeks and of Philip's own interests, since he was now planning a Persian expedition and realized that he would need military assistance from the Greeks as well as assurance that they would not overrun Macedonia in his absence. War against Persia could provide land and a new livelihood for the thousands of rootless mercenaries, a constant source of danger to the stability of the Greek states and also to him if they should be led against his kingdom. Such a war would supply necessary occupation for the Macedonians whom he had built into a war machine. When Philip began to formulate his ideas for a reorganization of Greece, he could count on the support of Thessaly and of many of the other Amphictionic states, of Epirus, and of his allies in the Peloponnesus such as Argos, Arcadia, Messenia, and Elis. Also in many cities there were pro-Macedonian elements, whether sincere or venal. The attitude of many states, however, was doubtful or hostile. Consequently, to prevent the possibility of outbreaks, garrisons were necessary. One was placed in Thebes and others in Ambracia to keep watch on western Greece, possibly in Chalcis to preserve order in Euboea and to guard the route southward,[43] and in Acrocorinth to ensure access to the Peloponnesus. These garrisons were probably established in the months immediately following Chaeronea, when occupation of key strategic sites seemed in keeping with the military situation.

In the Hellenic League Philip, undoubtedly having in mind the famous league established in 481 against Persia, brought into existence for the first time in Greek history an organization which, under his aegis, was to compel all Greek states to cooperate rather than to persist in their internecine rivalries. The appalling political chaos of a century, including the horrors and stupidities of the Peloponnesian War, the selfish hegemonies of the Spartans and Thebans, a Social War resulting from Athenian exploitation of the Second Athenian League, the sordid aspects and hypocrisies of the Sacred War against the Phocians, and the ever-increasing social and economic evils demonstrated all too clearly the need for some kind of unifying organ among the Greeks, but national pride and patriotism and the traditions of the glory of city-state autonomy blinded the eyes of many to anything beyond parochial interests. Isocrates, although at heart a pan-Athenian, had eloquently described the wretched conditions of the leading states, Thebes, Argos, and Sparta, and the bungling folly of contemporary Athenian imperialism, and had urged the adoption of Panhellenic thinking. Even Demosthenes finally broke loose from his balance of power mentality and spoke in Panhellenic terms, but his Panhellenism was directed solely against the Macedonian danger and surely would have degenerated into the old vicious scramble for hegemonies if that threat were eliminated.

Philip was fully aware of the vitality of this intense nationalistic pride and of its destructive nature, for his capitalizing on these provincial jealousies had contributed to his rise to power. He also knew that the Hellenes, although they enthusiastically fought and slaughtered one another, had an inbred conviction that they were superior to all other peoples. Consequently in his organization of the League of Corinth he made it entirely Hellenic, for the Macedonians, in Greek eyes, were merely barbarians. He, as a member of a family (Argead) officially recognized as Hellenic, therefore, served as liaison between Macedonians and Greeks. His role as hegemon, although very real, was in some ways beyond or above the regular machinery of the league; he may have hoped that in time this role could gradually become only advisory. Out of respect for Greek prejudices he carefully avoided in his relations with the league that hated title "king" and employed the term "hegemon," for that term had been known to the Greeks for generations as a designation for the dominant state. The ordinances approved by the congress at Corinth were all thoroughly Greek in character, adopted with the aim of suppressing the disorders which had plagued the Greeks so continuously.

The basis of the league was a Common Peace, a concept which the Greeks, beginning with the King's Peace of 386, had attempted unsuccessfully several times in the fourth century; but this peace of 338/7, which every member swore to maintain, had sanctions to make it effective. Not only were the states sharing in the peace bound by oath not to wage war on one another and on Philip and his descendants or to change their forms of government by violence, but the hegemon and the *synedrion* also were obligated to maintain order and, in particular, to prevent civil or social strife (*stasis*), a blight which had especially plagued Argos in recent years. In case of a dispute between two cities, the *synedrion* was to interfere and to arrange arbitration procedure. An extant inscription (Tod, no. 179), dated shortly after 337, records a case in which the *synedrion* had ordered Argos to arbitrate a quarrel between two islands. The sea was to be free, which presumably implied that the *synedrion* would take measures to suppress piracy and to prevent any state such as Athens from exploiting the sea for its own benefit to the detriment of the rights of others. The intention of the "constitution" of the league clearly was that the *synedrion*, representing all the Greek states, should play a significant role. To judge from the league of 302, the *synedrion* was to appoint its own chairman. Philip probably intended, as a precautionary measure, to attend the meetings of the *synedrion*, at least in its early days, but the machinery of the council could function whether the hegemon was present or not. Again, to judge from the league of 302, the regular meetings of the *synedrion* were to occur at the time and the place of the great Panhellenic festivals—Olympia, Delphi, Nemea, Corinth—an excellent arrangement since it was at such festivals that Panhellenic feeling was especially prevalent. Extraordinary meetings were to be held at Corinth.

The Hellenic League revealed Philip as a statesman and not as the destroyer depicted in Demosthenes' oratory. Established after the battle of Chaeronea, the league obviously was intended to strengthen Philip's position, but it also demonstrated an intimate understanding of Greek conditions. The four garrisons, the weakening of Thebes and Sparta, the fact that pro-Macedonians were dominant in many cities, and the vote of the *synedrion* to supply contingents for the Persian expedition—these and other factors all contributed to the increase of Philip's power and authority. The reality of his hegemony was obvious to all. If Philip had lived for another score of years and if, eradicating the shame of the King's Peace, he had liberated the Ionian Greeks and opened Asia Minor for Greek colonization, especially for the mercenaries, the Greeks might have become more reconciled to the league. If the *synedrion* had performed its functions satisfactorily, the hegemon might have assumed a less prominent role. Such speculations are really idle, for there is no way to know what Philip's intentions really were. He wanted the cooperation of the Greeks, but there is no evidence that he wished to tyrannize over them. Philip, however, was assassinated in 336, and the subsequent conquests of his son, Alexander the Great, changed the world situation so profoundly that the Hellenic League had little chance of survival. The anti-Macedonian outbreak immediately after Philip's death disclosed what the contemporary attitude of a large number of the Greeks was. Beneficial as an organization enforcing internal peace and cooperation would have been to the Greeks, their pride could not stomach being under the aegis of a "barbarian," and cities like Athens felt nothing but rage and humiliation at being placed on a level with other states and having to abandon the eternal quest for hegemony.

THE BATTLE of Chaeronea, the establishment of the Hellenic League, and the "world" conquests of Alexander the Great from 334 until his death in 323 marked a turning point in the history of the Greeks. The significance of Alexander in terms of Greek history is that he ushered in the Hellenistic Age—a period in which the Greek city-states played an increasingly minor role politically. In the years of the wars of the successors (*diadochoi*) of Alexander, and later when the Ptolemaic kingdom was established in Egypt, the Seleucid in Asia, and subsequently the Attalid in Asia Minor and the Euthydemid in Bactria and India, the Greeks flocked eastward as soldiers, administrators, scholars, businessmen, and colonists. In the homeland the Greeks struggled unsuccessfully to revive the glory of the city-states; they witnessed the rise to influence of leagues like the Achaean and Aetolian, and they fought intermittently with the Antigonid kingdom in Macedonia. The consequences of the movement of the Greeks to the east were significant: their relations with the natives; their living in new settlements and cities such as Alexandria in Egypt, Antioch on the Orontes, and Seleuceia on the Tigris ("the successor of Babylon and the precursor of Baghdad"); the spreading of the common Greek language, the Koinē, which became a *lingua franca* for the east and the language of the Septuagint into which the Old Testament was translated in Alexandria; the syncretism of religions; and the hellenization, at least externally, of many natives, well illustrated by St. Mark's story of "a Greek woman (Hellenis), a Syrophoenician by race," coming to Jesus for help. The Greeks and the Hellenistic kingdoms succumbed to the onslaught of Rome in the second and first centuries B.C, but Greek civilization, although humbled and somewhat altered, continued, even victoriously, as Horace's famous line (*Epistulae,* 2.1.156) emphasizes: *Graecia capta ferum victorem cepit*— "captured Greece her savage victor captured."

Notes

Abbreviations of Frequently Cited Journals

A.J.A.	*American Journal of Archaeology*
A.J.P.	*American Journal of Philology*
B.C.H.	*Bulletin de Correspondance Hellénique*
C.P.	*Classical Philology*
C.Q.	*Classical Quarterly*
J.H.S.	*Journal of Hellenic Studies*
T.A.P.A.	*Transactions of the American Philological Association*

Notes

1. The Early Aegean World

1. John Chadwick, *The Decipherment of Linear B,* 2nd ed. (Cambridge: Cambridge University Press, 1967). J. T. Hooker, *The Origin of the Linear B Script* (Salamanca, Spain: Ediciones Universidad de Salamanca, 1979). Leonard R. Palmer, *Mycenaeans and Minoans* (New York: Knopf, 1962), in an argument not generally accepted, states that the Linear B tablets at Cnossos should also be dated around 1200.

2. O. R. Gurney, *The Hittites,* 2nd ed. (Baltimore: Penguin Books, 1961).

3. André Parrot, *Le Palais,* vol. 2 of *Mission archéologique de Mari* (Paris: Geuthner, 1958), pt. 2, "Peintures murales," pp. 107–111.

4. Leonard Woolley, *A Forgotten Kingdom* (Baltimore: Penguin Books, 1953).

5. Michael Ventris and John Chadwick, *Documents in Mycenaean Greek,* 2nd ed. (Cambridge: Cambridge University Press, 1973), pp. 102–105. J. G. Macqueen, "Geography and History in Western Asia Minor in the Second Millennium B.C.," *Anatolian Studies,* 18 (1968), 169–185, especially 178–185. J. D. Muhly, "Hittites and Achaeans: Ahhijawa *Redomitus,*" *Historia,* 23 (1974), 129–145.

6. Carl W. Blegen, *Troy and the Trojans* (New York: Praeger, 1963).

7. Denys L. Page, *History and the Homeric Iliad* (Berkeley and Los Angeles: University of California Press, 1959), pp. 118–177. R. Hope Simpson and J. F. Lazenby, *The Catalogue of the Ships in Homer's Iliad* (Oxford: Clarendon Press, 1970).

8. Nancy K. Sandars, *The Sea Peoples: Warriors of the Ancient Mediterranean, 1250–1150 B.C.* (London: Thames and Hudson, 1978).

9. Rhys Carpenter, *Discontinuity in Greek Civilization* (Cambridge: Cambridge University Press, 1966), pp. 27–53. Reid A. Bryson and Thomas J. Murray, *Climates of Hunger: Mankind and the World's Changing Weather* (Madison: University of Wisconsin Press, 1977), pp. 4–16.

10. Oscar Broneer, "Athens in the Late Bronze Age," *Antiquity,* 30 (1956), 9–18. R. M. Cook, *Greek Painted Pottery* (Chicago: Quadrangle Books, 1960), pp. 5–13. Emily Vermeule, *Greece in the Bronze Age* (Chicago: University of Chicago Press, 1964), pp. 278–279.

11. J. T. Hooker, *Mycenaean Greece* (London: Routledge and Kegan Paul, 1976), pp. 166–180. John Chadwick, "Who were the Dorians?" *Parola del Pasato,* 166 (1976), 103–177.

12. Albert B. Lord, *The Singer of Tales* (Cambridge, Mass.: Harvard University Press, 1960), is very valuable for the historian and is followed

closely in the discussion above. James A. Notopoulos, "Homer, Hesiod and the Achaean Heritage of Oral Poetry," *Hesperia*, 29 (1960), 177–197. Geoffrey S. Kirk, *Homer and the Oral Tradition* (Cambridge: Cambridge University Press, 1976).

13. T. B. L. Webster, *From Mycenae to Homer*, 2nd ed. (New York: Norton, 1964), pp. 64–90.

14. M. I. Finley, *The World of Odysseus* (New York: Viking, 1965), pp. 17–45.

15. Alan J. B. Wace, *Mycenae: An Archaeological History and Guide* (Princeton: Princeton University Press, 1949). George E. Mylonas, *Mycenae and the Mycenaean Age* (Princeton: Princeton University Press, 1966).

16. John Chadwick, *The Mycenaean World* (Cambridge: Cambridge University Press, 1976), p. 24.

17. M. I. Finley, "The Mycenaean Tablets and Economic History," *The Economic History Review*, 2nd ser., 10 (1957–58), 128–141. Alan E. Samuel, *The Mycenaeans in History* (Englewood Cliffs, N.J.: Prentice-Hall, 1966).

2. The Dark Age

1. Strabo, book 13, passim. Jean Bérard, "La Migration Éolienne," *Revue Archéologique* (1959), 1–28.

2. J. M. Cook, "Old Smyrna, 1948–1951," *The Annual of the British School at Athens*, 53–54 (1958–59), 1–34.

3. Strabo, book 14, passim. Michel B. Sakellariou, *La Migration grecque en Ionie* (Athens: Institut français d'Athènes, 1958). Carl Roebuck, *Ionian Trade and Colonization* (New York: Archaeological Institute of America, 1959). Ionic was presumably a dialect gradually forming in Attica and Euboea in Mycenaean times.

4. H. E. Seebohm, *On the Structure of Greek Tribal Society* (London and New York: Macmillan, 1895). Gustave Glotz, *Histoire grecque*, vol. I (Paris: Presses Universitaires de France, 1925), pp. 113–152. Gustave Glotz, *The Greek City* (New York: Knopf, 1929), pp. 1–18. George D. Thomson, *Studies in Ancient Greek Society: The Prehistoric Aegean*, 3rd ed. (London: Lawrence and Wishart, 1978), pp. 102–109.

5. Denis Roussel, *Tribu et cité* (Paris: Belles Lettres, 1976).

6. Antony Andrewes, *The Greeks* (New York: Knopf, 1967), p. 78.

7. M. P. Nilsson, *Cults, Myths, Oracles, and Politics in Ancient Greece* (Lund: Gleerup, 1951), p. 150.

8. Margherita Guarducci, "L'Istituzione della fratria nella Graecia antica e nelle colonie greche d'Italia," *Memorie della R. Accademia Nazionale dei Lincei. Classe di Scienze Morali, Storice e Filologiche,* ser. VI, vol. VI, fasc. 1 (1937), pp. 5–103.

9. Antony Andrewes, "Phratries in Homer," *Hermes*, 89 (1961), 129–140.

10. Guarducci, "L'Istituzione della fratria," p. 12.

11. M. I. Finley, *The World of Odysseus* (New York: Viking, 1965), chap. 4, "Household, Kin, and Community." Thomson, *Studies*, pp. 109–112.

12. C. S. Orwin and C. S. Orwin, *The Open Fields*, 2nd ed. (Oxford: Clarendon Press, 1954). John Thirsk, "The Common Fields," *Past and Present*, 29 (December 1964), 3–25.

13. William Ridgeway, "The Homeric Land System," *J.H.S.*, 6 (1885), 319–339.

14. Gustave Glotz, *Ancient Greece at Work* (New York: Knopf, 1926), pp. 24–33.

3. The Age of Transition

1. Chester G. Starr, *The Origins of Greek Civilization 1100–650 B.C.* (New York: Knopf, 1961), pp. 335–345.

2. R. M. Cook, "Ionia and Greece in the Eighth and Seventh Centuries B.C.," *J.H.S.*, 66 (1946), 67–98. George M. A. Hanfmann, "Ionia, Leader or Follower?" *Harvard Studies in Classical Philology*, 61 (1953), 1–37.

3. D. W. S. Hunt, "Feudal Survivals in Ionia," *J.H.S.*, 67 (1947), 68–76.

4. Gustave Glotz, *The Greek City* (New York: Knopf, 1929), pp. 18–32.

5. Chester G. Starr, "The Decline of the Early Greek Kings," *Historia*, 10 (1961), 129–138.

6. James H. Oliver, *Demokratia, the Gods, and the Free World* (Baltimore: Johns Hopkins Press, 1960), chap. 1, "From Divinely Ordained Kingship to Civic Constitution," pp. 1–58.

7. George M. Calhoun, "Classes and Masses in Homer," *C.P.*, 29 (1934), 192–208; 301–316. Starr, *Origins of Greek Civilization*, pp. 302–305.

8. Roland Martin, *L'Urbanisme dans la Grèce antique* (Paris: Picard and Cie., 1956), pp. 30–47. R. E. Wycherley, *How the Greeks Built Cities*, 2nd ed. (Garden City, N.Y.: Doubleday, 1969), pp. 1–15.

9. Leonard Whibley, *Greek Oligarchies: Their Character and Organisation* (London: Methuen, 1896). Glotz, *The Greek City*, pp. 61–99. Victor Ehrenberg, *The Greek State* (New York: Barnes and Noble, 1960).

10. S. C. Humphreys, "Family Tombs and Tomb Cult in Ancient Athens: Tradition or Traditionalism?" *J.H.S.*, 100 (1980), 96–126, questions the belief that there was a common burial ground for members of a *genos*.

11. H. L. Lorimer, "The Hoplite Phalanx with Special Reference to the Poems of Archilochus and Tyrtaeus," *The Annual of the British School at Athens*, 42 (1947), 76–138, especially p. 81.

12. Robert J. Bonner and Gertrude Smith, *The Administration of Justice from Homer to Aristotle* (Chicago: University of Chicago Press, 1930), pp. 1–56.

4. Colonization

1. T. J. Dunbabin, *The Greeks and Their Eastern Neighbours: Studies in the Relations between Greece and the Countries of the Near East in the Eighth and Seventh Centuries B.C.* (London: Society for the Promotion of Hellenic Studies, 1957), and John Boardman, *The Greeks Overseas* (Baltimore: Penguin Books, 1964),

chap. 3, "The Eastern Adventure," pp. 57–126 provide an excellent background for conditions in the Near East in the period under consideration.

2. Leonard Woolley, *A Forgotten Kingdom* (Baltimore: Penguin Books, 1953), pp. 165–181.

3. Donald Harden, *The Phoenicians* (New York: Praeger, 1962).

4. Georges Roux, *Ancient Iraq* (Harmondsworth, Middlesex, England: Penguin Books, 1966), pp. 287–342.

5. Boardman, *Greeks Overseas*, pp. 127–174. M. M. Austin, *Greece and Egypt in the Archaic Age* (Cambridge, England: Proceedings of the Cambridge Philological Society, supplement no. 2, 1970).

6. For the colonizing movement to the west, the following pages owe much to T. J. Dunbabin, *The Western Greeks: The History of Sicily and South Italy from the Foundation of the Greek Colonies to 480 B.C.* (Oxford: Clarendon Press, 1948), A. G. Woodhead, *The Greeks in the West* (New York: Praeger, 1962), and Boardman, *Greeks Overseas,* pp. 175–231.

7. R. M. Cook, "Reasons for the Foundations of Ischia and Cumae," *Historia,* 11 (1962), 113–114. G. Buchner, "Pithekoussai, Oldest Greek Colony in the West," *Expedition,* 8. no. 4 (1966), 4–12.

8. Erik Sjöqvist, *Sicily and the Greeks: Studies in the Interrelationship between the Indigenous Populations and the Greek Colonists* (Ann Arbor: University of Michigan Press, 1973).

9. B. H. Warmington, *Carthage* (Baltimore: Penguin Books, 1964), pp. 22–26.

10. Philippe Gauthier, "Grecs et Phéniciens en Sicile pendant la période archaique," *Revue Historique* (1960), 257–274.

11. Rhys Carpenter, *Beyond the Pillars of Heracles: The Classical World Seen through the Eyes of Its Discoverers* (New York: Delacorte Press, 1966), pp. 38–67.

12. Hermann Bengtson, *Griechische Geschichte,* 4th ed. (Munich: C. H. Beck, 1969), p. 97.

13. Donald W. Bradeen, "The Chalcidians in Thrace," *A.J.P.,* 73 (1952), 356–380.

14. The account given here of this wave of colonization is greatly indebted to Carl Roebuck, *Ionian Trade and Colonization* (New York: Archaeological Institute of America, 1959), pp. 105–130; A. L. Mongait, *Archaeology in the U.S.S.R.* (Baltimore: Penguin Books, 1961), pp. 179–206; Boardman, *Greeks Overseas,* pp. 236–267.

15. For these pages on the Greeks in Egypt and the establishment of Naucratis, the account presented here owes much to John Boardman, *Greeks Overseas,* pp. 127–150, and to M. M. Austin, *Greece and Egypt in the Archaic Age,* which includes references to all pertinent previous work.

16. For an excellent work on Cyrene see François Chamoux, *Cyrène sous la monarchie des Battiades* (Paris: Boccard, 1953).

17. L. H. Jeffery, "The Pact of the First Settlers at Cyrene," *Historia,* 10 (1961), 139–147, especially 143–144.

18. A. J. Graham, *Colony and Mother City in Ancient Greece* (Manchester, England: Manchester University Press, 1964), pp. 225–226. The italicized words indicate textual difficulties. Charles W. Fornara, *Archaic Times to the End of the Peloponnesian War,* Translated Documents of Greece and Rome, vol. 1, no. 18 (Baltimore: Johns Hopkins University Press, 1967), gives a translation of the whole document.

19. A. J. Graham, "The Authenticity of the Horkion tōn Oikistērōn of Cyrene," *J.H.S.,* 80 (1960), 94–111, and Jeffery, "Pact of the First Settlers," 139–147.

5. Social, Economic, and Political Developments

1. On these and other economic matters, see such works as Gustave Glotz, *Ancient Greece at Work* (New York: Knopf, 1926), pt. 2, "The Archaic Period," pp. 61–143; Johannes Hasebroek, *Trade and Politics in Ancient Greece* (London: J. Bell and Sons, 1933); Moses I. Finkelstein, *"Emporos, Nauklēros,* and *Kapēlos:* A Prolegomena to the Study of Ancient Trade," *C.P.,* 30 (1935), 320–336; Carl Roebuck, *Ionian Trade and Colonization* (New York: Archaeological Institute of America, 1959); M. M. Austin and P. Vidal-Naquet, *Economic and Social History of Ancient Greece: An Introduction* (Berkeley: University of California Press, 1977); Chester G. Starr, *The Economic and Social Growth of Early Greece 800–500 B.C.* (New York: Oxford University Press, 1977).

2. William L. Westermann, *The Slave Systems of Greek and Roman Antiquity* (Philadelphia: The American Philosophical Society, 1955), pp. 1–5.

3. Antony Andrewes, *The Greek Tyrants* (New York: Harper & Row, 1963), pp. 31–36. W. G. Forrest, *The Emergence of Greek Democracy* (London: Weidenfeld and Nicolson, 1966), pp. 88–97. John Salmon, "Political Hoplites?" *J.H.S.,* 97 (1977), 84–101.

4. Robert J. Bonner and Gertrude Smith, *The Administration of Justice from Homer to Aristotle,* vol. I (Chicago: University of Chicago Press, 1930), pp. 67–82.

5. Rhys Carpenter, *A.J.P.,* 84 (1963), 76–85, review of L. H. Jeffery, *The Local Scripts of Archaic Greece* (Oxford: Clarendon Press, 1961). R. M. Cook and A. G. Woodhead, "The Diffusion of the Greek Alphabet," *A.J.A.,* 63 (1959), 175–178.

6. F. E. Adcock, "Literary Tradition and Early Greek Code-Makers," *Cambridge Historical Journal,* 2 (1927), 95–109. Andrew Szegedy-Maszak, "Legends of the Greek Lawgivers," *Greek, Roman, and Byzantine Studies,* 19 (1978), 199–209.

7. Andrewes, *Greek Tyrants,* pp. 20–30. Mary White, "Greek Tyranny," *Phoenix,* 9 (1955), 1–18. The literature on tyranny is immense. A good guide is Helmut Berve, *Die Tyrannis bei den Griechen,* vol. II, *Anmerkungen* (Munich: Beck, 1967), which gives an exhaustive presentation of sources and modern scholarship.

8. Andrewes, *Greek Tyrants,* pp. 34–36.

9. Mary White, "The Dates of the Orthagorids," *Phoenix*, 12 (1958), 2–14.

10. For the Cypselid tyranny in Corinth, see Édouard Will, *Korinthiaka* (Paris: Boccard, 1955), pp. 363–571; Andrewes, *Greek Tyrants*, pp. 43–53; Forrest, *Emergence of Greek Democracy*, pp. 104–122.

11. R. M. Cook, "Archaic Greek Trade: Three Conjectures. I. The Diolkos," *J.H.S.*, 99 (1979), 152–153.

12. B. P. Grenfell and A. S. Hunt, *The Oxyrhynchus Papyri*, XI, no. 1365 (London: Egypt Exploration Society, 1915). For problems of the genealogy of the family of Orthagoras, see N. G. L. Hammond, "The Family of Orthagoras," *C.Q.*, *49 (1956), 45–53.*

13. *Jean Defradas, Les Thèmes de la propaganda delphique*, 2nd ed. (Paris: Les Belles Lettres, 1972), pp. 21–118.

14. J. Jannoray, "Krisa, Kirrha et la Première Guerre Sacrée," *B.C.H.*, 61 (1937), 33–43.

15. This paragraph follows very closely George Forrest, "The First Sacred War," *B.C.H.*, 80 (1956), 33–52. The quotation is from p. 51.

16. Malcolm F. McGregor, "Cleisthenes of Sicyon and the Panhellenic Festivals," *T.A.P.A.*, 72 (1941), 266–287.

17. The account just given of the First Sacred War owes much to Forrest, "First Sacred War," and Marta Sordi, "La Prima Guerra Sacra," *Rivista di Filologia*, 81 (1953), 320–346. In "The Myth of the First Sacred War," *C.Q.*, 71 (1978), 38–73, Noel Robertson argues that the Sacred War of ca. 590 was only a fiction invented by Philip II of Macedonia and his partisans to provide a precedent for his policy in the "Third" and "Fourth" Sacred Wars of the mid-fourth century. Despite his learning, Robertson is mistaken to say that there are no direct references to this war before the 340s, for G. A. Lehmann, *Historia*, 29 (1980), 245–246, points out that Isocrates (14), *Plataicus*, 31 (to be dated in the period 373–371) specifically mentions it. It should also be stated that the elimination of the First Sacred War would remove the most logical—and only?—explanation for the formation of the Delphic Amphictiony.

18. Thomas Kelly, *A History of Argos to 500 B.C.* (Minneapolis: University of Minnesota Press, 1976). Salmon, "Political Hoplites?" p. 93, n. 37, rejects Kelly's dating.

19. McGregor, "Cleisthenes of Sicyon," pp. 277–278.

20. White, "Dates of the Orthagorids," pp. 2–14. D. M. Leahy, "The Dating of the Orthagorid Dynasty," *Historia*, 17 (1968), 1–23.

21. P. N. Ure, *The Origin of Tyranny* (Cambridge: Cambridge University Press, 1922), p. 267.

22. Denys Page, *Sappho and Alcaeus* (Oxford: Clarendon Press, 1955), pp. 149–243; Andrewes, *Greek Tyrants*, pp. 92–99.

23. Carl Roebuck, "Tribal Organization in Ionia," *T.A.P.A.*, 92 (1961), 495–507, especially 504–507.

24. Mary White, "The Duration of the Samian Tyranny," *J.H.S.*, 74 (1954), 36–43; Andrewes, *Greek Tyrants*, pp. 117–122.

25. June Goodfield, "The Tunnel of Eupalinus," *Scientific American* (June 1964), 104–112.

26. Will, *Korinthiaka,* pp. 506–507.

27. These conclusions owe much to White, "Greek Tyranny," pp. 1–18.

28. E. S. G. Robinson, "The Coins from the Ephesian Artemision Reconsidered," *J.H.S.,* 71 (1951), 156–167, especially 165.

29. R. M. Cook, "Speculations on the Origins of Coinage," *Historia,* 7 (1958), 257–262. C. M. Kraay, "Hoards, Small Change and the Origins of Coinage," *J.H.S.,* 84 (1964), 76–91.

6. Early Sparta

1. Max Cary, *The Geographic Background of Greek and Roman History* (Oxford: Clarendon Press, 1949), pp. 89–93. Paul Cartledge, *Sparta and Lakonia: A Regional History 1300–362 B.C.* (London: Routledge and Kegan Paul, 1979), pp. 13–23.

2. For the "credibility" problem see Chester G. Starr, "The Credibility of Early Spartan History," *Historia,* 14 (1965), 257–272.

3. Lionel Pearson, "The Pseudo-History of Messenia and Its Authors," *Historia,* 11 (1962), 397–426.

4. Luigi Moretti, "Olympionikai, I vincitori negli antichi agoni Olimpici," *Atti della Accademia Nazionale dei Lincei. Memorie, Classe di Scienze Morali, Storiche e Filologiche,* ser. VIII, vol. VIII, fasc. 2, (1957), pp. 53–198.

5. For the confused data about the resettling of the Asineans and Nauplians between 700 and 600, see G. L. Huxley, *Early Sparta* (Cambridge, Mass.: Harvard University Press, 1962), pp. 21, 60. W. G. Forrest, *A History of Sparta 950–192 B.C.* (New York: Norton, 1969), pp. 36–37.

6. Humfrey Michell, *Sparta* (Cambridge: Cambridge University Press, 1952; paperback ed., 1964), pp. 101–115. Pavel Oliva, *Sparta and Her Social Problems* (Amsterdam: Hakkert, 1971), pp. 23–28.

7. James H. Oliver, *Demokratia, the Gods, and the Free World* (Baltimore: Johns Hopkins Press, 1960), chap. 1, "From Divinely Ordained Kingship to Civic Constitution," pp. 1–58.

8. See, for example. C. G. Thomas, "On the Role of the Spartan Kings," *Historia,* 23 (1974), 257–270.

9. Michell, *Sparta,* pp. 126–131.

10. Ibid., p. 225.

11. Gustave Glotz, *Histoire Grecque,* vol. I (Paris: Presses Universitaires de France, 1925), pp. 367–370. Pierre Roussel, *Sparte* (1939; Paris: Boccard, 1960), pp. 118–124.

12. Michell, *Sparta,* pp. 281–297.

13. Michell, *Sparta,* pp. 165–204. Willem den Boer, *Laconian Studies* (Amsterdam: North-Holland, 1954), pp. 233–298.

14. Henri Jeanmaire, "La Cryptie Lacédémonienne," *Revue des Études Grecques,* 26 (1913), 121–150.

15. Alcman, *The Partheneion,* ed. Denys L. Page (Oxford: Clarendon Press, 1951). Huxley, *Early Sparta,* pp. 61–65.

16. J. A. O. Larsen in A. F. Pauly and Georg Wissowa, *Real-Encyclopädie der Classischen Altertumswissenschaft*, vol. 19, pt. 1 (Stuttgart: Metzler, 1937), see under "Perioikoi," pp. 816–833.

17. Roussel, *Sparte*, p. 161.

18. J. A. O. Larsen, "The Constitution of the Peloponnesian League," I and II, *C.P.*, 28 (1933), 257–276; 29 (1934), 1–19. Walter W. Snyder, "Peloponnesian Studies 404–371," Ph. D. dissertation, Princeton University, 1972.

7. Early Athens

1. I. T. Hill, *The Ancient City of Athens: Its Topography and Monuments* (London: Methuen, 1953; reprint ed., Chicago: Argonaut, 1969), pp. 1–3.

2. R. M. Cook, *Greek Painted Pottery* (Chicago: Quadrangle Books, 1960), pp. 5–22.

3. H. T. Wade-Gery, "Eupatridai, Archons, and Areopagus," in *Essays in Greek History* (Oxford: Blackwell, 1958), pp. 92–93.

4. T. J. Cadoux, "The Athenian Archons from Kreon to Hypsichides," *J.H.S.*, 68 (1948), 70–123.

5. John J. Keaney, "The Date of Aristotle's *Athenaion Politeia*," *Historia*, 19 (1970), 326–336.

6. James Day and Mortimer Chambers, *Aristotle's History of Athenian Democracy* (Berkeley: University of California Press, 1962).

7. Robert J. Bonner and Gertrude Smith, *The Administration of Justice from Homer to Aristotle*, vol. I (Chicago: University of Chicago Press, 1930), pp. 85–88.

8. Charles Hignett, *A History of the Athenian Constitution to the End of the Fifth Century B.C.* (Oxford: Clarendon Press, 1952), p. 76.

9. W. Robert Connor, *The New Politicians of Fifth Century Athens* (Princeton, N.J.: Princeton University Press, 1971), p. 12 and n. 11.

10. Wade-Gery, "Eupatridai," pp. 98–99.

11. Hignett, *Athenian Constitution*, pp. 62, 67.

12. Ronald S. Stroud, *Drakon's Law on Homicide* (Berkeley: University of California Press, 1968), pp. 6, 50.

13. Antony Andrewes, "Philochoros on Phratries," *J.H.S.*, 81 (1961), 1–15.

14. Hignett, *Athenian Constitution*, pp. 59–60.

15. R. M. Cook, *Greek Painted Pottery*, pp. 17–22; T. J. Dunbabin, *The Greeks and Their Eastern Neighbours* (London: Society for the Promotion of Hellenic Studies, 1957), pp. 19–23.

16. Bonner and Smith, *Administration of Justice*, pp. 134–135. Douglas M. MacDowell, *The Law in Classical Athens* (Ithaca, N.Y.: Cornell University Press, 1978), pp. 41–43.

17. B. L. Bailey, "The Export of Attic Black-Figure Ware," *J.H.S.*, 60 (1940), 60–70.

18. W. J. Woodhouse, *Solon the Liberator: A Study of the Agrarian Problem in Attika in the Seventh Century* (Oxford: Oxford University Press, 1938), pp. 164–165.

19. J. V. A. Fine, *Horoi: Studies in Mortgage, Real Security, and Land Tenure in Ancient Athens* (Princeton, N.J.: American School of Classical Studies at Athens; *Hesperia:* suppl. 9, 1951), pp. 178–180.

20. M. I. Finley, "The Servile Statuses of Ancient Greece," *Revue Internationale des Droits de l'Antiquité,* ser. 3, vol. VII (1960), 165–189; "Between Slavery and Freedom," *Comparative Studies in Society and History,* vol. VI (1963–64), 233–249; "La Servitude pour Dettes," *Revue Historique de Droit Français et Étranger,* ser. 4, 43 (1965), 159–184.

21. Ronald S. Stroud, *The Axones and Kyrbeis of Dracon and Solon* (Berkeley: University of California Press, 1979), especially pp. 41–44.

22. A. R. W. Harrison, *The Law of Athens,* vol. I, *The Family and Property* (Oxford: Clarendon Press, 1968), pp. 149–153. MacDowell, *Law in Classical Athens,* pp. 99–101.

23. George M. Calhoun, *The Growth of Criminal Law in Ancient Greece* (Berkeley: University of California Press, 1927), passim.

24. Eberhard Ruschenbusch, *"Patrios Politeia:* Theseus, Drakon, Solon und Kleisthenes in Publizistik und Geschichtsschreibung des 5 und 4 Jahrhenderts v. Chr.," *Historia,* 7 (1958), 398–424.

25. Hignett, *Athenian Constitution,* pp. 92–96; Day and Chambers, *Aristotle's History,* pp. 84–88.

26. K. H. Waters, "Solon's 'Price-Equalisation,'" *J.H.S.,* 80 (1960), 186.

27. Antony Andrewes, *The Greek Tyrants* (New York: Harper & Row, 1963), p. 104.

28. C. W. Eliot, "Where Did the Alkmaionidai Live?" *Historia,* 16 (1967), 279–286.

29. Cadoux, "Athenian Archons," pp. 90, 120.

30. Herodotus, 1.59–64; Aristotle, *Ath. Const.,* 14–16; Plutarch, *Solon,* 30–31.

31. H. T. Wade-Gery, "Miltiades," in *Essays in Greek History* (Oxford: Blackwell, 1958), p. 166.

32. D. M. Lewis, "Cleisthenes and Attica," *Historia,* 12 (1963), 25–27.

33. Donald W. Bradeen, "The Fifth-Century Archon List," *Hesperia,* 32 (1963), 196.

34. H. W. Parke, *Festivals of the Athenians* (Ithaca, N.Y.: Cornell University Press, 1977), pp. 125–126.

35. W. Robert Connor, "Theseus in Classical Athens," in *The Quest for Theseus,* ed. Anne G. Ward (London: Pall Mall Press, 1970), pp. 143–174.

36. G. K. Jenkins, *Ancient Greek Coins* (New York: Putnam 1972), pp. 43–49.

37. Benjamin D. Meritt, "An Early Archon List," *Hesperia,* 8 (1939), 59–65.

38. Mary White, "Greek Tyranny," *Phoenix,* 9 (1955), 16.

39. Felix Jacoby, *Atthis: The Local Chronicles of Ancient Athens* (Oxford:

Clarendon Press, 1949), pp. 152–196; C. W. Fornara, "The Cult of Harmodius and Aristogeiton," *Philologus,* 114 (1970), 150–180.

40. H. T. Wade-Gery, "The Laws of Kleisthenes," in *Essays in Greek History* (Oxford: Blackwell, 1958), pp. 142–143.

41. C. W. Eliot, *Coastal Demes of Attika: A Study of the Policy of Kleisthenes* (Toronto: Toronto University Press, 1962), p. 143.

42. Lewis, "Cleisthenes and Attica," pp. 30–31.

43. Day and Chambers, *Aristotle's History,* pp. 111–120.

44. Hignett, *Athenian Constitution,* p. 143.

45. R E. Wycherley, *The Stones of Athens* (Princeton, N.J.: Princeton University Press, 1978), pp. 52–53.

46. Wesley E. Thompson, "The Deme in Kleisthenes' Reforms," *Symbolae Osloenses,* 46 (1971), 72–79.

47. Cadoux, "The Athenian Archons," pp. 114–116.

48. Gustave Glotz, *The Greek City and Its Institutions* (New York: Knopf, 1930), pp. 171–173.

49. John J. Keaney, "The Text of Androtion F6 and the Origin of Ostracism," *Historia,* 19 (1970), 1–11, especially p. 3.

50. G. R. Stanton, "The Introduction of Ostracism and Alcmeonid Propaganda," *J.H.S.,* 90 (1970), 180–183.

51. A. R. Hands, "Ostraka and the Law of Ostracism: Some Possibilities and Assumptions," *J.H.S.,* 79 (1959), 69–79.

8. The Greeks and the Persians

1. The following pages on the early Iranians and the development of the Median and Persian kingdoms are largely based on the relevant chapters in books such as the following: J. B. Bury, S. A. Cook, and F. E. Adcock, eds., *Cambridge Ancient History,* vols. III and IV (Cambridge: Cambridge University Press, 1925 and 1926); Richard N. Frye, *The Heritage of Persia* (New York: Mentor Books, 1966); Roman Ghirshman, *Iran, from the Earliest Times to the Islamic Conquest* (Baltimore: Penguin Books, 1954); Albrecht Goetze, *Kleinasien* (Munich: C. H. Beck, 1957); Clément Huart and Louis Delaporte, *L'Iran antique: Élam et Perse et la civilisation iranienne* (Paris: Albin Michel, 1952); A. L. Mongait, *Archaeology in the USSR* (Baltimore: Penguin Books, 1961); A. T. Olmstead, *History of the Persian Empire* (Chicago: University of Chicago Press, 1948); Stuart Piggott, *Prehistoric India to 1000 B.C.* (Harmondsworth, Middlesex, England: Penguin Books, 1950).

2. D. L. Page, *A New Chapter in the History of Greek Tragedy* (Cambridge: Cambridge University Press, 1951).

3. Hermann Bengtson, *Griechische Geschichte,* 4th ed. (Munich: C. H. Beck, 1969), p. 130, n. 1.

4. Andrew R. Burn, *Persia and the Greeks: The Defense of the West, c. 546–478 B.C.* (New York: St. Martin's Press, 1962), p. 44.

5. Olmstead, *History of the Persian Empire,* p. 91.

6. This minority opinion of scholars like Olmstead, *History of the Persian Empire,* pp. 107–118, and Burn, *Persia and the Greeks,* pp. 90–95, is strengthened

by the recent article of E. J. Bickerman and H. Tadmore, "Darius I, Pseudo-Smerdis, and the Magi," *Athenaeum*, 66 (1978), 239–261.

7. Olmstead, *History of the Persian Empire*, p. 238.

8. H. T. Wade-Gery, "Miltiades," in *Essays in Greek History* (Oxford: Blackwell, 1958), pp. 161–163; see different interpretation in Burn, *Persia and the Greeks*, pp. 218–220.

9. J. A. O. Larsen, *Representative Government in Greek and Roman History* (Berkeley: University of California Press, 1955), p. 29.

10. Burn, *Persia and the Greeks*, p. 197 and n. 3.

11. K. J. Beloch, *Griechische Geschichte*, 2nd ed. (Berlin: de Gruyter, 1931), vol. II, pt. 2, p. 86.

12. Ernst Badian, "Archons and *Strategoi*," *Antichthon*, 5 (1971), p. 15, n. 44.

13. H. T. Wade-Gery, "Themistokles' Archonship," in *Essays in Greek History*, pp. 177–178; Burn, *Persia and the Greeks*, pp. 224–226.

14. Burn, *Persia and the Greeks*, pp. 227–232.

15. Ibid., p. 253.

16. Ibid., pp. 253–255.

17. *Aeschylus*, with an English translation by Herbert Weir Smyth, Loeb Classical Library (Cambridge, Mass.: Harvard University Press, 1922), Introduction, p. xxiii.

18. H. D. Westlake, "The Medism of Thessaly," *J.H.S.*, 56 (1936), 12–24.

19. W. P. Wallace, "Kleomenes, Marathon, the Helots, and Arkadia," *J.H.S.*, 74 (1954), 32–35.

20. Eugene Vanderpool, *Ostracism at Athens* (Cincinnati, Ohio: Cincinnati University Press, 1970), pp. 4, 11–13.

21. Burn, *Persia and the Greeks*, pp. 294–295.

22. Olmstead, *History of the Persian Empire*, pp. 230–237. Burn, *Persia and the Greeks*, p. 317.

23. P. A. Brunt, "The Hellenic League against Persia," *Historia*, 2 (1953), 135–163.

24. A. G. Woodhead, *The Greeks in the West* (New York: Praeger, 1962), pp. 74–81. Burn, *Persia and the Greeks*, chap. 15, "Military Monarchy in Sicily," pp. 297–304.

25. Noel Robertson, "The Thessalian Expedition of 480 B.C.," *J.H.S.*, 96 (1976), 100–120.

26. Translation of A. R. Burn, *Persia and the Greeks*, pp. 356–357.

27. Ibid., pp. 360–361.

28. Michael H. Jameson, "A Decree of Themistokles from Troizen," *Hesperia*, 29 (1960), 198–223; "A Revised Text of the Decree of Themistokles from Troizen," *Hesperia*, 31 (1962), 310–315.

29. Translation of A. R. Burn, *Persia and the Greeks*, pp. 364–366.

30. Ibid., p. 369.

31. Charles Hignett, *Xerxes' Invasion of Greece* (Oxford: Clarendon Press, 1963), pp. 464–465.

32. H. W. Parke, "Consecration to Apollo," *Hermathena*, 72 (1948), 85.

33. Brunt, "The Hellenic League," pp. 136–137.

34. Marcus N. Tod, *A Selection of Greek Historical Inscriptions,* vol. II (Oxford: Clarendon Press, 1948), no. 204.

35. Translation of A. R. Burn, *Persia and the Greeks,* pp. 512–513.

36. Parke, "Consecration to Apollo," pp. 93–95.

9. Delian League and Athenian Empire

1. J. A. O. Larsen, "The Constitution and Original Purpose of the Delian League," *Harvard Studies in Classical Philology,* 51 (1940), 175–213.

2. Russell Meiggs, *The Athenian Empire* (Oxford: Clarendon Press, 1973), pp. 45–49. N. G. L. Hammond, "The Origins and the Nature of the Athenian Alliance of 478/7 B.C.," *J.H.S.,* 87 (1967), 41–61. Phyllis Culham, "The Delian League: Bicameral or Unicameral?" *American Journal of Ancient History,* 3 (1978), 27–31.

3. A. G. Woodhead, "The Institution of the Hellenotamiae," *J.H.S.,* 79 (1959), 149–152. Meiggs, *Athenian Empire,* pp. 50–67. J. A. S. Evans, "The Settlement of Artaphrenes," *C.P.,* 71 (1976), 344–348.

4. Meiggs, *Athenian Empire,* pp. 62–63; 253.

5. B. D. Meritt, H. T. Wade-Gery, and M. F. McGregor, *The Athenian Tribute Lists,* vol. III (Princeton, N.J.: The American School of Classical Studies at Athens, 1950), pp. 234–243.

6. A. French, "The Tribute of the Allies," *Historia,* 21 (1972), 1–20.

7. Meritt, Wade-Gery, and McGregor, *Athenian Tribute Lists,* vol. III, pp. 226–227.

8. Felix Jacoby, *Die Fragmente der Griechischen Historiker* (Berlin: Weidmann, 1926), no. 70 (Ephoros), fragment 191.

9. J. Wolski, "Pausanias et le problème de la politique spartiate," *Eos,* 47 (1954–1956), 75–94.

10. Friedrich Cornelius, "Pausanias," *Historia,* 22 (1973), 502–504.

11. Mary White, "Some Agiad Dates: Pausanias and His Sons," *J.H.S.,* 84 (1964), 140–152. Meiggs, *Athenian Empire,* pp. 72–73; 465–468.

12. M. P. Milton, "The Date of Thucydides' Synchronism of the Siege of Naxos with Themistokles' Flight," *Historia,* 28 (1979), 257–275, argues that "Themistokles fled past the besieged island of Naxos not earlier than 466."

13. Meritt, Wade-Gery, and McGregor, *Athenian Tribute Lists,* vol. III, p. 158, n. 1.

14. Ibid., pp. 249; 267–268.

15. Meiggs, *Athenian Imperialism,* pp. 77–83.

16. *Inscriptiones Graecae, Editio Minor* (Berlin: de Gruyter, 1924), vol. I^2, 928.

17. Felix Jacoby, *"Patrios Nomos:* State Burial in Athens and the Public Cemetery in the Kerameikos," *J.H.S.,* 64 (1944), 37–66.

18. G. A. Papantoniou, "Once or Twice?" *A.J.P.,* 72 (1951), 176–181.

19. Meiggs, *Athenian Imperialism,* pp. 97; 469–472.

20. Georges Daux, "Remarques sur la Composition du Conseil Amphictionique," *B.C.H.,* 81 (1957), 95–120.

21. B. H. Fowler, "Thucydides I, 107–108 and the Tanagran Federal Issues," *Phoenix*, 11 (1957), 164–170.

22. Marta Sordi, "La posizione di Delfi e dell' Anfizionia nel decennio tra Tanagra e Coronea," *Rivista di Filologia e di Istruzione Classica*, 86 (1958), 48–65.

23. *M&L*, no. 39. Meritt, Wade-Gery, and McGregor, *Athenian Tribute Lists*, vols. I and II (1939 and 1949).

24. W. R. Connor, *Theopompus and Fifth-Century Athens* (Cambridge, Mass.: Harvard University Press, 1968), pp. 78–87.

25. J. M. Cook, "The Problem of Classical Ionia," *Proceedings of the Cambridge Philological Society*, n.s. 7 (1961), 9–18.

26. Robin Seager, *Historia*, 18 (1969), 129–141, struck by fourth-century concepts such as Common Peace and freedom of the seas in Plutarch's account, suggests that the Congress Decree may have been a forgery issued by opponents of Philip II of Macedonia after the Peace of Philocrates in 346 to aid Athenian orators in their eagerness for a Common Peace and in their hostility to Philip's increasing sea power. The arguments are interesting and partly persuasive, but, if correct, one would expect to find some reference to this Periclean endeavor in fourth-century Attic orators. It seems strange also for forgers, in search of an inspiring precedent, to have invented one that did not achieve its aim.

27. H. T. Wade-Gery and B. D. Meritt, "Athenian Resources in 449 and 431 B.C.," *Hesperia*, 26 (1957), 163–197. For a translation see C. W. Fornara, *Archaic Times to the End of the Peloponnesian War* (Baltimore: Johns Hopkins Press, 1977), pp. 93–95.

28. Meiggs, *Athenian Imperialism*, pp. 260–262.

29. Ibid., pp. 122–123.

30. Ibid., p. 180.

31. Victor Ehrenberg, "Polypragmosyne: A Study in Greek Politics," *J.H.S.*, 67 (1947), 46–67. Knut Kleve, "Apragmosunē and Polupragmosunē: Two Slogans in Athenian Politics," *Symbolae Osloenses*, 39 (1964), 83–88.

32. Victor Ehrenberg, "The Foundation of Thurii," *A.J.P.*, 69 (1948), 149–170.

33. G. E. M. de Ste. Croix, "Notes on Jurisdiction in the Athenian Empire," *C.Q.*, 55 (1961), 94–112; 268–280.

34. J. M. Balcer, *The Athenian Regulations for Chalkis: Studies in Athenian Imperial Law* (Wiesbaden: Steiner, 1978).

35. In Athenian public life the word translated above as "punishments" (*euthynai*) usually signified the examinations to which magistrates had to submit at the expiration of their terms of office, but most scholars, probably correctly, prefer the meaning "punishments" in the context of this document. Some scholars maintain that the term translated above as "appeal" (*ephesis*) should be interpreted as the initial transfer of any "capital" case to Athens, but the meaning "appeal" is better documented.

36. J. M. Balcer, "Imperial Magistrates in the Athenian Empire," *Historia*, 25 (1976), 257–287.

10. The Development of Athenian Democracy

1. Charles Hignett, *A History of the Athenian Constitution to the End of the Fifth Century B.C.* (Oxford: Clarendon Press, 1952), pp. 173–174.

2. Ernst Badian, "Archons and *Strategoi*," *Antichthon*, 5 (1971), 1–34. F. J. Frost, "Themistocles' Place in Athenian Politics," *California Studies in Classical Antiquity*, 1 (1968), 105–121.

3. W. R. Connor, *The New Politicians of Fifth-Century Athens* (Princeton: Princeton University Press, 1971) chaps. 1 and 2, pp. 3–84.

4. N. G. L. Hammond, "The Campaign and the Battle of Marathon," *J.H.S.*, 88 (1968), 49–50. Badian, "Archons and *Strategoi*," p. 29.

5. These remarks on Ephialtes owe much to James Day and Mortimer Chambers, *Aristotle's History of Athenian Democracy* (Berkeley: University of California Press, 1962), pp. 120–133, and Eberhard Ruschenbusch, "Ephialtes," *Historia*, 15 (1966), 369–376.

6. A. H. J. Greenidge, *A Handbook of Greek Constitutional History* (London: Macmillan, 1896), p. 164. Georg Busolt, *Griechische Geschichte bis zur Schlacht bei Chaeronea* (Gotha: Perthes, 1897), vol. III, pt. 1, p. 264, n. 1.

7. W. K. Pritchett, *The Greek State at War*, pt. 1 (Berkeley: University of California Press, 1971), pp. 3–29, especially pp. 23–24.

8. Hignett, *Athenian Constitution*, p. 346.

9. The attempts to argue that Pericles' law was made retroactive in 446/5 (Jacoby 328, Philochorus, fragment 119), as Plutarch (*Pericles*, 37) says in reference to a gift of grain to be distributed among the citizens from the Egyptian king, are not persuasive. Plutarch seemingly has confused the law with a revision of *deme* citizen registers (*diapsephismos*), a revision directed against aliens fraudulently enrolled, not against citizens legally enrolled in their phratries and in their *demes* on becoming eighteen.

10. J. W. Headlam-Morley, *Election by Lot at Athens*, 2nd ed., revised by D. C. MacGregor (Cambridge: Cambridge University Press, 1933), pp. 107–108.

11. Hignett, *Athenian Constitution*, pp. 347–348.

12. C. W. Fornara, *The Athenian Board of Generals from 501 to 404* (Wiesbaden: Steiner, 1971), pp. 19–27.

13. P. J. Bicknell, *Studies in Athenian Politics and Genealogy* (Wiesbaden: Steiner, 1972), pp. 101–112.

14. K. J. Dover, "Dekatos Autos," *J.H.S.*, 80 (1960), 61–77.

15. Headlam-Morley, *Election by Lot*, pp. 154–164.

16. On the Council of Five Hundred see especially P. J. Rhodes, *The Athenian Boule* (Oxford: Clarendon Press, 1972), and R. A. de Laix, *Probouleusis: A Study of Political Decision-Making* (Berkeley: University of California Press, 1973).

17. Rhodes, *Athenian Boule*, p. 26.

18. Gustave Glotz, *The Greek City and Its Institutions* (New York: Knopf, 1929), pp. 195–198.

19. J. A. O. Larsen, *Representative Government in Greek and Roman History* (Berkeley: University of California Press, 1955), pp. 15–18.

20. Rhodes, *Athenian Boule*, pp. 179–207.

21. Headlam-Morley, *Election by Lot*, pp. 1–40; Hignett, *Athenian Constitution*, pp. 221–232; A. H. M. Jones, *Athenian Democracy* (Oxford: Blackwell, 1957), pp. 41–72.

22. Glotz, *Greek City*, pp. 224–231, 184.

23. On the assembly in general see Glotz, *Greek City*, pp. 152–180; de Laix, *Probouleusis*, pp. 173–192.

24. A. R. W. Harrison, *The Law of Athens*, vol. I (Oxford: Clarendon Press, 1968), p. 68.

25. A. W. Gomme, *The Population of Athens in the Fifth and Fourth Centuries B.C.* (Oxford: Blackwell, 1933).

26. Hignett, *Athenian Constitution*, p. 236.

27. De Laix, *Probouleusis*, pp. 192–194.

28. Ibid., pp. 33–37; Glotz, *Greek City*, pp. 164–166.

29. Glotz, *Greek City*, pp. 178–180; Hignett, *Athenian Constitution*, pp. 209–213.

30. R. J. Bonner and Gertrude Smith, *The Administration of Justice from Homer to Aristotle*, vol. I (Chicago: University of Chicago Press, 1930), pp. 294–309; Harrison, *Law of Athens*, vol. II (1971), pp. 49–59.

31. Bonner and Smith, *Administration of Justice*, vol. II, pp. 24–25; Harrison, *Law of Athens*, vol. II, pp. 59–64.

32. Bonner and Smith, *Administration of Justice*, vol. II, pp. 25–38; D. M. MacDowell, *The Law in Classical Athens* (Ithaca, N.Y.: Cornell University Press, 1978), pp. 61–62.

33. R. J. Bonner, *Lawyers and Litigants in Ancient Athens* (Chicago: University of Chicago Press, 1927), chap. 4, "Prosecutors and Sycophants," pp. 59–71.

34. Bonner and Smith, *Administration of Justice*, vol. II, pp. 192–231; D. M. MacDowell, *Athenian Homicide Law in the Age of the Orators* (Manchester, England: Manchester University Press, 1963); MacDowell, *Law in Classical Athens*, pp. 109–122.

35. Translation of R. S. Stroud in his *Drakon's Law on Homicide* (Berkeley: University of California Press, 1968), pp. 6–7.

36. See K. J. Maidment in *Minor Attic Orators*, Loeb Classical Library (Cambridge, Mass.: Harvard University Press, 1941), General Introduction to the Tetralogies of Antiphon, pp. 34–37.

37. Harrison, *Law of Athens*, vol. II, pp. 222–229.

38. Bonner and Smith, *Administration of Justice*, vol. II, pp. 276–287.

39. Antonios D. Keramopoullos, *Ho Apotympanismos* (Athens: Estia, 1923).

40. H. C. Harrell, "Public Arbitration in Athenian Law," *University of Missouri Studies*, 11 (1936), 1–40; Bonner and Smith, *Administration of Justice*, vol. II, pp. 97–116; MacDowell, *Law in Classical Athens*, pp. 207–211.

41. Bonner and Smith, *Administration of Justice*, vol. I, pp. 357–362.

42. Harrison, *Law of Athens*, vol. II, pp. 239–241; MacDowell, *Law in Classical Athens*, pp. 35–40.

43. Bonner and Smith, *Administration of Justice,* vol. I, pp. 283–293.

44. Harrison, *Law of Athens,* vol. II, pp. 85–105; MacDowell, *Law in Classical Athens,* pp. 237–254.

45. A. L. Boegehold, "Toward a Study of Athenian Voting Procedure," *Hesperia,* 32 (1963), 366–374; Harrison, *Law of Athens,* vol. II, pp. 154–168.

46. Harrison, *Law of Athens,* vol. II, pp. 74–82.

47. See the excellent studies of M. I. Finley, "Athenian Demagogues," *Past and Present,* 21 (1962), 3–24; and *Democracy Ancient and Modern* (New Brunswick, N.J.: Rutgers University Press, 1973).

48. Gustave Glotz, *Ancient Greece at Work* (New York: Knopf, 1926), pp. 187–189.

49. M. I. Finley, "Was Greek Civilization Based on Slave Labour?" *Historia,* 8 (1959), 148, n. 13.

50. Ibid., p. 164.

11. The Peloponnesian War

1. J. H. Finley, *Thucydides* (Cambridge, Mass.: Harvard University Press, 1942), pp. 3–73.

2. Kathleen Freeman, *Ancilla to the Pre-Socratic Philosophers:* A complete translation of the fragments in Diels, *Fragmente der Vorsokratiker* (Oxford: Blackwell, and Cambridge, Mass.: Harvard University Press, 1948), p. 147.

3. E. R. Dodds, *The Greeks and the Irrational* (Berkeley: University of California Press, 1951), p. 179, with reference to the expression coined by Gilbert Murray in *Greek Studies* (Oxford: Clarendon Press, 1946), pp. 66–67.

4. H. I. Marrou, *A History of Education in Antiquity* (New York: Sheed and Ward, 1956), chaps. 4 and 5, pp. 36–60; E. A. Havelock, *The Liberal Temper in Greek Politics* (London: Jonathan Cape, 1957), pp. 284–285, 382, and passim.

5. Plato, *Apology,* 18b.

6. Finley, *Thucydides,* p. 42.

7. G. E. M. de Ste. Croix, *The Origins of the Peloponnesian War* (Ithaca, N.Y.: Cornell University Press, 1972), pp. 16–18.

8. F. M. Cornford, *Thucydides Mythistoricus* (London: Edward Arnold, 1907; reprinted by Routledge and Kegan Paul, 1965).

9. See, for example, Ste. Croix, *Origins of the Peloponnesian War,* pp. 200–203.

10. Ibid., pp. 225–289.

11. G. E. M. de Ste. Croix, "The Character of the Athenian Empire," *Historia,* 3 (1954/55), 1–41.

12. A. G. Woodhead, "Thucydides' Portrait of Cleon," *Mnemosyne,* ser. 4, 13 (1960), 289–317.

13. Ste. Croix, "Character of the Athenian Empire."

14. Russell Meiggs, *The Athenian Empire* (Oxford: Clarendon Press, 1972), pp. 324–339.

15. Ibid., pp. 340–343.

16. Ibid., pp. 335–336.

17. Woodhead, "Thucydides' Portrait of Cleon," pp. 306–317.

18. A. W. Gomme, *A Historical Commentary on Thucydides,* vol. III (Oxford: Clarendon Press, 1956), pp. 666–682.

19. Jean Hatzfeld, *Alcibiade: Étude sur l'histoire d'Athènes à la fin du cinquième siècle* (Paris: Presses Universitaires de France, 1940).

20. J. K. Davies, *Athenian Propertied Families 600–300 B.C.* (Oxford: Clarendon Press, 1971), p. 10.

21. Cornford, *Thucydides Mythistoricus,* pp. 174–187.

22. Book 8 of Thucydides covers the war from 413 into the events of 411. Since it is not a finished product like the earlier books, it is probably correct to believe that it is a series of reports which Thucydides collected while in exile—reports which he never was able to organize in his usual masterly manner. The interested reader should consult A. W. Gomme, A. Andrewes, and K. J. Dover, *A Historial Commentary on Thucydides,* vol. V, bk. 8 (Oxford: Clarendon Press, 1981). W. S. Ferguson's chapters 11 and 12 in *The Cambridge Ancient History,* vol. V (1927) are still excellent.

23. D. M. Lewis, *Sparta and Persia* (Leiden: E. J. Brill, 1977), pp. 102–107. See also Gomme, Andrewes, and Dover, *Historical Commentary,* on Thucydides 8.58.

24. P. J. Rhodes, "The Five Thousand in the Athenian Revolution of 411 B.C.," *J.H.S.,* 92 (1972), 115–127.

25. Lewis, *Sparta and Persia,* pp. 123–125.

26. Martin Ostwald, "The Athenian Legislation against Tyranny and Subversion," *T.A.P.A.,* 86 (1955), 103–128.

27. Antony Andrewes, "The Generals in the Hellespont, 410–407 B.C.," *J.H.S.,* 73 (1953), 2–9. C. W. Fornara, *The Athenian Board of Generals from 501 to 404* (Wiesbaden: Steiner, 1971), pp. 66–71.

28. Antony Andrewes, "The Arginousai Trial," *Phoenix,* 28 (1974), 112–122.

29. Stephen Usher, "Xenophon, Critias and Theramenes," *J.H.S.,* 88 (1968), 128–135.

30. Dionysius of Halicarnassus on *Lysias,* 34.

31. The following works on the restoration of the Athenian democracy are very useful: Paul Cloché, *La Restauration démocratique à Athènes en 403 avant J.-C.* (Paris: Ernest Leroux, 1915); Georges Mathieu, "La Réorganization du corps civique athénien à la fin du cinquième siècle," *Revue des Études Grecques,* 40 (1927), 65–116; Charles Hignett, *A History of the Athenian Constitution to the End of the Fifth Century B.C.* (Oxford: Clarendon Press, 1952), pp. 285–298.

12. The Fourth Century

1. A. W. Gomme, *The Population of Athens in the Fifth and Fourth Centuries B.C.* (Oxford: Blackwell, 1933), p. 26.

2. M. I. Finley, *Studies in Land and Credit in Ancient Athens, 500–200 B.C.: The Horos Inscriptions* (New Brunswick, N.J.: Rutgers University Press, 1952), pp. 79–87.

3. J. V. A. Fine, *Horoi: Studies in Mortgage, Real Security, and Land Tenure in*

Ancient Athens (Princeton, N.J.: American School of Classical Studies at Athens; *Hesperia:* suppl. 9, 1951), pp. 199–208.

4. Aristotle, *Ath. Const.* 41.3. The date is derived from various references in Aristophanes' *Ecclesiazusae,* produced probably in 392. The higher rate of pay mentioned in *Ath. Const.,* 62.2 refers to the figure current in Aristotle's time.

5. G. E. M. de Ste. Croix, "Demosthenes' *Timema* and the Athenian Eisphora in the Fourth Century B.C.," *Classica et Mediaevalia,* 14 (1953), 30–70, provides a useful account of many of the problems related to the *eisphora.* See also A. H. M. Jones, *Athenian Democracy* (Oxford: Blackwell, 1957), pp. 23–30.

6. Of the many studies dealing with social and economic aspects of fourth-century Athens, it will be sufficient to mention Gert Audring, "Über Grundeigentum und Landwirtschaft in der Krise der Athenischen Polis," in *Hellenische Poleis,* ed. E. C. Welskopf (Berlin: Akademie Verlag, 1974), pp. 108–131, and the perceptive review of the four volumes in the series by Robert Browning, "The Crisis of the Greek City—a New Collective Study," *Philologus,* 120 (1976), 258–266; Sally Humphreys, "Economy and Society in Classical Athens," *Annales della Scuola di Pisa,* ser. 2, vol. 39 (1970), 1–26; Alexander Fuks, "Isokrates and the Social-Economic Situation in Greece," *Ancient Society,* 3 (1972), 17–44; V. N. Andreyev, "Some Aspects of Agrarian Conditions in the Fifth to Third Centuries B.C.," *Eirene,* 12 (1974), 5–46; Jan Pečirka, "The Crisis of the Athenian Polis in the Fourth Century B.C.," *Eirene,* 14 (1976), 5–29.

7. For a fuller study of the attempted revolt of Cinadon, see E. David, "The Conspiracy of Cinadon," *Athenaeum,* 67 (1979), 239–259.

8. E. A. Costa, Jr., "Evagoras I and the Persians, ca. 411 to 391 B.C.," *Historia,* 23 (1974), 40–56.

9. I. A. F. Bruce, *An Historical Commentary on the "Hellenica Oxyrhynchia"* (Cambridge: Cambridge University Press, 1967), pp. 58–60.

10. G. T. Griffith, "The Union of Corinth and Argos (392–386 B.C.)," *Historia,* 1 (1950), 236–256.

11. For a general treatment of the concept of Common Peace, see T. T. B. Ryder, *Koine Eirene: General Peace and Local Independence in Ancient Greece* (London and New York: Oxford University Press, 1965), with a useful bibliography, pp. 174–179.

12. Hermann Bengtson, *Die Verträge der Griechisch-Römischen Welt von 700 bis 338 v. Chr.,* 2nd ed. (Munich: C. H. Beck, 1975), nos. 236 and 237.

13. See the interesting article of Victor Martin, "Sur une interprétation nouvelle de la 'Paix du Roi,'" *Museum Helveticum,* 6 (1949), 127–139. Cf. Hermann Bengtson, *Griechische Geschichte,* 4th ed. (Munich: C. H. Beck, 1969), pp. 269–271.

14. For the Chalcidian League, see A. B. West, *The History of the Chalcidic League* (1918; reprint ed., New York: Arno Press, 1973); Michael Zahrnt, *Olynth und die Chalkidier: Untersuchungen zur Staatenbildung auf der Chalkidischen Halbinsel im 5. und 4. Jahrhundert v. Chr.* (Munich: C. H. Beck, 1971).

15. K. J. Beloch, *Griechische Geschichte,* vol. III, pt. 2 (Berlin: de Gruyter,

1923), pp. 56–59; Fritz Geyer, *Makedonien bis zur Thronbesteigung Philipps II* (Munich: Oldenbourg, 1930), pp. 111–122.

16. Silvio Accame, *La Lega Ateniese del Sec. IV A.C.* (Rome: Signorelli, 1941); G. L. Cawkwell, "The Foundation of the Second Athenian Confederacy," *C.Q.*, 67 (1973), 47–60.

17. G. L. Cawkwell, "Notes on the Peace of 375/4," *Historia*, 12 (1963), 84–95.

18. The problem of the reestablishment of the Boeotian League is discussed fully in John Buckler, *The Theban Hegemony, 371–362 B.C.* (Cambridge, Mass.: Harvard University Press, 1980), pp. 15–45.

19. G. L. Cawkwell, "Epaminondas and Thebes," *C.Q.*, 66 (1972), 254–278, especially 264–265.

20. J. B. Bury, "The Double City of Megalopolis," *J.H.S.*, 18 (1898), 15–22.

21. J. A. O. Larsen, *Greek Federal States: Their Institutions and History* (Oxford: Clarendon Press, 1968), pp. 180–195.

22. Buckler, *Theban Hegemony*, suggests on p. 89 that Iphicrates' real aim was to hasten their departure.

23. Ibid., pp. 138–145.

24. Ibid., pp. 185–193.

25. Ibid., pp. 193–198.

26. For the chaotic history of Thessaly in the 360s, see H. D. Westlake, *Thessaly in the Fourth Century B.C.* (London: Methuen, 1935), pp. 126–159; Marta Sordi, *La Lega Tessala fino ad Alessandro Magno* (Rome: Istituto Italiano per la Storia Antica, 1958), pp. 191–234; Buckler, *Theban Hegemony*, pp. 110–129.

27. Despite certain absurdities in Aeschines' account (2.28–29), G. T. Griffith, *A History of Macedonia*, vol. II (Oxford: Clarendon Press, 1979), pp. 204–205, is probably correct in assigning the surrender of Philip as a hostage to this period rather than to the preceding year, as Buckler, *Theban Hegemony*, p. 118 argues by following Plutarch (*Pelopidas*, 26.4–5) and Diodorus (15.67.4).

28. The evidence for these events is so scattered that it seems best to refer to two works where the sources are carefully collected: K. J. Beloch, *Griechische Geschichte*, vol. III, pt. 1 (Berlin: de Gruyter, 1922), pp. 193–195, and Gustave Glotz, *Histoire Grecque*, vol. III (Paris: Presses Universitaires de France, 1936), pp. 167–169.

29. W. Dittenberger, *Sylloge Inscriptionum Graecarum*, 3rd ed. (1915; reprint ed., Hildesheim: Olms, 1960), no. 179.

30. On Epaminondas' naval plans, see Cawkwell, "Epaminondas and Thebes," pp. 270–274; Buckler, *Theban Hegemony*, pp. 160–175. It seems almost certain that financial aid must have come from Persia.

31. Dittenberger, *Sylloge Inscriptionum Graecarum*, no. 145. Sordi, *La Lega Tessala*, pp. 183–190.

32. Sordi, *La Lega Tessala*, pp. 207–223.

33. Dittenberger, *Sylloge Inscriptionum Graecarum*, nos. 175 and 176.

34. Geyer, *Makedonien*, p. 136.

35. Glotz, *Histoire Grecque*, III, pp. 182–185.

36. Ibid., p. 192.

37. On the Social War and the role of Mausolus, see Beloch, *Griechische Geschichte, III,* pt. 1, pp. 233–245, and Glotz, *Histoire Grecque*, III, pp. 188–201.

13. Macedonia and Greece

1. Of the many studies on early Macedonia, it will be sufficient to mention Fritz Geyer, *Makedonien bis zur Thronbesteigung Philipps II* (Munich: Oldenbourg, 1930); C. F. Edson, "Early Macedonia," in *Ancient Macedonia*, Papers read at the First International Symposium held in Thessaloniki, 26–29 August, 1968 (Thessaloniki: Institute for Balkan Studies, 1970), pp. 17–44; and N. G. L. Hammond, *A History of Macedonia*, vol. I, *Historical Geography and Prehistory* (Oxford: Clarendon Press, 1972), exhaustive, but somewhat uncritical in the use of the scattered and fragmentary sources. For an introduction to the remarkable excavations by Manolis Andronikos at Vergina, see Manolis Andronikos, "The Royal Tomb of Philip II," *Archaeology,* 31 (1978), 33–41, and N. G. L. Hammond, " 'Philip's Tomb' in Historical Context," *Greek, Roman, and Byzantine Studies,* 19 (1978), 331–350.

2. Edson, "Early Macedonia," p. 29.

3. This account of the *pezetairoi* is based on Edson, "Early Macedonia," pp. 30–32. Several scholars subsequently, for example, R. D. Milns, "The Army of Alexander the Great," in *Alexandre le Grand: Image et Réalité* in Entretiens sur l'Antiquité Classique, 22 (Vandoeuvres-Genève: Fondation Hardt, 1975), pp. 87–136, and G. T. Griffith, *A History of Macedonia,* vol. II, *550–336 B.C.* (Oxford: Clarendon Press, 1979), pt. 2, pp. 405–408 and appendix 3, "The pezetairoi," pp. 705–713, find a fragment of Theopompus (Jacoby, 115, fragment 348), "Theopompus says that picked men out of all the Macedonians, the tallest and strongest, served as the King's Guards, and they were called Foot Companions," a more convincing explanation of the nature (and origin?) of the *pezetairoi.* Theopompus, who was in Macedonia in the late 340s, presumably observed that Philip had a bodyguard of crack infantrymen called *pezetairoi,* but when one considers the prowess of Macedonian infantry under Philip, it seems reasonable to assume that the bodyguard was only an elite group of a much larger number of *pezetairoi.*

4. Geyer, *Makedonien*, pp. 94–97.

5. Edson, "Early Macedonia," pp. 38–41.

6. This account of the reigns of Amyntas III, Alexander II, and Perdiccas III largely follows the interpretation of Geyer, *Makedonien,* pp. 111–139. N. G. L. Hammond, *A History of Macedonia,* vol. II (Oxford: Clarendon Press, 1979), pp. 172–188, interprets these years somewhat differently.

7. J. R. Ellis, *Philip II and Macedonian Imperialism* (London: Thames and Hudson, 1976), pp. 47–48.

8. G. E. M. de Ste. Croix, "The Alleged Secret Pact between Athens and Philip II concerning Amphipolis and Pydna," *C.Q.,* 56 (1963), 110–119. Griffith, *History of Macedonia,* II, pt. 2, pp. 236–244, rejects the secret agreement but believes there were curious negotiations.

9. R. A. de Laix, *Probouleusis at Athens: A Study of Political Decision-Making* (Berkeley: University of California Press, 1973), pp. 80–81.

10. Ellis, *Philip II*, p. 66.

11. On the Macedonian army, see Griffith, *History of Macedonia*, II, pt. 2, pp. 405–449; M. M. Markle, "The Macedonian Sarissa, Spear, and Related Armor," *A.J.A.*, 81 (1977), 323–339.

12. Barclay V. Head, *Historia Numorum: A Manual of Greek Numismatics*, 2nd ed. (Oxford: Clarendon Press, 1911; reprint ed., Chicago: Argonaut, 1967), pp. 222–224.

13. On the Macedonian Government, see Griffith, *History of Macedonia*, II, pt. 2., pp. 383–404.

14. G. L. Cawkwell, "Eubulus," *J.H.S.*, 83 (1963), 47–67.

15. A. H. M. Jones, *Athenian Democracy* (Oxford: Blackwell, 1957), pp. 33–34.

16. W. Dittenberger, *Sylloge Inscriptionum Graecarum*, 3rd ed. (Leipzig: Hirzel, 1915), no. 241. In "Diodorus' Narrative of the Sacred War," *J.H.S.*, 57 (1937), 44–77, N. G. L. Hammond tries to establish a logical chronology.

17. Griffith, *History of Macedonia*, II, pt. 2, pp. 274–277.

18. Marta Sordi, *La Lega Tessala fino ad Alessandro Magno* (Rome: Istituto Italiano per la Storia Antica, 1958), pp. 249–260. Griffith, *History of Macedonia*, II, pt. 2, pp. 220–230.

19. J. R. Ellis, "Philip's Thracian Campaign of 352–351," *C.P.*, 72 (1977), 32–39. Griffith, *History of Macedonia*, II, pt. 2, pp. 281–285.

20. A. B. West, *The History of the Chalcidic League* (1918; reprint ed., New York: Arno Press, 1973), pp. 122–126.

21. Ellis, *Philip II*, pp. 93–95.

22. Sordi, *La Lega Tessala*, pp. 262–267.

23. P. A. Brunt, "Euboea in the Time of Philip II," *C.Q.*, 63 (1969), 245–265, especially 248–251.

24. See, for example, Arnold Schaefer, *Demosthenes und seine Zeit*, 2nd ed., vol. 2 (Leipzig: Teubner, 1886), p. 189, n. 1.

25. A. W. Pickard-Cambridge, *Demosthenes and the Last Days of Greek Freedom, 384–322 B.C.* (London and New York: G. P. Putnam's Sons, 1914), pp. 252–255. The author's treatment of the negotiations for the Peace of Philocrates and of the peace itself, pp. 228–300, is excellent.

26. Sordi, *La Lega Tessala*, pp. 275–293. Ellis, *Philip II*, pp. 137–143.

27. Pickard-Cambridge, *Demosthenes and the Last Days*, pp. 305–306.

28. See, for example, G. L. Cawkwell, "Demosthenes' Policy after the Peace of Philocrates," *C.Q.*, 56 (1963), 127–128, and Griffith, *History of Macedonia*, II, pt. 2, pp. 484–489.

29. Cawkwell, "Demosthenes' Policy," pp. 120–138, 200–213. Cf. Ellis, *Philip II*, pp. 150–151. Somewhat different conclusions in Brunt, "Euboea," pp. 245–265 and in Griffith, *History of Macedonia*, II, pt. 2, pp. 474–484, 496–504, 545–554.

30. Ellis, *Philip II*, pp. 156–159; Griffith, *History of Macedonia*, II, pt. 2, pp. 504–509.

31. D. E. W. Wormell, "The Literary Tradition concerning Hermias of Atarneus," *Yale Classical Studies*, 5 (1935), 57–92; Werner Jaeger, *Aristotle: Fundamentals of the History of His Development*, 2nd ed. (Oxford: Oxford University Press 1948, paperback 1962), pp. 105–123. Griffith, *History of Macedonia*, II, pt. 2, pp. 517–522.

32. Schaefer, *Demosthenes und seine Zeit*, pp. 447–449; F. R. Wüst, *Philipp II von Makedonien und Griechenland in den Jahren von 346 bis 338* (1938; reprint ed., New York: Arno Press, 1973), pp. 102–108; Griffith, *History of Macedonia*, II, pt. 2, pp. 554–566.

33. Wüst, *Philipp II von Makedonien und Griechenland*, pp. 108–113; Brunt, "Euboea," pp. 245–265. Griffith, *History of Macedonia*, II, pt. 2, pp. 545–554.

34. Wüst, *Philipp II von Makedonien und Griechenland*, pp. 133–136.

35. Ibid., pp. 136–140.

36. Griffith, *History of Macedonia*, II, pt. 2, pp. 581–584.

37. The dating of this meeting of the Amphictionic Council is a chronological crux. Wüst, *Philipp II von Makedonien und Griechenland*, pp. 153–155, places it in spring 339; P. Marchetti, *B.C.H.*, suppl. 4 (1977), pp. 83–89, in spring 340; Griffith, *History of Macedonia*, II, pt. 2, pp. 717–719, in autumn 340.

38. Wüst, *Philipp II von Makedonien und Griechenland*, pp. 160–161. Griffith, *History of Macedonia*, II, pt. 2, pp. 592–593.

39. Griffith, *History of Macedonia*, II, pt. 2, pp. 604–609.

40. Carl Roebuck, "The Settlements of Philip II with the Greek States in 338 B.C.," *C.P.*, 43 (1948), 73–92.

41. *Inscriptiones Graecae*, IV^2, 1, 68 (Berlin: de Gruyter, 1929).

42. J. A. O. Larsen, *Representative Government in Greek and Roman History* (Berkeley: University of California Press, 1955), p. 52.

43. Griffith, *History of Macedonia*, II, pt. 2, p. 612, n. 3, suggests that there was no garrison at Chalcis until probably 335.

Index

DATE DUE	
DEC 1 3 2002	
DEC 0 6 2004	